25th Italian Symposium on Advanced Database Systems (SEBD 2017)

Squillace Lido, Italy
25-29 June 2017

Editors:

Sergio Flesca
Elio Masciari

Sergio Greco
Domenico Sacca

ISBN: 978-1-5108-4725-5

Printed from e-media with permission by:

Curran Associates, Inc.
57 Morehouse Lane
Red Hook, NY 12571

Some format issues inherent in the e-media version may also appear in this print version.

Printed by Curran Associates, Inc. (2017)

Edited by:
Sergio Flesca
Elio Masciari
Sergio Greco
Domenico Sacca

Additional copies of this publication are available from:

Curran Associates, Inc.
57 Morehouse Lane
Red Hook, NY 12571 USA
Phone: 845-758-0400
Fax: 845-758-2633
Email: curran@proceedings.com
Web: www.proceedings.com

Preface

This volume collects the papers selected for presentation at the twenty-fifth Italian Symposium on Advanced Database Systems (SEBD 2017), held at Squillace Lido (Catanzaro), Italy, at Sun Beach Clubesse from the 25th to the 29th of June 2017.

The first edition of SEBD was held in 1993 and was very successful. Hence, the organizers were encouraged to repeat the experience year after year, until the symposium has became THE annual event of the Italian database research community. Database research played a crucial role for the growth of the computer science field since its early stage. When the first edition of SEBD was organized, the demands placed on the classical relational database systems already required new solutions to answer challenges posed by emerging applications. Twenty-five years later, we can say that, thanks to the solutions found so far, databases became a fundamental component of almost every computer science system, but new challenges continuously arise that actually lead to the Big-Data paradigm that is nowadays of great interest for both the research community and the industry.

However, even in this new paradigm, database related research issues play a fundamental role. Indeed Data mining and knowledge Discovery, Information Extraction, Semistructured Data Management and Intelligent Web Information Systems to cite a few, can be considered today as mature research fields whose results are fundamental in order to realize the Big Data metaphor. All these research field are addressed by the papers published in this volume. Fifty-seven contributions were originally submitted, of which forty-three have been accepted. Each submission was evaluated by three independent referees. Most of the contributions came from universities and the CNR (Italian National Research Council).

We hope that SEBD will continue to be a gathering forum where people from academic and industrial environments meet, discuss and exchange experiences on the theory and practice of information storage and management. Besides paper and demo presentations, the program also featured four invited talks by Serge Abiteboul, Ronald Fagin, Floris Geerts and Carlo Zaniolo, and two tutorials given by Sihem Amer-Yahia and Pierangela Samarati.

We would like to thank all the authors who submitted papers and all the conference participants. We are also grateful to the members of the Program Committee and the external referees for their thorough work in reviewing submitted contributions with expertise and patience, and the members of the SEBD Steering Committee.

A special thank is due to all the members of the Organizing Committee which made this event possible. We gratefully acknowledge the many sponsoring companies and institutions and the patronage of DIMES - Università della Calabria and ICAR-CNR.

June 25, 2017
Squillace Lido (CZ), Italy

Sergio Flesca
Sergio Greco
Elio Masciari
Domenico Saccà

Program Committee

Annalisa Appice	University Aldo Moro of Bari
Alessandro Artale	Free University of Bolzano-Bozen, Faculty of Computer Science
Ilaria Bartolini	University of Bologna
Devis Bianchini	University of Brescia
Andrea Calì	University of London, Birkbeck College
Alfredo Cuzzocrea	University of Trieste
Bettina Fazzinga	ICAR-CNR
Alfio Ferrara	Universita degli Studi di Milano
Elena Ferrari	University of insubria
Nicola Ferro	Department of Information Engineering - University of Padua
Sergio Flesca	Unical
Paolo Garza	Politecnico di Torino
Matteo Golfarelli	DISI - University of Bologna
Francesco Guerra	UniMo
Giovanna Guerrini	DISI- University of Genova
Gianluca Lax	DIIES - Universita' Mediterranea di Reggio Calabria
Davide Martinenghi	Politecnico di Milano
Elio Masciari	ICAR-CNR
Mirjana Mazuran	Politecnico di Milano
Giuseppe M. Mazzeo	Facebook
Massimo Mecella	Sapienza Universita di Roma
Anna Monreale	Computer Science Dep., University of Pisa
Vincenzo Moscato	Unina
Paolo Papotti	Arizona State University
Stefano Paraboschi	Universita di Bergamo
Francesco Parisi	DIMES - University of Calabria
Antonella Poggi	SAPIENZA Universita di Roma - Dipartimento di Informatica e Sistemistica "A. Ruberti"
Giuseppe Polese	University of Salerno
Domenico Potena	Universita Politecnica delle Marche
Alessandra Raffaetà	Universita' Ca' Foscari Venezia
Chiara Renso	ISTI-CNR, Pisa, Italy
Donatello Santoro	University of Basilicata
Riccardo Torlone	Roma Tre University
Irina Trubitsyna	University of Calabria, DIMES
Pierangelo Veltri	Laboratory of Bioinformatics, University of Catanzaro

Additional Reviewers

Caruccio, Loredana
Cinaglia, Pietro
Deufemia, Vincenzo
Leotta, Francesco
Mircoli, Alex
Nicolazzo, Serena
Nocera, Antonino
Sacca , Valeria
Storti, Emanuele

Table of Contents

Author Index

Keyword Index

Usage of network analysis to investigate Periodic Sharp Wave Complexes in EEGs of patients with sporadic CJD*

P. Lo Giudice[1], N. Mammone[2], F.C. Morabito[3], D. Ursino[3], U. Aguglia[4], V. Cianci[5], E. Ferlazzo[4], and S. Gasparini[4]

[1] DIIES, University "Mediterranea" of Reggio Calabria
[2] IRCCS Centro Neurolesi Bonino-Pulejo
[3] DICEAM, University "Mediterranea" of Reggio Calabria
[4] DSMC, University "Magna Graecia" of Catanzaro
[5] UOC Neurologia, Grande Ospedale Metropolitano di Reggio Calabria

(DISCUSSION PAPER)

Abstract. Creutzfeldt-Jacob Disease (CJD) is a rapidly progressive, uniformly fatal Transmissible Spongiform Encephalopathy. Sporadic CJD (sCJD) is the most common form of CJD. Electroencephalography (EEG) is one of the main methods to perform clinical diagnosis of CJD, mainly because of Periodic Sharp Wave Complexes (PSWCs). In this paper, we propose a new numerical coefficient and some network motifs, which characterize the presence of PSWCs in an EEG tracing. Furthermore, network motifs are able to detect what the most active and/or connected brain areas are in the tracing segments with PSWCs.

1 Introduction

Creutzfeldt-Jacob Disease (CJD) is a rapidly progressive, uniformly fatal Transmissible Spongiform Encephalopathy (TSE). It is characterized by the accumulation of a variant of the host encoded cellular prion protein in the brain [14]. CJD became well known to common people some years ago because one of its variants, known as vCJD, has been linked to the transmission of the causative agent of the bovine spongiform encephalopathy (BSE) to the human population, mainly in United Kingdom. Sporadic CJD (hereafter, sCJD) represents the most common form of CJD. An early and reliable diagnosis of CJD is extremely important to exclude other, potentially treatable, causes of rapidly progressive encephalopathies. However, the early diagnosis of this disease is complicated by the extreme heterogeneity of its clinical presentation. Electroencephalography (hereafter, EEG) has always been, and still is, one of the main methods to perform clinical diagnosis of neurological diseases in general [7], and of CJD in particular. In fact, in the EEG of patients with sCJD, it is often possible to observe three-phase periodic spikes with sharp waves known as "Periodic Sharp Wave Complexes" (hereafter, PSWCs). More specifically, PSWCs were reported

* Nadia Mammone's work was funded by the Italian Ministry of Health, Project Code GR-2011-02351397. This work was partially supported by Aubay Italia S.p.A.

to occur in the EEG tracings of about two-thirds of patients with sCJD. For this reason, they were included in the World Health Organization diagnostic classification criteria of sCJD [14, 13].

In the past, approaches to investigating PSWCs in the EEGs of patients with sCJD were mainly based on signal processing [14, 1, 12, 6]. By contrast, to the best of our knowledge, no network analysis based approach to investigating the CJD phenomenon has been previously proposed in the literature. Nevertheless, network analysis has been largely exploited in the investigation of brain, especially in those application scenarios where brain connectivity is extremely important [8]. For instance, in [9, 2], network analysis has been used to investigate Alzheimer's disease, whereas, in [10, 5], it has been employed to analyze Epilepsy. Since in sCJD (as well as in all the neurodegenerative diseases) the investigation of the connection level of the brain areas is extremely important, we argue that network analysis could play a key role in this research context. In this paper, we aim at providing a first contribution in this setting. Indeed, we propose a network analysis based approach to characterizing PSWCs in EEGs of patients with sCJD. Here, the term "characterizing" means two things, namely: *(i)* finding (if possible) a quantitative coefficient - that we call *connection coefficient* - capable of distinguishing the EEG tracing segments with PSWCs from the ones without PSWCs, and *(ii)* finding (possible) *network motifs* characterizing the presence (or, conversely, the absence) of PSWCs in an EEG tracing. In our opinion, these two contributions are worthwhile. Indeed: *(i)* A numeric coefficient can help to recognize PSWCs when they start to appear, thus allowing a much earlier diagnosis of sCJD. Furthermore, in the future, in presence of much more sophisticated electroencephalographs with 256 electrodes, the human eye could experiment much more difficulties in finding PSWCs. *(ii)* Motifs represent a further indicator of the presence of PSWCs. Furthermore, they could provide a characterization of the behavior of brain areas in presence of PSWCs. For instance, they could denote what the brain areas most connected and/or most active are in presence of PSWCs. This is, probably, the most important contribution of our approach because this information cannot be directly derived by a human expert.

This paper is organized as follows: in Section 2, we present some support data structures. In Section 3, first we illustrate our connection coefficient, then we introduce our concept of motif and, finally, we present our approach to motif extraction. Finally, in Section 4, we draw some conclusions.

2 Basic Support Data Structures

The EEGs to perform our investigation were provided by three different Italian centers (i.e., University "Magna Graecia" of Catanzaro, Neurologic Institute "Carlo Besta" of Milano, and Neurologic Institute of the University of Catania). They regard a group of ten patients with sCJD examined in the last 15 years in these three centers[6]. We segmented each EEG at disposal in such a way as to separate the tracing segments with PSWCs from those without PSWCs. As a consequence, for each EEG, we had several tracing segments, which could be grouped in two distinct sets, namely, those containing PSWCs and those not containing PSWCs.

Formally speaking, let $EEGSet$ be the set of EEGs at our disposal, let eeg be an EEG of $EEGSet$. Starting from eeg, it is possible to define a network $\mathcal{N}$ (resp., $\overline{\mathcal{N}}$) representing the set of segments of eeg with PSWCs (resp., without PSWCs). Specifically: $\mathcal{N} = \langle V, E \rangle$ and $\overline{\mathcal{N}} = \langle V, \overline{E} \rangle$. Here, V is the set of the nodes of $\mathcal{N}$ and $\overline{\mathcal{N}}$. Each node $v_i \in V$ corresponds to an electrode. In our EEGs, the electrodes were applied by following the 10-20 system. As a consequence, $|V| = 19$. E (resp., $\overline{E}$) is the set of the edges of $\mathcal{N}$ (resp., $\overline{\mathcal{N}}$). Each edge $e_{ij} \in E$ connects the nodes v_i and v_j. It can be represented as $e_{ij} = (v_i, v_j, w_{ij})$. Here, w_{ij} is a measure of "distance" between v_i and v_j, which is an indicator of their disconnection level. Actually, each measure representing this feature could be adopted in our model. In the experiments described in this paper, we adopted the *Permutation Disalignment Index* (PDI) between v_i and v_j, which is a new metric of cross-randomness between channels in multivariate electrophysiological time-series [3].

In order to make our model more "user-friendly" and "expressive" and, at the same time, more capable of discriminating strong and weak connections between brain areas, we decided to construct two new networks, namely $\mathcal{N}_\pi$ and $\overline{\mathcal{N}_\pi}$, obtained from $\mathcal{N}$ and $\overline{\mathcal{N}}$ by removing the edges with an "excessive" weight and by coloring the other ones on the basis of their weight. More specifically, blue edges denote strong connections (i.e., small weights), red edges represent intermediate ones and, finally, green edges indicate weak connections. Due to space limitations, we cannot report the technical details concerning the construction of $\mathcal{N}_\pi$ and $\overline{\mathcal{N}_\pi}$.

In Figure 1, we report the colored networks $\mathcal{N}_\pi$ and $\overline{\mathcal{N}_\pi}$ for a patient with sCJD. The disposal of the nodes in the networks reflects the 10-20 system, even if they are rotated 90 degrees clockwise. Observe how the filtering of the edges with the highest distance, along with the coloration of the other ones on the basis of the closeness of the corresponding nodes, make this model very expressive. The trends emerging from these figures have been confirmed in all the other EEGs at our disposal. In particular, we observe that: *(i)* for a specific EEG, $\mathcal{N}_\pi$ has more edges than $\overline{\mathcal{N}_\pi}$; furthermore, the edges of $\mathcal{N}_\pi$ are generally stronger than the ones of $\overline{\mathcal{N}_\pi}$; *(ii)* in both networks, the strongest edges can be found in the occipital area of the skull.

[6] We are aware that the number of patients under examination is low. However, this is due to the fact that sCJD is a very rare disease and, consequently, it is very difficult to collect data about it.

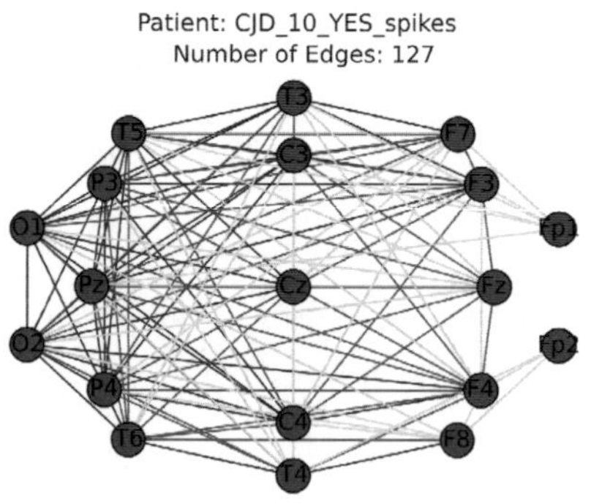

Fig. 1. Colored Networks $\mathcal{N}_\pi$ and $\overline{\mathcal{N}_\pi}$ for the patient CJD 10. Node labels reflect the electrode names in the 10/20 system

3 PSWC Characterization

3.1 Connection Coefficient

As pointed out in the Introduction, one of the main features to investigate in neurodegenerative patients is the connection level of brain areas. This feature is also relevant in the problem we are facing. In fact, in the literature, it was shown that, in presence of PSWCs, brain areas are more connected than in absence of them [11]. Furthermore, in Section 2, we have seen that the networks corresponding to the tracing segments with PSWCs are generally more and stronger connected than the networks corresponding to the tracing segments without PSWCs.

In network analysis, one of the most important (and, at the same time, simple and basic) tools for investigating network connection is the concept of *clique*. We recall that, given a network, a clique of dimension k represents a totally connected subnetwork with k nodes. On the basis of this reasoning, a quantitative coefficient for discriminating the networks corresponding to the tracing segments with PSWCs from the ones associated with the tracing segments without PSWCs could highly benefit from cliques.

In particular, this coefficient should take the following considerations into account: *(i)* Both the dimension and the number of cliques are important as connectivity indicators. *(ii)* The concept of clique is intrinsically exponential; in other words, a clique of dimension $n+1$ is exponentially more complex than a clique of dimension n.

Due to space limitations, we do not report here the technical description of connection coefficient. However, in Table 1, we report the values $cc_{\mathcal{N}_\pi}$ and $cc_{\overline{\mathcal{N}_\pi}}$ of this coefficient for $\mathcal{N}_\pi$ and $\overline{\mathcal{N}_\pi}$, along with the percentage of decrease observed when passing from $cc_{\mathcal{N}_\pi}$ to $cc_{\overline{\mathcal{N}_\pi}}$, for all the patients at our disposal.

From the analysis of these tables we can draw two important results. In fact:

- $cc_{\mathcal{N}_\pi}$ is always higher than $cc_{\overline{\mathcal{N}_\pi}}$ except for the patient CJD 19 for whom the two coefficients have the same value. However, $\mathcal{N}_{\pi_{19}}$ and $\overline{\mathcal{N}_{\pi_{19}}}$ are associated

Patient	$cc_{\mathcal{N}_\pi}$	$cc_{\overline{\mathcal{N}_\pi}}$	$\frac{cc_{\overline{\mathcal{N}_\pi}} - cc_{\mathcal{N}_\pi}}{cc_{\mathcal{N}_\pi}}$
CJD 02	66064	24640	-62.70%
CJD 04	20864	13312	-36.20%
CJD 05	69632	43008	-38.24%
CJD 08	196672	51712	-73.71%
CJD 09	49664	25856	-47.94%
CJD 10	20736	9728	-53.09%
CJD 13	12288	5376	-56.25%
CJD 16	9721	9216	-5.19%
CJD 19	524288	524288	0%
CJD 22	164352	78080	-52.49%

Table 1. Values of $cc_{\mathcal{N}_\pi}$, $cc_{\overline{\mathcal{N}_\pi}}$ and $\frac{cc_{\overline{\mathcal{N}_\pi}} - cc_{\mathcal{N}_\pi}}{cc_{\mathcal{N}_\pi}}$ for all the patients at our disposal

with a very particular EEG. Indeed, $\mathcal{N}_{\pi_{19}}$ is totally connected and, therefore, has only a unique clique coinciding with it. $\overline{\mathcal{N}_{\pi_{19}}}$, instead, is totally connected except for only one edge; as a consequence, it has only two cliques, each consisting of 18 nodes.
As a consequence, we can say that connection coefficient is really a quantitative parameter capable of distinguishing the tracing segments with PSWCs from the ones without PSWCs.

– The values obtained for $cc_{\mathcal{N}_\pi}$ and $cc_{\overline{\mathcal{N}_\pi}}$ confirm the previous results presented in the literature about the fact that brain areas are more connected to each other in presence of PSWCs than in absence of them [11].

3.2 Motifs

Motifs were already investigated and exploited in past approaches adopting network analysis. In those scenarios, motifs are considered as "patterns of interconnections occurring in complex networks at numbers that are significantly higher than those in randomized networks" [4] . In our approach, we use motifs in a completely different fashion. Indeed, we do not examine a unique complex network to find patterns frequently repeated therein. By contrast, we search for patterns appearing frequently in the networks corresponding to the tracing segments with PSWCs and being absent in the networks corresponding to the tracing segments without PSWCs, thus characterizing the former segment typology against the latter, and vice versa.

As will be clear in the following, our approach to deriving motifs exploits the support data structures introduced in Section 2, along with a further support network, strongly based on the clique concept, which we call clique network. The clique network $\mathcal{CN}$ (resp., $\overline{\mathcal{CN}}$) corresponding to $\mathcal{N}_\pi$ (resp., $\overline{\mathcal{N}_\pi}$) and to the set $\mathcal{C}$ (resp., $\overline{\mathcal{C}}$) of the cliques of $\mathcal{CN}$ (resp., $\overline{\mathcal{CN}}$), is defined as $\mathcal{CN} = \langle CV, CE \rangle$ and $\overline{\mathcal{CN}} = \langle \overline{CV}, \overline{CE} \rangle$. Here: *(i)* CV represents the set of the nodes of $\mathcal{CN}$; there is a node $v_i \in CV$ for each node $v_i \in V$. A weight w_i is associated with v_i; it represents the number of cliques of $\mathcal{C}$ in which v_i is involved; *(ii)* CE represents the set of the edges of $\mathcal{CN}$. There is an edge $(v_i, v_j, w_{ij}) \in CE$ if the edge (v_i, v_j) is present in at least one clique of $\mathcal{C}$. w_{ij} denotes the number of cliques of $\mathcal{C}$ in which (v_i, v_j) is present; *(iii)* $\overline{CV}$ and $\overline{CE}$ are analogous to CV and CE, but

Motifs					
Cz-Fz-P4	Fz-P4-Pz	Fz-O2-P4	F4-O2-T6	C4-F4-T6	F4-P4-T6
Cz-Fz-Pz	F7-P3-Pz	Cz-Fz-O2	F7-O2-P3	Fz-O2-Pz	P4-T3-T4
F7-Pz-T5	F7-Pz-T3	F7-O2-Pz	F7-O1-Pz	F7-O2-T5	F7-O2-T3
F7-O1-O2	Pz-T3-T4	T3-T4-T5	T3-T4-T6	O2-T3-T4	O1-T3-T4

Table 2. The basic motifs extracted by our approach

for $\overline{\mathcal{C}}$, instead of for $\mathcal{C}$. The edges of $\mathcal{CN}$ and $\overline{\mathcal{CN}}$ can be "colored" in a way analogous to the edges of $\mathcal{N}_\pi$.

After having introduced clique networks, we define more restrictive colored networks and clique networks by removing green edges from the networks defined previously. Specifically, we define $\mathcal{N}_{\pi\pi}$, $\overline{\mathcal{N}_{\pi\pi}}$, $\mathcal{CN}_{\pi\pi}$ and $\overline{\mathcal{CN}_{\pi\pi}}$. We also define the sets $NSet_\pi$ (resp., $\overline{NSet_\pi}$, $NSet_{\pi\pi}$, $\overline{NSet_{\pi\pi}}$, $CNSet_{\pi\pi}$, $\overline{CNSet_{\pi\pi}}$) comprising all the networks $\mathcal{N}_\pi$ (resp., $\overline{\mathcal{N}_\pi}$, $\mathcal{N}_{\pi\pi}$, $\overline{\mathcal{N}_{\pi\pi}}$, $\mathcal{CN}_{\pi\pi}$, $\overline{\mathcal{CN}_{\pi\pi}}$) associated with the EEGs of $EEGSet$. Finally, let t be a generic triad. We call $nocc_\pi$ (resp., $\overline{nocc_\pi}$, $nocc_{\pi\pi}$, $\overline{nocc_{\pi\pi}}$, $cnocc_{\pi\pi}$, $\overline{cnocc_{\pi\pi}}$) the number of occurrences of t in $NSet_\pi$ (resp., $\overline{NSet_\pi}$, $NSet_{\pi\pi}$, $\overline{NSet_{\pi\pi}}$, $CNSet_{\pi\pi}$, $\overline{CNSet_{\pi\pi}}$).

After having defined all support data structures and parameters, we are able to describe our motif extraction approach. It consists of two main steps, the former devoted to the extraction of basic motifs and the latter conceived to the construction of derived ones. Preliminarily, it is necessary to specify what is a basic motif in our context. Specifically: let t be a totally connected triad of $NSet_\pi$. If: (1) t is present *frequently* in $NSet_\pi$ and is *absent* in $\overline{NSet_\pi}$, and (2) this trend is confirmed (also only to a lesser extent) for $NSet_{\pi\pi}$ and $\overline{NSet_{\pi\pi}}$ and also for $CNSet_{\pi\pi}$ and $\overline{CNSet_{\pi\pi}}$, then t is a basic motif. In particular, t is a motif characterizing the tracing segments with PSWCs against the ones without PSWCs.

In order to quantify the concept of "frequently", we define a threshold $th_f = \alpha_f \cdot |NSet_\pi|$[7]. In this case, Condition (1) becomes $(nocc_\pi \geq th_h) \wedge (\overline{nocc_\pi} = 0)$, whereas Condition (2) becomes $(nocc_{\pi\pi} > \overline{nocc_{\pi\pi}}) \wedge (cnocc_{\pi\pi} > \overline{cnocc_{\pi\pi}})$.

In a dual fashion, it is possible to define the basic motifs associated with $\overline{NSet_\pi}$ and characterizing the tracing segments without PSWCs against the ones with PSWCs. In the following, we indicate by $\mathcal{M}_\pi$ (resp., $\overline{\mathcal{M}_\pi}$) the set of motifs extracted starting from the triads of $NSet_\pi$ (resp., $\overline{NSet_\pi}$). In an analogous way, it is possible to derive the basic motifs of the sets $\mathcal{M}_{\pi\pi}$, $\overline{\mathcal{M}_{\pi\pi}}$, $\mathcal{CM}_{\pi\pi}$ and $\overline{\mathcal{CM}_{\pi\pi}}$, obtained starting from the triads of $NSet_{\pi\pi}$, $\overline{NSet_{\pi\pi}}$, $CNSet_{\pi\pi}$ and $\overline{CNSet_{\pi\pi}}$. The basic motifs derived by our approach are reported in Table 2.

Once basic motifs have been extracted and a first version of $\mathcal{M}_\pi$, $\overline{\mathcal{M}_\pi}$, $\mathcal{M}_{\pi\pi}$, $\overline{\mathcal{M}_{\pi\pi}}$, $\mathcal{CM}_{\pi\pi}$ and $\overline{\mathcal{CM}_{\pi\pi}}$ has been obtained, it is possible to construct derived (and, possibly, much more complex and significant) motifs starting from them.

Our approach to constructing new derived motifs starts from the already known ones. It uses nodes common to two or more known motifs as "junction points". Formally speaking, let $m_1 = \langle V_1, E_1 \rangle$ and $m_2 = \langle V_2, E_2 \rangle$ be two motifs of $\mathcal{M}_\pi$ such that $V_1 \cap V_2 \neq \emptyset$. Then, it is possible to construct a candidate

[7] We experimentally set the value of α_f to 0.30.

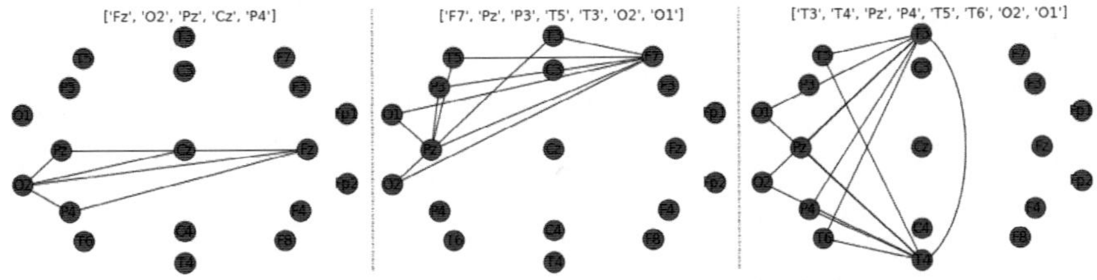

Fig. 2. The most significant motifs characterizing the tracing segments with PSWCs

motif as the union of m_1 and m_2: $m_{12} = \langle V_1 \cup V_2, E_1 \cup E_2 \rangle$. Once m_{12} has been constructed, analogously to what we have seen for basic motifs, it is necessary to evaluate $nocc_\pi$, $\overline{nocc_\pi}$, $nocc_{\pi\pi}$, $\overline{nocc_{\pi\pi}}$, $cnocc_{\pi\pi}$ and $\overline{cnocc_{\pi\pi}}$[8]. If, for these parameters, conditions (1) and (2) presented above hold, then m_{12} can be added to $\mathcal{M}_\pi$, i.e., $\mathcal{M}_\pi = \mathcal{M}_\pi \cup \{m_{12}\}$. Clearly, the addition of a new motif in $\mathcal{M}_\pi$ could lead to the possibility that new candidate motifs are constructed. As a consequence, the enrichment process of $\mathcal{M}_\pi$ is iterative and terminates when, during an iteration, no new motif is added to $\mathcal{M}_\pi$. In an analogous fashion, the derived motifs of $\overline{\mathcal{M}_\pi}$, $\mathcal{M}_{\pi\pi}$, $\overline{\mathcal{M}_{\pi\pi}}$, $\mathcal{CM}_{\pi\pi}$ and $\overline{\mathcal{CM}_{\pi\pi}}$ can be extracted.

In Figure 2, we report the most significant derived motifs extracted by our approach. The motif on the left derives from the tracing segments with PSWCs. It indicates that, in presence of PSWCs, the most active areas of the human brain reside in its right part. The other two motifs derive from the tracing segments without PSWCs. They indicate that, in absence of PSWCs, the most active areas of the human brain reside in its left part (motif on the center) and in its occipital part (motif on the right).

4 Conclusion

In this paper, we have proposed a network analysis based approach to characterizing PSWCs in EEGs of patients with sCJD. We have also introduced a new form of network motifs, well suited for this application context.

Clearly, this paper is only a first attempt of applying network analysis to characterize specific aspects of sCJD. In the future, we plan to investigate this possibility in more depth. As an example, the component of our approach performing motif extraction could be enriched in several directions. Furthermore, our approach does not currently perform analyses in the sub-bands α, β, δ and θ of an EEG; adding this feature could be extremely useful, in particular for the sub-band δ, which was proven to play a relevant role in the analysis of sCJD [14]. The ultimate goal of our research efforts could be a complete network analysis based decision support system, which can help a human expert in identifying patients with sCJD as early as possible starting from their EEGs.

[8] Clearly, for derived motifs, $nocc_\pi$, $\overline{nocc_\pi}$, $nocc_{\pi\pi}$, $\overline{nocc_{\pi\pi}}$, $cnocc_{\pi\pi}$ and $\overline{cnocc_{\pi\pi}}$ refer to the number of occurrences on motifs, instead of on triads.

References

1. U. Aguglia, A. Gambardella, E. Le Piane, D. Messina, G. Farnarier, R.L. Oliveri, M. Zappia, and A. Quattrone. Disappearance of periodic sharp wave complexes in Creutzfeldt-Jakob disease. *Neurophysiologie Clinique/Clinical Neurophysiology*, 27(4):277–282, 1997. Elsevier.
2. W. de Haan, Y.A. Pijnenburg, R.L. Strijers, Y. van der Made, W. van der Flier, P. Scheltens, and C.J. Stam. Functional neural network analysis in frontotemporal dementia and Alzheimer's disease using EEG and graph theory. *BMC neuroscience*, 10(1):1, 2009. BioMed Central.
3. N. Mammone, L. Bonanno, S. De Salvo, S. Marino, P. Bramanti, A. Bramanti, and F.C. Morabito. Permutation Disalignment Index as an Indirect, EEG-Based, Measure of Brain Connectivity In MCI And AD Patients. *International Journal of Neural Systems*, http://dx.doi.org/10.1142/S0129065717500204, In press.
4. R. Milo, S. Shen-Orr, S. Itzkovitz, N. Kashtan, D. Chklovskii, and U. Alon. Network motifs: simple building blocks of complex networks. *Science*, 298(5594):824–827, 2002. American Association for the Advancement of Science.
5. F. Miraglia, F. Vecchio, G. Curcio, G. Della Marca, C. Vollono, E. Mazzucchi, and P. Rossini. Cortical connectivity in fronto-temporal focal epilepsy from EEG analysis: A study via graph theory. *Clinical Neurophysiology*, 127(3):e47, 2016. Elsevier.
6. F.C. Morabito, M. Campolo, N. Mammone, M. Versaci, S. Franceschetti, F. Tagliavini, V. Sofia, D. Fatuzzo, A. Gambardella, A. Labate, L. Mumoli, G.G. Tripodi, S. Gasparini, V. Cianci, C. Sueri, E. Ferlazzo, and U. Aguglia. Deep Learning representation from electroencephalography of early-stage Creutzfeldt-Jakob Disease and Features for Differentiation from Rapidly Progressive Dementia. *International Journal of Neural Systems*, 3:1650039, 2016. World Scientific.
7. V.P. Oikonomou, A.T. Tzallas, and D.I. Fotiadis. A Kalman filter based methodology for EEG spike enhancement. *Computer Methods and Programs in Biomedicine*, 85(2):101–108, 2007. Elsevier.
8. M. Rubinov and O. Sporns. Complex network measures of brain connectivity: uses and interpretations. *Neuroimage*, 52(3):1059–1069, 2010. Elsevier.
9. K. Supekar, V. Menon, D. Rubin, M. Musen, and M.D. Greicius. Network analysis of intrinsic functional brain connectivity in Alzheimer's disease. *PLoS Computational Biology*, 4(6):e1000100, 2008. Public Library of Science.
10. S. Supriya, S. Siuly, and Y. Zhang. Automatic epilepsy detection from EEG introducing a new edge weight method in the complex network. *Electronics Letters*, 52(17):1430–1432, 2016. IET.
11. R.D. Traub and T.A. Pedley. Virus-induced electrotonic coupling: Hypothesis on the mechanism of periodic EEG discharges in Creutzfeldt-Jakob disease. *Annals of Neurology*, 10(5):405–410, 1981. Wiley Online Library.
12. P.S. Wang, Y.T. Wu, C.I. Hung, S.Y. Kwan, S. Teng, and B.W. Soong. Early detection of periodic sharp wave complexes on EEG by independent component analysis in patients with Creutzfeldt-Jakob disease. *Journal of Clinical Neurophysiology*, 25(1):25–31, 2008. LWW.
13. World Health Organization (WHO). Consensus on criteria for diagnosis of sporadic CJD. *Weekly Epidemiological Record*, 73:361–365, 1998.
14. H.G. Wieser, K. Schindler, and D. Zumsteg. EEG in Creutzfeldt–Jakob disease. *Clinical Neurophysiology*, 117(5):935–951, 2006. Elsevier.

Schema Profiling of Document Stores*

Enrico Gallinucci, Matteo Golfarelli, and Stefano Rizzi

DISI — CINI, University of Bologna, Italy

Abstract. In document stores, schema is a soft concept and the documents in a collection can have different schemata; this gives designers and implementers augmented flexibility but requires an extra effort to understand the rules that drove the use of alternative schemata when heterogeneous documents are to be analyzed or integrated. In this paper we outline a technique, called schema profiling, to explain the schema variants within a collection in document stores by capturing the hidden rules explaining the use of these variants; we express these rules in the form of a decision tree, called schema profile, whose main feature is the coexistence of value-based and schema-based conditions. Consistently with the requirements we elicited from real users, we aim at creating explicative, precise, and concise schema profiles; to quantitatively assess these qualities we introduce a novel measure of entropy.

Keywords: NoSQL, Schema Discovery, Decision Trees

1 Motivation and Outline

Recent years have witnessed an erosion of the relational DBMS predominance to the benefit of DBMSs based on alternative representation models (e.g., document-oriented and graph-based) which adopt a *schemaless* representation for data. Schemaless databases are preferred to relational ones for storing heterogeneous data with variable schemata and structural forms; typical schema variants within a collection consist in missing or additional attributes, in different names or types for an attribute, and in different structures for instances. The absence of a unique schema grants flexibility to operational applications but adds complexity to analytical applications, in which a single analysis often involves large sets of data with different schemata. Dealing with this complexity requires a notable effort to understand the rules that drove the use of alternative schemata, plus an integration activity to identify a common schema to be adopted for analysis —which is quite hard when no documentation is available.

In this paper we outline a technique to explain the schema variants within a collection in document stores by capturing the hidden rules explaining the use of these variants. We call this activity *schema profiling*. Schema profiling can be used for instance when trying to decode the behavior of an undocumented application that manages a document-base, or to support analytical applications

* This work was partly supported by the EU-funded project TOREADOR (contract n. H2020-688797).

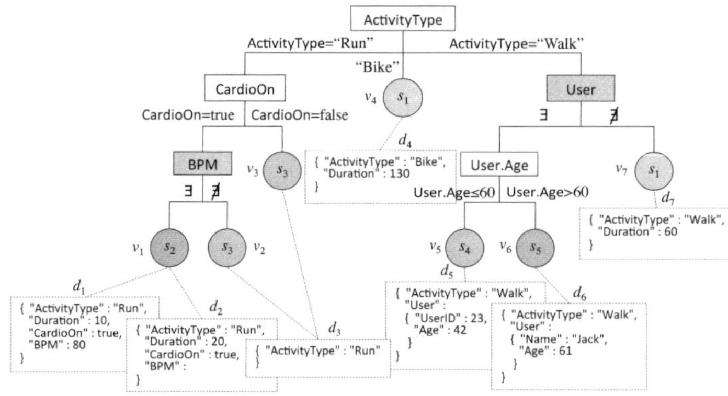

Fig. 1. A schema profile in the physical fitness domain

that query a document store following either a schema-on-write or schema-on-read approach [2].

A schema profile should describe the rules for assigning a document to a schema based on the document features; hence, modeling a schema profile as a *classifier* is a natural choice, which also allows the existing literature on classification to be reused. More specifically, since users need a comprehensible and compact representation of schema profiles, among the different types of classifiers we focus on decision trees.

Straightly reusing traditional decision trees for schema profiling would mean classifying documents based on the *values* of their attributes only. However, this would often lead to trees where a single rule explains different schemata, which would yield an imprecise information. To address this issues, in our approach documents are also classified using *schema-based conditions* related to the presence or absence of attributes. Consider for example Figure 1, showing a portion of a schema profile built in the domain of physical fitness to describe a collection of documents generated by training machines. Each internal node in the tree is associated with a document attribute a and can express either a value-based condition (white box; each outgoing arc is related to one or more values of a, e.g., User.Age < 60) or a schema-based condition (grey box; the two outgoing arcs represent the presence or absence of a in the document, e.g., $\exists$BPM). Each path in the tree models a *rule*; it leads to a leaf (represented as a circle) that corresponds to a schema found for the documents that meet all the conditions expressed along that path (document examples are shown in dashed boxes). So, for instance, schema s_1 is used in all the documents for which either ActivityType = "Bike", or ActivityType = "Walk" and field User is not present.

Another drawback of traditional decision trees is that they often give several rules for the same class. While this may be correct for some specific collections (e.g., schema s_1 in Figure 1 appears in two leaves, i.e., it is explained by two different rules), in general we wish to keep the number of rules to a minimum

```
{ "ActivityType" : "Run" ,
  "Duration" : 108 ,
  "CardioOn" : true,
  "Notes" : null ,
  "Details" :
  { "MusicTracks" : [ 4 , 8 ] ,
    "Comments":
    [{ "UserID" : 15 ,
        "Comment": "Well done!"
      },
      { "UserID" : 16,
        "Vote" : "6/10"
      }],
  },
  "User" :
  { "UserID" : 23 ,
    "Name" : "Jack" ,
    "Age" : 42 ,
    "FacebookID" : "jack42"
  }
}
```

(a)

```
{ ...
  "Comments" :
  { "type" : "array" ,
    "items" :
    [{ "type" : "object" ,
        "properties" :
        { "UserID" : { "type" : "number" } ,
          "Comment" : { "type" : "string" }
        }
      },
      { "type" : "object" ,
        "properties" :
        { "UserID" : { "type" : "number" } ,
          "Vote" : { "type" : "string" }
        }]
  },
  ...
}
```

(b)

Path	*Type*
ActivityType	primitive
Duration	primitive
CardioOn	primitive
Notes	primitive
Details	object
Details.MusicTracks	array
Details.Comments	array
User	object
User.UserID	primitive
User.Name	primitive
User.Age	primitive
User.FacebookID	primitive

(c)

Fig. 2. A JSON document representing a training session (a), a portion of its JSON schema (b), and its r-schema (c)

aimed at giving users a more concise picture of schema usage. This is achieved in our approach by introducing a novel measure called *schema entropy* that, together with the classical entropy measure, enables a better assessment of the quality of a schema profile.

2 From Documents to Schema Profiles

The central concept of a document store is the notion of a *document*. Following the most widely adopted format, a document is a JSON object. An *object* is formed by a set of *name/value* pairs called *elements*. A *value* can be either a primitive value (i.e, a number, a string, or a Boolean), an array of values, an object, or null. A collection D is a set of documents. Arrays have no constraint on their size and on the type of their values, i.e., an array can simultaneously contain numbers, strings, other arrays, as well as objects with different structures. Figure 2.a shows a document that represents a training session containing an array of objects with different schemata (element Comments).

The JSON schema initiative provides the specifications to define the schema of a document; however, as shown in Figure 2.b, the resulting schemata provide a complex representation of arrays and are quite verbose. Indeed, the schema of an array is defined as the ordered list of the schemata of its values, so two arrays share the same schema only if they contain the same number of values and these values share the same schemata in the same order. This schema-matching criterion would add unnecessary burden to our approach —also considering that the type variability of array elements is less relevant than that of the other attributes. So we adopt a more concise representation for the schema of a document, called *reduced schema*, which does not enter into the content of arrays, but simply denotes the presence of an array structure.

Definition 1 (R-Schema of a Document). *Given document d, the reduced schema (briefly,* r-schema*) of d, denoted $rs(d)$, is a set of* attributes*, each corresponding to one element in d. Attribute $a \in rs(d)$ is identified by a* pathname*, $path(a)$, and by a type, $type(a) \in \{\mathsf{primitive}, \mathsf{object}, \mathsf{array}\}$. While $path(a)$ is a string in dot notation reproducing the path of the element corresponding to a in d, $type(a)$ is the type of that element (type* primitive *generalizes numbers, strings, Booleans, and nulls).*

Note that, although r-schemata are defined as sets of attributes, their pathnames code the document structure (short of the internal structure of arrays).

Example 1. Figure 2 shows a sample document, its JSON schema (as per the specifications of the JSON schema initiative), and its r-schema. Note how, in the r-schema, the complexity and heterogeneity of array Comments is hidden in attribute Details.Comments with generic type array.

To put together the relevant information coded by different r-schemata, for the documents within a collection D we define a global r-schema that includes all the distinct attributes that appear in the r-schemata of the documents in D:

Definition 2 (R-Schema of a Collection). *Given collection D, we denote with $S(D)$ the set of distinct r-schemata of the documents in D (where two attributes in the r-schemata of two documents are considered equal if they have the same pathname and the same type). The* r-schema *of D is defined as $rs(D) = \bigcup_{d \in D} rs(d)$. Given $s \in S(D)$, we denote with $|D|_s$ the number of documents in D with r-schema s.*

Based on the concepts introduced above, we can now define schema profiles.

Definition 3 (Schema Profile). *A* schema profile *for collection D is a directed tree T where each internal node corresponds to some attribute $a \in rs(D)$ and expresses a condition that can be either* value-based *or* schema-based*: (i) a node expressing a schema-based condition has exactly two outgoing arcs, labelled as $\exists$ and $\nexists$ respectively; (ii) a node expressing a value-based condition has two or more outgoing arcs, each labelled with a condition over the domain of a. Value-based conditions can only be expressed on attributes of type* primitive*. Given node v, we denote with $D_v \subseteq D$ the set of documents that meet all the conditions expressed by the nodes in the path from the root to v, with $S(D_v) \subseteq S(D)$ the set of distinct r-schemata of the documents in D_v, and with $|D_v|_s$ the number of documents with r-schema $s \in S(D_v)$ belonging to D_v.*

Intuitively, each path in a schema profile models a *rule* that includes a set of conditions for selecting one or more r-schemata. We also remark that Definition 3 can accommodate both binary and n-ary trees.

Example 2. Figure 1 shows an n-ary schema profile with two schema-based conditions (User and BPM) and three value-based conditions (ActivityType, CardioOn, and User.Age). In this case, it is $D = \{d_1, \dots, d_7\}$ and $S(D) = \{s_1, \dots, s_5\}$. The schema profile has leaves $v_1, \dots, v_7$, with $D_{v_1} = \{d_1, d_2\}$. Note that document d_3 belongs to both v_2 and v_3, since attribute CardioOn is missing.

3 Evaluating Schema Profiles

The first stage of our work has been devoted to elicit user requirements for schema profiling with reference in two application domains: that of a company selling fitness equipment, whose documents contain the registration of workout sessions, and that of a software development company, whose documents contain the log of the errors generated by the deployed applications. The requirements we elicited can be summarized as follows: (i) a schema profile should be *explicative*, i.e., it should give priority to value-based conditions (which explain the difference between two r-schemata in terms of the values taken by an attribute) over schema-based ones (which merely acknowledge this difference); (ii) a schema profile should be *precise*, i.e., it should accurately characterize each single r-schema by avoiding mixing documents with different r-schemata in the same leaf of the tree; (iii) a schema profile should be *concise*, i.e., it should provide a small set of rules (a single rule for each r-schema).

Now we can informally state our final goal as that of finding a schema profile that achieves a trade-off between precision, conciseness, and explicativeness. The problem can be modeled as a classification one where the documents, properly extended with schema information, are the objects to be classified according to the schema labels. Since schema profiles are decision trees, to solve this problem we have extended the well-known C4.5 algorithm [6]. For space reasons we cannot give the details of the extension here, so in the following we just discuss how the above-mentioned requirements can be quantitatively characterized.

3.1 Explicativeness

We consider a schema profile to be explicative if it prefers value-based conditions over schema-based ones, because the latter acknowledge that there is a difference between two r-schemata but do not really explain its reason. Indeed, a value-based condition always relates two different attributes (for instance, with reference to Figure 1, attributes User.Age and UserID); this is because a condition on the values of an attribute a does not partition the documents based on the presence/absence of a. Conversely, a schema-based condition on a always partitions the documents based on the presence/absence of a so, in a sense, it merely explains itself.

So, to evaluate explicativeness we use the number of schema-based conditions in the schema profile T: the lower this number, the more explicative T.

3.2 Precision

A distinguishing feature of the classification approaches based on decision trees is the function they adopt to quantify the "purity" of the leaves where observations are classified, where a leaf is said to be *pure* if all its observations share the same class. The most common function used to this end is *entropy* [8].

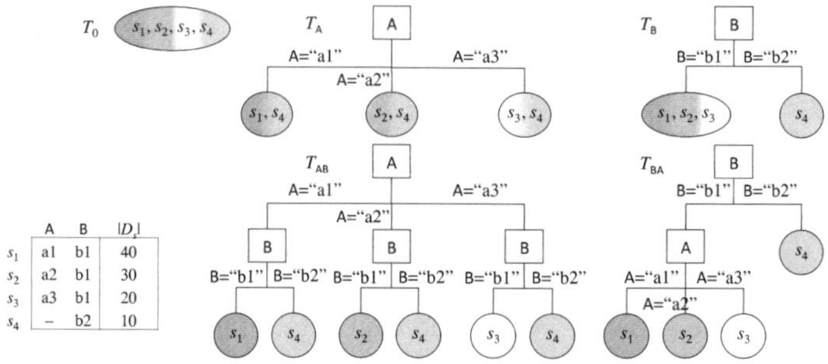

Fig. 3. A collection (on the left) and five possible schema profiles (see Example 3)

Definition 4 (Entropy). *Let $S(D)$ be the set of distinct r-schemata of the documents in collection D, and T be a schema profile for D with leaves $v_1, \ldots, v_m$. The entropy of T is*

$$entropy(T) = \sum_{j=1}^{m} \frac{|D_{v_j}|}{|D|} \cdot entropy(v_j)$$

where $\frac{|D_{v_j}|}{|D|}$ is the probability of leaf v_j, $entropy(v_j) = -\sum_{s \in S(D_v)} \frac{|D_{v_j}|_s}{|D_{v_j}|} \log \frac{|D_{v_j}|_s}{|D_{v_j}|}$ is the entropy *of leaf v_j, and $\frac{|D_{v_j}|_s}{|D_{v_j}|}$ is the probability of r-schema s within leaf v_j. Leaf v_j is said to be* pure *if $entropy(v_j) = 0$.*

Entropy is strictly related to precision: within a schema profile with null entropy, all the documents included in each leaf share the same r-schema, thus the schema profile has maximum precision.

Example 3. Let D be a collection with 100 documents, 4 r-schemata $s_1, \ldots, s_4$, and two attributes, A and B. The values of the attributes for the different r-schemata are listed in Figure 3 (symbol "–" means "any value"), together with five possible schema profiles. A degenerate schema profile T_0 made of a single root node v_0 has entropy $entropy(T_0) = entropy(v_0) = 1.85$ (because $D_{v_0} \equiv D$). Schema profiles T_{A} and T_{B} have $entropy(T_{\mathsf{A}}) = 0.46$ and $entropy(T_{\mathsf{B}}) = 1.38$, respectively. Both schema profiles T_{AB} and T_{BA} have null entropy because no leaf includes multiple r-schemata.

3.3 Conciseness

Entropy is focused on node purity, hence its minimization often leads to split observations of the same class among several leaves. While this is a secondary problem in generic classification problems, where the precision of the resulting model is more important than its readability, it becomes critical in schema profiling since it conflicts with the conciseness requirement. Indeed, in our context, each r-schema might end up for being explained by a wide set of rules, thus precluding users from getting a concise picture of schema usage. For instance, with reference to Example 3, though both schema profiles T_{AB} and T_{BA} have null entropy, the latter is clearly the one that best represents the collection, with each r-schema being reached by a single path in the tree.

To evaluate the conciseness of schema profiles, we propose a measure called *schema entropy*. Our requirement is to reduce the number of rules provided by maximizing the cohesion of the documents that share the same r-schema —a maximally concise schema profile is one where there is a single rule for each r-schema. So we invert the original definition of entropy to relate it to the purity of the r-schemata instead of the purity of the leaves: in terms of entropy, a leaf is pure if it contains only documents with the same r-schema; in terms of schema entropy, an r-schema is pure if all its documents are in the same leaf. The schema entropy of a degenerate schema profile where all the documents are included into a single node (the root) is 0; when documents are split into different leaves, the schema entropy can never decrease.

Definition 5 (Schema Entropy). *The schema entropy of T is*

$$sEntropy(T) = -\sum_{s\in S(D)} \frac{|D|_s}{|D|} \cdot sEntropy(s)$$

where $sEntropy(s) = \sum_{j=1}^{m} \frac{|D_{v_j}|_s}{|D|_s} \log \frac{|D_{v_j}|_s}{|D|_s}$ *is the* schema entropy *of r-schema* $s \in S(D)$.

Example 4. With reference to Example 3, it is $sEntropy(T_0) = sEntropy(T_{\mathsf{B}}) = sEntropy(T_{\mathsf{BA}}) = 0$ and $sEntropy(T_{\mathsf{A}}) = sEntropy(T_{\mathsf{AB}}) = 0.16$. Therefore, if both entropy and schema entropy are considered, T_{BA} is the best schema profile.

4 Related Work and Conclusions

Early work on schema discovery focused on describing semi-structured data retrieved from web pages based on the Object Exchange Model (e.g., [5]). As XML became a standard for data exchange on the web, work such as [1] emerged to help software tools in processing XML documents or in integrating data. With the replacement of XML with JSON, similar issues are now being addressed aimed at capturing and representing the intrinsic variety of schemata within a collection of JSON objects. In [3] a unique schema is built for the JSON objects returned by a single API service, while the union of all the attributes in a collection of JSON objects is modeled in [4] to measure the heterogeneity of a collection. In [7], a versioned schema model for a collection of JSON documents is built by creating a new version of the same attribute for every intensional variation found in the documents. Finally, in [9] the documents of a collection are clustered to identify groups of similar schemata; then, the schemata of each group are summarized into a *skeleton*, i.e., a tree containing the smallest set of core attributes according to a frequency-based formula.

In this paper we have outlined an approach to schema profiling for document stores. The idea is to capture the rules that explain the use of different schemata within a collection through a decision tree whose nodes express either value-based or schema-based conditions. Though our approach has some points in common with the above mentioned ones, its goal is completely different. The ultimate goal of the previous work is to provide a way to *describe* the intensional aspects of the documents, while ours is to *explain* the schema variants. Besides, no other approach considers the extensional point of view to describe schema variants. Finally, while all previous approaches produce in output some form of skeleton schema, we create a schema profile that classifies schema variants.

We made some experimental tests using both synthetic and real-world collections, with numbers of documents ranging from about 10000 to more than 5 millions, and it turned out that our approach achieves a good trade-off among precision, conciseness, and expressiveness. Specifically, to assess its accuracy we compared the schema profiles it delivers with a baseline (for synthetic collections the baseline is the set of rules used to generate the collection itself, while for real-world collections it has been provided by the users). For comparisons we adopt the weighted *tree edit-distance* (i.e., the length of the cheapest sequence of node-edit operations that transforms one tree into the other, weighted on the tree depth), which ranges between 0 and 1.17 for synthetic collections and between 0 and 1.33 for real-world collections. Finally, in terms of efficiency, we found that the total time to build a schema profile ranges from a few seconds to about 3 minutes, depending on the number of documents and on their number of attributes (on a 64-bits Intel Core i7 quad-core 3.4GHz).

References

1. Bex, G.J., Gelade, W., Neven, F., Vansummeren, S.: Learning deterministic regular expressions for the inference of schemas from XML data. ACM TWEB 4(4), 14 (2010)
2. Dong, X.L., Srivastava, D.: Big data integration. In: Proc. ICDE. pp. 1245–1248 (2013)
3. Izquierdo, J.L.C., Cabot, J.: Discovering implicit schemas in JSON data. In: Proc. ICWE. pp. 68–83 (2013)
4. Klettke, M., Störl, U., Scherzinger, S., Regensburg, O.: Schema extraction and structural outlier detection for JSON-based NoSQL data stores. In: Proc. BTW. vol. 2105, pp. 425–444 (2015)
5. Nestorov, S., Ullman, J., Wiener, J., Chawathe, S.: Representative objects: Concise representations of semistructured, hierarchical data. In: Proc. ICDE. pp. 79–90 (1997)
6. Quinlan, J.R.: C4.5: Programs for Machine Learning. Morgan Kaufmann (1993)
7. Ruiz, D.S., Morales, S.F., Molina, J.G.: Inferring versioned schemas from NoSQL databases and its applications. In: Proc. ER. pp. 467–480 (2015)
8. Shannon, C.E.: A mathematical theory of communication. ACM SIGMOBILE Mobile Computing and Communications Review 5(1), 3–55 (2001)
9. Wang, L., Zhang, S., Shi, J., Jiao, L., Hassanzadeh, O., Zou, J., Wangz, C.: Schema management for document stores. Proc. VLDB Endowment 8(9), 922–933 (2015)

A Model for Fine-Grained Data Citation*

Susan Davidson[1], Daniel Deutch[2], Tova Milo[2], and Gianmaria Silvello[3]

[1] University of Pennsylvania, USA
susan@seas.upenn.edu
[2] Tel Aviv University, Israel
{danielde,milo}@post.tau.ac.il
[3] University of Padua, Italy
silvello@dei.unipd.it

Abstract. An increasing amount of information is being collected in structured, evolving, curated databases, driving the question of how information extracted from such datasets via queries should be cited. Unlike traditional research products which have a fixed granularity, data citation is a challenge because the granularity varies. Different portions of the database, with varying granularity, may have different citations. Furthermore, there are an infinite number of queries over a database, so we cannot hope to explicitly attach a citation to every possible result set and/or query. We present the novel problem of *automatically generating citations for general queries* over a relational database, and explore a solution based on *citation views*, each of which attaches a citation to a view of the database. Citation views are then used to automatically construct citations for general queries.

1 Introduction

Citation is essential to traditional scholarship. It helps identify the cited material so that it can be retrieved, gives credit to the creator of the material, dates it, and so on. In the context of printed materials, such as books and journals, citation is well understood. However, the world is now digital, and an increasing amount of information is being collected in structured and evolving curated databases, driving database owners, publishers and standards groups to consider how such data should be cited [6].

Unlike traditional publications which have a fixed granularity to which citations can be attached – e.g. a conference proceedings, or a paper in a conference proceedings – data citation is a challenge because the granularity varies. For example, the content of a scientific database frequently represents the effort of a large number of members of the scientific community (some use cases are presented in Section 2). Different portions of the database, with varying granularity, are contributed and/or curated by different subgroups of these individuals. While a citation to the database as a whole is typically provided as a traditional publication, whose author list includes the owners and developers of

* This is an extended abstract of [5]. Please refer to the original paper for more details.

the resource, there is a growing belief that contributors/curators should be acknowledged when their data is extracted and used. That is, when the database is queried and a result set returned, the citation (i.e. a textual snippet to be used as a reference) for that data should include information about the contributors/curators of the result set as well as of the data used to compute it. The latter depends on the query.

Since there are a potentially infinite number of queries, each accessing and generating different subsets of the database, we cannot hope to explicitly attach a citation to every possible result set and/or query. Instead, we must find ways of specifying citations for some semantically meaningful portions of the database (possibly defined declaratively via queries), and use these to automatically construct citations for more general queries. Thus data citation is a *computational* problem, as argued in [3] and fleshed out in more detail here.

Our approach draws inspiration from results in two areas: *query rewriting using views*, which has been well studied in the context of query optimization, data integration [2], and *database provenance* [7].

We start with a notion of *citation views*, through which database owners specify how citations are attached to the output of some number of queries (views) over the database representing typical usage patterns. The citation to a general query is then constructed by *rewriting* it to a set of equivalent queries using the citation views, and combining the citations attached to these views to construct a citation to the query (Section 3). To construct the citation, we leverage the fact that citations and provenance are both forms of *annotation* that are manipulated through queries [4]. In particular, the *joint* $(\cdot)$ and *alternative* $(+)$ use of annotations within a rewriting are modeled using the *semirings* approach of [7] presented in Section 4. We close in Section 5 by discussing several open issues that must be addressed in developing a practical solution to this challenging problem.

2 Use cases

Currently, several data resources specify *how* citations to single resources, collections, result lists and data subsets should be constructed but do not generate the appropriate citation. Three such examples are Eagle-i[4] (an RDF dataset built to facilitate translational science research which allows researchers to share information about resources such as cell lines and software), Reactome[5], an open-source, curated and peer reviewed pathway relational database, and Drugbank[6], a relational database (available also as RDF and XML) combining detailed chemical, pharmacological and pharmaceutical data with comprehensive sequence, structure, and pathway information. Instructions are given on which snippets of information on the web page view of the resource should be included in a citation to the resource, but generating the citation is left to the user.

[4] `https://www.eagle-i.net/`
[5] `http://www.reactome.org/`
[6] `http://www.drugbank.ca/`

The example we will use throughout the remainder of this paper is the IUPHAR/BPS Guide to Pharmacology (GtoPdb).[7] GtoPdb is a relational database that contains expertly curated information about drugs in clinical use and some experimental drugs. Users view information through a hierarchy of web pages: The top level divides information by families of drug targets that reflect typical pharmacological thinking; lower levels divide the families into subfamilies and so on down to individual drugs. The content of a particular family "landing" page is curated by a committee of experts; a family may also have a "detailed introduction page" which is written by a set of contributors, who are not necessarily the same as the committee of experts for the family. Currently, citations for these views are hard-coded into the web pages – queries are issued against the underlying relational database to obtain content for the page as well as the committee members or contributors. Thus, GtoPdb in fact does generates citations, but only to a subset of the possible queries against the underlying relational database, i.e. those corresponding to web-page views of the data.

In the future, the owners of GtoPdb would like to allow users to issue *general queries* against the relational database and automatically generate a citation for the result. We address this problem in the remainder of the paper.

3 Citation Views and Rewriting

We assume that queries and views are expressed as Conjunctive Queries (see [1] for an overview). Given a database D, we start with a set of *view definitions*. Each view definition has an associated *citation query* C_V and *citation function* F_V. A *citation view* consists of a view query, a citation query, and citation function. The citation function takes as input the citation query result, and returns a citation. The citation becomes an annotation on each tuple in the view query result. The view and citation queries may be *parameterized*, which we discuss shortly.

Definition 1. *A* citation view *is a triple* (V, C_V, F_V) *where*

- V *is the* view definition *of form* $\lambda X.V(Y) :- Q$*;*
- C_V *is the* citation query *of form* $\lambda X.\ C_V(Y') :- Q'$*; and*
- F_V *is the* citation function *which transforms the output of the citation query (i.e. the bindings to variables* Y'*) into a citation in some desired format, such as JSON or XML.*

In V *and* C_V*:*

- Q *and* Q' *are conjunctions of atoms;*
- $X = [x_1, ..., x_n]$, $Y = [y_1, ..., y_m]$, $Y' = [y'_1, ..., y'_p]$ *are ordered sequences of variables;*
- $X \subseteq Y$ *are subsets of the variables in* Q*;*
- X *and* Y' *are subsets of the variables in* Q'.

[7] http://www.guidetopharmacology.org/

The terms $x_1, ..., x_n$ *are the* parameters *of* V *and* C_V*. Parameters are optional, in which case the* λ*-term may be dropped. If there is a* λ*-term the citation view is called* parameterized.

Each choice of values for the parameters may lead to a different view instance and different citation. We denote the view instance by applying the view to the input parameter values, e.g. if the view is

$$\lambda(x_1, \ldots, x_n)V(Y) :- Q$$

and is passed parameter values $(a_1, \ldots, a_n)$, we write

$$V(Y)(a_1, \ldots, a_n).$$

Since the citation query Q' is also parametrized by X, each valuation of X leads to a different result for Q'. The output of the citation function – the *citation* for the view – becomes an annotation on each tuple in the output of the instantiated view. Thus for every sequence of parameter values $(a_1, \ldots, a_n)$, the citation for all tuples in $V(Y)(a_1, \ldots, a_n)$ is $F_v(C_v(Y')(a_1, \ldots, a_n))$. Note that the citation views and queries have to be defined by the DBA and thus they can be considered a user choice. On the other hand, we can also foresee some methods to automatic define views and queries for instance by using query logs.

Example 1. We use as a running example a simplified database schema for GtoPdb, in which keys are underlined:

Family(<u>FID</u>, FName, Type)
FamilyIntro(<u>FID</u>, Text)
Person(<u>PID</u>, PName, Affiliation)
FC(<u>FID</u>, <u>PID</u>), FID references Family, PID references Person
FIC (<u>FID</u>, <u>PID</u>), FID references FamilyIntro, PID references Person
MetaData(Type, Value)

Intuitively, FC captures the committee members who curate the content of a family page while FIC captures the contributors who author the Family Introduction page of a family. The last table, MetaData, captures other information that may be useful to include in citations, such as the owner of the database ("Owner", "Tony Harmar"), the URL of the database ("URL", "guidetopharmacology.org") and the current version number of the database ("Version", "23").

To express citation views for GtoPdb we start by defining a small set of view definitions.

$$\begin{aligned}
\lambda F.V1(F,N,Ty) &:- Family(F,N,Ty)\\
\lambda F.V2(F,Tx) &:- FamilyIntro(F,Tx)\\
V3(F,N,Ty) &:- Family(F,N,Ty)
\end{aligned}$$

All views except $V3$ are parameterized. $V1$ and $V2$ restrict the output to a single tuple since the parameter, F, corresponds to the key FID in Family. $V3$ contains all tuples in Family. For each of the views, we define a citation query.

$$\begin{aligned}
\lambda F.\ C_{V1}(F,N,Pn) &:- Family(F,N,Ty), FC(F,C), Person(C,Pn,A)\\
\lambda F.\ C_{V2}(F,N,Tx,Pn) &:- Family(F,N,Ty), FamilyIntro(F,Tx),
\end{aligned}$$

$$
\begin{aligned}
& FIC(F,C), Person(C,Pn,A) \\
C_{V3}(X1,X2) \quad & :- \; MetaData(T1,X1), T1 = \text{"}Owner\text{"}, \\
& MetaData(T2,X2), T2 = \text{"}URL\text{"}
\end{aligned}
$$

Since V1 and its citation query C_{V1} are parameterized by F, each valuation of V1 results in a single tuple and each tuple may have a different citation. As an example, for the family with FID=11 the citation is a function of the result of C_{V1}(F,N,Pn)("11"), which consists of the family id, name and list of committee members. In contrast to $V1$ and $V2$, $V3$ is not parameterized, which means that all tuples have the same citation in V3. C_{V3} uses the MetaData table to obtain the url and owner of the database.

Database owners specify a set of citation views, from which the citation for a general query over the database will be constructed. Our approach is to rewrite as much of the query as possible using the view definitions, and combine their citations to construct a citation for the input query. We start by defining what a rewriting is.

Definition 2. *Let $\mathcal{R}$ be a set of relation names, Q be a query, and $\mathcal{V}$ be a set of views. The query Q' is a* rewriting *of Q using $\mathcal{V}$ if:*

- *the subgoals of Q' are either relation names in $\mathcal{R}$, views in $\mathcal{V}$, or comparison predicates;*
- *Q' is equivalent to Q;*
- *no subgoal of Q' can be removed and obtain an equivalent query; and*
- *no subset of subgoals of Q' can be replaced by a view in $\mathcal{V}$ and obtain an equivalent query.*

A rewriting is *total* if its subgoals contain only views and comparison predicates; otherwise, if its subgoals also contain relation names, it is *partial.* We illustrate the trade-offs between different rewritings in terms of the citations generated through an example.

Example 2. Let us consider a query which finds the name and text of the introduction of families with type "gpcr".

$Q(N,Tx) :- Family(F,N,Ty), FamilyIntro(F,Tx), Ty = \text{"}gpcr\text{"}$

Q can be rewritten in several ways, including:

$Q_1(N,Tx) :- V1(F,N,Ty), V2(F,Tx), Ty = \text{"}gpcr\text{"}$
$Q_2(N,Tx) :- V3(F,N,Ty), V2(F,Tx), Ty = \text{"}gpcr\text{"}$

These two rewritings are total and the difference between Q_1 and Q_2 is that the former uses V_1, while the latter uses V_3; C_{V1} produces a citation for each distinct family, whereas C_{V3} provides a single citation for the entire view. In this sense, $V3$ is more general than $V1$. In neither case is the comparison predicate $Ty = \text{"}gpcr\text{"}$ matched by the lambda term of the view.

4 Combining citations

As we have seen, a single query may be rewritten in multiple ways and each rewriting may use one or more views. The question is how the citation for the query result should be defined as a function of these rewritings. To do this, observe that citations and provenance are both forms of *annotation* that are manipulated through queries [4]. We therefore take inspiration from work on database provenance, in particular that of *provenance semirings* [7], to model the different ways in which citations views are combined.

In provenance semirings, provenance tokens (base annotations) are associated with each tuple in a relational instance (EDB). Restricting our attention to SPJU queries, there are two ways in which tuples are combined through queries:

- *Joint use*, as in a join which combines two tuples to form a new tuple. In this case, the provenance annotation of the new tuple is the '$\cdot$' of the annotations of the two input tuples.
- *Alternate use*, as when one or more tuples are "identified" via unions or projections to form a new tuple. In this case, the provenance annotation of the new tuple is the '$+$' of the annotations of all input tuples.

In citations, annotations are defined through the citation queries (and their corresponding functions). Citation views are combined in two different ways when providing a citation to general queries: they may appear *jointly* in equivalent rewritings of the query, or they may appear in *alternate* rewritings.

In the following, we will assign query output with citations that are the combination of results of citation functions, through $+$ and $\cdot$ based on the use of the views in the query. The resulting structure of citations is that of a *commutative semiring*: we start with a set of basic citations C, and introduce an abstract operation $+$ on it with the properties that $+$ is commutative, associative, and has some neutral element 0 in C. Similarly we introduce an operation $\cdot$ with the same properties, but with a different neutral element 1. Last, we impose that $\cdot$ is distributive over $+$.

We start by defining a citation for a *single binding* of a *single rewriting* of the query. This dictates a single output tuple, and a particular valuation to the parameters of the views. We define the citation of the output tuples as the joint use of citations for the views and the parameter valuations, denoted by "$\cdot$".

Definition 3. *Let Q be a query, let V be a set of citation views and let Q' be a (partial) rewriting of Q using $V1, ..., Vn \in V$. Further let B be a binding to the variables of Q', yielding an output tuple t. The citation for t w.r.t. Q, Q', V, B, denoted as $cite(t, Q, Q', V, B)$, is defined as $F_{V1}(C_{V1}(B1)) \cdot \ldots \cdot F_{Vn}(C_{Vn}(Bn))$ where Bi is the application of B to the variables occurring in an atom involving Vi in Q'.*

Example 3. Consider the rewriting Q_1 from Example 2, and consider the binding to its variables F="11", N="Calcitonin", Ty = "gpcr" and Tx="stuff". The resulting tuple is ("Calcitonin", "stuff"), and the citation we get *for this particular binding* is the citation assigned in $V1$ to family "11" (note that the lambda parameter of $V1$ is F), combined via $\cdot$ with the one assigned in $V2$ to the same family (i.e., $F_{V1} \cdot F_{V2}$): {ID: "11", Name: "Calcitonin", Committee: ["Hay", "Poyner"]} $\cdot$ {ID: "11", Name: "Calcitonin", Text: "The calcitonin peptide family ", Contributors: ["Brown", "Smith"]}.

So far we have only defined the citation for a single binding. Multiple bindings lead to multiple *alternative* citations, which we capture using $+$.

Definition 4. *Let Q, V, Q' be as in Definition 3, and let β_t be the set of all bindings for Q' that yield a tuple t. The citation for t w.r.t. Q, Q' (denoted as $cite(t, Q, Q', V)$) is denoted as $\Sigma_{B \in \beta_t} cite(t, Q, Q', V, B)$.*

Example 4. Recall $Q1$ and assume now that the family name N="Calcitonin" is shared by two families, with identifiers 11 and 12. This leads to two bindings to the variables of $Q1$, and intuitively to two ways of using the views to get the output tuple ("Calcitonin"). The citation for the tuple, in this case, will be a "+" over the expression in Example 3 and a similar expression for family id 12: {ID: "11", Name: "Calcitonin", Committee: ["Hay", "Poyner"]} $\cdot$ {ID: "11", Name: "Calcitonin", Text: "The calcitonin peptide family", Contributors: ["Brown", "Smith"]} + {ID: "12", Name: "Calcitonin", Text: "The calcitonin peptide family", Contributors: ["Brown", "Hey"]}

For example, "$\cdot$" could be a join of some sort and "+" could be union.

Finally, a query may have multiple rewritings, each leading to a possibly different citation. These are again alternatives, but the function used to combine the citations for them may be different than the one used for multiple bindings for a single rewriting. We therefore use $+^R$ ("+ for rewritings") to denote this function, whose operands are elements of the citation semiring (i.e. polynomials using + and $\cdot$). $+^R$ has a neutral value 0_R, and is associative and commutative. Note that this is a formal semantics, not a means of computation: going through all rewritings would be an impractical implementation.

There are many interpretations "$\cdot$" , "+", and $+^R$ that could be used. For "$\cdot$" and "+", union or join are natural interpretations. For $+^R$, the "minimum" in some ordering would also be natural. These ordering could reflect how "precise" or "comprehensive" the rewritings are relative to each other, or the "size" of the resulting citation.

5 Final Remarks

We presented an approach for automatically constructing citations to information extracted from a database via general queries. In this approach, owners of the database specify citations to a small set of (possibly parameterized) views of the database which represent typical usage patterns; they also give interpretations to the combining functions + , $\cdot$ and $+^R$. A query against the database is then rewritten using the views, and a citation for the result set constructed using the interpretations of the combining functions.

The described model can be used for constructing citations using only schema level information (as is done in query optimization using views) as well as using citation annotations attached to tuples (as is done with reasoning about provenance). Note that reasoning at the tuple level requires changes to an existing database both in terms of the schema (to capture citation annotations on view tuples) and in terms of query processing (to combine citation annotations).

While we have formally defined a model for citations for query results, we have not given efficient means for computing them. In particular, it is infeasible both in terms of run time and the size of the resulting citation to go through all rewritings and all assignments within each of them. A precursor for algorithms in this respect is further modeling of (some of) the "black boxes" of the model, which include the citation functions and the semiring operations. We have demonstrated initial ideas in this respect, such as the assumption of idempotence over + and its use in some cases. Even for restricted cases, designing efficient algorithms for computing citations is a non-trivial task. To this end, our future work will also study further connections to relevant classic problems in the literature such as query inclusion (which we have mentioned as useful for the preference relation); query rewriting using views; using logs to understand database usage and decide what citation views should be specified; caching and materialization; and the maintenance and presentation of data provenance.

Acknowledgments The authors would like to thank Peter Buneman and Val Tannen for many fruitful discussions. Peter Buneman initially formulated several of these ideas in the context of XML. This work has been partially funded by NSF IIS 1302212, NSF ACI 1547360, and NIH 3-U01-EB-020954-02S1; by the ERC under the FP7, ERC grant MoDaS, agreement 291071; by the ISF (1636/13); and by a grant from the Blavatnik Interdisciplinary Cyber Research Center.

References

1. S. Abiteboul, R. Hull, and V. Vianu. *Foundations of Databases.* Addison-Wesley, 1995.
2. F. A. Afrati, C. Li, and J. D. Ullman. Using views to generate efficient evaluation plans for queries. *Journal of Computer and System Sciences*, 73(5):703–724, 2007.
3. P. Buneman, S. B. Davidson, and J. Frew. Why data citation is a computational problem. *Communications of the ACM (CACM)*, 59(9):50–57, 2016.
4. J. Cheney, L. Chiticariu, and W. C. Tan. Provenance in databases: Why, how, and where. *Foundations and Trends in Databases*, 1(4):379–474, 2009.
5. S. B. Davidson, D. Deutsch, M. Tova, and G. Silvello. A Model for Fine-Grained Data Citation. In *8th Biennial Conference on Innovative Data Systems Research (CIDR 2017)*, 2017.
6. N. Ferro and G. Silvello. The Road Towards Reproducibility in Science: The Case of Data Citation. In C. Grana and L. Baraldi, editors, *Proc. 13th Italian Research Conference on Digital Libraries (IRCDL 2017).* Communications in Computer and Information Science (CCIS), Springer, Heidelberg, Germany, 2017.
7. T. J. Green, G. Karvounarakis, and V. Tannen. Provenance Semirings. In L. Libkin, editor, *Proc. of the 26th ACM SIGACT-SIGMOD-SIGART Symposium on Principles of Database Systems*, pages 31–40. ACM Press, New York, USA, 2007.

A Social Network Analysis based approach to deriving knowledge about research scenarios in a set of countries*

Paolo Lo Giudice[1], Paolo Russo[2], and Domenico Ursino[3]

[1] DIIES, University "Mediterranea" of Reggio Calabria
[2] NEGG
[3] DICEAM, University "Mediterranea" of Reggio Calabria

(DISCUSSION PAPER)

Abstract. In this paper, we propose a new Social Network Analysis based approach to providing a multi-dimensional picture of the research scenarios of a set of countries of interest and to detecting possible "research hubs" operating therein. This knowledge allows innovation managers to understand the impact of different socio-economic conditions on the research level of a country. Furthermore, it may help the design of policies for supporting the accumulation of scientific and technological capabilities. In the last part of this paper, we apply our approach to four North African countries (i.e., Algeria, Egypt, Morocco and Tunisia) in such a way as to show its potential.

1 Introduction

In the last years, scientometrics and bibliometrics received a growing interest both in research literature and as objective ways for evaluating the performances of researchers, universities, institutions, etc. [12, 10, 9, 7, 3]. The obvious consequence of this fact is that more and more innovative approaches to supporting these activities have been recently proposed. Social Network Analysis [13] and, more in general, graph theory, represent a prominent family of approaches adopted in the past in this context (see, for instance, [4, 5, 8, 6, 2]). Furthermore, it is possible to foresee that they will be even more adopted in the future.

This paper aims at providing a contribution in this setting. Indeed, it proposes a new Social Network Analysis based approach to extracting knowledge about research scenarios and spillovers [11] or, better, hubs in a set of countries. As for this paper, a *hub* is a research institution that operates as a guide or stimulus to research in its country and, at the same time, is capable of stimulating cooperations with institutions of other countries. Our hub definition is fitted to the scenario of our interest and strongly benefits from the observations, suggestions and experience of innovation management researchers, who guided

* The authors thank Proff. Fabio Landini and Roberto Mavilia of the Invernizzi Center for Research on Innovation, Organization, Strategy and Entrepreneurship of University "Bocconi", who supplied data for experiments and cooperated in the analysis of results.

us in its formulation. Our approach is general and can be directly applied to any set of countries. The only requirement is to have at disposal the set of the publications of all the research institutions of the countries to investigate. In this paper, we applied it to four North African countries (e.g., Algeria, Egypt, Morocco and Tunisia), and we exploited all the publications of all the research institutions of the four countries of interest in the time interval $[2003, 2013]$, as stored in the Web of Science repository [1]. The most important support data structure is a social network whose nodes represent institutions and whose edges denote collaborations among institutions. Starting from it, other important support data structures and accompanying parameters (some of which were never defined in the literature) are introduced.

This paper is organized as follows. In Section 2, we illustrate our approach. In Section 3, we apply it to the four North African countries mentioned above. Finally, in Section 4, we draw our conclusions and overview some possible future developments.

2 Description of our approach

Our approach operates on a set *Pub* of publications at our disposal and on a set C of countries to investigate. It will be described in the next subsections.

2.1 Hub characterization and detection

In this section, we aim at defining a method for detecting both hubs and their features in a set of countries. For this purpose, we preliminarily introduce a first support data structure. It is a social network: $G = \langle N, E \rangle$. N is the set of the nodes of G. A node $n_i \in N$ corresponds to exactly one institution registered in our database. Since there is a biunivocal correspondence between a node of N and the corresponding institution, in the following, we will use the symbol n_i to indicate both of them. Each node of N is labeled with an element of C depending on the country of the corresponding institution. We indicate by l_i the label of n_i. E is the set of the edges of G. There exists an edge $e_{ij} = (n_i, n_j, w_{ij}) \in E$ if there exists at least one publication involving one author of n_i and one author of n_j. w_{ij} is the weight of e_{ij}; it denotes the number of publications having at least one researcher of n_i and one researcher of n_j among their authors. If a paper has more than one author of the same institution n_i, then there is a self-edge linking n_i with itself.

Now, we are able to introduce the concept of hub. With regard to this fact, we point out that we do not aim at proposing a new concept, characterized by a mathematical foundation supporting it. Instead, we would like to introduce an informal and empirical, yet reasonable, concept, which can support innovation managers to make their decisions. In carrying out this activity, we strongly benefited from the observations, suggestions and experience of innovation management researchers, who guided us in its formulation. Taking this purpose into account, we can say that, in order to be a hub, an institution must satisfy the following conditions: *(i)* C_1: it should have published *a very high number* of papers; *(ii)* C_2: it should have published *a high number* of papers in cooperation with institutions different from the ones of its country; *(iii)* C_3: it should have published *many papers* in cooperation with institutions of its country.

To "quantify" conditions C_1, C_2 and C_3, we use three metrics, namely M_1, M_2 and M_3, respectively. M_1 coincides with the classical weighted degree centrality, M_2 coincides with the normalized weighted degree centrality and M_3 is analogous to the E-I index [13].

As theoretically conjectured in the past literature, and as verified for the countries composing our case study, M_1, M_2 and M_3 follow a power law distribution. Taking all these considerations into account, the set $\mathcal{H}^X$ of hubs for the countries into consideration can be defined as the set of those institutions simultaneously belonging to the top $X\%$ of the institutions with the highest values of M_1, M_2 and M_3 (we call I_1^X, I_2^X and I_3^X these three sets, when considered separately). In this definition, X is a threshold allowing the selection of the institutions having the highest values of M_1, M_2 and M_3. The choice to use X as a threshold parameter derives from the power law distributions characterizing all the three metrics. Reasonable values of X could be 10, 15 and 20. After several experiments, we decided to consider a default value of X equal to 20. As a consequence, in the following, when X is not specified, we intend that it is equal to 20. Below, we use the symbol $\mathcal{H}_k^X$ to indicate the hubs of a given country k.

2.2 Investigation of the research scenarios

In this section, we aim at analyzing the research scenarios of the countries into examination. Initially, we can introduce three indicators that could give us some knowledge about the research scenarios of the countries into consideration. The first one, RQ, is an indicator of the overall research quality in the countries of interest. In fact, it measures how many institutions of I_1 belong to these countries. The second one, FC, indicates how many institutions, among the top ones of the countries of interest, publish many papers with foreign institutions. The third one, TP, indicates how many institutions that publish very much with foreign institutions belong to the top institutions of the countries of interest.

In the investigation of the research scenario of a country k and of the role of its hubs, it appears very interesting to analyze its paper distribution. For this purpose, we introduce the average number $AvgPub_k^{\mathcal{H}}$ of the publications of its hubs. Another interesting issue to investigate is to verify if a hub of k publishes more with institutions of k (we call "internal" the corresponding publications) than with foreign ones (we call "external" the corresponding publications) or alone. To carry out this investigation, we introduce: *(i)* the average number $AvgHubPub_k^I$ of publications performed by the hubs of k with institutions of k; *(ii)* the average number $AvgHubPub_k^F$ of publications performed by the hubs of k with foreign institutions; *(iii)* the average number $AvgHubPub_k^A$ of publications performed alone by the hubs of k (we call them "alone publications" in the following).

A further interesting analysis is devoted to understand if, in their cooperation with foreign institutions, the hubs of a given country k privilege one or few countries. For this purpose, we specialize to our research context the Herfindahl Index. This index is very used in economics. It is defined as the sum of the squares of the market shares of the firms within the industry, where market shares are expressed as fractions. It can range from 0.0 to 1.0, moving from a huge number of very small firms to a single monopolistic producer. In our case, we extend the Herfindahl index to our context and define the Herfindahl Index HI_k associated with the papers published by the hubs of k to verify if these hubs published in cooperation with institutions of few (implying high values of HI_k) or many (implying low values of HI_k) countries.

2.3 Cooperation among hubs of the same country

In this section, we aim at investigating the cooperation levels of the hubs of a given country k. For this purpose, we preliminarily define a support data structure called *clique social network*. In particular, let G be the social network defined in Section 2.1 and let G_k be its "projection" on the country k. Let $\mathcal{C}_k$ be the set of cliques of G_k and let $\mathcal{H}_k$ be the set of the hubs of k. A *clique social network* CG_k has a node for each hub of $\mathcal{H}_k$ belonging to at least one clique of $\mathcal{C}_k$. Each node n_i of CG_k has associated a weight w_i denoting the number of cliques of $\mathcal{C}_k$ which it belongs to. An edge (n_i, n_j) of CG_k denotes that n_i and n_j together belong to at least one clique of $\mathcal{C}_k$.

Some measures capable of quantitatively representing the differences that characterize the cooperation among hubs are the following: *(i)* the number of cliques $|\mathcal{C}_k|$; *(ii)* the absolute dimension $d_{\mathcal{C}_k}$ of the largest clique in $\mathcal{C}_k$; *(iii)* the relative dimension $\frac{d_{\mathcal{C}_k}}{|\mathcal{H}_k|}$ of the largest clique in $\mathcal{C}_k$; *(iv)* the fraction $f^{\mathcal{H}}_{\mathcal{C}_k}$ of hubs belonging to at least one clique of $\mathcal{C}_k$. In order to avoid that results are biased by the number of publications (which can be very different in the different countries of interest), we defined a normalized version $\widehat{CG_k}$ of CG_k. Finally, we searched for some measures to compare clique social networks. After several experiments, we found that the most significant ones were: *(i)* the number of nodes; *(ii)* the number of edges; *(iii)* density[4].

2.4 Investigation about the quality of publications

All indicators introduced above are based only on the number of publications. Actually, it would be important to take also their quality into account. One way to do this consists in taking their impact factor into consideration; another way consists in considering the number of citations received by papers. Impact factors are measured only for journal papers. As a consequence, if we want to exploit this measure, we must define a new support data structure. This structure, that we indicate by G', is, once again, a social network. It is defined as $G' = \langle N', E' \rangle$.

[4] Actually, this last measure can be derived from the two other ones. However, it is very expressing and, consequently, we decided to explicitly consider it.

There is a node $n_i \in N'$ for each institution having at least one author, who published at least one journal paper. An edge $e'_{ij} = (n'_i, n'_j, w'_{ij})$ has a semantics similar to the one of e_{ij} except that the weight $w'_{ij} = \sum_{p \in (Pub_{ij} \cap JPub)} IF_p$ considers both the number of publications performed by n_i and n_j simultaneously and the corresponding impact factors. Paper citations are valid both for conference proceedings and for journal papers. However, in order to make our analyses about the quality of publications homogeneous, we chose to investigate only journal papers. In this case, we used the same support social network as the one exploited for impact factors, but the edge weights w'_{ij} was computed as: $w'_{ij} = \sum_{p \in (Pub_{ij} \cap JPub)} CitN_p$, where $CitN_p$ is the number of citations of p.

2.5 Characterization of hub neighborhoods

A first parameter useful to characterize hub neighbors is the average number $AvgPub$ of publications of the hub neighborhoods. A second parameter regards their average dimension $AvgDim$. Even in this case, we disaggregate data per country, and we call $AvgDim_k$ the corresponding parameter for the country k.

A next analysis regards the cooperation level among the institutions belonging to hub neighborhoods. To perform this task, we define a new support social network. We call it *nbh social network* and we represent it by means of the symbol $NbhG_i$. Given a neighborhood nbh_i, the corresponding nbh social network is defined as follows: $nbhG_i = \langle nbh_i, nbhE_i \rangle$. There is a node in $NbhG_i$ for each node of nbh_i; there is an edge $(n_i, n_j) \in nbhE_i$ if there exists at least one publication between an author of n_i and an author of n_j.

After having introduced this social network, we define a first parameter on it. This parameter is called $AvgCFrac$ and corresponds to the average fraction of the real number of cliques existing in hub neighborhoods against their possible number. It is an indicator of the cooperation level among hubs. As usual, we call $AvgCFrac_k$ the "projection" of $AvgCFrac$ on the country k. A second parameter about intra-neighborhood cooperation regards the average fraction $AvgCNbh$ of the number of cliques existing in hub neighborhoods against the number of neighborhood nodes. Again, we call $AvgCNbh_k$ the "projection" of $AvgCNbh$ on the country k. A final parameter measuring the cooperation level among hub neighbors is the average density $AvgDens$ of the nbh social network. As usual, we call $AvgDens_k$ the "projection" of $AvgDens$ on the country k.

3 Application of our approach to four North African countries

As pointed out in the introduction, we applied our approach to four North African countries, namely Algeria, Egypt, Morocco and Tunisia. As a consequence, in our case study, the set C of the countries to investigate (see Section 2) consisted of the following elements: $C = \{$'A', 'E', 'M', 'T', 'O'$\}$, where 'A' (resp., 'E', 'M', 'T', 'O') stands for 'Algeria' (resp., 'Egypt', 'Morocco', 'Tunisia', 'Others'). Clearly, 'O' indicates all the countries different from the four into

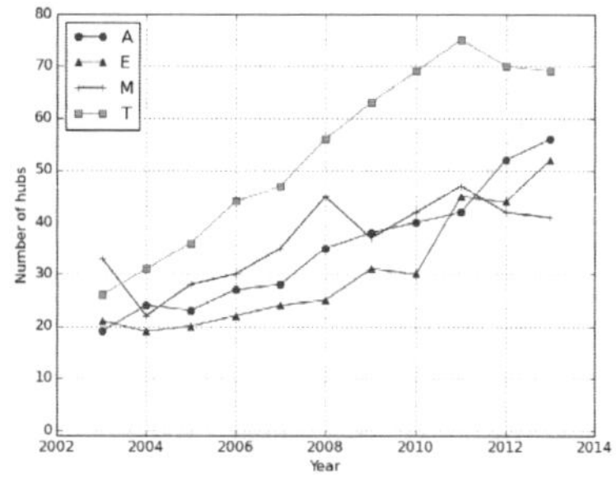

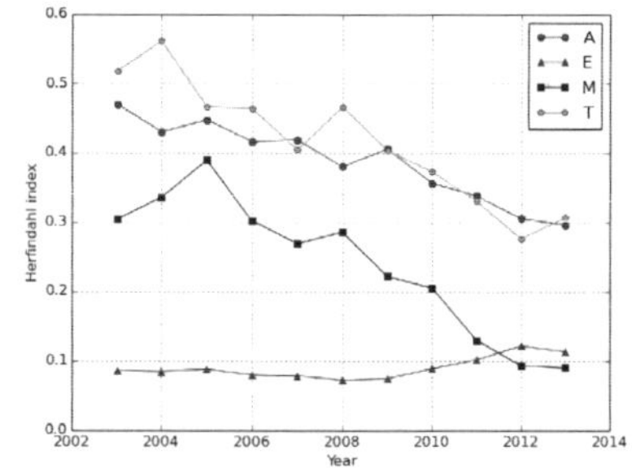

Fig. 1. Number of hubs for each country in the year interval [2003,2013]

Fig. 2. Herfindahl index over time for the four countries

examination. We chose these four countries because we had the possibility to access the corresponding data thanks to an academic partner that was carrying out a project aiming at investigating their research and innovation scenarios. Our dataset was stored in a MongoDB database. To give an idea of it, we report some of its features: *(i)* dimension = 10.27 GB; *(ii)* number of institutions = 278,696 ; *(iii)* number of authorships = 89,008,846; *(iv)* number of publications = 6,599,104; *(v)* number of research areas = 6; *(vi)* number of research fields = 251. Due to space limitations we can present only a very limited number of the results that we obtained.

In Figure 1, we report the variation of the number of hubs for each country. From the analysis of this figure, we can see that the country with the highest number of hubs is Tunisia. This result was unexpected also because both the extension and the number of citizens of Tunisia were smaller than the ones of the other three countries.

In Figure 2, we report the Herfindahl index HI_k for the four countries. From the analysis of this figure we can observe that Tunisia and Algeria have a high Herfindahl index, which implies that their hubs cooperate mostly with one or few countries. In particular, after some investigations, we have seen that Tunisia and Algeria cooperate mostly with France, which is reasonable if we consider that they are French past colonies. By contrast, Egypt has a very low Herfindahl index, i.e., its hubs cooperate with many countries. An interesting trend is the one of Morocco; in fact, it initially has a behavior like the ones of Tunisia and Algeria, whereas, in the last years, it shows a behavior like the one of Egypt.

To determine the cooperation levels among hubs for the four North African countries into consideration, for each country k, we performed the following tasks: *(i)* we considered the two time intervals $[2003, 2009]$ and $[2007, 2013]$; *(ii)* we computed the clique social networks $CG1_k$ (resp., $CG2_k$), corresponding to the first and the second time intervals, respectively; *(iii)* we measured the four parameters introduced in Section 2.2 for quantitatively evaluating clique social networks. Obtained results for the first time interval are reported in Table 1.

Country	$\lvert C1_k \rvert$	$d1_{C_k}$	$\frac{d1_{C_k}}{\lvert \mathcal{H}_k \rvert}$	$f1^{\mathcal{H}}_{C_k}$
Algeria	292	7	0.152	0.913
Egypt	38	13	0.351	0.973
Tunisia	130	8	0.116	0.942
Morocco	82	7	0.127	0.818

Table 1. Quantitative differences characterizing the cooperation behaviors of hubs in the four countries of interest in the time interval [2003, 2009]

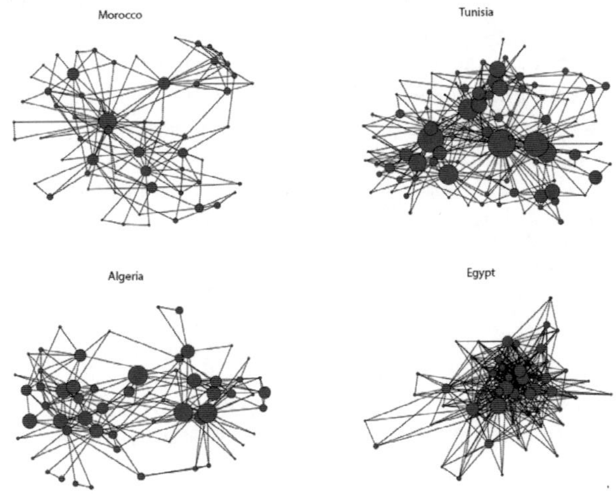

Fig. 3. Graphs $CG2_k$ for all the four countries

From the analysis of this table we can draw the following conclusions: *(i)* Egypt has the largest clique; this clique is much larger than the maximum cliques of the other countries; *(ii)* in Egypt almost all hubs belong to at least one clique. These results indicate that Egyptian hubs are more prone to cooperation than the hubs of the other countries.

In Figure 3, we report the graphs $CG2_k$ for all the four countries; in these graphs the dimension of nodes is proportional to the corresponding weight, i.e., to the number of cliques they belong to. The analysis of this figure confirms the previous conjecture; in fact, the number of edges in the Egyptian graph is much higher than in the other graphs. This fact, along with the presence of many not very large nodes, allows us to derive another important knowledge pattern, i.e., that research activities in Egypt are more "distributed" among hubs.

4 Conclusion

In this paper, we have proposed a new Social Network Analysis based approach to investigating the research scenarios of a set of countries of interest and to detecting possible hubs operating in these countries. Extracted knowledge allows the evaluation of the impact of different socio-economic conditions on research and favors the design of policies for supporting innovation in the countries of interest. We applied our approach to four North African countries. In the future, we plan to exploit techniques for analyzing information diffusion in social networks to understand how the possible mobility of top researchers from one institution to another can impact on the quality of both of them. Moreover, we plan to investigate the possible application of classification techniques to derive hub profiles in different countries. Furthermore, it is necessary to consider that a network changes over time. As a consequence, hubs could also change over time. The evolution of an institution's capability of becoming hub, remaining hub or no longer being a hub is a challenging task that we plan to investigate. Finally, we plan to analyze the possible application of prediction techniques to understand what kind of financial investment must be performed for maximizing the increase of both the number and the quality of hubs and publications in the countries of interest.

References

1. Web Of Science. `http://wokinfo.com/`, 2017.
2. A. Abbasi, L. Hossain, and L. Leydesdorff. Betweenness centrality as a driver of preferential attachment in the evolution of research collaboration networks. *Journal of Informetrics*, 6 (3):403–412, 2012.
3. J. Adams, K. Gurney, D. Hook, and L. Leydesdorff. International collaboration clusters in Africa. *Scientometrics*, 98(1):547–556, 2014. Springer.
4. T. Arif, R. Ali, and M. Asger. Scientific co-authorship social networks: A case study of computer science scenario in India. *Science*, 52 (12):38–45, 2012.
5. K. Badar, J.M. Hite, and Y.F. Badir. Examining the relationship of co-authorship network centrality and gender on academic research performance: the case of chemistry researchers in Pakistan. *Scientometrics*, 94 (2):755–775, 2013. Elsevier.
6. M. Bordons, J. Aparicio, B. González-Albo, and A.A. Díaz-Faes. The relationship between the research performance of scientists and their position in co-authorship networks in three fields. *Journal of Informetrics*, 9 (1):135–144, 2015.
7. K. Börner, L. dell'Asta, W. Ke, and A. Vespignani. Studying the emerging global brain: Analyzing and visualizing the impact of co-authorship teams. *Complexity*, 10 (4):57–67, 2005.
8. J. Kim and C. Perez. Co-authorship network analysis in industrial ecology research community. *Journal of Industrial Ecology*, 19 (2):222–235, 2015.
9. F. Landini, F. Malerba, and R. Mavilia. The structure and dynamics of networks of scientific collaborations in Northern Africa. *Scientometrics*, 105(3):1787–1807, 2015. Elsevier.
10. P. Liu and H. Xia. Structure and evolution of co-authorship network in an interdisciplinary research field. *Scientometrics*, 103 (1):101–134, 2015.
11. F. Montobbio and V. Sterzi. Inventing together: exploring the nature of international knowledge spillovers in Latin America. *Journal of Evolutionary Economics*, 21(1):53–89, 2011. Springer.
12. J. Singh. Distributed R&D, cross-regional knowledge integration and quality of innovative output. *Research Policy*, 37(1):77–96, 2008. Elsevier.
13. S. Wasserman and K. Faust. *Social network analysis: Methods and applications.* 1994. Cambridge University Press.

A Decidable Very Expressive n-ary Description Logic for Database Applications (extended abstract)

Alessandro Artale, Enrico Franconi, Rafael Peñaloza, Francesco Sportelli

KRDB Research Centre, Free University of Bozen-Bolzano, Italy
{artale, franconi, penaloza, sportelli}@inf.unibz.it

Abstract. We introduce $\mathcal{DLR}^+$, an extension of the n-ary propositionally closed description logic $\mathcal{DLR}$ to deal with attribute-labelled tuples (generalising the positional notation), projections of relations, and global and local objectification of relations, able to express inclusion, functional, key, and external uniqueness dependencies. The logic is equipped with both TBox and ABox axioms forming a $\mathcal{DLR}^+$ knowledge base (KB). We show how a simple syntactic restriction on the appearance of projections sharing common attributes in the KB makes reasoning in the language decidable with the same computational complexity as $\mathcal{DLR}$. The obtained $\mathcal{DLR}^{\pm}$ n-ary description logic is able to encode more thoroughly conceptual data models such as EER, UML, and ORM.

1 Introduction

We introduce the new description logic (DL) $\mathcal{DLR}^+$ extending the n-ary DL $\mathcal{DLR}$ [Calvanese *et al.*, 2008], in order to capture more database oriented constraints. While $\mathcal{DLR}$ is an expressive logic, it lacks a number of expressive means that can be added without increasing the complexity of reasoning—when used in a carefully controlled way. The added expressivity is motivated by the increasingly use of DLs as an abstract conceptual layer over relational databases, both to reason over such conceptual models during the database design phase, and to answer ontology-mediated queries over databases.

A $\mathcal{DLR}$ TBox can express axioms involving (i) propositional combinations of concepts and (compatible) n-ary relations, (ii) concepts as unary projections of n-ary relations, and (iii) relations with a component selected to be of a certain type. For example, if Pilot and RacingCar are concepts and DrivesCar, DrivesMotobike, DrivesVehicle are binary relations, we can write the following axioms:

$$\texttt{Pilot} \sqsubseteq \exists[1]\sigma_{2:\texttt{RacingCar}}\texttt{DrivesCar}$$
$$\texttt{DrivesCar} \sqcup \texttt{DrivesMotobike} \sqsubseteq \texttt{DrivesVehicle}\ .$$

$\mathcal{DLR}^+$ extends $\mathcal{DLR}$ in the following way.

- While $\mathcal{DLR}$ instances of n-ary relations are n-tuples of objects—whose components are identified by their position in the tuple—instances of relations in $\mathcal{DLR}^+$ are *attribute-labelled tuples*, i.e., tuples where each component is identified by an attribute and not by its position in the tuple (see, e.g., [Kanellakis, 1990]). For example, the relation Employee may have the signature:
  $$\texttt{Employee}(\texttt{firstname}, \texttt{lastname}, \texttt{dept}, \texttt{deptAddr})\ ,$$
  and an instance of Employee could be the tuple:
  $$\langle \texttt{firstname}:\texttt{John}, \texttt{lastname}:\texttt{Doe}, \texttt{dept}:\texttt{Purchase}, \texttt{deptAddr}:\texttt{London}\rangle\ .$$
- Attributes can be *renamed*, also with the goal to recover the positional perspectives on relations: $\texttt{firstname}, \texttt{lastname}, \texttt{dept}, \texttt{deptAddr} \rightleftarrows 1,2,3,4$.

– *Relation projections* allow to form new relations by projecting a given relation on some of its attributes. For example, if Person is a relation with signature Person (name, surname), it could be related to Employee as follows:
$\exists[\mathtt{firstname}, \mathtt{lastname}]\mathtt{Employee} \sqsubseteq \mathtt{Person}$
$\mathtt{firstname}, \mathtt{lastname} \rightleftarrows \mathtt{name}, \mathtt{surname}$.
– The *objectification* of a relation (also known as *reification*) is a concept whose instances are unique identifiers of the tuples instantiating the relation. Those identifiers could be unique only within an objectified relation (*local objectification*), or they could be uniquely identifying tuples independently on the relation they are instance of (*global objectification*). For example, the concept EmployeeC could be the global objectification of the relation Employee, assuming that there is a global one-to-one correspondence between pairs of values of the attributes firstname, lastname and EmployeeC instances:
$\mathtt{EmployeeC} \equiv \circledcirc\, \exists[\mathtt{firstname}, \mathtt{lastname}]\mathtt{Employee}$.
As an example of local objectification, let us consider the two (ternary) relations OwnsCar (name, surname, car) and DrivesCar (name, surname, car), and assume that anybody driving a car also owns it; that is, $\mathtt{DrivesCar} \sqsubseteq \mathtt{OwnsCar}$. The locally objectified events of driving a car and owning a car, defined by the axioms $\mathtt{CarDrivingEvent} \equiv \odot\, \mathtt{DrivesCar}$ and $\mathtt{CarOwningEvent} \equiv \odot\, \mathtt{OwnsCar}$, model the fact that a driving event by a person of a car is not necessarily the owning event by the same person and the same car. Indeed, they should be disjoint: $\mathtt{CarDrivingEvent} \sqcap \mathtt{CarOwningEvent} \sqsubseteq \bot$ should hold.

It turns out that $\mathcal{DLR}^+$ is an expressive description logic able to assert relevant constraints in the context of relational databases. In Section 3 we consider *inclusion dependencies*, *functional and key dependencies*, *external uniqueness* and *identification* axioms. For example, $\mathcal{DLR}^+$ can express the fact that the attributes firstname, lastname play the role of a multi-attribute key for the relation Employee:

$\exists[\mathtt{firstname}, \mathtt{lastname}]\mathtt{Employee} \sqsubseteq \exists^{\leqslant 1}[\mathtt{firstname}, \mathtt{lastname}]\mathtt{Employee}$,

and that the attribute deptAddr functionally depends on the attribute dept within the relation Employee:

$\exists[\mathtt{dept}]\mathtt{Employee} \sqsubseteq \exists^{\leqslant 1}[\mathtt{dept}]\,(\exists[\mathtt{dept}, \mathtt{deptAddr}]\mathtt{Employee})$.

While $\mathcal{DLR}^+$ turns out to be undecidable, in this paper we show how a simple syntactic condition on the appearance of projections sharing common attributes in the knowledge base makes the language decidable. The result of this restriction is a new language called $\mathcal{DLR}^{\pm}$. We prove that $\mathcal{DLR}^{\pm}$, while preserving most of the $\mathcal{DLR}^+$ expressivity, has a reasoning problem whose complexity does not increase w.r.t. the computational complexity of the basic $\mathcal{DLR}$ language. We also present in Section 5 the implementation of an API for the reasoning services in $\mathcal{DLR}^{\pm}$.

2 The Description Logic $\mathcal{DLR}^+$

A $\mathcal{DLR}^+$ *signature* is a tuple $\mathcal{L} = (\mathcal{C}, \mathcal{R}, \mathcal{O}, \mathcal{U}, \tau)$ where $\mathcal{C}$, $\mathcal{R}$, $\mathcal{O}$ and $\mathcal{U}$ are finite, mutually disjoint sets of *concept names*, *relation names*, *individual names*, and *attributes*, respectively, and τ is a *relation signature* function, associating a set of attributes to each relation name $\tau(RN) = \{U_1, \ldots, U_n\} \subseteq \mathcal{U}$ with $n \geqslant 2$.

The syntax of concepts C, relations R, formulas φ, and attribute renaming axioms ϑ is given in Figure 1, where $CN \in \mathcal{C}$, $RN \in \mathcal{R}$, $U \in \mathcal{U}$, $o \in \mathcal{O}$, q is a positive integer and $2 \leqslant k < \text{ARITY}(R)$. The *arity* of a relation R is the number of the attributes in its signature; i.e., $\text{ARITY}(R) = |\tau(R)|$, where we extend the signature function τ to arbitrary relations

$$
\begin{array}{lll}
C & \rightarrow & \top \mid \bot \mid CN \mid \neg C \mid C_1 \sqcap C_2 \mid C_1 \sqcup C_2 \mid \exists^{\lessgtr q}[U_i]R \mid \circledcirc R \mid \odot RN \\
R & \rightarrow & RN \mid R_1 \backslash R_2 \mid R_1 \sqcap R_2 \mid R_1 \sqcup R_2 \mid \sigma_{U_i:C} R \mid \exists^{\lessgtr q}[U_1,\ldots,U_k]R \\
\varphi & \rightarrow & C_1 \sqsubseteq C_2 \mid R_1 \sqsubseteq R_2 \mid CN(o) \mid RN(U_1{:}o_1,\ldots,U_n{:}o_n) \mid o_1 = o_2 \mid o_1 \neq o_2 \\
\vartheta & \rightarrow & U_1 \rightleftarrows U_2
\end{array}
$$

Fig. 1. Syntax of $\mathcal{DLR}^+$.

$$
\begin{array}{rll}
\tau(R_1 \backslash R_2) = & \tau(R_1) & \text{if } \tau(R_1) = \tau(R_2) \\
\tau(R_1 \sqcap R_2) = & \tau(R_1) & \text{if } \tau(R_1) = \tau(R_2) \\
\tau(R_1 \sqcup R_2) = & \tau(R_1) & \text{if } \tau(R_1) = \tau(R_2) \\
\tau(\sigma_{U_i:C} R) = & \tau(R) & \text{if } U_i \in \tau(R) \\
\tau(\exists^{\lessgtr q}[U_1,\ldots,U_k]R) = & \{U_1,\ldots,U_k\} & \text{if } \{U_1,\ldots,U_k\} \subset \tau(R) \\
\tau(R) = & \varnothing & \text{otherwise}
\end{array}
$$

Fig. 2. The signature of $\mathcal{DLR}^+$ relations.

as specified in Figure 2. Notice that, while global objectification ($\circledcirc R$) can be applied to arbitrary relations, local ones ($\odot RN$) can be applied just to relation names. We use the shortcut $\exists[U_1,\ldots,U_k]R$ for $\exists^{\geqslant 1}[U_1,\ldots,U_k]R$ for $k \geqslant 1$.

A $\mathcal{DLR}^+$ *TBox* $\mathcal{T}$ is a finite set of *concept inclusion* axioms of the form $C_1 \sqsubseteq C_2$ and *relation inclusion* axioms of the form $R_1 \sqsubseteq R_2$. We use $X_1 \equiv X_2$ as a shortcut for $X_1 \sqsubseteq X_2$ and $X_2 \sqsubseteq X_1$. A $\mathcal{DLR}^+$ *ABox* $\mathcal{A}$ is a finite set of *concept instance* axioms of the form $CN(o)$, *relation instance* axioms of the form $RN(U_1{:}o_1,\ldots,U_n{:}o_n)$, and *same/distinct individual* axioms of the form $o_1 = o_2$ and $o_1 \neq o_2$, with $o_i \in \mathcal{O}$. Restricting ABox axioms to concept and relation names only does not affect the expressivity of $\mathcal{DLR}^+$ due to the availability of TBox axioms.

A set of renaming axioms forms a *renaming schema*, inducing an equivalence relation $(\rightleftarrows, \mathcal{U})$ over the attributes $\mathcal{U}$, providing a partition of $\mathcal{U}$ into equivalence classes each one representing alternative ways to name attributes. We write $[U]_{\Re}$ to denote the equivalence class of the attribute U w.r.t. the equivalence relation $(\rightleftarrows, \mathcal{U})$. We allow only *well founded* renaming schemas, i.e., there is no equivalence class containing two attributes from the same relation signature. We use the shortcut $U_1 \ldots U_n \rightleftarrows U'_1 \ldots U'_n$ to group many renaming axioms with the meaning that $U_i \rightleftarrows U'_i$ for all $i = 1,\ldots,n$.

The renaming schema reconciles the named attribute and the positional perspectives on relations. They are crucial when expressing both inclusion axioms and set operators ($\sqcap$, $\sqcup$, $\backslash$) between relations, which make sense only over *union compatible* relations. Two relations R_1, R_2 are union compatible if their signatures are equal up to the attribute renaming induced by the renaming schema $\Re$; that is, $\tau(R_1) = \{U_1,\ldots,U_n\}$ and $\tau(R_2) = \{V_1,\ldots,V_n\}$ have the same arity n and $[U_i]_{\Re} = [V_i]_{\Re}$ for each $1 \leqslant i \leqslant n$. Notice that through the renaming schema relations can use just local attribute names that can then be renamed when composing relations. Also note that it is obviously possible for the same attribute to appear in the signature of different relations.

A $\mathcal{DLR}^+$ knowledge base (KB) $\mathcal{KB} = (\mathcal{T}, \mathcal{A}, \Re)$ is composed by a TBox $\mathcal{T}$, an ABox $\mathcal{A}$, and a renaming schema $\Re$.

Example 1. Consider the relation names R_1, R_2 where $\tau(R_1) = \{W_1, W_2, W_3, W_4\}$, $\tau(R_2) = \{V_1, V_2, V_3, V_4, V_5\}$, and the renaming axiom $W_1W_2W_3 \rightleftarrows V_3V_4V_5$. The TBox $\mathcal{T}_{\mathsf{exa}}$ consists of the axioms:

$$\exists[W_1, W_2]R_1 \sqsubseteq \exists^{\leqslant 1}[W_1, W_2]R_1 \tag{1}$$

$$\exists[V_3, V_4]R_2 \sqsubseteq \exists^{\leqslant 1}[V_3, V_4](\exists[V_3, V_4, V_5]R_2) \tag{2}$$

$$
\begin{aligned}
\top^{\mathcal{I}} &= \Delta \\
\bot^{\mathcal{I}} &= \varnothing \\
(\neg C)^{\mathcal{I}} &= \top^{\mathcal{I}} \backslash C^{\mathcal{I}} \\
(C_1 \sqcap C_2)^{\mathcal{I}} &= C_1^{\mathcal{I}} \cap C_2^{\mathcal{I}} \\
(C_1 \sqcup C_2)^{\mathcal{I}} &= C_1^{\mathcal{I}} \cup C_2^{\mathcal{I}} \\
(\exists^{\lesseqgtr q}[U_i]R)^{\mathcal{I}} &= \{d \in \Delta \mid \left|\{t \in R^{\mathcal{I}} \mid t[\rho(U_i)] = d\}\right| \lesseqgtr q\} \\
(\circledcirc R)^{\mathcal{I}} &= \{d \in \Delta \mid d = \imath(t) \wedge t \in R^{\mathcal{I}}\} \\
(\odot RN)^{\mathcal{I}} &= \{d \in \Delta \mid d = \ell_{RN}(t) \wedge t \in RN^{\mathcal{I}}\} \\
(R_1 \backslash R_2)^{\mathcal{I}} &= R_1^{\mathcal{I}} \backslash R_2^{\mathcal{I}} \\
(R_1 \sqcap R_2)^{\mathcal{I}} &= R_1^{\mathcal{I}} \cap R_2^{\mathcal{I}} \\
(R_1 \sqcup R_2)^{\mathcal{I}} &= \{t \in R_1^{\mathcal{I}} \cup R_2^{\mathcal{I}} \mid \rho(\tau(R_1)) = \rho(\tau(R_2))\} \\
(\sigma_{U_i:C} R)^{\mathcal{I}} &= \{t \in R^{\mathcal{I}} \mid t[\rho(U_i)] \in C^{\mathcal{I}}\} \\
(\exists^{\lesseqgtr q}[U_1, \dots, U_k]R)^{\mathcal{I}} &= \{\langle \rho(U_1) : d_1, \dots, \rho(U_k) : d_k \rangle \in T_\Delta(\{\rho(U_1), \dots, \rho(U_k)\}) \mid \\
& \quad 1 \leqslant \left|\{t \in R^{\mathcal{I}} \mid t[\rho(U_1)] = d_1, \dots, t[\rho(U_k)] = d_k\}\right| \lesseqgtr q\}
\end{aligned}
$$

Fig. 3. Semantics of $\mathcal{DLR}^+$ expressions.

$$\exists[W_1, W_2, W_3]R_1 \sqsubseteq \exists[V_3, V_4, V_5]R_2. \tag{3}$$

Intuitively, the axiom (1) expresses that W_1, W_2 form a multi-attribute key for R_1; (2) introduces a functional dependency in the relation R_2 where the attribute V_5 is functionally dependent from attributes V_3, V_4, and (3) states an inclusion between two projections of the relation names R_1, R_2 based on the renaming schema axiom.

The semantics of $\mathcal{DLR}^+$ is based on *labelled tuples* over a domain Δ: a $\mathcal{U}$*-labelled tuple over* Δ (or *tuple* for short) is a function $t\colon \mathcal{U} \to \Delta$. For $U \in \mathcal{U}$, we write $t[U]$ to refer to the domain element $d \in \Delta$ labelled by U, if the function t is defined for U—that is, if the attribute U is a label of the tuple t. Given $d_1, \dots, d_n \in \Delta$, the expression $\langle U_1 \colon d_1, \dots, U_n \colon d_n \rangle$ stands for the tuple t such that $t[U_i] = d_i$, for $1 \leqslant 1 \leqslant n$. The *projection* of the tuple t over the attributes $U_1, \dots, U_k$ (i.e., the function t restricted to be undefined for the labels not in $U_1, \dots, U_k$) is denoted by $t[U_1, \dots, U_k]$. The relation signature function τ can be applied also to labelled tuples to obtain the set of labels on which the tuple is defined. $T_\Delta(\mathcal{U})$ denotes the set of all $\mathcal{U}$-labelled tuples over Δ.

A $\mathcal{DLR}^+$ *interpretation* is a tuple $\mathcal{I} = (\Delta, \cdot^{\mathcal{I}}, \rho, \imath, L)$ consisting of a nonempty *domain* Δ, an *interpretation function* $\cdot^{\mathcal{I}}$, a *renaming function* ρ, a *global objectification function* $\imath$, and a family L containing one *local objectification function* ℓ_{RN_i} for each named relation $RN_i \in \mathcal{R}$.

The renaming function ρ is a total function $\rho\colon\mathcal{U} \to \mathcal{U}$ representing a canonical renaming for all attributes. We use $\rho(\{U_1, \dots, U_k\})$ to denote $\{\rho(U_1), \dots, \rho(U_k)\}$. The global objectification function is an injective function, $\imath\colon T_\Delta(\mathcal{U}) \to \Delta$, associating a *unique* global identifier to each tuple. The local objectification functions, ℓ_{RN_i} : $T_\Delta(\mathcal{U}) \to \Delta$, are associated to each relation name in the signature, and as the global objectification function they are injective: they associate an identifier—which is guaranteed to be unique only within the interpretation of a relation name—to each tuple. The interpretation function $\cdot^{\mathcal{I}}$ assigns a domain element to each individual $o^{\mathcal{I}} \in \Delta$, a set of domain elements to each concept name $CN^{\mathcal{I}} \subseteq \Delta$, and a set of $\mathcal{U}$-labelled tuples over Δ to each relation name conforming with its signature and to the renaming function $RN^{\mathcal{I}} \subseteq T_\Delta(\{\rho(U) \mid U \in \tau(RN)\})$. Note that the unique name assumption is not enforced. The interpretation function $\cdot^{\mathcal{I}}$ is unambiguously extended over concept and relation expressions as specified in Figure 3.

The interpretation $\mathcal{I}$ satisfies the concept inclusion axiom $C_1 \sqsubseteq C_2$ if $C_1^{\mathcal{I}} \subseteq C_2^{\mathcal{I}}$, and the relation inclusion axiom $R_1 \sqsubseteq R_2$ if $R_1^{\mathcal{I}} \subseteq R_2^{\mathcal{I}}$. It satisfies the concept instance axiom $CN(o)$ if $o^{\mathcal{I}} \in CN^{\mathcal{I}}$, the relation instance axiom $RN(U_1{:}o_1, \ldots, U_n{:}o_n)$ if $\langle \rho(U_1) : o_1^{\mathcal{I}}, \ldots, \rho(U_n) : o_n^{\mathcal{I}} \rangle \in RN^{\mathcal{I}}$, and the axioms $o_1 = o_2$ and $o_1 \neq o_2$ if $o_1^{\mathcal{I}} = o_2^{\mathcal{I}}$, and $o_1^{\mathcal{I}} \neq o_2^{\mathcal{I}}$, respectively. $\mathcal{I}$ satisfies a renaming schema $\Re$ if for every $U, V \in \mathcal{U}$, (i) $\rho(U) \in [U]_{\Re}$, and (ii) if $V \in [U]_{\Re}$, then $\rho(U) = \rho(V)$. $\mathcal{I}$ is a *model* of the KB $(\mathcal{T}, \mathcal{A}, \Re)$ if it satisfies the axioms in the TBox $\mathcal{T}$, in the ABox $\mathcal{A}$, and the renaming schema $\Re$.

KB satisfiability refers to the problem of deciding the existence of a model of a given KB; *concept satisfiability* (resp. *relation satisfiability*) is the problem of deciding whether there is a model of the KB with a non-empty interpretation of a given concept (resp. relation). A KB *entails* (or *logically implies*) an axiom if all models of the KB are also models of the axiom. For instance, the TBox in Example 1 entails that axiom (2) is redundant since V_3, V_4 are a key for R_2: $\mathcal{T}_{\mathsf{exa}} \models \exists[V_3, V_4]R_2 \sqsubseteq \exists^{\leqslant 1}[V_3, V_4]R_2$.

3 Expressiveness of $\mathcal{DLR}^+$

$\mathcal{DLR}^+$ is an expressive description logic able to assert relevant constraints in the context of relational databases, such as *inclusion dependencies* (inclusion axioms among arbitrary projections of relations), *equijoins*, *functional dependency* axioms, *key* axioms, *external uniqueness* axioms, *identification* axioms, and *path functional dependencies*.

An *equijoin* among two relations with disjoint signatures is the set of all combinations of tuples in the relations that are equal on their selected attribute names. Let R_1, R_2 be relations with $\tau(R_1) = \{U, U_1, \ldots, U_{n_1}\}$ and $\tau(R_2) = \{V, V_1, \ldots, V_{n_2}\}$; their equijoin over U and V is the relation $R = R_1 \underset{U=V}{\bowtie} R_2$ that uses the signature $\tau(R) = \tau(R_1) \cup \tau(R_2) \backslash \{V\}$, and is expressed by the $\mathcal{DLR}^+$ axioms:

$$\exists[U, U_1, \ldots, U_{n_1}]R \equiv \sigma_{U:(\exists[U]R_1 \sqcap \exists[V]R_2)} R_1$$
$$\exists[V, V_1, \ldots, V_{n_2}]R \equiv \sigma_{V:(\exists[U]R_1 \sqcap \exists[V]R_2)} R_2$$
$$U \rightleftarrows V \ .$$

A *functional dependency* axiom $(R : U_1 \ldots U_j \rightarrow U)$ (also called *internal uniqueness* axiom [Halpin and Morgan, 2008]) states that the values of the attributes $U_1 \ldots U_j$ uniquely determine the value of the attribute U in the relation R. Formally, the interpretation $\mathcal{I}$ satisfies this functional dependency axiom if, for all tuples $s, t \in R^{\mathcal{I}}$, $s[U_1] = t[U_1], \ldots, s[U_j] = t[U_j]$ imply $s[U] = t[U]$. Functional dependencies can be expressed in $\mathcal{DLR}^+$, assuming that $\{U_1, \ldots, U_j, U\} \subseteq \tau(R)$, with the axiom:

$$\exists[U_1, \ldots, U_j]R \sqsubseteq \exists^{\leqslant 1}[U_1, \ldots, U_j](\exists[U_1, \ldots, U_j, U]R).$$

A special case of functional dependencies are *key* axioms $(R : U_1 \ldots U_j \rightarrow R)$, which state that the values of the key attributes $U_1 \ldots U_j$ of a relation R uniquely identify tuples in R. A key axiom can be expressed in $\mathcal{DLR}^+$, assuming that $\{U_1 \ldots U_j\} \subseteq \tau(R)$, with the axiom:

$$\exists[U_1, \ldots, U_j]R \sqsubseteq \exists^{\leqslant 1}[U_1, \ldots, U_j]R \ .$$

The *external uniqueness* axiom $([U^1]R_1 \downarrow \ldots \downarrow [U^h]R_h)$ states that the join R of the relations $R_1, \ldots, R_h$ via the attributes $U^1, \ldots, U^h$ has the joined attribute functionally dependent on all the others [Halpin and Morgan, 2008]. This can be expressed in $\mathcal{DLR}^+$ with the axioms:

$$R \equiv R_1 \underset{U^1=U^2}{\bowtie} \cdots \underset{U^{h-1}=U^h}{\bowtie} R_h$$
$$R : U_1^1, \ldots, U_{n_1}^1, \ldots, U_1^h, \ldots, U_{n_h}^h \rightarrow U^1$$

where $\tau(R_i) = \{U^i, U^i_1, \ldots, U^i_{n_i}\}, 1 \leqslant i \leqslant h$, and R a new relation name with signature $\tau(R) = \{U^1, U^1_1, \ldots, U^1_{n_1}, \ldots, U^h_1, \ldots, U^h_{n_h}\}$.

Identification axioms as defined in $\mathcal{DLR}_{ifd}$ [Calvanese *et al.*, 2001] (an extension of $\mathcal{DLR}$ with functional dependencies and identification axioms) are a variant of external uniqueness axioms, constraining only the elements of a concept C; they can be expressed in $\mathcal{DLR}^+$ with the axiom:

$[U^1]\sigma_{U_1:C}R_1 \downarrow \ldots \downarrow [U^h]\sigma_{U_h:C}R_h$.

Path functional dependencies—as defined in the DL family $\mathcal{CFD}$ [Toman and Weddell, 2009]—can be expressed in $\mathcal{DLR}^+$ as identification axioms involving joined sequences of functional binary relations. $\mathcal{DLR}^+$ also captures *tree-based identification constraint (tid)* introduced in [Calvanese *et al.*, 2014] to capture fds in *DL-Lite*$_{RDFS,tid}$.

The rich set of constructors in $\mathcal{DLR}^+$ allows us to extend the known mappings in description logics of popular conceptual data models. The EER mapping as introduced in [Artale *et al.*, 2007] can be extended to deal with multi-attribute keys (by using identification axioms) and named roles in relations; the ORM mapping as introduced in [Franconi *et al.*, 2012; Sportelli and Franconi, 2016] can be extended to deal with arbitrary subset and exclusive relation constructs (by using inclusions among global objectifications of projections of relations), arbitrary internal and external uniqueness constraints, arbitrary frequency constraints (by using projections), local objectification, named roles in relations, and fact type readings (by using renaming axioms); the UML mapping as introduced in [Berardi *et al.*, 2005] can be fixed to deal properly with association classes (by using local objectification) and named roles in associations.

4 The $\mathcal{DLR}^\pm$ fragment of $\mathcal{DLR}^+$

Since a $\mathcal{DLR}^+$ KB can express inclusions and functional dependencies, the reasoning is undecidable [Chandra and Vardi, 1985]. In this section we present $\mathcal{DLR}^\pm$, a decidable syntactic fragment of $\mathcal{DLR}^+$ limiting the co-occurence of relation projections in a KB.

Given a $\mathcal{DLR}^+$ knowledge base $(\mathcal{T}, \mathcal{A}, \mathfrak{R})$, the *projection signature* is the set $\mathscr{T}$ containing the signatures $\tau(RN)$ of the relations $RN \in \mathcal{R}$, the singleton sets associated with each attribute name $U \in \mathcal{U}$, and the relation signatures that appear explicitly in projection constructs in some axiom from $\mathcal{T}$, together with their implicit occurrences due to the renaming schema. Formally, $\mathscr{T}$ is the smallest set where (i) $\tau(RN) \in \mathscr{T}$ for all $RN \in \mathcal{R}$; (ii) $\{U\} \in \mathscr{T}$ for all $U \in \mathcal{U}$; and (iii) $\{U_1, \ldots, U_k\} \in \mathscr{T}$ for all $\exists^{\lesseqgtr q}[V_1, \ldots, V_k]R$ appearing as sub-formulas in $\mathcal{T}$ and $\{U_i, V_i\} \subseteq [U_i]_{\mathfrak{R}}$ for $1 \leqslant i \leqslant k$.

The *projection signature graph* is the directed acyclic graph $(\supset, \mathscr{T})$ whose sinks are the attribute singletons $\{U\}$. Given a set of attributes $\tau = \{U_1, \ldots, U_k\} \subseteq \mathcal{U}$, the *projection signature graph dominated by* τ, denoted as $\mathscr{T}_\tau$, is the sub-graph of $(\supset, \mathscr{T})$ containing all the nodes reachable from τ. Given two sets of attributes $\tau_1, \tau_2 \subseteq \mathcal{U}$, $\text{PATH}_{\mathscr{T}}(\tau_1, \tau_2)$ denotes the set of paths in $(\supset, \mathscr{T})$ between τ_1 and τ_2. Notice that $\text{PATH}_{\mathscr{T}}(\tau_1, \tau_2) = \varnothing$ both when a path does not exist and when $\tau_1 \subseteq \tau_2$. The notation $\text{CHILD}_{\mathscr{T}}(\tau_1, \tau_2)$ means that τ_2 is a child of τ_1 in $(\supset, \mathscr{T})$. We now introduce $\mathcal{DLR}^\pm$.

Definition 1. *A* $\mathcal{DLR}^\pm$ knowledge base *is a* $\mathcal{DLR}^+$ *knowledge base that satisfies the following syntactic conditions:*

1. *the projection signature graph* $(\supset, \mathscr{T})$ *is a multitree: i.e., for every node* $\tau \in \mathscr{T}$, *the graph* $\mathscr{T}_\tau$ *is a tree; and*
2. *for every projection construct* $\exists^{\lesseqgtr q}[U_1, \ldots, U_k]R$ *appearing in* $\mathcal{T}$, *if* $q > 1$ *then the length of the path* $\text{PATH}_{\mathscr{T}}(\tau(R), \{U_1, \ldots, U_k\})$ *is 1.*

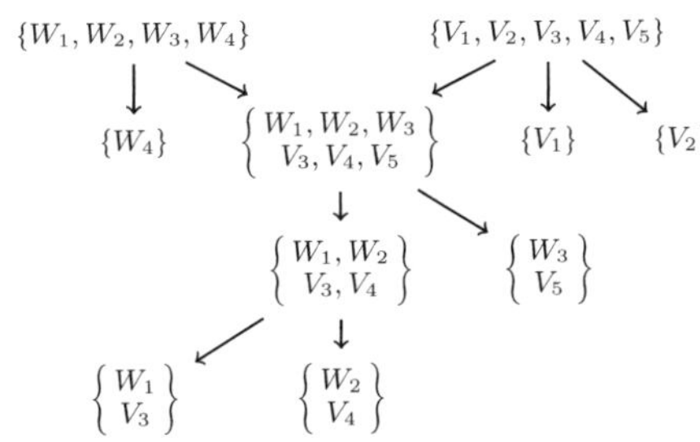

Fig. 4. The projection signature graph of Example 1.

The conditions in $\mathcal{DLR}^{\pm}$ restrict $\mathcal{DLR}^{+}$ in the way that multiple projections of relations may appear in a KB: intuitively, there can not be projections of a relation sharing a common attribute. Moreover, observe that in $\mathcal{DLR}^{\pm}$ PATH$_{\mathcal{T}}$ is necessarily functional, due to the multitree restriction. Figure 4 shows that the projection signature graph of the knowledge base from Example 1 is indeed a multitree. Note that in the figure we have collapsed equivalent attributes in a unique equivalence class, according to the renaming schema. Furthermore, since all its projection constructs have $q = 1$, this knowledge base belongs to $\mathcal{DLR}^{\pm}$.

$\mathcal{DLR}$ is included in $\mathcal{DLR}^{\pm}$, since the projection signature graph of any $\mathcal{DLR}$ knowledge base is always a degenerate multitree with maximum depth equal to 1. Not all the database constraints as introduced in Section 3 can be directly expressed in $\mathcal{DLR}^{\pm}$. While functional dependency and key axioms can be expressed directly in $\mathcal{DLR}^{\pm}$, equijoins, external uniqueness axioms, and identification axioms introduce projections of a relation which share common attributes, thus violating the multitree restriction. However, in $\mathcal{DLR}^{\pm}$ it is still possible to reason over both external uniqueness and identification axioms by encoding them into a set of saturated ABoxes (as originally proposed in [Calvanese *et al.*, 2001]) and check whether there is a saturation that satisfies the constraints. Therefore, we can conclude that $\mathcal{DLR}_{ifd}$ extended with unary functional dependencies is included in $\mathcal{DLR}^{\pm}$, provided that projections of relations in the knowledge base form a multitree projection signature graph. Since (unary) functional dependencies are expressed via the inclusions of projections of relations, by constraining the projection signature graph to be a multitree, the possibility to build combinations of functional dependencies as the ones in [Calvanese *et al.*, 2001] leading to undecidability is ruled out. Concerning the ability of $\mathcal{DLR}^{\pm}$ to capture conceptual data models, only the mapping of ORM schemas is affected by the $\mathcal{DLR}^{\pm}$ restrictions: the projections involved in the ORM schema should satisfy the $\mathcal{DLR}^{\pm}$ multitree restriction.

The main result of this work is that reasoning in $\mathcal{DLR}^{\pm}$ is an EXPTIME-complete problem. The lower bound comes by observing that $\mathcal{DLR}$ is a sublanguage of $\mathcal{DLR}^{\pm}$, the upper bound is proved by providing a mapping from $\mathcal{DLR}^{\pm}$ KBs to $\mathcal{ALCQI}$ KBs.

5 Implementation

We have implemented the framework discussed in this paper. DLRtoOWL is a Java library fully implementing $\mathcal{DLR}^{\pm}$ reasoning services. The library is based on the tool ANTLR4 to parse serialised input, and on OWLAPI4 for the OWL2 encoding. The system includes JFact, the Java version of the popular Fact++ reasoner. DLRtoOWL provides a Java $\mathcal{DLR}$ API package to allow developers to create, manipulate, serialise, and reason with $\mathcal{DLR}^{\pm}$ knowledge bases in their Java-based application, extending in a compatible way the standard OWL API with the $\mathcal{DLR}^{\pm}$ TELL and ASK services. During the development of this new library we strongly focused on performance. Since the OWL encoding is only possible if we have already built the $\mathcal{ALCQI}$ projection signature multitree, in principle the program should perform two parsing rounds: one to create the multitree and the other one to generate the OWL mapping. We faced this issue using dynamic programming: during the first (and only) parsing round we store in a data structure each axiom that we want to translate in OWL and, after building the multitree, by the dynamic programming technique we build on-the-fly a Java class which generates the required axioms.

References

[Artale *et al.*, 2007] A. Artale, D. Calvanese, R. Kontchakov, V. Ryzhikov, and M. Zakharyaschev. Reasoning over extended ER models. In *Proc. of the 26th Int. Conf. on Conceptual Modeling (ER'07)*, volume 4801 of *Lecture Notes in Computer Science*, pages 277–292. Springer, 2007.

[Berardi *et al.*, 2005] D. Berardi, D. Calvanese, and G. De Giacomo. Reasoning on UML class diagrams. *Artificial Intelligence*, 168(1–2):70–118, 2005.

[Calvanese *et al.*, 2001] Diego Calvanese, Giuseppe De Giacomo, and Maurizio Lenzerini. Identification constraints and functional dependencies in description logics. In *Proceedings of the Seventeenth International Joint Conference on Artificial Intelligence, IJCAI-01*, pages 155–160. Morgan Kaufmann, 2001.

[Calvanese *et al.*, 2008] Diego Calvanese, Giuseppe De Giacomo, and Maurizio Lenzerini. Conjunctive query containment and answering under description logic constraints. *ACM Trans. Comput. Logic*, 9(3):22:1–22:31, June 2008.

[Calvanese *et al.*, 2014] Diego Calvanese, Wolfgang Fischl, Reinhard Pichler, Emanuel Sallinger, and Mantas Simkus. Capturing relational schemas and functional dependencies in RDFS. In *Proceedings of the 28th AAAI Conference on Artificial Intelligence (AAAI)*, pages 1003–1011. AAAI Press, 2014.

[Chandra and Vardi, 1985] Ashok K. Chandra and Moshe Y. Vardi. The implication problem for functional and inclusion dependencies is undecidable. *SIAM Journal on Compututing*, 14(3):671–677, 1985.

[Franconi *et al.*, 2012] Enrico Franconi, Alessandro Mosca, and Dmitry Solomakhin. ORM2: formalisation and encoding in OWL2. In *International Workshop on Fact-Oriented Modeling (ORM 2012)*, pages 368–378, 2012.

[Halpin and Morgan, 2008] Terry Halpin and Tony Morgan. *Information Modeling and Relational Databases*. Morgan Kaufmann, 2nd edition, 2008.

[Kanellakis, 1990] Paris C. Kanellakis. Elements of relational database theory. In A.R. Meyer, M. Nivat, M.S. Paterson, D. Perrin, and J. van Leeuwen, editors, *The Handbook of Theoretical Computer Science*, volume B, chapter 17, pages 1075–1144. North Holland, 1990.

[Sportelli and Franconi, 2016] Francesco Sportelli and Enrico Franconi. Formalisation of ORM derivation rules and their mapping into OWL. In *ODBASE Conference 2016*, pages 827–843, 2016.

[Toman and Weddell, 2009] David Toman and Grant E. Weddell. Applications and extensions of PTIME description logics with functional constraints. In *IJCAI 2009, Proceedings of the 21st International Joint Conference on Artificial Intelligence*, pages 948–954, 2009.

Structural Characterization of Graph Navigational Languages* (Extended Abstract)

Valeria Fionda[1] and Giuseppe Pirrò[2]

[1] DeMaCS, University of Calabria, Italy
fionda@mat.unical.it
[2] Institute for High Performance Computing and Networking, ICAR-CNR, Italy
pirro@icar.cnr.it

Abstract. Graph navigational languages define binary relations in terms of pair of nodes in a graph subject to the existence of a path satisfying a certain regular expression. The goal of this paper is to give a novel characterization of navigational languages in terms of the structure of the graph embracing the results of a query. We define novel graph-based query evaluation semantics and efficient algorithms able to represent and capture intermediate nodes/edges linking pairs of nodes in the answer. We enhance the language of Nested Regular Expressions (NREs) with our machineries, thus defining the language of Structural NREs (sNREs).

1 Introduction

Graph data pervade everyday's life; social networks, biological networks, and Linked Open Data on the Web are just a few examples of its spread and flexibility. The limited support that relational query languages offer in terms of recursion stimulated the design of graph query languages where *navigation* is a first-class citizen. Regular Path Queries (RPQs) and their variants allowing conjunction (CRPQs) and inverse (C2RPQs) [5], and Nested Regular Expressions (NREs) [11] are some examples. More recently, also SPARQL has been extended with a (limited) navigational core called property paths (PPs). The complexity of query evaluation for these languages is now well understood; the only tractable languages are 2RPQs and NREs while the introduction of conjunction (C2RPQs) makes the problem intractable (NP-complete) and the evaluation of PPs still suffers from some problems (mixing set and bag semantics) [2].

Queries expressible with these languages ask for *pairs of nodes* connected by a path conforming to a regular language over binary relations. As an example, Syd can find that one of his co-authors at distance 3 is Mark; nevertheless, no information about the structure (i.e., intermediate nodes/edges) of the graph where the pair (Syd, Mark) appears is given. This missing piece of information

* An extended version of this work titled "Explaining Graph Navigational Queries" will appear in proc. of the 14th Extended Semantic Web Conference (ESWC).

would allow to understand why a query has returned a certain set of (pairs of) nodes and is useful in contexts where one needs to connect the dots, such as in bibliographic networks, generic exploratory search or query debugging [6]. The broad goal of this paper is to introduce Structural Nested Regular Expressions (sNREs in short), an enhancement of Nested Regular Expressions (NREs) tackling query answering from the point of view of the structure of the graph where the results of a query appear. The challenge that we face with sNREs is to *define formal semantics and efficient algorithms that allow navigational queries to return graphs while keeping query evaluation tractable.*

Related Work. There exists a solid body of work about graph query languages. The core of such languages are Regular Path Queries (RPQs) that have been extended with other features, among which, conjunction (CRPQs) [5], inverse (C2RPQs) and the possibility to return and compare paths (EXPQs) [4]. These additions do add expressive power at the cost of making query evaluation intractable (combined complexity). Languages such as Nested Regular Expressions (NREs) [11] allow existential tests in the form of nesting, in a similar spirit to PDL and XPath while offering tractable query evaluation. Other strands of research (e.g., [10, 3]) feature more expressive languages than NREs with a higher computational cost. Our work differs from related research in one main respect: We *do not* focus on increasing the expressiveness of existing languages with new features (e.g., path variables and path variable constraints) as done with CRPQs, ECRPQs. Our goal is to provide a *novel structural characterization of graph navigational languages* taking as a yardstick the language of NREs. Such characterzation amount at studying how NREs can be enhanced to also return structural information (i.e., graphs) without hindering the complexity of query evaluation.

Contributions and Outline. We make the following main contributions: *(i)* a structural characterization of Nested Regular Expressions that we call Structural NREs (sNREs), which to the best of our knowledge is the first graph navigational language able to return graphs as the answer to a navigational query; *(ii)* formal semantics based on novel operators that work with graphs besides pairs of nodes; *(iii)* efficient algorithms for query evaluation under the novel semantics.

The remainder of the paper is organized as follows. Section 2 presents the sNREs language. Section 3 presents query evaluation algorithms and a study of their complexity. We conclude and sketch future work in Section 4.

2 Structural Nested Regular Expressions

We focus our attention on the Resource Description Framework (RDF). An RDF triple is a tuple of the form $\langle s, p, o \rangle \in \mathbf{I} \times \mathbf{I} \times \mathbf{I} \cup \mathbf{L}$, where $\mathbf{I}$ (IRIs) and $\mathbf{L}$ (literals) are countably infinite sets; for ease of exposition we do not consider blank nodes. An RDF graph G is a set of triples. The set of terms of a graph will be $terms(G) \subseteq \mathbf{I} \cup \mathbf{L}$; $nodes(G)$ will be the set of terms used as a subject or object of a triple while $triples(G)$ is the set of triples in G. Since SPARQL property paths offer very limited expressive power we will consider the language of Nested Regular Expressions (NREs) [11] as reference language.

Nested Regular Expressions. NREs, originally proposed as the navigational core of SPARQL, allow to express existential tests along the nodes in a path via nesting (in the same spirit of XPath) while keeping the (combined) complexity of query evaluation tractable. NREs allow to specify *pairs of nodes* in a graph G, subject to the existence of a path satisfying a certain regular condition among them. Each NRE *nexp* over an alphabet of symbols Σ defines a *binary relation* $[\![nexp]\!]^G$ when evaluated over a graph G. The result of the evaluation of an NRE *is a set of pairs of nodes.* In the spirit of NREs, several extensions have been defined (e.g., EPPs [7]). Although adding expressive power to NREs (e.g., EPPs add path conjunction and (safe) negation), these languages all return pairs of nodes. This motivates the introduction of sNREs, which to the best of our knowledge is the first language tackling the problem of returning graphs from the evaluation of navigational queries while remaining tractable.

2.1 The sNREs Language

The syntax of sNREs is defined by the following grammar:

$$snrexp := \tau\#exp \quad (\tau \in \{full, filt, set\})$$
$$exp := a \mid \hat{}a \mid exp/exp \mid exp|exp \mid exp^* \mid exp[exp_1]$$

where a$\in\Sigma$, ^ denotes backward navigation, / path concatenation, | path union, and $[exp_1]$ an existential test in the form of a nested expression. It is interesting to note that, syntactically, sNREs differs from NREs (and other navigational languages) only for the construct τ. sNREs offers a flexible way of choosing the desired output. τ allows to specify different evaluation semantics that output: *(i)* pairs of nodes (i.e., *set*) as in NREs; *(ii)* structural information in terms of the whole portion of the graph "touched" during the evaluation (*full*); *(iii)* structural information in terms of (union of) paths leading to some result (*filt*).

On the expressiveness of sNREs. We compare sNREs with NREs and other languages that deal with paths/subgraphs. As for NREs, it is easy to see that *the output* of a sNREs query, when specifying structural information via *full* or *filt*, is richer than that of its corresponding NREs. This occurs because graph navigation is only referenced in the semantics of NREs *as the means* to get the resulting set of nodes. sNREs enrich NREs in terms of output produced via our reconstruction algorithms (see Section 3) thus indirectly allowing to ask a larger class of requests. As an example with sNREs one can ask to retrieve *co-directors* and get as by-product *movies co-directed.*

Languages like ERPQs [4] or ρ-queries [1] are clearly more expressive than sNREs as they allow to manipulate paths via e.g., regular relations. Nevertheless this higher expressiveness comes at the cost of a higher complexity for query evaluation. Our goal in this paper is to focus on providing a structural characterization of low-complexity languages like NREs and showing that one can get more (i.e., structural information) with no additional computational cost.

2.2 Structural Graphs

Structural Graphs are used to formally capture the output of the evaluation of a sNRE and are the building blocks of the novel sNREs query semantics.

Definition 1 (Structural Graph). *Given a graph G, a sNRE expression ex and a set of starting node $S \subseteq nodes(G)$, a structural graph is a quadruple $\Gamma=(V, E, S, T)$ where $V \subseteq nodes(G)$, $E \subseteq triples(G)$ and $T \subseteq V$ is a set of ending nodes, that is, nodes reachable from nodes in S via paths satisfying ex.*

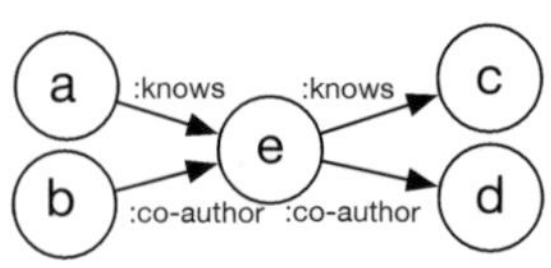

Fig. 1. An example graph.

Consider the graph G in Fig. 1 and the sNRE η=(`:knows/:knows`)|(`:co-author/:co-author`). The answer with the semantics based on pairs of nodes (i.e., NREs semantics) is the set of pairs of nodes: (a,c), (b,d). Under the sNREs semantics, since there are two starting nodes a and b from which the evaluation produces results, one possibility would be to consider the Structural Graph (SG) capturing all results, that is, $\Gamma=(nodes(G), triple(G), \{a,b\}, \{c,d\})$. However, one may note that there exists a path (via the node e) from a to d in the SG even if the pair (a,d) does not belong to the answer. This could lead to misinterpretation of the query results and their structural information. To avoid these situations, we define G-sound and G-complete SGs.

Definition 2 **(G-Soundness)**. *Given a graph G and a sNRE expression ex, a SG is G-sound if, and only if, all ending nodes are reachable from all the starting nodes via some paths satisfying ex.*

Definition 3 **(G-Completeness)**. *Given a graph G and a sNRE expression ex, an SG is G-complete if, and only if, all nodes in a graph G reachable from some starting nodes, via some paths satisfying ex, are in the ending nodes.*

The SG Γ in the above example violates G-soundness because the only path existing (via the node e) from a to d (and from b to c) in Γ does not satisfy the expression η. The following lemma guarantees G-soundness and G-completeness.

Lemma 4 **(G-Sound and G-Complete SGs)**. *Structural Graphs having a single starting node $v \in nodes(G)$ are G-sound and G-complete.*

We are now ready to define answer graphs that capture the output of sNREs.

Definition 5 (**Answer Graph**). *Given a sNRE expression ex and a graph G, an answer graph $\mathcal{E}$ is a set of G-sound and G-complete structural graphs.*

The answer graph of our previous example is the set $\mathcal{E}=\{\Gamma_a, \Gamma_b\}$ s.t.:

1. $\Gamma_a=(\{a,e,c\}, \{\langle a,$ `:knows`$, e\rangle, \langle e,$ `:knows`$, c\rangle\}, a, \{c\})$
2. $\Gamma_b=(\{b,e,d\}, \{\langle a,$ `:co-author`$, e\rangle, \langle e,$ `:co-author`$, c\rangle\}, b, \{d\})$.

Note that $\mathcal{E}$ is an answer graph according to both $full$ and $filt$ semantics since there are no edges that do not contribute to reach some result node.

Formal Semantics. We devised two different evaluation semantics for sNREs that match the syntactic constructs $filt$ and $full$. In particular, the $full$ semantics considers all the parts of G that were visited during the evaluation of an expression, while the second one $filt$, only the portion of G that actually contributed to build the answer; in other words, the set of SGs such that each Γ_v only considers paths that starts from $v \in nodes(G)$ and satisfy the expression (i.e., union of all the successful paths). For sake of space we do not report the semantics that are available in an extended version of this paper [9].

3 Algorithms and Complexity

We now describe algorithms for the evaluation of sNREs expressions under the novel semantics. The interesting result is that the evaluation of a sNRE expression e in this new setting can be done efficiently. Let e be a sNRE expression and G a graph. Let $|e|$ be the size of e, Σ_e the set of edge labels appearing in it, and $|G|=|nodes(G)| + |triples(G)|$ be the size of G. Algorithms that build answer graphs according to the $full$ or $filt$ semantics are automata-based and work in two steps. The first step is shared and leverages *product automata*; the second step requires a *marking phase* only for the $filt$ semantics and is needed to include nodes and edges that are relevant for the answer.

Building Product Automata. The idea is to associate to e (and to each $[exp]$) a non deterministic finite state automaton with ϵ transitions $\mathcal{A}_e$ ($\mathcal{A}^{exp}$, resp.). Such automata can be built according to the standard Thomson construction rules over the alphabet $Voc(e)=\Sigma_e \cup \bigcup_{[e_1]\in e}$, that is, by considering also $[e_1]$ in e as basic symbols. The product automaton is a tuple $G \times \mathcal{A}_e = \langle Q^e, Voc(e), \delta^e, Q_0^e, F^e \rangle$ where Q^e is a set of states, $\delta^e{:}Q^e \times (Voc(e) \cup \epsilon) \rightarrow 2^{Q^e}$ is the transition function, $Q_0^e \subseteq Q^e$ is the set of initial states, and $F^e \subseteq Q^e$ is the set of final states. The building of the product automaton $G \times \mathcal{A}_e$ is based on the algorithm used by [11] based on the labeling of the nodes of G wrt nested subexpressions in e.

Building Answer Graphs. We now discuss algorithms that leverage product automata (of the sNRE expression e and all nested subexpressions) to produce answer graphs according to the $full$ and $filt$ semantics. To access the elements of a structural graph Γ (see Definition 1) we use the notation $\Gamma.x$, with $x \in \{V, E, S, T\}$. The main algorithm is Algorithm 1, which receives the sNRE expression and the type of answer graph to be built. In case of the $filt$ semantics the data structure `reached`, which maintains a set of states (n_i, q_j), is initialized via the procedure `mark` (line 3) reported in Algorithm 2; otherwise, it is initialized as the union of: *(i)* all the states of the product automaton $G \times \mathcal{A}_e$; *(ii)* all the states of the product automata ($G \times \mathcal{A}_{exp}$) of all the nested expressions in e (line 5). The procedure `mark` fills the set `reached` with all the states in all the product automata that contribute to obtain an answer; these are the states in a path from an initial state to a final state in the product automata. As shown in Algorithm 2, `reached` is populated by navigating the product automata backward from the final states to the initial ones.

Input : sNRE e, graph G, output (*full* or *filt*)
Output: $\mathcal{E}$: an answer graph as set of SGs Γ_s

1: build the product automaton $G \times \mathcal{A}_e$
2: **if** *filt* /* filtered semantics */ **then**
3: reached $= \underline{\textbf{mark}}(G \times \mathcal{A}_e, \emptyset)$
/* reached keeps nodes in $G \times \mathcal{A}_e$ that are in a path to a final state */
4: **else**
5: reached $= Q^e \cup \bigcup_{[exp] \text{ in } e} Q^{exp}$
6: **for all** $(s, q_o) \in Q_0^e$ **do**
7: $\Gamma_s = \langle \{s\}, \emptyset, s, \emptyset \rangle$
8: $\texttt{seen}_{(s,q_o)} = \{s\}$
/* seen for each state s_j keeps nodes in $G \times \mathcal{A}_e$ from which it has been reached */
9: $\mathcal{E} = \bigcup_{(s,q_o) \in Q_0^e} \{\Gamma_s\}$
10: visit $= \bigcup_{(s,q_o) \in Q_0^e} \{((s, q_0), \{s\})\}$
/* visit keeps nodes to be visited */
11: $\underline{\textbf{buildA}}(G \times \mathcal{A}_e$, reached, $\mathcal{E}$, visit)

Algorithm 1: BuildAnsG

Input: product automaton $G \times \mathcal{A}$, set of states `reached`
Build: set of states `reached`

reached $=$ reached $\cup \bigcup_{(n,q_f) \in F^e} \{(n, q_f)\}$
visit $= \bigcup_{(n,q_f) \in F^e} \{(n, q_f)\}$ s.t. $q_f \in F$
visitN $= \emptyset$
while visit $\neq \emptyset$ **do**
  for all (n, q) in visit **do**
    for all transition $\delta((n', q'), x) \in G \times \mathcal{A}^e$ s.t. $(n, q) \in \delta((n', q'), x)$ **do**
      if $(n', q') \notin$ reached **then**
        visitN $=$ visitN $\cup \{(n', q')\}$
        reached $=$ reached $\cup \{(n', q')\}$
      for all $[exp]$ in x **do**
        $\underline{\textbf{mark}}(G \times \mathcal{A}^{exp}$, reached)
  visit $=$ visitN
  visitN $= \emptyset$
return reached

Algorithm 2: mark($G \times \mathcal{A}^e$, `reached`)

Then, the set of SGs composing an answer graph $\mathcal{E}$ are initialized (lines 6-7; 9) by adding to $\mathcal{E}$ an SG Γ_s for each initial state (s, q_0) of $G \times \mathcal{A}_e$. Moreover, the data structure `seen` is also initialized (line 8) by associating to each state (s, q_0) the node s (associated to the initial state (s, q_0)) from which it has been visited. Hence, `seen` maintains for each state, reached during the visit of the product automata, the starting nodes from which this state has already been visited.

The usage of `seen` avoids to visit the same state more than once for each starting node. The data structure `visit` is also initialized with the initial states of $G \times \mathcal{A}_e$ (line 10); it contains all the states to be visited in the subsequent step plus the set of starting nodes for which these states have to be visited. Then, the SGs are built via `buildA` (Algorithm 3). All the states in `visit` are considered (line 2) only once for the set $B_{n,q}$, which keeps starting nodes for which states in `visit` have to be processed (line 3). Then, for each state $(n, q) \in$`visit` all its transitions are considered (line 7); in particular, for each state $(n', q') \in$`reached`, reachable from some $(n, q) \in$ `visit` via some transitions (line 8), the set of "new" starting nodes (D) for which (n', q') has to be visited in the subsequent step is computed with a possible update of the sets `visit` and `seen` (lines 9-12).

Input: product automaton $G \times \mathcal{A}^{\bar{e}}$, set of states `reached`, Answer Graph $\mathcal{E}$, list of states to visit `visit`

```
1  visitN = ∅
2  for all (n, q) in visit do
3      B_{n,q} = ⋃_{((n,q),S)∈visit} S
4      for all s ∈ B_{n,q} do
5          if q ∈ F^ē then
6              add n to Γ_s.T
7      for all transition δ^ē((n, q), x) do
8          for all (n′, q′) ∈ δ^ē((n, q), x) s.t (n′, q′) ∈ reached do
9              D = B_{n,q} \ seen_{(n,q)}
10             if D ≠ ∅ then
11                 visitN = visitN ∪ {((n′, q′), D)}
12                 seen_{(n′,q′)} = seen_{(n′,q′)} ∪ D
13             if x ∈ Σ_e then
14                 for all s ∈ B_{n,q} do
15                     add n′ to Γ_s.V
16                     add (n, x, n′) to Γ_s
17             else if x is a [exp] then
18                 let (n, q_0) ∈ Q_0^{exp}
19                 seen_{(n,q_0)} = seen_{(n,q_0)} ∪ B_{n,q}
20                 buildA(G × A^{exp}, reached, E, {(n, q), B_{n,q}})
21 buildA(G × A^ē, reached, E, visitN)
```

Algorithm 3: buildA($G \times \mathcal{A}$, `reached`, $\mathcal{E}$, `visit`)

If the transition is labeled with a predicate symbol in G (line 13), the SGs corresponding to nodes $s \in B_{n,q}$ are populated by adding the corresponding nodes and edges (lines 14-16). Otherwise, if the transition is a nested expression the building of the answer graph $\mathcal{E}$ proceeds recursively by visiting the product automata associated to all nested (sub)expressions.

Theorem 6. *Given a graph G and a sNRE expression e, the answer graph $\mathcal{E}$ (according to both semantics) can be computed in time $\mathcal{O}(|nodes(G)| \times |G| \times |e|)$.*

Proof (Sketch). The answer graph built according to the *full* semantics can be constructed by visiting $G \times \mathcal{A}_e$ (Algorithm 3). In particular, for each starting state (n, q), the states and transitions of $G \times \mathcal{A}_e$ are all visited at most once (and the same also holds for the automata corresponding to the nested expressions of e). The starting and ending nodes of each answer graph are set during the visit of the product automaton. For each node s corresponding to a starting state $(s, q_o) \in Q_0^e$ a structural graph is created (Algorithm 1, lines 6-7); the set of nodes reachable from s is set to be $\Gamma_s.T = \{\texttt{n} \mid (\texttt{n}, q) \in F^e$ and (n, q) is reachable from $(s, q_o)\}$ (Algorithm 3 lines 5-6). Thus, each structural graph can be computed by visiting each transition and each node exactly once with a cost $O(|Q^e| + \sum_{[exp] \in e} |Q^{exp}| + |\delta^e| + \sum_{[exp] \in e} |\delta^{exp}|) = O(|G| \times |e|)$. Since the number of SGs to be constructed is bound by $|nodes(G)|$, the total cost of building the answer graph $\mathcal{E}$, is $\mathcal{O}(|nodes(G)| \times |G| \times |e|)$. This bounds also take into account the cost of building product automata. In the case of the *filt* semantics, the marking phase does not increase the complexity bound; this is because the set `reachable`, which keeps reachable states, is built by visiting at most once all nodes and transitions in all the product automata, with a cost $O(|G| \times |e|)$. □

Note that in Algorithm 3, the amortized processing time per node is lower than $|G| \times |e|$ when visiting the product automaton since the Breadth First

Search(es) from each starting state are concurrently run according to the algorithm in [12]. Finally, the SGs in the $\mathcal{E}$ built via Algorithm 1 are both G-sound and G-complete. It is easy to see by the definition of the product automaton, that there exists a starting state (n, q_0) that is connected to a final state (n', q_f) in $G \times \mathcal{A}_e$ and, thus, a path from n to n' in Γ_n iff, there exists a path connecting n to n' in G satisfying e.

4 Concluding Remarks and Future Work

We have studied the novel problem of characterizing graph languages from the point of view of the structure of the graph where queries are evaluated. We picked the language of NREs as yardstick because of its attractive computational properties and showed how we can get more (in terms of structural information) at the same computational cost. We had to face challenges in terms of formalization of novel semantics that can deal with graphs and non-trivial (automata-based) algorithms that can capture structural information in an efficient way. In an extended version of this work [9] we discuss an experimental evaluation and an instantiation of the framework to tackle the problem of explaining graph queries. This works opens some challenging research questions such as: (i) consider a more expressive navigational core [7] and enhance it with structural information; (ii) add negative information (e.g., parts of a query that failed) (iii) provide structural information according to user-specified preferences [8].

References

1. K. Anyanwu and A. Sheth. p-Queries: Enabling Querying for Semantic Associations on the Semantic Web. In *WWW*, pages 690–699. ACM, 2003.
2. M. Arenas, S. Conca, and J. Pérez. Counting Beyond a Yottabyte, or how SPARQL 1.1 Property Paths will Prevent Adoption of the Standard. In *WWW*, pages 629–638, 2012.
3. M. Arenas, G. Gottlob, and A. Pieris. Expressive Languages for Querying the Semantic Web. In *PODS*, 2014.
4. P. Barceló, L. Libkin, A. W. Lin, and P. T. Wood. Expressive Languages for Path Queries over Graph-Structured Data. *ACM TODS*, 37(4):31, 2012.
5. D. Calvanese, G. De Giacomo, M. Lenzerini, and M. Y. Vardi. Containment of Conjunctive Regular Path Queries with Inverse. In *KR*, pages 176–185, 2000.
6. M. P. Consens, J. W. S. Liu, and F. Rizzolo. Xplainer: Visual explanations of xpath queries. In *ICDE*, pages 636–645. IEEE, 2007.
7. V. Fionda, Pirrò G., and M. P. Consens. Extended Property Paths: Writing More SPARQL Queries in a Succinct Way. In *AAAI*, 2015.
8. V. Fionda and G. Pirrò. Querying Graphs with Preferences. In *CIKM*, pages 929–938. ACM, 2013.
9. V. Fionda and G. Pirrò. Explaining Graph Navigational Queries. In *ESWC*, 2017.
10. L. Libkin, J. Reutter, and D. Vrgoč. Trial for RDF: adapting graph query languages for RDF data. In *PODS*, pages 201–212, 2013.
11. J. Pérez, M. Arenas, and C. Gutierrez. nSPARQL: A Navigational Language for RDF. *Journal of Web Semantics*, 8(4), 2010.
12. M. Then, M. Kaufmann, F. Chirigati, T. Hoang-Vu, K. Pham, A. Kemper, T. Neumann, and H. T. Vo. The More the Merrier: Efficient Multi-Source Graph Traversal. *VLDB Endowment*, 8(4):449–460, 2014.

Googling the Deep Web

Andrea Calì[1], Davide Martinenghi[2], and Riccardo Torlone[3]

[1]Birkbeck, University of London, UK, email: andrea@dcs.bbk.ac.uk
[2]Politecnico di Milano, Italy, email: davide.martinenghi@polimi.it
[3]Università Roma Tre, Italy, email: torlone@dia.uniroma3.it

Abstract. The Deep Web is constituted by data that are accessible through Web pages, but not indexable by search engines as they are returned in dynamic pages. In this paper we propose a conceptual framework for answering keyword queries on Deep Web sources represented as relational tables with so-called access limitations. We formalize the notion of optimal answer and characterize queries for which an answer can be found.

Keywords: Keyword Query, Access Pattern, Deep Web.

1 Introduction

It is well known that the data available on the Web through forms and in general in dynamic pages constitutes a corpus of data that is way larger than the Web data that are indexed by search engines. The former are commonly referred to as *Deep Web*, that is, data "hidden" in local databases whose content can only be accessed through queries. This happens for instance when we search for a flight on the Web site of an airline company – the data make sense only for a short time, after which they become obsolete due to the frequent changes of prices and availability. This immediately poses an interesting challenge, i.e., how to automatically retrieve relevant information from the Deep Web – a problem that has been investigated in recent years (see, e.g., [2, 4, 15] for discussion).

Usually, a data source in the Deep Web is modeled at the logical level by a relational table in which some columns, called *input* attributes, represent fields of a form that need to be filled in so as to retrieve data from the source, while all the others, called *output* attributes, represent values that are returned to the user. Consider for instance the following relations in which the i superscript denotes the input attributes.

$r_1 =$

$Dept^i$	Emp	
IT	John	t_{11}
AI	Mike	t_{12}

$r_2 =$

Emp^i	$Proj$	
John	P1	t_{21}
Ann	P2	t_{22}
Mike	P2	t_{23}

$r_3 =$

$Proj^i$	Emp	$Role$	
P1	John	DBA	t_{31}
P1	Ann	Analyst	t_{32}

Relation r_1 represents a form that, given a department, returns all the employees working in it; relation r_2 a form that, given an employee, returns all the projects he/she works on; and relation r_3 a form that, given a project, returns the employees working in it along with their role. These access modalities are commonly referred to as *access limitations*, in that data can only be queried according to given patterns.

Different approaches have been proposed in the literature for querying databases with access limitations: conjunctive queries [3], natural language [13], and SQL-like statements [11]. In this paper, we address the novel problem of accessing the Deep Web by just providing a set of keywords, in the same way in which we usually search for information on the Web with a search engine.

Consider for instance the case in which the user only provides the keywords "DBA" and "IT" for querying the portion of the Deep Web represented by the relations above. Intuitively, he/she is searching for employees with the DBA role in the IT department. Given the access limitations, this query can be concretely answered by first accessing relation r_1 using the keyword *IT*, which allows us to extract the tuple t_{11}. Then, using the value *John* in t_{11}, we can extract the tuple t_{21} from relation r_2. Finally, using the value *P1* in t_{21}, we can extract the tuples t_{31} and t_{32} from relation r_3. Now, since t_{31} contains *DBA*, it turns out that the set of tuples $\{t_{11}, t_{21}, t_{31}\}$ is a possible answer to the input query in that the set is connected (every two tuples in it share a constant) and contains the given keywords. However, the tuple t_{21} is somehow redundant and can be safely eliminated from the solution, since the set $\{t_{11}, t_{31}\}$ is also connected and contains the keywords. This example shows that, in this context, the keyword query answering problem can be involved and tricky, even in simple situations.

In the rest of this paper, we formally investigate this problem in depth. We first propose, in Section 2, a precise semantics of (optimal) answer to a keyword query in the Deep Web. We then tackle, in Section 3, the problem of finding an answer to a keyword query by assuming that the domains of the keywords are known in advance. This allows us to perform static analysis to immediately discard irrelevant cases from our consideration. Section 4 ends the paper with some conclusions and future works.

Related work To the best of our knowledge, ours is the first comprehensive approach to the problem of querying the Deep Web using keywords. Other works addressed keyword search on relational data previously extracted from the Deep Web [?]. This paper reports results previously published in [?], the paper where we illustrate our techniques for keyword search in the Deep Web.

The problem of query processing in the Deep Web has been widely investigated in the last years, with different approaches and under different perspectives including: data crawling [16], integration of data sources [9], query plan optimization [3], and generic structured query models [11]. However, none of them has tackled the problem that we have addressed in this paper.

The idea of querying structured data using keywords emerged more than a decade ago [1] as a way to provide high-level access to data and free the user from the knowledge of query languages and data organization. Since then, a lot of work has been done in this field (see, e.g., [18] for a survey) but never in the context of the Deep Web. This problem has been investigated in the context of various data models: relational [12], semi-structured [14], XML [8], and RDF [17]. Within the relational model, the common assumption is that an answer to a keyword query is a graph of minimal size in which the nodes represent tuples, the edges represent foreign key references between them, and the keywords occur in some node of the graph [10]. Our definition of query answer follows this line but it is more general, since it is only based on the presence of common values between tuples, while not forcing the presence of foreign keys.

The various approaches to keyword query answering over relational databases are commonly classified into two categories: *schema-based* and *schema-free*. Schema-based approaches [1, 10] make use, in a preliminary phase, of the database schema to build SQL queries that are able to return the answer. Conversely, schema-free approaches [7, 12] rely on exploration techniques over a graph-based representation of the whole database. Since the search for an optimal answer consists in finding a minimal *Steiner tree* on the graph, which is known to be an NP-Complete problem [6], the various proposals rely on heuristics aimed at generating approximations of Steiner trees. Our approach makes use of the schema of the data sources but cannot be classified in any of the approaches above since, given the access limitations, it rather relies on building a minimal query plan of accesses to the data sources.

2 Preliminaries and problem definition

We model data sources as relations of a relational database and we assume that, albeit autonomous, they have "compatible" attributes. For this, we fix a set of *abstract domains* $\mathbf{D} = \{D_1, \ldots, D_m\}$, which, rather than denoting concrete value types (such as string or integer), represent data types at a higher level of abstraction (for instance, *car* or *country*). Therefore, in an abstract domain an object is uniquely represented by a value. The set of all values is denoted by $\mathcal{D} = \bigcup_{i=1}^{n} D_i$. For simplicity, we assume that all abstract domains are disjoint. We then say that a *(relation) schema* r, customarily indicated as $r(A_1, \ldots, A_k)$, is a set of attributes $\{A_1, \ldots, A_k\}$, each associated with an abstract domain $dom(A_i) \in \mathbf{D}$, $1 \leq i \leq k$. A *database schema* $\mathcal{S}$ is a set of *schemas* $\{r_1, \ldots, r_n\}$.

As usual, given a schema r, a *tuple* t over r is a function that associates a value $c \in dom(A)$ with each attribute $A \in r$, and a *relation instance* $r^{\mathcal{I}}$ of r is a set of tuples over r. For simplicity, we also write $dom(c)$ to indicate the domain of c. A (database) instance $\mathcal{I}$ of a database schema $\mathcal{S} = \{r_1, \ldots, r_n\}$ is a set of relation instances $\{r_1^{\mathcal{I}}, \ldots, r_n^{\mathcal{I}}\}$, where $r_i^{\mathcal{I}}$ denotes the relation instance of r_i in $\mathcal{I}$.

For the sake of simplicity, in the following we assign the same name to attributes of different schemas that are defined over the same abstract domain.

Definition 1 (Access pattern). *An* access pattern Π *for a schema* $r(A_1, \ldots, A_k)$ *is a mapping* $\Pi : \{A_1, \ldots, A_k\} \rightarrow M$, *where* $M = \{i, o\}$ *is called* access mode, *and* i *and* o *denote* input *and* output, *respectively;* A_i *is correspondingly called an* input *(resp.,* output*) attribute for* r *wrt* Π.

Henceforth, we denote input attributes with an 'i' superscript, e.g., A^i. Moreover, we assume that each relation has exactly one access pattern.

Definition 2 (Binding). *Let* $A'_1, \ldots, A'_\ell$ *be all the input attributes for* r *wrt* Π*; any tuple* $\mathscr{b} = \langle c_1, \ldots, c_\ell \rangle$ *such that* $c_i \in dom(A'_i)$ *for* $1 \leq i \leq \ell$ *is called a* binding *for* r *wrt* Π.

Definition 3 (Access). *An* access *is a pair* $\langle \Pi, \mathscr{b} \rangle$*, where* Π *is an access pattern for a schema* r *and* $\mathscr{b}$ *is a binding for* r *wrt* Π*. The* output *of such an access on an instance* $\mathcal{I}$ *is the set* $\mathcal{T}$ *of all tuples in the relation* $r^{\mathcal{I}} \in \mathcal{I}$ *over* r *that match the binding, i.e., such that* $\mathcal{T} = \sigma_{A_1=c_1,\ldots,A_\ell=c_\ell}(r)$*.*

Intuitively, we can only access a relation if we can provide a binding for it, i.e., a value for every input attribute.

Definition 4 (Access path). *Given an instance* $\mathcal{I}$ *for a database schema* $\mathcal{S}$*, a set of access patterns* $\mathbf{\Pi}$ *for the relations in* $\mathcal{S}$*, and a set of values* $\mathcal{C} \subseteq \mathcal{D}$*, an* access path *on* $\mathcal{I}$ *(for* $\mathcal{S}$*,* $\mathbf{\Pi}$ *and* $\mathcal{C}$*) is a sequence* $\xrightarrow{\mathscr{b}_1}_{r_1^{\mathcal{I}}} \mathcal{T}_1 \xrightarrow{\mathscr{b}_2}_{r_2^{\mathcal{I}}} \cdots \xrightarrow{\mathscr{b}_n}_{r_n^{\mathcal{I}}} \mathcal{T}_n$*, where, for* $1 \leq i \leq n$*, (i)* $\mathscr{b}_i$ *is a binding for a relation* $r_i \in \mathcal{S}$ *wrt a pattern* $\Pi_i \in \mathbf{\Pi}$ *for* r_i*, (ii)* $\mathcal{T}_i$ *is the output of access* $\langle \Pi_i, \mathscr{b}_i \rangle$ *on* $\mathcal{I}$*, and (iii) each value in* $\mathscr{b}_i$ *either occurs in* $\mathcal{T}_j$ *with* $j < i$ *or is a value in* $\mathcal{C}$*.*

Definition 5 (Reachable portion). *A tuple* t *in* $\mathcal{I}$ *is said to be* reachable *given* $\mathcal{C}$ *if there exists an access path* P *(for* $\mathcal{S}$*,* $\mathbf{\Pi}$ *and* $\mathcal{C}$*) such that* t *is in the output of some access in* P*; the* reachable portion $reach(\mathcal{I}, \mathbf{\Pi}, \mathcal{C})$ *of* $\mathcal{I}$ *is the set of all reachable tuples in* $\mathcal{I}$ *given* $\mathcal{C}$*.*

In the following, we will write $\mathcal{S}^{\mathbf{\Pi}}$ to refer to schema $\mathcal{S}$ under access patterns $\mathbf{\Pi}$.

Example 1. Consider the following instance $\mathcal{I}$ of a schema $\mathcal{S}^{\mathbf{\Pi}} = \{r_1(A^i, B), r_2(B^i, A), r_3(A^i, B, C)\}$.

$r_1 =$

A^i	B	
a_1	b_1	t_{11}
a_2	b_3	t_{12}

$r_2 =$

B^i	A	
b_1	a_2	t_{21}
b_2	a_2	t_{22}
b_1	a_4	t_{23}

$r_3 =$

A^i	B	C	
a_2	b_1	c_1	t_{31}
a_3	b_2	c_2	t_{32}
a_4	b_4	c_1	t_{33}

Then, for instance, $\{t_{11}\}$ is the output of the access with binding $\langle a_1 \rangle$ wrt $r_1(A^i, B)$, and $\xrightarrow{\langle a_1 \rangle}_{r_1^{\mathcal{I}}} \{t_{11}\} \xrightarrow{\langle b_1 \rangle}_{r_2^{\mathcal{I}}} \{t_{21}, t_{23}\}$, is an access path for $\mathcal{S}$, $\mathbf{\Pi}$ and $\mathcal{C} = \{a_1\}$, since, given $\mathcal{C}$, we can extract t_{11} from r_1 and, given $\{b_1\}$ from t_{11}, we can extract t_{21} and t_{23} from r_2. The reachable portion of $\mathcal{I}$, given $\mathcal{C}$, is $reach(\mathcal{I}, \mathbf{\Pi}, \mathcal{C}) = \{t_{11}, t_{12}, t_{21}, t_{23}, t_{31}, t_{33}\}$, while $\{t_{22}, t_{32}\} \cap reach(\mathcal{I}, \mathbf{\Pi}, \mathcal{C}) = \emptyset$. Figure 1a shows the reachable portion $\mathcal{I}'$ of $\mathcal{I}$ given $\mathcal{C}$ along with the access paths used to extract it, with dotted lines enclosing outputs of accesses. ■

The definition of answer to a keyword query in our setting requires the preliminary notion of join graph.

Definition 6 (Join graph). *Given a set* $\mathcal{T}$ *of tuples, the* join graph *of* $\mathcal{T}$ *is a node-labeled undirected graph* $\langle N, E \rangle$ *constructed as follows: (i) the nodes* N *are labeled with tuples of* $\mathcal{T}$*, with a one-to-one correspondence between tuples of* $\mathcal{T}$ *and nodes of* N*; and (ii) there is an arc between two nodes* n_1 *and* n_2 *whenever the tuples labeling* n_1 *and* n_2 *have at least one value in common.*

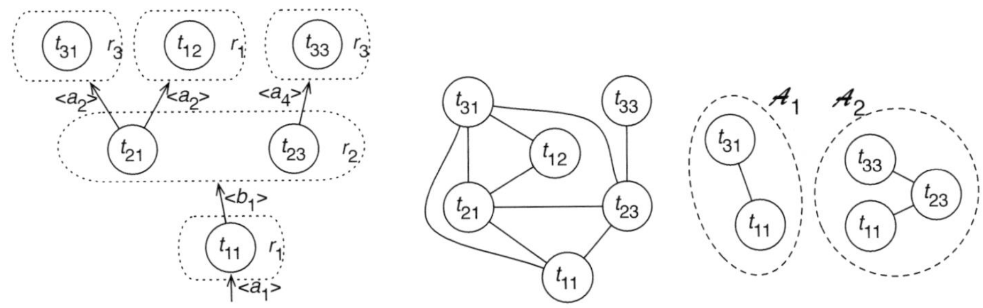

(a) Reachable portion $\mathcal{I}'$, given $\{a_1\}$. (b) Join graph of $\mathcal{I}'$. (c) Two answers to KQ q.

Fig. 1: Illustration of Examples 1, 2, and 3.

Example 2. Consider instance $\mathcal{I}$ of Example 1 and the reachable portion $\mathcal{I}'$ of $\mathcal{I}$ given $\{a_1\}$, shown in Figure 1a. The join graph of $\mathcal{I}'$ is shown in Figure 1b. ■

A *keyword query* (KQ) is a non-empty set of values in $\mathcal{D}$ called *keywords*.

Definition 7 (Answer to a KQ). *An answer to a KQ q against a database instance $\mathcal{I}$ over a schema $\mathcal{S}^{\mathbf{\Pi}}$ is a set of tuples $\mathcal{A}$ in $reach(\mathcal{I}, \mathbf{\Pi}, q)$ such that: (i) each keyword $k \in q$ occurs in at least one tuple t in $\mathcal{A}$; (ii) the join graph of $\mathcal{A}$ is connected; (iii) no proper subset $\mathcal{A}' \subset \mathcal{A}$ satisfies both Conditions (i) and (ii) above.*

It is straightforward to see that there could be several answers to a KQ; below we give a widely accepted criterion for ranking such answers [18].

Definition 8. *Let $\mathcal{A}_1, \mathcal{A}_2$ be two answers to a KQ q on an instance $\mathcal{I}$. We say that $\mathcal{A}_1$* is better than *$\mathcal{A}_2$ if $|\mathcal{A}_1| \leq |\mathcal{A}_2|$. The* optimal *answers are those of minimum size.*

Example 3. Consider a KQ $q = \{a_1, c_1\}$ over the instance $\mathcal{I}$ of Example 1. Figure 1a shows two possible answers: $\mathcal{A}_1 = \{t_{11}, t_{31}\}$ and $\mathcal{A}_2 = \{t_{11}, t_{23}, t_{33}\}$. $\mathcal{A}_1$ is better than $\mathcal{A}_2$ and is the optimal answer to q. ■

3 Detecting non-answerable queries

For convenience of notation, we sometimes write c: D to denote value c and indicate that $dom(c) = D$. In addition, in our examples, the name of an attribute will also indicate its abstract domain.

3.1 Compatible queries

In order to focus on meaningful queries, we semantically characterize queries for which an answer might be found.

Definition 9 (Compatibility). *A KQ q is said to be* compatible *with a schema $\mathcal{S}$ if there exist a set of access patterns $\mathbf{\Pi}$ and an instance $\mathcal{I}$ over $\mathcal{S}^{\mathbf{\Pi}}$ such that there is an answer to q against $\mathcal{I}$.*

Example 4. The KQ $q_1 = \{a\colon A, c\colon C\}$ is not compatible with schema $\mathcal{S}_1 = \{r_1(A,B), r_2(C,D)\}$, since no set of tuples from $\mathcal{S}$ containing all the keywords in q_1 can ever be connected, independently of the access patterns for $\mathcal{S}_1$. Conversely, q_1 is compatible with $\mathcal{S}_2 = \{r_1(A,B), r_3(B,C)\}$, as witnessed by a possible answer $\{r_1(a,b), r_3(b,c)\}$ and patterns $\mathbf{\Pi}$ such that $\mathcal{S}_2^{\mathbf{\Pi}} = \{r_1(A^i,B), r_3(B,C)\}$.

Similarly, KQ $q_2 = \{a\colon A, a'\colon A\}$ is compatible with a schema $\mathcal{S}_3 = \{r_1(A,B)\}$, as witnessed by a possible answer $\{r_1(a,b), r_1(a',b)\}$ and patterns $\mathbf{\Pi}$ such that $\mathcal{S}_3^{\mathbf{\Pi}} = \{r_1(A^i,B)\}$. However, q_2 is not compatible with a schema $\mathcal{S}_4 = \{r_4(A)\}$, since a unary relation, alone, can never connect two keywords. ■

Checking compatibility of a KQ with a schema essentially amounts to checking reachability on a graph. The main idea is that in order for an answer to ever be possible, we must find an instance that exhibits a witness (i.e., a set of tuples) satisfying all the conditions of Definition 7.

3.2 Answerable queries

A stricter requirement than compatibility is given by the notion of answerability.

Definition 10 (Answerability). *A KQ q is* answerable *against a schema $\mathcal{S}^{\mathbf{\Pi}}$ if there is an instance $\mathcal{I}$ over $\mathcal{S}^{\mathbf{\Pi}}$ such that there is an answer to q against $\mathcal{I}$.*

Example 5. Consider KQ $q = \{a\colon A, c\colon C\}$ and schema $\mathcal{S}_1^{\mathbf{\Pi}} = \{r(A^i,B), s(B,C,D^i)\}$. Although q is compatible with $\mathcal{S}_1$, it is not answerable against $\mathcal{S}_1^{\mathbf{\Pi}}$, since no tuple from $\mathcal{S}_1$ can be extracted under $\mathbf{\Pi}$ (no values for domain D are available). Conversely, q is answerable against $\mathcal{S}_2^{\mathbf{\Pi}} = \{r(A^i,B), s(B^i,C,D)\}$, since an answer like $\{r(a,b), s(b,c,d)\}$ could be extracted by first accessing r with binding $\langle a\rangle$, thus extracting value b, and then s with binding $\langle b\rangle$. ■

In order to check answerability, we need to check that all the required relations can be accessed according to the access patterns. To this end, we first refer to a schema enriched with unary relations representing the keywords in the KQ. [1]

Definition 11 (Expanded schema). *Let q be a KQ over a schema $\mathcal{S}^{\mathbf{\Pi}}$. The* expanded schema $\mathcal{S}_q^{\mathbf{\Pi}}$ *of $\mathcal{S}^{\mathbf{\Pi}}$ wrt. q is defined as $\mathcal{S}_q^{\mathbf{\Pi}} = \mathcal{S}^{\mathbf{\Pi}} \cup \{r_c(C) | c \in q\}$, where r_c is a new unary relation, not occurring in $\mathcal{S}^{\mathbf{\Pi}}$, whose only attribute C is an output attribute with abstract domain $dom(C) = dom(c)$.*

Then, we use the notion of dependency graph (d-graph) to denote output-input dependencies between relation arguments, indicating that a relation under access patterns needs values from other relations.

[1] If other values are known besides the keywords, this knowledge may be represented by means of appropriate unary relations with output mode in the schema.

Definition 12 (d-graph). *Let q be a KQ over a schema $\mathcal{S}^{\Pi}$. The* d-graph $G_q^{\mathcal{S}^{\Pi}}$ *is a directed graph $\langle \mathcal{N}, \mathcal{E} \rangle$ defined as follows. For each attribute A of each relation in the expanded schema $\mathcal{S}_q^{\Pi}$, there is a node in $\mathcal{N}$ labeled with A's access mode and abstract domain. There is an arc $u \frown v$ in $\mathcal{E}$ whenever: (i) u and v have the same abstract domain; (ii) u is an output node; and (iii) v is an input node.*

Some relations are made invisible by the access patterns and can be discarded.

Definition 13 (Visibility). *An input node $v_n \in \mathcal{N}$ in a d-graph $\langle \mathcal{N}, \mathcal{E} \rangle$ is* visible *if there is a sequence of arcs $u_1 \frown v_1, \ldots, u_n \frown v_n$ in $\mathcal{E}$ such that (i) u_1's relation has no input attributes, and (ii) v_i's and u_{i+1}'s relation are the same, for $1 \leq i \leq n-1$. A relation is visible if all of its input nodes are.*

Example 5 (cont.). Consider the KQ and the schemas from Example 5. The d-graphs $G_q^{\mathcal{S}_1^{\Pi}}$ and $G_q^{\mathcal{S}_2^{\Pi}}$ are shown in Figures 2a and Figure 2b, respectively. ■

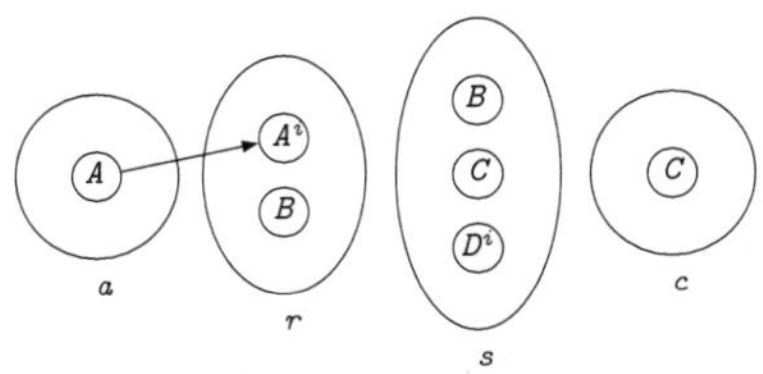

(a) D-graph $G_q^{\mathcal{S}_1^{\Pi}}$ from Example 5; s is not visible.

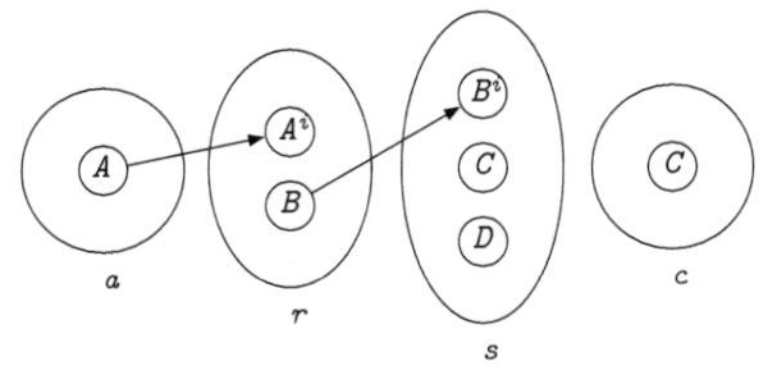

(b) D-graph $G_q^{\mathcal{S}_2^{\Pi}}$ from Example 5; all relations are visible.

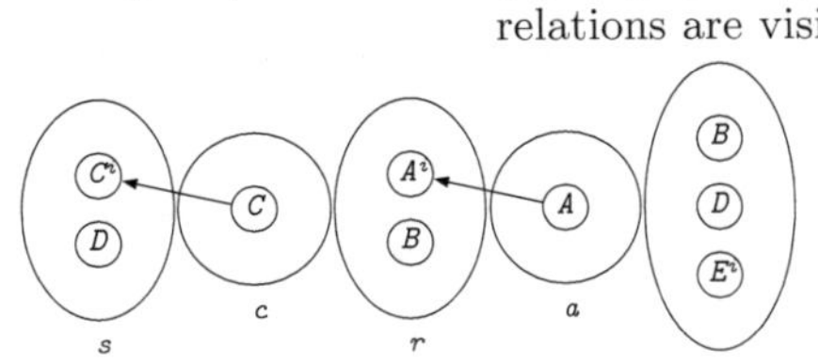

(c) D-graph $G_q^{\mathcal{S}^{\Pi}}$ from Example 6; u is not visible.

Fig. 2: D-graphs from the Examples.

Answerability of a KQ q is checked by means of compatibility with a schema in which all non-visible relations have been eliminated.

Example 6. Consider a KQ $q = \{a\colon A, c\colon C\}$ and a schema $\mathcal{S}^{\Pi} = \{r(A^i, B), s(C^i, D), u(B, D, E^i)\}$. Relation u is not visible in $G_q^{\mathcal{S}^{\Pi}}$ (Figure 2c). Then, q is not answerable in $\mathcal{S}^{\Pi}$, since q is not compatible with schema $\{r(A, B), s(C, D)\}$ (i.e., $\mathcal{S}$ without relation u). ■

4 Conclusions and future work

We have defined the problem of keyword search in the Deep Web. We are currently working on minimizing the number of accesses to the data sources.

We believe that several interesting issues can be studied in the framework defined in this paper. We plan, e.g., to leverage known values (besides the keywords) and ontologies to speed up the search for an optimal answer as well as to consider the case in which nodes and arcs of the join graph are weighted to model source availability and proximity, respectively.

References

1. Sanjay Agrawal, Surajit Chaudhuri, and Gautam Das. Dbxplorer: A system for keyword-based search over relational databases. In *ICDE*, pages 5–16, 2002.
2. Meghyn Bienvenu et al. Dealing with the deep web and all its quirks. In *Proc. of VLDS*, pages 21–24, 2012.
3. Andrea Calì and Davide Martinenghi. Querying data under access limitations. In *ICDE*, pages 50–59, 2008.
4. Andrea Calì and Davide Martinenghi. Querying the deep web. In *EDBT*, pages 724–727, 2010.
5. Andrea Calì, Davide Martinenghi, and Riccardo Torlone. Keyword search in the deep web. In *Proc. of the 9th AMW*, 2015.
6. M. R. Garey, R. L. Graham, and D. S. Johnson. The complexity of computing Steiner minimal trees. *SIAM J. on Applied Mathematics*, 32(4):835–859, 1977.
7. Konstantin Golenberg, Benny Kimelfeld, and Yehoshua Sagiv. Keyword proximity search in complex data graphs. In *SIGMOD*, pages 927–940, 2008.
8. Lin Guo, Feng Shao, Chavdar Botev, and Jayavel Shanmugasundaram. Xrank: ranked keyword search over xml documents. In *SIGMOD*, pages 16–27, 2003.
9. Bin He, Zhen Zhang, and Kevin Chen-Chuan Chang. Metaquerier: querying structured web sources on-the-fly. In *Proc. of SIGMOD*, pages 927–929, 2005.
10. Vagelis Hristidis and Yannis Papakonstantinou. Discover: Keyword search in relational databases. In *VLDB*, pages 670–681, 2002.
11. Hasan M. Jamil and Hosagrahar V. Jagadish. A structured query model for the deep relational web. In *CIKM*, pages 1679–1682, 2015.
12. Benny Kimelfeld and Yehoshua Sagiv. Finding and approximating top-k answers in keyword proximity search. In *PODS*, pages 173–182, 2006.
13. Jens Lehmann et al. Deqa: Deep web extraction for question answering. In *ISWC'12*, pages 131–147. Springer-Verlag, 2012.
14. Guoliang Li et al. EASE: an effective 3-in-1 keyword search method for unstructured, semi-structured and structured data. In *SIGMOD*, pages 903–914, 2008.
15. Jayant Madhavan, Loredana Afanasiev, Lyublena Antova, and Alon Y. Halevy. Harnessing the deep web: Present and future. In *CIDR*, 2009.
16. Sriram Raghavan and Hector Garcia-Molina. Crawling the hidden web. In *VLDB*, pages 129–138, 2001.
17. Thanh Tran et al. Top-k exploration of query candidates for efficient keyword search on graph-shaped (rdf) data. In *ICDE*, pages 405–416, 2009.
18. Jeffrey Xu Yu, Lu Qin, and Lijun Chang. Keyword search in relational databases: A survey. *IEEE Data Eng. Bull.*, 33(1):67–78, 2010.

Forecasting via Distributed Density-Based Clustering
(Discussion Paper)

Roberto Corizzo[1], Gianvito Pio[1], Michelangelo Ceci[1,2] and Donato Malerba[1,2]

[1]University of Bari Aldo Moro
Department of Computer Science - Via Orabona, 4 - 70125 Bari, Italy

[2]CINI - Consorzio Interuniversitario Nazionale per l'Informatica - Bari
{roberto.corizzo,gianvito.pio,michelangelo.ceci,donato.malerba}@uniba.it

1 Introduction

The generation of massive amounts of data in different forms (such as activity logs and measurements produced by sensor networks) increased the need of novel data mining algorithms which are capable to build accurate models efficiently and in a distributed fashion. In the recent years, several approaches able to distribute the workload to several machines have been proposed for the classical clustering, classification and regression tasks. However, they often suffer from strong limitations in their applicability, i.e. they are limited to data organized in a specific structure, are able to analyze only low-dimensional data, or suffer from overhead and scalability issues when the number of instances and attributes increase considerably. For example, to the best of our knowledge, in the literature there are very few density-based clustering algorithms (mostly inspired by the well known algorithm DBSCAN) able to work with an arbitrary number of features and with good scalability performances. Moreover, most of them are exploitable only for pure clustering purposes. At this respect, in this paper we propose a novel density-based clustering algorithm, implemented in the Apache Spark framework, which is able to handle large-scale and high-dimensional data by exploiting the Locality Sensitive Hashing (LSH). Moreover, the proposed approach is able to exploit the identified clusters, built on historical data, to forecast the values assumed by a target variable in the future. Therefore, the proposed method can be adopted also for forecasting purposes.

The rest of the paper is structured as follows: in Section 2, we briefly review existing methods to solve the classical density-based clustering task as well as recently proposed clustering methods which are able to handle large-scale data in parallel on multiple processors. In Section 3, we propose our distributed density-based clustering solution, which is able to work on high-dimensional and large-scale data, and describe our approach to exploit the identified clusters for forecasting purposes. In Section 4, we report the results of our experimental evaluation, showing that the proposed method is able to obtain accurate predictions and appears very efficient in dealing massive amounts of high-dimensional data. Finally, in Section 5 we draw some conclusions and outline some future work.

2 Background on Density-based Clustering

Density-based clustering was introduced in [9] with the algorithm DBSCAN. This approach is able to identify arbitrarily shaped clusters (not only spherical, as partitioning-based approaches) without requiring the number of clusters to be extracted as an input parameter. However, it requires two other parameters, i.e., *eps* and *minPts*. Since several concepts about density-based algorithms are common to those adopted in this paper, here we recall some useful basic notions:

- The neighborhood of an object p is defined as $N(p) = \{q \mid dist(p,q) < eps\}$;
- An object p is a *core object* w.r.t. *eps* and *minPts* if $|N(p)| \geq minPts$;
- An object p is directly density-reachable from an object q if $p \in N(q)$ and q is a *core object*;
- An object p_w is density-reachable from an object p_1 if there exists a chain of objects $p_1, p_2, \ldots, p_w$, such that for each pair of objects $\langle p_i, p_{i+1} \rangle$, p_{i+1} is directly density-reachable from p_i w.r.t. *eps* and *minPts*;
- An object p is density-connected to an object q if there is an object o such that both p and q are density-reachable from o w.r.t. *eps* and *minPts*;
- A *cluster* is a non-empty subset of objects, such that for each pair of objects $\langle p, q \rangle$, p is density-connected to q;
- Non-core objects belonging to at least one cluster are called *border objects*, whereas objects not belonging to any cluster are called *noise objects*.

The algorithm DBSCAN starts with an arbitrary object o and, if it is a core object, retrieves all the objects which are density-reachable from o w.r.t. *eps* and *minPts*. This procedure returns a cluster and the algorithm proceeds with the next unclustered object. This algorithm has been proved to identify accurate and arbitrary shaped clusters and is almost independent of the order of the analysis of the objects. Several variants have been proposed in the literature, aiming at facing different limitations of the original DBSCAN (e.g., [2, 5] for the estimation of the value of the input parameters) or at extending its applicability, for example, to streams of data [1] or to spatio-temporal data [3].

In order to be able to process large datasets, other works focused on the computational complexity, which is originally $O(n^2 \cdot m)$ (where n is the number of objects and m is the number of features), dominated by the computation of the neighborhood of each node. An example can be found in [14], where the authors proposed an approximated variant of DBSCAN, based on Locality Sensitive Hashing (LSH) [7] which requires $O(n \cdot m)$ steps to compute the neighborhood of the nodes. Still focusing on the possibility to process large datasets, in [12] a parallel implementation of DBSCAN for MapReduce has been proposed. This method is based on the partitioning of objects according to each dimension, thus it suffers from a computational viewpoint with high-dimensional data. For this reason, the authors limit their experiments to 2D datasets. The same limitation affects other existing methods implemented in the Apache Spark framework [8].

In this context, the algorithm proposed here attacks the issues raised by high-dimensional and large-scale datasets through an approach which is computationally efficient and distributed in all its steps and that, inspired by works on predictive clustering [13], can be exploited for forecasting purposes.

3 The Proposed Method

In this Section, we describe our distributed density-based clustering method, which is able to work with high-dimensional and large-scale datasets and that can be exploited for forecasting purposes. In Figure 1 we show the general workflow of the proposed approach, while in the following subsections we describe in detail each step of the method, briefly analyzing their computational complexity and showing that they can be easily parallelized in the Apache Spark framework.

3.1 Computation of the Neighborhood Graph and Core Objects

Given a dataset D of n objects described by m features ($m-1$ descriptive attributes and one target attribute), the first goal is to identify groups of similar objects according to their features. Most clustering algorithms, including density-based algorithms, strongly rely on the computation of similarity/distance measures among pairs of objects. This task has an inherent cost of $O(n^2 \cdot m)$, which can be reduced significantly only by resorting to approximated strategies. In this paper, inspired by [14], we adopt the Locality Sensitive Hashing (LSH), which is able to identify an approximation of the neighborhood graph (where nodes are linked when their similarity is greater than 1-*eps*) among the instances in $O(n \cdot m)$, preserving the neighborhood relationships. In particular, LSH adopts a hash function which maps similar objects (according to cosine similarity) to the same *bucket* with high probability. Objects falling in the same bucket of a given object are considered as belonging to its neighborhood. Here, we exploit a parallel implementation of LSH available for the Apache Spark framework[1].

Once the neighborhood graph has been computed, we identify the set of core objects, according to the definitions provided in the previous section, that is, we identify the set $cores = \{o \text{ s.t. } |N(o)| \geq minPts\}$. Let E be the set of edges of the neighborhood graph identified by LSH, represented as a distributed data structure of pairs of nodes. This step can be implemented as an *aggregateByKey* operation (to find the set of neighbors for each node) followed by a *filter* operation (to select only those nodes o such that $|N(o)| \geq minPts$). Therefore, this step is fully parallelizable and, since each edge of the neighborhood graph is analyzed once, its computational complexity is $O(|E|)$.

[1] `https://github.com/soundcloud/cosine-lsh-join-spark`

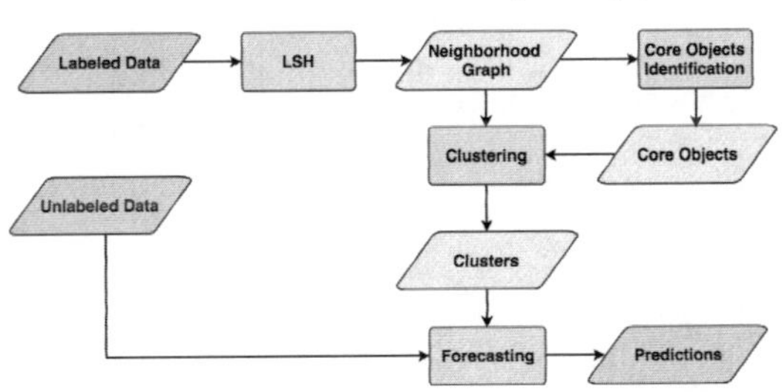

Fig. 1. Workflow of the proposed method.

3.2 Distributed Density-based Clustering

Given the set of core nodes and the neighborhood graph, our density-based clustering algorithm exploits the property of *density-connection*, described in Section 2, to simultaneously identify multiple density-based clusters. It is noteworthy that in this phase we do not need node attributes, therefore we can distribute over the available machines only the neighborhood graph, making the proposed algorithm efficient also in terms of memory requirements. An intuitive pseudo-code description of our clustering method is shown in Algorithm 1.

In detail, the algorithm initially assigns a different cluster ID to each core node, and the $ID = 0$ to boundary and noise nodes (lines 1-10). This step can be implemented in a distributed fashion by a single *map* operation over the set of nodes, therefore its complexity is $O(n)$. Subsequently, each core node *sends a message* containing its cluster ID to its neighbouring nodes having a lower cluster ID (lines 15-27). Each node receives multiple *messages* from its adjacent

Algorithm 1 Density-based clustering exploiting the neighborhood graph.

Require:
- $G = \langle V, E \rangle$: the neighborhood graph, where V are the nodes and E are the edges representing the neighborhood relationship between pairs of nodes;
- *cores*: set of core nodes from which to start the propagation of cluster IDs;
- *labelChangeRate*: minimum percentage of label changes to perform a new iteration.

Ensure:
- the updated graph G, where nodes V are associated to their cluster ID.

```
1: {Initialization of the cluster ID for core objects}
2: clusterid ← 1
3: for all v ∈ V do
4:    if v ∈ cores then
5:       v.clusterID ← clusterID
6:       clusterID ← clusterID + 1
7:    else
8:       v.clusterID ← 0
9:    end if
10: end for
11:
12: {Propagation of cluster IDs according to reachability of nodes}
13: threshold ← labelChangeRate * |E|
14: repeat
15:    changes ← 0
16:    {Reset messages for all the nodes}
17:    for all v ∈ V do
18:       v.messages ← ∅
19:    end for
20:
21:    {Each node receives multiple messages from (core, clustered) neighboring nodes}
22:    for all e = ⟨src, dst⟩ ∈ E do
23:       if src ∈ cores and src.clusterID > dst.clusterID then
24:          dst.messages ← dst.messages ∪ {src.clusterID}
25:          changes ← changes + 1
26:       end if
27:    end for
28:
29:    {Aggregate multiple messages received by each node}
30:    for all v ∈ V do
31:       v.clusterID ← max(v.messages)
32:    end for
33: until (changes < threshold)
34: return G
```

nodes and aggregates them by taking the highest cluster ID (lines 29-32)[2]. We repeat this process until the cluster assignments appear stable, i.e. when the messages exchanged among nodes through the edges of the neighborhood graph are less then a given percentage $labelChangeRate$ of the whole set of edges. This process is coherent with the general concepts at the basis of classical density-based clustering approaches, since clusters can only be built from core nodes and since the propagation of cluster IDs is performed only from core nodes.

This iterative process can be easily parallelized, since each edge of the graph can be analyzed independently of the other to evaluate whether a message has to be sent. Moreover, the final aggregation step of the received messages can be performed by a single *reduce* operation. Therefore, the computational cost of this phase is dominated by $O(u \cdot |E|)$, where u is the number of performed iterations. We also emphasize the fact that, contrary to existing methods (e.g., [8]) our approach does not require a final merging procedure necessary to aggregate the results computed on different machines, which is usually executed on a single *driver* machine.

3.3 Exploiting Clusters for Forecasting Purposes

Inspired by predictive clustering approaches [13], we exploit the k identified clusters for forecasting purposes (see Figure 2). In particular, we re-associate each node to its features through a *join* operation and compute a representative m-dimensional vector (including the target attribute[3]) for each cluster, by performing a column-wise average of the vectors associated to objects falling in the cluster. This operation can be easily parallelized by aggregating the clustering result over the cluster IDs and by performing a single *map* operation to obtain the representative vectors for each cluster. Since each object can fall in at most one cluster, the complexity of this operation is $O(n \cdot m)$. The prediction of the value of the target attribute for unlabeled instances can then be performed by

[2] This is only an implementation choice. Indeed, we could keep the lowest cluster ID without any change in the results, since the *density-connection* is symmetric.

[3] Here we assume that the target attribute is numerical. However, we can handle also categorical attributes by adopting a strategy based on majority voting.

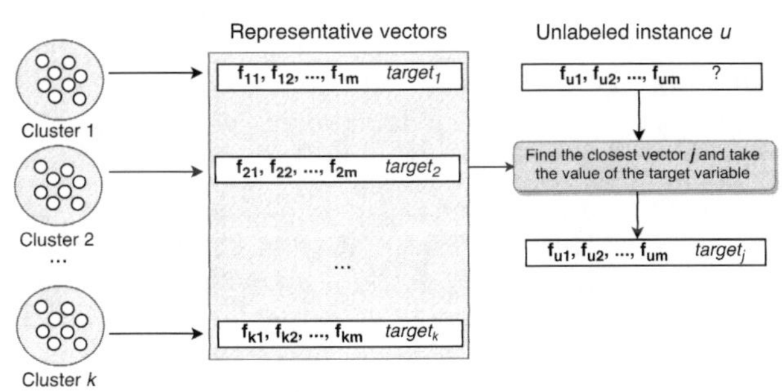

Fig. 2. Outline of the forecasting step.

comparing their $(m-1)$-dimensional feature vector (excluding the target attribute, since it is unknown for unlabeled instances) to all the representative vectors associated to the clusters, in order to find the closest cluster. The value assumed by the target attribute of the closest representative vector is finally associated to the unlabeled instance. Also this step can be easily parallelized through a *map* operation over the set of unlabeled instances which compares their vector to all the k representative vectors. Therefore, the computational complexity of the prediction phase is $O(k * m)$ for each unlabeled instance.

4 Experiments

We performed the experiments by adopting the self-adaptive online training strategy, where data are represented as a time-based sliding window [11] of size d (past d days of historical data). We considered different values of d $(30, 60$ and $90)$, and set the forecasting horizon as one-day-ahead. Each configuration was run five times, with different random picks of test days. Results are evaluated in terms of the average Root Mean Square Error (RMSE).
The considered approaches, each run in its best configuration, are:
• **Our method**, optimized by means of a grid search on a separate set of days, in order to identify the best values of the parameters *eps* and *minPts*;
• **K-Means** algorithm, implemented in the Apache Spark framework, extended with our forecasting strategy. A grid search has been performed using a separate set of days, in order to identify the best value of the parameter k;
• **ARIMA** [4], a pure forecasting method which automatically selects the best forecasting model, on the basis of the Akaike Information Criterion (AIC);
• **AVG**, a baseline approach which predicts the value of the target attribute as the average value assumed over the training instances.

The considered datasets are described in the following:
• **PVItaly.** This dataset contains data about the energy production of photovoltaic power plants, aggregated hourly, collected at regular intervals by sensors located on 17 plants in Italy, from January 1st 2012 to May 4th 2014.
• **PVNREL.** This dataset originally consists of simulated photovoltaic data of 6,000 plants, aggregated hourly, for the year 2006. The experiments were performed on a reduced version of the dataset, consisting of 48 plants belonging to the 16 States with the highest Global Horizontal Irradiation.
• **Bike Sharing (BS).** This dataset[4] contains data of the *Capital bikeshare* system, aggregated hourly, about the process of rental and returning of bikes, from/to possibly different positions, collected in 2011 and 2012 [10].

Descriptive attributes of *PVItaly* and *PVNREL* regard environmental and meteorological factors, whereas the target attribute is the hourly energy production (pre-processing steps applied to these datasets can be found in [6]). Descriptive attributes of *Bike Sharing* regard weather and seasonal information, whereas the target attribute is the hourly count of rented bikes. See Table 1 for additional information about the dataset characteristics and the considered parameters.

[4] `https://archive.ics.uci.edu/ml/datasets/Bike+Sharing+Dataset`

Table 1. Characteristics and parameter values for each dataset. LSH parameters are set as follows: *dimensions*=5, *numPermutations*=20, *maxNeighbors*=2·*minPts*.

				Window size (days)								
				30			60			90		
	instances	**test set**	**features**	**min Pts**	**eps**	**training set**	**min Pts**	**eps**	**training set**	**min Pts**	**eps**	**training set**
PVItaly	254,486	323	19	3	0.03	9690	3	0.03	19,380	5	0.02	29,070
PVNREL	331,968	912	17	10	0.97	27,360	10	0.95	54,720	10	0.95	82,080
BS	17,379	24	15	3	0.02	720	3	0.02	1,440	3	0.02	2,160

Table 2. Forecasting results (RMSE) with different training window sizes. Best results for each dataset and configuration are highlighted in bold.

	PVItaly			**PVNREL**			**BS**		
	Window size (days)			Window size (days)			Window size (days)		
	30	60	90	30	60	90	30	60	90
Our Method	**0.1371**	**0.1341**	**0.1379**	**0.1525**	**0.1488**	**0.1499**	0.1204	0.1142	0.1188
K-Means (w/forecasting)	0.1471	0.1474	0.1469	0.2338	0.2335	0.2349	**0.1096**	**0.1096**	**0.1136**
ARIMA	0.1508	0.1704	0.1925	0.2736	0.2843	0.3001	0.1646	0.1739	0.2240
AVG	0.2032	0.2058	0.2065	0.2635	0.2640	0.2647	0.1625	0.1638	0.1656

In the results shown in Table 2, we can observe that the simple baseline approach *AVG* actually appears comparable to *ARIMA* in the datasets PVNREL and BS. However, they are strongly outperformed by our method and the extended version of *K-Means*. Our density-based method leads to the best results in PVItaly and PVNREL, whereas it appears comparable to *K-Means* in BS. Moreover, it can be observed that, on PVNREL and BS, the proposed method is able to exploit the possible availability of more instances in the training phase. At this respect, in order to evaluate whether we can handle a massive amount of data, without incurring in time complexity issues, we performed a scalability test with the large version of the dataset PVNREL, on a cluster of 4 worker machines and one driver machine, each with 4 cores and 32GB of RAM, by progressively increasing the number of edges in the neighborhood graph up to 130 millions. In Figure 3, we can observe that *i)* the proposed algorithm scales linearly with respect to the number of edges, therefore it is able to deal massive amounts of data, and *ii)* the possible overhead introduced by the distribution of data to (and by the collection of the results from) different machines appears negligible.

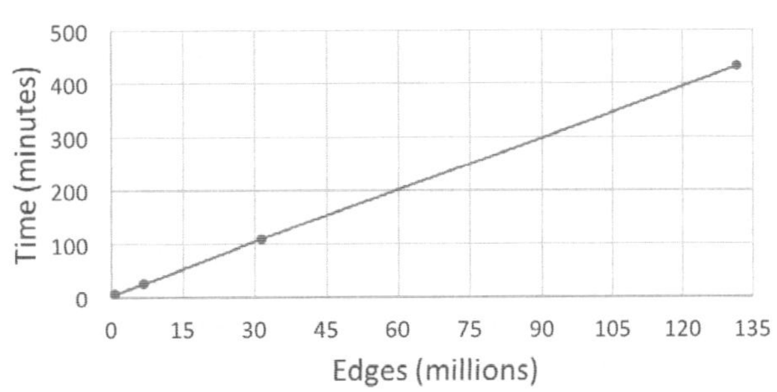

Fig. 3. Scalability test with increasing number of edges in the neighborhood graph.

5 Conclusions

In this paper, we proposed a distributed density-based clustering approach, which can be fruitfully exploited for forecasting purposes. The algorithm, implemented in the Apache Spark framework, is fully parallel, does not require any final merging procedure and is computationally efficient. Experimental results show that it is able to obtain good predictive performance and that it scales linearly with respect to the number of edges in the neighborhood graph. For future work, we intend to extend the forecasting capabilities to the multi-target setting and to perform more extensive comparisons with existing parallel solutions.

Acknowledgments

We would like to acknowledge the support of the European Commission through the projects MAESTRA - Learning from Massive, Incompletely annotated, and Structured Data (Grant Number ICT-2013-612944) and TOREADOR - Trustworthy Model-aware Analytics Data Platform (Grant Number H2020-688797).

References

1. Aggarwal, C.C., Han, J., Wang, J., Yu, P.S.: A framework for clustering evolving data streams. In: Proc. of VLDB - Volume 29. pp. 81–92. VLDB Endowment (2003)
2. Ankerst, M., Breunig, M.M., Kriegel, H.P., Sander, J.: OPTICS: Ordering Points to Identify the Clustering Structure. In: ACM SIGMOD '99. pp. 49–60 (1999)
3. Birant, D., Kut, A.: ST-DBSCAN: An algorithm for clustering spatial–temporal data. Data & Knowledge Engineering 60(1), 208–221 (2007)
4. Box, G.E.P., Jenkins, G.: Time Series Analysis, Forecasting and Control. Holden-Day, Incorporated (1990)
5. Campello, R.J.G.B., Moulavi, D., Zimek, A., Sander, J.: Hierarchical density estimates for data clustering, visualization, and outlier detection. ACM Trans. Knowl. Discov. Data 10(1), 5:1–5:51 (Jul 2015)
6. Ceci, M., Corizzo, R., Fumarola, F., Malerba, D., Rashkovska, A.: Predictive modeling of pv energy production: How to set up the learning task for a better prediction? IEEE Transactions on Industrial Informatics PP(99), 1–1 (2016)
7. Charikar, M.S.: Similarity estimation techniques from rounding algorithms. In: Proc. of ACM symposium on Theory of computing. pp. 380–388. ACM (2002)
8. Cordova, I., Moh, T.S.: Dbscan on resilient distributed datasets. In: High Performance Computing & Simulation (HPCS). pp. 531–540. IEEE (2015)
9. Ester, M., Kriegel, H.P., et al.: A density-based algorithm for discovering clusters in large spatial databases with noise. In: Kdd. vol. 96(34), pp. 226–231 (1996)
10. Fanaee-T, H., Gama, J.: Event labeling combining ensemble detectors and background knowledge. Progress in Artificial Intelligence pp. 1–15 (2013)
11. Gama, J.: Knowledge Discovery from Data Streams. Chapman and Hall / CRC Data Mining and Knowledge Discovery Series, CRC Press (2010)
12. He, Y., Tan, H., Luo, W., Mao, H., Ma, D., Feng, S., Fan, J.: MR-DBSCAN: an efficient parallel density-based clustering algorithm using MapReduce. In: Parallel and Distributed Systems (ICPADS). pp. 473–480. IEEE (2011)
13. Stojanova, D., Ceci, M., Appice, A., Dzeroski, S.: Network regression with predictive clustering trees. Data Min. Knowl. Discov. 25(2), 378–413 (2012)
14. Wu, Y.P., Guo, J.J., Zhang, X.J.: A linear DBSCAN algorithm based on LSH. In: Int. Conf. on Machine Learning and Cybernetics. vol. 5, pp. 2608–2614 (2007)

In Codice Ratio: Scalable Transcription of Historical Handwritten Documents (Extended Abstract)

Serena Ammirati[1], Donatella Firmani[1], Marco Maiorino[2], Paolo Merialdo[1], Elena Nieddu[1], and Andrea Rossi[1]

[1] Roma Tre University
serena.ammirati,donatella.firmani@uniroma3.it,merialdo@dia.uniroma3.it, ema.nieddu,and.rossi.516@gmail.com
[2] Vatican Secret Archives (Archivum Secretum Apostolicum Vaticanum)
m.maiorino@asv.va

Abstract. Huge amounts of handwritten historical documents are being published by digital libraries world wide. However, for these raw digital images to be really useful, they need to be annotated with informative content. State-of-the-art Handwritten Text Recognition (HTR) approaches require an impressive training effort by expert paleographers. Our contribution is a scalable, end-to-end transcription work-flow – that we call *In Codice Ratio* – based on fine-grain segmentation of text elements into characters and symbols, with limited training effort. We provide a preliminary evaluation of *In Codice Ratio* over a corpus of letters by pope Honorii III, stored in the Vatican Secret Archive.

1 Introduction

Large document collections are sources of important correlations between entities such as people, events, places, and organizations. Previous studies [7] have shown that it is possible to detect macroscopic patterns of cultural change over periods of centuries by analyzing large textual time series. Such automatic methods promise to empower scholars with a quantitative and data-driven tool to study culture and society, but their power has been limited by the amount of digitally transcribed sources. Indeed, the World Wide Web only contains a small part of the traditional archives. (It is evocative to think that it may only contain a few millimeters out of the 85km of linear shelves in the Vatican Secret Archives.) Recently, many historical archives have begun to digitize their assets, sharing high-resolution images of the original documents. Notable examples include the Bibliothque Nationale de France[3], the Virtual Manuscript Library of Switzerland[4], and the Vatican Apostolic Library[5]. In this scenario, expert paleographers

[3] http://gallica.bnf.fr
[4] http://www.e-codices.unifr.ch/en
[5] http://www.digitavaticana.org

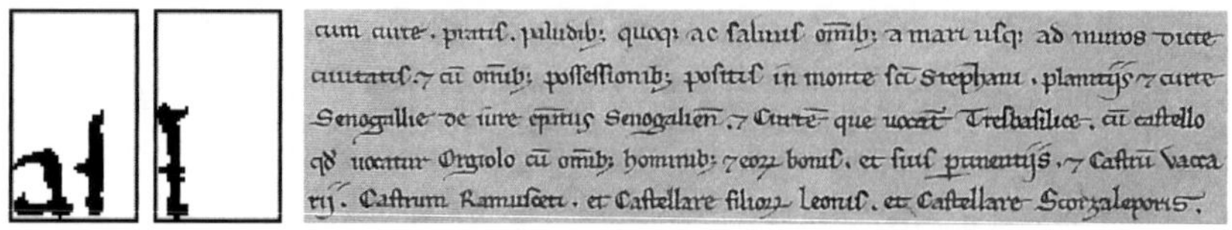

(a) (b)

Fig. 1: (a) Fragments. (b) Sample text from the manuscript *Liber septimus regestorum domini Honorii pope III*, in the Vatican Registrers.

can largely benefit from computer-assisted transcription technologies. This includes not only full transcriptions, but also partial transcription and other kinds of automatically produced meta-data, useful for indexing and searching.

Popular automatic tools for transcribing the text content of digital images include Optical Character Recognition (OCR) systems, which work great for typewritten text but are not suitable for handwritten text recognition (HTR). Since most digitized documents by historical archives are manuscripts, HTR has recently gained more and more attention by researchers worldwide. Handwritten text is more challenging to recognize than typewritten one because characters have less regular shapes, and are often combined into single units known as a *ligatures*. Therefore, while OCR systems are trained to recognize individual typewritten glyphs, most state-of-the-art HTR systems use holistic approaches: all text elements (sentences, words, and characters) of a single text line are recognized as a whole, without any prior segmentation of the line into these elements. So-called *segmentation free* models [13] can be automatically obtained using well known training techniques, but they require the whole transcripts of a number of these unsegmented images. In order to use these technologies, users with experience in handwritten documents transcription are required to transcribe manually significant portions of the original documents. Currently available HTR technologies are still far from offering scalable automated solutions.

Our contribution. The approach of our project *In Codice Ratio* is in the middle of a spectrum, where on the one side there are OCR systems and on the other segmentation free HTR technologies, which recognize bigger handwritten elements. Rather than relying on well-segmented glyphs (as in typewriting) or training to recognize whole words, we focus on overlapping "fragments" of words composed of zero, one, or two (rarely three) characters, as in Figure 1a. For each word, we compute possible *cut-points* yielding different ways for segmenting the word into fragments. Then, we choose the best among different segmentation options using OCR and language models. Cut points are managed similarly to *on-line* HTR systems [6], where the text is written on a touch-screen and a sensor captures all the pen tip movements. Since we do not have access to pen movements, we need a number of labelled fragments[6] for training our model.

[6] A fragment can also have empty transcriptions when it does not contain any character.

Training with fragments has two advantages over training with words (as in segmentation free HTR):

- the number of fragments needed for training is much smaller, because it does not need to deal with the impressive variety of lexicon;
- fragments can be labeled by volunteers in large transcription projects, with little or no expertise, provided with adequate examples.

To this end, we set up a simple crowd-sourcing application.

Proof of Concept. Our hybrid work-flow takes the best of two worlds: we can handle challenging ligatures as in state-of-the-art HTR, and at the same time we require limited training effort like typical OCR systems. Our system is not mature enough for a thorough experimental evaluation, but for sake of demonstration, we take into account the "Vatican Registrers" corpus in the Vatican Secret Archives. The Vatican Registers is a huge collection of volumes (more than 18.000 pages) produced in the 13-th century, and containing official correspondence of the Roman Curia, such as political letters, opinions on legal questions, and documents addressed to various religious institutes throughout Europe. Such records are of unprecedented historical relevance, have not been transcribed yet, and have a regular writing style (see Figure 1b). For these reasons, we believe that they can motivate our work.

Our crowd-sourcing application enrolled 120 high-school students in the city of Rome, that did the labelling as a part of their work-related learning program. The program is jointly organized by the engineering and humanities departments of Roma Tre University, and includes frontal lessons in a variety of topics, such as paleography, history and machine learning, thus also serving as school guidance.

2 Related Works

The idea of exploiting large textual corpora to detect macroscopic cultural trends has been discussed for many years [11], promising to empower historians and other humanities scholars with a tool for the study of culture and society.

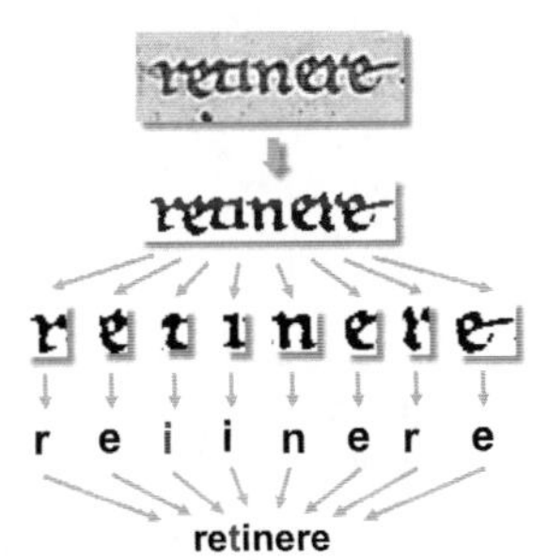

Fig. 2: Our workflow.

Data-driven history. Many studies have been published over the past few years [4, 10] about a quantitative and data-driven approach to the study of cultural change and continuity. A seminal study of 5 million English-language books published over the arc of 200 years [9] showed the potential of this approach, for example, measuring the time required by various technologies to become established or the duration of celebrity for various categories of people.

Handwriting text recognition. HTR can be defined as the ability to transform handwritten input represented as graphical marks into symbolic representation as ASCII text. According to the mode of data acquisition used, HTR can be classified into off-line and on-line. In off-line systems the handwriting is given as an image or scanned text, without time sequence information. In on-line systems the handwriting is given as a temporal sequence of coordinates that represents the pen tip trajectory. For high quality text images, current HTR state-of-the-art prototypes provide accuracy levels that range from 40 to 80% at the word level [12, 2]. On the other hand, on-line systems are more accurate [1, 5, 6], reaching 90% word-level accuracy in some cases.

Crowd-sourcing. Expected users of HTR technology belong mainly to two groups:

- individual researchers with experience in handwritten documents;
- volunteers which collaborate in large transcription projects.

Recent HTR project [14, 8] expose HTR tools through specialised crowd-sourcing web portals, supporting collaborative work.

Other works. Language modeling for on-line handwriting recognition bears many similarities with OCR and speech recognition, which often employ statistical n-gram models on the character or word level [15].

3 System Work-Flow

Our system first segments every word into small (possibly overlapping) fragments, then recognizes characters in fragments, and finally the entire word. The main steps are schematically shown in Figure 2.

1. **Pre-processing.** In this phase the color image of a page is cropped into lines and words. The image is also transformed into a bi-chromatic one.
2. **Cut-level operations.** For each word we guess cut-points for characters and build the so-called segmentation lattice data structure [6], such that each path in the lattice represent a way of **segmenting** the word.
3. **Fragment-level operations.** For each pair of cut-points we crop the corresponding text fragment and classify it, choosing among known characters.
4. **Word-level operations.** We finally return the best path in the labelled lattice, which represent a way for **transcribing** the word.

3.1 Transcription Algorithms

In this section we describe the inner phases of our system. Inner phases are designed for the Carolingian minuscule script, which is used in the manuscript for our proof of concept (see Figure 1b of Section 1).

Cut-level operations. The input for on-line HTR consists of pen up/pen down switching movements, therefore *cut-points* for character boundaries can be selected at certain positions of each stroke. Since we do not have access to stroke sequences, we design a simple heuristic based on black pixel distribution *local minima*, as shown in Figure 3a for a sample occurrence of the word "culpam". Then, we consider all the possible segmentation options induced by the cut-points and let the further phases select the best one. We build a *segmentation lattice* where each start-end path represents a segmentation option.

- Each cut-point corresponds to a node. The leftmost cut-point is the *start* node, and the rightmost the *end* node.
- Each edge corresponds to the fragment of word bounded by its endpoints.

We observed experimentally that edges corresponding to fragments smaller than 8 pixels or larger than 34 pixels can be safely dropped our further consideration. The segmentation lattice for our "culpam" example is shown in Figure 3b. In the figure, edges have labels, as will be clarified in the next section.

Fragment-level operations. We call *fragment* any squared portion of a word that is bounded by two cut-points, including incomplete characters, combinations of incomplete characters, or multiple characters together. Each edge of the segmentation lattice corresponds to a different fragment, and each path corresponds to a different segmentation option of the word into fragments. Our next step is a OCR step, where each fragment/edge of the segmentation lattice is labeled with the result of a character classifier. There are many principled ways for the classification task at hand. We decide to use a *convolutional* Neural Network (NN), that is one of the most common and popular approaches [3]. Since the NN return a *score distribution*, rather than a unique answer, we add multiple edges between the same two nodes. Some of the fragments are submitted to a crowd-sourcing application, for training the NN. The application guides the workers, providing sample images of characters and highlighting variations in shape and style. Therefore, workers without experience in transcription can give answers based on their perceived similarity of fragments to sample images. We refer to the resulting data structure as *labeled lattice*.

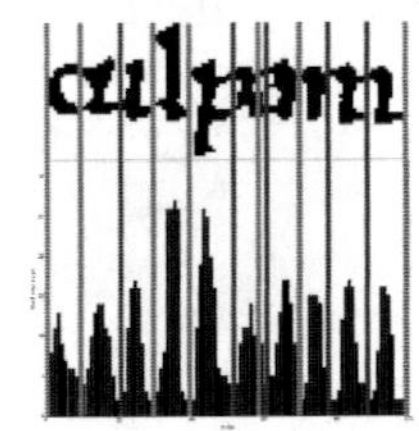

(a)

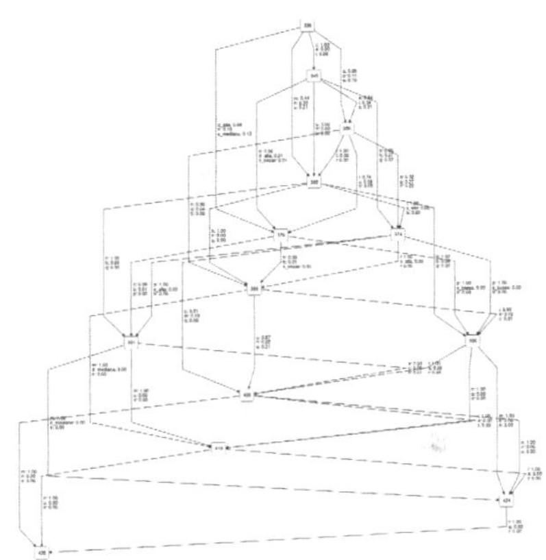

(b)

Fig. 3: Cut-points for the word "culpam" and corresponding lattice. We use green for actual character boundaries, and red otherwise.

Word-level operations. Labeled paths represent candidate transcriptions for the current word. In order find the best transcription recognition result, we use language models (LM). A statistical LM is a representation of a certain language as a probability distribution over sequences of words or characters.

In other words, a LM expresses the likelihood that certain sequences of words or characters appear in texts written in the language under analysis. To this end, we downloaded a large medieval Latin corpus ($\approx 1.5M$ words) and computed 3-grams frequencies. Then, we select the best path maximizing the corresponding **word** probability. For instance, for the path "culham" in Figure 3b we have[7] $p(\$culham^\wedge) = p(c|\$)p(u|\$c)p(l|cu)p(h|ul)p(a|lh)p(m|ha)p(^\wedge|am)$, where \$ and $^\wedge$ are special symbols denoting the beginning and the end of a word. Every term in the product can be computed directly from language models.

4 Experiments

We describe in this section our preliminary experimental results, which serves us as a *proof of concept* for *In Codice Ratio*. Ideas and methods in the proof have been realized in collaboration with the Vatican Secret Archives, with the aim of demonstrating in principle the practical potential of our system.

Fig. 4: Sample words, for our proof of concept.

Dataset. The "Vatican Registrers" corpus consists of 43 parchment registers, for a total of 18650 pages (i.e., writing facades). All the registers are written with the same script: the so-called *Cancelleresca*. Our dataset consists of 30 pages ($\approx 15K$ characters) of register 12 by Pope Honorii III, that is the only Pope with un-transcribed registers and therefore is of most interest for the VSR.

Results and future works. Our NN shows 95% accuracy and recall for our dataset, with 4.6% error. Typical errors of the NN are the following.

- Characters "f" and "s" are easily confused, due to their similar shapes. Specifically, $\approx$ 20% of "s" are labelled as "f" and 25% of "f" as "s".
- Characters "l" is often mis-classified as other "upper" characters, due to spurious ink in the fragment. Specifically, $\approx$ 72% of "l" are labelled as "b" and only $\approx$ 17% of "l" are labelled as such.

Other characters are labelled correctly more than 96% of the times.

We select 3 words, showing strengths and limits of our method, dubbed "culpam", "criminis" and "uiuscemod(i)"[8]. In Table 1 we show the top three paths in the labelled lattice, according to word probability. For "criminis", the right transcription is first in the ranking. For "uiuscemod", the right transcription is not contained in any path, but the maximum probability path "uiufemod" is correct except for the ligature "sc", which is labelled as "f" as mentioned earlier in this section. This specific problem is due to errors in the training set, where a number of "sc" fragments has been selected as "f" by workers. In the near

[7] Using 2-nd order Markov assumption.

[8] "uiuscemod" and "i" are processed as separate words.

future, we plan to repeat the training phase by removing such wrong items. Finally, "culpam" is overthrown by "cullum" because of more serious errors in the OCR process ("p" and "a" are labelled as "l" and "u', respectively). While word probability does not help (3-gram "llu" is more frequent than "lpa" in our LM), we are confident to correct this kind of error in future works. Furture works include the following.

- More sophisticated path selection criteria, for instance, taking into account NN output score (second "l" has lower score than "p").
- More advanced language model tools, such as Hidden Markov Models. This is currently being developed with promising result.
- Excluding labels that do not fit in current line margins, such as excluding an "l" where the lower margin contains black pixels, such as for "p".

5 Conclusions

In Codice Ratio is an automatic transcription workflow with low training effort. Our proof of concept is done on a high-resolution digitized copy of the registers by pope Honorii III. Manuscript pages first undergo a series of transformations, that extract a clean version of the text image. Then, preprocessed pages are decomposed into fragments containing basic text elements, such as characters and symbols. Some fragments are labelled by unskilled crowd-sourcing workers, which are asked simply to select matching images to template symbols selected by paleographers. Labelled symbols are used to train a Neural Networks, that is in charge of automatically compute labels for all the un-labelled fragments. Automatically computed labels are aggregated at the word-level into a segmentation lattice, in which all the traversing paths represent candidate transcriptions for the word. Selection of the best path is done based on language models. Our proof of concept suggests that *In Codice Ratio* can be applied to the large collection of Vatican Registers in the Vatican Secret Archives, subject to specifics improving, that are matter of ongoing work.

path	prob
culpam	
cullum	$1 \cdot 10^{-4}$
culpam	$8 \cdot 10^{-7}$
culluni	$3 \cdot 10^{-7}$
criminis	
criminis	$8 \cdot 10^{-7}$
crinunis	$6 \cdot 10^{-8}$
crinuius	$4 \cdot 10^{-8}$
uiuscemod(i)	
uiufemod	$2 \cdot 10^{-2}$
uuifemod	$2 \cdot 10^{-3}$
uiiifemod	$5 \cdot 10^{-4}$

Table 1: Path probabilities for the words in Figure 4.

Acknowledgments

We thank Gaetano Bonofiglio, Veronica Iovinella e Andrea Salvoni for their work on the OCR neural network. We thank Matteo Mariani for helping with all the pre-processing steps. We also thank Gianlorenzo Didonato for developing the front-end of the *In Codice Ratio* crowd-sourcing application. Finally, we are indebted to all the teacher and students of Liceo Keplero and Liceo Montale who joined the work-related learning program, and did all the labelling effort.

References

1. Character recognition experiments using unipen data. In *Proceedings of the Sixth International Conference on Document Analysis and Recognition*, ICDAR '01, pages 481–, Washington, DC, USA, 2001. IEEE Computer Society.
2. R. Bertolami and H. Bunke. Hidden markov model-based ensemble methods for offline handwritten text line recognition. *Pattern Recognition*, 41(11):3452 – 3460, 2008.
3. D. Ciregan, U. Meier, and J. Schmidhuber. Multi-column deep neural networks for image classification. In *Computer Vision and Pattern Recognition (CVPR), 2012 IEEE Conference on*, pages 3642–3649. IEEE, 2012.
4. I. Flaounas, O. Ali, T. Lansdall-Welfare, T. De Bie, N. Mosdell, J. Lewis, and N. Cristianini. Research methods in the age of digital journalism: Massive-scale automated analysis of news-contenttopics, style and gender. *Digital Journalism*, 1(1):102–116, 2013.
5. S. Jaeger, S. Manke, J. Reichert, and A. Waibel. Online handwriting recognition: the npen++ recognizer. *International Journal on Document Analysis and Recognition*, 3(3):169–180, 2001.
6. D. Keysers, T. Deselaers, H. A. Rowley, L.-L. Wang, and V. Carbune. Multi-language online handwriting recognition. *IEEE Transactions on Pattern Analysis and Machine Intelligence*, 2016.
7. T. Lansdall-Welfare, S. Sudhahar, J. Thompson, J. Lewis, F. N. Team, and N. Cristianini. Content analysis of 150 years of british periodicals. *Proceedings of the National Academy of Sciences*, 114(4):E457–E465, 2017.
8. A. Marcus, A. Parameswaran, et al. Crowdsourced data management: Industry and academic perspectives. *Foundations and Trends® in Databases*, 6(1-2):1–161, 2015.
9. J.-B. Michel, Y. K. Shen, A. P. Aiden, A. Veres, M. K. Gray, , J. P. Pickett, D. Hoiberg, D. Clancy, P. Norvig, J. Orwant, S. Pinker, M. A. Nowak, and E. L. Aiden. Quantitative analysis of culture using millions of digitized books. *Science*, 331(6014):176–182, 2011.
10. F. Moretti. *Distant reading*. Verso Books, 2013.
11. R. Reddy and G. StClair. The million book digital library project. `http://www.rr.cs.cmu.edu/mbdl.htm`, 2016. Accessed December 19, 2016.
12. V. Romero, V. Alabau, and J. M. Benedí. Combination of n-grams and stochastic context-free grammars in an offline handwritten recognition system. In *Proceedings of the 3rd Iberian Conference on Pattern Recognition and Image Analysis, Part I*, IbPRIA '07, pages 467–474, Berlin, Heidelberg, 2007. Springer-Verlag.
13. V. Romero, J. A. Snchez, V. Bosch, K. Depuydt, and J. de Does. Influence of text line segmentation in handwritten text recognition. In *2015 13th International Conference on Document Analysis and Recognition (ICDAR)*, pages 536–540, Aug 2015.
14. J. A. Sánchez, G. Mühlberger, B. Gatos, P. Schofield, K. Depuydt, R. M. Davis, E. Vidal, and J. De Does. transcriptorium: a european project on handwritten text recognition. In *Proceedings of the 2013 ACM symposium on Document engineering*, pages 227–228. ACM, 2013.
15. A. Stolcke et al. Srilm-an extensible language modeling toolkit. In *Interspeech*, volume 2002, page 2002, 2002.

Trusted Volunteer Computing

Michele Ianni[1] and Elio Masciari[2]

[1] DIMES, Università della Calabria mianni@dimes.unical.it
[2] ICAR CNR elio.masciari@icar.cnr.it

Abstract. Technology becomes more and more advanced everyday, both from the software and from the hardware perspective. Brand new devices, more powerful and capable of the generation preceding them, are steadily released. Everybody owns laptops, smartphones and many other devices with great compute capabilities, able to easily solve problems a few years ago considered almost impossible. These devices are, however, most of the time underused, resulting in an incredible waste of computational resources. The needs of professional people and scientists are evolving too, alongside the advances of technology. In many fields, from financial and biomedical simulation to insurance predictions, from 3D rendering to mathematical computations etc huge compute capabilities are still required. Despite the always growing presence of powerful devices and their increasingly cheap prices, in many situations using only our own devices is not enough. The contrast between underused devices and needs of computational resources led to the birth of a new approach: volunteer computing. This approach brings a user to be part of a network, sharing his idle CPU (or GPU) cycles in order to solve a subtask of a problem thus contributing, along with many other users, to the solution of a bigger task. In a very large number of cases, however, volunteer computing needs to tackle some serious security concerns. Many tasks, in fact, deal with sensitive information whose disclosure, even in a minimal part, must be avoided. For this reason still many problems are usually not handled by collaborative networks, since it is not possible, in many cases, to hide confidential data from inputs of every subtask. In this paper we present a way to solve the problem described. Through the use of trusted computing we are able to manage complex problems in a distributed network of volunteer computing devices without the risks related to the spread of sensitive data.

1 Introduction

Nowadays we are constantly surrounded by an always growing number of so called smart devices [18]. Everything we use seems to need great compute capabilities and Internet connection to work properly. Many everyday life objects, from fridges to cars, from light bulbs to toasters are integrating computers and providing functionality that several years ago where almost unthinkable. We are facing a new era, the era of Internet of Things [15], everything is always connected thus accessible from everywhere. The object that best represents this revolution is the smartphone. Everybody owns at least one of them, they are always connected and capable to perform tasks with remarkable performances. The hardware vendors are unceasingly releasing new generations every season, with new devices that easily overwhelm their predecessors, both for compute capabilities and new functionality added. The industry of personal computers follows an analogous rhythm, releasing more and more powerful devices with incredible constancy. These devices are becoming affordable and everybody, due to the hard rules imposed by our consumer society, have an induced need not only to buy them, but even upgrading to newer models as soon as the pressure related to the menace of losing their social position becomes unbearable. However this then begs the question: do we really need all those compute capabilities? Or at least, do we need them continuously? The answer is pretty obvious: our devices are, most of the time, underused. The average user does not take advantage of all the power embedded in his devices and the waste of resources is huge. On the other side there exist a lot of people who really need a huge amount of compute capabilities, that goes far beyond the considerable power of a brand new laptop. Computer scientists, 3D artists, financial analysts to cite a few, most of the time are involved in problems that require a lot of time to be solved and they are forced to spend time and money to obtain results. From this contrast between compute resources need and waste a new paradigm has born: volunteer computing. It is a type of distributed computing in which a user is part of a larger network. He donates idle CPU (or GPU) cycles, or even storage sometimes, in order to contribute to one or more "projects". Volunteer computing frameworks usually have a master/slave structure. When a problem (called job) have to be solved, one server is responsible of splitting the job in subtasks which are distributed across the nodes of the network (the volunteer computers). A client application runs on the volunteer's computer and receives the subtask from the remote server. After completing the assigned subtask the result is sent back to the server who merges the partial results to provide a solution for the initial job. In many cases the system keeps track of the volunteers work in order to implement a reward policy. Volunteer computing is a well known paradigm that spans across many different application areas. The first volunteer computing project was the Great Internet Mersenne Prime Search [23], which was started in January 1996. From that date many other projects arose [20, 19, 1, 9]. A special mention, due to the several hundred thousand volunteers involved, goes to SETI@home project [7], whose purpose is to analyze radio signals, searching for signs of extraterrestrial intelligence, and Folding@home [17] which aims to determine the mechanisms of protein folding, a subject of significant academic interest with major implications for medical research into many types of disease. One of the biggest steps in volunteer computing history has been made in 2002 with the born of BOINC [4], the Berkeley Open Infrastructure for Network

Computing. It is a project, founded at University of California, Berkeley Space Sciences Laboratory, whose aim is to provide a complete middleware system for volunteer computing. BOINC includes everything needed to start a project using volunteer computing, from the client application to the server software.

Although it is easy, thanks to the middleware available, to start a new project, volunteer computing is still not expressing its full potential. This is because this computing paradigm is based on the distribution of problem inputs among users and there is a serious problem related to data distribution: *privacy*. Many projects perfectly suitable for volunteer computing: from financial simulations to insurance predictions, from health databases scraping or biomedical modeling to marketing analysis and so forth most of the time deal with sensitive information that must remain secret. In many cases the sensitive data is so tightly connected to the rest of the information that is impossible to hide the former without altering significantly the result of the computation. Most of the times it is not possible to distribute even a small subset (the input for a subtask) of the data, because sensitive information can be inferred by its observation or because the solution of the subtask itself cannot be computed without the rest of the dataset.

Example: In our past experience with distributed computing we faced the problem of distributed rendering. In order to solve the rendering equation a ray tracing algorithm (or variants of it) is used [13]. The algorithm correctly computes the value of luminosity of every pixel in the scene by taking into account all the objects and lights that can affect the color of the given pixel. In distributed rendering, even if the rendering of a single tile (a subset of the entire scene) is requested to a volunteer, he needs to know all the information present in the entire scene (objects, lights) in order to solve the rendering problem for the pixels in the tile. It is easy to figure many cases in which the scene to be rendered must be kept secret, we just need to think about the work of architects, engineers, graphics, 3D artists and so on.

All these security concerns are crucially narrowing the potential of volunteer computing. The current middleware projects, in fact, are not suitable to deal properly with sensitive data. Our contribution in this paper is to introduce the use of trusted computing to extend the power of volunteer computing by making possible to deal with sensitive data in a safe way. The proposed solution described in this paper is related to the use of Intel® Software Guard Extensions [3], but the same concepts are applicable for other environments (e.g. ARM TrustZone [2]) with slight modifications on which we are currently working on.

2 Intel® Software Guard Extensions

It is very common to deal with software applications that need to work with sensitive data. Operating system's security policy based on permissions are often not enough to protect secrets. Despite they prevent a user from accessing other user's files they cannot avoid the access to the sensitive information to processes running with higher privileges, including the operating system itself and a plethora of various types of malicious software. To protect the secret data even in the presence of privileged malware, Intel® designed Software Guard Extensions (SGX): a security technology introduced in autumn 2015 in their CPUs based on the Skylake x86 microarchitecture. SGX is a set of CPU instructions that permit the allocation of private regions of usermode address space, called *enclaves* by leveraging trusted hardware. These regions are protected from processes running even at higher privilege levels and provide confidentiality and integrity [12]. Several protection are guaranteed by Intel® SGX:

- Enclave memory is encrypted and cannot be read or written from outside even by processes with high privileges and independently by the CPU mode. The encryption key, stored in an inaccessible region within the CPU, is changed every power cycle.
- The only way to enter in an enclave is through a dedicated instruction, there is no other way to jump inside an enclave.
- Enclaves cannot be debugged by software or hardware debuggers.
- Data within enclaves can only by accessed by code in the same enclave.

One of the main drawbacks of this technology is that the applications running in SGX enclaves are severely restricted compared to normal programs. The Trusted Computing Base (TCB) of SGX is minimal, it consists of the CPU (hardware logic, microcode, registers, cache memory) and the software components used for attestation (see section 4). More in detail the operating system is not part of the TCB, this means that is not possible to use kernel services or system calls directly. This is because the operating system is untrusted and a syscall involves the transfer of control flow from trusted code running in an enclave to untrusted OS code. The latter could be a malicious kernel exposing crafted system calls capable of compromising the security of the enclave. As a workaround SGX includes instructions, called OCALLs, that offer the opportunity to temporarily exit the enclave and calling untrusted code to perform general purpose operations like system calls, I/O etc. Several studies (Graphene [14], SCONE [8], Haven [10], Panoply [22]) have been released on this topic and many of them aim at overcoming the burden of switching from enclaves to untrusted OS. The solutions proposed in those projects are based on a syscall forwarding mechanism that handle the calls to system services inside the enclave and execute them outside taking care of switch between two different context and the transfer of the data needed to perform the operation requested. This allows the shielded execution, within a SGX enclave, of unmodified legacy applications written for traditional operating systems. In our paper we are assuming that, if required by the algorithm that runs inside the enclave and handles the sensitive data, one of this syscall forwarding mechanism is implemented and we can run arbitrary code within the enclave.

3 Trusted volunteer computing system architecture

The proposed architecture is based on a Client-Server model. The clients of the system are all the users sharing their compute capabilities in the network. Their work is coordinated by one or more servers which are in charge of splitting the task to be executed in subtasks and distributing them among the clients. Usually in volunteer computing networks the server is responsible of many other actions: collecting the results from the clients and merging them to obtain the result of the main task, verifying the correctness of the results provided, enforcing client management policies based on several factors, such that performances or reliability, of the volunteer devices, just to cite a few. All these server duties are well known topics fully covered in literature [21, 6, 5].
The volunteers of the network, who wish to share their computational resources, can achieve this goal by using a client application on their devices. We focus our attention on protecting the client application, since they tend to run on platforms that may not have the same degree of control and security as servers. Nevertheless, the techniques described here can also be applied in order to protect assets on the server.
The client application consists of two different parts: a trusted and an untrusted module. The trusted part of the application runs within the SGX enclave and handles the sensitive data. It is kept as small as possible, it is composed only by the algorithms which need to deal directly with the secret assets. The untrusted part of the application is made up of all the rest: graphical user interface, libraries and all the functionality needed to communicate with the rest of the network performing tasks such as signaling presence in the network, handling connections, managing the amount and the type of the resources shared with the volunteer network. The trusted and untrusted components of the client application communicate to each other through well-defined entry-points. These are designed to ensure that no secrets are allowed to leak out from the enclave. The integrity and confidentiality of the data inside the enclave is guaranteed by the the hardware/software protections of SGX.
The subtasks to be resolved are sent by the remote server to the client application. The sensitive data is encrypted (see section 4) and is forwarded by the untrusted part of the client application to the trusted part. After the completion of the subtask the results, encrypted, are sent back to the remote server which merges them with the other results coming from other clients to finally get the result of the main task.

4 Provisioning and attestation issues

Since our goal is to provide a way to deal with sensitive information in volunteer computing networks, we need to tackle some security issues related to the

transfer of this data between server and client. Our threat model is based on the assumption that every client on the network is untrusted, thus we need to provide a way to secure the communication among all the parties involved. The SGX enclave must have the assurance of communicating with a legit remote server and vice versa (this process is called *attestation*). They also need to establish a secure channel to talk each other and to transfer the sensitive data (*provisioning* phase). To address the issues described we make use of the services provided by Intel® SGX [3, 16]. On the client machine is running, in fact, the SGX Platform Software (PSW) that includes also a Quoting Enclave containing an asymmetric attestation key representing the SGX TCB.
In response to the first request of connection from a client application to the remote server the latter will send to the client an attestation request containing a nonce for liveness purposes. This request aim at verifying that the software runs on a legit SGX enclave as well as ensuring the validity of the enclave and collecting information about the identity of software being attested. It is the untrusted part of the client, as explained in section 3 that handles the connection with the remote server. This part of the application receives the attestation request and forwards it to the trusted part, running inside the enclave. At this point the trusted part sends a local attestation to the Quoting Enclave through the untrusted part. The local attestation consists of a report structure along with a manifest that include the nonce and a temporary public key C_P that is used later by the remote server. The Quoting Enclave creates a remote-attestation by verifying, and signing (with the asymmetric attestation key) the local one. The result of this process is called *Quote* and is sent (always through the untrusted part) to the remote server. A verification server is used by the remote server to verify the received Quote. To avoid some privacy concerns related to this scheme [24] Intel® adopts an extension called Intel® Enhanced Privacy ID (EPID) [11]. EPID signatures are anonymous and thanks to a group signature scheme, nobody can uniquely identify the platform where the application is running by looking at objects signed by the application itself. At the end of the attestation process the remote server is sure to communicate with a legit secure enclave. The entire client application running alongside the secure enclave is now part of the volunteer computing network and it is ready to share its computational resources to solve the subtasks provided by the remote server. It is still mandatory, however, to ensure that the communication between client and server is conducted through a secure channel and is necessary to create this channel along the remote attestation process to avoid the provisioning of sensitive data to not attested enclaves. To create this channel the temporary public key C_P, created by the trusted enclave and delivered to the server inside the Quote is used. The remote server generates an encryption key E, encrypts it with C_P and sends the result of this operation to the application. Only the trusted part of the client, running within the enclave, knows the private key associated with C_P and can obtain the encryption key E. The sensitive data, as well as the results of

the subtasks, can be encrypted using E, permitting the secure communication between the client and the remote server.

5 Conclusions and future work

In this paper we described a new way to further enhance the power of volunteer computing networks. By the leverage of Intel® Software Guard Extension we provided a way to build trusted volunteer computing systems without the problems related to the spread of secret information. Using the system proposed it is possible to use computational resources of untrusted devices for solving tasks that deal with sensitive data. As a future development of the approach described we are working on extending these ideas to other Trusted Execution Environments (e.g. ARM TrustZone), since they are integrated in most of the new smartphones.

References

[1] Albert D Alexandrov et al. "Superweb: Towards a global web-based parallel computing infrastructure". In: *Parallel Processing Symposium, 1997. Proceedings., 11th International.* IEEE. 1997, pp. 100–106.

[2] Tiago Alves, Don Felton, et al. "Trustzone: Integrated hardware and software security". In: *ARM white paper* 3.4 (2004), pp. 18–24.

[3] Ittai Anati et al. "Innovative technology for CPU based attestation and sealing". In: *Proceedings of the 2nd international workshop on hardware and architectural support for security and privacy.* Vol. 13. 2013.

[4] David P Anderson. "Boinc: A system for public-resource computing and storage". In: *Grid Computing, 2004. Proceedings. Fifth IEEE/ACM International Workshop on.* IEEE. 2004, pp. 4–10.

[5] David P Anderson, Carl Christensen, and Bruce Allen. "Designing a runtime system for volunteer computing". In: *SC 2006 Conference, Proceedings of the ACM/IEEE.* IEEE. 2006, pp. 33–33.

[6] David P Anderson, Eric Korpela, and Rom Walton. "High-performance task distribution for volunteer computing". In: *e-Science and Grid Computing, 2005. First International Conference on.* IEEE. 2005, 8–pp.

[7] David P Anderson et al. "SETI@ home: an experiment in public-resource computing". In: *Communications of the ACM* 45.11 (2002), pp. 56–61.

[8] Sergei Arnautov et al. "SCONE: Secure linux containers with Intel SGX". In: *12th USENIX Symp. Operating Systems Design and Implementation.* 2016.

[9] Arash Baratloo et al. "Charlotte: Metacomputing on the web". In: *Future Generation Computer Systems* 15.5 (1999), pp. 559–570.

[10] Andrew Baumann, Marcus Peinado, and Galen Hunt. "Shielding applications from an untrusted cloud with haven". In: *ACM Transactions on Computer Systems (TOCS)* 33.3 (2015), p. 8.

[11] Ernie Brickell and Jiangtao Li. "Enhanced privacy ID from bilinear pairing for hardware authentication and attestation". In: *International Journal of Information Privacy, Security and Integrity 2* 1.1 (2011), pp. 3–33.

[12] Victor Costan and Srinivas Devadas. "Intel SGX Explained." In: *IACR Cryptology ePrint Archive* 2016 (2016), p. 86.

[13] Andrew S Glassner. *An introduction to ray tracing.* Elsevier, 1989.

[14] *Graphene Library OS for Intel SGX.* `https://github.com/oscarlab/graphene/wiki/Introduction-to-Intel-SGX-Support`. Accessed: 2017-03-12.

[15] Jayavardhana Gubbi et al. "Internet of Things (IoT): A vision, architectural elements, and future directions". In: *Future generation computer systems* 29.7 (2013), pp. 1645–1660.

[16] Simon Johnson et al. "Intel software guard extensions: EPID provisioning and attestation services". In: *White Paper* (2016).

[17] Stefan M Larson et al. "Folding@ Home and Genome@ Home: Using distributed computing to tackle previously intractable problems in computational biology". In: *arXiv preprint arXiv:0901.0866* (2009).

[18] Stefan Poslad. *Ubiquitous computing: smart devices, environments and interactions.* John Wiley & Sons, 2011.

[19] Ori Regev and Noam Nisan. "The popcorn market. online markets for computational resources". In: *Decision Support Systems* 28.1 (2000), pp. 177–189.

[20] Luis FG Sarmenta. "Bayanihan: Web-based volunteer computing using Java". In: *International Conference on Worldwide Computing and Its Applications.* Springer. 1998, pp. 444–461.

[21] Luis FG Sarmenta. "Volunteer computing". PhD thesis. Massachusetts Institute of Technology, 2001.

[22] Shweta Shinde et al. "Panoply: Low-TCB Linux Applications With SGX Enclaves". In: *24th Annual Network and Distributed System Security Symposium, NDSS 2017, San Diego, California, USA, February 26-March 1, 2017.* 2017.

[23] George Woltman, Scott Kurowski, et al. "The great internet mersenne prime search". In: *Online],(1997, March 23) available http://www. mersenne. org* (2004).

[24] *Working Document on Trusted Computing Platforms and in particular on the work done by the Trusting Computing Group (TCG group).* Article 29 Data Protection Working Party. European Commission, Brussels, 2004.

Labour Market Intelligence for Supporting Decision Making

Roberto Boselli[1,2], Mirko Cesarini[1,2], Fabio Mercorio[1,2], and Mario Mezzanzanica[1,2]

[1] Dept. of Statistics and Quantitative Methods, Univ. of Milano-Bicocca, Italy
[2] CRISP Research Centre, Univ. of Milano-Bicocca, Italy
(discussion paper)

Abstract. Over the past decade, a growing number of employers has been using the Web for advertising job opportunities through Web job vacancies, that usually specify a job position, along with a set of skills a candidate should possess. Reasoning with these Web job advertisements can effectively support the decision marking processes of several labour market stakeholders, including public organisations, educational and employment agencies, and analysts as well. Here, Labour Market Intelligence refers to the design and definition of automated methodologies and tools for supporting real-time labour market monitoring at a very fine-grained level. This, in turn, represents a competitive advantage to labour market stakeholders with respect to classical survey-based analyses, as they are quite expensive and may require up to one year before being available. In this paper we discuss how Web job vacancies have been collected from selected websites, processed, and classified over a standard taxonomy through machine learning algorithms, extracting the most relevant skills from raw texts. Then, we show how our approach has been applied to some real-life studies and we discuss the benefits provided to end users.

Keywords: Machine Learning, Text Classification, Big Data

1 Introduction

In recent years, the diffusion of Web-centric services is growing exponentially, and this allows a significant part of European Labour demand to be conveyed through specialised Web portals and services. This also contributed to introduce the term "Labour Market Intelligence" (LMI), that refers to the use and design of AI algorithms and frameworks to Labour Market Data for supporting decision making. This is the case of *Web job vacancies*, that are job advertisements containing two main text fields: a *title* and a *full description*. The title shortly summarises the job position, while the full description field usually includes the position details and the relevant skills the employee should hold.

There is a growing interest in designing and implementing real LMI application to Web Labour Market data for supporting the policy design and evaluation activities through evidence-based decision-making. In 2016, the European Commission's highlighted the importance of Vocational and Educational activities, as they are "valued for fostering job-specific and transversal skills, facilitating the transition into employment and maintaining and updating the skills of the workforce according to sectorial, regional and local needs".[1] In 2014, the Cedefop EU Agency[2] launched a call-for-tender[3] aimed at collecting Web job vacancies from five EU countries and extracting the requested skills from the data. The rationale behind the project is to turn data extracted from Web job vacancies into knowledge (and thus value) for policies design and evaluation through a fact-based decision making. In 2016, the EU launched the ESSnet Big Data project, involving 22 EU member states with the aim of "integrating big data in the regular production of official statistics, through pilots exploring the potential of selected big data sources and building concrete applications".

The rationale behind all these initiatives is that reasoning over Web job vacancies represents an added value for both *public and private* labour market operators to deeply understand the Labour Market dynamics, occupations, skills, and trends: (*i*) by reducing the time-to-market with respect to classical survey-based analyses (official Labour Market surveys results actually require up to one year before being available); (*ii*) by overcoming the linguistic boundaries through the use of standard classification systems rather than proprietary ones; (*iii*) by representing the resulting knowledge over several dimensions (e.g., territory, sectors, contracts, etc) at different level of granularity and (*iv*) by evaluating and comparing international labour markets to support fact-based decision making.

Paper's Goal. This paper would summarise some results of our research activities and outcomes in Web Labour Market Intelligence in two distinct research projects: *WollyBI*[4] and *Cedefop*[3], by focusing on (i) job vacancy classification and skill extraction tasks, and (ii) the support to decision making activities that our approach provided to the involved stakeholders.

2 Web Labour Market in the Literature

LMI is an*emerging* cross-disciplinary field of studies that is attracting research interests in both industrial and academic communities, as we summarise below.

Scientific Literature. Since the early 90s, *text classification* (TC) has been an active research topic. It has been defined as "the activity of labelling natural language texts with thematic categories from a predefined set" [12]. Most popular techniques are based on the *machine learning* paradigm, according to which an automatic text classifier is created by using an inductive process able to learn, from a set of pre-classified documents, the characteristics of the categories of interest. Recently, text classification has proven to give good results in categorizing many real-life Web-based data such as, for instance, news and

---

[1] The Commission Communication "A New Skills Agenda for Europe" COM(2016) 381/2, available at https://goo.gl/Shw7bI

[2] Cedefop European agency supports the development of European Vocational Education and Training (VET) policies and contributes to their implementation - http://www.cedefop.europa.eu/

[3] "Real-time Labour Market information on skill requirements: feasibility study and working prototype". Cedefop Reference number AO/RPA/VKVET-NSOFRO/Real-time LMI/010/14. Contract notice 2014/S 141-252026 of 15/07/2014 https://goo.gl/qNjmrn

[4] www.wollybi.com

social media [7], and sentiment analysis [11]. On the other side, skills extraction from Web job vacancies can be framed in the Information Extraction field [6] and Named Entity Recognition [13]. The latter has been applied to solve numerous domain specific problems in the areas of Information Extraction and Normalization [14]. In the last years, public administrations started exploring new ways for supporting knowledge management (see, e.g., [2]) as well as for obtaining detailed and fresh information about the Labour Market. Here, administrative information collected by public administrations has been used for studying the Italian Labour Market dynamics performing both data quality [5,9] and knowledge discovery activities [10,4] through AI techniques (see, e.g.[8]). Unfortunately, administrative data are collected when people is hired (and only in countries where the state collect such information), therefore they do not provide information about the labour demand.

Industries. This problem is also relevant for business purposes, and this motivates the growing of several commercial products providing job seekers and companies with skill-matching tools. Concerning firms, they strongly need to automatize Human Resource (HR) department activities; as a consequence, a growing amount of commercial skill-matching products has been developed in the last years, for instance BurningGlass, Workday, Pluralsight, EmployInsight, and TextKernel. To date, the only commercial solution that uses standard taxonomies as thesauri is Janzz: a Web based platform to match labour demand and supply in both public and private sectors. It also provides APIs access to its knowledge base, but it is not aimed at classifying job vacancies. Worth of mentioning is Google Job Search API, a pay-as-you-go service announced in 2016 for classyfying job vacancies through the Google Machine Learning service over O*NET, that is the US standard occupation taxonomy. Though this commercial service is still a closed alpha, it is quite promising and also sheds the light on the needs for reasoning with Web job vacancies using a common taxonomy.

All these approaches are quite relevant and effective, and they also make evidence of the importance of the Web for labour market information. Nonetheless, they differ from our approach in two aspects. First, we aim to classify *job vacancies* according to a target classification system for building a (language independent) knowledge base for analyses purposes, rather than matching resumes on job vacancies. Second, our approach aims to build a knowledge-graph for supporting the fact-based decision making activities for LMI.

3 An Approach to deal with Web Job Vacancies

Background on Web Labour Market Information. A Web job offer extracted can be seen as a document mainly composed of a pair of texts: a title and a (full job) description. The title summarises the working position offered by the employer, while the description usually provides the position details, including all the required relevant skills, according to the employer preferences.

One of the most important classification system designed for this purposes is ISCO: The *International Standard Classification of Occupations* is a four-level classification that represents a standardised way for organising the labour market occupations. ESCO is the multilingual classification system of European Skills, Competences, Qualifications and Occupations, it is the European standard for supporting the whole labour market intelligence over 24 EU languages. Basically, the ESCO data model includes the whole ISCO structure, and extends it through (i) a further level of fine-grained occupation descriptions and (ii) a taxonomy of skills, and competences.

Web job vacancy classification through Text Classification. Text categorization aims at assigning a Boolean value to each pair $(d_j, c_i) \in D \times C$ where D is a set of documents and C a set of predefined categories. A *true* value assigned to (d_j, c_i) indicates document d_j to be set under the category c_i, while a *false* value indicates d_j cannot be assigned under c_i. In our scenario, we consider a set of job vacancies $\mathcal{J}$ as a collection of documents each of which has to be assigned to one (and only one) ISCO occupation code. We can model this problem as a text classification problem, relying on the definition of [12]. Formally speaking, let $\mathcal{J} = \{J_1, \ldots, J_n\}$ be a set of Job vacancies, the classification of $\mathcal{J}$ under $|O|$ ESCO occupation labels consists of $|O|$ independent problems of classifying each job vacancy $J \in \mathcal{J}$ under a given ESCO occupation code o_i for $i = 1, \ldots, |O|$. Then, a *classifier* for o_i is a function $\psi : \mathcal{J} \times O \rightarrow \{0, 1\}$ that approximates an unknown target function $\dot{\psi} : \mathcal{J} \times O \rightarrow \{0, 1\}$. Clearly, as we deal with a single-label classifier, $\forall j \in \mathcal{J}$ the following constraint must hold: $\sum_{o \in O} \psi(j, o) = 1$. Notice that in this way we can also *extend* the ESCO skills taxonomy through the skills extracted from the job vacancies, as well as to *weight* both occupations and skills with respect to the frequency through which they appear in the Web Labour Market.

Building up the Machine Learning Model. We build a machine learning model for classifying multilingual Web job vacancies exploiting a *single-label classifier* using both titles and descriptions. Indeed, titles often does not contain enough information for performing a correct classification as we shown in [1]. Several machine learning techniques have been evaluated for developing the text classifier, and they have been comparatively evaluated on a data set of 75,546 job vacancies in Italian. The evaluated techniques are: Support Vector Machines (SVMs), in particular SVM Linear, SVM RBF Kernel, Random Forests (RFs), and Artificial Neural Networks (ANNs).

Table 1: Classifiers Evaluation of the classifiers trained on the train set and evaluated on the test set. Precision, Recall, and F1-Score values are the weighted average of the values computed for each ISCO code.

Classifier	Precision	Recall	F1-Score
SVM Linear	**0.93**	**0.93**	**0.93**
SVM RBF Kernel	0.90	0.88	0.88
Random Forest	0.67	0.67	0.67
Neural Networks	0.92	0.92	0.92

Focusing on the Italian Labour Market Information, a set of 57,740 vacancies previously classified by domain experts belonging to ENRLMM[5] was used.

[5] The European Network on Regional Labour Market Monitoring

The set of already classified vacancies are split into *train*, *validation*, and *test* sets. Then, a grid-search was performed over each classifier parameter space to identify the values maximizing the classification effectiveness (using training and validation sets). Tab. 1 shows the scores computed over the test set.

Skills Identification. The text pieces stating the required skills usually concentrate on a small portion of job vacancy descriptions. Thus, these relevant text pieces are extracted through a look-up search of sentinel expressions selected by domain experts involved within the projects. The domain expert kept adding new sentinel expressions until the number of n-grams identified in the next step grows (i.e., the set converged to a stable set). Then, the n-gram *Document Frequency* (DF), i.e., the number of vacancies where the n-gram is found, is computed considering as a scope both (1) the whole dataset and (2) the vacancy subsets homogeneous w.r.t. the ISCO occupation code.

The n-gram produced by the previous step underwent a string similarity comparison with respect to ESCO skill concept labels. The pair <*skill candidate* n-gram, ESCO Skill label> matching the following criteria were suggested for domain experts approval. The string similarity was computed as the mean value among the following well-known string metrics: Levenshtein distance, Jaccard similarity, and the Sørensen-Dice indexes[6]. The pairs having a similarity lower than 70% are dropped while the others are proposed to the domain experts for evaluation. Each <*candidate* n-gram, ESCO Skill label> above the threshold has been reviewed by a domain expert to decided whether to consider an n-gram as: (1) a skill described in ESCO; (2) a skill not enlisted in ESCO (i.e., a *novel* skill); (3) or to reject the proposed n-gram as a skill concept. The outcome of this process can be seen as a dictionary of n-gram related skills and their corresponding ESCO skill concept (when available). Finally, the n-gram dictionary produced by the previous steps and the mappings among the ESCO skill concepts have been used to look for skills among the downloaded vacancies.

LM Knowledge as a Graph. The resulting knowledge on LM is then modelled as a graph. In Fig. 1 we report *a selection of* the graph-db data model according to the Neo4j property graph structure. The model is basically composed of two main node labels, *occupations* and *skills*. The former are the ISCO occupation codes whilst the latter are the union of both ESCO skills and the skills recognised as *novel* in the skill extraction phase, as described above. Then, two distinct directed relationships are allowed between skills and occupations to model that a skill s belongs to a given occupation o. The :BELONG relation would represent an occupation o requiring an ESCO skill s with a relevance of w in the ESCO taxonomy. This relationship measures the importance of the skill for a given occupation according to a set of labour market experts. Differently, the :BELONG_DATA relation models that w job vacancies have asked for skill s in the Web job vacancy text.

Such a knowledge graph allowed us to perform a several path-traversal analyses, such as *Skill2Job*, to identify the most promising occupations that one could

[6] Though the latter is not a proper distance metric, it has been selected as we do not ask string metrics to satisfy the triangle inequality

be interested into given a set of skills, the *Gap Analysis* to identify the most important skills that one should acquire given a set of skills that a candidate already holds. Due to the space restrictions, here we only give the idea of how the graph-structure can be used to identify occupation groups on the basis of the skills they have in common, distinguishing between groups according to the *ESCO* and *real data*. To this end, we employed a local-clustering-coefficient metric to identify all the occupations that share *at least k%* skills in common (i.e., having a clustering coefficient equals to 1). We employed a weigthed Jaccard metric to compute the similarity between occupations on the basis of skills in common. Fig. 2 shows the ESCO skills category asked for a group of occu-

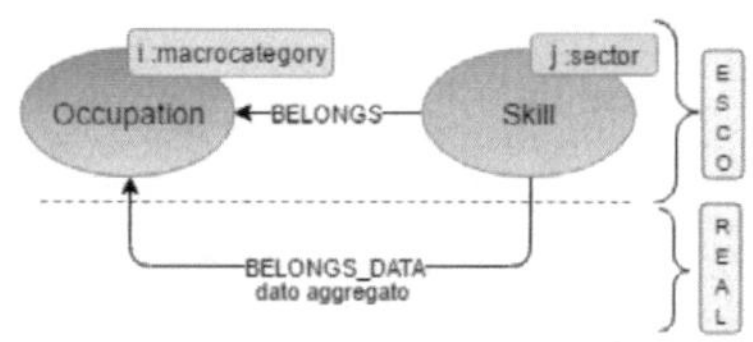

Fig. 1: Extraction of the Graph-DB data model employed

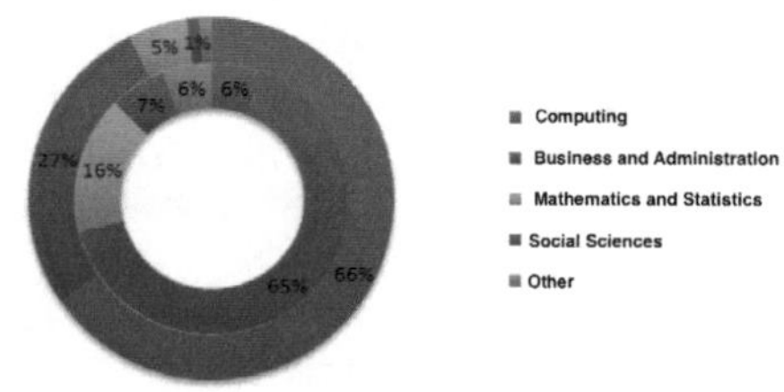

Fig. 2: It includes the following ESCO occupations: *Statistical, mathematical and related associate professionals*, *Financial Analysts* and *Mathematicians, actuaries and statisticians* having at least 60% skills in common.

pations related to *mathematicians and statisticians*. The outer circle refers to ESCO skills whose relevance has been computed using the :BELONGS relation, whilst the inner circle refers to ESCO skills with a relevance computed using the :BELONG_DATA relation (i.e., Web job vacancies). As one might note, *computing* skills account for 6% according to the ESCO experts, whilst this value grows up to 66% in the real data that mainly specifies skills such as SQL, Relational Databases, Python and Data Warehouse. Conversely, the *Business & Administration* sector seems to be overstimated by ESCO taxonomy, that indicates up to 56 B&A related skills whilst only few on them are actually repeatedly asked by companies. This analysis would allow one to measure the gap between (1) an LMI system built through an expert-driven approach as in the ESCO case, where labour market experts indicates a list of skills that are relevant in an occupation profile, and (2) a data-driven system, where skills are recognised as important on the basis of the real labour market expectations.

4 Some Results and Concluding Remarks

The WollyBI Experience. WollyBI is a SaaS tool for collecting and classifying Web job vacancies on the ISCO/ESCO standard taxonomies, and extracting the most requested skills from job descriptions. It has been designed to provide five distinct entry points to the user on the basis of the analysis purposes, that are, *Geographical Area*, *Skill*, *Firm*, *Occupation*, and *free OLAP queries*.

Competition Analysis for Strategic Decision Making. WollyBI supported a recruitment agency to identify and measure the market share with respect to its competitors, that included the most relevant recruitment Agencies in Italy, namely: GiGroup, Adecco, ManPower, RandStad, ObiettivoLavoro, and Umana. In Fig. 4 we report the market share distribution over the top-10 ISCO occupations, by analysing the Italian Web Job Vacancies since February 2013 to April 2015. Clearly, due to undisclosure agreements, the agency labels reported in Fig. 4 have been anonymized. We analysed about 850K Web job vacancies posted by these agencies. This competition analysis has been validated as helpful to the customer (Agency B) as it allowed to (i) *measure* the position in the market and the *gap* with respect to their competitors; (ii) to *drive* the identification of strategic decisions to improve its market share and, in turn, to identify the corresponding strategies that allow achieving the desired goals. Just to give a few examples, our analysis revealed that Agency B is leader in recruiting "shop sales assistants" whilst its market share ranges between 9% and 15% in the remaining professions. Thanks to this results, Agency B has been made in state to design its strategic intervention through fact-based decision-making.

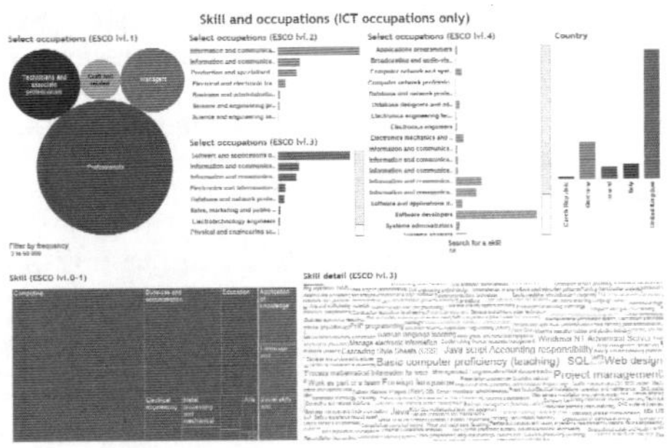

Fig. 3: Snapshot from the prototype as deployed to the Cedefop Agency

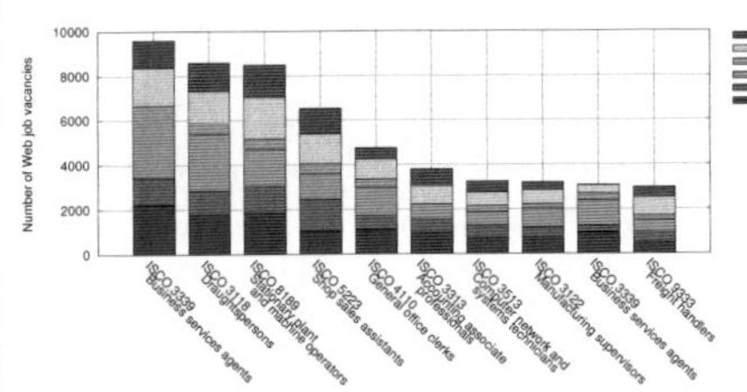

Fig. 4: Top-10 ISCO occupations and relative distribution over the six recruitment agencies analysed.

The Cedefop Experience. In 2014, the experience of WollyBI put the basis of a prototype system we realised within a call-for-tender for the Cedefop EU Agency aimed at collecting Web job vacancies from five EU countries and extracting the requested skills from the data. The rationale behind the project is to turn data extracted from Web job vacancies into knowledge (and thus value) for policies design and evaluation through fact-based decision making. The architecture of the system basically relies on WollyBI, that is now running on the Cedefop data centre since June 2016, gathering and classifying job vacancies from 5 EU countries, namely: United Kingdom, Ireland, Czech Republic, Italy and Germany. To date, the system collected 7+ million job vacancies over the 5 EU countries, and it accounts among the research projects that a selection of Italian universities addressed in the context of big data [3]. In Fig. 3 we report a snapshot from the project dashboard that allows to surf the data over the ISCO taxonomy and the ESCO skills extracted from the data.

Concluding Remarks and Research Directions. In this paper we described our approach to Web Labour Market Intelligence, focusing on the realisation of a machine learning model for classifying job vacancies and showing the benefits of a graph-based representation of the knowledge base. Our research goes toward two directions. From an application point of view, we have been commited by Cedefop for extending the prototype to the whole EU community to all 28 EU Countries, building the system for the EU Web Labour Market Monitoring[7]. From a methodological perspective, reasoning with Web job vacancies raises some interesting research issues, such as the automatic synthesis of the labour market knowledge through word embeddings, the identification of AI heuristic-search algorithms for path-traversal over big knowledge-graph, as well as the design of novel AI techniques for data cleasing in a big data scenario.

References

1. Amato, F., Boselli, R., Cesarini, M., Mercorio, F., Mezzanzanica, M., Moscato, V., Persia, F., Picariello, A.: Challenge: Processing web texts for classifying job offers. In: IEEE International Conference on Semantic Computing (2015)
2. Amato, F., Colace, F., Greco, L., Moscato, V., Picariello, A.: Semantic processing of multimedia data for e-government applications. J. Vis. Lang. Comput. 32 (2016)
3. Bergamaschi, S., Carlini, E., Ceci, M., Furletti, B., Giannotti, F., Malerba, D., Mezzanzanica, M., Monreale, A., Pasi, G., Pedreschi, D., et al.: Big data research in italy: A perspective. Engineering 2(2), 163–170 (2016)
4. Boselli, R., Cesarini, M., Mercorio, F., Mezzanzanica, M.: Inconsistency knowledge discovery for longitudinal data management: A model-based approach. In: SouthCHI13 special session on Human-Computer Interaction & Knowledge Discovery. Springer (2013)
5. Boselli, R., Mezzanzanica, M., Cesarini, M., Mercorio, F.: Planning meets data cleansing. In: The 24th International Conference on Automated Planning and Scheduling (ICAPS 2014). pp. 439–443. AAAI (2014)
6. Chang, C.H., Kayed, M., Girgis, M.R., Shaalan, K.F.: A survey of web information extraction systems. IEEE Transactions on Knowledge and Data Engineering 18(10), 1411–1428 (2006)
7. Khan, F.H., Bashir, S., Qamar, U.: Tom: Twitter opinion mining framework using hybrid classification scheme. Decision Support Systems 57, 245 – 257 (2014)
8. Mercorio, F.: Model checking for universal planning in deterministic and non-deterministic domains. AI Communications 26(2), 257–259 (2013)
9. Mezzanzanica, M., Boselli, R., Cesarini, M., Mercorio, F.: Data quality through model checking techniques. In: Intelligent Data Analysis (IDA), LNCS. pp. 270–281. Springer (2011)
10. Mezzanzanica, M., Boselli, R., Cesarini, M., Mercorio, F.: A model-based evaluation of data quality activities in KDD. Information Processing & Management 51(2), 144–166 (2015)
11. Pang, B., Lee, L., Vaithyanathan, S.: Thumbs up?: sentiment classification using machine learning techniques. In: ACL-02 conference on Empirical methods in natural language processing. Association for Computational Linguistics (2002)
12. Sebastiani, F.: Machine learning in automated text categorization. ACM computing surveys (CSUR) 34(1), 1–47 (2002)
13. Tjong Kim Sang, E.F., De Meulder, F.: Introduction to the conll-2003 shared task: Language-independent named entity recognition. In: Conference on Natural Language Learning at HLT-NAACL (2003)
14. Zhao, M., Javed, F., Jacob, F., McNair, M.: Skill: A system for skill identification and normalization. In: In the Twenty-Seventh AAAI Conference on Innovative Applications of Artificial Intelligence. pp. 4012–4018. AAAI (2015)

[7] "Real-time Labour Market information on Skill Requirements: Setting up the EU system for online vacancy analysis AO/DSL/VKVET-GRUSSO/Real-time LMI 2/009/16. Contract notice - 2016/S 134-240996 of 14/07/2016 https://goo.gl/5FZS3E

Knowledge-based access to art collections: the KIRA system

Flora Amato, Vincenzo Moscato, Antonio Picariello, and Giancarlo Sperlì

DIETI - University of Naples "Federico II", via Claudio 21, 80125, Naples, Italy
CINI - ITEM National Lab, Via Cinthia, 80126, Naples, italy

{flora.amato,vmoscato,picus,giancarlo.sperli}@unina.it

Abstract. This discussion paper represents an extended abstract of a recent publication where we presented KIRA (*Knowledge-based Information Retrieval from Art collections*), a system to query, browse and analyze cultural digital contents from a set of distributed and heterogeneous repositories. KIRA relies on a Big Data infrastructure with the following features: capability to gather information from different data sources; advanced data management techniques and technologies; ability to provide useful and personalized data to users based on their preferences and context. KIRA thus provides retrieval and presentation functionalities to search information of interest and present it to the users in a suitable format and according to their needs. Using ad-hoc APIs, our system can also support several applications: mobile multimedia guides, web portals to promote the Cultural Heritage, multimedia recommender and storytelling systems and so on. We discuss the main ideas that characterize the system, showing its use for several applications.

Keywords: Knowledge Management, Big Data, Information Retrieval

1 Introduction

The enhancement and promotion of worldwide Cultural Heritage (CH) using Information and Communication Technologies (ICT) represents nowadays an important research issue, with a variety of potential applications. ICT have radically changed the modern CH scenery: simple traditional Information Systems for the management of cultural artifacts have left the place to complex systems that expose rich information extracted from heterogeneous data sources (e.g. Digital Libraries and Open Archives, Multimedia Art Collections, Social Media, Web Encyclopedias, etc.). A large number of proposals, which focus on how ICT solutions should be applied to the CH domain for different purposes, has been presented in the literature [1]. Indeed, several recent European projects (e.g. Ariadne, Europeana, etc.) have already suggested a set of methodologies/technologies together with the best ways and practices to manage and organize the cultural knowledge for different contexts and applications.

In spite of the great effort, some research problems have to be still faced during the design of a modern Cultural Heritage Information System, especially if we consider high change rate, large volume, and intrinsic heterogeneity of cultural data: i) the adoption of architectural models for *Big Data* management [2]; ii) the access, retrieval, integration and analysis of information from distributed and very heterogeneous art repositories [3]; iii) the transformation of the captured data into useful knowledge and the related management in according to the different "views" of a cultural item exploiting the LD/LOD (*Linked Data/Linked Open Data*) paradigm [4]; iv) the access to the knowledge based on the user profile and the *context*.

This paper represents an extended abstract of the work [5], where we describe KIRA (*Knowledge-based Information Retrieval from Art collections*), a system to query, browse and analyze cultural digital contents from a set of distributed and heterogeneous art repositories. In particular, the system prototype has been developed within the Cultural Heritage Information Systems (CHIS) National project, promoted by DATABENC[1]. KIRA is able to manage all the digital contents related to *Cultural Items*. More in details, in our vision each *Cultural Heritage environment* (e.g. museums, archaeological sites, old town centers, etc.) is grounded on a set of cultural *Points of Interest* (PoI), which correspond to one or more cultural items (e.g. specific ruins of an archaeological site, sculptures and/or pictures exhibited within a museum, historical buildings and famous squares in an old town center and so on). In order to meet variety, velocity and volume of the managed information, KIRA is characterized by the following technical features that are typical of a *Big Data* platform:

- capability to gather information from distributed and heterogeneous data sources (e.g. Social Media , Digital Libraries and Open Archives, Multimedia Collections, Web Encyclopedias, Web Data Services, etc.);
- advanced data management techniques and technologies;
- advanced information retrieval services and ability to provide useful and personalized data to users based on their preferences and context.

The paper is organized as follows. Section 2 describes the proposed data model. Section 3 presents a system description with several implementation details. Section 4 reports a possible application of our system and discusses some conclusions and the future work.

2 Data Model for Cultural Items

The introduced data model relies on the concept of "Cultural Item" (CI): examples of CIs are specific ruins of an archaeological site, sculptures and/or pictures exhibited within a museum, historical buildings in an old town center and so on.

[1] The High Technology District for Cultural Heritage (DATABENC) management of the Campania Region, in Italy (www.databenc.it).

In the CH domain, a CI can be opportunely described with respect to a variety of annotation schemata, for example the archaeological view, the architectural perspective, the archivist vision, the historical background, etc., which usually exploit different sets of "metadata" and possibly domain taxonomies or ontologies [6]. In a simplified way, we consider a *ontology* $O = (V, E)$ as a network of concepts belonging to the CH domain, where a node $v \in V$ represents a "concept" and an edge $e \in E$ a relationship between two concepts. Thus, we define an *annotation schema* and a *semantic annotation* for a CI.

Definition 1 (Annotation Schema). *Given a set of ontologies* $\mathcal{O}$, *an* Annotation Schema *is a tuple* $\lambda_{\mathcal{O}} = (A_1, \ldots, A_n, B_1, \ldots, B_m)$, *where* $A_1, \ldots, A_n$ *are attributes for which* $\forall i \in [1,n], \exists O = (V,E) \in \mathcal{O}$ *s.t.* $dom(A_i) \subseteq V$, *and* $B_1, \ldots, B_m$ *are attributes for which* $\forall j \in [1,m], \nexists O = (V,E) \in \mathcal{O}$ *s.t.* $dom(B_j) \subseteq V$.

The attributes $A_1, \ldots, An$ are *Ontological Attributes* (OAs) and correspond to concepts that are relevant for the specific domain(s) being modeled. In turn, *Non-Ontological Attributes* $B_1, \ldots, B_m$ (NOAs) can contain other useful information, such as multimedia items (e.g. audio, video, images, texts and 3D models, etc.) characterized by a set of low-level features and other metadata. In particular, we can adopt both "literals" or a set of URIs (*Uniform Resource Identifiers*), which allow to access the related cultural information according to the LD/LOD paradigms, as values of the annotation attributes. In addition, a CI may be associated with a specific "Point of Interest" (POI), defined by a set of geographic coordinates, and corresponding either to a single point or to a set of lines and more complex polygons of the considered environment.

Definition 2 (Semantic Annotation). *Given a set of ontologies* $\mathcal{O}$, *an annotation schema* $\lambda_{\mathcal{O}}$ *and cultural item* CI, *a* Semantic Annotation *of* CI *is a tuple* $\lambda_{\mathcal{O}}(\text{CI}) = (a_1, \ldots, a_n, b_1, \ldots, b_m)$, *where* $\forall i \in [1,n], a_i \in dom(A_i)$ *and* $\forall j \in [1,m], b_i \in dom(B_i)$

Using various sets of ontologies and semantic annotations [7], we can thus describe a cultural item from different points of view supporting several applications. A large set of relationships can also be instantiated among cultural items and the entire system *Knowledge Base* (KB) can be modeled as a *graph*[2].

Definition 3 (Knowledge Base). *The* Knowledge Base *is a graph* $G = (C, R)$: *each node* $c \in C$ *can be a cultural item or an ontological attribute (concept) [8], while each edge* $r \in R$ *represents a relationship derived from a semantic annotation or established between two cultural items.*

Figure 1 shows how a portion of knowledge related to the Paestum ruins can be easily represented in our model.

[2] All possible relationships in the model are opportunely defined "a-priori" and the related meaning can be found in a proper thesaurus.

Leveraging different annotation schemes and ontologies, our model allows achieving interoperability goals. The KB content can be easily exported in the most used formats (e.g. XML, RDF, OWL) and according to the most diffused harvesting standards for CH applications (e.g., EDM, Italian ICCD, etc.). On the other hand, the LD/LOD paradigm permits us to deal with several problems related to data consistency and copyright constraints[3].

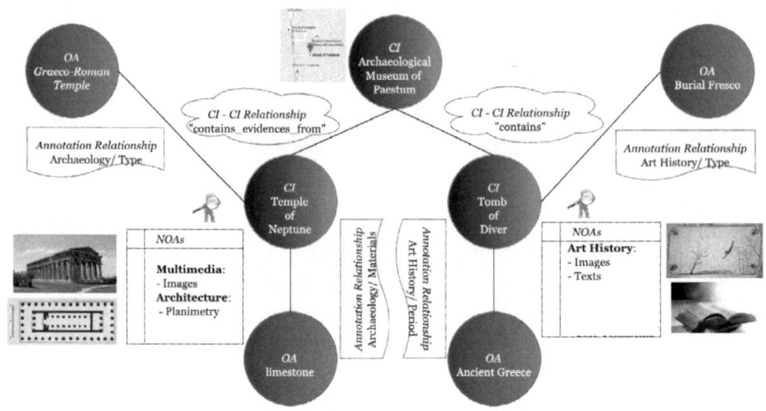

Fig. 1: KIRA - Data Model for CIs

3 System Description

3.1 Architecture

KIRA has to deal with the large and heterogeneous amount of information: annotations and descriptions provided by cultural heritage foundations, web encyclopedias and open archives, multimedia contents coming from social media networks and digital libraries, opinions and comments of users from common online social networks, etc. For this reason, KIRA presents a layered architecture typical of a Big Data platform [2], exploiting the related stack of technologies (see [5] for more details). In the *data source layer*, each data source is properly "wrapped" in order to extract the information of interest that is then represented as required by the described data model. In particular, each Wrapper is specialized for a particular kind of source (i.e. Social Media Networks, Digital Repositories, Open Archives) and must address all the interoperability issues, providing a

[3] Some cultural items descriptions are accessible only using URI, thus the data management issues are in charge to the related source.

set of functionalities to access data sources and gather all the desired data, possibly leveraging the available APIs[4]. In the *data storage and management layer*, data are stored in the Knowledge Base in compliance with the above-described data model, and managed also exploiting the LD/LOD paradigm. In addition, specific semantics to be attached to the data is provided using the annotation schemes, including ontologies, vocabularies, taxonomies, etc. related to the Cultural Heritage domain. The KB leverages different Data Repositories realized by advanced data management technologies (e.g. Distributed File Systems, NoSQL and relational systems) and provides a set of basic APIs to read/write data by an Access Method Manager. As a basis for the *data processing layer* our system provides a Query Engine that can be invoked by user applications to search data of interest using information retrieval facilities. In particular, our system supports all the basic functionalities for multimedia and semantic information retrieval by means of proper Information Filters. The *data analytics layer* is based on different Analytics Services allowing to create personalized "dashboards" for a given cultural environment. In addition, it provides basic data mining, graph analysis and machine learning algorithms useful to infer new knowledge and provided mechanisms for personalized and *context-aware* access to data.

3.2 Functionalities and Implementation Details

One of the most important functionalities provided by KIRA consists in the capability of gathering the different kinds of data from different sources: User Data, Social Data, Digital Repository and Multimedia Data.

User Data basically include preferences and needs that are useful to define the related *profiles*: data on users (e.g. favorite artistic genre and artists) constitutes the *Personally Identifiable Information* (PII) that is stored in the Knowledge Base and can be used as additional filter in the retrieval. As to *Social Data*, the current prototype only considers information coming from Twitter. In particular, KIRA retrieves user comments and posts information about a given CI by exploiting the related APIs. Social data can be used in several applications requiring a "social vision" of cultural items. We collect *Digital Repositories' Data*, information describing cultural items from on-line digital repositories (e.g. museums, libraries, open archives, multimedia collections, etc.). The wrapper for this kind of sources can import such data descriptions and convert them into a JSON format. *Multimedia data* (e.g. images, texts, video, etc.) related to a given cultural item can be similarly collected using the wrapper facilities. In particular, the descriptions in terms of basic metadata are captured and stored within

[4] Data integration problems for heterogeneous data sources are addressed by means of classical schema mapping techniques, record linkage and data fusion techniques [3], according to the specific data source. Eventually, data stream management problems have to be considered.

KIRA, while raw multimedia data can be opportunely linked and, in other cases, temporarily imported into the system for content-based analysis [9][5].

The data gathered by the Wrappers are then stored and managed by the Knowledge Base. One of the basic functionalities of the KB is to export the related content into the *Europeana Data Model*[6] (EDM) format (see [5] for more details). Metadata semantics is provided by the set of annotation schemes (in XML, RDF or OWL formats). All the data can be represented as sequences of triples ($\langle$ subject, predicate, object $\rangle$) in according to the described data model. The KB is based on several technologies that are briefly described in the following[7].

The data describing basic properties of CIs (e.g. name, short description, etc.) and basic information on users profiles are stored into a *key-value data store* (i.e. *Redis*). The complete description in terms of all the metadata of CIs using the different annotation schemes are in turn saved using a *wide column data store* (i.e. *Cassandra*). We use a table for each kind of CIs having a column for each "metadata family"; column values can be literals or URIs. The *document store* technology (i.e. *MongoDB*) is used to deal with JSON messages, complete user profiles and descriptions of internal resources (multimedia data and textual documents, etc.) associated with a cultural item. All the relationships among cultural items within a cultural environment and interactions with users (behaviors) are managed by means of a *graph database* (i.e. *Titan*). The entire cartography related to a cultural environment together with POIs is managed by a GIS (i.e. *PostGIS*), which provides the functionalities to filter and visualize on a map the geographic area around a given $\mathcal{PoI}$. Multimedia data management is realized using the *Windsurf* library [9]. We exploit an *RDF store* (i.e. different *Allegrograph* instances) to memorize data views in terms of triples related to a given cultural environment and useful for specific applications, providing a SPARQL endpoint for the applications. All system configuration parameters, internal catalogs and thesauri are stored in a relational database (i.e. *PostegreSQL*). Finally, semantics of data can be specified by linking values of high-level metadata to some available internal (managed by Sesame) or external ontological schemes.

This heterogeneous Knowledge Base provides basic *Restful APIs* to read-/write data and further functionalities for importing/exporting data in the most common diffused Web standards. The search of data useful for the applications can be eased by using different information filters that implement the right queries to the various databases. The implementation of such filters is based

[5] Note that multimedia data that are managed by the system are suitably filtered before the storing process. The number and kinds of multimedia data required by the application are tuned by means of configuration parameters.

[6] http://pro.europeana.eu/edm-documentation

[7] We chose to adopt such heterogeneous technologies in order to meet the specific requirements of the applications dealing with the huge amount of data at stake. For example, Social Networking applications typically benefit of graph database technologies because of their focus on data relationships. In turn, more efficient technologies (key-value ore wide-column stores) are required by Tourism applications to quickly and easily access the data of interest.

on *Apache Spark*, and we distinguish four kinds of query on the KB: i) *query by keywords/tags*: through such a query a user/application can search a set of CIs using keywords (as in Google search engine) or specific tags (the query is then "expanded" with similar search terms leveraging the system thesauri); ii) *query by metadata*: by this query a user/application can search a set of CIs using specific metadata of internal or external annotation schemes (the query for OAs is semantically "expanded" with the concepts of managed ontologies that are similar to the target one); iii) *query by example*: through such a query a user/application can search a set of multimedia contents – related to CIs – that are similar to a target one (the query processing is base on the *Windsurf multimedia libraries*); iv) *query by user preferences*: user profiles are exploited to find the set of cultural items that are more similar to user preferences using co-clustering techniques [10].

4 System Running Example and Conclusions

We describe a possible application of our system to support the development of a multimedia guide for the *Paestum archeological site*. The ancient buildings, together with the museum and its main artifacts, constitute the set of cultural items for our case study. Tourists, both from their places and while visiting ruins, can browse these cultural items and enjoy a useful multimedia guide describing them, or be recommended other nearby places, comments of other users and other information of interest. When users search a specific cultural item, as

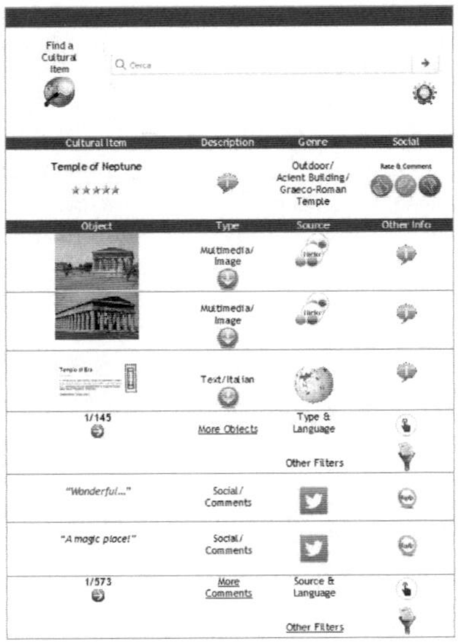

Fig. 2: KIRA - System Query Interface

an example the Temple of Neptune, our system provides a basic description with the related multimedia objects (i.e. audio, images, video and texts) and detailed users' comments. The list of proposed cultural items with descriptions and multimedia objects depends on the user's preferences and system settings: images rather than voice, or expert-level rather than layman-level descriptions of the art pieces; specific metadata and annotation schemes. In addition, *query by example* facilities can be exploited to determine other images that are similar to a given multimedia object. In addition, a *semantic search* can be performed on specific ontological attributes to find other cultural items of the same type. At the same time, users can choose to retrieve some interesting information, to read comments, opinions and ratings about the visited cultural items and to express their own ratings and opinions. Figure 2 shows a running example (obtained by assembling different screenshots) concerning the search of $\mathcal{CI}$s related to the Paestum ruins. Users can browse the data by means of an appropriate GUI; they can filter objects belonging to a given $\mathcal{CI}$ using different criteria: type of multimedia data, language, etc. Future work will be devoted to collect the huge amount of data related to all the different cultural objects of the Campania region and to experiment our system from the efficiency and effectiveness points of view with respect to the information retrieval and filtering tasks providing a comparison with other systems.

References

1. C. Guccio, M. F. Martorana, I. Mazza, and I. Rizzo, "Technology and public access to cultural heritage: the italian experience on ict for public historical archives," in *Cultural Heritage in a Changing World.* Springer, 2016, pp. 55–75.
2. C. P. Chen and C.-Y. Zhang, "Data-intensive applications, challenges, techniques and technologies: A survey on big data," *Information Sciences*, vol. 275, pp. 314–347, 2014.
3. X. L. Dong and D. Srivastava, "Big data integration," in *Data Engineering (ICDE), 2013 IEEE 29th International Conference on.* IEEE, 2013, pp. 1245–1248.
4. A. Zaveri, A. Rula, A. Maurino, R. Pietrobon, J. Lehmann, and S. Auer, "Quality assessment for linked data: A survey," *Semantic Web*, vol. 7, no. 1, pp. 63–93, 2016.
5. F. Amato, V. Moscato, A. Picariello, and G. Sperlì, "Kira: a system for knowledge-based access to multimedia art collectionsl," in *Proceedings of the IEEE 11th International Conference on Semantic Computing, (ICSC 2017).* IEEE, 2017.
6. M. Doerr, S. Gradmann, S. Hennicke, A. Isaac, C. Meghini, and H. van de Sompel, "The europeana data model (edm)," in *World Library and Information Congress: 76th IFLA general conference and assembly*, 2010, pp. 10–15.
7. F. Amato, A. De Santo, V. Moscato, F. Persia, A. Picariello, and S. Poccia, "Partitioning of ontologies driven by a structure-based approach," 2015, pp. 320–323.
8. F. Amato, A. Mazzeo, A. Penta, and A. Picariello, "Using nlp and ontologies for notary document management systems," 2008, pp. 67–71.
9. I. Bartolini and M. Patella, "Multimedia queries in digital libraries," in *Data Management in Pervasive Systems.* Springer, 2015, pp. 311–325.
10. I. Bartolini, V. Moscato, R. Pensa, A. Penta, A. Picariello, C. Sansone, and M. L. Sapino, "Recommending multimedia visiting paths in cultural heritage applications," *Multimedia Tools and Applications*, vol. 75, no. 7, pp. 3813–3842, 2016.

Process Conformance Checking by Relaxing Data Dependencies

Montserrat Estañol[1,2], Mirjana Mazuran[3] Xavier Oriol[1], Letizia Tanca[3], and Ernest Teniente[1] *

[1] Universitat Politècnica de Catalunya, Barcelona, Spain
{estanyol|xoriol|teniente}@essi.upc.edu
[2] SIRIS Lab, Research Division of SIRIS Academic, Spain
[3] Politecnico di Milano, Milan, Italy
{mirjana.mazuran|letizia.tanca}@polimi.it

Abstract. Given the events modeled by a business process, it may happen in the presence of alternative execution paths that the data required by a certain event determines somehow what event is executed next. Then, the process can be modeled by using an approximate functional dependency between the data required by both events. We apply this approach in the context of conformance checking: given a business process model with a functional dependency (FD) that no longer corresponds to the observed reality, we propose corrections to the FD to make it exact or at least to improve its confidence and produce a more accurate model.

1 Introduction

Conformance checking aims at determining whether the actual execution of a business process, as recorded within an event log, conforms to its model. This approach helps bridge the gap between process specifications and their implementation, by detecting deviations between models and reality [1]. Several approaches take data into consideration when looking for these misalignments [2,6,8,9,11]. They assume that the data is provided through global attributes, and do not deal with structured data, which instead is usually considered in business process specification. Moreover, these approaches are able to highlight the deviations between the real executions and the process model, but do not propose alternatives to modify the model so that it becomes correct again.

In contrast, our work addresses conformance checking by considering an artifact-centric perspective of process definition where the data is represented by a UML class diagram and the processes are described in BPMN. So, we use standard and common formalisms for conceptual representation of data and processes, and are aligned with recent proposals aimed at specifying business process conceptually to facilitate understanding of these models by the domain experts [4, 5]. We assume in this paper that the activities in the BPMN diagram and in the event log are the same (no new activity is taking place in the

* This work is supported by project TIN2014-52938-C2-2-R, project 2014 SGR 1534, H2020 IT2Rail grant. 636078 and Italian project SHELL CTN01 00128 111357.

actual execution of the business process) and we concentrate on analyzing the correctness of the conditions specfied in the condition points of a BPMN.

With our approach, not only can we identify current deviations between the model and the actual execution of the process, but we can also propose modifications to the models to correct this misalignment. This is achieved by analyzing, for each event in the log, the functional dependency holding between its contextual data and the next branch after it.

The following example illustrates our contribution. Assume that a Taxi Service has developed an application to coordinate its taxi drivers. When they are in service, they may receive offers for new rides. Then, depending on the distance and the price of the offer, the drivers decide to accept/reject it. The BPMN model in Figure 1 shows this behavior.

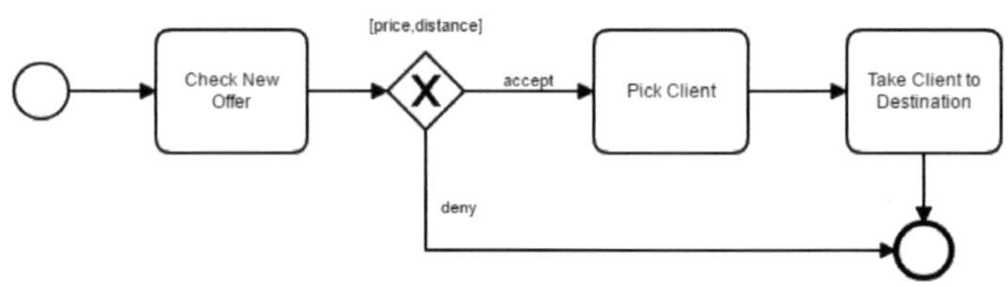

Fig. 1. BPMN model to handle taxi requests

In order to execute artifact-centric approaches, activities need to handle data. In particular, the data required by previous activities is shown in the UML diagram in Figure 1. Note that it contains information regarding the taxi and its driver, and also regarding the offers and the clients that make them. Additionally, we include an OCL operation that defines how the activity *check new offer* shown in the BPMN updates the data represented in the class diagram [4].

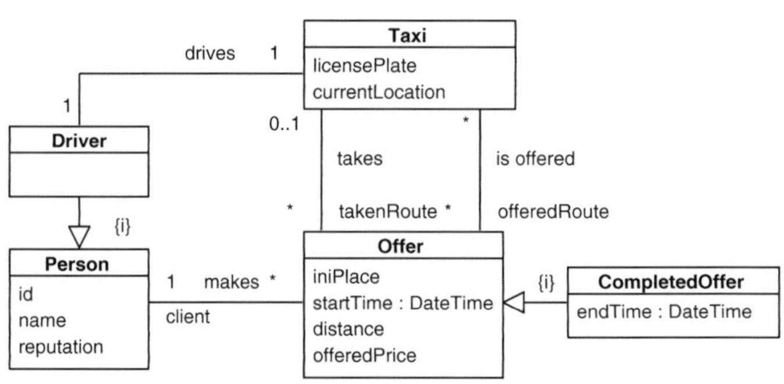


```
Operation: checkNewOffer(Offer o, Taxi t)
post: t.offeredRoute->includes(o)
```

Fig. 2. UML diagram describing data/operations required to handle a request

When the application is running, it may come up with the log in Table 1, which shows the attributes related to the *new offer* event (as given by the class *Offer* in Figure 1), and the name of the branch taken in the BPMN diagram (i.e. the decision made by the Taxi driver).

Table 1. Price, distance, and acceptance relation

timestamp	*price*	*distance*	*client reputation*	*driver reputation*	*Next event*
21-03-17 12:01:01	78,13	4,8	4	2	Pick client
21-03-17 14:45:12	35,12	34	2	3	Refuse client
21-03-17 14:56:27	34,14	35	5	4	Pick client
21-03-17 11:51:21	37,89	32	1	3	Refuse client

From the log we observe that some offers with distances and prices similar to those that are accepted are instead rejected, thus actually taxi drivers DO NOT necessarily decide to accept or reject an offer just based on the distance and price: clearly, this implies that the previous BPMN model is incorrect. At a closer observation of the data in the log, we eventually note that the decision depends also on the client's reputation. While this seems rather obvious with few data, in practice, with huge amounts of data, a manual analysis is unfeasible, and error prone because of the difficulty of the analysis itself.

In this paper we propose an approach that uses the techniques for evolving approximate functional dependencies proposed in [10] to compute *to what extent* the event log conforms to the business process model specified, and to identify the attributes (possibly missing from the BPMN diagram) that determine the next branch taken in a decision point of a process execution.

2 Preliminaries

Conformance Checking It receives as input a business process model and the *footprints* of the processes executed in the information system in terms of an event log. An execution of a process (also known as *process instance* or *case*) is represented as a sequence of activities called *trace*. We assume, without loss of generality, that each trace can be identified with a (surrogate) *id*, and each activity within the trace with a *timestamp* and *activity name*. An event log is a set of traces, representing the behavior observed in the information system during the execution of the process.

Definition 1 (Trace, Event Log). *Let $A \subseteq \mathcal{U}_A$ be a set of events A over a universe of events $\mathcal{U}_A$. A trace $\sigma \in A^*$ is a sequence of events. An event log $L \in \mathcal{P}(A^*)$ is a set of traces, where $\mathcal{P}(A^*)$ represents the power set of A^*.*

Functional Dependencies Let r be an instance of relation $R(A_1, A_2, ..., A_n)$, $|r|$ denotes the number of tuples in r, $t[A_i]$ the value of the attribute A_i in the tuple t and $\pi_X(r)$ is the projection of r on the attributes of X. A functional dependency F over R has the form $F : X \rightarrow Y$ where X and Y are two subsets of the attributes of R. Given an instance r of R, r satisfies an FD F defined on R if, for every pair of tuples t_1, t_2 in r, if $t_1[X] = t_2[X]$ then $t_1[Y] = t_2[Y]$. An instance r is inconsistent with respect to F if it does not satisfy it. Each FD can be characterized by its *confidence* $c_{F,r}$ and its *goodness* $g_{F,r}$ [10]:

Definition 2. *Let r be an instance of a relation R, X and Y two subsets of the attributes of R and $F : X \to Y$ a functional dependency over R. Then:*

$$c_{F,r} = |\pi_X(r)|/|\pi_{XY}(r)| \text{ and } g_{F,r} = |\pi_X(r)| - |\pi_Y(r)|$$

Depending on the confidence value we have the following definition:

Definition 3. *Given a relation R, an instance r of R, a functional dependency F over R and its confidence $c_{F,r}$, we say that F is an* exact functional dependency *iff $c_{F,r} = 1$, otherwise it is an* approximate functional dependency.

3 Our Approach

We start from the signature of the events of the BPMN to be analyzed and from the database storing the data of the process. Then, we automatically build the *enriched log table*, which is a new database table that essentially contains the contextual data of the initial event applied, together with the subsequent events. At runtime, the enriched log is filled with the real data of the processes. Then, to have the data ready for analysis, we have to discretize the continuous values of the *enriched log* since we are not interested in how a particular continuous value determines the next event, but on how a *kind* of values does. The resulting *discrete enriched log* is the basis for our conformance checking analysis.

3.1 Enriching the Log

The enriched log table should contain all necessary attributes to store the *contextual data* of each event execution, plus an additional attribute to store the name of the successive event. The contextual data consist of the values given in the event's input, together with all those values from the database that can be obtained through joins following the *foreign keys*.

We obtain these contextual attributes by looking at the UML types of the event's arguments. Then, we pick the attributes in the relational tables implementing these UML types and chase the *foreign keys* of these tables recursively to obtain more tables (and attributes). Note that, since this process is essentially a chase of *foreign keys*, we need to pay special attention to *foreign key* cycles. Indeed, chasing *foreign key* cycles never stops, thus, we should eventually break these cycles at some predefined point. Intuitively, this is done by deciding how many nested levels of joins we want to perform.

This process can be performed at compile time since the contextual attributes are fully determined by the user's given operation signature, the database schema, and the mapping between the UML schema and the underlying relational schema. At runtime we store each execution of the transition under study in a single row (tuple) of the enriched log. That is, whenever we detect an execution of the targeted transition, we query the database using the given event argument values to obtain the values for all its attributes. In the same row, we also store the next event applied by the user.

3.2 Discretization

The existence of a functional dependency (FD) depends, of course, on the data, and indeed, two different discretizations of the data may affect the fact that the dependency holds or not in the obtained table. Consider the FD $F : Distance \rightarrow Outcome$, meaning that a taxi driver decides to accept or reject a request only based on the distance. Suppose that the attribute *Distance* has been discretized to assume the values $\{short, long\}$ and that the data satisfy the FD. If we change the discretization of the *Distance* to the domain $\{short, medium, long\}$, then it is likely that the data will not satisfy the FD any longer, because now some tuples having *medium* distance will belong to the *accepted* category, while others with different, but still medium, distance, will be among the *rejected* ones.

These observations also hold for FDs that involve more than one attribute. Consider $F : Distance, Price \rightarrow Outcome$, that is, a taxi driver decides to accept or reject a request based on the distance and price of the offer. It is also possible that we find an "appropriate" discretization of the two attributes *Distance* and *Price* such that the tuples satisfy the FD. Note that most discretization techniques are univariate, that is, they consider only one feature at a time and can be used to discretize *Distance* and *Price* independently of one another. However, the two attributes are involved in the FD together, thus a multivariate discretization, performed on the two attributes together, would be more appropriate.

One way to perform multivariate discretization is by means of clustering techniques: data can be clustered according to the values of the attributes *Distance* and *Price*, thus, each cluster contains data with a certain combination of ranges of the domains of the two attributes. Then each cluster can be given a label that is the symbolic representation of such combination of domain ranges. This label can be interpreted as *a single categorical attribute*, that takes the place of the two attributes *Distance* and *Price*. Therefore, a FD is influenced by the discretization process, but can also be used, conversely, to guide the discretization task. In fact, given a FD, we can try and find a discretization of the antecedent such that the FD would hold on the current data: for the FD to hold on the data, the antecedent must have at least the same amount of distinct values as the consequent (ideally each of them should be related to exactly one of the distinct values of the consequent) or more (more than one distinct value of the antecedent is related to the same value of the consequent). If this is true, then the confidence of the FD will be 1 (thus an exact FD) otherwise it will be less than 1 (thus an approximate FD). The greater the amount of distinct values of the antecedent and of the consequent, the worse the goodness of the FD.

Let r be an instance of a relation R, $F : X \rightarrow Y$ an FD defined on it and $K = |\pi_Y(r)|$ the number of distinct values of the consequent of the FD. The process of discretization, under the guidance of F, consists in finding K homogeneous clusters of the tuples based on their values of X. If such clustering exists it represents a multivariate discretization of X such that F holds on the discretized data.

3.3 Applying Functional Dependency Evolution

Given a FD that is no longer valid, there are two ways to capture the modeled reality again: (i) try to change the way the attributes in the FD antecedent are discretized, so that the dependency holds again, (ii) keep the same discretization and "strengthen" the antecedent of the FD by adding an attribute to it. Consider the example of Section 3.2 and suppose both price and distance vary in the range [1,98] (both 1 and 98 are included) and that, initially, the taxi service company has a conceptual discretization of these ranges such that, for the *distance*, [1,32] means *short* and [33,98] means *long*, while for the *offeredPrice* [1,65] means *low* and [66,98] means *high*. Moreover, $F : distance, offeredPrice \rightarrow accepted$ is defined on the data. Suppose the initial data, without discretization are

					initial discretization				K=2: C1 and C2			K=3: C1, C2 and C3		
	dist	price	rep	accept	dist	price	rep	accept	label	reput	accept	label	reput	accept
(A)	30	80	3	1	short	high	3	1	C1	3	1	C1	3	1
	25	68	2	1	short	high	2	1	C1	2	1	C1	2	1
	90	10	4	0	long	low	4	0	C2	4	0	C2	4	0
	80	30	4	0	long	low	4	0	C2	4	0	C2	4	0
	70	20	3	0	long	low	3	0	C2	3	0	C2	3	0
(B)	20	10	4	1	short	low	4	1	C2	4	1	C3	4	1
	45	15	4	1	long	low	4	1	C2	4	1	C3	4	1
(C)	30	10	2	0								C3	2	0
	35	20	2	0								C3	2	0
	(1)				(2)				(3)			(4)		

Fig. 3. Taxi service running example

the tuples in Figure 3(1)(A). After discretization we obtain the data in (2)(A) satisfying F with c_F=1 and g_F=0. By running the K-means algorithm (with K=2) we find two homogeneous clusters: C_1 with centroid *distance*=29 and $offeredPrice$=79.333 where all tuples have *accepted*=1 and C_2 with centroid *distance*=75 and $offeredPrice$=25 where all tuples have *accepted*=0. Thus, $C1$ represents (accepted) offers with short distance and high price while $C2$ represents (rejected) offers with long distance and low price. We can also discretize the data assigning them the label of the cluster to which they belong (as shown in Figure 3(3)(A)).

Now, suppose that the two tuples in Figure 3(1)(B) arrive. The first tuple still satisfies the FD but the second one does not. Therefore, the FD is not satisfied any longer. By running the K-means algorithm again on the data we find C_1 (centroid *distance*=29, $offeredPrice$=79.333), where all tuples have *accepted*=1; and C_2 (centroid *distance*=75, $offeredPrice$=25), where 60% of tuples have *accepted*=0 and the rest *accepted*=1, i.e., a non-homogeneous cluster. Thus, C_1 still represents accepted offers with short distance and high price while C_2 mixes tuples having different ranges of distance and price and different outcomes.

Now, we can choose different strategies: (i) accept approximate FDs, and decide that c_F=2/3 is still a good confidence for the FD: nothing should be changed in this case; (ii) try to find a different discretization of the data such that the FD would hold on them: the data discretization should be changed; (iii) choose to evolve the FD by looking for attributes that can be added to its antecedent in order to repair it: the FD should be changed.

Suppose that we decide that the new confidence of the FD is too low and try to re-cluster the data with K=3. Then, we find 3 homogeneous clusters whose centroids are: C_1: *distance*=27.5 and $offeredPrice$=74 with *accepted*=1; C_2: *distance*=80 and $offeredPrice$=20 with *accepted*=0; C_3: *distance*=32.5 and $offeredPrice$=12.5 with *accepted*=1. In fact, if we associate each tuple with the label of the cluster it belongs to (see Figure 3(4)(A-B)), instead of *distance* and $offeredPrice$, we can see that the functional dependency F holds on these data with c_F=1 and g_F=1. As data continue to arrive the confidence of the FD might continue to decrease: we could try to change the discretization again but there might be a point where this would not be possible anymore. For example, suppose the two new tuples shown in Figure 3(1)(C) are added to the data: a homogeneous clustering is found only at K=9, when each cluster contains only one tuple! Thus, no discretization can bring the data to satisfy the FD. At this point we can choose to change the FD, looking for a minimal set of attributes that can be added to its antecedent in order to restore a high confidence value. To this end we apply the technique for evolving FD in [10] and add one attribute of the relation at a time to the antecedent of F, evaluate the confidence of the newly built FD and decide what is the confidence value we consider acceptable. Consider the tuples in Figure 3(4): since with the discretization we have performed the data no longer satisfies F, we try adding *reputation* to the antecedent of F. The obtained FD: $label, reputation \rightarrow accepted$ has confidence 1 and goodness 4, hence the reputation allows us to discriminate in particular inside the C_3 cluster. By remembering its centroid (*distance*=32.5 and $offeredPrice$=12.5) we can say, intuitively, that it contains medium-distance offers with low price. Thus, by repairing the FD, we are saying that these offers are accepted if the client has high reputation and are rejected otherwise.

4 Related Work

Several proposals perform conformance checking over process models and logs considering the data. Most of them use procedural models [6, 9, 11] and are usually based on Petri nets with data, although they are scalable to other representations such as BPMN or EPC. More specifically, [11] deals with event logs with deviating behavior and more complex control-flow constructs. [7] follows a different approach by splitting the log when doing the conformance checking, to achieve better efficiency. All of [6, 9] incorporate resources into the conformance checking, but [6, 9] also consider time constraints in the process. On the other hand, [2, 8] perform conformance checking and process discovery on declarative process models which consider data. They are based on the Declare language, which has formal semantics and a graphical representation and it allows defining many different types of dependencies between tasks. All these approaches do not deal with structured data, but rather they consider data as a set of global attributes. Moreover, none of them deals with variable discretization. In terms of the data itself, note that the approaches performing conformance checking highlight the deviations between the real executions, as recorded in the log, and the process model, but do not propose alternative conditions like we do. [8, 11] do discover data conditions from the log, but both are focused on discovery, not on conformance. In addition, [8] uses a declarative specification instead of a procedural one, like we do. Our method for analyzing, for each event in the log, the (approximate) functional dependency holding between its contextual data and the next branch is based on [10], which employs the two measures *confidence* and *goodness* to evaluate the degree of approximation of a FD. This is rather efficient because it only requires to count tuples. However, we plan to study whether other measures of approximation [3] produce suggestions of model modifications that are "closer" to the intention of the designer.

5 Conclusions

Our approach for conformance checking of artifact-centric BPMN models determines whether the actual execution of a business process conforms to the model and, by analyzing the data dependencies, proposes changes to the model accordingly.

References

1. van der Aalst, W.M.P.: Process Mining: Discovery, Conformance and Enhancement of Business Processes (2011)
2. Burattin, A., Maggi, F.M., Sperduti, A.: Conformance checking based on multi-perspective declarative process models. Expert Syst. Appl. 65, 194–211 (2016)
3. Caruccio, L., Deufemia, V., Polese, G.: Relaxed functional dependencies - A survey of approaches. IEEE Trans. Knowl. Data Eng. 28(1), 147–165 (2016)
4. De Giacomo, G., Oriol, X., Estañol, M., Teniente, E.: Linking data and BPMN processes to achieve executable model. In: CAiSE (2017), accepted for publication
5. Estañol, M., Sancho, M., Teniente, E.: Verification and validation of UML artifact-centric business process models. In: CAiSE. pp. 434–449 (2015)
6. de Leoni, M., van der Aalst, W.M.P.: Aligning event logs and process models for multi-perspective conformance checking: An approach based on integer linear programming. In: 11th BPM. pp. 113–129 (2013)
7. de Leoni, M., Munoz-Gama, J., Carmona, J., van der Aalst, W.M.P.: Decomposing alignment-based conformance checking of data-aware process models. In: On the Move to Meaningful Internet Systems: OTM. pp. 3–20 (2014)
8. Maggi, F.M., Dumas, M., García-Bañuelos, L., Montali, M.: Discovering data-aware declarative process models from event logs. In: 11th BPM. pp. 81–96 (2013)
9. Mannhardt, F., de Leoni, M., Reijers, H.A., van der Aalst, W.M.P.: Balanced multi-perspective checking of process conformance. Computing 98(4), 407–437 (2016)
10. Mazuran, M., Quintarelli, E., Tanca, L., Ugolini, S.: Semi-automatic support for evolving functional dependencies. In: EDBT. pp. 293–304 (2016)
11. Rozinat, A., van der Aalst, W.M.P.: Decision mining in prom. In: 4th International Conference on Business Process Management. pp. 420–425 (2006)

Ensuring the Integrity of Wikipedia: A Data Science Approach

Francesca Spezzano

Computer Science Department
Boise State University
francescaspezzano@boisestate.edu

Abstract. In this paper, we present our research on the problem of ensuring the integrity of Wikipedia, the world's biggest free encyclopedia. As anyone can edit Wikipedia, many malicious users take advantage of this situation to make edits that compromise pages' content quality. Specifically, we present DePP, the state-of-the-art tool that detects article pages to protect with an accuracy of 93% and we introduce our research on identifying spam users. We show that we are able to classify spammers from benign users with 80.8% of accuracy and 0.88 mean average precision.

1 Introduction

Wikipedia is the world's biggest free encyclopedia read by many users every day. Thanks to the mechanism by which anyone can edit, its content grows and is kept constantly updated. However, malicious users can take advantage of this open editing mechanism to seriously compromise the quality of Wikipedia articles.

The main form of content damaging is vandalism, defined by Wikipedia itself as "any addition, removal, or change of content, in a deliberate attempt to compromise the integrity of Wikipedia"[1]. Other forms of damaging edits are page spamming [2] and dissemination of false information, e.g. through hoax articles [11].

In this paper, we discuss two research efforts which have the common goal of ensuring the content integrity of Wikipedia.

First, we introduce DePP, the state-of-the-art tool detecting article pages to protect [12]. Page protection is a mechanism used by Wikipedia to place restrictions on the type of users that can make edits to prevent vandalism, libel, or edit wars [3]. Our DePP system achieves an accuracy of 93% and significantly improves over baselines.

Second, we present our work on spam users identification [8]. We formulate the problem as a binary classification task and propose a set of features based on user editing behavior to separate spam users from benign ones. Our results show that we reach 80.8% classification accuracy and 0.88 mean average precision and beat ORES, the most recent tool developed by Wikimedia to assign damaging scores to edits.

2 Related Work

Detecting damaging edits. Plenty of work has been done on detecting damaging edits, particularly vandalism (see [7] for a survey). Currently, ClueBot NG [4] and STiki [5] are the state-of-the-art tools used by Wikipedia to detect vandalism. ClueBot NG is a bot based on an artificial neural network which scores edits and reverts the worst-scoring edits. STiki is an intelligent routing tool which suggests potential vandalism to humans for definitive classification. It works by scoring edits on the basis of metadata and reverts, and computing a reputation score for each user.

Recently, Wikimedia Foundation launched a new machine learning-based service, called Objective Revision Evaluation Service (ORES) [6] which measures the level of general damage each edit causes. More specifically, given an edit, ORES provides three probabilities predicting (i) whether or not it causes damage, (ii) if it was saved in good-faith, and (iii) if the edit will eventually be reverted. These scores are available through the ORES public API [1].

Regarding spam edits detection specifically, previous work concentrated on the problem of predicting whether a link contained in an edit is spam or not, whereas, in this paper, we predict whether a user is a spammer or not by considering her edit history. [14] created the first Wikipedia link-spam corpus, identified Wikipedia's link spam vulnerabilities, and proposed mitigation strategies based on explicit edit approval, refinement of account privileges, and detecting potential spam edits through a machine learning framework. The latter strategy, described by the same authors in [13], relies on features based on (i) article metadata and link/URL properties, (ii) HTML landing site analysis, and (iii) third-party services used to discern spam landing sites. This tool was implemented as part of STiki and has been used on Wikipedia since 2011. Nowadays, this STiki component is inactive due to a monetary cost for third-party services.

An Early Warning System for Vandals. In our previous work [10], we addressed the problem of vandalism in Wikipedia from a different perspective. We studied for the *first* time the problem of early prediction of vandal users. The proposed system, called VEWS (Vandal Early Warning System) [2], leverages differences in the editing behavior of vandals vs. benign users and detect vandals with an accuracy of over 85% and outperforms both ClueBot NG and STiki. Moreover, as an early warning system, VEWS detects, on average, vandals 2.39 edits before ClueBot NG. The combination of VEWS and Cluebot NG results in a fully automated system that does not leverage any human input (e.g. edit reversion) and further increases the performances.

Page protection. When a page article is heavily vandalized, administrators may decide to protect the page by restricting its access. To the best of our knowledge, little research has been done on the topic of page protection in Wikipedia.

[1] `http://ores.wikimedia.org`

[2] Dataset and code are available at `http://www.cs.umd.edu/~vs/vews/`

Hill and Shaw [9] studied the impact of page protection on user patterns of editing. They also created a dataset (they admit it may not be complete) of protected pages to perform their analysis. There are not currently bots on Wikipedia that can search for pages that may need to be protected. WikiMedia does have a script [3] available in which administrative users can protect a set of pages all at once. However, this program requires that the user supply the pages, or the category of pages to be protected and is only intended for protecting a large group of pages at once. There are some bots on Wikipedia that can help with some of the wiki-work that goes along with protecting or removing page protection. This includes adding or removing a template to a page that is marked as protected or no longer marked as protected. These bots can automatically update templates if a page protection has expired.

3 Detecting Pages to Protect

The first problem we address consists in deciding whether or not a page should be protected by Wikipedia administrators. Page protection consists in placing restrictions on the type of users that can edit a Wikipedia page. Common motivations that an administrative user may have in protecting a page include (i) consistent vandalism or libel from one or more users, and (ii) avoiding edit wars [3]. There are different levels of page protection for which different levels of users can make edits (or, in general, perform actions on the page): fully protected pages can be edited (or moved) only by administrators, semi-protected pages can be edited only by autoconfirmed users, while move protection does not allow pages to be moved to a new title, except by an administrator. Page protections can also be set for different amounts of time, including 24 or 36 hours, or indefinitely.

Currently, English Wikipedia contains over five million pages. Only a small percentage of those pages are currently protected, less than 0.2 percent. However, around 17 pages become protected every day (according to the number of protected pages from May 6 through Aug 6, 2016). This ratio shows how it is difficult for administrative users to monitor over all Wikipedia pages to determine if any need to be protected. Users can request pages to be protected or unprotected but an administrative user would have to analyze the page to determine if it should be protected, what level of protection to give, and for how long the protection should last, if not indefinitely. All this work is currently *manually* done by administrators.

To overcome this problem, we propose `DePP`, the *first* automated tool to detect pages to protect in Wikipedia [12]. `DePP` is a machine learning-based tool that works with two novel set of features based on (i) users page revision behavior and (ii) page categories. More specifically, the first group of features includes the following six base features:

E1 *Total average time between revisions*;

[3] `https://www.mediawiki.org/wiki/Manual:Pywikibot/protect.py`

E2 *Total number of users making 5 or more revisions*;
E3 *Total average number of revisions per user*;
E4 *Total number of revisions by non-registered users*;
E5 *Total number of revisions made from mobile device*;
E6 *Total average size of revisions.*

In addition to the above base features, we also include an additional set of features taking into account the page editing pattern over the time. We define these features by leveraging the features E1-E6 as follows. For each page, we consider the edits made in the latest 10 weeks and we split this time interval into time frames of two weeks (last two weeks, second last two weeks, etc.). Then, we compute features E1 to E6 within each time frame. The idea of these features is to monitor features E1-E6 over time to see if some anomaly starts to happen at some point. For instance, if a page is new we may observe a lot of edits of larger size in a short time after the page is created as users are building the content of the page. Later when the content is stable, we may observe fewer edits of smaller size representing small changes in the page. On the other hand, if the content of the page was stable and suddenly we observe a lot of edits from many users, it may indicate the page topic became controversial and the page may need protection.

The second group of features use information about page categories and includes:

NC *Number of categories a page is marked under*;
PC *Probability of protecting the page given its categories*: given all the pages in the training set T and a page category c, we compute the probability $\texttt{pr}(c)$ that pages in category c are protected as the percentage of pages in T having category c that are protected. Then, given a page p having categories $c_1, \ldots, c_n$, we compute this feature as the probability that the page is in at least one category whose pages have a high probability to be protected as $PC(p) = 1 - \prod_{i=1}^{n}(1 - \texttt{pr}(c_i))$.

In addition to the above two features, we define another group of features that shows how much features E1-E6 vary for a page p w.r.t. the average of these values among all the pages in the same categories as p. Specifically, given the set of pages in the training set T, we computed the set C of the top-100 most frequent categories. Additionally, for each category $c \in C$, we averaged the features E1-E6 among all the pages (denoted by T_c) having category c in the training set. Then, for each page p we computed 600 features (6 times 100), one for each feature Ei ($1 \leq i \leq 6$) and for each category $c \in C$ as follows:

$$C(Ei, c) = \begin{cases} |Ei(p) - \texttt{avg}_{p' \in T_c}(Ei(p'))| & \text{if } p \text{ is in category } c \\ 0 & \text{otherwise} \end{cases}$$

where $Ei(p)$ is the value of the feature Ei for the page p. The aim of this group of features is to understand if a page is anomalous w.r.t. other pages in the same category.

	Accuracy
B1	55.964%
B2	65.617%
B3	73.361%
B1+B2+B3	78.089%
DePP	**93.237%**

Table 1. DePP accuracy results and comparison with baselines. Everything is computed with random forest.

All the features that we propose are language independent as they do not consider page content. As a consequence, DePP is general and able to work on any version of Wikipedia.

To test our DePP system we built a balanced dataset [4] containing all edit protected articles until to Apr. 7, 2016 (6,799 pages) and an almost equal number of randomly selected unprotected pages (6,824), for a total of 13.6K article pages, and up to the last 500 most recent revisions for each selected page. For protected pages, we only gathered the revisions up until the most recent protection. If there was more than one recent protection, we gathered the revision information between the two protections. This allowed us to focus on the revisions leading up to the most recent page protection. Revision information that we collected included the user who made the revision, the timestamp of the revision, the size of the revision, the categories of the page, and any comments, tags or flags associated with the revision.

The DePP accuracy in the prediction task on 10-fold cross validation is reported for random forest (the best performing algorithm as compared to Logistic Regression, SVM, and K-Nearest Neighbor) in Table 1. As we can see, DePP is able to classify pages to protect from pages that do not need protection with an accuracy of 93.237%. As no automated tool detecting which page to protect exists in Wikipedia, we defined some baselines to compare our results. One of the main reasons for protecting a page on Wikipedia is to stop edit wars, vandalism or libel from happening, or continuing to happen on a page. Thus, we used the following baselines: [B1] *Number of revisions tagged as "Possible libel or vandalism"*; [B2] *Number of revisions that Cluebot NG or STiki reverted as possible vandalism*; [B3] *Number of edit wars between two users in the page.*

As we can see in Table 1, DePP significantly beats each individual baseline and the combination of all the three.

4 Spam Users Identification

Another problem that compromises the content quality of Wikipedia articles is spamming. Wikipedia, like most forms of online social media, receives continuous spamming attempts every day. Since all non-protected pages are open for editing by any type of user, inevitably happens that malicious users have the opportunity to post spam messages into any open page. These messages remain

[4] Dataset available at http://bit.ly/wiki_depp

on the page until they are discovered and removed by another user. Specifically, Wikipedia recognizes three main types of spam, namely "advertisements masquerading as articles, external link spamming, and adding references with the aim of promoting the author or the work being referenced"[2].

Currently, no specific tool is available on Wikipedia to identify neither spam edits or spam users. Tools like Cluebot NG and STiki are tailored toward vandalism detection, while ORES is designed to detect damaging edits in general. As in the case of page protection, the majority of the work to protect Wikipedia from spammers is done *manually* by Wikipedia users (patrollers, watchlisters, and readers) who monitor recent changes in the encyclopedia and, eventually, report suspicious spam users to administrators for definitive account blocking.

To fight spammers on Wikipedia, we study the problem of identifying spam users from benign ones [8]. Our work is closer in spirit to [10] as the aim is to classify users by using their editing behavior instead of classifying a single edit as vandalism [4,5], spam [13] or generally damaging [6].

We propose a machine learning-based framework using a set of features which are based on research that has been done regarding typical behaviors exhibited by spammers: similarity in edit size and links used in revisions, similar time-sensitive behavior in edits, social involvement of a user in the community through contribution to Wikipedias talk page system, and chosen username. We did not consider any feature related to edit content so that our system would be language independent and capable of working for all Wikipedia versions. Moreover, we do not rely on third-party services, so there is no overhead cost as in [13].

The list of features we considered in our system are as follows:

User edit sizes based features : average size of edits, standard deviation of edit sizes, and variance significance (previous feature normalized by user average edit size).

Edit timing behavior based features : average and standard deviation of time between edits.

Links in edits based features : Unique link rating (the ratio of unique links posted by a user to the total number of links posted by the user) and link ratio in edits (number of edits that a user makes which contain links).

Talk page edit ratio : this is the ratio of talk pages edited by a user that correspond with the main article pages that a user edits.

Username based features : Zafarani and Liu [15] showed that aspects of users' usernames themselves contain information that is useful in detecting malicious users. Thus, in addition to the features based on users' edit behaviors, we also considered four additional username related features: number of digits in a username, ratio of digits in a username, number of leading digits in a username, and unique character ratio in a username.

To test our framework, we built a new dataset [5] containing 4.2K (half spammer and half benign) users and 75.6K edits as follows. We collected all Wikipedia

[5] Dataset available at `http://bit.ly/wiki_spammers`

	Our Features	ORES	Our Features + ORES
Accuracy	**80.8%**	69.7%	**82.1%**
MAP	**0.88**	0.695	**0.886**

Table 2. Spammers identification accuracy and Mean Average Precision (MAP) results in comparison with ORES. Everything is computed with XGBoost.

users (up to Nov. 17, 2016) who were blocked for spamming from two lists maintained on Wikipedia: "Wikipedians who are indefinitely blocked for spamming"[6] "Wikipedians who are indefinitely blocked for link spamming" [7]. The first list contains all spam users blocked before Mar 12, 2009, while the second one includes all link-spammers after Mar 12, 2009 to today. We gathered a total of 2,087 spam users (we only included users who did at least one edit) between the two lists considered.

In order to create a balanced dataset of spam/benign users, we randomly select a sample of benign Wikipedia users of roughly the same size as the spammer user set (2,119 users). To ensure these were genuine users, we cross-checked their usernames against the entire list of blocked users provided by Wikipedia [8]. This list contains all users in Wikipedia who have been blocked for any reason, spammers included. For each user in our dataset, we collected up to their 500 most recent edits. For each edit we gathered the following information: edit content, time-stamp, whether or not the edit is done on a Talk page, and the damaging score provided by ORES.

We run 10-fold cross validation on several machine learning algorithms, namely SVM, Logistic Regression, K-Nearest Neighbor, Random Forest, and XGBoost, to test the performances of our features. Experimental results are shown in Table 2 for the best performing algorithm (XGBoost). Here we can see that our system is able to classify spammers from benign users with 80.8% of accuracy and it is a valuable tool in suggesting potential spammers to Wikipedia administrators for further investigation as proved by a mean average precision of 0.88.

We compared our tool with ORES only, as the tool proposed in [13] is no longer used and Cluebot NG and STiki are designed specifically for vandalism and not spam. To compare our system with ORES, we considered the edit damaging score. More specifically, given a user and all her edits, we computed both the average and maximum damaging score provided by ORES and used these as features for classification. Results on 10-fold cross validation with XGBoost (the best performing classifier) are reported in Table 2, as well. As we can see, ORES performances are poor for the task of spammer detection (69.7% of accuracy

[6] `http://en.wikipedia.org/wiki/Category:Wikipedians_who_are_indefinitely_blocked_for_spamming`

[7] `http://en.wikipedia.org/wiki/Category:Wikipedians_who_are_indefinitely_blocked_for_link-spamming`

[8] `http://en.wikipedia.org/wiki/Special:BlockList`

and a mean average precision of 0.695). However, combining our features with ORES further increases the accuracy to 82.1%.

5 Conclusions

In this paper, we addressed the problem of ensuring the integrity of Wikipedia pages and presented our research on detecting pages to protect and identifying spam users. Our experimental results show that we are able to classify (i) article pages to protect with an accuracy of 93% and (ii) spammers from benign users with 80.8% of accuracy and 0.88 mean average precision.

Both the methods proposed do not look at edit content and, as a consequence, they are generally applicable to all versions of Wikipedia.

References

1. http://en.wikipedia.org/wiki/Wikipedia:Vandalism.
2. http://en.wikipedia.org/wiki/Wikipedia:Spam.
3. http://en.wikipedia.org/wiki/Wikipedia:Editwarring.
4. http://en.wikipedia.org/wiki/User:ClueBot_NG.
5. http://en.wikipedia.org/wiki/Wikipedia:STiki.
6. http://meta.wikimedia.org/wiki/Objective_Revision_Evaluation_Service.
7. B. Thomas Adler, Luca de Alfaro, Santiago Moisés Mola-Velasco, Paolo Rosso, and Andrew G. West. Wikipedia vandalism detection: Combining natural language, metadata, and reputation features. In *Computational linguistics and intelligent text processing*, pages 277–288, 2011.
8. Thomas Green and Francesca Spezzano. Spam users identification in wikipedia via editing behavior. In *International AAAI Conference Web and Social Media*, pages 532–535, 2017.
9. Benjamin Mako Hill and Aaron D. Shaw. Page protection: another missing dimension of wikipedia research. In *International Symposium on Open Collaboration*, pages 15:1–15:4, 2015.
10. Srijan Kumar, Francesca Spezzano, and VS Subrahmanian. Vews: A wikipedia vandal early warning system. In *ACM SIGKDD Conference on Knowledge Discovery and Data Mining*, pages 607–616, 2015.
11. Srijan Kumar, Robert West, and Jure Leskovec. Disinformation on the web: Impact, characteristics, and detection of wikipedia hoaxes. In *International World Wide Web Conference*, pages 591–602, 2016.
12. Kelsey Suyehira and Francesca Spezzano. Depp: A system for detecting pages to protect in wikipedia. In *International Conference on Information and Knowledge Management*, pages 2081–2084, 2016.
13. Andrew G West, Avantika Agrawal, Phillip Baker, Brittney Exline, and Insup Lee. Autonomous link spam detection in purely collaborative environments. In *International Symposium on Wikis and Open Collaboration*, pages 91–100, 2011.
14. Andrew G. West, Jian Chang, Krishna Venkatasubramanian, Oleg Sokolsky, and Insup Lee. Link spamming wikipedia for profit. In *Annual Collaboration, Electronic messaging, Anti-Abuse and Spam Conference*, pages 152–161, 2011.
15. Reza Zafarani and Huan Liu. 10 bits of surprise: Detecting malicious users with minimum information. In *International Conference on Information and Knowledge Management*, pages 423–431, 2015.

Exposing the Deep Web in the Linked Data Cloud

Andrea Calì[1], Giuseppe De Santis[2], Tommaso Di Noia[2] and Nicola Mincuzzi[2]

[1]London Knowledge Lab, Birkbeck, University of London
andrea@dcs.bbk.ac.uk
[2]SisInf Lab, Politecnico di Bari
{g.desantis6,n.mincuzzi}@studenti.poliba.it,tommaso.dinoia@poliba.it

Abstract. The Deep Web is constituted by dynamically generated pages, usually requested through a HTML form; it is notoriously difficult to query and to search, as its pages are obviously non-indexable. More recently, Deep Web data have been made accessible through RESTful services that return information usually structured in JSON or XML format. We propose techniques to make the Deep Web available in the Linked Data Cloud, and we study algorithms for processing queries, posed in a transparent way on the Linked Data, on the underlying Deep Web sources. The tool we developed mainly focuses on exposing RESTful services as Linked Data datasets thus allowing a smoother semantic integration of different structured information sources in a global data- and knowledge-space.

1 Introduction

Slowly but steadily, the Web has moved from a huge collection of unstructured textual documents to a gigantic repository of structured data. At a first stage, the original static Web pages have been replaced by dynamic ones fed by information coming from Deep web data sources which cannot be directly queried. Then we assisted to the flourishing of new services that expose structured data by exploiting standard Web technologies thus making possible their composition for the creation of new integrated applications (mash-ups [10]) and knowledge spaces. Among the various technological proposals and approaches for data publication on the Web which survived to the present days, the two most relevant ones are for sure: RESTful services [5] and Linked Data (LD) [2]. The former is a very agile way of exposing data in a request/response way over HTTP and has been widely adopted by programmers thanks to its easiness of implementation. Data are usually returned in XML or JSON documents after the invocation of a service. Among the issues related to pure a RESTful approach we may mention:

- no explicit semantics attached to the returned data[1];

[1] Actually, with JSON-LD this issue could be solved but this format is not widely adopted yet.

- lack of a unique query language to invoke services. Each service exposes its own API which can considerably differ from each other even when they refer to the same knowledge domain;
- manual integration of different data sources.

On the other side, the Linked Data (LD) approach bases on the idea that data can be delivered on the Web together with their explicit semantics by means of common vocabularies. Following the Linked Data principles[2], datasets should be accessible through a SPARQL endpoint. Moreover, by using federated queries[3] an agent is able to automatically integrate data coming from different sources thus creating a data space at a Web scale. Unfortunately, also the Linked Data approach comes with its drawbacks:

- the effort in setting up a SPARQL endpoint is felt more difficult than a RESTful approach from service providers. Nowadays, it is much easier to find a JSON-based service than a LD-based one.
- programmers are more used to JSON services than to SPARQL endpoints;
- service providers are usually not interested in exposing all the data they have but only a small portion.

Based on the above points we can see that while from the *practical* point of view the champion is the RESTful approach, if we look at the *knowledge* point of view Linked Data represents a much better alternative. This was the leading observation that inspired us in the development of `PoLDo`. With `PoLDo` we can expose an already existing RESTful service, even a third-party one, as a SPARQL endpoint thus making it part of the Linked Data cloud. Thanks to a configurable query planner, `PoLDo` is able to break down a SPARQL query into a sequence of RESTful service invocations. Starting from the retrieved data it then builds the answer to the original SPARQL query.

The remainder of this paper is structured as follows. In the next section we report on some relevant related work on accessing the Deep Web while in Section 3 we describe `PoLDo` together with an explanatory example. Conclusion closes the paper.

2 Related Work

The term *Deep Web* (sometimes also called *Hidden Web*) [9,8,3,4] refers to the data content that is created dynamically as the result of a specific search on the web. For example, when we query a Yellow Pages website, the generated output is the result of a query posed on an underlying database, and cannot be indexed by a search engine. In this respect, the Deep Web content resides outside web pages, and is only accessible through interaction with the web site – typically via HTML forms.

[2] `https://www.w3.org/DesignIssues/LinkedData.html`
[3] `https://www.w3.org/TR/sparql11-federated-query/`

As an example of Deep Web source, the whitepages.com website presents a form where, when searching by name, the last name is a required field. In order to look for a person named Joseph Noto, living in New Jersey, we would fill the form which in relational terms, corresponds to issuing a SQL query to the underling database. Therefore, a Deep Web source can be naturally modeled as a relational table (or a set of relational tables) where not all queries are allowed; in fact, *access limitations* exist on such relations. In particular, they can be queried only according to so-called *access patterns*, each of which enforces the selection on some of the attributes (which corresponds to filling the corresponding field in the form with a value). It is believed that the size of the Deep Web is several orders of magnitude larger [7] than that of the so-called *Surface Web*, i.e., the web that is accessible and indexable by search engines. The information stored in the Deep Web is invaluable, but at the same time hard to collect automatically on a reasonably large scale.

Two main approaches for accessing the Deep Web exist [8]. In the *vertical data integration* approach, each Deep Web site is a data source, and sources are integrated and unified by a *global schema* representing the domain of interest. Normally, in this approach one deals with a relatively small number of sources, storing data related to a single domain of interest. In the *Surfacing* approach, instead, answers are pre-computed from Deep Web sources by posing suitable queries, and then the results are indexed as normal static pages in a search engine. Accessing the Deep Web requires a variety of techniques and tools from several areas of computer science. In this paper we survey some of the most relevant approaches to querying and searching the Deep Web. One important problem in accessing the Deep Web is the automatic understanding of the semantics of the so-called *query interfaces*, that is, the forms that provide access to Deep Web sources. Several approaches have been developed, based on heuristics or learning from samples; some techniques involve domain-specific knowledge encoded in ontological rules. Processing structured query over Deep Web sources is the key problem in the integration of such sources. Interestingly, when Deep Web sources are modeled, as mentioned, as relations with access patterns (i.e., having certain attributes that are necessarily to be selected in order to query the source), answering a simple conjunctive (select-project-join) query on such sources may require, in the worst case, the evaluation of a *recursive* Datalog query. This raises the issue of reducing the number of accesses to sources while answering a query.

The problem of answering a query over sources with access patterns falls into the setting of vertical data integration, where a limited number of Deep Web sources, whose interface is known (having been possibly understood automatically), are queried in a structured way. But if we want to search via keyword search the Deep Web together with the ordinary, "shallow" Web, we cannot rely on a set of known sources, and therefore we have to adopt the surfacing approach. Surfacing the Deep Web poses several challenges because it is not easy to get a good coverage of the content of a source while at the same time limiting the number of sampling accesses on it. Keyword search on relational databases has

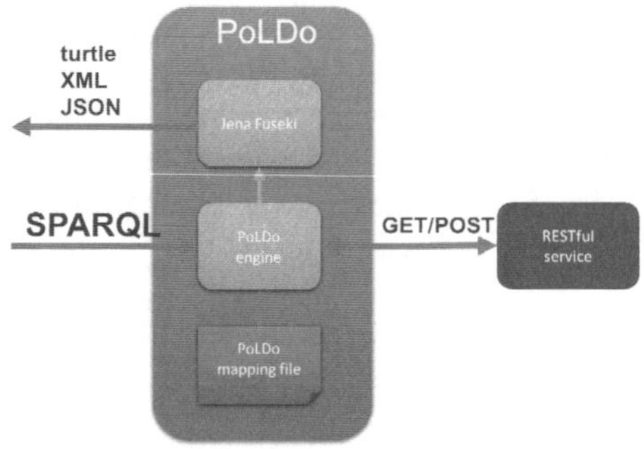

Fig. 1. A high level view for the architecture of `PoLDo`

been traditionally studied in several works in the literature (see e.g., [1,6]). It is interesting to consider keyword search also on Deep Web sources, in the context of vertical Deep Web integration. In this case, a suitable notion of answer to keyword queries is needed.

3 PoLDo

The high level architecture of `PoLDo` is represented in Fig. 1. The engine is responsible of getting the SPARQL query and breaking it down to a sequence of RESTful calls to a remote service. The transformation is made possible thanks to a mapping file that maps Linked Data URIs to the elements of the signature of the remote call. While querying the remote service, `PoLDo` feeds an RDF local triple store (Jena Fuseki in its current implementation) which is in charge of processing the actual SPARQL query. More in details, we have:

`PoLDo` **engine** It receives the SPARQL query and extracts all the constants from the graph template in the WHERE clause. Then, by using the algorithm in [3], it uses the constants to query the external service and to get the data that will be used to create a local RDF representation of the data space. Thanks to the information encoded in the `PoLDo` mapping file, the engine is able to feed a local repository of RDF triples.

Jena Fuseki The triple store is used to save a LD version of the data which are incrementally retrieved from the RESTful service. The availability of a third-party triple store makes `PoLDo` able to support the full specification of SPARQL query language. Furthermore, it is able to return the data in all the formats supported by Jena Fuseki.

`PoLDo` **mapping file** This file contains information about how to map the URIs of the SPARQL query to inputs and outputs of the service. Moreover, it also describes the entities represented by inputs and outputs as well as their mutual relations.

3.1 PoLDo mapping language

PoLDo mapping file allows the designer to create a link between URIs contained in the SPARQL queries processed by the engine and, at the same time, to enrich their semantics by explicitly adding information about the corresponding OWL class or property that can be defined also in an external vocabulary (e.g. DBpedia). Mapping rules can also be created to describe RDF triples containing information on how to relate values of an input parameter with the outputs of the service invocation. All the rules contained in the PoLDo mapping file are, in turn, represented as RDF triples which refers to a corresponding RDF-S ontology. The main element of the PoLDo ontology is the class `poldo:Service` (see Fig. 2). It describes each service in terms of its base URL (`poldo:hasUrl`), the

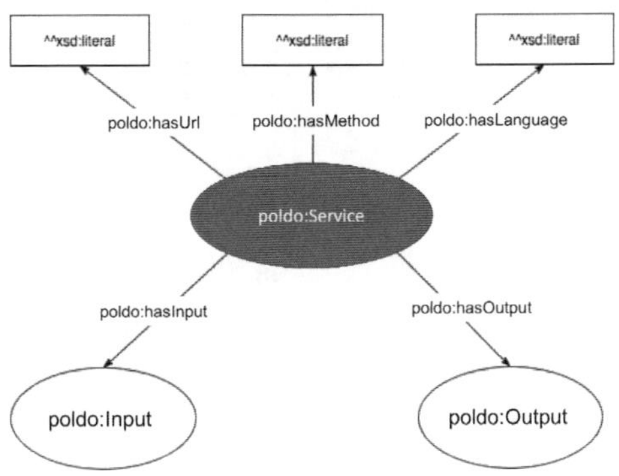

Fig. 2. The class `poldo:Service` in the PoLDo mapping ontology.

HTTP method GET or POST (`poldo:hasMethod`), the language of the answer to the service call, e.g. XML or JSON (`poldo:hasLanguage`) and its inputs and outputs (`poldo:hasInput` and `poldo:hasOutput`). The ontological description of `poldo:Input` and `poldo:Output` are represented respectively in Fig. 3 and Fig. 4. As we can see, both inputs and outputs of a services can be mapped as instances of a class or as a property. Indeed, especially when the type of the corresponding value is different from a string, we may have cases when the parameter is better represented by a property rather than the subject or object of a triple. We may think at a geographical service returning places based on their coordinates. In this case, coordinates are better mapped to the properties `geo:lat` and `geo:long` of the Basic Geo vocabulary[4]. The modeling of `poldo:Input` and `poldo:Output` classes try to catch all possible cases in the description of the inputs and outputs of a service. For instance, the parameter `poldo:hasFixedValue` is used when we need a key to access the RESTful service. As for `poldo:Output` we just highlight that it possible to model the

[4] `https://www.w3.org/2003/01/geo/`

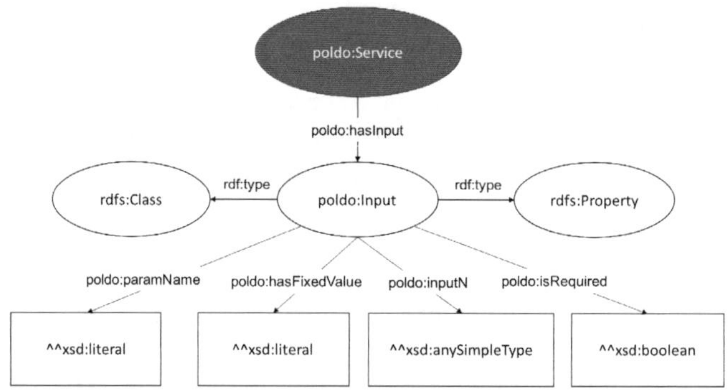

Fig. 3. The class `poldo:Input` in the `PoLDo` mapping ontology.

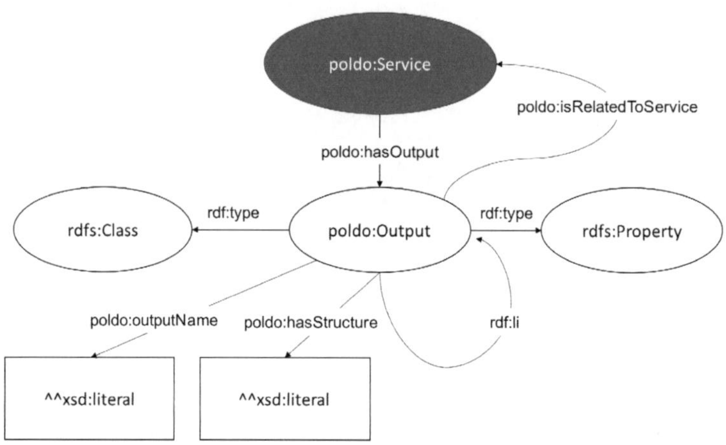

Fig. 4. The class `poldo:Output` in the `PoLDo` mapping ontology.

situation when the service returns a single value or a list of values by means of the `poldo:hasStructure` and `rdf:li` statements.

3.2 `PoLDo` engine

The main component of `PoLDo` is its query planner implemented in the `PoLDo` engine module. It uses the algorithm presented in [3] to iteratively query the RESTful services and build a local cache containing the RDF version of the data whose transformation follows the rules available in the `PoLDo` mapping file.

For a better understanding of the overall approach, we now describe how `PoLDo` engine works by means of an example. Suppose we have two services related to music events in a city as in the following.

service	**input**	**output**
`http://example.com/api/returnSinger`	city	title, singer
`http://example.com/api/returnPlace`	singer	city, country

Given a city, the first service returns the title of the events in that city together with the performing artist. The second service returns the birth place of an artist. The corresponding mapping file will then contain the following triples:

```
1   :returnArtist a poldo:Service ;
                 poldo:hasURL ''http://example.com/api/returnSinger'' ;
2                poldo:hasLanguage ''JSON'' ;
```

```
1   :returnArtist a poldo:Service ;
2                 poldo:hasURL ''http://example.com/api/returnSinger'' ;
3                 poldo:hasLanguage ''JSON'' ;
4                 poldo:hasMethod  ''GET'' ;
5                 poldo:hasInput :city ;
6                 poldo:hasOutput :title ;
7                 poldo:hasOutput :singer .
...
8   :returnPlace a poldo:Service ;
9                poldo:hasURL ''http://example.com/api/returnPlace'' ;
10               poldo:hasLanguage ''JSON'' ;
11               poldo:hasMethod  ''GET'' ;
12               poldo:hasInput :singer ;
13               poldo:hasOutput :city ;
14               poldo:hasOutput :country ;
...
15  :singer a dbo:Person .
16  :title a dbo:Event .
17  :city a dbo:Place .
18  :country a dbo:Country .
19  :singer dbo:birthPalce :city, :country .
20  :title dbo:artist :singer;
```

Now suppose we want to know the name of singers born in a specific city. The corresponding SPARQL query is then:

```
SELECT ?singer
WHERE {
   ?singer dbo:birthPlace ?city .
   ?city rdfs:label ''modena'' .
   ?singer a dbo:Person .
   ?city a dbo:Place .
}
LIMIT 1
```

The only entry points `PoLDo` engine has to query the services are constant symbols, in our case `modena` whose corresponding entity is declared to be a `dbo:Place` in the SPARQL query. By looking at the mapping file, the engine discovers it can query the service `:returnArtist`. Then, by using the outputs (constants) of the first service, the engine may query `:returnPlace` and, if lucky, it can get that one of the artists returned by `:returnArtist` was born in `modena`. If this is not the case, the engine uses the constants returned by `:returnPlace` to query again `:returnArtist` thus continuing its search of the answer for the original SPARQL query. It is worth noticing that while iteratively querying the services, `PoLDo` builds RDF triples by creating fresh entities corresponding to the arriving constants and by enriching and connecting them thanks to the rules states in rows 15-20 of the above mapping file. All the triples are saved in the triple store which is then natively queried by means of the original SPARQL query.

PoLDo engine stops querying the original services in the following cases: (i) the answer to the query is found; (ii) there are no more fresh constants and then the answer to the original query can not be found; (iii) the execution time exceeds a timeout set by the designer.

4 Conclusion

In this paper we presented PoLDo, that acts as a middleware between a RESTful service and SPARQL endpoint. By means of PoLDo we are allowed to expose the Deep Web data available via RESTful services as Linked Data that can be easily integrated in the so called Linked Data Cloud. The tool we developed adopts algorithms and techniques coming from the Deep Web literature to make possible the composition of services at a data level. Via a mapping file, PoLDo is able to interpret a SPARQL query in terms of a sequence of remote calls to external services and to translate the returned data in a temporary RDF graph which is locally stored in a triple store. The approach we developed is for sure a step forward the creation of a global, semantics-enabled, integrated, gigantic data graph as in the original view of the Semantic Web.

Acknowledgments. Andrea Calí acknowledges partial support by the EPSRC project "Logic-based Integration and Querying of Unindexed Data" (EP/E010865/1) and by the EU COST Action IC1302 KEYSTONE.

References

1. S. Agrawal, S. Chaudhuri, and G. Das. Dbxplorer: A system for keyword-based search over relational databases. In *ICDE*, pages 5–16, 2002.
2. C. Bizer, T. Heath, and T. Berners-Lee. Linked data - the story so far. *Int. J. Semantic Web Inf. Syst*, 5(3):1–22, 2009.
3. A. Calì and D. Martinenghi. Querying data under access limitations. In *Proceedings of the 24th IEEE International Conference on Data Engineering (ICDE 2008)*, pages 50–59. IEEE Computer Society Press, 2008.
4. K. Chen-Chuan Chang, B. He, and Z. Zhang. Toward large scale integration: Building a metaquerier over databases on the web. In *Proc. of CIDR*, pages 44–55, 2005.
5. R. T. Fielding and R. N. Taylor. Principled Design of the Modern Web Architecture. *ACM Transactions on Internet Technology*, 2(2):115–150, 2002.
6. V. Hristidis and Y. Papakonstantinou. Discover: Keyword search in relational databases. In *Proceedings of the 28th International Conference on Very Large Data Bases*, VLDB '02, pages 670–681. VLDB Endowment, 2002.
7. G. Kabra, Z. Zhang, and K. Chen-Chuan Chang. Dewex: An exploration facility for enabling the deep web integration. In *Proc. of ICDE*, pages 1511–1512, 2007.
8. J. Madhavan, L. Afanasiev, L. Antova, and A. Y. Halevy. Harnessing the deep web: Present and future. In *Proc. of the 4th Conf. on Innovative Database Research (CIDR 2008)*, 2009.
9. D. Martinenghi. Access pattern. In H. C. A. van Tilborg and S. Jajodia, editors, *Encyclopedia of Cryptography and Security, 2nd Edition*, pages 17–20, 2011.
10. A. Soylu, F. M dritscher, F. Wild, P. D. Causmaecker, and P. Desmet. Mashups by orchestration and widgetbased personal environments: Key challenges, solution strategies, and an application. *Program*, 46(4):383 – 428, 2012.

A Novel Algorithm for Local Alignment of Protein Interaction Networks: MODULA
Extended Abstract

Pietro H Guzzi[1], Pierangelo Veltri[1], Swarup Roy[2], and Jugal K Kalita[2]

[1] Dept Surgical Medical Sciences Unicz, Italy,
hguzzi,veltri@unicz.it
[2] Department of Information Technology, North-Eastern Hill University,India
swarup@nehu.ac.in
[3] Department of Computer Science
University of Colorado, Colorado Springs, USA
jkalita@uccs.edu

Abstract. Biological networks are usually used to model interactions among biological macromolecules in a cells. For instance protein-protein interaction networks (PIN) are used to model and analyse the set of interactions among proteins. The comparison of networks may result in the identification of conserved patterns of interactions corresponding to biological relevant entities such as protein complexes and pathways. Several algorithms, known as network alignment algorithms, have been proposed to unravel relations between different species at the interactome level. Algorithms may be categorized in two main classes: merge and mine and mine and merge. Algorithms belonging to the first class initially merge input network into a single integrated and then mine such networks. Conversely algorithms belonging to the second class initially analyze separately two input networks then integrate such results. In this paper we present MODULA (Network **Modul**e based PPI **A**ligner), a novel approach for local network alignment that belong to the second class. The algorithm at first identifies compact modules from input networks. Modules of both networks are then matched using functional knowledge. Then it uses high scoring pairs of modules as seeds to build a bigger alignment. In order to asses MODULA we compared it to the state of the art local alignment algorithms over a rather extensive and updated dataset. [4]

1 Introduction

Complex biological systems are often represented as networks and studied computationally. In PPI networks [1, 2], also known as protein interaction networks (PINs), the proteins are represented by nodes and interactions between them are represented by edges. Studies suggest that molecular networks are conserved through evolution [3, 4], and that highly connected proteins are more likely to

[4] This work has been presented in IEEE BIBM 2015.

be essential for survival than proteins with lower connectivity. As a result, the interactions between protein pairs as well as the overall composition of the network are important for the overall functioning of an organism. Understanding conserved substructures through comparative analysis of these networks can provide basic insights into a variety of biochemical processes. The ultimate goal of network alignment is to transfer knowledge of protein function from one species to another. Since sequence similarity metrics such as BLAST bit scores are not conclusive evidence of similar function, the purpose of aligning two PPI networks is to supplement sequence similarity with topological information so as to identify orthologs as accurately as possible. PIN alignment is relatively a young research area and successes of PIN network alignment so far include uncovering large shared sub-networks between species as diverse as *S. cerevisiae* and *H. sapiens*, and reconstructing phylogenetic relationships between species based solely on the amount of overlap discovered between their PPI networks [3]. Comparing two biological networks is a particularly challenging problem, since many interesting questions we might ask of these networks are computationally intractable to answer . Most papers in the literature report promising results in creating alignments that do indeed show large regions of biological or topological similarity between the PPI networks of various species, but few do both well [5, 6].

In this work, we try to align two or more PPI networks from different species. That is, we want to find a mapping from the nodes of one network to the nodes of another, in such a way as to maximize the topological and biological similarity of the pairs of nodes which are aligned to one another. This allows for the identification of orthologous proteins that are conserved during evolution as well as similar modules or pathways in the networks themselves.

We focus in particular on local network alignment. Existing approach for local network alignment fall in two main classes: (i) mine and merge approach, (ii) merge and mine approach. Algorithms of the first class at first analyze single networks, then integrate results. Conversely algorithms of the second class build an initial integrated network and then analyze such network [2, 7, ?]. We propose MODULA, a novel local alignment method based on merge and mine approach. MODULA performs alignment using compact PIN modules or complexes extracted from two different species and explore best matching modules from them. Below we present the background of the study and few related works.

2 Problem Formulation and Related Work

Literature contains different formalizations of PIN alignment and we here follow the formalization we developed in a previous work by Mina and Guzzi [7].

Given two input graphs, $G_a = \{V_a, E_a\}$ and $G_b = \{V_b, E_b\}$, a correspondence between two regions of G_a and G_b can be expressed as a set of node pairs

$$S_i = \{(x^a, y^b) \mid x^a \in V_a \cup \eta,\ y^b \in V_b \cup \eta\} \qquad (1)$$

where η is a fictitious symbol that means the associated protein has no ortholog in the other species.

Let

$$S_i^a = \{x^a \mid (x^a, y^b) \in S_i\}$$
$$S_i^b = \{y^b \mid (x^a, y^b) \in S_i\}$$

be the sets of proteins belonging to V_a and V_b, respectively, involved in S_i. Let G_i^a (G_i^b) be the subgraph induced by S_i^a (S_i^b) on G_a (G_b).

The **pairwise local network alignment problem** consists of finding all the correspondences S_i (i.e. groups of nodes) in order to maximize a cost function based on two criteria: (i) a similarity criterion that guarantees that matched subgraphs are topologically similar; and (ii) a model criterion drives the analysis toward the identification of specific topologies, and depends on the specific module to be uncovered (i.e. protein complex, linear pathway).

Literature contains many algorithms that have been proposed to detect conserved modules in PINs [8]. There exist different way to categorize such algorithms, we here distinct them on two main classes on the basis of the overall strategy: *mine and merge*, i.e. algorithms that first analyze each PIN separately, and then project solutions reciprocally from a PIN to the others [9, 10]; *merge and mine*, i.e. algorithms that fist integrate PINs into a single graph and then analyze such graph [11–13, 7].

Mine and merge analysis are usually less expensive in terms of computational resources, as evidenced by Erten et al. [9]. In general, merge and mine algorithms are more complicated due to difficulties in formulating and accounting for approximate matches, and the existence of multiple mappings between proteins in different species [9]. Moreover, they are computationally expensive, since in order to merge the input networks it is necessary to compare their topologies. The main drawback of these approaches is that these algorithms are more sensible to noise in input networks and to redundancy of information in input networks. Conversely, merge and mine algorithms are less sensible to these problems but they present in general a higher computational cost in the building of the initial integrated graph (also referred to as alignment graph). The interested reader may find a detailed discussion of these approaches in Mina and Guzzi[7].

A common problem in both groups is the requirement of additional information used to seed to build the alignment. Such seed are ortholog pairs and the absence of such information would require the exploration of all the possible combinations of protein pairs should be considered. Consequently many algorithms require as input two networks and a list of protein pairs, (for instance list of putative orthologs), to start the computation. List of pairs may be obtained from existing databases of orthologs, or gathering sequence similarity information using tools, using semantic similarity [14].

3 A New Alignment Approach

In this section we propose a new local alignment method MODULA that explore a matching between two different biologically significant compact protein inter-

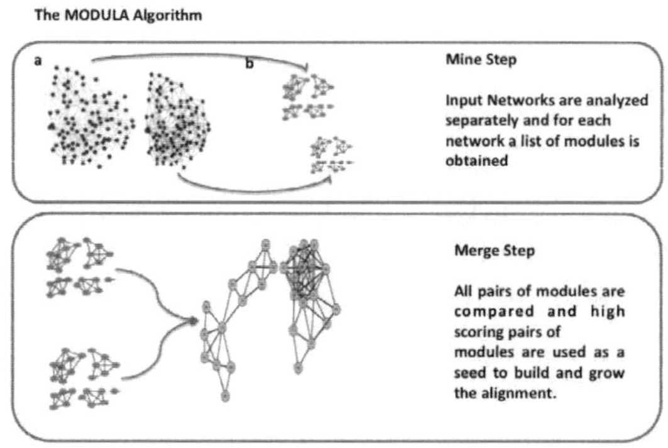

Fig. 1. Basic steps of MODULA.

action network modules from different species to find orthologous modules conserved functional similarity during evolution. Interestingly, the same approach may be extended for detecting conserved functional modules in multiple species. Broadly, MODULA is a two step process as describe below.

At first it identify compact network modules (or subgraphs) from input networks G_i and G_j using any state-of-the-art protein complex finding method. Then, every detected modules from G_i are compared and matched with each modules in G_j using any existing global alignment method.Finally, The best matching pairs are considered as aligned conserved modules.

The overall idea of the method is shown in Fig. 1. More formally, the step wise representation of MODULA is given in Algorithm 1.

3.1 The Algorithm

As an input other than two PINs from two different species, MODULA requires an user defined threshold τ to satisfy a minimum similarity score for global alignment between a pair of modules. To start with, MODULA needs compact modules or complexes. It uses existing network modules finding methods to detect biologically significant compact protein complexes (C_i and C_j). In our work, we use *ClusterOne* [15], an overlapping complex finding method from PINs. Recent study revels that ClusterOne is an effective technique in detecting biologically significant protein complexes [16]. For each module $M_i \in C_i$ is compared with each module $M_j \in C_j$ using any suitable global alignment method. We use here Magna++ for alignment [17]. MODULA considers only best match out of all pair matches. If the best match score is above threshold τ, it will be considered as best local alignment and added into the list L of all such alignments. The process continues for rest of the pairs.

Next, we assess the performance of our proposed method in light of several real data.

Algorithm 1: MODULA: The PIN Alignment Algorithm

Data: G_i (PIN-I); G_j (PIN-II); τ (Minimum Similarity Score)
Result: L (Aligned sub-networks)

```
Ci ← FindModules (Gi);
Cj ← FindModules (Gj);
// Ci and Cj list of compact modules detected by PIN complex finding method
for each Mi ∈ Ci do
    for each Mj ∈ Cj do
        if Max (Alignment (Mi, Mj)) > τ then
            L= L ⋃ (Mi,Mj);
        end
    end
end
Return(L) ;
```

3.2 Experimental Evaluation

In order to assess performances of MODULA we compared it with respect to state of the art algorithms showing a sensible improvement of performances. In order to compare results, we expressed the performances of the algorithms in terms of the ability to recover known protein complexes conserved in two aligned species. Consequently, given a solution and a known complex, we measures this ability in terms of their overlap by using two classical measures: precision (π) and recall (ρ). Precision is defined as the fraction of proteins in the solution also present in the complex, while recall is the ration of proteins in the complex that are in common with the solution. Usually these measures are integrated into the F_1-score defined as the harmonic mean of precision and recall. Formally, these measures are defined as follows:

$$\pi = \frac{TP}{TP+FP}, \; \rho = \frac{TP}{TP+FP}, \; F_1 - score = \frac{2\pi\rho}{\pi+\rho}$$

where TP is the number of proteins found in a solution that are also in the complex. Analogously, FP and FN are the number of false positives and false negatives. The F_1-score ranges in the interval [0, 1], with 1 corresponding to perfect agreement. In our analysis, we match each known complex of a species to all the solutions of a given alignment, and we select as best match the solution with highest F_1-score. For each species we selected a dataset of known complexes as benchmark dataset. Within each dataset we identified many complexes with similar biological functions and highly overlapping with each other. This might lead to a biased evaluation since a solution might overlap with more than a known complex, and therefore be counted more than once. Moreover, these overlapping complexes are often quite small (3-4 proteins).

Comparison has been made against Align-MCL algorithms since it has been demonstrated AlignMCL outperformed other local alignment algorithms and also showed a more stability when different PINs of the same organisms are used. In order to compare MODULA with state-of-the-art methods, we use same datasets as used in the [13] comprises of interaction networks of mouse, yeast, human, worm and fly available in I2D database (release of 2011) [18]. The datasets

Table 1. Characteristics of Networks (Datasets) Used.

Species	Proteins	Interactions
D. Melanogaster [DM]	9854	37979
H. Sapiens [HS]	14567	138258
M. Musculus [MM]	4261	9547
C. Elegans [CE]	4755	9995
S. Cerevisiae [SC]	6182	147408

used here are presented in Table 1. However, for detail description of the dataset one may refer [13].

Initially, we clustered these networks using ClusterOne algorithm. Then for each alignment we built a comprehensive scoring matrix in which we compared all the pairs of generated modules. Finally, we used such pairs of high scoring modules to build a single aligned module. The resulting alignment is made by considering all the modules.

Table 2 summarizes results. Results shows that for this preliminary set of experiments, MODULA is able to recover more known complexes with respect to Align-MCL.

Table 2. Number of known complexes recovered by the different algorithms.

Alignment	Number of known complexes hit		Number of known complexes hit	
-	AlignMCL	MODULA	AlignMCL	MODULA
DM-SC	33	**35**	15	**16**
DM-HS	54	**55**	19	**25**
DM-CE	34	34	7	**9**
DM-MM	35	**42**	7	**16**

4 Conclusion

PPI networks are largely used to analyze biological mechanisms inside cells. Recently, many different experiments have generated a lot of data causing the growth of existing networks in terms of nodes and edges. Consequently, the need for the development of novel tools and methodologies for data management and analysis arose. In particular, one of the most exciting area is represented by the comparative analysis of protein interaction networks.

In this paper we proposed MODULA, a local network alignment algorithms that improves existing state of the art. The quality of the algorithm has been assessed. Results show that MODULA outperforms the other algorithms in discovering conserved functional modules (protein complexes).

A future work consists of comparing the solutions of different algorithms to determine their agreement. Additional assessments will be performed comparing the semantic similarity of the solutions.

References

1. M. Cannataro, P. H. Guzzi, and P. Veltri, "Protein-to-protein interactions," *ACM Computing Surveys*, vol. 43, no. 1, pp. 1–36, Nov. 2010.
2. ——, "Impreco: Distributed prediction of protein complexes," *Future Generation Computer Systems*, vol. 26, no. 3, pp. 434–440, 2010.
3. T. Milenković and N. Pržulj, "Topological characteristics of molecular networks," in *Functional Coherence of Molecular Networks in Bioinformatics*. Springer, 2012, pp. 15–48.
4. P. H. Guzzi, M. T. Di Martino, G. Tradigo, P. Veltri, P. Tassone, P. Tagliaferri, and M. Cannataro, "Automatic summarisation and annotation of microarray data," *Soft Computing*, vol. 15, no. 8, pp. 1505–1512, 2011.
5. P. H. Guzzi and T. Milenković, "Survey of local and global biological network alignment: the need to reconcile the two sides of the same coin," *Briefings in Bioinformatics*, p. bbw132, 2017.
6. M. T. Di Martino, P. H. Guzzi, D. Caracciolo, L. Agnelli, A. Neri, B. A. Walker, G. J. Morgan, M. Cannataro, P. Tassone, and P. Tagliaferri, "Integrated analysis of micrornas, transcription factors and target genes expression discloses a specific molecular architecture of hyperdiploid multiple myeloma," *Oncotarget*, vol. 6, no. 22, pp. 19 132–47, 2015.
7. M. Mina and P. H. Guzzi, "Improving the robustness of local network alignment: Design and extensive assessmentof a markov clustering-based approach," *IEEE/ACM Trans. Comput. Biology Bioinform.*, vol. 11, no. 3, pp. 561–572, 2014. [Online]. Available: http://doi.ieeecomputersociety.org/10.1109/TCBB.2014.2318707
8. J. Ji, A. Zhang, C. Liu, X. Quan, and Z. Liu, "Survey: Functional module detection from protein-protein interaction networks," *IEEE Transactions on Knowledge and Data Engineering*, vol. 99, no. PrePrints, p. 1, 2012.
9. S. Erten, X. Li, G. Bebek, J. Li, and M. Koyutürk, "Phylogenetic analysis of modularity in protein interaction networks." *BMC bioinformatics*, vol. 10, p. 333, Jan. 2009.
10. P. Jancura, E. Mavridou, E. Carrillo-de Santa Pau, and E. Marchiori, "A methodology for detecting the orthology signal in a PPI network at a functional complex level." *BMC bioinformatics*, vol. 13 Suppl 1, no. Suppl 10, p. S18, Jan. 2012.
11. G. Ciriello, M. Mina, P. H. Guzzi, M. Cannataro, and C. Guerra, "AlignNemo: A Local Network Alignment Method to Integrate Homology and Topology." *PloS one*, vol. 7, no. 6, p. e38107, Jan. 2012.
12. J. Flannick, A. Novak, C. B. Do, B. S. Srinivasan, and S. Batzoglou, "Automatic parameter learning for multiple local network alignment." *Journal of computational biology*, vol. 16, no. 8, pp. 1001–22, Aug. 2009.
13. M. Mina and P. H. Guzzi, "Alignmcl: Comparative analysis of protein interaction networks through markov clustering," in *2012 IEEE International Conference on Bioinformatics and Biomedicine Workshops, BIBMW 2012, Philadelphia, USA, October 4-7, 2012*, 2012, pp. 174–181. [Online]. Available: http://doi.ieeecomputersociety.org/10.1109/BIBMW.2012.6470300

14. P. Guzzi, M. Mina, C. Guerra, and M. Cannataro, "Semantic similarity analysis of protein data: assessment with biological features and issues," *Briefings in bioinformatics*, vol. 13, no. 5, pp. 569–585, 2012.
15. T. Nepusz, H. Yu, and A. Paccanaro, "Detecting overlapping protein complexes in protein-protein interaction networks," *Nature methods*, vol. 9, no. 5, pp. 471–472, 2012.
16. P. Sharma, H. A. Ahmed, S. Roy, and D. K. Bhattacharyya, "Unsupervised methods for finding protein complexes from ppi networks," *Network Modeling Analysis in Health Informatics and Bioinformatics*, vol. 4, no. 1, pp. 1–15, 2015.
17. V. Vijayan, V. Saraph, and T. Milenković, "Magna++: Maximizing accuracy in global network alignment via both node and edge conservation," *Bioinformatics*, p. btv161, 2015.
18. K. R. Brown and I. Jurisica, "Unequal evolutionary conservation of human protein interactions in interologous networks," *Genome biology*, vol. 8, no. 5, p. R95, 2007.

Chatbots as a Novel Access Method for Government Open Data*

Simone Porreca, Francesco Leotta, Massimo Mecella, and Tiziana Catarci

Sapienza Università di Roma
Dipartimento di Ingegneria Informatica
Automatica e Gestionale Antonio Ruberti
porreca.1673726@studenti.uniroma1.it,
{leotta,mecella,catarci}@diag.uniroma1.it

Abstract. In this discussion paper, we propose to employ chatbots as a user-friendly interface for open data published by organizations, specifically focusing on public administrations. Open data are especially useful in e-Government initiatives but their exploitation is currently hampered to end users by the lack of user-friendly access methods. On the other hand, current UX in social networks have made people used to chatting. Building on cognitive technologies, we prototyped a chatbot on top of the OpenCantieri dataset published by the Italian Ministero delle Infrastrutture e Trasporti, and we argue that such a model can be extended as a generally available access method to open data.

1 Introduction

Open data generally refers to the idea that some data should be freely available to everyone to use and republish as they wish, without restrictions from copyright, patents or other mechanisms of control. In particular, according to the Open Definition, "a piece of data is open if anyone can freely access, use, modify, and share for any purpose (subject, at most, to requirements that preserve provenance and openness)"[1]. Some characteristics should be granted to provide open data, namely *(i)* accessibility – all the users can freely access to data, mostly free or at a very low cost, *(ii)* machine readability – data can be naturally "understood" and processed by machines, *(iii)* rights – data are released under certain licenses that bound softly the usage, the transformation and the distribution of those data.

* An extended version of this paper appears as S. Porreca, F. Leotta, M. Mecella, S. Vassos and T. Catarci: Accessing Government Open Data through Chatbots. *Proc. Int. Workshop on the Practice of the Open Web (practi-O-web 2017), at ICWE 2017*, Rome, Italy, June 2017, Springer. This work has been partly supported by the Italian projects *NEPTIS*, *SM&ST* and *RoMA*, and the EU RISE prioject *FIRST*. The work of Francesco Leotta has been partly supported by the Lazio regional project *Sapientia* (FILAS-RU-2014-1186).

[1] cf. http://opendefinition.org/

Much related to open data, *open government* is the governing doctrine that supports the right of citizens to access the documents and proceedings of the government for an effective public oversight. Enabling interested citizens to get more directly involved in the legislative process, making government information available to the public as machine readable open data, can facilitate government transparency, accountability and public participation. Opening up official information can support technological innovation and economic growth by enabling third parties to develop new kinds of digital applications and services.

Several national governments have created sites to distribute a portion of the data they collect, e.g., the European Commission has created two portals for the European Union: the EU Open Data Portal[2] giving access to open data from the EU institutions, agencies and other bodies, and the Public Data portal[3] providing datasets from local, regional and national public bodies across Europe. In October 2015, the Open Government Partnership (OGP) launched the International Open Data Charter, a set of principles and best practices for the release of governmental open data formally adopted by seventeen countries (including Italy[4]) during the OGP Global Summit in Mexico.

Despite all these initiatives, access from citizens to such open data is not always as large as expected. Technical issues often inhibit easy access from citizens, if no specific user-friendly applications are built on top of such open data for easy access and navigation. In this discussion paper, we present the disruptive idea of adopting chatbots as user-friendly access and querying method to open data. Nowadays persons are used to chat with friends over popular applications (e.g., WhatsApp or Facebook Messenger), and the typical interaction is indeed based on the paradigm ask – get a response. Citizens accessing open data would appreciate the same paradigm in querying the data, for which a chatbot can be a much more natural way of interaction than traditional web applications.

Developing chatbots over open data poses many challenges, such as interpreting the natural language adopted by users in querying the dataset, and translating into effective queries over the dataset. In this paper, we present a prototype of such a system built using the cognitive platform by IBM, namely Bluemix and related APIs, in order to evaluate the technical feasibility of the proposed idea.

The following of this paper is organized as it follows: Section 2 provides some background information and relevant work; Section 3 describes the architecture used to build a chatbot over the Open Cantieri dataset, published by the Italian Ministero delle Infrastrutture e Trasporti at `http://opencantieri.mit.gov.it`, by using a cognitive platform, and Section 4 describes the realization aspects. Finally Section 5 concludes the paper, by remarking future work, including a user evaluation to assess the usability of the approach, and to prove the argued simplicity of use.

---

[2] cf. `http://data.europa.eu/euodp/en/data/`

[3] cf. `http://publicdata.eu/`

[4] cf. `https://www.opengovpartnership.org/country/italy`

2 Background and relevant work

Chatbots are computer programs able to hold up a conversation with a user, either in textual or vocal form. Given the growing complexity of information systems, chatbots are specifically designed to support the user interaction and to make it as natural as possible. They do not only represent a faster and more natural way to access information, but they will also be a significant key factor in the process of humanizing machines in the near future [1,2].

In order to correctly and efficiently design a chatbot, many techniques have to be not trivially combined, including pattern matching, parsing, artificial intelligence, machine learning, and ontologies. There are numerous approaches and methodologies proposed for this; in this work, we followed the approach that divides the chatbot architecture in three parts: *responder*, *classifier* and *graphmaster* [1]. The responder is the interface by which users access the system. It is responsible for taking the input and validate the output. The classifier is located between the responder and the graphmaster. It is dedicated to normalize the input to pass to the graphmaster and processing the output coming from the latter (e.g., interacting with a database). Finally, the graphmaster is the agent responsible to elaborate the correct output to the corresponding input. It represents the pattern matching element of the chain.

Tim Berners-Lee suggested a 5-star deployment scheme for open data[5], being a star when an organization makes data available on the Web (whatever format) under an open license, 2 stars when it makes data available as structured data (e.g., Excel file instead of image scan of a table), 3 starts when data are available in a non-proprietary open format (e.g., CSV as well as of Excel), 4 stars by using URIs to denote things, so that people can point at them and 5 stars when data are linked to other data to provide context [3]. Technologies supporting this vision of linked open data are those ones commonly referred as Semantic Web, including RDF/RDFS, OWL (ontologies) and SPARQL (for querying). In Italy, the AgID - Agenzia per l'Italia Digitale, publishes every year guidelines for Public Administrations on how to publish their data as open, including a model for metadata consisting of 4 levels [6]. In this work, we have built our prototype on the basis of a dataset which can be ranked at most at level 3 of the above classification.

During the last years, some attempts to apply chatbots to query and retrieve data have been made. In [4], a chatbot was constructed on top of some open data. Here the first step is to extract plain text from documents stored as PDF files by employing an optical character recognition (OCR) software. At this point, a set of possible questions about the extracted contents were constructed using a "Overgenerating Transformations and Rankings" algorithm, which was implemented using the question generation framework presented in [5]. Finally, the

[5] cf. `http://5stardata.info/en/`

[6] cf. `http://www.agid.gov.it/agenda-digitale/open-data`

matching patterns, essential to the chatbot's answering capability, are defined through Artificial Intelligence Markup Language (AIML).

Authors in [6] presents a system, called OntBot, which employs a mapping technique to transform an ontology into a relational database and then uses that knowledge to construct answers. Therefore, likewise our solution, OntBot does not need to handwrite all the knowledge base that stands behind the system. The main drawback of traditional chatbots, implemented for example through AIML, is the fact that the knowledge base has to be constructed ad-hoc by handwriting thousands of possible responses. OntBot, likewise our system, does not construct answers by looking for a matching one inside the database. Instead, it retrieves information from the database, which will be then used to build up the response.

3 Case study and proposed architecture

Open Cantieri, offered by the Italian Ministero delle Infrastrutture e dei Trasporti (MIT), is an open, complete and up-to-date repository about the realization status and history of the public infrastructures. All the available data are generated and published by public sources. Open Cantieri offers a unified platform, with specific views, in which all these different datasets are collected together. The platform is a collection of open data in a very raw form: datasets can be downloaded as single CSV files, sometimes grouped in archives. Very often, unfortunately, different files do not employ the same keys to represent concepts (e.g., cities are represented using their code in some files whereas their names is used in others) and manual mapping between different representations was needed. More generally, the files do not follow any standard on field names and reported values.

Figure 1 shows the architecture of the proposed solution. The user interface to the system is implemented as a Facebook Messenger application. The back-end core of the system is deployed on the IBM Bluemix cloud computing platform. In particular, a Java Server Page (JSP) handles the requests and constructs the corresponding responses by orchestrating two Bluemix service instances: *(i)* an instance of Watson Conversation, specifically created and trained, which is responsible for processing, and *(ii)* an instance of Compose for MySQL, which handles the connection and the query to the back-end database. In particular, the user interacts through the chat interface, e.g., issuing a question as "How much money have been invested in public infrastructures in the south of Italy in 2015?" (step 1). The sentence is forwarded to the JSP, which handles it in order to construct the appropriate response (step 2). The Watson Conversation instance receives a request constructed starting from the user's input, and generates the corresponding response (step 3). According to the provided response, the JSP page defines an SQL query to be issued to the database through Compose (step 4). Once all the elements needed to construct the output are collected, the JSP will proceed to generate the response to be shown through the Facebook Messenger chat.

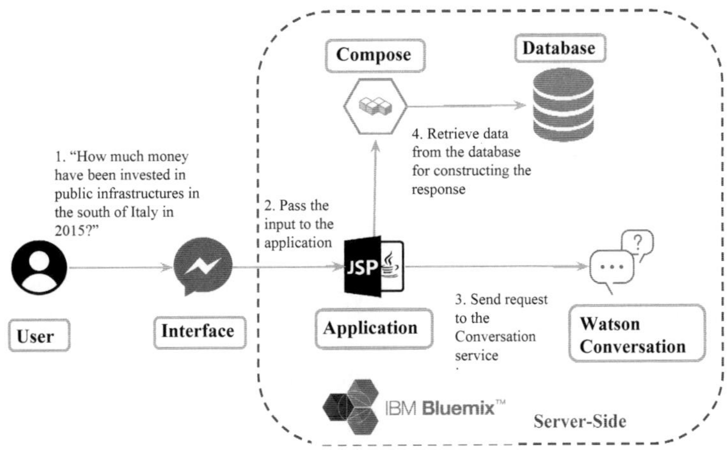

Fig. 1. Architecture

In order to generate the response, Watson Conversation performs the following operations (the reader should also refer to following subsections): intents and entities extraction; verification of which node, within the Dialog Tree, has conditions satisfied by these information; and, finally, return of the nodes response. In our specific case, the intent is triggered by "How much money", which is associated to the intention of knowing the investment amount about the highway management, regarding the intent "#Investment". The entities are: "South of Italy", which is a specific value of the entity "@Geographical_Region" and "2015", which is a value of "Year". In the Conversation response, the application is able to find all the essential information for constructing the output. First of all, a flag, called "DB_Search", is retrieved from the Conversation response in order to understand if a database search is required. This is achieved by constructing the SQL query, starting from the information obtained from Watson Conversation, and by send it to Compose for MySQL, which will retrieve the desired data from the database. The SQL query is specifically constructed with the "Text" included into the Conversation response, which is one of many JSON variables returned with the response itself. Once all the elements needed to construct the output are collected, the application will proceed to generate the users output and send it back through the interface.

In the following, we describe the single components.

3.1 Watson Developer Cloud and Conversation

IBM Watson Developer Cloud (WDC) offers a set of services for developing Cognitive Applications, which consists of programs able to take advantage of the most modern technologies in artificial intelligence, machine learning, and natural language processing. Each WDC service provides a REST API for interacting with it, and most of these services also includes Software Development Kits (SDKs) for various programming languages. In our work we used the Java one.

Inside IBM WDC, the Watson Conversation service allows to create an application that understands natural language input and uses machine learning to respond to users in a way that simulates a conversation between humans. When an instance of this service is created, it is able to contains several *workspaces*. A workspace is a container for all the artifacts that define the conversation flow and it is responsible for the natural language processing operations. A workspace includes the following elements:

Intents. An intent represents the intention and the purpose behind user input. It could be associated with the "goal" the user wants to achieve with every request and thus it is important to define one intent for each type of user request the application has to support. Each intent is prefixed with the character "#" and, during its creation, the developer is encouraged to provide "positive examples", in order to allow the system to construct the corresponding model. A positive example is a sentence that clarifies the way in which the intent could be presented to the system. By collecting at least five positive examples, the instance of the Conversation service will be able to perform a deep learning process, which will train the service itself to recognize that specific intent. The most important fact is to distinctly define each intent from the others. The "borders" between intents should be clear in order to allows the system to correctly recognize them inside user requests. If there is the need for an intent to have more "interpretations", depending on a particular user request, it is possible to make use of another Watson Conversation's element: the Entity.

Entities. An entity is an element, corresponding to a term or an object, that could be used in order to better specify the intention behind a user request. They are frequently used in combination with intents to increase their range of possible interpretations and meanings. Each entity is prefixed with the character "@" and is associated with a set of values. Each value of a specific entity represents an object or a term that belongs to the same category defined by the entity itself. In this way, an entity called "day of the week", could be include values as "Monday", "Thursday", etc. Associated with each value, the developer has the possibility to insert synonyms, in order to be sure that the system will recognize a specific value of the entity even if the user provides it with a different word.

Dialog. The dialog represents the flow of the conversation, divided in several branches, which defines how the application responds when it recognizes the defined intents and entities. The dialog is composed by several nodes, structured in a tree-like graph. At a very basic level, each node is defined by two main elements: the condition and the response. When the condition, composed by elements like intents and entities, is satisfied, the node is considered "activated" and hence its response will be returned as output. The response could be a sentence, another node, or it can be defined by the developer. In order to maintain the state of the conversation through each interaction with the user, the instance service keeps a JSON variable called "context". In this element there are several variables, which can be customized by the developer, and, among them, there is the "Dialog Stack", which contains the stack of all the nodes visited during the conversation and the first one, the "Contextual Node", is the ID of the node that should be returned when the user will start another interaction, within the same session, with the instance of the service Watson Conversation.

3.2 Compose for MySQL

IBM Compose for MySQL is a platform able to simplify the maintenance and the management of a MySQL database; it automatically executes some common operations as backups, scaling and health check. Even though the database can be accessed as a normal MySQL database, the main benefit offered by Compose is that no management aspects (such as security issues or scaling) has to be manually handled.

4 Realization aspects

As seen in the previous sections, at a certain point of the interaction with the user, the system (through the Compose component) requires to retrieve data from a database in order to build answers. As stated above, the Open Cantieri dataset does not follow any standard, thus a database schema able to rationalize the information contained in the different CSVs has been defined. The result of this operation is a schema that does not match anymore in terms of tables and columns with the original file, making it necessary to proceed to an ETL (Extract, Transform and Load) operation.

Once the database was set up, we had to configure the Watson Conversation service to be able *(i)* to understand user requests, *(ii)* to find out if a database search is needed to fulfill the request, and *(iii)* to present a response template to the user. The response template is filled by the JSP using the data retrieved from the database through the Compose component.

In order to define and create a Watson Conversation instance, we need to define intents and entities useful for our purposes. An intent, in our case, represents an argument the user is interested to, e.g., the highway management or the airport system. In order to correctly define them, we have collected all the possible ways in which a user could refer to them, and then we passed these ones as positive examples in the intent's creation process. An entity, on the other hand, corresponds to the values that may concern a specific intent, e.g., the concessionaire societies for the highway management or the airports of the airport system. All these elements were then used in order to construct the dialog of the Watson Conversation instance. Here, we had to figure out all the possible questions the user might ask and the ways in which he might do it. The user may, for example, specify an argument, and then ask for more specific data about it through other questions. He may specify, as argument, the highway s management and then asks for the name of all the concessionaire societies. The user may, at anytime, specify a new argument or asks for more questions, in a human-like conversation. The system can also recognize when the user insert an invalid input and it will help him to correct it.

5 Concluding remarks

We have presented our preliminary idea of combining a chatbot with open data. It involves the employment of several novel instruments and services that are increasingly employed by the researchers and practitioners involved in the development of smart services. Our intent was to take advantage of these new technologies in order to make something new, able to improve the accessibility of open government data.

Open data should be accessible to the public; with our prototype, we would like to showcase a new mean to consult them, in such a way that allows the user to easily retrieve and analyze them.

Future work will include an extensive validation of the approach on a sample of users. Additionally, structured data represents only a face of government complexity. Next steps will include automatic analysis of procedures in order to provide users with a mean to explore bureaucracy in a simpler manner. The conjunction of structured data with unstructured ones may provide public administrations a useful tool to turn open data into something directly usable by citizens.

References

1. S.A. Abdul-Kader, J. Woods. Survey on Chatbot Design Techniques in Speech Conversation Systems International Journal of Advanced Computer Science and Applications, 6 (7), 2015, `https://thesai.org/Downloads/Volume6No7/Paper_12-Survey_on_Chatbot_Design_Techniques_in_Speech_Conversation_Systems.pdf`.
2. Y.P. Yang. An Innovative Distributed Speech Recognition Platform for Portable, Personalized and Humanized Wireless Devices Computational Linguistics and Chinese Language Processing, 9 (2), pp. 77-94, 2004.
3. C. Bizer, T. Heath, T. Berners-Lee. Linked DataThe Story So Far. International Journal on Semantic Web and Information Systems, 5 (3), pp. 122, 2009.
4. L. Pichponreay, C.H. Choi, W.S. Cho, J.H. Kim, K.H. Lee. Smart Answering Chatbot based on OCR and Overgenerating Transformations and Ranking. Proc. ICUFN 2016, IEEE, DOI: 10.1109/ICUFN.2016.7536948
5. M. Heilman, N.A. Question Generation via Overgenerating Transformations and Ranking. Language Technologies Institute, Carnegie Mellon University, Technical Report CMU-LTI-09-013, 2009, `http://www.cs.cmu.edu/~ark/mheilman/questions/papers/heilman-smith-qg-tech-report.pdf`.
6. H. Al-Zubaide, A.A. Issa. OntBot : Ontology based ChatBot. Proc. ISIICT 2011, IEEE, DOI: 10.1109/ISIICT.2011.6149594

Exploiting multiple heterogeneous data sets for improving geotagging quality
Discussion paper

Laura Di Rocco[1], Roberto Marzocchi[2,3], Barbara Catania[1], Tiziano Cosso[3], and Giovanna Guerrini[1]

[1] DIBRIS, Università degli Studi di Genova
[2] DICCA, Università degli Studi di Genova
[3] Gter srl

Abstract. Geotagging is the process of associating with textual data items the geographic position they denote, usually in the form of geographical coordinates (latitude and longitude). Automatic geotagging is often trivial relying on one of the many available gazetteers, such as OpenStreetMap (OSM)[1]. However, such knowledge bases are not free of errors, and, while this simple match works for popular locations, automatic annotation of less relevant venues and events may be significantly inaccurate. The goal of this work is to increase geotagging quality (in terms of completeness and accuracy) by also identifying and jointly exploiting diverse data sources as gazetteers. This will also allow us to cope with ambiguity by additionally performing semantic queries in various open knowledge bases.

1 Introduction

The ability to geolocate a user (i.e., to assign a geographic position) enables a number of location-aware applications and services. Similarly, associating geolocation information to data enables managing and analyzing them on the basis of the geographic dimension. When no explicit georeferencing (e.g., in the form of location metadata coming from the application providing data) is available, geolocation can be implicit and can be inferred, with variable degree of confidence, by the data itself, which may contain, for example, names of entities with known spatial location. Georeferencing by place name is an informal and the most common form of georeferencing approach. We commonly use place names in conversations, correspondence, reporting, and documentation.

Data are said to be implicitly (or indirectly) georeferenced [6] when they are not associated with explicit geospatial references (such as positioning on maps or spatial coordinates), rather they are referenced by place names, geocodes, and addresses. The term geotagging highlights the fact that additional steps are required to identify the locations on maps.

[1] `openstreetmap.org`

More precisely, geotagging is the computational process of transforming a textual location description[2] into a location on the Earth's surface (spatial representation in numerical coordinates). The geotagging process therefore produces a function that, given a toponym, returns the corresponding coordinates.

Automatically geotagging is usually trivial using one of the many available curated geographical knowledge bases. Dictionaries of placenames are called gazetteers [4]. Gazetteers contain descriptive information about named places, which can include their geographic locations, categories, etc. However, such gazetteers are not free of errors, and while automatic annotation is actually easy for popular locations, automatic annotation of less important venues and events may be significantly inaccurate. This low accuracy is not only introduced by human mistakes in the strings, but it is inherent in the data which could be ambiguous due to the multiple, context-dependent, interpretations toponym. For example, even for the case of very popular toponym as "Eiffel Tower", there is a replica in the city of Paris, Texas, USA, yielding a second match, with different geographical metadata.

The quality problems that may affect geotagging can be classified in three categories: (i) accuracy/correctness issues: datasets can contain human mistakes; (ii) completness issues: no metadata are available; (iii) consistency issues leading to ambiguity: when names of places are generic and there are no additional information to devise whether a name refers to a village or to a mountain and so on. These ambiguity problems are usually difficult to solve even with human intervention.

In this paper, we propose to cope with these issues by jointly exploiting heterogeneous datasets and relying on strong assumptions on the geographical domain, in terms of: (i) a specific geographical area, and (ii) a specific domain of interest the geonames refer to.

Diverse data sources are exploited in order to achieve a fast and accurate automatic geotagging, allowing to cope with both human induced errors, gazetteer incompleteness, and ambiguity. In particular, we combine the usage of a geotagging approach relying on a crowdsourced gazetteer containing toponyms related to the specific domain, with semantic searches on dataset, like DBpedia[3], in order to disambiguate toponyms and achieve a higher accuracy.

The advantage of using a combined approach is due to the specific characteristics of the different datasets. Crowdsourced gazetteers help us in addressing the problems related to the use of vernacular and very specific names. On the other hand, semantic sources help to exploit a semantic layer with the aim of achieving an higher precision and a lower ambiguity. As a specific use case, we will consider data from an outdoor tourism domain.

Related work. Geotagging consists of toponym recognition and toponym resolution. Toponym recognition assigns a possible geographical metadata (e.g., matching the toponym in a gazetteer) to geographical name. Toponym resolu-

[2] In the rest of the paper, we will use the words *toponym*, that means placename, and *geoname*, as synonyms, to refer to textual location descriptions.

[3] `dbpedia.org/`

tion, instead, eliminates the geo/non-geo ambiguity (e.g., Washington can be a city in the USA or the name of a person). There are different strategies to do this: (i) finding names in the text that exist in a gazetteer [1, 5]; (ii) using Name Entity Recognition techniques [8, 9]; (iii) using a geographic ontology (for understanding the context) [9, 8]. In general, a lot of studies in geotagging are related to the analysis of social media data [3, 2]. Moreover, implicit georeferencing information has been exploited, for instance, for localizing news on maps [10].

Outline of the paper. The remainder of the paper is structured as follows: Section 2 states the problem and presents the proposed solution, Section 3 illustrates the specific scenario, and Section 4 concludes by discussing future work.

2 Problem Statement and Proposed Approach

In this section, we first present the formalization of the problem, starting from a simple geotagging function and extending it to cope with issues that may impact geotagging quality. Then, we present a specific istantiation of the proposed approach.

Geotagging function. Given a set of input toponyms, belonging to some texts or to an input dataset, we want to define a geotagging function associating geographical metadata with these toponyms.

Let $C \subseteq \mathbb{R}^2$ be a set of geographical coordinates corresponding to locations in the physical world, and T be a set of toponyms, i.e., strings denoting locations. Let G be a gazetteer, i.e., a set of pairs of the form (t, c), where $t \in T$ is a toponym referring to a specific location $c \in C$ (coordinates).

The simplest geotagging function f_G relying on a gazetteer G is defined as: $f_G : T \longrightarrow C$, where $f_G(t) = c$ s.t. $\exists!(t, c) \in G$. We notice that f_G is partial since it is undefined for t if (i) $t \notin \pi_1(G)$ or (ii) several pairs in G for t are found.

Assuming that our dataset is split into specific known geographic bounding boxes define as $BB \subseteq C \times C$, e.g., country or geographical regions. We can now define the geotagging process related to a specific geographical area as a bounding box $b \in BB$ represented as a pair of coordinates. We define a function g relying on G that, given a specific toponym $t \in T$ and a specific $b \in BB$ returns its coordinates $c \in C$. More formally, $g_G : T \times BB \longrightarrow C$ where $g_G(t, b) = c$ if $(t, c) \in G$ and c is included in bounding box b. The g function is partial but the point (ii), explained above, is partial solved.

In Figure 1, we graphically depict the geotagging function for a specific bounding box.

Issues in geotagging and proposed approach. There are a number of issues in realizing the geotagging function g_G: (i) typos and alternatives names, (ii) G incompleteness, (iii) ambiguity. To avoid these issues, in the following we discuss how we extend the geotagging function g_G.

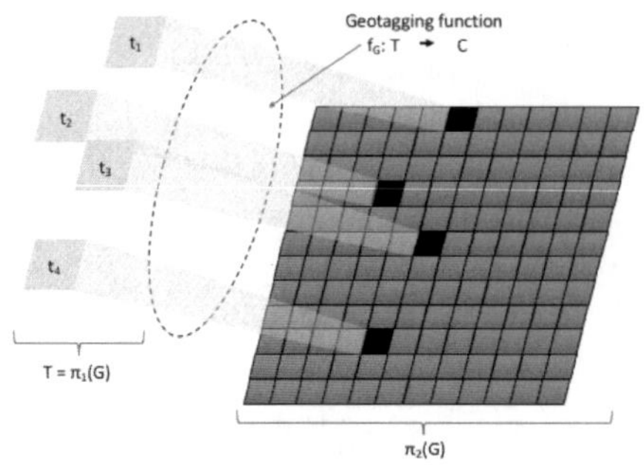

Fig. 1. The geotagging function g_G.

Naming differences and typos. To solve typos and alternative name problems that toponyms can have, we introduce a correction function γ. For example, we can have different toponyms like "Tour Eiffel", "Eiffel Tower" or "eifel tower" and we would be able to geotag correctly "Tour Eiffel" in all these cases. To do this, we define γ as follow:

$$\forall t \in T \ \gamma(t) = t \text{ if } \gamma(t) \subseteq \pi_1(G)$$

$$\gamma(t) = t' \text{ otherwise}$$

where $t' \in T$ is the toponym closest to t according to a string similarity function (and s.t. t and t' similarity according to such function is above a fixed threshold).

Therefore, we define function h_G as follows:

$$h_G(t, b) = g_G(\gamma(t), c)$$

Dataset incompleteness and ambiguity. The problem in the application of function h_G is that, in a real scenario, it is difficult to have a set G complete for a specific set of toponyms T. Since individual datasets are incomplete, we propose the combined use of different datasets for which an order has been specified. The use of a sequence of gazetteers works like a filter on T. Performing geotagging on different gazetteers, we can also disambiguate toponyms. Ambiguity arises when several alternative geographical coordinates are found for one toponym. The same name may indeed denote different geolocated objects.

Let $\mathcal{G} = G_1, ..., G_n$ be a sequence of gazetteers, we define a new function k on $\mathcal{G}$ as:

$$k_{\mathcal{G}}(t, b) = c \text{ if } h_{G_i}(t, b) = c \wedge \forall j < i.(t, c) \notin G_j$$

Note, therefore, to cope with ambiguity, we rely on two approaches:
- the usage of bounding box $b \in BB$ in order to reduce the geographical area in which we search a toponym (see g_G).
- the usage of multiple gazetteers G_i in order to understand exactly which toponym we found (see $k_{\mathcal{G}}$).

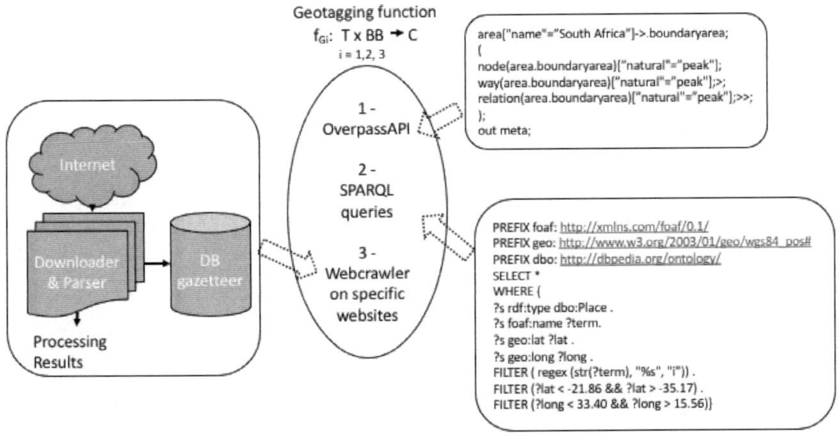

Fig. 2. Graphical representation of the geotagging function $k_{\mathcal{G}}$.

Instantiation of geotagging function $k_{\mathcal{G}}$ We describe a specific solution exploiting three different gazetteers. The described solution relies on the assumption that toponyms refers to a specific domain of interest. In details, as we can see in Figure 2, the istantiation of $\mathcal{G}$ is:
1. G_1 : OpenStreetMap(OSM)
2. G_2 : DBpedia.
3. G_3 : specific domain websites.

Our function $k_{\mathcal{G}}$ cycles on $\mathcal{G}$ in order. In the follow, we describe in detail G_1, G_2 and G_3. The way we query these gazetteers is the implementation of h_{G_i}. The bounding boxes provided as input to the functions for different G_i are the same.

OpenStreetMap We use OSM and OverpassAPI as a geotagger. The use of OSM helps us to extract vernacular toponyms. Moreover, knowing a specific tag of the toponym, we are able to assert the correctness of our preliminary solution. In this specific case our correction function γ is the Levenshtein distance[7]. After this process, for each toponym three different results may be obtained : (i) a single solution, (ii) more that one solutions, (iii) no solutions. As discussed before, toponyms in (i) are solved, while for the other ones, the new gazetteers will be used.

DBpedia We use DBpedia for data geotagging. We query DBpedia with a SPARQL endpoint (see the query in Figure 2). The use of semantic information helps us to disambiguate in case of multiple matches coming from the previous step. Moreover, in case of extraction of new toponyms, if we extract more than one solution, we are able to choose the correct one. This is because we know the meaning of this object. With this gazetteer, the correction function γ in the filter option of our SPARQL query. We use regex function in order to find similar strings.

Web sites We query specific information from the web that we know being related to our specific domain. We create a web crawler on websites related to the specific domain and we extract from them the coordinates of our toponyms. This implementation is still in progress and we cannot provide more details about it.

3 An Application to the Outdoor Tourism Domain

As an application of the proposed approach, we consider a dataset containing toponyms related to the touristic outdoor domain. The dataset used in this application is a private dataset. We are, thus, not allowed to share the data.

The entire dataset contains more or less 50000 toponyms from all over the world. The toponyms are split in three different types of area: data from administrative areas (e.g., Ande), countries (e.g., South Africa) and geographical areas (e.g., Caucaso). Therefore, the possibility to split the dataset in subsets related to a specific geographic bounding box is due to information provided in the dataset itself (and provided by the data owner). These toponyms are not uniformly distributed over the world. In order to provide some information related to the sparsity of the dataset, in South Africa we have ~300 toponyms, in the Ande area we have ~3000 toponyms and in Causaso we have ~100 toponyms.

The data are structured and each data item contains the following fields: toponym name, toponym name without typology, main locality (nullable field) and altitude (nullable field). These data have been collected over 30 years from different sources (e.g. books, journals, website, ecc.). These data are very noisy and imprecise but the expertise of the owner of the data can give us the assurance that the data are related to the touristic outdoor domain only.

Since we have toponyms from all over the world, our algorithm works on separate subsets of this domain. In case of administrative areas and countries, we have specific BBs retrieved from geographical gazetteers. The geographical area has a different problem: we must choose *a priori* the relative BB. In this case we can have two different problems that could increment errors retrieving toponyms: (i) we can take a BB that does not correctly cover the entire area, therefore loosing some toponyms, (ii) we can take a "big" BB and increment the ambiguity in retrieving toponyms.

Following the process explained in Section3, first of all we clean the OSM data by filtering out geographic information that are not useful in the outdoor touristic domain. Relying on this external knowledge, we perform a first level of geotagging. When we obtain only one solution, we can already assume that we found the correct geographical location. Unfortunately, we have a lot of toponyms without a location. On this new subset of data, we will use the second gazetteer. With a specific SPARQL query on DBpedia, we obtain new results without ambiguity. We can see in Figure 3 an example of ambiguity coming from the

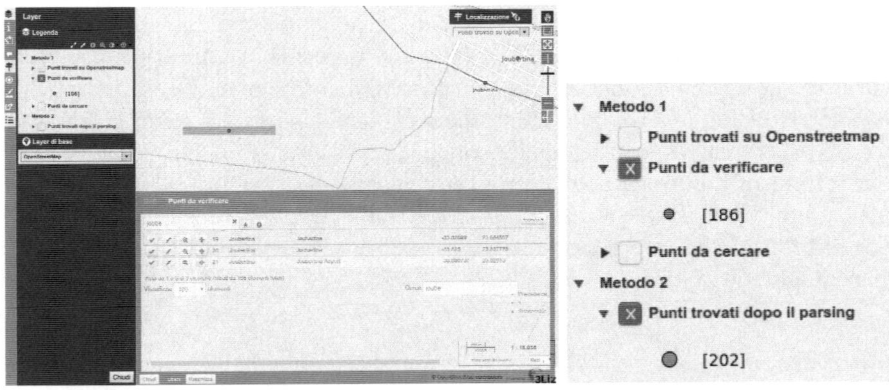

Fig. 3. Our user interface with an example of ambiguity.

first geotagging step with OSM. We provide two examples to better illustrate the method:
1- Toponym Cockscomb: It does not exist in OSM. We retrieve this information from DBpedia. This is an example of incompleteness that we solve using different gazetteers.
2- Toponym Joubertina: Three different points are retrieved in OSM. We found it in DBpedia as a village. This is an example of ambiguity. We solve it with the combined use of a correction function γ and multiple gazetteers.

Gazetteers, OSM and DBpedia, are not enough to geotag the entire set of toponyms. The third gazetteer will allow us to find the remaining location.

Using the geotagging function, we obtain a set of toponyms with the corresponding location metadata. As a real scenario, we do not want to compute error measures such as precision and recall, but we use a web visual interface (as the one shown in Figure 3) available on the web platform `www.gishosting.gter.it`, implemented using the QuantumGIS open source software, in order to get a feedback from the end user of the dataset.

We notice that we are able to show the user the possible location of a toponym. In this case, the end user can assess the correctness of geographical coordinates.

We report information related to the percentage of toponyms that we are able to retrieve. We cannot report all the results because this is work in progress and we have to perform the analysis on the whole world, but on the set of toponyms of South Africa, we geotag 50% of the toponyms with OSM and 20% with DBpedia solving some of the arising ambiguities.

4 Conclusions

In this paper we have proposed the joint use of different datasets for improving the quality of geotagging and we have applied the proposed approach in a specific scenario. The motivation of this work is to meet the needs of the data owner.

We introduced a geotagging function $k_{\mathcal{G}}$, taking as input a toponym and a specific geographic bounding box. The function, iterating over multiple gazetteers, returns the geographical metadata associated with a toponym. Our function does not perform a simple string matching rather it uses a specific correction function for each gazetteer. The consciousness of the specific geographical domain allows us to select and to decide how to use the relevant gazetteers.

This approach is still work in progress. Our future efforts will be the implementation of the web crawler to increase completeness and to complete the experimental evaluation.

References

[1] E. Amitay, E. Amitay, N. Har'El, N. Har'El, R. Sivan, R. Sivan, A. Soffer, and A. Soffer. Web-a-where: geotagging web content. *Proceedings of SIGIR '04 conference on Research and development in information retrieval*, pages 273–280, 2004.

[2] Z. Cheng, J. Caverlee, and K. Lee. You are where you tweet: A content-based approach to geo-locating twitter users. In *Proceedings of the 19th ACM International Conference on Information and Knowledge Management*, pages 759–768. ACM, 2010.

[3] J. Gelernter and N. Mushegian. Geo-parsing messages from microtext. *Transactions in GIS*, 15(6):753–773, 2011.

[4] M. F. Goodchild and L. L. Hill. Introduction to digital gazetteer research. *International Journal of Geographical Information Science*, 22(10):1039–1044, 2008.

[5] C. Grover, R. Tobin, K. Byrne, M. Woollard, J. Reid, S. Dunn, and J. Ball. Use of the Edinburgh geoparser for georeferencing digitized historical collections. *Philosophical Transactions of the Royal Society A: Mathematical, Physical and Engineering Sciences*, 368(1925):3875–3889, 2010.

[6] L. L. Hill. *Georeferencing: The geographic associations of information*. Mit Press, 2009.

[7] G. Navarro. A guided tour to approximate string matching. *ACM computing surveys (CSUR)*, 33(1):31–88, 2001.

[8] R. S. Purves, P. Clough, C. B. Jones, A. Arampatzis, B. Bucher, D. Finch, G. Fu, H. Joho, A. K. Syed, S. Vaid, and B. Yang. The design and implementation of spirit: A spatially aware search engine for information retrieval on the internet. *Int. J. Geogr. Inf. Sci.*, 21(7):717–745, Jan. 2007.

[9] N. Stokes, Y. Li, A. Moffat, and J. Rong. An empirical study of the effects of NLP components on Geographic IR performance. *International Journal of Geographical Information Science*, 22(3):247–264, 2008.

[10] B. E. Teitler, M. D. Lieberman, D. Panozzo, J. Sankaranarayanan, H. Samet, and J. Sperling. Newsstand: A new view on news. In *Proceedings of the 16th ACM SIGSPATIAL international conference on Advances in geographic information systems*, page 18. ACM, 2008.

Comparing Performances of Big Data Stream Processing Platforms with RAM^{3}S (extended abstract)

Ilaria Bartolini and Marco Patella

DISI - Alma Mater Studiorum, Università di Bologna
{ilaria.bartolini,marco.patella}@unibo.it

Abstract. Nowadays, Big Data platforms allow the analysis of massive data streams in an efficient way. However, the services they provide are often too raw, thus the implementation of advanced real-world applications requires a non-negligible effort for interfacing with such services. This also complicates the task of choosing which one of the many available alternatives is the most appropriate for the application at hand. In this paper, we present a comparative study of the three major open-source Big Data platforms for stream processing, as performed by using our novel RAM^{3}S framework. Although the results we present are specific for our use case (recognition of suspect people from massive video streams), the generality of the RAM^{3}S framework allows both considering such results as valid for similar applications and implementing different use cases on top of Big Data platforms with very limited effort.

1 Introduction

The huge amount of information produced by modern society could help in several important tasks of public life, such as security, medicine, environment, and smarter use of cities, but is rarely exploited due to aspects of privacy, ethics, and availability of appropriate technology, among the others. The emerging Big Data paradigm provides opportunities for the management and analysis of such large quantities of information, but the services such systems provide are often too raw, since they focus on issues of fault tolerance, increased parallelism, etc.

In order to help bridging the technological gap between facilities provided by Big Data analysis platforms and advanced applications, in this paper we focus on the real-time analysis of massive multimedia streams, where data come from multiple data sources (like sensors, cameras, etc.) that are widely located on the territory. The goal of such analysis is the discovery of new and hidden information from the output of data sources as they occur, thus with very limited latency. A strong technological support is therefore needed to analyze the information generated by the growing presence of multimedia sensors. Such technologies have to meet strict requirements: rapid processing, high accuracy, and minimal human intervention. In this context, Big Data techniques can help this automated analysis, e.g., to enable corrective actions or to signal a state of security alarm for citizens.

To this end, we exploit our RAM^{3}S (Real-time Analysis of Massive MultiMedia Streams) framework for the automated real-time analysis of multimedia streams to compare the performance of three different open source engines for the analysis of streaming Big Data. In particular, we focus on the study of face detection for the automatic identification of "suspect" people: this can be useful, for example, in counter-terrorism, protection against espionage, intelligent control of the territory, or smart investigations.[1]

Although the problem of stream analysis is not novel per se [5,2], its application in presence of several *multimedia* (MM) streams is questionable, due to the very nature of MM data, which are complex, heterogeneous, and of large size. This makes the analysis of MM streams computationally expensive, so that, when deployed on a single centralized system, computing power becomes a bottleneck. Moreover, the size of the knowledge base could also prevent its storage on a single computation node.

In order to allow efficient analysis of massive multimedia streams in real scenarios, we advocate scaling out the underlying system by using platforms for Big Data management. Since we deal with online applications, we are interested in analyzing the data as soon as these are available, in order to exploit their "freshness". Therefore, we concentrate on platforms for Big Data analytics following the *stream processing* paradigm, as opposed to systems for *batch processing* [6]. While in the latter, whose main representative is Apache Hadoop (`hadoop.apache.org`), data are first stored on a physical support (usually on a Distributed File System, *DFS*) and then analyzed, for the case of stream processing data are not stored and the efficiency of the system depends on the amount of data processed, keeping low latency, at the second, or even millisecond, level.

2 Big Data Analysis Platforms

In this section, we describe the alternatives available for the analysis of Big Data under the stream processing paradigm. This is necessary to grasp common characteristics present in such systems, that will be exploited to guarantee the generality of the proposed framework.

Apache Spark Streaming Apache Spark [10] (`spark.apache.org`) is an open source platform, originally developed at the University of California, Berkeley's AMPLab. The main idea of Spark is that of storing data into a so-called Resilient Distributed Dataset (*RDD*), which represents a read-only fault-tolerant collection of (Python, Java, or Scala) objects partitioned across a set of machines that can be stored in main memory. RDDs are immutable and their operations are lazy. The "lineage" of every RDD, i.e., the sequence of operations that produced it, is kept so that it can be rebuilt in case of failures, thus guaranteeing fault-tolerance. Every Spark application is therefore a sequence of operations on such RDDs, with the goal of producing the desired final result. There are two types of

[1] Although we instantiated RAM^{3}S for a very specific task, it is independent of the particular application at hand, thus demonstrating its wide applicability which is however out of the scope of this paper.

operations that can be performed on a RDD: a *transformation* is any operation that produces a new RDD, built from the original one; on the other hand, an *action* is any operation that produce a single value or writes an output on disk. The kernel of Spark is Spark Core, providing functionalities for distributed task dispatching, scheduling, and I/O. The program invokes the operations on Spark Core exploiting a functional programming model. Spark Core then schedules the function's execution in parallel on the cluster. This assumes the form of a Directed Acyclic Graph (DAG), where nodes are operations on RDDs performed on a computing node and arcs represent dependencies among RDDs.

The Streaming version of Spark introduces receiver components, in charge of receiving data from multiple sources, like Apache Kafka, Twitter, or TCP/IP sockets. Real-time processing is made possible by introducing a new object, the *D-Stream*, a sequence of RDDs, sampled every n time units. Every D-Stream can be now introduced in the Spark architecture as a "regular" RDD to be elaborated, thus realizing micro-batching. A Spark Streaming application is built by two main components: A *receiver* contains the data acquisition logic, defining the `OnStart()` and `OnStop()` methods for initializing and terminating the data input; every receiver occupies a core in the architecture; in a *driver* the program specifies the receiver(s) creating the D-Streams and the sequence of operations transforming the data, terminated with an action storing the final result.

Apache Storm Apache Storm (`storm.apache.org`) is an open source platform, originally developed by Backtype and afterwards acquired by Twitter. The basic element that is the subject of computation is the *tuple*, a serializable user defined type. The Storm architecture is composed of two types of nodes: *spouts* are nodes that generate the stream of tuples, binding to an external data source (like a TCP/IP socket or a message queue), while *bolts* are nodes that perform stream analysis; ideally, every bolt node should perform a transformation of limited complexity, so that the complete computation is performed by the coordination of several bolt nodes. Every bolt is characterized by the `prepare()` and the `execute(Tuple)` methods; the former is used when the bolt is started, while the latter is invoked every time a `Tuple` object is ready to be processed.

A Storm application simply defines a *topology* of spout and bolt nodes in the form of a DAG, where nodes are connected by way of streams of tuples flowing from one node to the other. The overall topology, therefore, specifies the computation pipeline. A key concept in Storm is the *acknowledgment* of input data, in order to provide fault-tolerance, so that if a node emits a tuple but this is not acknowledged, this can be re-processed, e.g., forwarding it to another node. This amounts to an "at-least-once" semantics, guaranteeing that every datum is always processed. This allows low latency, but does not ensure the uniqueness of the final result.

Apache Flink Apache Flink (`flink.apache.org`) is an open source platform, originally started as a German research project [1], that was later transformed into an Apache top-level project. Its core is a distributed streaming dataflow that accepts programs in form of a graph (*JobGraph*) of activities consuming and producing data. Each JobGraph can be executed according to a single distribution option, chosen among the several available for Flink (e.g., single JVM, YARN, or cloud). This allows Flink to perform both batch and stream processing, by simply turning data buffering on and off. Data processing by Flink is based on the *snapshot algorithm* [3], using marker messages to save the state of the whole distributed system without data loss and duplication. Flink saves the topology state in main memory (or on DFS) at fixed time intervals. The use of the snapshot algorithm provides Flink with a "exactly-once" semantics, guaranteeing that every datum is processed at least one time and no more than that. Clearly, this allows both a low latency and a low overhead, and also maintains the original flow of data. Finally, Flink has a "natural" data flow control, since it uses fixed-length data queues for passing data between topology nodes.

The main difference between Storm and Flink is that, in the former, the graph topology is defined by the programmer, while the latter does not have this requirement, since each node of the JobGraph can be deployed on every computing node of the architecture.

3 The RAM^{3}S Framework

The RAM^{3}S framework provides a general infrastructure for the analysis of multimedia streams on top of Big Data platforms. By exploiting RAM^{3}S, researchers can apply their multimedia analysis algorithms to huge data streams, effectively scaling out methods that were originally created for a centralized scenario, without incurring the overhead of understanding issues peculiar to distributed systems. To be both general and effective, we designed RAM^{3}S as a "middleware" software layer between the underlying Big Data platforms and the top data stream application.

The core of RAM^{3}S consists of two interfaces that, when appropriately instantiated, can act as a general stream analyzer: the `Analyzer` and the `Receiver` (see below).

Receiver	Analyzer
`start(): void`	`Analyzer(KnowledgeBase)`
`stop(): void`	`analyze(MMObject): boolean`

The `Analyzer` is the component in charge of the analysis of individual multimedia objects. In particular, every multimedia object is compared to the underlying KB to see whether an alarm should be generated or not. On the other hand, the `Receiver` should break up a single incoming multimedia stream into individual objects that can be analyzed one by one. The interface of the `Receiver` component is very simple: only the `start()` and the `stop()` methods should be defined, specifying how the data stream acquisition is initiated and terminated. The output of the `Receiver` component is a sequence of `MMObject` instances. The `Analyzer` component includes only a constructor and a single `analyze()` method. The constructor has a single parameter, the KB which will be used for the analysis of individual objects. On the other hand, the `analyze()` method takes as input a single `MMObject` instance and outputs a boolean, indicating whether the comparison of the input `MMObject` "matches" the KB or not.

3.1 Applying the Framework to the Use Case

Our scenario of suspect people recognition is illustrated in Figure 1. Each camera sends its video flow to a single `Receiver`, that performs the task of frame splitting and generates a stream of still images (instances of the `MMObject` interface). The `Analyzer` receives a flow of images, and performs the face detection task first, by exploiting an Haar cascade detector [8], followed by face recognition, by way of an eigenfaces algorithm [7]: both techniques are provided by the OpenIMAJ library (`openimaj.org`).

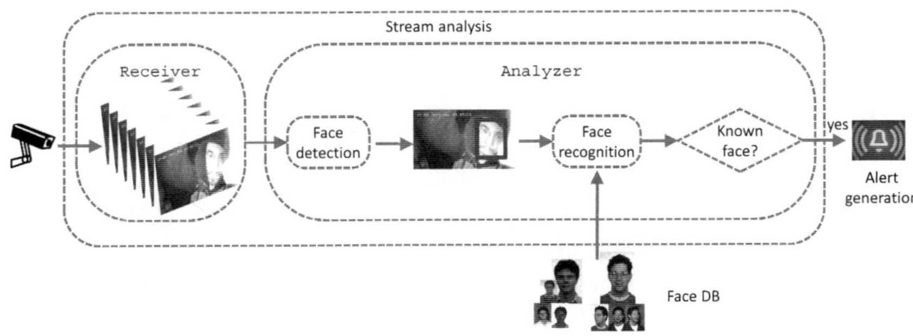

Fig. 1. Instantiation of the RAM^{3}S framework classes for suspect face recognition.

3.2 Interface to Big Data Platforms

The software framework described so far (and its application to the use case) is directly applicable to a centralized framework, by instantiating a `Receiver` for each input data stream and a single `Analyzer`, collecting outputs of the `Receivers`. In Figure 2, we show how RAM^{3}S has been appropriately extended in order to work as components of the distributed Big Data platforms.

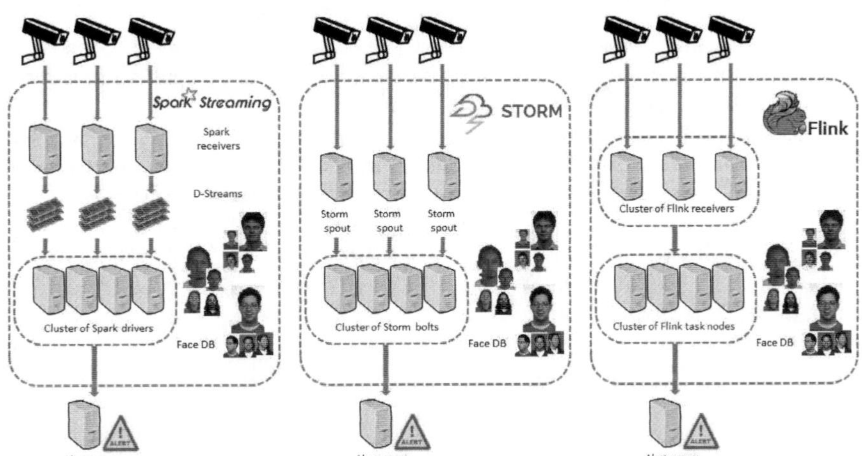

Fig. 2. Architecture for Big Data platforms: Spark (a), Storm (b), and Flink (c).

Apache Spark For Spark (Figure 2 (a)), every camera sends its video stream to a `Receiver`, corresponding to a single Spark receiver: the output of the receiver is buffered to build the D-stream. The buffer consists of n `MMObject` instances, where n is a system parameter. Every time the buffer is full, a D-stream is completed and it is sent to the cluster of Spark drivers. The `OnStart()` and `OnStop()` methods of the Spark receiver correspond to the `start()` and `stop()` methods of the `Receiver` interface. Any Spark driver includes an `Analyzer`. The logic of Spark drivers should iterate the `analyze()` method for all the n `MMObject` instances included in the input D-stream. The output of the Spark driver is the boolean "or" of the n boolean results of the `analyze()` method. Finally, this alarm is sent to the alert server.

Apache Storm For Storm (Figure 2 (b)), as before, every camera sends its video stream to a `Receiver`, encapsulated into a Storm spout. Now, however, every `MMObject` generated by the spout is immediately sent to the cluster of Storm bolts. Storm bolts correspond to single `Analyzer` objects. The `prepare()` method is equivalent to the `Analyzer` constructor, while `execute()` matches the `analyze()` method, which is executed for any received `MMObject`. Any time the `Analyzer` receives a `MMObject`, it has to acknowledge the emitting Receiver to respect the Storm semantics. With respect to the Spark solution, we have the advantage of a real stream processing architecture: latency is likely to be reduced, since we do not have to wait the completion of a D-stream to begin the analysis of any single `MMObject`.

Apache Flink Finally, for Flink (Figure 2 (c)) the configuration is apparently rather similar to the Storm case: cameras send their video streams to a cluster of Flink receivers, each including a single `Receiver` which sends individual instances of `MMObject` to the cluster of Flink task nodes. A single Flink task node consists of an `Analyzer`, executing the `analyze()` method for any received `MMObject`, finally sending an alarm to the alert server. With respect to the Storm architecture, although for ease of presentation Figure 2 (c) shows Flink receivers separated from Flink task nodes, we remind that this difference is only virtual, since each activity of the Flink JobGraph can be executed on any computing node, i.e., there are no "receiver" nodes and "task" nodes, but any single computing node can host either a receiver or a task node at any given moment. This gives to the Flink architecture high resiliency and versatility, since it can easily accommodate node faults (for both receivers and task nodes) and addition/deletion of input data streams (which would require modification of the topology in Storm).

4 Experiments

The goal of our experiments is to evaluate the efficiency of the proposed architectures, comparing them on a fair basis. The open source platforms for real-time data analysis described in Section 2 have been implemented both in a local environment with a cluster of 12 PCs and on the Google Cloud Platform (`cloud.google.com`). The first example, realized in our datalab (`www-db.disi.`

unibo.it/research/datalab/), mimics the case where streams from surveillance cameras are processed locally by a commodity cluster of low-end computers, while the latter represents the scenario where all video streams are transmitted to a center of massively parallel computers.

For tests on the local cluster, we used (up to) 12 PCs with a Pentium 4 CPU @ 2.8 GHz, equipped with 1GB of RAM, interconnected with a 100Mbps Ethernet network. For tests on the cloud architecture, we used (up to) 128 machines of type n1-standard-1 with 1 vCPU (2.75 GCEU) and 3.75GB of RAM. Our real dataset for the face detection/recognition task consists of the YouTube Faces Dataset (YTFD) [9], including 3,425 videos of 1,595 different people, with videos having different resolutions (480x360 is the most common size) and a total of 621,126 frames containing at least a face (on average, 181.3 frames/video). In order to be able to freely vary the input frame rate, the incoming stream of video frames was implemented as a RabbitMQ queue fed with sequences of still images.

Figure 3 shows the sustainable input rate (the maximum frame rate such that the input buffer does not overflow) obtained for the two scenarios. Results show that Apache Storm consistently outperforms the other two frameworks on both scenarios. We believe this behavior is due to the simplest at-least-once semantics of Storm (with respect to the exactly-once semantics of Flink) and to the fact that the Storm topology has to be explicitly defined by the programmer, while for Flink the topology is decided by the streaming optimizer; this superior flexibility of Flink comes at the cost of a slightly diminished efficiency. On the other hand, Apache Spark exhibits the worst performance, although its results are quite similar to those of Apache Flink for the cloud scenario. This is largely expected, since Spark is not a real streaming engine and the management of D-Streams is the main reason of its inferior input rates.

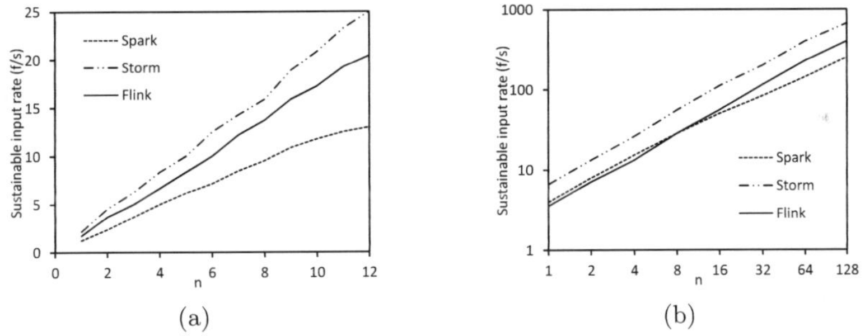

Fig. 3. Sustainable input rate when varying the number n of computing nodes for the local cluster (a) and cloud (b).

Figure 4 illustrates the latency for the three architectures on the local and the cloud scenarios. Latency of the system is the measured as the (average) time interval between an image exiting the FIFO queue and the corresponding alert signal received by the alert server, when using the maximum input rate sustainable by an architecture composed of a single node. For Apache Spark, the delay is the average delay of images included in a single D-Stream. Since a micro-batch period of 30 seconds was considered, this can be computed as 30/2 plus the average latency. Figure 4 only plots the average latency, omitting the 15 seconds from the total delay. Apache Storm consistently achieves the lowest latency, with Apache Flink always very close. For both streaming-native platforms, latency times are largely unaffected by the number of nodes: this same behavior is also common to the non-discounted latency of Apache Spark (not shown here to avoid cluttering of figures). The discounted latency of Spark, on the other hand, clearly takes advantage of the increased number of nodes, reaching latency values similar to Storm for high numbers of nodes.

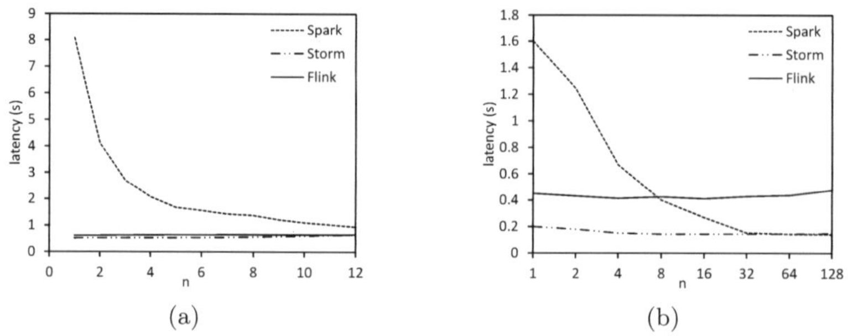

Fig. 4. Latency when varying n for the local cluster (a) and cloud (b).

Comparing performance of the three Big Data platforms, Spark attains the lower throughput and highest latency, clearly due to its micro-batch design: when looking at its good latency performance on the cloud environment, we should remember that the time for building the D-stream is not considered there. Comparing Storm and Flink, the former attains slightly better results, both in terms of throughput and in latency: as already pointed out in Section 3.2, Flink is likely to be superior to Storm when issues related to fault tolerance and correctness of the final result are considered; this clearly comes at the expenses of slightly inferior results when only performance is an issue. Similar considerations, albeit for a slightly different scenario (counting JSON events from Apache Kafka), were recently obtained in [4].

References

1. A. Alexandrov, R. Bergmann, et al. The Stratosphere Platform for Big Data Analytics. In *VLDBJ*, 23(6), 2014.
2. A. Bifet, G. Holmes, et al. MOA: Massive Online Analysis. In *JMLR*, 99, 2010.
3. K. M. Chandy and L. Lamport. Distributed Snapshots: Determining Global States of Distributed Systems. In *TOCS*, 3(1), 1985.
4. S. Chintapalli, D. Dagit, et al. Benchmarking Streaming Computation Engines at Yahoo!. *Yahoo! Engineering blog*, 2015.
5. M.M. Gaber, A. Zaslavsky, and S. Krishnaswamy. Mining Data Streams: A Review. In *SIGMOD Record*, 34(2), 2005.
6. H. Hu, Y. Wen, T.-S. Chua, and X. Li. Toward Scalable Systems for Big Data Analytics: A Technology Tutorial. In *IEEE Access*, 2, 2014.
7. M. Turk and A.P. Pentland. Face Recognition Using Eigenfaces. In *CVPR 1991*, Lahaina, HI.
8. P. Viola and M. Jones. Rapid Object Detection Using a Boosted Cascade of Simple Features. In *CVPR 2001*, Kauai, HI.
9. L. Wolf, T. Hassner, and I. Maoz. Face Recognition in Unconstrained Videos with Matched Background Similarity. In *CVPR 2011*, Colorado Springs, CO.
10. M. Zaharia, M. Chowdhury, et al. Spark: Cluster Computing with Working Sets. In *HotCloud '10*, Boston, MA.

A genetic algorithm to discover relaxed functional dependencies from data

Loredana Caruccio, Vincenzo Deufemia, and Giuseppe Polese

University of Salerno, Department of Computer Science,
via Giovanni Paolo II n.132, 84084 Fisciano (SA), Italy
{lcaruccio,deufemia,gpolese}@unisa.it

Abstract. Approximate functional dependencies are used in many emerging application domains, such as the identification of data inconsistencies or patterns of semantically related data, query rewriting, and so forth. They can approximate the canonical definition of functional dependency (FD) by relaxing on the data comparison (i.e., by considering data similarity rather than equality), on the extent (i.e., by admitting the possibility that the dependency holds on a subset of data), or both. Approximate FDs are difficult to be identified at design time like it happens with FDs. In this paper, we propose a genetic algorithm to discover approximate FDs from data. An empirical evaluation demonstrates the effectiveness of the algorithm.

Keywords: Functional Dependency, Genetic Algorithm, Discovery from data

1 Introduction

In the last decades, functional dependencies have been extended to deal with new problems, such as data cleansing [2], record matching [9], query rewriting upon schema evolutions [6], or to express constraints for complex data types, such as multimedia [7]. To this end, the canonical definition of FD has been extended either by using approximate paradigms rather than equality to compare attribute values, or by admitting subsets of data on which the FD does not hold. In the literature such extensions are referred to as *relaxations*, and these new dependencies are indicated with the term *relaxed functional dependencies* (RFDs) [3]. The relaxation degree is expressed by means of thresholds, indicating either the required similarity degree for the RFD to hold, or the minimum percentage of data on which the RFD must hold.

While FDs were originally specified at database design time, as properties of a schema that should hold on every instance of it, in order to reduce the designer effort and to dynamically adapt the RFDs to the evolution of the application domain, it is necessary to automatically discover them from data. This is made possible also thanks to the availability of big data collections, and to the contributions of several research areas, such as machine learning and knowledge discovery [18].

Most of the discovery algorithms described in the literature are intended for FDs [23], whereas few RFD definitions are equipped with algorithms for discovering them from data [18]. In this paper, we propose a genetic algorithm (GA) to identify a broad class of RFDs, including both relaxation criteria. In general, GAs are efficient for global searches in large search spaces, for which deterministic methods are not suitable. They perform operations inspired to natural species evolutions, such as natural selection, crossover, and mutation. In particular, by using these operations, the proposed algorithm iteratively generates new candidate RFDs, but only a subset of them, determined by means of a fitness function, survives to the evolution process. The fitness function exploits the support and confidence quality measures, mainly used for evaluating association rules. An empirical evaluation demonstrates the effectiveness of the algorithm.

The paper is organized as follows. Section 2 reviews the RFD discovery algorithms existing in the literature. Section 3 provides some background definitions about RFDs and formulates the problem of RFD discovery. Section 4 presents the proposed genetic algorithm named GA-RFD for discovering RFDs from data, whose performance are reported in Section 5. Finally, summary and concluding remarks are included in Section 6.

2 Related Work

In the literature there are two main categories of methods to automatically discover FDs from data, namely top-down and bottom-up methods. The formers exploit an attribute lattice to generate candidate FDs, which are successively tested to verify their validity. The whole process is made efficient by exploiting valid FDs to prune the search space for new candidate FDs. Examples of top-down approaches include the algorithms TANE [14], FD_Mine [27], FUN [21], and DFD [1]. On the other hand, bottom-up methods derive candidate FDs from two attribute subsets, namely *agree-sets* and *difference-sets*, which are built by comparing the values of attributes for all possible combinations of pairs of tuples. Examples of bottom-up approaches include the algorithms DepMiner [19], FastFD [26], and FDep [11]. Recently, an hybrid algorithm has been proposed in order to obtain better performance in all cases [24].

Although a recent survey listed thirdy-four different types of RFDs [3], very few of them are equipped with algorithms for discovering them from data [18]. These are reviewed in the following.

Approximate functional dependencies (AFDs) are FDs holding for 'most' rather than 'all' the tuples of a relation r [16]. The amount of tuples satisfying the AFDs can be calculated by means of several measures [12], among which the g_3 error measure is the most frequently used [16]. The latter represents the minimum fraction of tuples that must be removed from a relation instance r in order to make a candidate AFD valid. Most approaches for AFD discovery use a small portion of tuples (sampling) $s \subset r$ to decide whether an AFD holds on r [16]. The method proposed in [15] exploits the error measure of super keys to determine the approximate satisfaction of AFDs.

Like AFDs, *conditional functional dependencies* (CFDs) are FDs holding for a subset of tuples, but in this case the subset is identified by specifying conditions [2]. Among the approaches for discoverying CFDs from data, the algorithm proposed in [8] exploits an attribute lattice derived from partitions of attribute values, in order to generate candidate CFDs. Alternatively, the greedy algorithm proposed in [13] tries to derive CFDs by finding close-to-optimal tableau, where the closeness is measured by means of support and confidence. In [10] the authors adapt three algorithms used for FD discovery, namely FD_Miner, TANE, and FastFD, to the discovery of CFD.

Matching dependencies (MDs) are RFD_c defined in terms of similarity predicates to accommodate errors, and different representations in unreliable data sources [9]. They have been mainly proposed for object identification. The most recent algorithm for MD discovery evaluates the utility of candidate MDs for a given database instance, determining the corresponding similarity threshold pattern. The utility is measured by means of support and confidence MDs, whereas thresholds are determined by analyzing the statistical distribution of data.

Differential dependencies (DDs) are RFD_c based on differential constraints on attribute values [25]. Among the algorithms proposed for their discovery, the one proposed in [25] exploits reduction algorithms, which detect DDs by first fixing the RHS differential function for each attribute in r, and then finding the set of differential functions that left-reduce the LHS. The performances of the algorithm are improved by means of pruning strategies based on the subsumption order of differential functions, implication of DDs, and instance exclusion. Another approach for DD discovery tries to reduce the problem search space by assuming a user-specified distance threshold as upper limit for the distance intervals of LHS [17]. The algorithm is based on a distance-based subspace clustering model, and exploits pruning strategies to efficiently discover DDs when high threshold values are specified.

As opposed to these discovery algorithms, which focus each on a specific RFD, the discovery algorithm proposed in [5] aims to identify the entire class of RFDs [3] relaxing on the tuple comparison method. In particular, the approach relies on lattice-based algorithms conceived for FD discovery, which are feeded with similar subsets of tuples derived from previously computed differential matrices.

The algorithm proposed in this paper further extends the class of discovered RFDs, by also including those relaxing on the extent.

3 Discovery Relaxed Functional Dependencies from Data

3.1 Relaxed Functional Dependencies

Before defining RFDs we need to introduce the concept of *similarity constraint*, which expresses the similarity of two values on a specific domain, and it is represented through a function ϕ. In particular, given two attributes A and B on a domain D, $\phi(A, B)$ evaluates the similarity of A and B. As an example, ϕ can be defined in terms of a similarity metric $\approx$, like for instance the edit distance, such that $a \approx b$ is true if a and b are "close" enough w.r.t. a predefined threshold.

Given a relational schema R defined over a fixed set of attributes, and $R_1 = (A_1, \ldots, A_k)$ and $R_2 = (B_1, \ldots, B_m)$ two relation schemas of $\mathcal{R}$, an RFD φ on $\mathcal{R}$ is denoted by

$$\mathbb{D}_{c_1} \times \mathbb{D}_{c_2} : (X_1, X_2)_{\Phi_1} \xrightarrow{\Psi \geq \epsilon} (Y_1, Y_2)_{\Phi_2} \tag{1}$$

where

- $\mathbb{D}_{c_1} \times \mathbb{D}_{c_2} = \{(t_1, t_2) \in dom(R_1) \times dom(R_2) \mid (\bigwedge_{i=1}^{k} c_{1_i}(t_1[A_i])) \wedge (\bigwedge_{j=1}^{m} c_{2_j}(t_2[B_j]))\}$ where $c_1 = (c_{1_1}, \ldots, c_{1_k})$ and $c_2 = (c_{2_1}, \ldots, c_{2_m})$, with c_{1_i} and c_{2_j} predicates on $dom(A_i)$ and $dom(B_j)$, respectively, that filter the tuples on which φ applies;
- $X_1, Y_1 \subseteq attr(R_1)$, and $X_2, Y_2 \subseteq attr(R_2)$, with $X_1 \cap Y_1 = \varnothing$ and $X_2 \cap Y_2 = \varnothing$;
- Φ_1 (Φ_2, resp.) is a set of constraints $\phi[X_1, X_2]$ ($\phi[Y_1, Y_2]$, resp.) on attributes X_1 and X_2 (Y_1 and Y_2, resp.). For any pair of tuples $(t_1, t_2) \in \mathbb{D}_{c_1} \times \mathbb{D}_{c_2}$, the constraint $\phi[X_1, X_2]$ ($\phi[Y_1, Y_2]$, resp.) indicates true, if the similarity of t_1 and t_2 on attributes X_1 and X_2 (Y_1 and Y_2, resp.) agrees with the constraint specified by $\phi[X_1, X_2]$ ($\phi[Y_1, Y_2]$, resp.).
- Ψ is a coverage measure defined on $\mathbb{D}_{c_1} \times \mathbb{D}_{c_2}$, which quantifies the satisfiability degree of φ on r, and can be defined as a function $\Psi : dom(X) \times dom(Y) \rightarrow \mathbb{R}$ measuring the amount of tuples in r violating or satisfying φ.
- ϵ is a threshold indicating the lower bound (or upper bound in case the comparison operator is $\leq$) for the result of the coverage measure.

Given $r_1 \subseteq \mathbb{D}_{c_1}$ and $r_2 \subseteq \mathbb{D}_{c_2}$ two relation instances on (R_1, R_2), (r_1, r_2) *satisfies* the RFD φ, denoted by $(r_1, r_2) \models \varphi$, if and only if: $\forall\ (t_1, t_2) \in (r_1, r_2)$, if $\phi[X_1, X_2]$ indicates true for each constraint $\phi \in \Phi_1$, then *almost always* $\phi[Y_1, Y_2]$ indicates true for each constraint $\phi \in \Phi_2$. Here, *almost always* means that $\Psi(\pi_{X_1}(r_1)\pi_{X_2}(r_2), \pi_{Y_1}(r_1)\pi_{Y_2}(r_2)) \geq \epsilon$.

For RFDs defined on single relation schemas (i.e., $R_1 = R_2$), if $X_1 = X_2$ and $Y_1 = Y_2$, then we will simplify the RFD notation given in (1) by using $\mathbb{D}_c$, X, and Y to refer to the Cartesian product $\mathbb{D}_{c_1} \times \mathbb{D}_{c_2}$, and to the pairs $(X,\ X)$ and $(Y,\ Y)$, respectively. Moreover, if the RFD has to be satisfied by all tuples in r, then the symbol $\Psi_{err(0)}$ is shown on the arrow. Such coverage measure corresponds to the expression $\psi(X, Y) = 0$, where $\psi(X, Y)$ measures the number of tuples violating the RFD. As an example, the canonical FD can also be written as: $\mathbb{D}_{\text{TRUE}} : X_{\text{EQ}} \xrightarrow{\Psi_{err(0)}} Y_{\text{EQ}}$, where TRUE is a sequence of tautologies, hence $\mathbb{D}_{\text{TRUE}} = dom(R_1)$, whereas EQ is the equality constraint.

As an example, in a database of body measures it is likely to have a similar shoe size for people having a similar height. Thus, the following RFD might hold $\mathbb{D}_{\text{TRUE}} : \textsf{Height}_{\approx} \xrightarrow{\Psi_{err(0)}} \textsf{Shoe Size}_{\approx}$, where $\approx$ is a differential function. On the other hand, there might be exceptions to this dependencies, since few people might have close heights but more different shoe sizes. This can be modeled by introducing a different coverage measure into the RFD, making it approximate $\mathbb{D}_{\text{TRUE}} : \textsf{Height}_{\approx} \xrightarrow{\psi(Height, ShoeSize) \leq 0.02} \textsf{Shoe Size}_{\text{EQ}}$, where $\psi(Height, ShoeSize) \leq 0.02$ indicates that at most for 2% of tuples the RFD does not hold.

3.2 The RFD discovery problem

Given a relation r, the discovery of RFDs is the problem of finding a minimal cover set of valid RFDs that hold in r. This problem introduces further complexity to the already complex task of FD discovery from data, due to the significantly larger search space, which derives from the several similarity/distance functions that may be defined over each attribute [17]. Consequently, it is necessary to devise tractable algorithms capable of extracting RFDs with meaningful similarity constraints.

In this paper, we analyze the problem of RFD discovery from data given a set of thresholds for both attribute comparison and coverage measure. Although this reduces the overall complexity of the problem, it still remains more complex than the FDs discovery one. In fact, as said in Section 3.1, an RFD $X \rightarrow Y$ holds on a relation r iff whenever the distance between two tuples t_1 and t_2 in r is below a threshold value α_A on each attribute A belonging to X, then their distance is below a threshold value α_B on each attribute B belonging to Y, with a degree of certainty greater than a threshold value ϵ. For this reason, we have to analyze the similarity between portions of tuple pairs rather than their equality. This does not permit to exploit the equivalence classes of attribute values, usually used for FD discovery. Indeed, an attribute value might be similar to other attribute values that are not similar to each other.

4 Identifying Relaxed Functional Dependencies with a Genetic Algorithm

The proposed algorithm discovers RFDs by comparing tuples pairwise, based on the similarity of subsets of their attributes. In particular, pairs of tuples with a similarity higher than a threshold are represented with the value 1, and 0 otherwise. In this way, we reduce the RFD discovery problem to a search one, which is solved through a GA. The latter implements a simulation in which a population of candidate solutions to an optimization problem evolves towards better solutions. The process usually starts from a population of randomly generated individuals (Initialization), which evolves by stochastically selecting multiple individuals from the current population (based on a fitness function), and modified (recombined and possibly randomly mutated) to form a new population. The algorithm terminates when either a maximum number of generations has been produced, or a satisfactory fitness level has been reached for the population. In the first case, a satisfactory solution may or may not have been reached.

4.1 GA-RFD

In this section, we explain the GA to discover RFDs, which is named GA-RFD. In particular, in the following we first explain how the discovery problem has been encoded for GA processing, then we define the fitness function to evaluate the satisfactory degree of individuals, and finally, we present the GA-RFD algorithm.

Encoding. Given the thresholds for attribute comparison and coverage measure, the problem of RFD discovery reduces to find all possible dependencies $X \rightarrow Y$ satisfying the following rule: tuples that are similar on the LHS must correspond to those that are similar on the RHS. Such a rule must hold for almost all set of tuples that are similar on the LHS attributes, according to the threshold specified for the coverage measure.

In order to accomplish this with a GA, the dataset has to be modeled in a way that highlights similarity between tuple pairs. For this reason, in the proposed methodology we transform an input dataset in terms of a *difference dataset*. The latter contains the input dataset attributes as columns, the input dataset tuple pairs as rows, and the similarity between tuple pairs as values. In particular, given an attribute X_i and a tuple pair (t_1, t_2), the difference dataset will have the value 1 if $t_1[X_i]$ is similar to $t_2[X_i]$ according to the threshold associated to X_i, and the value 0 otherwise.

Example 1. Let us consider the sample dataset shown in Table 1a, and the similarity thresholds: 1 for the attributes Height and Shoe Size, and 10 for the attribute Weight. By using the absolute difference as a distance function, we can derive the difference dataset shown in Table 1b.

Table 1 A dataset of body measures.

Tuple ID	Height	Weight	Shoe size
1	175	70	40
2	175	75	39
3	175	69	40
4	176	71	40
5	178	81	41
6	169	73	37
7	170	62	39

(a) A sample dataset.

Pair ID	Height	Weight	Shoe Size
(1,2)	1	1	1
(1,3)	1	1	1
(1,4)	1	1	1
(1,5)	0	0	1
(1,6)	0	1	0
(1,7)	0	1	1
(2,3)	1	1	1
(2,4)	1	1	1
(2,5)	0	1	0
(2,6)	0	1	0
(2,7)	0	0	1
(3,4)	1	1	1
(3,5)	0	0	1
(3,6)	0	1	0
(3,7)	0	1	1
(4,5)	0	1	1
(4,6)	0	1	0
(4,7)	0	1	1
(5,6)	0	1	0
(5,7)	0	0	0
(6,7)	1	0	0

(b) The difference dataset.

In order to construct individuals in the population we use an array of integers representing the attribute indices in the difference dataset. In particular, each item i of the array corresponds to a specific attribute X_i in the dataset. In particular, since all the RFDs can be reduced w.l.o.g. to a format with a single attribute on the RHS, each individual of size k will represent a candidate RFD, where the $k-1$ attributes on the LHS correspond to the first $k-1$ items in the array, and the last one corresponds to the attribute on the RHS. It is worth to notice that the algorithm can be iterated with several values for k in order to consider RFDs with different sizes on the LHS.

Example 2. The individual $[3,1]$ for the dataset in Table 1a will represent the candidate RFD: Shoe Size → Height.

Fitness Function. In order to discover RFDs we exploit the concepts of *support* and *confidence* commonly used in the context of association rule mining. In particular, several studies have demonstrated the relationship existing between FDs and association rules [14]. Formally, let X and Y be two sets of items, the *support* of a set X, denoted with $sup(X)$, represents the ratio of the transactions in the dataset containing X, whereas the confidence represents the ratio $sup(X \cup Y)/sup(X)$.

In our context, $sup(X)$ represents the ratio of tuple pairs that are similar on all attributes in X. In this way, we can use the *confidence* as the fitness function to determine if a candidate RFD $X \rightarrow Y$ is valid: $conf(X \rightarrow Y) = \frac{supp(X \cup Y)}{supp(X)}$. This fitness function returns 1 if and only if whenever tuple pairs are similar on attributes in X, then they are similar also on Y. In order to validate a candidate RFD the proposed algorithm associates the threshold specified for the coverage measure to the fitness function.

Example 3. If we consider the individual $[3,1]$ of Example 2, representing the candidate RFD: Shoe Size → Height, the associated support and confidence are: $sup(\text{Shoe Size}) = \frac{13}{21}$, $sup(\{\text{Shoe Size}, \text{Height}\}) = \frac{6}{21}$, $conf(\text{Shoe Size} \rightarrow \text{Height}) = \frac{6}{21} \times \frac{21}{13} = \frac{6}{13} = 0.46$. This candidate RFD will not be considered as valid, unless the coverage threshold specified in input is less than 0.46.

Algorithm 1 The general GA-RFD algorithm

```
procedure GA-RFD(difference dataset D, extent threshold β, int maxgen, int
    pop_size, int k, double p1, double p2)
    Set pop, final_pop, new_pop
    int gen ← 0
    final_pop ← INITIALIZE(pop_size, k, numCols(D))
    while gen ≤ maxgen do
        if (allOf(final_pop, β)) then
            break
        end if
        new_pop ← SELECT(final_pop, β)
        pop ← ∅
        pop ← CROSSOVER(new_pop, k, p1)
        pop ← MUTATE(pop, k, numCols(D), p2)
        final_pop ← new_pop ∪ pop
        g ← g + 1
    end while
    return final_pop
end procedure
```

Algorithm. The pseudo-code of the main procedure of GA-RFD is shown in Algorithm 1. It first produces the initial population through the INITIALIZE procedure, and then, within a cycle, it selects only the individuals that reach the fitness function objective (SELECT procedure), makes crossover on selected individuals according to a fixed probability p_1 (CROSSOVER procedure), mutates some of them according to a fixed probability p_2 (MUTATE procedure). The new population is evaluated in the next iteration of the cycle. GA-RFD terminates if and only if either the population is composed of individuals, each one representing a valid RFD according to the β-threshold for the coverage measure, which determines the fitness objective; or the number of iterations exceeds the specified maximum number.

The INITIALIZE procedure shown in Algorithm 2 creates a set of individuals representing the initial population, according to the size *pop_size* specified as input. The used random values are ranged in the number of columns of the dataset, since each individual element will represent a column index.

The SELECT procedure shown in Algorithm 3 analyzes the individuals of the population *pop* and constructs a new population (*selected_pop*) by including individuals with a probability related to the fitness function objective β.

Algorithm 2 The INITIALIZE procedure

```
procedure INITIALIZE(int pop_size, int k, int numCols)
    Set pop
    for i ≤ pop_size do
        List x
        for j ≤ k do
            add randInt(1,numCols) to x
        end for
        add x to pop
    end for
    return pop
end procedure
```

Algorithm 3 The SELECT procedure

```
procedure SELECT(Set pop, double β)
    Set selected_pop → {}
    double fitness, confidence
    for each c ∈ pop do
        confidence = supp(c.{X∪Y}) / supp(c.X)
        if confidence ≥ β then
            fitness = 1
        else
            fitness = confidence/β
        end if
        if rand() < fitness then
            selected_pop = selected_pop ∪ {c}
        end if
    end for
    return selected_pop
end procedure
```

The CROSSOVER procedure shown in Algorithm 4 creates a new population of individuals (*new_pop*) by crossing individual pairs. We use a one-point crossover to recombine individuals; the *crosspoint* is selected randomly. In this procedure we use the function *swap*, which changes a sublist of two individuals by swapping one to each other.

The MUTATE procedure shown in Algorithm 5 creates a new population of individuals (*new_pop*) by mutating one value in each individual. The individual element that has to be changed (*gene*) and the new value (*new_gene*) are selected randomly. In this procedure we use the function *swapValue*, which changes a value in a individual by swapping it with the new value. The MUTATE procedure permits to detect candidate RFDs that do not directly depend on the initial population. It has associated a low probability, which limits the randomness of the whole methodology.

Algorithm 4 The CROSSOVER procedure

```
procedure CROSSOVER(Set pop, int k, double p)
    Set new_pop → {}
    int crosspoint
    for each c1,c2 ∈ pop with c1 ≠ c2 do
        if rand() < p then
            crosspoint = randInt(1,k)
            for i ≤ crosspoint do
                swap(c1,c2, i)
            end for
            add c1 to new_pop
            add c2 to new_pop
        end if
    end for
    return new_pop
end procedure
```

Algorithm 5 The MUTATE procedure

```
procedure CROSSOVER(Set pop, int k, int numCols, double p)
    Set new_pop
    int gene, new_gene
    for each c ∈ pop do
        if rand() < p then
            gene = randInt(1,k)
            new_gene = randInt(1,numCols)
            swapValue(c, gene, new_gene)
        end if
        add c to new_pop
    end for
    return new_pop
end procedure
```

5 Empirical Evaluation

In this section we describe the performed empirical evaluation to verify the effectiveness of the proposed GA-RFD algorithm. In particular, we first evaluate the performance of the algorithm when used to discover FDs, then we evaluated the RFD discovery performance.

The evaluation has been performed on a version of GA-RFD implemented in the Python language, and on a machine with an AMD Opteron (TM) CPU, 8 GB RAM, and Linux Ubuntu 16.10 OS. Moreover, we used two real-world datasets, also employed for evaluating several FD discovery algorithms [22], and the sample dataset introduced in Example 1. The probability parameters for the crossover and mutate procedures have been set to 0.85 and 0.3, respectively.

Evaluation by discovering FDs. This experiment compares the performances of GA-RFD with those of the FD discovery algorithms with the aim of evaluating the effectiveness of GA-RFD with respect to well-known results, as in the case of *iris* and *bridges* datasets [23]. Here, we do not evaluate the time performances, since FD and RFD discovery problems are not comparable. In order to reduce the problem to discover canonical FDs we assigned the value 0 to all tuple comparison thresholds and the value 1 to the coverage threshold. Table 2 reports the FDs discovered on the analyzed datasets. For the *iris* and *bridge* datasets GA-RFD achieves the same results obtained by other FD discovery algorithms [23].

Table 2 Results obtained by GA-RFD algorithm to discovery FDs.

Dataset	#Columns	#Rows	Size(KB)	#FDs
sample-dataset	3	7	1	2
iris	5	150	5	4
bridges	13	108	6	142

Evaluation by discovering RFDs. In order to verify the effectiveness of GA-RFD, we dirtied some values in the datasets used in the previous experiment with the aim of verifying whether the number of canonical FDs also changes. In other words, we simulated the presence of dirtiness in data, and analyzed GA-RFD overtakes errors in dependency discovery. For this reason, we evaluated how the number of RFDs changes by varying either the tuple comparison thresholds or the coverage measure threshold. It is worth to notice that, we have used this methodology in order to highlight the usefulness of the proposed algorithm w.r.t. the results shown in Table 2. In fact, in real contexts we use GA-RFD with different thresholds, those indicating similar tuples, and the one specifying the satisfiability degree.

Table 3 reports for each dataset: (*i*) the number of errors introduced in the dataset, (*ii*) the number FDs of discovered on the dataset with dirty data, (*iii*) the number of discovered RFDs by associating a threshold ≤1 to one attribute in order to manage similarities in the value comparison[1], (*iv*) the number of RFDs discovered with a coverage threshold of 0.9.

Table 3 Results obtained by using a threshold 1 on the comparison of attribute values, and the results obtained using a coverage threshold of 0.9.

Datasets	n. errors	FDs	RFDs by relaxing on tuple comparison	RFDs by relaxing on extent
sample-dataset2	1	1	2	1
iris2	2	3	4	3
bridges2	2	144	143	254

We can observe that the errors introduced in *sample-dataset2* and *iris2* have reduced the number of discovered FDs. On the contrary, for *bridge2* such a number increases, since a minimal FD ϕ_1 has been violated by errors and three new FDs, whose LHS has more attributes than LHS(ϕ_1), have been discovered. The relaxation on attribute comparison has allowed to capture the errors introduced in the datasets. However, for *bridge2* a new dependency has been discovered

[1]In particular, we have associated the threshold 1 to the first attribute in the *sample-dataset2*, and to the fifth attribute in both *iris2* and *bridges2*. The other attributes have associated threshold 0.

beyond those reported in 2. Regarding the relaxation of tuple coverage, for *sample-dataset2* the threshold is too narrow to capture the introduced error; for *iris2* we obtained less but more general dependencies than those reported in 2; for *bridge2* many more dependencies were discovered, due to the fact that the introduced errors is not significant compared to the size of the dataset, and to the number of dependencies holding in it, as reported in 2.

6 Conclusion and Future Work

In this paper we have proposed GA-RFD, a GA for discovering RFDs from data. It analyzes tuple pairs similarity through a *difference dataset*, and validates RFDs by calculating the confidence on each candidate RFD. A preliminary evaluation of the algorithm has been carried out to assess the effectiveness of the approach.

In the future, we would like to further improve this approach in order to automatically discover the RFDs and the threshold ranges of validity, without requesting their specification to the user. Furthermore, we would like to investigate the discovery of GA-RFD in the context of user interaction logs, especially in web applications, aiming to mine user intent [4]. To this end, mashup repositories are a further interesting application domain, since they are precious sources of data concerning mashup component usage, which can be useful to opportunely advise the development of new mashups [20].

References

1. Abedjan, Z., Schulze, P., Naumann, F.: DFD: Efficient functional dependency discovery. In: Proceedings of the 23rd ACM International Conference on Information and Knowledge Management. pp. 949–958. CIKM '14 (2014)
2. Bohannon, P., Fan, W., Geerts, F., Jia, X., Kementsietsidis, A.: Conditional functional dependencies for data cleaning. In: Proceedings of the 25th International Conference on Data Engineering. pp. 746–755. ICDE '07 (2007)
3. Caruccio, L., Deufemia, V., Polese, G.: Relaxed functional dependencies – A survey of approaches. IEEE TKDE 28(1), 147–165 (2016)
4. Caruccio, L., Deufemia, V., Polese, G.: Understanding user intent on the web through interaction mining. Journal of Visual Languages & Computing 31, Part B, 230 – 236 (2015)
5. Caruccio, L., Deufemia, V., Polese, G.: On the discovery of relaxed functional dependencies. In: Proceedings of the 20th International Database Engineering & Applications Symposium. pp. 53–61. IDEAS '16 (2016)
6. Caruccio, L., Polese, G., Tortora, G.: Synchronization of queries and views upon schema evolutions: A survey. ACM Transactions on Database Systems (TODS) 41(2), 9 (2016)
7. Chang, S.K., Deufemia, V., Polese, G., Vacca, M.: A normalization framework for multimedia databases. IEEE TKDE 19(12), 1666–1679 (2007)
8. Chiang, F., Miller, R.J.: Discovering data quality rules. Proceedings of the VLDB Endowment 1(1), 1166–1177 (2008)
9. Fan, W., Gao, H., Jia, X., Li, J., Ma, S.: Dynamic constraints for record matching. The VLDB Journal 20, 495–520 (2011)

10. Fan, W., Geerts, F., Lakshmanan, L.V.S., Xiong, M.: Discovering conditional functional dependencies. In: Proceedings of the 25th International Conference on Data Engineering, ICDE'09. pp. 1231–1234 (2009)
11. Flach, P.A., Savnik, I.: Database dependency discovery: A machine learning approach. AI Commun. 12(3), 139–160 (1999)
12. Giannella, C., Robertson, E.: On approximation measures for functional dependencies. Inform. Syst. 29(6), 483–507 (2004)
13. Golab, L., Karloff, H., Korn, F., Srivastava, D., Yu, B.: On generating near-optimal tableaux for conditional functional dependencies. Proceedings of the VLDB Endowment 1(1), 376–390 (2008)
14. Huhtala, Y., Kärkkäinen, J., Porkka, P., Toivonen, H.: TANE: An efficient algorithm for discovering functional and approximate dependencies. The Computer Journal 42(2), 100–111 (1999)
15. King, R., Oil, J.: Discovery of functional and approximate functional dependencies in relational databases. J. Applied Math. and Decision Sciences 7(1), 49–59 (2003)
16. Kivinen, J., Mannila, H.: Approximate inference of functional dependencies from relations. Theor. Comput. Sci. 149(1), 129–149 (1995)
17. Kwashie, S., Liu, J., Li, J., Ye, F.: Mining differential dependencies: A subspace clustering approach. In: Wang, H., Sharaf, M.A. (eds.) Proceedings of Australasian Database Conference. pp. 50–61. ADC '14 (2014)
18. Liu, J., Li, J., Liu, C., Chen, Y.: Discover dependencies from data - A review. IEEE Transactions on Knowledge and Data Engineering 24(2), 251–264 (2012)
19. Lopes, S., Petit, J.M., Lakhal, L.: Efficient discovery of functional dependencies and armstrong relations. In: Proceedings of the 7th International Conference on Extending Database Technology. pp. 350–364. EDBT '00 (2000)
20. Mario Andrés Paredes-Valverde, Giner Alor-Hernández, A.R.G.R.V.G.E.J.D.: A systematic review of tools, languages, and methodologies for mashup development. Software Practice & Experience 45(13), 365397 (2015)
21. Novelli, N., Cicchetti, R.: Fun: An efficient algorithm for mining functional and embedded dependencies. In: Proceedings of 8th International Conference Database Theory, pp. 189–203. ICDT '01 (2001)
22. Papenbrock, T., Bergmann, T., Finke, M., Zwiener, J., Naumann, F.: Data profiling with Metanome. Proceedings of the VLDB Endowment 8(12), 1860–1863 (2015)
23. Papenbrock, T., Ehrlich, J., Marten, J., Neubert, T., Rudolph, J.P., Schönberg, M., Zwiener, J., Naumann, F.: Functional dependency discovery: An experimental evaluation of seven algorithms. Proceedings of the VLDB Endowment 8(10), 1082–1093 (2015)
24. Papenbrock, T., Naumann, F.: A hybrid approach to functional dependency discovery. In: Proceedings of the 2016 International Conference on Management of Data. pp. 821–833. ACM (2016)
25. Song, S., Chen, L.: Differential dependencies: Reasoning and discovery. ACM Transactions on Database Systems 36, 16 (2011)
26. Wyss, C., Giannella, C., Robertson, E.: FastFDs: A heuristic-driven, depth-first algorithm for mining functional dependencies from relation instances. In: Procs of Intl Conf. on Data Warehousing and Knowl. Disc. pp. 101–110. DaWaK '01 (2001)
27. Yao, H., Hamilton, H.J., Butz, C.J.: FD_Mine: Discovering functional dependencies in a database using equivalences. In: Proceedings of IEEE International Conference on Data Mining. pp. 729–732. ICDM '02 (2002)

A compiler for stratified Datalog programs: preliminary results*

Bernardo Cuteri and Francesco Ricca

DeMaCS, Università della Calabria, Rende (CS), Italy
{cuteri,ricca}@mat.unical.it

Abstract. Deductive databases originated from the confluence between logic programming and databases. The core language of deductive databases is Datalog, which has recently found a renewed interest and new applications in several real-world problems. The evaluation of Datalog is traditionally implemented in monolithic systems that are general-purpose in the sense that they are able to process an entire class of programs. In this paper, we follow a different approach; we present a tool that is able to compile a given (non-ground) Datalog program, possibly with stratified negation, into a problem-specific executable implementation. Preliminary results show the performance benefits that can be obtained by a compilation-based approach.

Keywords: Compilation, Stratified programs, Deductive databases

1 Introduction

Deductive databases allow to manipulate data declaratively by means of logic programming. The target language of this work is Datalog [4, 12]: a simple, yet flexible logic programming language which is at the core of most deductive database systems. Datalog is sufficiently expressive to model many practical problems, and it recently found new applications in a variety of emerging domains such as data integration, information extraction, networking, program analysis, security, and cloud computing [6]. The evaluation of Datalog programs is traditionally performed by systems that are *general-purpose* in the sense that they are able to process an entire class of programs. In this paper, we follow a different approach; we consider a compilation strategy for the evaluation of Datalog programs. Moreover, we consider an extension of Datalog that includes stratified negation and allows the representation of a striclty larger class of problems. This language is also called *stratified Datalog.*

A Datalog program with stratified negation [4] P is a set of rules of the form $Head :- Body$, where $Body$ is a conjunction of possibly negated literals, and $Head$ is an atom. A literal is either a positive or a negative atom, while

* Partially supported by the Italian Ministry for Economic Development (MISE) under project "PIUCultura - Paradigmi Innovativi per l'Utilizzo della Cultura" (n. F/020016/01-02/X27)".

an atom is either a propositional variable or a n-ary predicate p with a list of terms $t_1, ..., t_n$. A term is either a constant or a variable. If a variable appears in the head of a rule or in a negative literal, it must then appear also in some positive literal of the same rule (safety), and recursion trough negation is not allowed (stratification). Programs are virtually split into two distinct parts: the intensional part (i.e. the set of possibly non-ground rules) that describes the problem, and the extensional part (i.e. the set of ground facts) that represent an instance of the problem. As an example, the following program models the well-known Reachability problem:

```
reaches(X,Y) :- edge(X, Y).
reaches(X,Y) :- edge(X,Z), reaches(Z,Y).
```

Facts of the form `edge(i,j)` for each arc `(i,j)` model the input graph. It is custom in the logic programming community to refer to the instensional part as the *encoding*, and to the extensional part as the *instance*. In applications, it is common to use the same uniform encoding several times with different instances.

A general-purpose system (often needlessly) processes the same encoding every time a new instance is processed. By compiling the encoding in a specialized procedure, one can wire it inside the evaluation procedure so that one does not have to process it every time. Moreover, specialized evaluation strategies can be adopted on a per-rule basis possibly increasing evaluation performance.

Datalog represents the kernel sub-language of Answer Set Programming (ASP) [2]. Notably, the grounder modules of ASP systems are based on algorithms for evaluating stratified Datalog programs [7], and, basically, any monolithic ASP system is also an efficient engine for this class of programs.

Actually, the idea of compiling Datalog programs is not new [1, 4, 8]; however, a new complexity-wise optimal compilation-based approach has been recently proposed in [11]. There, Liu and Stoller describe a method for transforming Datalog programs (with rules having at most two literals in the body) into efficient specialized implementations.

We extend the approach in [11] in order to handle *rules with bodies of any size, stratified negation and inequalities*. Moreover, *we implemented a concrete system* entirely developed in C++. In our prototype implementation, both the compiler and its output (the compiled logic programs) are written in C++.

To assess the k of our tool, we performed an experimental analysis where we compare our implementation against existing general-purpose systems capable of handling stratified logic programs.

2 Compilation of stratified logic programs

In this section, we first overview the evaluation strategy adopted by our system, and then we present the compilation strategy by means of an example.

Evaluation strategy. Stratified logic programs are evaluated in our approach by following the classical bottom-up schema [12]. Basically, rules are applied

Algorithm 1 Reachability compiled program

```
...{Data structures initializations and facts reading}
while Wedge ≠ ∅ do {Evaluation of rule (1)}
    edge = Wedge.pop()
    Redge.insert(edge)
    EdgeZMap.insertKeyValue({edge[1]}, {edge[0]})
    Wreaches.insert({edge[0], edge[1]})
end while
while Wreaches ≠ ∅ do {Evaluation of rule (2)}
    reaches = Wreaches.pop()
    Rreaches.insert(reaches)
    for X : edgeZMap.at(reaches[0]) do
        Wreaches.insert({X, reaches[1]})
    end for
end while
while Wvertex ≠ ∅ do {Evaluation of rule (3)}
    vertex = Wvertex.pop()
    Rvertex.insert(vertex)
    if not Rreaches.contains({2, vertex[0]}) then
        Rnoreaches.insert({vertex[0]})
    end if
end while
Model = Redge ∪ Rreaches ∪ Rvertex ∪ Rnoreaches
```

starting from the known facts to deduce new facts until no new information can be derived. The notion of *dependency graph* of the input program is used both to improve efficiency of the evaluation and to determine a correct order of evaluation of rules in presence of negation. More in details, given program P the dependency graph $DG =< V, E >$ of P has a vertex $p \in V$ for each intensional predicate p, and a (direct) edge of the form $(b, h) \in E$ whenever b occurs in the body and h in the head of a rule of P. Edges are labeled as negative if the body literal is negated. The dependency graph is, then, partitioned into strongly connected components (SCC)s. A SCC is a maximal subset of the vertices, such that every vertex is reachable from every other vertex. We say that a rule $r \in P$ defines a predicate p if p appears in the head of r. For each strongly connected component (SCC) of DG, the set of rules defining all the predicates in C is called the module of C. The dependency graph yields a topological order $[C_1], ..., [C_n]$ over the SCCs: for each pair (C_i, C_j) with $i < j$, there is no path in the dependency graph from C_i to C_j. Program modules corresponding to components are evaluated by following a topological order. If two predicates do not belong to the same SCC it means that they do not depend on each other, thus their defining rules can be evaluated separately (possibly increasing evaluation performance). Since, by definition, stratified programs admit no negative edge inside any SCC (i.e. no loop can contain a negative edge), an evaluation performed according to a topological order ensures a sound computation of the semantics of programs with negation. Since the rules of a program module (possibly) need to be processed several times, the evaluation of modules is optimized employing the semi-naïve evaluation technique [12]. Basically, at each iteration n, only the significant information derived during iteration $n-1$ is used.

Compilation by example. The strategy described above is quite standard, and it is employed also by general-purpose implementations. In our approach the same strategy is used to produce a specialized implementation. In the following, we exemplify how the compilation of a program module is done in our system. Consider once more the program P^{GR} that models the Reachability problem with an extra rule to derive all vertices that do not reach vertex 2:

```
(1) reaches(X,Y) :- edge(X, Y).
(2) reaches(X,Y) :- edge(X,Z), reaches(Z,Y).
(3) noReach(Y) :- vertex(Y), not reaches(2,Y).
```

The dependency graph analysis basically ensures that the rule (3) is evaluated after rule (1) and (2). Then , the core part of the compilation process applied to P^{GR}, in pseudo-code is presented in Algorithm 1. There, $Wedge$, $Wreaches$ and $Wvertex$ denote working sets while *Redge*, *Rreaches*, *Rvertex* and *Rnoreaches* denote result sets (cfr.[11]). Working sets and result sets are implemented in efficient indexed data structures that provide associative access and efficient insertions and deletions of ground atoms. In the example, we first loop on the working set of predicate *edge* which was previously loaded with facts. In every iteration, we retrieve and remove an element from the working set (*pop*) and we insert it in the result set. At line 5 we insert an edge atom into an auxiliary map (note that, attributes in atom variables, such as *edge*, are accessed in the example by position, where the first attribute has index 0). Auxiliary maps are used to index predicate ground atoms that appear in the body of some rule and might be involved in join operations with other predicates of the same body. In our example, rule (2) induces an indexing of predicate *edge* on attribute Z. At line 6, we derive an instance of reaches because of rule (1) and we insert it in its working set. After the edge loop completes, we can loop on $Wreaches$ and once again we retrieve and remove an atom from the working set and we insert it into the result set. At this point (line 11) we loop over joining edge atoms retrieved from the auxiliary map *EdgeZMap*. Inside the loop, we generate the head ground atom and we insert it in Wreaches. In the last loop (line 15), we iterate over vertex ground atoms and we add into *Rnoreaches* all vertices that do not reach vertex 2 because of rule (3). Note that we do not need an extra auxiliary map for $reaches$ because we can directly use Rreaches instead. Finally, the model of the program is given by the union of all result sets.

We remark that, there are tasks involved in the evaluation of programs that are carried out by the compiler and do not appear in the execution code. For instance, the computation of SCCs and the individuation of which data structures are needed in the evaluation. Thus, the product of the compilation does not have to perform such tasks because they are done only once and for all in the compilation process, while a general-purpose solver has to deal with such tasks once for every instance. At low level, another advantage, comes from the possi-

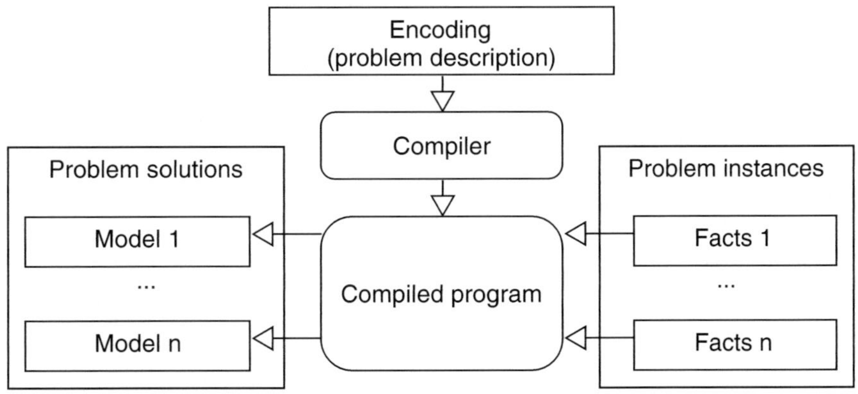

Fig. 1. Datalog compiler architecture.

bility to declare data structures as variables and exploit direct access (reducing pointers dereferencing), which results in faster C++ code.

Datalog Compiler. The compiler is written in C++ and the output is first written in C++ and then compiled into an executable program (using standard C++ compilers). Figure 1 shows a high-level architecture of Datalog compilation and evaluation as designed in our system. The resulting executable program can be run on any instance of the compiled logic program.

3 Experimental analysis

To assess the potential of our tool, we performed an experimental analysis where we compared our system against existing general-purpose systems that can evaluate stratified logic programs by using bottom-up strategies, namely: *Clingo* [5], *DLV* [9] and *I-DLV* [3]. *Clingo* and *DLV* are two well-known ASP solvers, while *I-DLV* is a recently-introduced grounder. Even though the target language of

Table 1. Average execution times in seconds and number of solved instances grouped by solvers and domains, best performance outlined in bold face.

		compiled		Clingo		DLV		I-DLV	
Benchmark	**Inst.**	**Time**	**Sol.**	**Time**	**Sol.**	**Time**	**Sol.**	**Time**	**Sol.**
LargeJoins	23	272	**22**	418	21	263	21	258	21
Recursion	21	**139**	**21**	331	20	444	21	332	21
Stratified negation	5	109	5	154	5	255	5	**88**	**5**
Totals	49	**197**	**48**	352	46	343	47	273	47

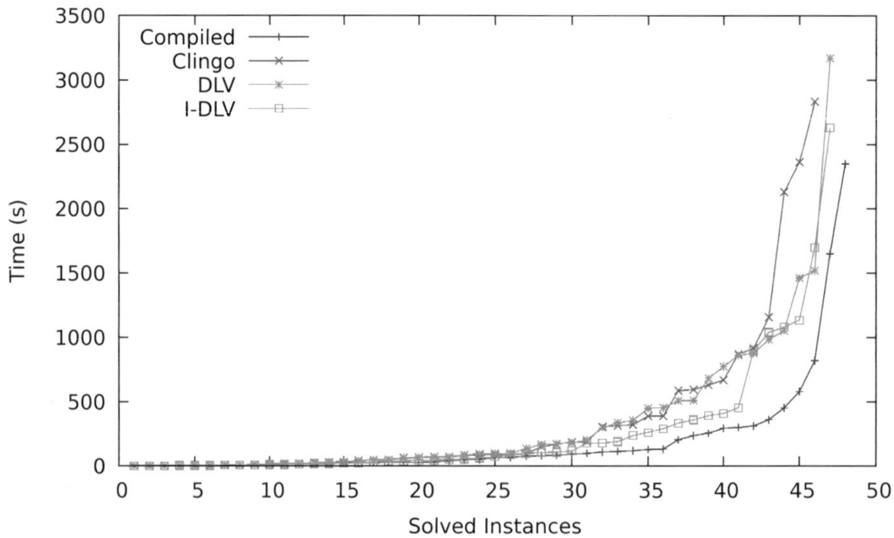

Fig. 2. Overall performance: Cactus plot of the execution times.

such systems is *ASP* they can also be considered as rather efficient implementations for stratified logic programs. The experimental analysis has been carried out on benchmarks from OpenRuleBench [10], which is a well-known suite for rule engines. The execution times reported for our system include compilation times to provide a fair comparison with general-purpose tools.

Results are summarized in Table 1 and in Figure 2. By looking at the table, we observe that our tool solves more instances than any alternative on the overall, and is the fastest on average in Large Joins and Recursion sets. In Stratified negation, our tool is on par with the others in terms of solved instances, but is slower on average than *I-DLV*. This might be explained by the fact that there are still some optimizations, such as join reordering, that general-purpose systems adopt, but we did not consider yet in our prototype implementation. An aggregate view on the results is reported in Figure 2 showing that our tool performs well on the overall. For completeness, we report that compilation required 2.6s on average (over all benchmarks). This performance is acceptable given that compilation is intended as a one-time process in our approach.

4 Conclusions and future works

In this paper, we presented a new compiler for stratified Datalog programs.[1] The prototype takes as input a stratified Datalog program and generates a specialized implementation for a given program. Experimental results are very encouraging. Ongoing work concerns the improvement of data structures generated by our

[1] The tool can be downloaded from http://goo.gl/XhZXWh.

compiler and the inclusion of other known optimization techniques used by ASP grounders [7]. Since, notably, the grounder modules of ASP systems are based on algorithms for evaluating stratified Datalog programs and we are obtaining promising results for Datalog, we then expect to be able to obtain similar improvements by applying compilation to the grounding of ASP programs. As for future works, we aim at applying compilation-based techniques to the instantiation of ASP programs.

References

1. Arni, F., Ong, K., Tsur, S., Wang, H., Zaniolo, C.: The deductive database system LDL++. TPLP 3(1), 61–94 (2003)
2. Brewka, G., Eiter, T., Truszczynski, M.: Answer set programming at a glance. Commun. ACM 54(12), 92–103 (2011)
3. Calimeri, F., Fuscà, D., Perri, S., Zangari, J.: *I* -dlv: The new intelligent grounder of dlv. In: AI*IA. LNCS, vol. 10037, pp. 192–207. Springer (2016)
4. Ceri, S., Gottlob, G., Tanca, L.: Logic Programming and Databases. Springer (1990)
5. Gebser, M., Kaminski, R., Kaufmann, B., Ostrowski, M., Schaub, T., Wanko, P.: Theory solving made easy with clingo 5. In: ICLP 2016 TCs. pp. 2:1–2:15 (2016)
6. Huang, S.S., Green, T.J., Loo, B.T.: Datalog and emerging applications: an interactive tutorial. In: Proceedings of SIGMOD 2011. pp. 1213–1216. ACM (2011)
7. Kaufmann, B., Leone, N., Perri, S., Schaub, T.: Grounding and solving in answer set programming. AI Magazine 37(3), 25–32 (2016)
8. Kifer, M., Lozinskii, E.L.: On compile-time query optimization in deductive databases by means of static filtering. ACM TDS 15(3), 385–426 (1990)
9. Leone, N., Pfeifer, G., Faber, W., Eiter, T., Gottlob, G., Perri, S., Scarcello, F.: The DLV system for knowledge representation and reasoning. ACM TOCL 7(3), 499–562 (2006)
10. Liang, S., Fodor, P., Wan, H., Kifer, M.: Openrulebench: an analysis of the performance of rule engines. In: Proceedings of WWW 2009. pp. 601–610. ACM (2009)
11. Liu, Y.A., Stoller, S.D.: From datalog rules to efficient programs with time and space guarantees. ACM Trans. Program. Lang. Syst. 31(6), 21:1–21:38 (2009)
12. Ullman, J.D.: Principles of Database and Knowledge-Base Systems. Computer Science Press (1988)

Querying OWL 2 QL ontologies under the SPARQL Metamodeling Semantics Entailment Regime

Gianluca Cima, Giuseppe De Giacomo, Maurizio Lenzerini, Antonella Poggi

Sapienza Università di Roma
lastname@dis.uniroma1.it

Abstract. OWL 2 QL is the profile of OWL 2 targeted to Ontology-Based Data Access (OBDA) scenarios, where large amount of data are to be accessed, and thus answering conjunctive queries over data is the main task. However, this task is quite restrained wrt the classical KR *Ask-and-Tell* framework based on querying the whole theory, not only facts (data). If we use SPARQL as query language, we get much closer to this ideal. Indeed, SPARQL queries over OWL 2 QL, under the so-called *Direct Semantics Entailment Regime*, may comprise any assertion expressible in the language, i.e., both ABox atoms and TBox atoms, including inequalities expressed by means of DifferentIndividuals. Nevertheless this regime is hampered by the assumption that variables in queries need to be *typed*, meaning that the same variable cannot occur in positions of different types, e.g., both in class and individual position (*punning*). In this paper we dismiss this limiting assumption by resorting to a recent meta modeling semantics and show that query answering in the resulting entailment regime is polynomially compilable into Datalog (and hence PTIME wrt both TBox and ABox).

Introduction

DL-Lite is a family of Description Logics specifically designed for achieving tractability in answering conjunctive queries (CQs) expressed over ontologies. In particular, when the ontology is expressed in one of the logics of the family, i.e., *DL-Lite*$_R$, query answering can be reduced to standard evaluation of first-order queries over a database, and can therefore make use of SQL engines. By virtue of these characteristics, *DL-Lite*$_R$ is at basis of OWL 2 QL, the OWL 2 profile especially designed for Ontology-Based Data Access (OBDA) applications, where the aim is to use an ontology to access a typically big amount of data residing in external data sources.

SPARQL is the de-facto standard language for expressing queries over OWL 2 ontologies. The key form of SPARQL query is the so-called basic graph pattern, that is a conjunction of atoms, where each atom has the form of an axiom expressible in the ontology. So, any axiom that can appear in the ontology can also appear in the conjunctive query pattern corresponding to the SPARQL query. This is coherent with the classical knowledge representation *Ask-and-Tell* framework [10], which is based on "*ask* anything that can be *told* to a knowledge base". Notice that when the Ask-and-Tell framework is specialized to OBDA, it reflects the idea of *querying whole OWL 2 QL theories*, specifying patterns spanning both through the TBox (the intensional knowledge represented in the ontology), and the ABox (the *facts* at the extensional level of the ontology), with no limitation on the use of variables, and therefore with a distinct metamodeling and metaquerying flavor, see, e.g., [9].

Starting from the seminal work [2], there has been a huge amount of work aiming at designing optimized algorithms for query answering in OBDA, and developing systems implementing such algorithms. So, it is natural to ask whether, after such body of work, the problem of querying `OWL 2 QL` theories is solved. Surprisingly, the answer to this question is negative, for the following reasons.

First, the queries studied in the great majority of the works on OBDA contain only ABox atoms. In other words, the CQs expressible in the current OBDA systems are able essentially to specify patterns in the data, and retrieve individual objects satisfying such patterns. Obviously, the intensional knowledge represented in the ontology (TBox axioms) is taken into account when answering the query, but in most of the results, the assumption is that TBox atoms do not appear in queries.

Second, the syntax and the semantics of `SPARQL` conjunctive queries over `OWL 2 QL` ontologies are defined by means of the so-called *Direct Semantics Entailment Regime (DSER)* [3], which interprets the ontology under the *Direct Semantics (DS)*, i.e., as a first-order theory, and defines the solutions to a query as the set of tuples of `IRIs` occurring in the ontology that, once substituted to the variables within the query, make the resulting set of axioms *logically implied* by the ontology. The fact that DS interprets the ontology as a first order theory has an important implication: although the syntactic rules for defining an ontology allow *punning*, that is the capability of using the same name in positions of different *type* (i.e., in an object and in a predicate position, or in a class and in a property position), the semantics imposes that occurrences of the same name in different positions are treated as is they were occurrences of different names. A direct consequence of this choice is that the use of variables in the queries is limited by the so-called *typing constraint*, by which no variable can appear both in object position (i.e., as an argument of a class or of a property), and in predicate position (i.e., as class or property). The result is that we cannot join variables denoting classes with those denoting individuals, thus preventing the specification of interesting queries related to metamodeling, e.g., the one asking for all classes that are instances of another class [9].

Third, although `OWL 2 QL` allows specifying inequalities between `IRIs`, by means of axioms of the form `DifferentIndividuals`(e_1 e_2), imposing that e_1 and e_2 denote distinct objects of the domain, the inequality predicate is completely dismissed in the work on query answering over `OWL 2 QL` ontologies. Notably, it is a folk theorem that extending the approach to cover the inequality predicate is completely trivial, but we argue in this paper that this is not the case in general, and in particular when querying whole theories. Indeed, inequalities between ontology entities can be logically implied by an `OWL 2 QL` ontology, as shown in the following simple example. Consider the ontology consisting of the axioms:

```
ClassAssertion(:Male :p).
ClassAssertion(:Male :peter).
ClassAssertion(:Female :petra).
SubClassOf(:Female :Person).
SubClassOf(:Male :Person).
DisjointClasses(:Female :Male)
```

and suppose we want to retrieve all classes that contain at least two distinct instances, by means of the SPARQL query:

```
select $x where {ClassAssertion($x $y).ClassAssertion($x $z).
                 DifferentIndividuals($y $z)}
```

It is easy to see that, since :Male and :Female are disjoint, :petra and :peter denote distinct domain objects in every model. Hence, the answer to the query is {:Person, owl:Thing}. This clearly shows that the presence of inequalities within queries requires forms of reasoning taking into account the whole ontology.

The goal of this paper is to present the first approach to querying OWL 2 QL theories, which unleashes the potentiality of the metamodeling characteristics inherent in OWL 2 QL, and of the metaquerying capabilities of SPARQL. To this aim we introduce a new entailment regime, called *Metamodeling Semantics Entailment Regime (MSER)*, which generalizes DSER by (*i*) adopting the Metamodeling Semantics (MS) for OWL 2 QL, introduced in [9], and (*ii*) relaxing the typing constraint of DSER, thus allowing the same variable to occur in positions of different type, e.g., in object and class position.

The main contribution of this paper is to show that both checking the consistency of an OWL 2 QL ontology and answering SPARQL queries over an OWL 2 QL ontology under MSER are polynomially compilable into Datalog (and hence PTIME wrt both TBox and ABox). It is easy to verify that querying OWL 2 QL ontologies with SPARQL under DSER (but *without inequality axioms*) can be polynomially reduced to evaluating a Datalog program. Our result shows that the same is true for the more general problem of querying OWL 2 QL theories under MSER, with inequalities. Moreover, our Datalog reduction provides the first algorithm for querying OWL 2 QL theories with SPARQL basic graph patterns without any restriction.

Related work. Related to our work are results on query answering in *DL-Lite*$_{\mathrm{R}}$ [2, 1, 6], i.e., the logic underpinning OWL 2 QL, and, in particular, results of [5] showing that answering conjunctive queries with inequalities in *DL-Lite*$_{\mathrm{R}}$ is in general undecidable. We point out, however, that such a negative result is due to the fact that existential variables and union are assigned the standard logical meaning, which is not the case in SPARQL. Few recent works [7, 4, 9, 8] have investigated the problem of answering SPARQL queries over OWL 2 QL theories. However, none of such works considers queries possibly containing inequalities. Moreover, all such works interpret ontologies according to DS and thus do not consider queries that violate the typing constraint, with the exception of [9, 8], which consider the problem of querying OWL 2 QL theories comprising metaclasses and metaproperties, as allowed by the OWL 2 standard, and, hence, to overcome the limitations of DS, introduce and use MS[1]. In particular, their study show that the problem of answering untyped queries is in general intractable (in data complexity), even in the absence of inequalities. However, they considered a variant of MSER, that assigns to existential variables and union the classical logical meaning.

[1] In fact, in [9], the authors use the name *Higher Order Semantics (HOS)* to denote what we call here Metamodeling Semantics. We prefer the latter because, even though the proposed semantic structure has a second-order flavor, its expressive power does not exceed first-order.

Preliminaries

OWL 2 QL. Ontology *entities*, such as individuals, classes, object properties, etc., are denoted by *expressions*. *Atomic expressions* correspond to element in the ontology vocabulary. The *vocabulary* $V_{\mathcal{O}}$ of an ontology $\mathcal{O}$ is defined as the tuple $(V_N, V_C, V_{OP}, V_{DP}, V_{DT}, \mathrm{L_{QL}})$, where *(i)* V_N is the set of IRIs occurring in $\mathcal{O}$ extended with the OWL 2 QL reserved vocabulary, *(ii)* V_C (resp., V_{OP}, V_{DP}), is the subset of V_N consisting of the IRIs that appear in class (resp., object property, data property) positions in $\mathcal{O}$, or are reserved IRIs (*Internationalized Resource Identifiers*) denoting classes (resp., object properties, data properties) *(iii)* V_{DT} is a subset of the datatypes in OWL 2 QL, and *(iv)* $\mathrm{L_{QL}}$ is the set of literals occurring in some logical axiom of $\mathcal{O}$. *Complex expressions* are built on the basis of $V_{\mathcal{O}}$. We denote by $Exp^{\mathcal{O}}$ the *finite* set of *expressions* that can be built on $V_{\mathcal{O}}$. Thus, for example, if $e \in V_{OP}$, then ObjectInverseOf(e) and ObjectSomeValuesFrom(e_1 e_2) are complex expressions in $Exp^{\mathcal{O}}$. For the sake of simplicity, in the following, we use the Description Logic (DL) syntax for denoting OWL 2 QL expressions. For example, we respectively denote by e^- and $\exists e_1.e_2$ the two above mentioned expressions. Also, we denote by $\top_C, \top_R, \top_D, \bot_C, \bot_R, \bot_D$, respectively, the OWL 2 QL reserved IRIs: owl:Thing, owl:topObjectProperty,owl:topDataProperty,owl:Nothing,owl:bottom-ObjectProperty,owl:bottomDataProperty.

An OWL 2 QL theory, or OWL 2 QL ontology (or simply *ontology* in the following) is a finite set of OWL 2 QL *(logical) axioms*. As we do for expressions, we write axioms using the DL syntax, which we modify as described next. Inclusions axioms are written as $e_1 \sqsubseteq_* e_2$, where the subscript * is C, R, A, or D, depending on whether the inclusion is an inclusion between classes, object properties, data properties, or datatypes, respectively. Similarly, disjointness axioms are written as $e_1 \sqsubseteq_* \neg e_2$. Also, axioms asserting that an object property e is reflexive (irreflexive), are written ref(e), (resp., irr(e)). We classify logical axioms into *(i) positive TBox axioms*, i.e., inclusion and reflexivity axioms, *(ii) negative TBox axioms*, i.e., disjointness and irreflexivity axioms, and *(iii) ABox axioms*, i.e., axioms of the forms $C(a)$, $R(a, b)$, $A(a, b)$, $a \neq b$. Axioms not in the above list can be expressed by appropriate combinations of the ones listed.

OWL 2 Metamodeling Semantics The OWL 2 Metamodeling Semantics (MS) was introduced in [9] and is based on the notion of interpretation structure, which plays the same role as the "interpretation domain" in classical first-order logic. Specifically, an *interpretation structure* is a tuple $\Sigma = \langle \Delta_o, \Delta_v, \cdot^I, \cdot^E, \cdot^R, \cdot^A, \cdot^T \rangle$ where:

- Δ_o, the *object domain*, and Δ_v, the *value domain* are two disjoint nonempty sets, forming the interpretation domain $\Delta = \Delta_o \cup \Delta_v$;
- $\cdot^E : \Delta_o \to \mathcal{P}(\Delta_o)$ is a partial function;
- $\cdot^R : \Delta_o \to \mathcal{P}(\Delta_o \times \Delta_o)$ is a partial function;
- $\cdot^A : \Delta_o \to \mathcal{P}(\Delta_o \times \Delta_v)$ is a partial function;
- $\cdot^T : \Delta_o \to \mathcal{P}(\Delta_v)$ is a partial function;
- $\cdot^I : \Delta_o \to \{\mathtt{T}, \mathtt{F}\}$ is a total function s.t. for each $d \in \Delta_o$, if $\cdot^E, \cdot^R, \cdot^A, \cdot^T$ are undefined for d, then $d^I = \mathtt{T}$.

Thus, the interpretation structure is not simply a set, but a mathematical representation of a world made up by elements which have complex inter-relationships, where such inter-relationships are represented by the various functions constituting Σ. Also, an *interpretation* $\mathcal{I}$ for $\mathcal{O}$ is a pair, $\langle \Sigma, \mathcal{I}_o \rangle$, where Σ is an interpretation structure and $\mathcal{I}_o$ is the *interpretation function* for $\mathcal{I}$, i.e., a function that maps every expression in $Exp^{\mathcal{O}}$ into an object in Δ_o, and every literal in L_{QL} into a value in Δ_v, according to an appropriate set of conditions. For example, one condition imposes that $\bot_C$ is interpreted as an object associated through $\cdot^E$ to an empty set. As another example, if an entity e is interpreted as an object regarded as a relation R_e, then the expression e^- is interpreted as the inverse of R_e. For the full list of conditions, please refer to [9]. Finally, to define the semantics of logical axioms, MS resorts to the usual notion of satisfaction of an axiom with respect to an interpretation $\mathcal{I}$. Thus, for example, $\mathcal{I} \models (e_1 \sqsubseteq_C e_2)$ if $(e_1^{\mathcal{I}_o})^E$ and $(e_2^{\mathcal{I}_o})^E$ are defined, and $(e_1^{\mathcal{I}_o})^E \subseteq (e_2^{\mathcal{I}_o})^E$ where e_1, e_2 are expressions. As another notable example, $\mathcal{I} \models e_1 \neq e_2$ if $e_1^{\mathcal{I}_o} \neq e_2^{\mathcal{I}_o}$.

SPARQL. We concentrate on conjunctive queries (simply called *queries* in the following), expressed using SPARQL. Let $\mathcal{O}$ be an ontology and $\mathcal{V}$ a set of variables. We start by introducing the notion of query atom. A *query atom over* $\mathcal{O}$ (simply called *atom* in the following) has the same form of an axiom with the difference that its arguments belong to the set of *terms over* $\mathcal{O}$ *and* $\mathcal{V}$. The set of terms, denoted $Exp^{\mathcal{O}}_{\mathcal{V}}$, is defined similarly to $Exp^{\mathcal{O}}$, with the difference that its base set is $V^{\mathcal{O}}_N \cup \mathcal{V}$, rather than simply $V^{\mathcal{O}}_N$. Note that, similarly to axioms, atoms can be classified into TBox atoms and ABox atoms.

A conjunctive query q over an ontology is an expression of the form

$$\texttt{select}\ x_1 \ldots x_n\ \texttt{where}\ \{B\} \tag{1}$$

where $n \geq 1$, $x_1, \ldots, x_n$ are variables, called *distinguished variables*, n is the *arity* of the query, and B, called *body of the conjunctive query* q and denoted by *body*(q), is a non-empty conjunction of atoms. In the following we will use the notation $q(\boldsymbol{x}, \boldsymbol{y}) : \boldsymbol{x} \leftarrow B$, or simply $q(\boldsymbol{x}, \boldsymbol{y})$, to denote a query of the form above, where $\boldsymbol{x} = (x_1, \ldots, x_n)$ and $\boldsymbol{y}$ is the tuple of variables that occur in B and do not belong to $\boldsymbol{x}$. Note that in SPARQL jargon, a conjunction of atoms is a *basic graph pattern*, i.e., a conjunction of RDF triples involving variables. However, for the sake of clarity and without loss of generality, instead of using the RDF syntax, we use here the DL syntax.

Queries are interpreted by relying on the notion of SPARQL *entailment regime*, as defined in the SPARQL 1.1. W3C standard specification[2]. Specifically, a SPARQL entailment regime defines (*i*) the syntax and the semantics of axioms constituting the queried ontology, (*ii*) the syntax of conjunctive queries considered legal for the regime, and (*iii*) the semantics of such queries, i.e., what are the answers to a query. The most typical SPARQL Entailment Regime for OWL 2 QL ontologies is the Direct Semantics Entalment Regime (DSER). However, based on its limitations discussed in the introduction, we introduce here a new entailment regime, called *Metamodeling Semantics Entailment Regime (MSER)*, which generalizes DSER as described in the following. As for (*i*), MSER assumes to deal with OWL 2 QL ontologies interpreted according to MS, which generalizes the Direct Semantics adopted by DSER. As for (*ii*), it considers as legal the whole set of queries defined above, while DSER restricts to queries where variables can occur only in positions of the same type. Thus, for example, in

[2] www.w3.org/TR/sparql11-entailment/

DSER, a variable occurring in object position cannot also occur in class position (e.g. in $\sqsubseteq_C$ axioms). As for *(iii)*, MSER defines the answers to a query similarly to DSER, except that it uses MS for logical entailment. Specifically, given a tuple of variables $\boldsymbol{z} = (z_1, \ldots, z_n)$, a tuple of `IRIs` $\boldsymbol{w} = (w_1, \ldots, w_n)$, and a conjunction of atoms B, we denote by $\sigma[\boldsymbol{z} \rightarrow \boldsymbol{w}](B)$ the conjunction of atoms obtained from B by substituting each z_i in $\boldsymbol{z}$ with w_i in $\boldsymbol{w}$, for $i \in \{1, \ldots, n\}$. Now, let $\mathcal{O}$ be an ontology and $q(\boldsymbol{x}, \boldsymbol{y})$ a conjunctive query. An n-tuple of `IRIs` $\boldsymbol{t}$ is an *answer to* $q(\boldsymbol{x}, \boldsymbol{y})$ *over* $\mathcal{O}$ *under MSER* if there exists an m-tuple of `IRIs` $\boldsymbol{v}$ such that

$$\mathcal{O} \models \sigma[(\boldsymbol{x}, \boldsymbol{y}) \rightarrow (\boldsymbol{t}, \boldsymbol{v})](body(q)).$$

Also, $Ans(q, \mathcal{O})$ denotes the set of answers to q over $\mathcal{O}$ under MSER. It is worth noting that, in MSER as in DSER, the variables $\boldsymbol{y}$, although projected out from the answer, are required to be *bound* to the same m-tuple of constants $\boldsymbol{v}$, in every model of $\mathcal{O}$. Thus, $\boldsymbol{y}$ are treated as distinguished variables, and not as existential ones in classical logic.

Reducing consistency checking and query answering to Datalog evaluation

In this section, we show that consistency checking and query answering over `OWL 2 QL` ontologies under MSER can be reduced to the evaluation of a Datalog program. Note that, for the sake of simplicity, from now on we implicitly assume to deal with ontologies that do not contain data properties. But our results can be immediately extended to ontologies containing data properties as well.

Intuitively, the key ideas of our approach are the following. First, we define a finite number of inference rules which capture reasoning in `OWL 2 QL`, i.e. which are sound and complete with respect to logical implication in `OWL 2 QL`. Second, we define a translation function τ from the set of legal `OWL 2 QL` axioms to the set of instances of a database schema S^{ql}, where S^{ql} comprises a distinct relation for each distinct *form* of axiom, whose arity is the number of atomic expressions that occur in axioms of that form. Then, for example, inclusion axioms of the form $c_1 \sqsubseteq_C \exists r_2^-.c_2$, where c_1, c_2 are atomic classes, and r_2 is an atomic object property, are translated into tuples (c_1, r_2, c_2) of the relation `isacCI`. Third, we use τ to translate each inference rule to a Datalog rule over the predicates of S^{ql} and obtain a set of Datalog rules $\mathcal{P}^{ql}$.

Because of the lack of space, we cannot report on the whole set of inference rules, nor the whole set of Datalog rules P^{ql}, but we next provide an overview on the main sets of rules it consists of. Thus, we define, in Table 1, the translation function τ from the set of `OWL 2 QL` axioms and atoms to the set of atoms over the schema $\mathcal{S}^{ql}$, where $x, y, c, c_1, c_2, r_1, r_2$ denote elements of V_N or variables in $\mathcal{V}$ and S^{ql} consists of the predicates that occur in the columns of Table 1 labeled with $\tau(\alpha)$ and of the binary predicates `existR` and `existI`. Then, $\mathcal{P}^{ql}$ consists of the sets of rules $\mathcal{P}^{ql}_{\mathcal{T}}$, $\mathcal{P}^{ql}_{\mathcal{T},\mathcal{A}}$, $\mathcal{P}^{ql}_{\neq}$, and $\mathcal{P}^{ql}_{\exists}$. The former are obtained by using τ to translate `OWL 2 QL` inference rules for deriving logically implied TBox axioms, ground ABox axioms, and inequalities, respectively, while the latter is obtained by translating inference rules that allow deriving first-order assertions that are not expressible in `OWL 2 QL` but can be logically implied

α	$\tau(\alpha)$	α	$\tau(\alpha)$	α	$\tau(\alpha)$
$c_1 \sqsubseteq_C c_2$	isacCC(c_1, c_2)	$c_1 \sqsubseteq_C \neg c_2$	disjcCC(c_1, c_2)	$r_1 \sqsubseteq_R r_2$	isarRR(r_1, r_2)
$c_1 \sqsubseteq_C \exists r_2.c_2$	isacCR(c_1, r_2, c_2)	$c_1 \sqsubseteq_C \neg\exists r_2$	disjcCR(c_1, r_2)	$r_1 \sqsubseteq_R r_2^-$	isarRI(r_1, r_2)
$c_1 \sqsubseteq_C \exists r_2^-.c_2$	isacCI(c_1, r_2, c_2)	$c_1 \sqsubseteq_C \neg\exists r_2^-$	disjcCI(c_1, r_2)	$r_1 \sqsubseteq_R \neg r_2$	disjrRR(r_1, r_2)
$\exists r_1 \sqsubseteq_C c_2$	isacRC(r_1 c_2)	$\exists r_1 \sqsubseteq_C \neg c_2$	disjcRC(r_1, c_2)	$r_1 \sqsubseteq_R \neg r_2^-$	disjrRI(r_1, r_2)
$\exists r_1 \sqsubseteq_C \exists r_2.c_2$	isacRR(r_1, r_2, c_2)	$\exists r_1 \sqsubseteq_C \neg\exists r_2$	disjcRR(r_1, r_2)	$refl(r)$	refl(r)
$\exists r_1 \sqsubseteq_C \exists r_2^-.c_2$	isacRI(r_1, r_2, c_2)	$\exists r_1 \sqsubseteq_C \neg\exists r_2^-$	disjcRI(r_1, r_2)	$irr(r)$	irref(r)
$\exists r_1^- \sqsubseteq_C c_2$	isacIC(r_1 c_2)	$\exists r_1^- \sqsubseteq_C \neg c_2$	disjcIC(r_1, c_2)	$c(x)$	instc(c, x)
$\exists r_1^- \sqsubseteq_C \exists r_2.c_2$	isacIR(r_1, r_2, c_2)	$\exists r_1^- \sqsubseteq_C \neg\exists r_2$	disjcIR(r_1, r_2)	$r(x, y)$	instr(r, x, y)
$\exists r_1^- \sqsubseteq_C \exists r_2^-.c_2$	isacII(r_1, r_2, c_2)	$\exists r_1^- \sqsubseteq_C \neg\exists r_2^-$	disjcII(r_1, r_2)	$x \neq y$	diff(x, y)

Table 1: Function τ

by $\mathcal{O}$, such as assertions of the form $\exists y \mid r(e, y)$, or $\exists y \mid r(y, e)$. In particular, we use the predicates existR and existI to encode such assertions, and the key point is that the use of such predicates allows us to avoid introducing existential variables within the head of the rule. Thus, the above mentioned assertions are translated into the tuples existR(r,e) and existI(r,e). Note that this, together with the fact that we consider inequalities and we interpret $\mathcal{O}$ under a more general semantics, significantly distinguishes our reduction to Datalog from the one proposed in [4]. In Table 2, we provide examples of Datalog rules belonging to each of the sets mentioned above, together with the inference rule they are obtained from.

	Datalog rule	Inference rule
$\mathcal{P}^{ql}_{\mathcal{T}}$	isacCI(c_1,r_2,c_2):-isacCC(c_1,c_3),isacCI(c_3,r_2,c_2)	$\mathcal{O} \models c_1 \sqsubseteq c_3,\ \mathcal{O} \models c_3 \sqsubseteq_C \exists r_2.c_2 \Rightarrow \mathcal{O} \models c_1 \sqsubseteq \exists r_2.c_2$
$\mathcal{P}^{ql}_{\mathcal{T},\mathcal{A}}$	instr(r_1,x,y):-instr(r_2,y,x),isarRI(r_2,r_1)	$\mathcal{O} \models r_2(y,x),\ \mathcal{O} \models r_2 \sqsubseteq_R r_1^- \Rightarrow \mathcal{O} \models r_1(x,y)$
$\mathcal{P}^{ql}_{\neq}$	diff(x,y):-disjrRR(r_1,r_2),instr(r_1,x,z),instr(r_2,y,z)	$\mathcal{O} \models r_1 \sqsubseteq \neg r_2,\ \mathcal{O} \models r_2(x,z),\ \mathcal{O} \models r_1(y,z) \Rightarrow \mathcal{O} \models x \neq y$
$\mathcal{P}^{ql}_{\exists}$	existR(r,x):-instr(r,x,y)	$\mathcal{O} \models r(x,y) \Rightarrow \mathcal{O} \models \exists z r(x,z)$

Table 2: Examples of rules in $\mathcal{P}^{ql}$

Finally, we show that both the problems of checking the consistency of $\mathcal{O}$ under MS and of answering q over $\mathcal{O}$ under MSER can be reduced to the evaluation a Datalog program. Note that, as customary in Datalog, we assume to deal with programs including a "special" intensional predicate, called *answer predicate*, here denoted Ans, and we assume that, given an instance D of a schema $\mathcal{S}$, the answer to a program Π over D, denoted $\Pi(D)$, is the extension of the answer predicate within the instance D' of $\mathcal{S}$ that results from the evaluation of Π over D.

Thus, let $D^{\mathcal{O}}$ be the set of facts computed by applying τ to each axiom in $\mathcal{O}$. Obviously, by construction, $D^{\mathcal{O}}$ is an instance of S^{ql} over elements of V_N. Also, let $\mathcal{P}^{inc}$ be the following fixed set of rules:

```
Ans():-instc(x,z),instc(y,z),disjc(x,y),
Ans():-instr(x,z,v),instc(y,z,v),disjr(x,y),
Ans():-instr(x,z,z),irref(x),
Ans():-⊥C(x),
Ans():-⊥R(x)
```

Intuitively, the rules of $\mathcal{P}^{inc}$ check for the existence of specific *violation patterns* in $D^{\mathcal{O}}$. Then, we have the following.

Theorem 1. *An ontology $\mathcal{O}$ is consistent under MS iff* $(\mathcal{P}^{ql} \cup \mathcal{P}^{inc})(D^{\mathcal{O}}) = \emptyset$.

Now, let q be a query over $\mathcal{O}$ and let r^q be the rule $\texttt{Ans}(\boldsymbol{x}) : -\tau(body(q))$, where, with a little abuse of notation, we denote by $\tau(B)$ the conjunction of the assertions obtained by applying τ to each atom in B. It is easy to see that, by construction, $\tau(B)$ is expressed over the alphabet of S^{ql} and involve only elements of V_N and $\mathcal{V}$. Also, let $\Pi^q = \mathcal{P}^{ql} \cup \mathcal{P}^q$.

Theorem 2. *Let $\mathcal{O}$ be a consistent ontology and q a conjunctive query. Then,*

$$Ans(q, \mathcal{O}) = \Pi^{\mathcal{O},q}(D^{\mathcal{O}}).$$

In a nutshell, the correctness of the two theorems relies on (*i*) the soundness and completeness of the set of OWL 2 QL inference rules, (*ii*) the semantics of MSER which treats existential variables as if they were distinguished, and, finally, (*ii*) the property that for every tuple t of elements of V_N, that is an instance of a predicate in $S^{ql} \setminus \{\texttt{existR}, \texttt{existI}\}$, t belongs to the minimum model of the Datalog program if and only if either $\mathcal{P}^{inc} \neq \emptyset$ and $\mathcal{O}$ is unsatisfiable, or t can be translated, via the inverse funtion of τ, into an axiom that belongs to every model of the ontology.

Clearly, the above theorems provide algorithms that are PTIME in the size of the ontology, and can be readily used by exploiting any off-the-shelf Datalog engine.

References

1. A. Artale, D. Calvanese, R. Kontchakov, and M. Zakharyaschev. The dl-lite family and relations. *CoRR*, abs/1401.3487, 2014.
2. D. Calvanese, G. De Giacomo, D. Lembo, M. Lenzerini, and R. Rosati. Tractable reasoning and efficient query answering in description logics: The *DL-Lite* family. *J. of Automated Reasoning*, 39(3):385–429, 2007.
3. B. Glimm. Using SPARQL with RDFS and OWL entailment. In *RW-11*, pages 137–201. 2011.
4. G. Gottlob and A. Pieris. Beyond SPARQL under OWL 2 QL entailment regime: Rules to the rescue. In *Proc. of IJCAI 2015*, pages 2999–3007, 2015.
5. V. Gutiérrez-Basulto, Y. A. Ibáñez-García, R. Kontchakov, and E. V. Kostylev. Queries with negation and inequalities over lightweight ontologies. *J. of Web Semantics*, 35:184–202, 2015.
6. S. Kikot, R. Kontchakov, and M. Zakharyaschev. Conjunctive query answering with OWL 2 QL. In *Proc. of KR 2012*, 2012.
7. R. Kontchakov, M. Rezk, M. Rodriguez-Muro, G. Xiao, and M. Zakharyaschev. Answering SPARQL queries over databases under OWL 2 QL entailment regime. In *Proc. of ISWC 2014*, pages 552–567, 2014.
8. M. Lenzerini, L. Lepore, and A. Poggi. Answering metaqueries over hi(owl 2 ql) ontologies. In *Proc. of IJCAI 2016*, 2016.
9. M. Lenzerini, L. Lepore, and A. Poggi. A higher-order semantics for metaquerying in owl 2 ql. In *Proc. of KR 2016*, 2016.
10. H. J. Levesque. Foundations of a functional approach to knowledge representation. *Artificial Intelligence*, 23:155–212, 1984.

Keyword-based access to relational data: To reproduce, or to not reproduce?

Alex Badan, Luca Benvegnù, Matteo Biasetton, Giovanni Bonato, Alessandro Brighente, Stefano Marchesin, Alberto Minetto, Leonardo Pellegrina, Alberto Purpura, Riccardo Simionato, Matteo Tessarotto, Andrea Tonon, and Nicola Ferro

University of Padua, Italy
{alex.badan, luca.benvegnu.2, matteo.biasetton, giovanni.bonato, alessandro.brighente, stefano.marchesin, alberto.minetto, leonardo.pellegrina, alberto.purpura, riccardo.simionato.1, matteo.tessarotto.1, andrea.tonon.3}@studenti.unipd.it
ferro@dei.unipd.it

Abstract. We investigate the problem of the reproducibility of keyword-based access systems to relational data. These systems address a challenging and important issue, i.e. letting users to access in natural language databases whose schema and instance are possibly unknown. However, neither there are shared implementations of state-of-the-art algorithms nor experimental results are easily replicable. We explore the difficulties in reproducing such systems and experimental results by implementing from scratch several state-of-the-art algorithms and testing them on shared datasets.

1 Introduction

Structured data are an intrinsic and pervasive constituent of Big Data. Raw figures estimate the existence of about 14 billion raw tables, coming from 5.4 million schemas and comprising more than 5.4 million attributes [8] and Gartner puts the relational database market at $26 billion with about 9% annual growth for an expected $40 billion market in 2018. The Deep Web alone is estimated to be 500 times the size of the surface or indexable Web [4, 19] while [7] estimates in excess of one billion structured data sets as of February 2011: more than 300 million sources just come from a subset of all English-language HTML tables [8] and HTML lists [12], a total that does not account for the non-English Web.

Structured queries are not end-user oriented and far away from a natural expression of user information needs by means of keywords [6, 20], given that their formulation is based on a quite complex syntax and requires some knowledge about the structure of the data to be queried. Furthermore, structured queries are issued assuming that a correct specification of the user information need exists and that answers are perfect – i.e. they follow the "exact match" search paradigm. On the other hand, end-users are more oriented towards a "best match" search paradigm where their often vague information needs are progressively refined by the search process itself. Keyword-based access to relational data [21] is the key technology to lower the barriers of access to such huge amounts of structured data since it matches user keywords or their interpretations to the data structures and domains of selected attributes in order to retrieve and rank database tuples according to their degree of relevance to user information needs. Over the past years, these facts triggered the research community and big data technology vendors to put a lot of effort into developing new approaches for keyword search over structured databases and it is still a primary research and industrial concern [1].

One of the major obstacles to the take up of keyword-based access systems is the lack of a fully-fledged reference architecture [3] which allows for a coherent and unifying vision of the different modules comprising such systems. As a consequence, there is a also lack of commonly shared open source platforms implementing state-of-the-art algorithms for keyword-based access to relational data. This situation is very different from the case of *Information Retrieval (IR)* where there are shared platforms openly available such as Lucene[1] or Terrier[2]. On the contrary, for keyword-based access system, you mostly need to re-implement each system from scratch, somehow "wasting" resources in re-developing existing solutions. Moreover, the lack of shared implementations also raises serious concerns about the *reproducibility* [13–15] of the obtained experimental results, since there is no way to know if a new implementation corresponds to the reference one or in which respect a new implementation is better than a reference one.

Therefore, as part of a student project at the course on databases in the master degree in computer engineering at the University of Padua [2], academic year 2015-2016, we considered several state-of-the-art algorithms, we implemented them from scratch, and we experimented them on the shared datasets provided by [10]. The goal is two-fold: (i) to understand the difficulties and pitfalls in implementing these state-of-the-art algorithms; (ii) to compare against the results of [10] for the same algorithms on the same datasets in order to get an idea of how difficult are these results to be reproduced. All the implemented algorithms and the experimental data are available online[3] as open source.

The paper is organized as follows: Section 2 describes the considered algorithms, their implementation and the main issues encountered; Section 3 introduces the experimental setup; Section 4 reports and discusses the experimental results; and, Section 5 draws conclusions and discusses future work.

2 Implemented Keyword-based Search Algorithms

There are two main approaches to keyword search over relational data: *graph-based* approaches model relational databases as graphs where nodes are tuples

[1] `http://lucene.apache.org/`
[2] `http://www.terrier.org/`
[3] `https://bitbucket.org/ks-bd-2015-2016/ks-unipd/`

and edges are foreign-primary key relationships between those tuples; *schema-based* approaches exploit schema information to formulate SQL queries generate from the user keyword queries. For a broader perspective on keyword search over relational databases, please refer to [18, 21].

As discussed in [2], we have implemented several state-of-the-art algorithms, both graph-based and schema-based. Each group of students was responsible for the implementation of a specific algorithm and all the groups worked independently. All the algorithms are implemented in Java using PostgreSQL[4] as relational engine.

BANKS-I *Browsing ANd Keyword Searching I (BANKS-I)* [5] is a graph-based algorithm: it starts from the nodes containing keywords and traverses all the edges in reverse direction, the so-called backward expansion, by using the Dijkstra's single source shortest path algorithm. When multiple paths intersect at a common node r in the graph, the resulting tree with root r is examined to check whether its leaves contain all the user keywords and it is weighted accordingly. Then, it returns the most relevant trees, until a predefined number of results has been reached.

We start with a pre-processing step which creates the required graph in main memory and, then, we use this graph for answering all the different queries. We create this graph in a schema-agnostic way by deducing the structure of a database from its information schema; in this way our implementation is easily portable to different databases. For each node in the graph, we save in main memory only the identifier of a tuple while an external file is used to store the information contained in the tuple itself, in order to avoid further queries to the database. The graph is represented as an hash map, where keys are identifiers node/tuple and values are lists of adjacent nodes, by using the efficient implementation provided by the fastutil library[5].

[5] lacked details on how to efficiently run multiple instances of the Dijkstra's algorithm, even if these aspects considerably affect the memory usage and the execution time. Moreover, some corner cases were not described: for example, trees with nodes containing all the user keywords, where there is no need to run the Dijkstra's algorithm, or trees composed of only a root and a child node, which we decided to consider as valid if both nodes contain a keyword.

We optimize the execution of multiple instances of Dijkstra's algorithm (one for each keyword node) by computing the next node to be returned by the algorithm only when it is actually required. i.e. only when we have to process a result tree to be returned, which typically involves only an handful of nodes instead of executing the Dijkstra's algorithm on the whole graph.

We also developed an improved version of BANKS-I by observing that it tends to return trees containing more nodes than necessary, which are also potentially irrelevant. Therefore, we penalize longer paths by incrementing the weight of each edge proportionally to the depth of the path.

[4] `https://www.postgresql.org/`

[5] `http://fastutil.di.unimi.it/`

BANKS-II *Browsing ANd Keyword Searching II (BANKS-II)* [17] improves over BANKS-I by allowing forward search from potential roots towards other keyword nodes. The algorithm uses two concurrent iterators, called outgoing and ingoing: both iterators use the Dijkstra's single source shortest path approach but the outgoing iterator expands towards other matching sets using the forward expansion while the ingoing iterator implements the same backward expansion strategy of BANKS-I. In addition, BANKS-II prefers expansion of paths with less branching by using a spreading activation mechanism, which assigns an activation score to every explored vertex and prioritizes the most promising paths to avoid wasteful exploration of the graph.

As in the previous case, a pre-processing step creates the required graph in main memory using a schema-agnostic approach. In this case, instead of using adjacency lists, we implement the graph in an object-oriented way by developing our own `Graph`, `Vertex`, and `Edge` classes. In particular, `Vertex` objects are stored in the `Graph` object using a two-layered Java `HashMap`: the name of a table in the database is used as key to a second `HashMap` which associates an unique identifier to a tuple `Vertex`. Since [17] does not mandate a specific way of weighting edges, we assigned uniform weights.

[17] lacked some details on the update of the distances of the reached ancestors and the spread of activations when adding a new node (ATTACH and ACTIVATE methods); we opted for a recursive solution. In our implementation, the outgoing and ingoing iterators explore the `Graph`, by using the Java `TreeSet` class and defining a custom `compare` method to order nodes by their activation. We decided to use `TreeSets` instead of a priority queue as suggested by [17] to update more efficiently the activation parameter of the nodes already stored in the `TreeSet`. As soon as a new result for the user query is found, i.e. a rooted tree connecting all the matching keywords, we store it in a Java `PriorityQueue` which ranks the results by the overall sum of the weights of the edges in the tree. Finally, to increase performance, we used two heuristic solutions: we set a maximum distance of the results trees (dmax = 8) as suggested by [17] and to avoid wasteful spreading towards the graph we set a minimum threshold value for the activation of a node even if not explicitly stated in [17].

DPBF *Dynamic Programming Best-First (DPBF)* [11] is a graph-based algorithm which relies on minimum cost Steiner trees to merge trees with the same root and different sets of keywords until a tree contains all searched keywords is found. In the pre-processing stage we create the graph from the database, using specific knowledge of the schema, and serialize it to a file for the subsequent processing. The graph is represented using a Java `HashMap` associating each `Vertex` to the list of its adjacent neighbours. Furthermore, we also keep an additional Java `HashMap` where keys are query keywords and values are sets of vertexes associated to those keywords.

As in the case of the other algorithms, also [11] does not specify the actual data structure to be used to represent the graph, even it actually impacts on performances. Moreover, [11] presents just a specific case of graph exploration and tree merging but it lacks details on the general case, i.e. the most important for reproducibility purposes.

We also developed an improved version of DPBF by modifying the order of the different steps of the algorithm. Indeed, when DPBF creates a new root adding a level to the tree, it then merges the trees containing different keywords under this new root. However, this step produces a large number of trees, some of which containing the very same keywords and representing the same candidate solution, but, in the end, the algorithm will keep only the trees with the lower weight. Therefore, we swap these two operations: first, we merge trees and remove all the duplicate candidate solutions with higher weight and then we add a new root to the trees, as before. In this way we reduce the number of possible found solutions but we converge to the optimal ones faster, especially in the case of complex schemas.

DISCOVER-II DISCOVER-II [16] is a schema-based algorithm which uses IR-style document-relevance ranking strategies. For each table, the IR engine module extracts and ranks the tuple sets corresponding to the query keywords which, in turn, are used to generate the *Candidate Networks (CNs)*, i.e. join of tuples which are potential answers to the issued query. The CN Generator involves a combination of not-free and free tuple sets – the former contains at least one keyword, the latter contains no keywords but allows us to connect not-free tuple sets via foreign-key joins. The final step is to identify the top-k results by combining the top-k results from each CN in a sort-merge manner.

In our implementation, we build the graph using a schema-agnostic approach, as in the previous cases, and use a `Graph` class, which is a container for tuple sets and their primary key/foreign key links. The full text extension of PostgreSQL and generalized inverted indexes (GIN) are used to implement the IR engine module. Moreover, to improve performance, we store the tuple sets for a given query as a materialized view to have them readily available during the subsequent execution of the algorithm. The Execution Engine module receives as input the set of CNs along with the non-free tuple sets, it repeatedly contacts the database to identify the top-k query results. We compute a bound on the maximum possible score of a tuple tree derived from a CN and discard the CN when this bound does not exceed the score of the already produced CNs. The CNs for a user query are evaluated in ascending size order, so that smallest CN, i.e. the least expensive to process and the most likely to produce high-score tuple trees, are evaluated first.

3 Experimental Setup

We adopted the same evaluation framework of [10], which is based on the Cranfield approach [9] widely used in IR. In particular, we used the Mondial and IMDb datasets. Each dataset, available online[6], contains 50 topics assessed using binary relevance.

[6] `https://www.cs.virginia.edu/~jmc7tp/resources.php`

Mondial has a complex schema and consists of 28 relations, containing 17,000 tuples, 56,000 foreign keys and 12,000 unique terms for a total size of 16 Mbyte; IMDb has a simple schema and consists of 6 relations, containing 1,673,000 tuples, 6,075,000 foreign keys, and 1,748,000 unique terms for a total size of 459 Mbyte.

We kept only the topics where all the studied algorithms retrieved at least one result (relevant or not). Therefore, we removed topics 31–36, 38 and 41 from Mondial, that is we used 42 topics, and we removed topics 21–22, 24, 26–27, 29–35, 38–39, 41, 46, 48 and 50 from IMDb, that is we used 32 topics. We set a maximum retrieval depth of 20 results.

We used a six-processor 3.33 GHz Intel(R) Xeon(R) machine with 96GB of RAM running Java 1.8 and PostgreSQL 9.1. We set a maximum execution time of 1 hours and maximum 15 Gbytes of memory to be used.

We used the following measures for evaluating effectiveness. *Precision at Ten (P@10)* is the classic precision measure with cut-off at the first 10 retrieved documents: $\text{Prec}(n) = \frac{1}{n}\sum_{i=1}^{i} r_i$, where r_i is 1 if a relevant result is found; 0 otherwise. Note that several topics have only 1 relevant document and this affects P@10 which can only be 0.1 in this cases. *Average Precision (AP)* represents the "gold standard" measure in IR, known to be stable and informative, with a natural top-heavy bias and an underlying theoretical basis as approximation of the area under the precision/recall curve: $AP = \frac{1}{RB}\sum_{i \in \mathcal{R}} \text{Prec}(i)$, where $\mathcal{R}$ is the sets of ranks at which relevant results have been retrieved and RB is the recall base, i.e. the total number of relevant documents.

4 Experimental Results

4.1 Efficiency

Figure 1 shows the memory occupation and execution times for running the queries: each sub-figure reports a boxplot computed over the different queries. Figure 1(e) reports the mean performance.

Memory-wise BANKS-I and DPBF are the most demanding algorithms on both Mondial and IMDb while their UNIPD variants improve on this, especially in the case of IMDb when there are lots of data and we save between 15% and 40% in memory occupation. DISCOVER-II performs very well on Mondial and better than BANKS-I and DPBF on IMDb. BANKS-II always outperforms all the other algorithms, requiring a very small memory footprint. Finally, Figure 1(a) and 1(b) show quite a bit variance in the memory occupation across the different queries and, especially in the case of IMDb, there are quite high outliers. This indicates that the algorithms are quite affected by the topic and collection at hand and that the performance can vary quite a lot. The most robust algorithm in this respect is BANKS-II, which has a very low variance.

[10] reports in Table 10 at page 38 the memory occupation for creating the graph and the initial memory required by a search technique, so these figures does not seem directly comparable with the memory occupation per query execution

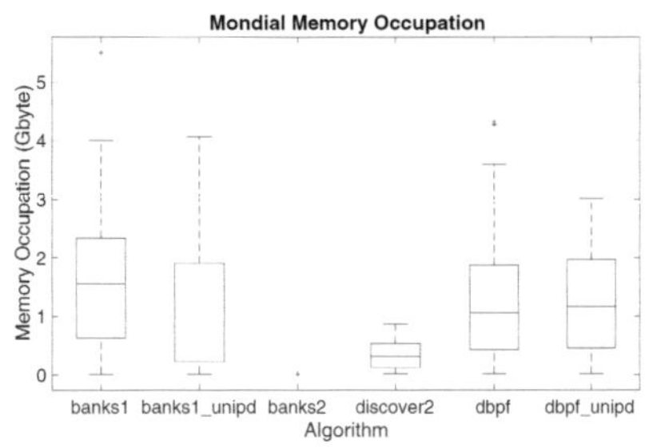

(a) Mondial memory occupation.

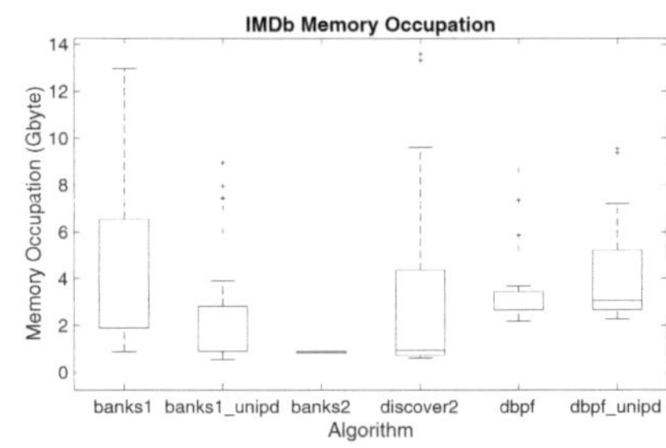

(b) IMDb memory occupation.

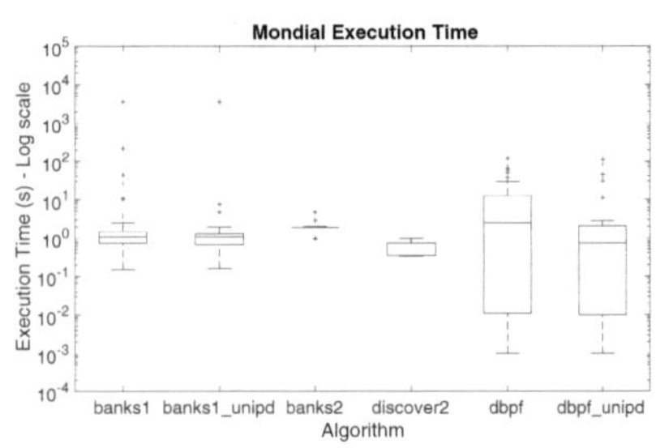

(c) Mondial execution time.

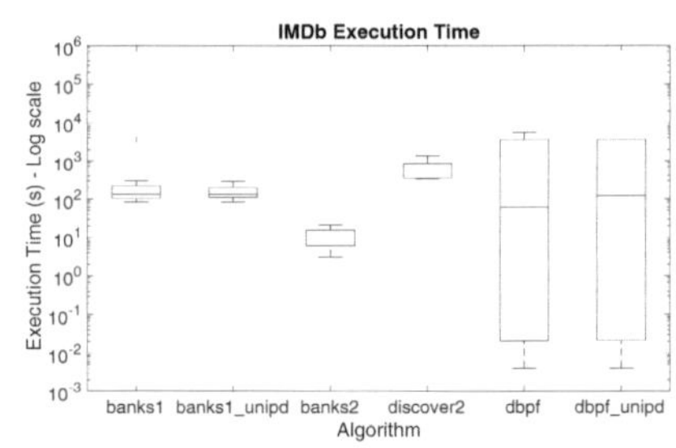

(d) IMDb execution time.

Algorithm	Mondial		IMDb	
	Memory (Gbyte)	Time (s)	Memory (Gbyte)	Time (s)
BANKS-I	1.597	93.939	4.602	576.835
BANKS-I UNIPD	1.174	86.865	2.630	149.971
BANKS-II	0.020	1.837	0.856	10.423
DISCOVER-II	0.358	0.482	2.976	653.302
DPBF	1.270	14.337	3.481	1,544.736
DPBF UNIPD	1.192	8.355	4.025	1,366.078

(e) Average memory occupation and execution time.

Fig. 1. Efficiency: memory occupation and execution time for running the queries.

we report in Figure 1. However, we may try some very qualitative observation: [10] reports, in the case of Mondial, a memory occupation in the range of tens of megabytes while Figure 1(a) shows a memory occupation in the range of gigabytes, except for BANKS-II and DISCOVER-II; in the case of IMDb, both [10] and Figure 1(b) report a memory occupation in the range of gigabytes, except for BANKS-II in our case. As discussed in Section 2, most of the papers lack any details on the actual data structures to be used and this leads to the differences we observed above.

Time-wise, on Mondial DISCOVER-II is the fastest algorithm followed by BANKS-II, the DPBF variants, and, finally, the BANKS-I variants; on IMDb, BANKS-II is the fastest algorithm, followed by the BANKS-I variants, DISCOVER-II, and DPBF. Figure 1(c) and 1(d) show how, in general, there is less variance in the execution times than in memory occupation, even if DPBF exhibit the largest spread of performance and BANKS-I suffers from several high outliers in the case of Mondial. We can note how the UNIPD variant of BANKS-I improves around 8% and 75% on Mondial and IMDb, respectively; this indicates that the optimization on the length of the paths is most effective with larger amounts of data, as in the case of IMDb, when we also save about 40% in memory occupation. The UNIPD variant of DPBF performs similarly on IMDb but it saves about 42% of execution time on Mondial; this indicates that the optimization in the merging steps is most effective for more complex schemas, as expected.

Since we used a different hardware than [10], execution times are not directly comparable in a quantitative way, even if it is possible to discuss trends in a qualitative manner. Tables 8(a) and 8(b) at page 37 of [10] report the mean execution times for Mondial and IMDb, respectively. In the Mondial case, according to [10], DISCOVER-II is the fastest algorithm, followed by DPBF, BANKS-II, and BANKS-I; we also note that [10] reports execution times one/two orders of magnitude bigger than ours. In the case of IMDb, according to [10], DISCOVER-II is the fastest algorithm, followed by BANKS-I, DPBF, and BANKS-II; in this case [10] reports execution times 2-3 times bigger than ours. Overall, there is some agreement in the ranking of algorithms on Mondial but there is quite disagreement in the case of IMDb. As in the case of the memory occupation, we think all these differences in the execution times are due to quite different choices at implementation level.

4.2 Effectiveness

Figure 2 shows the effectiveness of different algorithms under examination in terms of AP and P@10: each sub-figure reports a boxplot computed over the different queries while Figure 2(e) reports the mean performances for AP and P@10 on each collection. Note that, since by construction of the dataset many queries have just one relevant result, in many cases it is not possible to have P@10 bigger than 0.10.

In the case of AP, on Mondial the BANKS-I variants are the top performing algorithms, followed by the DPBF versions, BANKS-II, and DISCOVER-II. In particular, the UNIPD variants of both BANKS-I and DPBF outperform the original versions and BANKS-I UNIPD is the top performer. On IMDb, the BANKS-I versions are the top performing algorithms, followed by BANKS-II, DPBF, and DISCOVER-II; in this case the UNIPD variants perform very similarly to the original algorithms. So we can deduce, that the UNIPD variants of BANKS-I and DPBF provide benefits in terms of memory occupation and/or execution time, as shown in Figure 2, and they keep or even improve the effectiveness in terms of AP.

The boxplots of Figures 2(a) and 2(b) indicate quite a lot of variance in the performances and, especially, distributions skewed towards 1.0 AP. This is a very different behaviour with respect to the one typically observed in IR evaluation and it might be more an indicator of overfitting and/or design issues in the dataset rather than high performances of these algorithms.

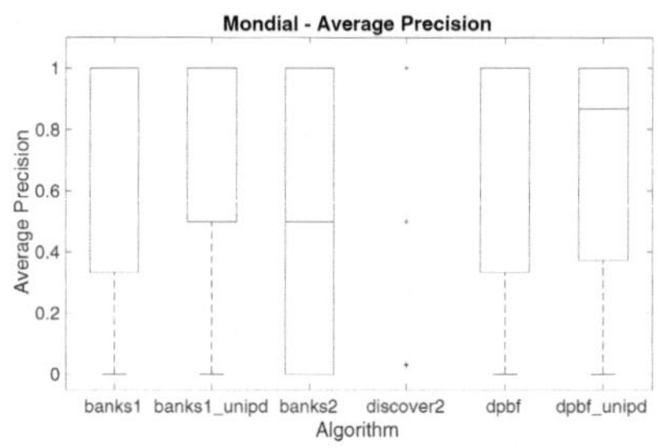

(a) Mondial AP.

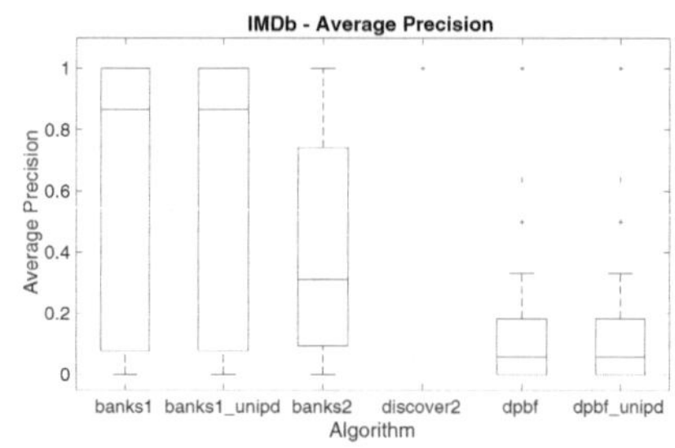

(b) IMDb AP.

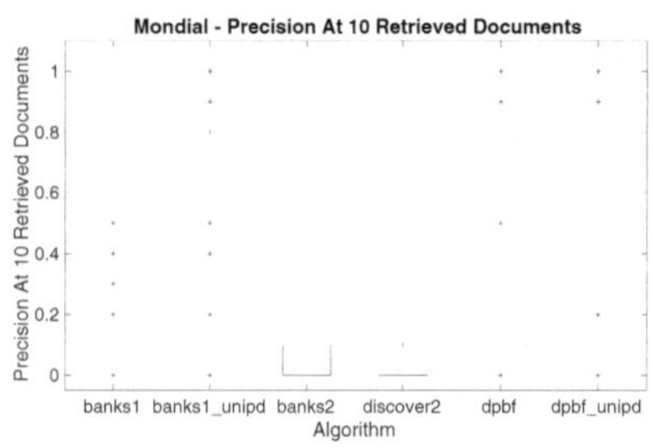

(c) Mondial P@10.

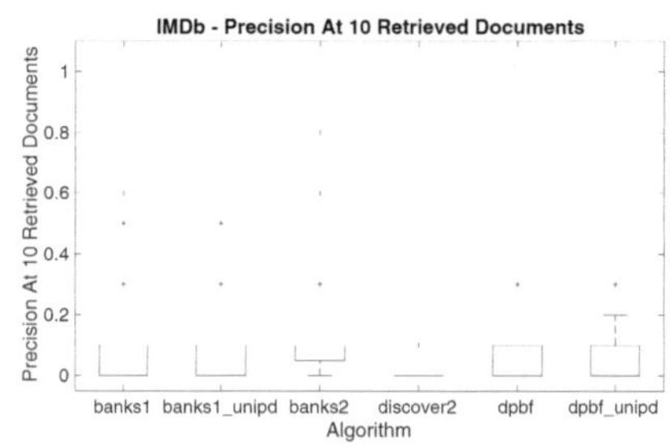

(d) IMDb P@10.

Algorithm	Mondial		IMDb	
	MAP	Mean P@10	MAP	Mean P@10
BANKS-I	0.7166	0.1214	0.6245	0.1313
BANKS-I UNIPD	0.7553	0.2000	0.6240	0.1281
BANKS-II	0.5220	0.0667	0.4100	0.1375
DISCOVER-II	0.0498	0.0143	0.0312	0.0031
DPBF	0.6575	0.2167	0.1393	0.0500
DPBF UNIPD	0.6699	0.2381	0.1376	0.0469

(e) Mean performances for Mondial and IMDb.

Fig. 2. Efficiency: precision at 10 retrieved documents and average precision.

If we compare Figures 2(a) and 2(b) with Figure 7 at page 40 of [10], we can observe several differences. On Mondial, [10] identifies DPBF as the top algorithm, followed by BANKS-II, DISCOVER-II, and BANKS-I; on IMDb, [10] ranks the algorithms as BANKS-I, DISCOVER-II, DPBF, and no results for BANKS-II. These trends are quite different from those emerging in our experiments. For example, if we look at mean performance of BANKS-I, on Mondial [10] roughly[7] reports 38% of MAP while we have around 71% and, on IMDb, 20% against 62% in our case; we can find similar discrepancies in the case of the other algorithms.

[7] There are no tables in [10] with precise values for MAP and P@10 and we have to "deduce" them from the histograms in their figures.

We think that the cause of these differences is two-fold. Firstly, we used only the topics where all the algorithms retrieved at least one result while [10] does not specify how topics without results are considered and averaged. Secondly, the difficulty in reproducing the results of [10] indicates that the issues we encountered in implementing the various algorithms have led to implementations that are non-identical to those of [10]. However, these differences may be due to our own choices to address the lack of details previously pointed out but also the implementations of [10] may be based on choices and assumptions not explicitly reported which made them different from the original algorithms; so, overall, it is not easy to determine which is the closer implementation of the original algorithms, also because those of [10] are not available online as open source.

When it comes to P@10, on Mondial, the DPBF versions are the top algorithm, followed by the BANKS-I versions, BANKS-II, and DISCOVER-II; also in this case, the UNIPD variants of both BANKS-I and DPBF improve with respect to their original versions and DPBF UNIPD is the top performer. On IMDb, BANKS-II is the top performer, followed by the BANKS-I versions, the DPBF versions, and DISCOVER-II; also in this case the UNIPD variants perform very similarly to the original algorithms.

Also in the case of P@10, if we compare our results with those of [10], we can find several differences and it is hard to reproduce the same results.

5 Discussion and Future Work

In this paper, we have tried to reproduce several state-of-the-art algorithms for keyword-based search over relational databases and compare our results with those of [10], which represents one of the most comprehensive studies so far.

As discussed in Section 2, we found that, in general, the papers describing these algorithms lack many details on both the exact data structures to be used and some specific steps of each algorithm. This lack of details is also confirmed by the diversity of choices made by the student groups, which worked independently: for example, even if they all had to represent a graph, they all adopted a different approach to this problem.

As discussed in Section 4, we obtained experimental results different from those of [10] in terms of both efficiency and effectiveness. So, we discovered that it is extremely hard to reproduce these experiments.

It could be argued that keyword-based search over relational databases is a research topic and master students may be not experienced enough yet to properly deal with it, leading to implementations with bugs or misinterpretations of an algorithm. Our implementation will certainly contain bugs and/or errors, nevertheless a striking question arises: how difficult should be to re-implement keyword-based search over relational databases algorithms? Our master students attended courses on algorithms and data structures, advanced algorithms, databases and, about half of them, information retrieval; so you can guess that they have quite a good mix of competencies to study and implement algorithms whose core is basically navigation in graphs. The fact that they found so difficult, if not impossible, to reproduce the results suggests that these algorithms are not explained clearly enough and that the barrier to just start working on this topic is very high. Think about a PhD student: how long she/he should take to just get started on the topic? Would one year (or more) be a reasonable amount of time?

Overall, this experience further stresses the issues we discussed in the introduction: keyword-based search over relational databases completely lacks a reference architecture and, as a consequence, also a reference implementation of state-of-the-art algorithms. If these algorithms turn out to be so difficult to implement from scratch, it becomes even more compelling to have reference implementations available, where all the possible care and expertise have been put in correctly implementing them.

Therefore, this work represents a first step towards shared and common implementations of such algorithms. Indeed, notwithstanding all the limitations that a student project may have, we implemented several algorithms which are online available[8] under a very liberal open source license, and everyone is now free to start from, correct, improve and compare against these implementations.

Our future works concerns revising and consolidating all these independent implementations into a single an coherent framework to begin providing a "reference" implementation of keyword-based search algorithms.

References

1. D. Abadi, R. Agrawal, A. Ailamaki, M. Balazinska, P. A. Bernstein, M. J. Carey, S. Chaudhuri, J. Dean, A. Doan, M. J. Franklin, J. Gehrke, L. M. Haas, A. Y. Halevy, J. M. Hellerstein, Y. E. Ioannidis, H. V. Jagadish, D. Kossmann, S. Madden, S. Mehrotra, T. Milo, J. F. Naughton, R. Ramakrishnan, V. Markl, C. Olston, B. C. Ooi, C. Rè, D. Suciu, M. Stonebraker, T. Walter, and J. Widom. The Beckman Report on Database Research. *SIGMOD Record*, 43(3):61–70, 2014.
2. A. Badan, L. Benvegnù, M. Biasetton, G. Bonato, A. Brighente, A. Cenzato, P. Ceron, G. Cogato, S. Marchesin, A. Minetto, L. Pellegrina, A. Purpura, R. Simionato, N. Soleti, M. Tessarotto, A. Tonon, F. Vendramin, and N. Ferro. Towards open-source shared implementations of keyword-based access systems to relational data. In *Proc. 1st International Workshop on Keyword-Based Access and Ranking at Scale (KARS 2017) – Proc. of the Workshops of the EDBT/ICDT 2017 Joint Conference (EDBT/ICDT 2017)*. CEUR Workshop Proceedings (CEUR-WS.org), ISSN 1613-0073, `http://ceur-ws.org/Vol-1810/`, 2017.
3. S. Bergamaschi, N. Ferro, F. Guerra, and G. Silvello. Keyword-based Search over Databases: A Roadmap for a Reference Architecture Paired with an Evaluation Framework. *LNCS Transactions on Computational Collective Intelligence (TCCI)*, 9630:1–20, 2016.
4. M. K. Bergman. The Deep Web: Surfacing Hidden Value. *The Journal of Electronic Publishing*, 7(1), August 2001.
5. G. Bhalotia, A. Hulgeri, C. Nakhe, S. Chakrabarti, and S. Sudarshan. Keyword Searching and Browsing in Databases using BANKS. In *Proc. 18th International*

[8] `https://bitbucket.org/ks-bd-2015-2016/ks-unipd`

Conference on Data Engineering (ICDE 2002), pages 431–440. IEEE Computer Society, Los Alamitos, CA, USA, 2002.
6. M. Bron, K. Balog, and M. de Rijke. Example Based Entity Search in the Web of Data. In *Advances in Information Retrieval. Proc. 35th European Conference on IR Research (ECIR 2013)*, pages 392–403. Lecture Notes in Computer Science (LNCS) 7814, Springer, Heidelberg, Germany, 2013.
7. M. J. Cafarella, A. Halevy, and J. Madhavan. Structured Data on the Web. *Communications of the ACM (CACM)*, 54(2):933–947, February 2011.
8. M. J. Cafarella, A. Halevy, D. Z. Wang, E. Wu, and Y. Zhang. WebTables: Exploring the power of tables on the Web. *Proceedings of the VLDB Endowment (PVLDB)*, 1:538–549, 2008.
9. C. W. Cleverdon. The Cranfield Tests on Index Languages Devices. *Aslib Proceedings*, 19(6):173–194, 1967.
10. J. Coffman and A. C. Weaver. An Empirical Performance Evaluation of Relational Keyword Search Techniques. *IEEE Transactions on Knowledge and Data Engineering (TKDE)*, 1(26):30–42, 2014.
11. B. Ding, J. Xu Yu, S. Wang, L. Qin, X. Zhang, and X. Lin. Finding Top-k Min-Cost Connected Trees in Databases. In *Proc. 23rd International Conference on Data Engineering (ICDE 2007)*, pages 836–845. IEEE Computer Society, Los Alamitos, CA, USA, 2007.
12. H. Elmeleegy, J. Madhavan, and A. Halevy. Harvesting Relational Tables from Lists on the Web. *Proceedings of the VLDB Endowment (PVLDB)*, 2:1078–1089, 2009.
13. N. Ferro. Reproducibility Challenges in Information Retrieval Evaluation. *ACM Journal of Data and Information Quality (JDIQ)*, 8(2):8:1–8:4, February 2017.
14. N. Ferro, N. Fuhr, K. Järvelin, N. Kando, M. Lippold, and J. Zobel. Increasing Reproducibility in IR: Findings from the Dagstuhl Seminar on "Reproducibility of Data-Oriented Experiments in e-Science". *SIGIR Forum*, 50(1):68–82, June 2016.
15. N. Ferro and G. Silvello. The Road Towards Reproducibility in Science: The Case of Data Citation. In *Proc. 13th Italian Research Conference on Digital Libraries (IRCDL 2017)*. Communications in Computer and Information Science (CCIS), Springer, Heidelberg, Germany, 2017.
16. V. Hristidis, L. Gravano, and Y. Papakonstantinou. Efficient IR-Style Keyword Search over Relational Databases. In *Proc. 29th International Conference on Very Large Data Bases (VLDB 2003)*, pages 850–861. Morgan Kaufmann Publisher, Inc., San Francisco, CA, USA, 2003.
17. V. Kacholia, S. Pandit, S. Chakrabarti, S. Sudarshan, R. Desai, and H. Karambelkar. Bidirectional Expansion For Keyword Search on Graph Databases. In *Proc. 31st International Conference on Very Large Data Bases (VLDB 2005)*, pages 505–516. ACM Press, New York, USA, 2004.
18. H. Wang and C. C. Aggarwal. A Survey of Algorithms for Keyword Search on Graph Data. In *Managing and Mining Graph Data*, pages 249–273. Springer-Verlag, New York, USA, 2010.
19. A. Wright. Searching the Deep Web. *Communications of the ACM (CACM)*, 51(10):14–15, October 2008.
20. W. Wu. Proactive Natural Language Search Engine: Tapping into Structured Data on the Web. In *16th International Conference on Extending Database Technology (EDBT 2013)*, pages 143–148. Academic Press, New York, USA, 2013.
21. J. X. Yu, L. Qin, and L. Chang. *Keyword Search in Databases.* Morgan & Claypool Publishers, USA, 2010.

A Model for Handling Multiple Social Networks and its Implementation (discussion paper*)

Francesco Buccafurri, Gianluca Lax, Serena Nicolazzo, and Antonino Nocera

DIIES, University Mediterranea of Reggio Calabria
Via Graziella, Località Feo di Vito
89122 Reggio Calabria, Italy
E-mail:{bucca,lax,s.nicolazzo,a.nocera}@unirc.it

Abstract. Nowadays, users join several on-line social networks (OSNs) so that design and development applications able to work on multiple OSNs is a challenging issue. However, OSNs present relevant differences from both the adopted terminology (similar concepts have different names) and the supported technology (for example, in the APIs provided for data extraction). Consequently, the heterogeneity of OSNs does not allow the design of applications with suitable abstraction with respect to the specific OSNs processed. In this paper, we define a model aimed at generalizing concepts, actions and relationships of existing social networks, which can be exploited as a middleware to implement applications working on multiple social networks.

Keywords Multiple Social Networks, Facebook, Twitter, API.

1 Introduction

Over the past decade, online social networks have became part of people's live. Nowadays, most people have a profile in one or more online social networks like `Facebook`, `Twitter`, `Linkedin`, `MySpace`, in which they spend a lot of time. This is recognized as an important phenomenon from a social and economic point of view, and, thus, in design and development processes of (Web) applications. Indeed, often applications should be based on behaviors of a community, or take advantage from these, so that modern Web applications should be social by default. In many cases, both personal information and social interactions coming from social network profiles can be part of innovative solutions. Among these, social Web applications are the most significant example, in which both people's identities and contents they produced are involved in the business process and data are mostly owned by users, strongly interlinked and inherently polymorphic

* This is a short version of the paper titled "A model to support design and development of multiple-social-network applications" [3], which appears in Information Science journal.

[1]. Indeed, despite the conceptual uniformity of the social-network universe, in terms of structure, basic mechanisms, main features, etc., each social network has in practice its own terms, resources, actions: for example, connected people in Facebook are *friends*, whereas they are *followers* or *followings* in Twitter. Consequently, there is the need of delaying the binding between abstract concepts and concrete API calls, when applications operate across multiple social networks: the abstract request of finding connected people is implemented differently in Facebook and Twitter (this argument is discussed in Section 2). This is a strong handicap for the design and implementation of applications enabling internetworking functions among multiple social networks, and, then, for the achievement of the above goal. As a matter of fact, little exists in terms of models and languages to support social-network-based programming in large, according to software engineering principles of genericity and polymorphism.

On the other hand, the power of the social-network substrate can be fully exploited only if we move from a single-social-network to a multiple-social-network perspective, still keeping the user-centered vision, so that the above issue becomes crucial. The recent literature has highlighted that the aforementioned multiple-social-network perspective opens a lot of new problems in terms of analysis [12] but also new opportunities from the application point of view [14, 8, 15, 18]. Even though each single social network is an extraordinary source of knowledge, the information power of the social-network Web can be considerable increased if we see it as a huge global social network, composed of autonomous components with strong correlation and interaction. Thus, social-network-based programming should work at this abstraction level.

In this paper, we do an important step to cover the gap highlighted above, by defining and implementing a model aimed at generalizing concepts, actions and relationships of existing social networks. This paper is organized as follows. Section 2 introduces the characteristics of the multiple-social-network scenario that we model. We give a formal definition of the graph-based conceptual model in Section 3. To validate our approach, in Section 4, we show how our model has been profitably applied to two very relevant applications in the context of social network analysis. Finally, our conclusions are summarized in Section 5.

2 Design specification

One of the motivation of this study is the strong heterogeneity in the representation of concepts among different social networks. For instance, contacts are represented by *friends* in Facebook and the relationship is symmetric, while they are represented by *followers* and *followings* in Twitter and the corresponding relationship is not symmetric. Again, the concept of appreciation becomes *+1* in Google+ and *endorsement* in about.me. Importantly, similar concepts can mapped to each other but they have in general different features. Thus, an integration step is necessary for our purpose. In this section, we prepare this integration step by grouping the main technical entities into a number of categories to which the formal model presented in the next section maps. In particular, we aim at modeling the following entities.

Profile. Social network sites are built around user profiles, a form of individual (or group) homepage, which provides a description of each registered user. For example, in `Twitter`, at the moment of registration, a user can create his profile typing his name, username, password and email address in the registration form. After, he can upload a profile picture and start following other people. Moreover he can complete his profile adding a short biography, a position (the place where he lives) and a link to his website or to one of his accounts on other social networks. Another social network, `about.me`, is characterized by its one-page user profiles, each with a large background image and short biography. At the moment of registration a user has to fill the suitable form with his username, email, password for the site and at a second step short biography, a short description, a profile image and a background image.

Links to external social networks. An important feature provided by all the social networks considered in this paper is the possibility for a user to add in his profile a link toward one of his accounts in another social site or external website. This feature is typically enabled during the creation of the user profile. It is of particular interest in this paper because it encodes the basic information allowing the possibility of seeing different social sites as members of a Multiple-Social-Network environment.

Friendship. After creating a profile, participants are asked to invite their friends to the site or to look at others' profiles and add those people to their list of friends. In `Twitter`, a user can follow another user, becoming his *follower.* Only if this user follows him back the relationship is bidirectional. Differently from `Twitter`, `Facebook` requires approval for two people to be linked as friends. When someone links another as a friend, the recipient receives a message asking for confirmation. Indeed, `Facebook` friendship is bidirectional, hence, once a user accepts a friendship request of another user they become mutual friends.

Resources. A Social network resource is a Web asset such as a status update, a photo, a web link or a video created and loaded by a user in his profile. As for `LinkedIn`, a user can add a resource like a new item or a new file in his profile. He can also embed a comment, a photo, a web link or a video in a new status update. Also skills representing specific technical expertise can be seen as a typology of resource, which are posted by users to describe their ability. This way, his *connections* can like it, comment it and share it on their "wall".

Actions on resources. So far, we stated that in addition to the content that members add when they create their own profiles, social network sites typically provide the possibility to share resources. After a resource is published by a user, several actions can be performed on this resource: other users can appreciate it, or re-share it, or it can be associated with a user through a mention on his profile. Hereafter, we list the main actions a user can do on a resource according to the different social networks analyzed in this paper.

Once a user write a *tweet* in `Twitter`, it will appear on the homepage of all his followers, who can *reply* to it, make it one of their *favourites* or *retweet* it (that is, forwarding it again on their own timeline). A *tweet* can contain also a user *mention*. It can be done using the symbol `@` followed by the referenced username. To categorize *tweets* by keyword, people use the hashtag symbol `#` before a relevant keyword or phrase (no spaces) in their *tweets*.

Clicking on *like* option on `LinkedIn` presents some differences w.r.t. the `Facebook` *like* function. Indeed, on `LinkedIn`, when users click on the *like* link underneath the various updates, this immediately forwards that particular update out to all of the user first level *connections*. The *share* option, instead, allows users to either redistribute the article (and partially modify it) as an update to their *connections*, post it to a group (or multiple groups), or forward it in a private message. Similarly to what happens in `Twitter`, also in `LinkedIn` while a user publishes a resource he can mention one of his *connections* with the `@` symbol. He can also use a keyword as hashtag using the `#` symbol.

As for `Flickr`, by clicking on a photostream image, it is possible to open it in the interactive *photopage*, thus allowing users to comment it and to embed it on external websites. Moreover, images can be added to a user favourite list or to user galleries. The main `Google+` page consists of a "stream" of updates, conversations and shared content. A user can make comments underneath content shared by other users, and he can appreciate contents clicking "+1" on it. `Google+` provides the referencing functionality in its posts. A user can mention another user using the `+` or `@` signs.

As for `LiveJournal`, users can interact with resources in different ways. For instance, a user can leave a comment on a post of another user or share it in his blog. He can also add to "Memories" a post. The Memories feature on `LiveJournal` allows the organization of favorite resources with a keyword-based archive system. Thanks to this functionality, a user can also add tags, or descriptive keywords, to his own resources.

All the features of the OSNs described in this section are mapped by our model, and this is formalized in the next section.

3 The conceptual model

To model at an abstract level the entities described in the previous section, we use a graph. The set of nodes is partitioned into three disjoint sets P, R, and B, which correspond to the set of social profiles, the set of resources, and the set of bundles (which are resource containers), respectively.

An element of P models the *profile* of a user on a social network. It consists in the tuple ⟨`url, socialNetwork, screen-name, [personalInformation], [picture]`⟩, where `url` is the Web address that identifies and localizes the profile, and `socialNetwork` is the commercial name of the social network which the profile belongs to, `screen-name` is the name chosen by the user who registered the profile to appear in the home-page of the profile or when posting a resource, and, finally, `personalInformation` and `picture` are the information and the image which the user inserted as related to the profile. The two last elements of the tuple are optional (i.e., they can be null).

The set R models *resources* of the Web or created by users. A resource is represented by a tuple $\langle$`url, type, [description], [date]`$\rangle$, where `url` is the Web address to access the resource, `type` indicates the type of the resource content, and finally, `description` and `date`, which are optional, represent the string, inserted by the who published the resource, describing the resource itself and the publishing date, respectively. For example, the most viewed video on YouTube is a resource represented as $\langle$`'https://www.youtube.com/watch?v=9bZkp7q19f0', 'video/mp4', 'PSY - GANGNAM STYLE', '07/15/2012'`$\rangle$.

Our model includes the *bundle* set B. Indeed, commonly users do not handle a single resource, but most of the actions they do (e.g., publishing or sharing) involve more resources simultaneously. For example, a user can publish more photos or videos, can include a comment, and so on. In our model, we include all resources handled simultaneously by a user in a bundle. A bundle is represented by a tuple $\langle$`uri, [description], [date]`$\rangle$, where `uri` is the identifier of the bundle, `description`, which is optional, is the string chosen by the user to be shown with those resources and, finally, `date` represents the publishing date. As we will see next, we represent the inclusion of a resource into a bundle by means of *containing* edges.

In our model, relationships among profiles, resources and bundles are represented by direct edges of a graph. The set E of these edges is partitioned into 8 disjoint sets, named F, M, Pu, S, T, Re, L, and Co.

The *follow* edge set $F \subseteq E = \{p_s, p_t \mid p_s, p_t \in P\}$ models the fact that in the (source) profile p_s, it has been declared a certain type of relationship towards the (target) profile p_t. This kind of edge models different relationships. For example, on `Facebook` or `Flickr`, it models friendships, on `LinkedIn`, job contacts, and, on `Twitter`, *followers*. Observe that, typically, this kind of relationship occurs between users of the same social network, because it is presumable that a social network does not have interest in promoting links to profiles of another (competitor) social network.

The *me* edge set $M \subseteq E = \{p_s, p_t \mid p_s, p_t \in P\}$ denotes that the user with profile p_s has declared in this profile to have a second profile p_t. This edge allows a user to provide a link to its profile (typically) on a different social network or (sometimes) on the same social network (as a sort of alias).

The *publishing* edge set $Pu \subseteq E = \{p_s, b_t \mid p_s \in P, b_t \in B\}$ indicates that the user with profile p_s has published in this profile a bundle b_t. This edge models one of the typical actions a user does when enriches his/her profile by publishing resources.

The *shared* edge set $S \subseteq E = \{b_s, b_t \mid b_s, b_t \in B\}$ specifies that the bundle b_s (published by a user) is derived from an already published bundle b_t. This type of edge is used when a user shares an existing bundle. Indeed, this action is represented by two edges: a publishing edge (as described before) and a shared edge from the new bundle to the existing one.

The *tagging* edge set $T \subseteq E = \{p_s, br_t, w \mid p_s \in P, br_t \in B \cup R$ and w is a word$\}$, denotes that the user with profile p_s assigned the word w to describe a bundle or a resource br. By means of the tag mechanism, users contribute to resource labelling, which is necessary to carry out several actions on resources, such as searching or classification.

The *referencing* edge set $Re \subseteq E = \{b_s, p_t \mid b_s \in B, p_t \in P\}$ models the fact that a bundle b_s includes a reference to the profile p_t. For example, this occurs when a *tweet* includes a user account name.

The *like* edge set $L \subseteq E = \{p_s, pbr_t \mid p_s \in P, pbr_t \in B \cup R \cup P\}$ describes the information that a user with the profile p_s expressed a preference/appreciation for a bundle, a resource or another user profile pbr_t.

The *containing* edge set $Co \subseteq E = \{b_s, r_t \mid b_s \in B, r_t \in R\}$ indicates that a bundle b_s contains the resource r_t. For example, when a user publishes a photo p and includes a comment c, this action is modeled by creating a bundle b with a description c, a resource p, and finally, a *containing* edge from b to p.

Concerning how to practically map real-life data from social networks to each component of the model, the reader can refer to [3]. In the next section, we show how this model has been exploited at application level.

4 Case studies

Evaluating the accuracy of a model is a difficult task because often a golden standard misses [2]. In these cases, evaluation can be done by humans (e.g., [13, 11]) or by applying the model to an application and evaluating the results (e.g., [16]). In this section, following the latter approach, we describe how our model has been profitably applied to two applications very relevant in the context of social network analysis.

The first application we discuss regards the extraction of information from a multiple-social-network scenario. It is well known that any analysis activity on social network users needs a preliminary task implementing the extraction of data from social networks. In the past, several visit strategies have been adopted, such as Breadth First Search [19], Random Walk [10] or Metropolis- Hastings Random Walk [17]. In all these cases, data analysis focused on a single social network and data extraction was a quite simple task because there was not the problem of receiving data from different sources.

When data extraction involves different social networks, having a model that is able to handle indifferently data from different social networks is a very useful tool. In this case, it is possible to exploit a crawling task implementing the following steps.

1. Selecting the starting account (seed). This step is very important to provide data useful to the specified application. Usually, the starting account is randomly selected from an available pool of accounts. For particular analysis, the seed can be selected from those accounts having some characteristics, for example, being a power user (i.e., they have a number of contacts much higher than the average user [9]).
2. Building the sub-graph. In this step, the information about this account is created: it includes the user account, contacts, published resources, and so

on. This step is strongly facilitated by our model. Indeed, by following the procedures described in Section **??**, we map all information extracted from the different social networks to the components of our model (i.e., profiles, resources, bundles, and their relationships).
3. Selecting the next account. There exist several strategies to implement this step. A first possibility is to randomly select another profile (uniform sampling), and this is feasible whenever a social network uses an identifier for accounts and the domain of identifiers is known and limited. This occurs for example for Facebook and Twitter [7]. Another possibility consists in selecting one profile (i.e., a node of the graph) connected with the last visited profile by a *follow* edge or a *me* edge (see, for example, [10, 17]). Again, it is also possible to select more than one (even all) of the profiles referred above, as done for example in [4, 19]. Once one or more profiles have been selected, Steps 2 and 3 are iterated until the desired amount of data have been extracted or a stop condition has been reached.

The model defined here has been successfully used in the SNAKE system [6], a tool supporting the extraction of data from social network accounts.

The second application that benefited from our model concerns the problem of identifying users on the Web. A common approach to address this problem utilizes profile matching techniques typically based on a set of identification properties, such as username, to find user corresponding identity. In [5], an improvement of this approach is proposed. In particular, a new notion of profile similarity is defined, by combining a string similarity between the associated usernames with a contribution based on a suitable recursive notion of common-neighbor similarity. The computation of the second contribution requires to compare profiles coming from different social networks, which could be quite heterogeneous. The use of our model allowed us to simplify this issue and to handle all profiles in a uniform way. We can state that the success of the technique described in [5] strongly relied on the model described in this paper.

5 Conclusion

It is a matter of fact that the multiplicity of social networks together with users' membership overlap, result in a multiplicative effect in terms of information power. Indeed, correlation, integration, negotiation of information coming from different social networks offer a lot of strategic knowledge whose benefits are still unexplored. In this paper, we have defined and implemented a model aimed at creating a middleware on top of existing online social networks. The goal is to provide a (conceptual) layer able to facilitate design and implementation of applications relying on the internetworking nature of online social networks. By means of two case studies, we showed the effectiveness of the proposed model.

References

1. G. Bell. *Building social web applications.* "O'Reilly Media, Inc.", 2009.

2. J. Brank, M. Grobelnik, and D. Mladenić. A survey of ontology evaluation techniques. In *In Proceedings of the Conference on Data Mining and Data Warehouses (SiKDD 2005)*, 2005.
3. F. Buccafurri, G. Lax, S. Nicolazzo, and A. Nocera. A model to support design and development of multiple-social-network applications. *Information Sciences*, 331:99–119, 2016.
4. F. Buccafurri, G. Lax, A. Nocera, and D. Ursino. Moving from social networks to social internetworking scenarios: The crawling perspective. *Information Sciences*, 256:126–137, 2014. Elsevier.
5. F. Buccafurri, G. Lax, A. Nocera, and D. Ursino. Discovering missing me edges across social networks. *Information Sciences*, 319:18–37, 2015.
6. F. Buccafurri, G. Lax, A. Nocera, and D. Ursino. A system for extracting structural information from social network accounts. *Software: Practice and Experience*, 2015. DOI: 10.1002/spe.2280.
7. M. Gjoka, M. Kurant, C. Butts, and A. Markopoulou. Walking in Facebook: A case study of unbiased sampling of OSNs. In *Proc. of the International Conference on Computer Communications (INFOCOM'10)*, pages 1–9, San Diego, CA, USA, 2010. IEEE.
8. M. N. Jelassi, C. Largeron, and S. B. Yahia. Efficient unveiling of multi-members in a social network. *Journal of Systems and Software*, 94:30–38, 2014.
9. S.-H. Lim, S.-W. Kim, S. Park, and J. H. Lee. Determining content power users in a blog network: an approach and its applications. *Systems, Man and Cybernetics, Part A: Systems and Humans, IEEE Transactions on*, 41(5):853–862, 2011.
10. L. Lovász. Random walks on graphs: A survey. *Combinatorics, Paul Erdos is Eighty*, 2(1):1–46, 1993.
11. A. Lozano-Tello and A. Gómez-Pérez. Ontometric: A method to choose the appropriate ontology. *Journal of Database Management*, 2(15):1–18, 2004.
12. V. S. A. Menezes, G. Zimbrão, and J. M. Souza. Group and link analysis of multi-relational scientific social networks. *Journal of Systems and Software*, 86(7):1819–1830, 2013.
13. P. Mika. Ontologies are us: A unified model of social networks and semantics. In *The Semantic Web–ISWC 2005*, pages 522–536. Springer, 2005.
14. D. T. Nguyen, H. Zhang, S. Das, M. T. Thai, and T. N. Dinh. Least cost influence in multiplex social networks: Model representation and analysis. In *Data Mining (ICDM), 2013 IEEE 13th International Conference on*, pages 567–576. IEEE, 2013.
15. A. Papadimitriou, P. Symeonidis, and Y. Manolopoulos. Fast and accurate link prediction in social networking systems. *Journal of Systems and Software*, 85(9):2119–2132, 2012.
16. R. Porzel and R. Malaka. A task-based approach for ontology evaluation. In *ECAI Workshop on Ontology Learning and Population, Valencia, Spain*, 2004.
17. D. Stutzback, R. Rejaie, N. Duffield, S. Sen, and W. Willinger. On unbiased sampling for unstructured peer-to-peer networks. In *Proc. of the International Conference on Internet Measurements*, pages 27–40, Rio De Janeiro, Brasil, 2006. ACM.
18. Z. Sun, L. Han, W. Huang, X. Wang, X. Zeng, M. Wang, and H. Yan. Recommender systems based on social networks. *Journal of Systems and Software*, 99:109–119, 2015.
19. S. Ye, J. Lang, and F. Wu. Crawling online social graphs. In *Proc. of the International Asia-Pacific Web Conference (APWeb'10)*, pages 236–242, Busan, Korea, 2010. IEEE.

Decomposing and Pruning Primary Key Violations from Large Data Sets*
(discussion paper)

Marco Manna, Francesco Ricca, and Giorgio Terracina

DeMaCS, University of Calabria, Italy
{manna,ricca,terracina}@mat.unical.it

Abstract. The problem of computing the certain answer to a conjunctive query over a relational instance subject to primary key constraints is a classical hard problem in database research. On the theoretical side, we present a decomposition and pruning strategy that reduces, in polynomial time, the original problem to a collection of smaller problems of the same sort that can be solved independently. From a practical perspective, we discuss an experiment on large data sets that shows the effectiveness of the overall technique and its implementation in ASP.

1 Introduction

Integrity constraints provide means for ensuring that database evolution does not result in a loss of consistency or in a discrepancy with the intended model of the application domain. A relational database that do not satisfy some of these constraints is said to be inconsistent. In practice it is not unusual that one has to deal with inconsistent data [5], and when a conjunctive query (CQ) is posed to an inconsistent database, a natural problem arises that can be formulated as: *How to deal with inconsistencies to answer the input query in a consistent way?* This is a classical problem in database research and different approaches have been proposed in the literature. One possibility is to clean the database [7] and work on one of the possible coherent states; another possibility is to be tolerant of inconsistencies by leaving intact the database and computing answers that are "consistent with the integrity constraints" [2].

In this paper, we adopt the second approach – which has been proposed by [2] under the name of *consistent query answering* (CQA) – and focus on the relevant class of *primary key* constraints. Formally, in our setting: (1) a database D is *inconsistent* if there are at least two tuples of the same relation that agree on their primary key; (2) a *repair* of D is any maximal consistent subset of D; and (3) a tuple $\mathbf{t}$ of constants is in the *consistent answer* to a CQ q over D

* The paper —overviewing the results presented in [13]— has been partially supported by the Italian Ministry for Economic Development (MISE) under project "PIUCultura – Paradigmi Innovativi per l'Utilizzo della Cultura" (n. F/020016/01-02/X27), and under project "Smarter Solutions in the Big Data World (S2BDW)".

if and only if, for each repair R of D, tuple $\mathbf{t}$ is in the (classical) answer to q over R. Intuitively, the original database is (virtually) repaired by applying a minimal number of corrections (deletion of tuples with the same primary key), while the consistent answer collects the tuples that can be retrieved in every repaired instance.

CQA under primary keys is coNP-complete in data complexity [3], when both the relational schema and the query are considered fixed. Due to its complex nature, traditional RDBMs are inadequate to solve the problem alone via SQL without focusing on restricted classes of CQs [2, 8, 14, 15, 11]. Actually, in the unrestricted case, CQA has been traditionally dealt with logic programming [3, 4, 9, 12]. However, it has been argued [10] that the practical applicability of logic-based approaches is restricted to data sets of moderate size. Only recently, an approach based on Binary Integer Programming [10] has revealed good performances on large databases (featuring up to one million tuples per relation) with primary key violations.

In this paper, we show that logic programming can still be effectively used for computing consistent answers over large relational databases. We describe a decomposition strategy that reduces (in polynomial time) the computation of the consistent answer to a CQ over a database subject to primary key constraints into a collection of smaller problems of the same sort. At the core of the strategy is a cascade pruning mechanism that dramatically reduces the number of key violations that have to be handled to answer the query. Moreover, we implement the new strategy using Answer Set Programming (ASP) [6], and we prove empirically the effectiveness of our ASP-based approach on existing benchmarks from the database world. The experiment empirically demonstrate that our approach is efficient on large data sets, and can even perform better than state-of-the-art methods.

2 The Framework

We are given two disjoint countably infinite sets of *terms* denoted by $\mathbf{C}$ and $\mathbf{V}$ and called *constants* and *variables*, respectively. We denote by $\mathbf{X}$ sequences of variables $X_1, \ldots, X_n$, and by $\mathbf{t}$ sequences of terms $t_1, \ldots, t_n$. We also denote by $[n]$ the set $\{1, \ldots, n\}$, for any $n \geqslant 1$.

A (*relational*) *schema* is a triple $\langle \mathcal{R}, \alpha, \kappa \rangle$ where $\mathcal{R}$ is a finite set of *relation symbols* (or *predicates*), $\alpha : \mathcal{R} \rightarrow \mathbb{N}$ is a function associating an *arity* to each predicate, and $\kappa : \mathcal{R} \rightarrow 2^{\mathbb{N}}$ is a function that associates, to each $r \in \mathcal{R}$, a nonempty set of positions from $[\alpha(r)]$, which represents the *primary key* of r. Moreover, for each relation symbol $r \in \mathcal{R}$ and for each position $i \in [\alpha(r)]$, $r[i]$ denotes the i-th *attribute* of r. Throughout, let $\Sigma = \langle \mathcal{R}, \alpha, \kappa \rangle$ denote a relational schema. An *atom* (over Σ) is an expression of the form $r(t_1, \ldots, t_n)$, where $r \in \mathcal{R}$, and $n = \alpha(r)$. An atom is called a *fact* if all of its terms are constants of $\mathbf{C}$. Conjunctions of atoms are often identified with the sets of their atoms. For a set A of atoms, the variables occurring in A are denoted by $var(A)$. A *database* D (over Σ) is a finite set of facts over Σ. Given an atom $r(\mathbf{t}) \in D$, we denote by $\hat{\mathbf{t}}$ the sequence $\mathbf{t}|_{\kappa(r)}$. We say that D is *inconsistent* (w.r.t. Σ) if it contains two different atoms of the form $r(\mathbf{t}_1)$ and $r(\mathbf{t}_2)$ such that $\hat{\mathbf{t}}_1 = \hat{\mathbf{t}}_2$. Otherwise, it is *consistent*. A *repair* R of D (w.r.t. Σ) is any maximal consistent subset of D. The set of all the repairs of D is denoted by $rep(D, \Sigma)$. A *substitution* is a mapping $\mu : \mathbf{C} \cup \mathbf{V} \rightarrow \mathbf{C} \cup \mathbf{V}$ which is the identity on $\mathbf{C}$. Given a set A of atoms, $\mu(A) = \{r(\mu(t_1), \ldots, \mu(t_n)) \,:\, r(t_1, \ldots, t_n) \in A\}$. The restriction of μ to a set $S \subseteq \mathbf{C} \cup \mathbf{V}$, is denoted by $\mu|_S$. A *conjunctive query* (CQ) q (over Σ) is an expression of the form $\exists \mathbf{Y}\, \varphi(\mathbf{X}, \mathbf{Y})$, where $\mathbf{X} \cup \mathbf{Y}$ are variables of $\mathbf{V}$, and φ is a conjunction of atoms (possibly with constants) over Σ. To highlight the free variables of q, we often write $q(\mathbf{X})$ instead of q. If $\mathbf{X}$ is empty, then q is called a *Boolean conjunctive query* (BCQ). Assuming that $\mathbf{X}$ is the sequence $X_1, \ldots, X_n$, the *answer* to q over a database D, denoted $q(D)$, is the set of all n-tuples $\langle t_1, \ldots, t_n \rangle \in \mathbf{C}^n$ for which there exists a substitution μ such that $\mu(\varphi(\mathbf{X}, \mathbf{Y})) \subseteq D$ and $\mu(X_i) = t_i$, for each $i \in [n]$. A BCQ is *true* in D, denoted $D \models q$, if $\langle\rangle \in q(D)$. The *consistent answer* to a CQ $q(\mathbf{X})$ over a database D (w.r.t. Σ), denoted $ans(q, D, \Sigma)$, is the set of tuples $\bigcap_{R \in rep(D,\Sigma)} q(R)$. Clearly, $ans(q, D, \Sigma) \subseteq q(D)$ holds. A BCQ q is *consistently true* in a database D (w.r.t. Σ), denoted $D \models_\Sigma q$, if $\langle\rangle \in ans(q, D, \Sigma)$.

3 Dealing with Large Datasets

We present a strategy suitable for computing the consistent answer to a CQ over an inconsistent database subject to primary key constraints. The new strategy reduces in polynomial time that problem to a collection of smaller ones of the same sort. Given a database D over a schema Σ, and a BCQ q, we identify a set $F_1, \ldots, F_k$ of pairwise disjoint subsets of D, called fragments, such that: $D \models_\Sigma q$ *iff there is* $i \in [k]$ *such that* $F_i \models_\Sigma q$. At the core of our strategy we have: (1) a cascade pruning mechanism to reduce the number of "crucial" inconsistencies, and (2) a technique to identify a suitable set of fragments from any (possibly unpruned) database. For the sake of presentation, we start with principle (2). (Proofs are given in [13].)

Given a database D, a *key component* K of D is any maximal subset of D such that if $r_1(\mathbf{t}_1)$ and $r_2(\mathbf{t}_2)$ are in K, then both $r_1 = r_2$ and $\hat{\mathbf{t}}_1 = \hat{\mathbf{t}}_2$ hold. Namely, K collects only atoms that agree on their primary key. Hence, the set of all key components of D, denoted by $comp(D, \Sigma)$, forms a partition of D. If a key component is a singleton, then it is called *safe*; otherwise it is *conflicting*. Let $comp(D, \Sigma) = \{K_1, \ldots, K_n\}$. It can be verified that $rep(D, \Sigma) = \{\{\underline{a}_1, \ldots, \underline{a}_n\} \,:\, \underline{a}_1 \in K_1, \ldots, \underline{a}_n \in K_n\}$. Let us now fix throughout this section a BCQ q over Σ. For a repair $R \in rep(D, \Sigma)$, if q is true in R, then there is a substitution μ such that $\mu(q) \subseteq R$. But since $R \subseteq D$, it also holds that $\mu(q) \subseteq D$. Hence, $sub(q, D) = \{\mu|_{var(q)} \,:\, \mu \text{ is a substitution and } \mu(q) \subseteq D\}$ is an overestimation of the substitutions that map q to the repairs of D.

Inspired by the well-known notions of conflict-hypergraph and conflict-join graph, we now introduce the notion of conflict-join hypergraph. Given a database D, the *conflict-join hypergraph* of D (w.r.t. q and Σ) is denoted by $H_D =$

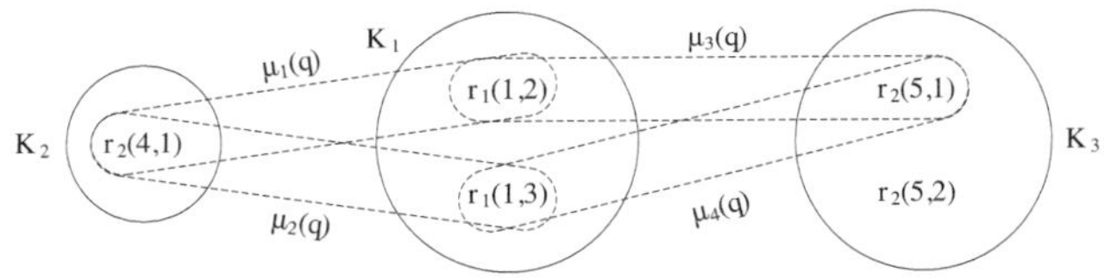

Fig. 1. Conflict-join hypergraph.

$\langle D, E\rangle$, where D are the vertices, and E are the hyperedges partitioned in $E_q = \{\mu(q) : \mu \in sub(q, D)\}$ and $E_\kappa = \{K : K \in comp(D, \Sigma)\}$. A *bunch* B of vertices of H_D is any minimal nonempty subset of D such that, for each $e \in E$, either $e \subseteq B$ or $e \cap B = \emptyset$ holds. Intuitively, every edge of H_D collects the atoms in a key component of D or the atoms in $\mu(q)$, for some $\mu \in sub(q, D)$. Moreover, each bunch collects the vertices of some connected component of H_D. An example follows to fix these preliminary notions.

Example 1. Consider the schema $\Sigma = \langle \mathcal{R}, \alpha, \kappa\rangle$, where $\mathcal{R} = \{r_1, r_2\}$, $\alpha(r_1) = \alpha(r_2) = 2$, and $\kappa(r_1) = \kappa(r_2) = \{1\}$. Consider also the database $D = \{r_1(1,2), r_1(1,3), r_2(4,1), r_2(5,1), r_2(5,2)\}$, and the BCQ $q = r_1(X,Y), r_2(Z,X)$. The conflicting components of D are $K_1 = \{r_1(1,2), r_1(1,3)\}$ and $K_3 = \{r_2(5,1), r_2(5,2)\}$, while its safe component is $K_2 = \{r_2(4,1)\}$. The repairs of D are $R_1 = \{r_1(1,2), r_2(4,1), r_2(5,1)\}$, $R_2 = \{r_1(1,2), r_2(4,1), r_2(5,2)\}$, $R_3 = \{r_1(1,3), r_2(4,1), r_2(5,1)\}$, and $R_4 = \{r_1(1,3), r_2(4,1), r_2(5,2)\}$. Moreover, $sub(q, D)$ contains the substitutions: $\mu_1 = \{X \mapsto 1, Y \mapsto 2, Z \mapsto 4\}$, $\mu_2 = \{X \mapsto 1, Y \mapsto 3, Z \mapsto 4\}$, $\mu_3 = \{X \mapsto 1, Y \mapsto 2, Z \mapsto 5\}$, and $\mu_4 = \{X \mapsto 1, Y \mapsto 3, Z \mapsto 5\}$. The conflict-join hypergraph $H_D = \langle D, E\rangle$ is as in Figure 1. Solid (resp., dashed) edges form the set E_κ (resp., E_q). Since μ_1 maps q to R_1 and R_2, and μ_2 maps q to R_3 and R_4, we conclude that $D \models_\Sigma q$. Finally, D is the only bunch of H_D. □

In Example 1 we observe that K_3 can be safely ignored in the evaluation of q. In fact, even if both $\mu_3(q)$ and $\mu_4(q)$ contain an atom of K_3, μ_1 and μ_2 are sufficient to prove that q is consistently true. This might suggest to focus only on the set $F = K_1 \cup K_2$, and on its repairs $\{r_1(1,2), r_2(4,1)\}$ and $\{r_1(1,3), r_2(4,1)\}$. Also, since $F \models_\Sigma q$, F represents the "small" fragment of D that we need to evaluate q. The practical advantage of considering F instead of D should be already clear: (1) the repairs of F are smaller than the repairs of D; and (2) F has less repairs than D. We are now ready to introduce the notion of fragment. Consider a database D. For any set $C \subseteq comp(D, \Sigma)$ of key components of D, we say that the set $F = \bigcup_{K \in C} K$ is a (*well-defined*) *fragment* of D. According to this notion, the set $F = K_1 \cup K_2$ in Example 1 is a fragment of D. The following theorem, states a useful property that holds for any fragment.

Theorem 1. *Consider a database D, and two fragments $F_1 \subseteq F_2$ of D. If $F_1 \models_\Sigma q$, then $F_2 \models_\Sigma q$.*

Note that D is indeed a fragment of itself. Hence, if q is consistently true, then there is always the fragment $F = D$ such that $F \models_\Sigma q$. But now the question is: *How can we identify a convenient set of fragments of D?* The naive way would be to use as fragments the bunches of H_D. Soundness is guaranteed by Theorem 1. Regarding completeness, we rely on the following result.

Theorem 2. *Consider a database D. If $D \models_\Sigma q$, then there is a bunch B of H_D such that $B \models_\Sigma q$.*

By combining Theorems 1 and 2 we are able to reduce, in polynomial time, the original problem into a collection of smaller ones of the same sort. However, this technique alone is not sufficient to deal with large data sets. Indeed, it involves the entire database by considering all the bunches of the conflict-join hypergraph. We now introduce an algorithm that can realize that K_3 is "redundant" in Example 1. Formally, a key component K of a database D is *redundant* (w.r.t. q) if *for each fragment F of D, $F \models_\Sigma q$ implies $F \setminus K \models_\Sigma q$.* In practice, a key component is redundant independently from the fact that some other key component is redundant or not. More formally, given a database D and a set C of redundant components of D, it holds that $D \models_\Sigma q$ iff $\left(D \setminus \bigcup_{K \in C} K\right) \models_\Sigma q$. Therefore, if we can identify all the redundant components of D, then after removing from D all these components, what remains is either: (1) a nonempty set of (minimal) bunches, each of which entails consistently q whenever $D \models_\Sigma q$; or (2) the empty set, whenever $D \not\models_\Sigma q$. More formally: given a database D, each key component of D is redundant iff $D \not\models_\Sigma q$.

However, assuming that PTIME $\neq$ NP, any algorithm for the identification of all the redundant components of D cannot be polynomial because, otherwise, we would have a polynomial procedure for solving the original problem. Our goal is therefore to identify sufficient conditions to design a pruning mechanism that detects in polynomial time as many redundant conflicting components as possible. To give an intuition of our pruning mechanism, we look again at Example 1. Actually, K_3 is redundant because it contains an atom, namely $r_2(5,2)$, that is not involved in any substitution (see Figure 1). Assume now that this is the criterion that we use to identify redundant components. Since we know that $D \models_\Sigma q$ iff $D \setminus K_3 \models_\Sigma q$, this means that we can now forget about D and consider only $D' = K_1 \cup K_2$. But once we focus on $sub(q, D')$, we realize that it contains only μ_1 and μ_2. Then, a smaller number of substitutions in $sub(q, D')$ w.r.t. those in $sub(q, D)$ motivates us to reapply our criterion. Indeed, there could also be some atom in D' not involved in any of the substitutions of $sub(q, D')$. This is not the case in our example since the atoms in D' are covered by $\mu_1(q)$ or $\mu_2(q)$. However, in general, in one or more steps, we can identify more and more redundant components. We can now state the main result of this section.

Theorem 3. *Consider some conflict-join hypergraph $H_D = \langle D, E \rangle$, and a key component K of D. If $K \setminus \bigcup_{e \in E_q} e \neq \emptyset$, then K is redundant.*

As discussed just before Theorem 3, an indirect effect of removing a redundant component K from D is that all the substitutions in the set $S = \{\mu \in sub(q, D) : \mu(q) \cap K \neq \emptyset\}$ can be in a sense ignored. In fact, $sub(q, D \setminus K) = sub(q, D) \setminus S$. Whenever a substitution can be safely ignored, we say that it is unfounded. Let us formalize this new notion. Consider a database D. A substitution μ of $sub(q, D)$ is *unfounded* if: for each fragment F of D, $F \models_{\Sigma} q$ implies that, for each repair $R \in rep(F, \Sigma)$, there exists a substitution $\mu' \in sub(q, R)$ different from μ such that $\mu'(q) \subseteq R$. We now show how to detect as many unfounded substitutions as possible.

Theorem 4. *Consider a database D, and some $\mu \in sub(q, D)$. If there exists a redundant component K of D such that $\mu(q) \cap K \neq \emptyset$, then μ is unfounded.*

Clearly, Theorem 4 alone is not helpful since it relies on the identification of redundant components. However, if combined with Theorem 3, it forms the desired cascade pruning mechanism. For example, both substitutions μ_3 and μ_4 in Example 1 are unfounded, since K_3 is redundant.

4 Experimental Evaluation

Benchmark Setup. The assessment of our approach was done using a benchmark employed in [10] for testing CQA systems on large inconsistent databases. It comprises 40 instances of a database schema with 10 tables, organized in four families of 10 instances each of which contains tables of size varying from 100k to 1M tuples; also it includes 21 queries of different structural features split into three groups depending on whether CQA complexity is coNP-complete (queries $Q_1, \cdots, Q_7$), PTIME but not FO-rewritable [14] (queries $Q_8, \cdots, Q_{14}$), and FO-rewritable (queries $Q_{15}, \cdots, Q_{21}$). We compare our approach, named *Pruning*, with two alternative ASP-based approaches. In particular, we considered one of the first encoding of CQA in ASP that was introduced in [4], and an optimized technique that was introduced more recently in [12]; these are named *BB* and *MRT*, respectively. *BB* and *MRT* can handle a larger class of integrity constrains than *Pruning*, and only *MRT* features specific optimization that apply also to primary key violations handling. We constructed the three alternative encodings for all 21 queries of the benchmark, and we run them on the ASP solver WASP 2.0 [1], configured with the iterative coherence testing algorithm.

Analysis of the results. Concerning the capability of providing an answer to a query within the time limit of 600 seconds, we report that *Pruning* was able to answer the queries in all the 840 runs in the benchmark with an average time of 14.6s. *MRT*, and *BB* solved only 778, and 768 instances within 600 seconds, with an average of 80.5s and 52.3s, respectively.

The scalability of *Pruning* is studied in detail for each query in Figures 2(d-f), each plotting the average execution times per group of queries of the same theoretical complexity. It is worth noting that *Pruning* scales almost linearly in all queries, and independently from the complexity class of the query. This is because *Pruning* can identify and deal efficiently with the conflicting fragments.

We now analyze the performance of *Pruning* from the perspective of a measure called *overhead*, which was employed in [10] for measuring the performance of CQA systems. Given a query Q the overhead is given by $\frac{t_{cqa}}{t_{plain}}$, where t_{cqa}

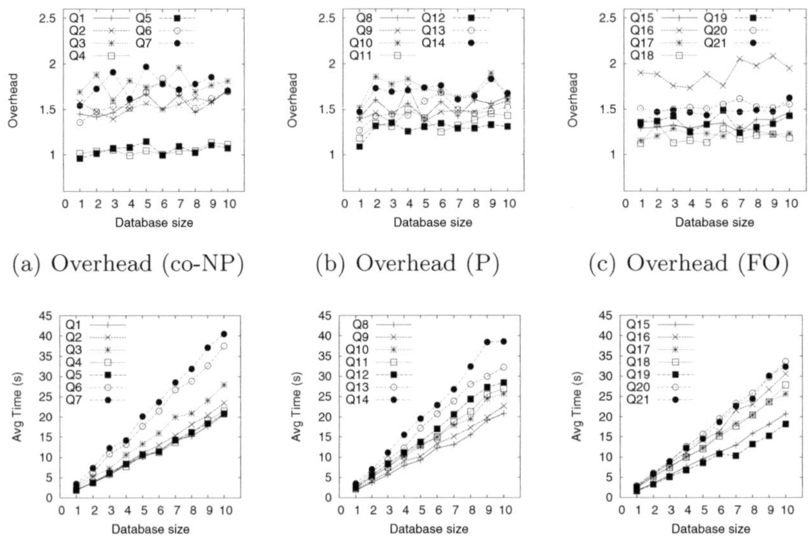

(a) Overhead (co-NP) (b) Overhead (P) (c) Overhead (FO)

(d) Scalability (co-NP) (e) Scalability (P) (f) Scalability (FO)

Fig. 2. Scalability and overhead of consistent query answering with Pruning encoding.

is time needed for computing the consistent answer of Q, and t_{plain} is the time needed for a plain execution of Q where the violation of integrity constraints are ignored. Note that the overhead measure is independent of the hardware and the software employed, since it relates the computation of CQA to the execution of a plain query on the same system. Thus it allows for a direct comparison of *Pruning* with other methods having known overheads. Following what was done in [10] (a comparison with [10] can be found in [13]), we computed the average overhead measured varying the database size for each query, and we report the results by grouping queries per complexity class in Figures 2(a-c). The overheads of *Pruning* is always below 2.1, and the majority of queries has overheads of around 1.5. The behavior is basically ideal for query Q5 and Q4 (overhead is about 1). The state of the art approach described in [10] has overheads that range between 5 and 2.8 on the very same dataset. Thus, our approach allows to obtain a very effective implementation of CQA in ASP with an overhead that is often more than two times smaller than the one of state-of-the-art approaches. We complemented this analysis by measuring also the overhead of *Pruning* w.r.t. the computation of safe answers, which provide an underestimate of consistent answers that can be computed efficiently (in polynomial time) by means of stratified ASP programs. We report that the computation of the consistent answer with *Pruning* requires only at most 1.5 times more in average than computing the safe answer. This further outlines that *Pruning* is able to maintain reasonable the impact of the hard-to-evaluate component of CQA. Finally, we have analyzed the impact of our technique in the various solving steps of the evaluation. We report that for *Pruning* the solver analyzes a few non-factual rules (below 1% in average), whereas *MRT* and *BB* have 5% and 63% of non-factual rules, respectively. Since the hard part of the computation is performed by the solver on non-factual rules, this also outlines the benefits of the pruning technique.

5 Conclusion

Logic programming approaches to CQA were recently considered not competitive [10] on large databases affected by primary key violations. In this paper, we overview a strategy that dramatically reduces the primary key violations to be handled to answer the query. The strategy is encoded naturally in ASP, and an experiment on benchmarks already employed in the literature demonstrates that our ASP-based approach is efficient on large datasets, and performs better than state-of-the-art methods in terms of overhead. As far as future work is concerned, we plan to extend the *Pruning* method for handling inclusion dependencies, and other tractable classes of tuple-generating dependencies.

References

1. Alviano, M., Dodaro, C., Ricca, F.: Anytime computation of cautious consequences in answer set programming. TPLP 14(4-5), 755–770 (2014)
2. Arenas, M., Bertossi, L.E., Chomicki, J.: Consistent query answers in inconsistent databases. In: Proc. of PODS '99. pp. 68–79 (1999)
3. Arenas, M., Bertossi, L.E., Chomicki, J.: Answer sets for consistent query answering in inconsistent databases. TPLP 3(4-5), 393–424 (2003)
4. Barceló, P., Bertossi, L.E.: Logic programs for querying inconsistent databases. In: Proc. of PADL'03. LNCS, vol. 2562, pp. 208–222 (2003)
5. Bertossi, L.E., Hunter, A., Schaub, T. (eds.): Inconsistency Tolerance, LNCS, vol. 3300. Springer, Berlin / Heidelberg (2005)
6. Brewka, G., Eiter, T., Truszczynski, M.: Answer set programming at a glance. Commun. ACM 54(12), 92–103 (2011)
7. Elmagarmid, A.K., Ipeirotis, P.G., Verykios, V.S.: Duplicate record detection: A survey. IEEE Trans. Knowl. Data Eng. 19(1), 1–16 (2007)
8. Fuxman, A., Miller, R.J.: First-order query rewriting for inconsistent databases. J. Comput. Syst. Sci. 73(4), 610–635 (2007)
9. Greco, G., Greco, S., Zumpano, E.: A logical framework for querying and repairing inconsistent databases. IEEE Trans. Knowl. Data Eng. 15(6), 1389–1408 (2003)
10. Kolaitis, P.G., Pema, E., Tan, W.C.: Efficient querying of inconsistent databases with binary integer programming. PVLDB 6(6), 397–408 (2013)
11. Koutris, P., Wijsen, J.: Consistent query answering for primary keys. SIGMOD Record 45(1), 15–22 (2016)
12. Manna, M., Ricca, F., Terracina, G.: Consistent query answering via asp from different perspectives: Theory and practice. TPLP 13(2), 227–252 (2013)
13. Manna, M., Ricca, F., Terracina, G.: Taming primary key violations to query large inconsistent data via ASP. TPLP 15(4-5), 696–710 (2015)
14. Wijsen, J.: On the consistent rewriting of conjunctive queries under primary key constraints. Inf. Syst. 34(7), 578–601 (2009)
15. Wijsen, J.: Certain conjunctive query answering in first-order logic. ACM Trans. Database Syst. 37(2), 9:1–9:35 (2012)

The Projective Clustering Ensemble problem for Advanced Data Clustering

EXTENDED ABSTRACT

Carlotta Domeniconi[1], Francesco Gullo[2], and Andrea Tagarelli[3]

[1] George Mason University, USA cdomenic@gmu.edu
[2] UniCredit, R&D Dept., Italy gullof@acm.org
[3] University of Calabria, Italy andrea.tagarelli@unical.it

Abstract. After more than five decades, a huge number of models and algorithms have been developed for data clustering. While most attention has been devoted to data types, algorithmic features, and application targets, in the last years there has also been an increasing interest in developing advanced data-clustering tools. In this respect, projective clustering and clustering ensembles represent two of the most important directions: the former is concerned with the discovery of subsets of the input data having different, possibly overlapping subsets of features associated with them, while the latter allows for the induction of a prototype consensus clustering from an available ensemble of clustering solutions.

In this paper we discuss the current state-of-the-art research in which the problems of projective clustering and clustering ensembles have been revisited and integrated in a unified framework, called Projective Clustering Ensemble (PCE). We discuss how PCE has originally been formalized as either a two-objective or a single-objective optimization problem, and how the limitations of such early approaches have been overcome by a metacluster-based formulation. We also summarize main empirical results, and provide pointers for future research.

1 Introduction

Given a set of data objects as points in a multi-dimensional space (or *feature space*), the problem of *clustering* consists in discovering a number of homogeneous subsets of data, called *clusters*, which are well-separated from each other [8]. Clustering is a key step for a myriad of data-management/data-mining tasks that require the discovery of unknown relationships and patterns in large datasets. Although most clustering approaches usually provide single clustering solutions and/or use the same (typically large) feature space, latest advances have focused on two main advanced aspects: (i) dealing with high dimensionality, and (ii) handling multiple clustering solutions.

Several problems of practical interest are inherently high-dimensional, i.e., they involve data objects represented by large sets of features. A common scenario with high-dimensional data is that several clusters may exist in different subspaces that correspond to different combinations of features. In fact, it is unlikely that all features of the data objects are equally relevant to form meaningful clusters.

Another challenge in the clustering process is that in many real-life domains multiple, and potentially meaningful groupings of the input data are available, hence providing different views of the data. For instance, in genomics, multiple clustering solutions

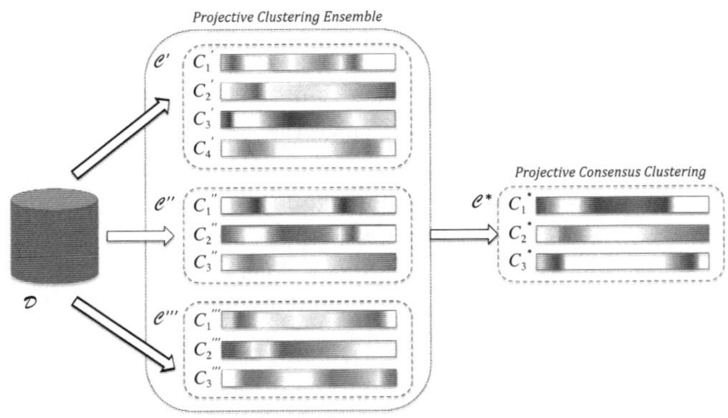

Fig. 1: Illustration of a projective clustering ensemble and derived consensus clustering. Each gradient refers to the cluster memberships over all objects. Colors denote different feature subspaces associated with the projective clusters [5].

would be needed to capture the multiple functional roles of genes. In text mining, documents discuss multiple topics, thus their grouping by content should reflect different informative views which correspond to multiple (possibly alternative) clusterings.

Recent advances in data clustering have led to the definition of the problems of *projective clustering*—to deal with high dimensionality—and *clustering ensembles*—to handle multiple clustering solutions. The goal of projective clustering [9] is to discover *projective clusters*, i.e., subsets of the input data having different, and possibly overlapping subsets of features (subspaces) associated with them. Projective clustering aims to solve issues that typically arise in high-dimensional data, such as sparsity and concentration of distances [7]. The problem of clustering ensembles [12], also known as *consensus clustering* or *aggregation clustering*, is stated as follows: given a set of clustering solutions, or *ensemble*, one must derive a *consensus clustering* that properly summarizes the solutions of the ensemble. The input ensemble is typically generated by varying one or more aspects of the clustering process, such as the clustering algorithm, the parameter setting, and the number of features, objects or clusters.

Projective clustering and clustering ensembles have recently been treated in a unified framework [2,3,4,5,6]. The underlying motivation of that study is that many real-world problems are high-dimensional *and* lack a-priori knowledge. Examples include clustering of multi-view data, privacy preserving clustering, news or document retrieval based on pre-defined categorizations, and distributed clustering of high-dimensional data. To address both issues simultaneously, the problem of *Projective Clustering Ensembles* (PCE) is hence formalized, whose goal is to compute a *projective consensus clustering* from an ensemble of projective clustering solutions. Intuitively, each projective cluster is characterized by a distribution of memberships of the objects as well as a distribution over the features that belong to the subspace of that cluster. Figure 1 illustrates an example of projective clustering ensemble with three projective clustering solutions, which are obtained according to different views over the same dataset. A projective cluster is graphically represented as a rectangle filled with a color gradient, where higher intensities correspond to larger membership values of objects to the cluster. Clusters of the same clustering may overlap with their gradient (i.e., objects can have multiple assignments with different degrees of membership), and colors change to denote that different groupings of objects are associated with different feature subspaces. A projective consensus clustering is derived by suitably "aggregating" the ensemble members: the first projective consensus cluster is derived by summarizing C'_1, C''_2, and C'''_2, the second from C'_2, C''_3, and C'''_3, and the third from C'_4, C''_1, and C'''_1. Note that the resulting color in each projective consensus cluster would merge colors in the original projective clusters, which means that a projective consensus cluster is associated with a subset of features shared by the objects in the original clusters.

In this paper we provide an overview of the PCE problem. We discuss how PCE has been originally formalized as either a two-objective or a single-objective optimization problem, and how the limitations of the early approaches have been overcome by a metacluster-based method that is able to jointly consider the object-based and feature-based cluster representations in a single-objective optimization problem. We also summarize main empirical results obtained on benchmark datasets. We finally provide pointers for future research in such a challenging context.

2 Projective Clustering Ensembles (PCE)

Let $\mathcal{D}$ be a set of data objects, where each $\mathbf{o} \in \mathcal{D}$ is an $|\mathcal{F}|$-dimensional point defined over a feature space $\mathcal{F}$.[4] A *projective cluster* C defined over $\mathcal{D}$ is a pair $\langle \mathbf{\Gamma}_C, \mathbf{\Delta}_C \rangle$. $\mathbf{\Gamma}_C$, termed the *object-based* representation of C, is a $|\mathcal{D}|$-dimensional real-valued vector whose components $\Gamma_{C,\mathbf{o}} \in [0,1]$, $\forall \mathbf{o} \in \mathcal{D}$, represent the *object-to-cluster* assignment of $\mathbf{o}$ to C, i.e., the probability $\Pr(\mathbf{o}|C)$ that the object $\mathbf{o}$ belongs to C. $\mathbf{\Delta}_C$, termed the *feature-based* representation of C, is an $|\mathcal{F}|$-dimensional real-valued vector whose components $\Delta_{C,f} \in [0,1]$, $\forall f \in \mathcal{F}$, represent the *feature-to-cluster* assignments of the f-th feature to C, i.e., the probability $\Pr(f|C)$ that the feature f is *informative* for cluster C (f belongs to the subspace associated with C).

The object-based ($\mathbf{\Gamma}_C$) and the feature-based ($\mathbf{\Delta}_C$) representations of a projective cluster C implicitly define the *projective cluster representation matrix* (for short, *projective matrix*) X_C of C. X_C is a $|\mathcal{D}| \times |\mathcal{F}|$ matrix that stores, $\forall \mathbf{o} \in \mathcal{D}$, $f \in \mathcal{F}$, the probability of the intersection of the events "*object* $\mathbf{o}$ *belongs to* C" and "*feature* f *belongs to the subspace associated with* C". Under the assumption of independence between the two events, such a probability is equal to $\Pr(C|\mathbf{o}) = \Gamma_{C,\mathbf{o}}$ joint with $\Pr(f|C) = \Delta_{C,f}$. Hence, given $\mathcal{D} = \{\mathbf{o}_1, \ldots, \mathbf{o}_{|\mathcal{D}|}\}$ and $\mathcal{F} = \{1, \ldots, |\mathcal{F}|\}$, the matrix X_C can formally be defined as $\mathrm{X}_C = \mathbf{\Gamma}_C^{\mathrm{T}} \, \mathbf{\Delta}_C$.

A *projective clustering solution*, denoted by $\mathcal{C}$, is defined as a set of projective clusters that satisfy $\sum_{C \in \mathcal{C}} \Gamma_{C,\mathbf{o}} = 1$, $\forall \mathbf{o} \in \mathcal{D}$, and $\sum_{f \in \mathcal{F}} \Delta_{C,f} = 1$, $\forall C \in \mathcal{C}$. The semantics of any projective clustering $\mathcal{C}$ is that for each projective cluster $C \in \mathcal{C}$, the objects belonging to C are close to each other if (and only if) they are projected onto the subspace associated with C.

A *projective ensemble* $\mathcal{E}$ is defined as a set of projective clustering solutions. No information about the ensemble generation strategy (algorithms and/or setups), nor original feature values of the objects within $\mathcal{D}$ are provided along with $\mathcal{E}$. Moreover, each projective clustering solution in $\mathcal{E}$ may contain in general a different number of clusters.

The goal of PCE is to derive a *projective consensus clustering* that properly summarizes the projective clustering solutions within the input projective ensemble.

[4] Vectorial notation here denotes row vectors.

2.1 Single-objective PCE

The earliest PCE formulation proposed in [5] is based on a single-objective function:

$$\mathcal{C}^* = \arg\min_{\mathcal{C}} \sum_{C \in \mathcal{C}} \sum_{\mathbf{o} \in \mathcal{D}} \Gamma_{C,\mathbf{o}}^{\alpha} \, X_{C,\mathbf{o}}, \tag{1}$$

$$\text{where} \qquad X_{C,\mathbf{o}} = \sum_{f \in \mathcal{F}} \left(\Delta_{C,f} - \Lambda_{\mathbf{o},f}\right)^2, \quad \Lambda_{\mathbf{o},f} = \frac{1}{|\mathcal{E}|} \sum_{\hat{\mathcal{C}} \in \mathcal{E}} \sum_{\hat{C} \in \hat{\mathcal{C}}} \Gamma_{\hat{C},\mathbf{o}} \, \Delta_{\hat{C},f}, \tag{2}$$

and $\alpha > 1$ is a positive integer. To solve the above optimization problem, the *EM-based Projective Clustering Ensembles (EM-PCE)* method is proposed in [5]. EM-PCE iteratively looks for the optimal values of $\Gamma_{C,\mathbf{o}}$ (resp. $\Delta_{C,f}$) while keeping $\Delta_{C,f}$ (resp. $\Gamma_{C,\mathbf{o}}$) fixed, until convergence.

Weaknesses of single-objective PCE. The objective function in (1) does not allow for a perfect balance between object- and feature-to-cluster assignments when measuring the error of a candidate projective consensus clustering solution. This weakness is formally shown in [3] and avoided by adjusting (1) with a corrective term. The resulting formulation of the problem based on the corrected objective function is the following:

$$\mathcal{C}^* = \arg\min_{\mathcal{C}} \sum_{C \in \mathcal{C}} \sum_{\mathbf{o} \in \mathcal{D}} \Gamma_{C,\mathbf{o}}^{\alpha} \left(\frac{1}{2|\mathcal{E}|} X_{C,\mathbf{o}} + \frac{1}{|\mathcal{D}| - 1} X'_{C,\mathbf{o}} \right), \tag{3}$$

$$\text{where} \qquad X'_{C,\mathbf{o}} = \sum_{\mathbf{o}' \neq \mathbf{o}} \left(1 - \frac{\Gamma_{C,\mathbf{o}'}}{|\mathcal{E}|} \sum_{\hat{\mathcal{C}} \in \mathcal{E}} \sum_{\hat{C} \in \hat{\mathcal{C}}} \Gamma_{\hat{C},\mathbf{o}} \, \Gamma_{\hat{C},\mathbf{o}'} \right).$$

The above optimization problem is tackled in [3] by proposing two different methods. The first one, called *E-EM-PCE*, follows the same scheme as the EM-PCE algorithm for the early single-objective PCE formulation. The second method, dubbed *E-2S-PCE*, consists of two sequential steps that handle the object-to-cluster and the feature-to-cluster assignments separately.

2.2 Two-objective PCE

PCE is formulated in [5] also as a two-objective problem, whose functions account for the object-based (function Ψ_o) and the feature-based (function Ψ_f) representations:

$$\mathcal{C}^* = \arg\min_{\mathcal{C}} \left\{ \Psi_o(\mathcal{C}, \mathcal{E}), \, \Psi_f(\mathcal{C}, \mathcal{E}) \right\}, \tag{4}$$

$$\text{where} \qquad \Psi_o(\mathcal{C}, \mathcal{E}) = \sum_{\hat{\mathcal{C}} \in \mathcal{E}} \overline{\psi}_o(\mathcal{C}, \hat{\mathcal{C}}), \qquad \Psi_f(\mathcal{C}, \mathcal{E}) = \sum_{\hat{\mathcal{C}} \in \mathcal{E}} \overline{\psi}_f(\mathcal{C}, \hat{\mathcal{C}}). \tag{5}$$

Functions $\overline{\psi}_o$ and $\overline{\psi}_f$ are defined as $\overline{\psi}_o(\mathcal{C}', \mathcal{C}'') = \frac{1}{2}(\psi_o(\mathcal{C}', \mathcal{C}'') + \psi_o(\mathcal{C}'', \mathcal{C}'))$ and $\overline{\psi}_f(\mathcal{C}', \mathcal{C}'') = \frac{1}{2}\left(\psi_f(\mathcal{C}', \mathcal{C}'') + \psi_f(\mathcal{C}'', \mathcal{C}')\right)$, respectively, where

$$\psi_o(\mathcal{C}', \mathcal{C}'') = \frac{1}{|\mathcal{C}'|} \sum_{C' \in \mathcal{C}'} \left(1 - \max_{C'' \in \mathcal{C}''} J(\mathbf{\Gamma}_{C'}, \mathbf{\Gamma}_{C''})\right),$$

$$\psi_f(\mathcal{C}', \mathcal{C}'') = \frac{1}{|\mathcal{C}'|} \sum_{C' \in \mathcal{C}'} (1 - \max_{C'' \in \mathcal{C}''} J(\mathbf{\Delta}_{C'}, \mathbf{\Delta}_{C''})),$$

and $J(\mathbf{u}, \mathbf{v}) = (\mathbf{u}\,\mathbf{v}^{\mathrm{T}})/(\|\mathbf{u}\|_2^2 + \|\mathbf{v}\|_2^2 - \mathbf{u}\,\mathbf{v}^{\mathrm{T}})$ denotes the Tanimoto coefficient.

The problem defined in (4) is solved by the *MOEA-PCE* method, in which a *Pareto*-based *Multi-Objective Evolutionary Algorithm* is exploited to avoid combining the two objective functions into a single one.

Weaknesses of two-objective PCE. Experimental evidence in [5] has shown that the two-objective PCE formulation is more accurate than the single-objective one. Nevertheless, the original two-objective PCE still suffers from an important conceptual issue: it does not take into consideration the interrelation between the object-based and the feature-based cluster representations. This can be overcome by employing a *metacluster-based* PCE formulation, which we discuss next.

2.3 Metacluster-based PCE

Metacluster-based PCE is defined in terms of the following single-objective function [4]:

$$\mathcal{C}^* = \arg\min_{\mathcal{C}} \ \Psi_{of}(\mathcal{C}, \mathcal{E}), \qquad (6)$$

where Ψ_{of} is a function designed to measure the "distance" of a projective clustering solution $\mathcal{C}$ from $\mathcal{E}$ in terms of both data clustering and feature-to-cluster assignment: $\Psi_{of}(\mathcal{C}, \mathcal{E}) = \sum_{\hat{\mathcal{C}} \in \mathcal{E}} \overline{\psi}_{of}(\mathcal{C}, \hat{\mathcal{C}})$, where $\overline{\psi}_{of}(\mathcal{C}', \mathcal{C}'') = \frac{1}{2}(\psi_{of}(\mathcal{C}', \mathcal{C}'') + \psi_{of}(\mathcal{C}'', \mathcal{C}'))$, $\psi_{of}(\mathcal{C}', \mathcal{C}'') = \frac{1}{|\mathcal{C}'|} \sum_{C' \in \mathcal{C}'} (1 - \max_{C'' \in \mathcal{C}''} \hat{J}(\mathrm{X}_{C'}, \mathrm{X}_{C''}))$, and $\hat{J}$ is the Tanimoto coefficient between the linearized versions of the matrices to be compared.

The PCE formulation reported in (6) is well-suited to measure the quality of a candidate consensus clustering in terms of both object-to-cluster and feature-to-cluster assignments as a whole. As shown in [4], this enables us to overcome the conceptual disadvantages of both early single-objective and two-objective PCE.

To solve the metacluster-based PCE problem, a two-step is defined in [4]. The method, called CB-PCE, first discovers a suitable metacluster structure, and then computes optimal object- and feature-based representations of each metacluster.

2.4 Enhanced metacluster-based PCE

Although the early metacluster-based PCE formulation in (6) mitigates the issues of two-objective PCE, such a formulation has still some limitations. By some rearrangement and omitting constant terms, the objective function in (6) can be rewritten as:

$$\Psi_{of}(\mathcal{C}, \mathcal{E}) = \underbrace{\sum_{\hat{\mathcal{C}} \in \mathcal{E}} \sum_{\hat{C} \in \hat{\mathcal{C}}} \min_{C \in \mathcal{C}} \left(1 - \hat{J}(\mathrm{X}_C, \mathrm{X}_{\hat{C}}\right)}_{\Psi'_{of}(\mathcal{C}, \mathcal{E})} + \underbrace{\sum_{C \in \mathcal{C}} \sum_{\hat{\mathcal{C}} \in \mathcal{E}} \min_{\hat{C} \in \hat{\mathcal{C}}} \left(1 - \hat{J}(\mathrm{X}_C, \mathrm{X}_{\hat{C}}\right)}_{\Psi''_{of}(\mathcal{C}, \mathcal{E})}. \qquad (7)$$

As formally shown in [6], both Ψ'_{of} and Ψ''_{of} suffer from conceptual drawbacks: the optimization of Ψ'_{of} favors projective clustering solutions composed of clusters coming all from the same input ensemble solution, while the optimization of Ψ''_{of} favors the replication of the same projective cluster within the output consensus projective clustering.

Table 1: Datasets used in the experimental evaluation

dataset	*objects*	*features*	*classes*
Iris	150	4	3
Wine	178	13	3
Glass	214	10	6
Ecoli	327	7	5
Yeast	1,484	8	10
Multiple-Features	2,000	585	10
Segmentation	2,310	19	7
Abalone	4,124	7	17
Waveform	5,000	40	3
Letter	7,648	16	10
Isolet	7,797	617	26
Gisette	13,500	5,000	2
p53-Mutants	300	5,409	2
Amazon	120	10,000	4
Arcene	200	10,000	2

dataset	*objects*	*features*	*classes*
Shapes	160	1,614	9
Tracedata	200	275	4
ControlChart	600	60	6
Twopat	800	128	4
N30	1,356	20	8
D75	1,365	75	7
S2500	2,262	20	8

To solve these issues, an enhanced metacluster-based PCE formulation is proposed in [6]: Given a projective ensemble $\mathcal{E}$ defined over objects $\mathcal{D}$ and features $\mathcal{F}$, and an integer $K > 0$, find a projective clustering solution $\mathcal{C}^*$ such that $|\mathcal{C}^*| = K$ and

$$\mathcal{C}^* = \arg\min_{\mathcal{C}} \sum_{C \in \mathcal{C}} \sum_{\hat{\mathcal{C}} \in \mathcal{E}} \sum_{\hat{C} \in \hat{\mathcal{C}}} x(\hat{C}, C)\, T(\hat{C}, C) \tag{8}$$

$$\begin{aligned} s.t. \quad & \sum_{C \in \mathcal{C}} \Gamma_{C,\mathbf{o}} = 1, \forall \mathbf{o} \in \mathcal{D}, \ \sum_{f \in \mathcal{F}} \Delta_{C,f} = 1, \forall C \in \mathcal{C}, \\ & x(\hat{C}, C) \in \{0,1\}, \quad \forall \hat{\mathcal{C}} \in \mathcal{E},\ \forall \hat{C} \in \hat{\mathcal{C}},\ \forall C \in \mathcal{C}, \\ & \sum_{C \in \mathcal{C}} x(\hat{C}, C) \geq 1, \quad \forall \hat{\mathcal{C}} \in \mathcal{E},\ \forall \hat{C} \in \hat{\mathcal{C}}, \qquad (9) \\ & \sum_{\hat{C} \in \hat{\mathcal{C}}} x(\hat{C}, C) \geq 1, \quad \forall \hat{\mathcal{C}} \in \mathcal{E},\ \forall C \in \mathcal{C}. \qquad (10) \end{aligned}$$

The above (**NP**-hard [6]) problem is solved by E-CB-PCE, i.e., a more effective and more efficient variant of the method devised for early metacluster-based PCE.

3 Experiments

In this section we report the main experimental findings on the various state-of-the-art PCE methods, i.e., MOEA-PCE [2,5], EM-PCE [2,5], E-EM-PCE [3], E-2S-PCE [3], CB-PCE [4], and E-CB-PCE [6].

Datasets. The evaluation was performed on 22 publicly-available benchmark datasets, whose main characteristics are shown in Table 1.[5]

Projective-ensemble generation. Projective ensembles were generated by running the well-established projective-custering LAC algorithm [1] on the selected datasets. The diversity of the projective clustering solutions was ensured by randomly choosing the initial centroids and varying the LAC's parameter h. For each dataset, we generated 10 different projective ensembles; all results were averaged over these 10 ensembles.

[5] The first 15 datasets are from the UCI Machine Learning Repository (http://archive.ics.uci.edu/ml), the next four ones are from the UCR Time Series Classification/Clustering Page (http://www.cs.ucr.edu/ eamonn/timeseries data), whereas the last three ones are synthetic datasets from http://dme.rwth-aachen.de/en/OpenSubspace/evaluation.

Table 2: Average gains of E-CB-PCE w.r.t. the other methods

criterion	*MOEA-PCE*	*EM-PCE*	*E-EM-PCE*	*E-2S-PCE*	*CB-PCE*
$F1_{of}$	0	.014	.021	.025	.020
$F1_o$	.029	.049	.054	.108	.023
$F1_f$	.005	.056	.055	.060	.078
$\overline{F1}_{of}$	.147	.186	.194	.237	.019
$\overline{F1}_o$	.021	.046	.055	.100	.021
$\overline{F1}_f$	.022	.066	.067	.076	-.010
avg	.037	.070	.074	.101	.025

Assessment criteria. The quality of a projective consensus clustering $\mathcal{C}$ was assessed by using both external and internal evaluations: the former compares $\mathcal{C}$ against a reference classification, whereas the latter is based on the average similarity w.r.t. the solutions of the input projective ensemble. Three variants of the classic *F1-measure* were used as external criteria, aiming at comparing projective clustering solutions in terms of their object-based representation ($F1_o$), feature-based representation ($F1_f$), or both ($F1_{of}$), respectively. The same criteria were used for internal evaluation too. The difference in this case is that the target consensus clustering $\mathcal{C}$ is compared against all solutions in the input ensemble, and an aggregated score is ultimately derived from all individual scores. Again, three variants were employed, accounting for object-based representation ($\overline{F1}_o$), feature-based representation ($\widehat{F1}_f$), or both ($\overline{F1}_{of}$), respectively. For a more detailed definition of all $F1_o$, $F1_f$, $F1_{of}$, $\overline{F1}_o$, $\overline{F1}_f$, and $\overline{F1}_{of}$ criteria, please refer to [6].

Results. Table 2 shows the accuracy of all methods for each assessment criterion, averaged on all the selected datasets.[6] In particular the table shows the average gain achieved by the E-CB-PCE method, which was recognized as the most accurate one. E-CB-PCE was more accurate than both MOEA-PCE and CB-PCE on 16 out of 22 datasets on average, while achieving average gains up to 0.147 ($\overline{F1}_{of}$ assessment criterion) and 0.078 ($F1_f$ assessment criterion) w.r.t. MOEA-PCE and CB-PCE, respectively. Larger improvements were produced by E-CB-PCE w.r.t. the early single-objective PCE methods, i.e., EM-PCE, E-EM-PCE, and E-2S-PCE.

Table 3 shows the runtimes (in milliseconds) of the various algorithms involved in the comparison. E-CB-PCE was slower than EM-PCE on most datasets, while clearly outperforming MOEA-PCE. The runtimes of E-CB-PCE were one or two orders of magnitude smaller than those of MOEA-PCE on average, up to four orders on Isolet. Only on one dataset, MOEA-PCE was more efficient than E-CB-PCE (Glass), even though the runtimes of the two methods remained of the same order of magnitude. Compared to CB-PCE, E-CB-PCE was faster on 11 out of 22 datasets.

4 Conclusions and Future Work

We provided an overview of research work on projective clustering ensembles (PCE). We discussed the major reasons behind the formulation of PCE as a new topic in the data clustering field, which required novel computational approaches and algorithmic solutions. We formally presented a summary of existing formulations of PCE, and reported major findings learned from experimental evaluation studies.

Our research work paved the way for the development of data clustering frameworks that can support a variety of current and emerging applications in several domains of data management and analysis. For instance, in the complex network systems

[6] Dataset-by-dataset scores are available in [6].

Table 3: Execution times (milliseconds)

dataset	*MOEA-PCE*	*EM-PCE*	*E-EM-PCE*	*E-2S-PCE*	*CB-PCE*	**E-CB-PCE**
Iris	2,056	37	109	253	74	1,492
Wine	2,558	29	88	163	144	1,223
Glass	7,712	56	615	248	500	9,177
Ecoli	14,401	59	685	625	1,147	9,337
Yeast	227,878	757	20,438	21,560	30,384	83,008
Mult.-Feat.	490,602	116,334	151,582	88,713	1,562,139	114,368
Segmentation	233,951	1,854	17,385	40,014	25,692	31,780
Abalone	3,411,116	4,105	156,959	430,974	275,053	857,164
Waveform	125,247	4,912	15,905	91,844	10,487	2,179
Letter	2,248,695	9,591	126,222	772,883	70,458	135,832
Isolet	20,676,754	10,100	10,000	8,488	66,136	1,447
Gisette	966,108	34,260	38,216	29,700	93,148	1,450
p53-Mutants	58,695	22,209	22,168	19,347	65,501	1,490
Amazon	395,988	21,556	21,619	20,914	135,446	12,737
Arcene	120,537	21,557	21,499	17,405	81,433	2,413
Shapes	211,654	17,752	19,152	12,473	282,857	106,180
Tracedata	12,777	1,062	1,108	960	9,000	4,716
ControlChart	50,798	1,522	5,397	2,801	13,900	20,708
Twopat	31,850	2,946	5,706	4,606	9,788	5,344
N30	164,969	1,340	13,781	16,243	22,904	44,517
D75	135,297	4,558	13,414	15,477	32,938	30,631
S2500	290,408	2,717	29,223	44,008	39,039	55,607

area, one interesting direction is to exploit PCE for addressing problems of dimensionality reduction and community detection in time-evolving attributed networks. Another problem that can benefit from our framework is outlier detection in high dimensional data, which has many of the same challenges as clustering. Some work has been done on outlier ensembles (e.g., [10]) and on subspace outlier detection (e.g., [11]), but a unified framework encompassing both does not exist.

References

1. Domeniconi, C., Gunopulos, D., Ma, S., Yan, B., Al-Razgan, M., Papadopoulos, D.: Locally Adaptive Metrics for Clustering High Dimensional Data. Data Mining and Knowledge Discovery 14(1), 63–97 (2007)
2. Gullo, F., Domeniconi, C., Tagarelli, A.: Projective Clustering Ensembles. In: Proc. IEEE Int. Conf. on Data Mining (ICDM). pp. 794–799 (2009)
3. Gullo, F., Domeniconi, C., Tagarelli, A.: Enhancing Single-Objective Projective Clustering Ensembles. In: Proc. IEEE Int. Conf. on Data Mining (ICDM). pp. 833–838 (2010)
4. Gullo, F., Domeniconi, C., Tagarelli, A.: Advancing data clustering via projective clustering ensembles. In: Proc. ACM SIGMOD Int. Conf. on Management of Data. pp. 733–744 (2011)
5. Gullo, F., Domeniconi, C., Tagarelli, A.: Projective Clustering Ensembles. Data Min. Knowl. Discov. 26(3), 452–511 (2013)
6. Gullo, F., Domeniconi, C., Tagarelli, A.: Metacluster-based projective clustering ensembles. Machine Learning 98(1), 181–216 (2015)
7. Hinneburg, A., Aggarwal, C.C., Keim, D.A.: What Is the Nearest Neighbor in High Dimensional Spaces? In: Proc. VLDB Conf. pp. 506–515 (2000)
8. Jain, A., Dubes, R.: Algorithms for Clustering Data. Prentice-Hall (1988)
9. Kriegel, H.P., Kröger, P., Zimek, A.: Clustering high-dimensional data: A survey on subspace clustering, pattern-based clustering, and correlation clustering. TKDD 3(1), 1:1–1:58 (2009)
10. Rayana, S., Akoglu, L.: Less is more: Building selective anomaly ensembles. TKDD 10(4), 42:1–42:33 (2016)
11. Sathe, S., Aggarwal, C.C.: Subspace outlier detection in linear time with randomized hashing. In: Proc. IEEE Int. Conf. on Data Mining (ICDM). pp. 459–468 (2016)
12. Strehl, A., Ghosh, J.: Cluster Ensembles — A Knowledge Reuse Framework for Combining Multiple Partitions. Journal of Machine Learning Research 3, 583–617 (2002)

Exploiting Recurrent Retrieval Needs in Querying Heterogeneous and Dynamic Graph Dataspaces

Discussion paper

Barbara Catania, Francesco De Fino, Giovanna Guerrini

University of Genoa, Italy
{firstname.lastname}@dibris.unige.it

Abstract. Querying data sources containing heterogeneous and dynamic information is a complex task: high quality answers need to be produced in a limited response time. Dynamic contexts preclude user involvement in interpreting the request and thus solutions should be devised, relying either on additional knowledge about the current execution (e.g., query context or user profile) or previous executions of the same request [?]. The aim of this discussion paper is to exploit similar requests recurring over time for improving query processing, in terms of result quality and processing time, and to provide a general framework for representing and managing information collected in the executions of (sets of) recurring queries. Our approach relies on the enabling concept of *Profiled Graph Query Pattern* (PGQP), which represents a set of (previously executed) queries associated with information about their executions. Differently from apparently similar proposals (materialized views, smart caching), the proposed approach approximately matches queries with profiled patterns with the aim of retrieving various kinds of information, related to past executions of similar queries, and improving the processing of the query at hand.

1 Introduction

The last few years have been characterized by the growth of highly heterogeneous and dynamic data sources, shared across the network. These sources usually contain both structured and unstructured data, strongly correlated and often highly dynamic. Such data are often exploited much below their potential due to difficulties in accessing them. Indeed, users can specify their request only vaguely because the format and the structure of the data encoding the relevant information is unknown. As an example, consider a smart city explorer, that is, a set of information published by a municipality to users that may retrieve, e.g., information about attractions, points of interests, and shops. In this specific context, data may come from different, heterogeneous and very dynamic datasets. At different instants of time, also user position or the environment itself (including data) may be changed.

Processing complex requests on diverse and dynamic sources requires: (i) request interpretation; (ii) source selection; (iii) actual processing of the request on the relevant, and usually big in size, sources. Besides being costly, the overall process may not guarantee the user is satisfied by the obtained result due to various problems: the request could be incorrectly interpreted or processed on inaccurate, incomplete, unreliable data; additionally, processing time could be inadequate to the query urgency. A common solution to reduce query processing time is to rely on approximate processing approaches, which provide a faster answer at the cost of a lower accuracy. On the other hand, user involvement in the interpretation of the request [?], is not adequate in dynamic contexts, where urgent requests hamper user interaction. In [?], we claimed that, to cope with the difficulties raised by the heterogeneity and dynamic nature of the considered environments, user profiles and request contexts, data and processing quality, and similar requests recurring over time could be exploited.

In this paper, we focus on *similar requests recurring over time* for improving approximate processing of requests, assumed to be already interpreted and represented according to a graph-based formalism [?]. Recurring retrieval needs have been considered in query processing for a very long time in terms of *materialized views* [?,?]. The idea is to precompute the results of some recurring queries as materialized views, select some of such views (view selection problem) and re-use them (view-based query processing) for the execution of new requests. Unfortunately, the usage of materialized views in the contexts described above suffers from some problems: (i) views associate a result with a given query, however in the reference contexts other or additional information could be of interest (e.g., the set of used data sources or, under pay-as-you-go integration approaches [6], query-to-data mappings); (ii) view updates are very frequent in dynamic environments, reducing the efficiency of the overall system; (iii) view-based query processing techniques usually rely on a precise semantics while heterogeneity tends to favour approximation-based approaches. Recurring retrieval needs are also at the basis of *smart caching* approaches. Here the main issue concerns the definition of suitable cache replacement policies. Some of the proposed approaches rely on approximate query matching [?,?] but, similarly to materialized views, cached queries are usually associated with query results.

The framework we propose aims at representing and managing recurring queries in order to improve query processing, in terms of result quality and processing time, getting over the limitations of current materialized views and smart caching approaches by relying on the enabling concept of *Profiled Graph Query Pattern* (PGQP). The idea is to take advantage of prior processing in order to obtain *shortcuts* to different points in the query processing stack. The approach we provide generalizes smart caching methods allowing various kinds of information to be associated with cached queries in order to improve query processing even further.

The remainder of the paper is organized as follows. PGQPs are introduced in Section ??. The main phases of the proposed framework are presented in Sections ?? and ??. Finally, Section ?? concludes by outlining some future developments.

2 Profiled Graph Query Patterns

The framework we propose is based on a graph-based representation of data spaces and user retrieval needs [?]. In particular, for the sake of simplicity and for guaranteeing a tractable combined and data complexity (fundamental requirements for dealing with massive in size graph databases), we assume the data space is represented in terms of a set of *graph data sources*, i.e., graphs where nodes can also be labeled with variables, for representing situations in which the node identity is not known [?], due to the heterogeneous nature of data and the possible lack of information. Furthermore, we assume a graph query is specified as a directed, labeled graph with variables belonging to the set of *Unions of Acyclic Conjunctive Queries* (UACQ) [?].

An example of a UACQ query is shown in Figure ??(a). The query represents the following request: find the authors of the figurative artworks the user is watching (i.e., they are located close to her position), together with such artworks, a biography of the authors, and information about places in Genoa where the authors are currently exposing their artworks. Since the user request is related to her current position, it needs to be interpreted and processed before such position changes. Additionally, data sources, and, in particular, information about exhibitions are dynamic due to frequent exhibit schedule updates.

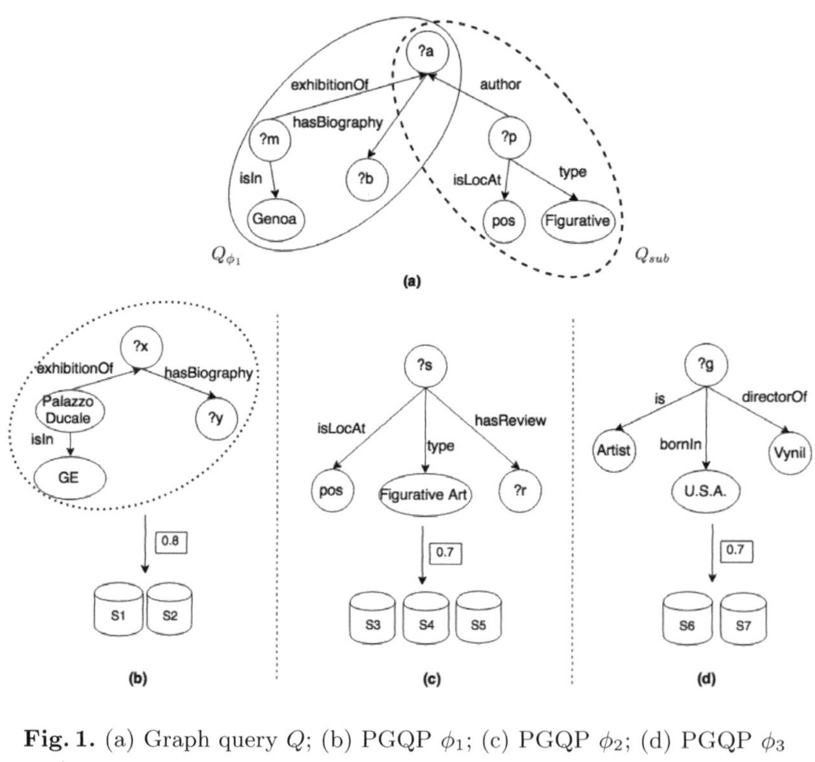

Fig. 1. (a) Graph query Q; (b) PGQP ϕ_1; (c) PGQP ϕ_2; (d) PGQP ϕ_3

For representing and managing (sets of) recurring user requests, the proposed framework relies on the enabling concept of *Profiled Graph Query Pattern* (PGQP), introduced in [?]. Each PGQP corresponds to a graph query, associated with data or metadata related to its past processing, together with some values quantifying the accuracy of such association. More formally, a PGQP ϕ can be defined as a triple $< Q, \mathcal{I}, v >$ where $Q \in UACQ$, $\mathcal{I}$ is a set of processing information, generated during the past processing of Q over the data space, and $v \in [0, 1]$ is a value which quantifies the accuracy of associating Q with I (we will detail this concept later).

Several kinds of information can be associated with PGQPs; when previously computed results are associated with a graph query, a PGQP becomes a slight extension of a materialized view. In general, however, any kind of metadata collected during query processing (e.g., the set of used data sources, query-to-data mappings under pay-as-you-go integration approaches [?]) can be considered. Any specific instantiation of the general definition makes PGQPs a shortcut to different points of the query processing stack.

Example 1. Consider an instantiation of the PGQP concept defined above targeted to source selection and assume that each PGQP graph query is associated with the specific data sources exploited during its past processing. Figure **??**(b),(c),(d) shows some examples of PGQPs. Specifically, PGQP ϕ_1 represents the following request, represented as a UACQ query: find the authors ($?x$) which are exposing at Palazzo Ducale in GE (which is an acronym for Genoa), together with a biography ($?x$) of such authors. Such query is associated with sources S_1 and S_2, meaning that past executions of the PGQP query relied on such sources for computing the query result. Data source S_1 may correspond to a dynamic data source containing information about art exhibitions of various artists (leftmost part of updated ϕ_1); on the other hand, S_2 may correspond to a static data source S_3 (such as dbpedia) containing biographies of artists. Value 0.8 is the accuracy measure associated with ϕ_1 which specifies that the results computed during past executions relying on data sources S_1 and S_2 could be considered 80% accurate. An important difference with respect to the materialized view approach is thus that the selected PGQP is not associated with query results (that would have required a frequent recomputation, given the dynamicity of data sources, e.g., in art exhibits) but with the sources contributing data to the result. Additionally, even by associating query results to PGQPs, graph ϕ_1 interpreted as a view would not have been selected since (referring for instance to the approach in [?]) the match between "Genoa" and "GE" is approximate and, thus, graph ϕ_1 cannot contribute to compute Q results. ◇

Figure **??** summarizes the overall PGQP-based framework we envision, assuming a set of PGQPs is available. It relies on two main phases: (i) the aim of the first phase (PGQP-based Query Processing) is to decompose a given query into a set of sub-queries which could be executed by relying on information association with PGQPs, execute them, and compute the final results. For each sub-query, an accuracy value should also be computed that quantifies how good is any generated partial result with respect to the original request; (ii) the aim of

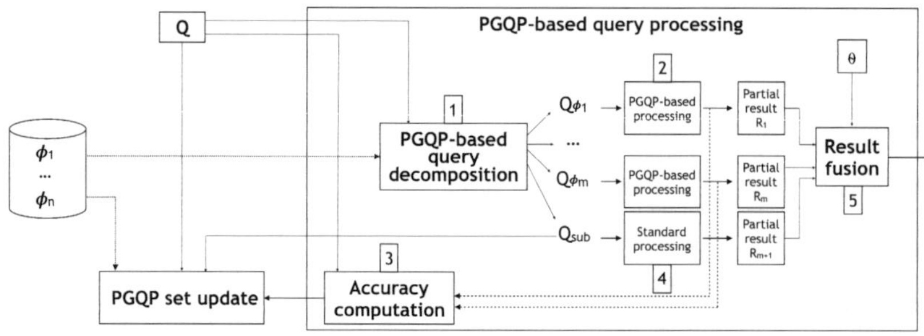

Fig. 2. PGQP-aware framework

the second phase (PGQP Set Management) is to refresh the PGQP set, possibly taking into account new information generated during query processing.

3 PGQP-Based Query Processing

Given a query Q, PGQP-based query processing relies on information associated with PGQPs to rewrite Q into an equivalent one and to process it improving evaluation performance and result quality. Six main steps can be identified.

1. PGQP-based query decomposition. Given a query Q and a set $\mathcal{S}$ of PGQPs, defined in terms of graph queries, we first determine whether it is possible to rely on $\mathcal{S}$ for executing Q. This is possible if Q can be approximated by a new query, obtained by composing a set of Q subgraphs, which best match PGQPs, with the portion of Q which cannot be represented in terms of $\mathcal{S}$. More formally, denoting with $\phi_i.1$ the query represented by the PGQP, we look for a subgraph Q_{sub} of Q, a PGQP subset $\mathcal{S}_{\subseteq} \subseteq \mathcal{S}$, and a fusion operator θ such that Q can be rewritten in a new approximate query $Q_a = \theta(\{Q_{\phi_i} | \phi_i \in \mathcal{S}_{\subseteq}\}, Q_{sub})$, where Q_{ϕ_i} denotes the (sub)graph of Q for which an approximate match with (a subgraph of) $\phi_i.1$ exists, and Q_a satisfies some optimality criteria. PGQPs in $\mathcal{S}_{\subseteq}$ are selected by combining approaches for *approximate supergraph matching* and graph view selection. PGQPs ϕ_i in $\mathcal{S}_{\subseteq}$ are selected according to a ranking value. Such value could be generated by combining the similarity between Q and $\phi_i.1$, computed through the similarity function δ underlying the matching process and quantifying how close Q and $\phi_i.1$ are, and the PGQP accuracy measure $\phi_i.3$, according to specific functions.

2. PGQP-based processing. Each graph query Q_{ϕ_i} can be executed taking into account information related to its prior executions, that is, information associated with the query represented by ϕ_i in $\mathcal{S}$. To this aim, specific PGQP-based processing algorithms should be designed, depending on the information associated with PGQPs.

3. Accuracy computation. The evaluation of each Q_{ϕ_i} subquery returns in general an approximate result, for which an accuracy value should be computed. This value is influenced by three main components: (i) the similarity between Q_{ϕ_i} and $\phi_i.1$; (ii) the usage of either a precise or an approximate PGQP-based query processing algorithm; (iii) result cardinality, in case we want to deal also with the empty or few answers problem [?], since it may impact user satisfaction. The accuracy values associated with the result obtained by the processing of each Q_{ϕ_i} are then used to update the accuracy values associated with $\phi_i.1$. See Section **??** for additional details.

4. Residual query execution. Query Q_{sub}, which represents the residual part of Q, has to be executed based on a traditional graph query processing algorithm (see, e.g. [?]). Processing information is collected during the execution and also, in this case, an accuracy measure has to be associated with the result. In case a precise query processing algorithm is used, such measure will be equal to 1.

5. Partial result merging. At the end of the processing, all partial results derived from the execution of each Q_{ϕ_i} and from the evaluation of the residual query Q_{sub} are merged through a fusion operator θ and the final result is returned to the user.

Example 2. Consider again Figure **??** and assume that $\delta(Q, \phi_1.1) = \delta(Q, \phi_2.1) = 0.8 > \delta(Q, \phi_3.1) = 0.4$. Suppose we want to select just one PGQP and that the ranking value $r(\phi)$, associated with each PGQP ϕ_i, is computed by multiplying the similarity and the accuracy values. In this case, PGQP ϕ_1 is selected for the PGQP-based processing, since $r(\phi_1) = 0.64, r(\phi_2) = 0.56$, and $r(\phi_3) = 0.28$. Thus, the decomposition step 1 will return: (i) $\mathcal{S}_{\subseteq} = \{\phi_1\}$; (ii) Q_{ϕ_1} defined as shown in Figure **??**(a); (iii) Q_{sub} defined as shown in Figure **??**(a); (iv) θ defined as the join between the partial results of Q_{ϕ_1} (tuples for variables $?a$, $?m$, $?b$) and Q_{sub} (tuples for variables $?a$, $?p$).

Suppose that the evaluation of Q_{ϕ_1} in step 2 generates the result R_1: $\{?a =$ "Andy Warhol", $?m =$ "Palazzo Ducale", $?b =$ "Bio"$\}$. In step 3, an accuracy value is computed for the result R_1, say 0.9. The evaluation of Q_{sub} in step 4 returns another partial result R_2, for example R_2: $\{?a =$ "Andy Warhol", $?p =$ "Shot Marilyn"$\}$. Finally, in step 5, R_1 and R_2 are joined, generating the final result $\{?a =$ "Andy Warhol", $?m =$ "Palazzo Ducale", $?b =$ "Bio", $?p =$ "Shot Marilyn"$\}$. ◇

4 PGQP Set Update

The PGQP-based query processing of a query produces various information that need to be reflected into the PGQP set to keep it up-to-date. More precisely, we envision two main groups of updates, namely *online updates*, executed as side effects of query processing, and *offline updates*, which periodically delete or refresh PGQPs which are considered unreliable.

Online Updates. PGQP-based query processing may generate two different types of information: (i) in step 3, an accuracy value is computed for each sub-query executed by relying on a PGQP ϕ_i; such value can be used to update the aggregate accuracy value associated with ϕ_i; suitable aggregation measures should be defined to this purpose and are current under investigation; (ii) in step 5, new processing information $\mathcal{I}$ are generated from the processing of the residual query Q_{sub}, together with an accuracy value v; such information can be interpreted as a new PGQP $\phi = (Q_{sub}, \mathcal{I}, v)$, which should be used for updating the PGQP set in case Q_{sub} is assumed to be recurrent. Various approaches can be exploited to detect recurrent queries. A simple and optimistic approach could be that of assuming any new query is recurrent, then monitoring the usage of the related PGQP to refine such decision. If Q_{sub} is recurrent, ϕ should be added to the set and made available for future query processing.

Offline Updates. Due to dynamicity of the environment, PGQPs, after their creation, may become unreliable for three main reasons: (i) the query they represent may be no more considered as recurrent (see above); (ii) the accuracy value becomes very low, meaning that the usage of the PGQP lead to the generation of inaccurate results; (iii) the associated information may become imprecise due to the variability of the data space. For this reason, periodically the PGQP set should be refreshed. Different policies could be provided. As an example, any PGQP with an accuracy value lower than a given threshold could be considered unreliable and could be refreshed by executing the PGQP query, using a standard graph query processing approach: similarly to the execution of a residual query, new information gathered during query processing, as well as the computed result accuracy value, could be used to update the PGQP considered unreliable. Additionally, all PGQPs could be periodically refreshed to take care of data source dynamicity.

Example 3. Consider again query Q in Figure **??**(a). Based on what we stated in Example **??**, we know that, after the PGQP-based processing of Q_{ϕ_1}, an accuracy value equal to 0.9 is computed. This value is used to perform an online update with the aim of updating the accuracy value associated with Q_{ϕ_1}, taking into account this further PGQP-based execution. For example, the two values could be multiplied (since they can be interpreted as the probability of two independent events). Additionally, after the execution of the residual query Q_{sub}, PGQP $< Q_{sub}, \{S_8, S_9\}, 0.75 >$ could be added to the PGQP set, assuming it is recurring. Now assume that the resulting accuracy value is lower than a given threshold: this means that the processing information represented inside the PGQP led to inaccurate query results. In this case, query $\phi_1.1$ could be re-executed and the information collected during query processing used to refresh ϕ_1. For example, a new data source S_3 could be identified as relevant, while a previously identified data source, e.g., S_2, may become useless. $\diamond$

5 Discussion

This paper presents a first step towards the design of query processing approaches for recurring retrieval needs. Several issues still need to be investigated, concerning specific framework instantiations, characterization of specific information to be associated with graph queries in PGQPs and related PGQP-based query processing approaches, and suitable approaches for detecting recurring queries and refreshing the PGQP set. We are currently working on an instantiation of the framework tailored to source selection for linked open data. The idea is to associate each PGQP with information about the data sources used in the past for query execution (as discussed in the presented examples), thus providing an alternative approach with respect to index-based source selection for linked open data [?] in all contexts in which queries are recurring.

References

1. Agrawal, S., Chaudhuri, S., Das, G. and Gionis, A. Automated ranking of database query results. In CIDR, 2003.
2. Barceló, P. Querying graph databases. In *Proc. of PODS*, pp. 175–188, 2013.
3. Catania, B., De Fino, F. and Guerrini, G. Recurring retrieval needs in diverse and dynamic dataspaces: issues and reference framework. In *GraphQ Workshop*, 2017.
4. Catania, B., Guerrini, G., Belussi, A., Mandreoli, F., Martoglia, R., and Penzo, W. Wearable queries: adapting common retrieval needs to data and users. In *DBRank Workshop*, 2013.
5. Das Sarma, A., Dong, X. and Halevy, A. Bootstrapping Pay-As-You-Go data integration systems. In *Proc. of SIGMOD*, 2008.
6. Fan, W., Wang, X. and Wu, Y. Answering pattern queries using views. *IEEE Trans. Knowl. Data Eng.*, 28(2):326–341, 2016.
7. Goasdoué, F., Karanasos, K., Leblay, J., and Manolescu, I. View selection in semantic web databases. *PVLDB*, 5(2): 97–108, 2011.
8. O.Hartig and M. T. Özsu. Linked Data query processing. In *Proc. of ICDE*, pp. 1286–1289, 2014.
9. Mass, Y., Ramanath, M., Sagiv, Y., and Weikum, G. IQ: the case for iterative querying for knowledge. In *Proc. of CIDR* , pp. 38-44, 2011.
10. Melnik, S., Garcia-Molina, H. and Rahm, E. Similarity flooding: a versatile graph matching algorithm and its application to schema matching. In *Proc. of ICDE*, pp. 117–128, 2002.
11. Ntarmos, N., Triantafillou, P., and Wang, J. GraphCache: a caching system for graph queries. In *Proc. of EDBT*, pp. 13-24, 2017
12. Papailiou, N., Tsoumakos, D., Karras, P., and Koziris, N. Graph-aware, workload-adaptive sparql query caching. In *Proc. of SIGMOD*, pp. 1777-1792, 2015.
13. Tian, Y. and Patel, J.M. TALE: a tool for approximate large graph matching. In *Proc. of ICDE*, pp. 963-972, 2008.
14. Zhang, K. and Shasha, D. Simple fast algorithms for the editing distance between trees and related problems. *SIAM Journal on Computing*, 18(6):1245–1262, 1989.
15. Zhao, P. and Han, J. On graph query optimization in large networks. *PVLDB*, 3(1): 340-351, 2010.
16. Weikum, G. Data and knowledge discovery. GRDI 2020, 2011.

An Influence Maximization based approach to the Engagement of Silent Users in Online Social Networks

EXTENDED ABSTRACT

Roberto Interdonato[1,2], Chiara Pulice[3], and Andrea Tagarelli[1]

[1] DIMES, University of Calabria, Italy
[2] Department of Information Technology, Uppsala University, Sweden
[3] UMIACS, University of Maryland, USA

Abstract. We discuss a targeted influence maximization (TIM) approach, based on the linear threshold (LT) diffusion model, which is designed to support the engagement of silent members, a.k.a. lurkers, of an online social network. A key aspect of this approach is the objective function of the underlying optimization problem, which is defined in terms of the lurking scores associated with the nodes in the final active set, or delurking capital. The resulting TIM problem shares the computational intractability with classic influence maximization (IM) problems. However, since the proposed objective function is shown to be monotone and submodular under the LT model, a greedy algorithm (with a guaranteed approximation ratio) is provided to compute a k-node set that maximizes the delurking capital in the network, for a given lurking threshold. Results have demonstrated the significance of our approach. A comparative evaluation with state-of-the-art algorithms for non-targeted and targeted LT-based IM has also shown the superiority of our approach in terms of the estimated overall delurking capital.

1 Introduction

Computer science research in online social networks (OSNs) has traditionally focused on users that are actively involved in the OSN life. However, online social environments are often characterized by the presence of a crowd which does not actively contribute, rather it takes a silent role. Such silent members of an OSN are also known as *lurkers*, since they gain benefit from others' information without significantly giving back to the community [8,2,9]. The study of lurking behaviors in OSNs is nonetheless important, since lurkers acquire knowledge from the community, and as such they can be social capital holders. Within this view, a major goal is to *delurk* such users, i.e., to encourage them to more actively be involved in the OSN. This can in principle be accomplished by nurturing and persuading lurkers to be more actively engaged in the community, also thanks the support of other, possibly influential users [9].

In [5] we proposed the first computational framework that addresses the problem of delurking in OSNs. Our key idea was to conceptualize a delurking approach under a graph-based *information diffusion model*. Research on information diffusion in OSNs (e.g., [1,14,4]) is well-established due to a plethora of methods that have been developed in the last years, mostly upon the two seminal models, namely Independent Cascade

(IC) and Linear Threshold (LT) [6]. These assume that an information diffusion process would unfold in a static, directed graph, where each node can be "activated" or not (under a progressive assumption) and each edge is associated with a weight expressing the diffusion probability or influence degree from one node to another. Moreover, in an *influence maximization* (IM) framework (e.g., [6,3,13]) the general objective is to find a set of initially activated users (also called early adopters, or seed users) which can maximize the spread of information through the network.

Our approach refers to a special case of IM, namely *targeted IM*; in particular, a specific instance of targeted IM, in which lurkers are regarded as the target of the diffusion process. Existing *lurker ranking* algorithms [10,11,12] can profitably be exploited to mine lurking behaviors in the network, and hence to associate users with a value (*lurking score*) indicating her/his lurking status. Given a budget k, our goal is to find a set of k nodes that are capable of maximizing the likelihood of "activating" the target lurkers. Intuitively, the activation of a node means that a user is influenced by other users so to "become aware of" or "adopt" a piece of information. Note that this outcome of a diffusion process has a nice analogy in the lurking analysis setting under consideration: the information to spread corresponds to a delurking trigger action, activating nodes regarded as lurkers can be seen as delurking those users, while the lurking score of a user would represent the gain deriving from delurking that user.

A key novelty in the formulated optimization problem is the objective function, which is defined in terms of the cumulative amount of the lurking scores associated with the nodes in the final active set, or *delurking capital*. Our delurking-oriented targeted IM problem shares the computational intractability with classic IM problems. However, since the proposed objective function is shown to be monotone and submodular under the LT model, we provide a greedy algorithm (with typical $1 - 1/e - \epsilon$ approximation ratio), named DEvOTION, which computes a k-node set that maximizes the delurking capital in the network, for a given minimum lurking threshold.

We evaluated DEvOTION over OSN datasets of different characteristics and sizes, assessing its performance in terms of estimation of the delurking capital, execution time, and seed characteristics. We also compared DEvOTION with state-of-the-art IM algorithms, namely SimPath [3] and TIM+ [13], and a query-based targeted IM algorithm, namely KB-TIM [7].

2 Delurking-oriented Targeted Influence Maximization

2.1 Problem statement

Let $\mathcal{G}_0 = \langle \mathcal{V}, \mathcal{E} \rangle$ be the directed graph representing a social network, with set of nodes $\mathcal{V}$ and set of edges $\mathcal{E}$. We denote with $\mathcal{G} = \mathcal{G}_0(b, \ell) = \langle \mathcal{V}, \mathcal{E}, b, \ell \rangle$ a directed weighted graph representing the information diffusion graph associated with the social network $\mathcal{G}_0$, where $b : \mathcal{E} \rightarrow \mathbb{R}^*$ is an edge weighting function, and $\ell : \mathcal{V} \rightarrow \mathbb{R}^*$ is a node weighting function.

We assume that the node and edge weighting functions in the diffusion graph $\mathcal{G}$ are completely specified based upon the availability of a *lurker ranking* solution. This is produced by a method that is designed to identify and characterize lurkers in an OSN, i.e., a method enabled to assign every user with a score that expresses the status of lurking behavior taken by that user. The intuition is that for any edge (u, v) in $\mathcal{G}$, the weight $b(u, v)$ will indicate how much node u has contributed to the v's lurking score calculated by the lurker ranking method, which resembles a measure of "influence" produced by u to v. Also, the node weight $\ell(v)$ will indicate the status of v as lurker, such as the higher the lurker ranking score of v the higher should be $\ell(v)$. We refer the reader to [11,10] for details about the lurker ranking method and to [5] for definitions of node and edge weighting functions.

We denote with $LS \in [0, 1]$ a threshold value that indicates the *minimum lurking score* that a node in the network is required to have in order to be regarded as a target node. Moreover, given any seed set $S \subseteq \mathcal{V}$, we denote with $\mu(S)$ the *final active set*, i.e., the set of nodes that are active at the end of the diffusion process starting from S.

Upon the above defined quantities, we introduce a measure that will be essential to the definition of our targeted IM problem. This measure, which we denote as *delurking capital* cumulated via S, is proportional to the amount of the lurking scores over all target nodes that are activated by the seed set S.

Definition 1. *Given a set $S \subseteq \mathcal{V}$, the* **delurking capital** $DC(\mu(S))$ *associated with the final active set $\mu(S) \subseteq \mathcal{V}$ is defined as:*

$$DC(\mu(S)) = \sum_{\substack{v \in \mu(S) \setminus S \, \wedge \\ \ell(v) \geq LS}} \ell(v) \tag{1}$$

Note that in Eq. (1) we do not consider nodes that belong to the seed set S. The ratio behind this choice is that the selection of the seed set should not be biased by nodes with highest lurking scores; this will be made clear next in the definition of our objective function, which in fact relies on $DC(\mu(S))$.

Definition 2. Delurking-oriented Targeted Influence Maximization Problem. *Given $\mathcal{G} = \langle \mathcal{V}, \mathcal{E}, b, \ell \rangle$, a diffusion model on $\mathcal{G}$, a budget k, and a lurking threshold LS, find a seed set $S \subseteq \mathcal{V}$ with $|S| \leq k$ of nodes (users) such that, by activating them, the final active set $\mu(S) \subseteq \mathcal{V}$ will have the maximum delurking capital:*

$$S = \underset{S' \subseteq \mathcal{V} \ s.t. \ |S'| \leq k}{\text{argmax}} \quad DC(\mu(S')) \tag{2}$$

The problem in Def. 2 preserves the complexity of the IM problem and, as a result, it is computationally intractable, i.e., it is still NP-hard. However, as for the classic IM problem, a greedy solution can be designed provided that the natural diminishing property holds for the considered problem. It is well-known that for many diffusion models, including LT, the function $\sigma(A)$ mapping any subset $A \subseteq \mathcal{V}$ of nodes to the size of the final active set $\mu(A)$ satisfies monotonicity and submodularity by exploiting the *equivalent live-edge graph model* [6].

Proposition 1. The delurking capital function DC defined in Eq. (1), mapping any active set $\mu(A) \subseteq \mathcal{V}$ to its overall delurking capital, is monotone and submodular, for any $LS \in [0, 1]$, under the LT model.

The above theoretical result enables the development of an approximate algorithm with guarantee for our problem, as discussed later in Sect. 2.3.

2.2 Choosing the information diffusion model

The LT model deals with situations in which exposure to multiple sources is needed for a user before taking a decision. More specifically, a node v can be influenced by each neighbor u according to a weight $b(u, v)$ such that $\sum_{u \in N^{in}(v)} b(u, v) \leq 1$, where $N^{in}(v)$ is the in-neighbor set of node v. At the very beginning of the diffusion process, each node v is assigned a threshold uniformly at random from $[0, 1]$. This represents the weighted fraction of v's neighbors that must become active in order for v to become active itself. Intuitively, the higher is this threshold, the harder will be the task of enrolling v in a new trend, since the total influence weight must exceed its threshold.

We chose LT for modeling the process of influence propagation to pursue the goal of engaging lurkers. Unlike IC or IC-based models, the ability of LT to reflect the cumulative effect of exposure to multiple sources of influence can be profitably exploited to maximize the likelihood of changing the status of a user into a more active role in the OSN. Of course, this can actually lead to delurking provided that the information to be diffused towards the target lurkers is of any type that concerns a well-established delurking action [9]. In this regard, note that our approach is general as it can involve any type of delurking action in the form of piece of information to flow through the network (e.g., informative rewards, welcome messages, guidelines from experts, etc).

2.3 The DEvOTION algorithm

Our proposed greedy method, named DEvOTION (stands for **DE**lurking **O**riented **T**argeted **I**nfluence maximizati**ON**), exploits the search for shortest paths in the diffusion graph, following the lead of the study in [3], however in a backward fashion. Along with the information diffusion graph $\mathcal{G}$, the budget integer k, and the minimum lurking score LS, DEvOTION takes in input a real-valued threshold η. This parameter is used to control the size of the neighborhood within which paths are enumerated: in fact, the majority of influence can be captured by exploring the paths within a relatively small neighborhood; for higher η values, less paths are explored (i.e., paths are pruned earlier) leading to smaller runtime but with decreased accuracy in spread estimation.

The key idea of DEvOTION is to perform a backward visit of the graph starting from the nodes identified as target (i.e., the nodes u with $\ell(u) \geq LS$). In order to yield a seed set S of size at most k, DEvOTION works as follows. During each iteration, DEvOTION computes the set (say T) of nodes that reach the target ones and keeps track of the node with the highest marginal gain (i.e., delurking capital DC). The former allows an efficient reset of the spread of each non-seed node contained in T. The latter is found at the end of each iteration upon backward visit of all nodes in $TargetSet$ that do not belong to the current seed set S. This visiting subroutine takes a path $\mathcal{P}$, its probability pp, and the lurking score of the end node in the path (i.e., a target node), and extends $\mathcal{P}$ as much as possible (i.e., as long as pp is not lower than η). Initially, a path is formed by one target node, with probability 1; then, the path is extended by exploring the graph backward, adding to it one, unexplored in-neighbor v at time, in a depth-first fashion. The path probability is updated according to the LT-equivalent "live-edge" model [3,6], and so the delurking capital. The process is continued until no more nodes can be added to the path.

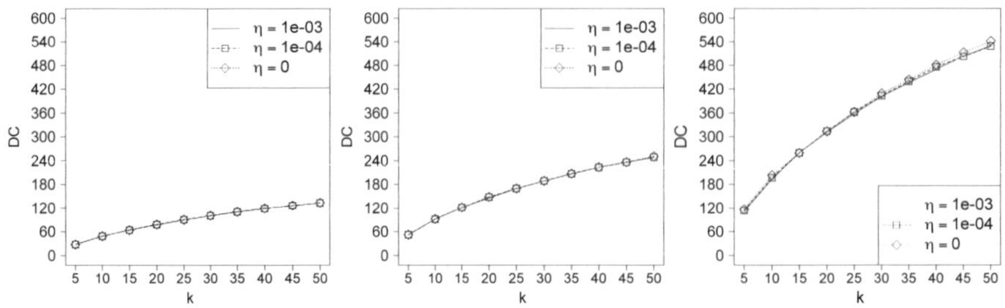

(a) LS-*perc* $= 5\%$ (b) LS-*perc* $= 10\%$ (c) LS-*perc* $= 25\%$

Fig. 1. Delurking capital in function of k and η on Instagram.

3 Experimental Evaluation

3.1 Evaluation methodology

We assessed the sensitivity of DEvOTION to the various parameters, i.e., the size of seed set (k), the lurking threshold (LS) for the selection of the target set, and the path pruning threshold (η). We also comparatively evaluated DEvOTION with SimPath [3] and TIM+ [7], two well-known state-of-the-art algorithms for IM problems, and with KB-TIM [13], a query-based targeted IM algorithm.

We used *FriendFeed* (493K, 19MM edges), *GooglePlus* (108K nodes, 14MM edges) and *Instagram* (18K nodes, 618K edges) network datasets, which are publicly available [11,12]. All experiments were carried out on an Intel Core i7-3960X CPU@3.30GHz, 64GB RAM machine.

3.2 Results

Sensitivity to parameters. We evaluated the performance of DEvOTION in terms of delurking capital obtained by varying all three parameters involved, i.e., k, LS-*perc*, η. We initially focused on η, by varying it from $1.0e$-03 to 0; note that $\eta = 1.0e$-03 is the default value used in other IM algorithms (e.g.,[3]), while $\eta = 0$ indicates no path pruning. We generally observed that no significant gain in DC is obtained for lower values of η. This fact achieves particular importance when it is coupled with the time performance results shown in Fig. 2: several orders of magnitude in the runtime are saved when $\eta > 0$. Within this view, $\eta = 1.0e$-03 might be be preferred to $\eta = 1.0e$-04 when trade-off between DC performance and runtime has to be ensured.

Concerning the other two parameters, as expected, the delurking capital increases with both the size of the seed set (k) and the size of the target set; we controlled the latter through a parameter LS-*perc* which corresponds to a percentage value that determines the setting of LS such that the selected target set corresponds to the top-LS-*perc* of the distribution of node lurking scores. An important remark is that on all datasets a significant fraction of delurking capital, for a given choice of LS-*perc*, can be achieved just using low k. This appears evident, especially for lower LS-*perc*, in Fig. 1 by observing the increasing slope of the line fitting the DC curves as LS-*perc* increases.

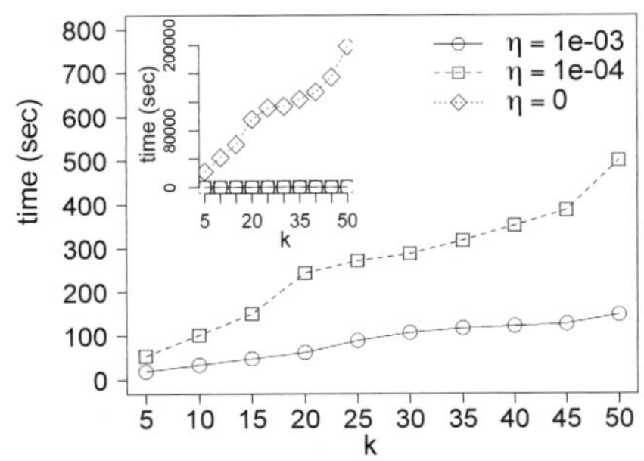

Fig. 2. Execution time of DEvOTION in function of k, with $LS\text{-}perc = 5\%$ and for varying η, on Instagram. The inset shows the overall results that include $\eta = 0$, while the main plot zooms in to focus on $\eta > 0$.

Concerning the other two datasets (results not shown), we observed that low values of k are enough to obtain a DC value close to or with the same order of magnitude of DC values achieved by using highest k.

Comparison with SimPath. SimPath shares with DEvOTION the kind of algorithmic approach to LT-based influence maximization, which includes the involvement of parameter η for controlling the enumeration of the paths through the diffusion graph. Results of the comparative evaluation for $\eta = 1.0e\text{-}04$, in terms of DC performances, are summarized in Table 1.

A first important remark that stands out is that the delurking capital obtained by SimPath is always lower than the one obtained by DEvOTION, for all datasets and configurations. The largest increment in DC is obtained for FriendFeed, with percentage of increment up to 10.8% (for $LS\text{-}perc = 5\%$). Significant increment is observed also w.r.t. the other datasets, with percentages of increment up to 4.27% (for $LS\text{-}perc = 5\%$) on GooglePlus, and up to 5.69% (for $LS\text{-}perc = 5\%$) on Instagram.

Impact of parameter η in the evaluation turns out to be marginal. Nevertheless, it should be noted that even though performance corresponding to $\eta = 1.0e\text{-}3$ (results not shown) are slightly lower in terms of DC, the increment w.r.t. SimPath is generally higher, indicating that DEvOTION is more robust than SimPath to path pruning.

As the size of target set increases, a general decreasing trend can be observed in the gap between DEvOTION and SimPath DC values. This is not surprising since a larger target set means a larger overlap with the entire node set, thus letting the seed nodes picked up by a non-targeted algorithm reach a larger part of the target set.

Regarding comparison in terms of running times, DEvOTION turns out to be two orders of magnitude faster than SimPath, for the same choice of η. Considering the largest dataset, FriendFeed, DEvOTION shows average running time of $47,278$ seconds smaller than SimPath in its faster configuration ($\eta = 1.0e\text{-}03$, $LS\text{-}perc = 5\%$), and of $182,131$ seconds in its slowest configuration ($\eta = 1.0e\text{-}04$, $LS\text{-}perc = 25\%$).

Comparison with TIM+. TIM+ follows an approach to influence maximization that was designed to improve efficiency in previously existing algorithms, including

Table 1. Summary of delurking capital performances of competitors against DEvOTION.

	FriendFeed			GooglePlus			Instagram		
	5%	10%	25%	5%	10%	25%	5%	10%	25%
incr. vs. SimPath	10.80%	9.32%	3.97%	4.27%	3.02%	1.06%	5.69%	4.10%	1.60%
incr. vs. TIM+	9.85%	8.82%	3.49%	4.22%	2.96%	1.01%	4.43%	3.11%	1.12%
incr. vs. KB-TIM	58.87%	34.48%	35.23%	40.66%	36.07%	33.86%	5.44%	6.79%	10.20%

SimPath. Therefore, it was not surprising to find out that TIM+ is indeed faster than DEvOTION. Taking FriendFeed as case in point, there is an average saving of 204 seconds for the fastest configurations ($\eta = 1.0e\text{-}03$ and $LS\text{-}perc = 5\%$ for DEvOTION, $\epsilon = 1.0$ for TIM+) , and of 6100 seconds for the slowest configurations ($\eta = 1.0e\text{-}04$ and $LS\text{-}perc = 25\%$ for DEvOTION, $\epsilon = 0.1$ for TIM+).

Nevertheless, DEvOTION always outperforms TIM+ in terms of DC on all datasets and for all configurations. The performance gain achieved by DEvOTION is more significant on FriendFeed, with average percentage of increment of 9.85% (for $LS\text{-}perc = 5\%$), 8.82% ($LS\text{-}perc = 10\%$) and 3.49% ($LS\text{-}perc = 25\%$). Analogously to what we observed for the evaluation with SimPath and for the same reason, the gap in performance between DEvOTION and TIM+ decreases for larger target sets. Smaller but significant increment is also obtained on GooglePlus (average of 4.22% for $LS\text{-}perc = 5\%$) and Instagram (average of 4.43% for $LS\text{-}perc = 5\%$).

Comparison with KB-TIM. DEvOTION always performs significantly better than KB-TIM in terms of DC, on all datasets and with all configurations. Surprisingly, the gain in performance between DEvOTION and KB-TIM is larger than the one observed for other non-targeted competitors (i.e., SimPath, TIM+). Again, as previously seen for the comparative evaluation with IM algorithms, the highest increment corresponds to FriendFeed. As shown in Table 1, the percentage of average increment in DC ranges from 35.23% (for $LS\text{-}perc = 25\%$) to 58.87% (for $LS\text{-}perc = 5\%$). The increment is from 33.86% (for $LS\text{-}perc = 25\%$) to 40.66% (for $LS\text{-}perc = 5\%$) for GooglePlus, and from 5.44% (for $LS\text{-}perc = 5\%$) to 10.20% (for $LS\text{-}perc = 25\%$) for Instagram.

It should be noted that the comparison between DEvOTION and KB-TIM on Instagram is the only one following an opposite trend, w.r.t. other datasets and competitors, with the size of the target set: larger increments are achieved for larger target sets. This is probably due to the structural characteristics of Instagram and it is confirmed by a greater overlap between the seed sets of DEvOTION and KB-TIM than the seed overlap observed for the other datasets, as we shall discuss in the next section. As regards the execution times, KB-TIM performs comparably to TIM+, thus running always faster than DEvOTION and SimPath.

3.3 Discussion

Empirical evidence has shed light on the significance and effectiveness of DEvOTION. The method has shown to be robust w.r.t. the pruning of paths to be explored in the graph. A significant fraction of delurking capital can be achieved already with a small seed set, even for large network datasets. Compared with state-of-the-art IM and targeted IM algorithms, DEvOTION always obtains better quality seed sets, confirming its efficacy and uniqueness to solve a delurking-oriented targeted IM task.

4 Conclusions

We discussed the first computational approach to delurking, i.e., to engaging users that take on a lurking role in OSNs. We presented a novel targeted IM problem in which the objective function to be maximized is defined in terms of delurking capital of the target users. We proved that the proposed objective function is monotone and submodular, by using the LT-equivalent live-edge graph model, and developed an approximate algorithm, DEvOTION, to solve the problem under consideration.

The presented approach is independent on the particular strategy of delurking (being it based on rewards, welcome messages, etc.). We paved the way for the development of web-based systems that, by embedding our approach, can effectively support engagement of users. Also, the presented approach can easily be generalized to deal with other targeted IM scenarios, therefore we envisage further developments from various perspectives, including human-computer interaction and marketing.

References

1. Bakshy, E., Rosenn, I., Marlow, C., Adamic, L.A.: The role of social networks in information diffusion. In: Proc. World Wide Web Conf. (WWW), pp. 519–528 (2012)
2. Edelmann, N.: Reviewing the definitions of "lurkers" and some implications for online research. Cyberpsychology, Behavior, and Social Networking **16**(9), 645–649 (2013)
3. Goyal, A., Lu, W., Lakshmanan, L.V.S.: SIMPATH: An Efficient Algorithm for Influence Maximization under the Linear Threshold Model. In: Proc. IEEE Int. Conf. on Data Mining (ICDM), pp. 211–220 (2011)
4. Guille, A., Hacid, H., Favre, C., Zighed, D.A.: Information diffusion in online social networks: a survey. SIGMOD Record **42**(2), 17–28 (2013)
5. Interdonato, R., Pulice, C., Tagarelli, A.: The DEvOTION algorithm for delurking in social networks. Trends in Social Network Analysis, LNSN, Springer, 28 pages (2017)
6. Kempe, D., Kleinberg, J.M., Tardos, E.: Maximizing the spread of influence through a social network. In: Proc. ACM Conf. on Knowledge Discovery and Data Mining (KDD), pp. 137–146 (2003)
7. Li, Y., Zhang, D., Tan, K.: Real-time targeted influence maximization for online advertisements. PVLDB **8**(10), 1070–1081 (2015)
8. Preece, J.J., Nonnecke, B., Andrews, D.: The top five reasons for lurking: improving community experiences for everyone. Computers in Human Behavior **20**(2), 201–223 (2004)
9. Sun, N., Rau, P.P.L., Ma, L.: Understanding lurkers in online communities: a literature review. Computers in Human Behavior **38**, 110–117 (2014)
10. Tagarelli, A., Interdonato, R.: "Who's out there?": Identifying and Ranking Lurkers in Social Networks. In: Proc. Int. Conf. on Advances in Social Networks Analysis and Mining (ASONAM), pp. 215–222 (2013)
11. Tagarelli, A., Interdonato, R.: Lurking in social networks: topology-based analysis and ranking methods. Social Netw. Analys. Mining **4**(230), 27 (2014)
12. Tagarelli, A., Interdonato, R.: Time-aware analysis and ranking of lurkers in social networks. Social Netw. Analys. Mining **5**(1), 23 (2015)
13. Tang, Y., Xiao, X., Shi, Y.: Influence maximization: near-optimal time complexity meets practical efficiency. In: Proc. ACM Conf. on Management of Data (SIGMOD), pp. 75–86 (2014)
14. Weng, L., Ratkiewicz, J., Perra, N., Gonçalves, B., Castillo, C., Bonchi, F., Schifanella, R., Menczer, F., Flammini, A.: The role of information diffusion in the evolution of social networks. In: Proc. ACM Conf. on Knowledge Discovery and Data Mining (KDD), pp. 356–364 (2013)

Querying finite or arbitrary models? No matter! Existential rules may rely on both once again*
(discussion paper)

Giovanni Amendola[1], Nicola Leone[2], and Marco Manna[2]

[1] School of Informatics, University of Edinburgh, UK
gamendol@exseed.ed.ac.uk
[2] DeMaCS, University of Calabria, Italy
{leone,manna}@mat.unical.it

Abstract. Ontology-based query answering asks whether a Boolean query is satisfied by all models of a logical theory consisting of an extensional database paired with an ontology. The introduction of existential rules (i.e., Datalog rules extended with existential quantifiers in rule-heads) as a means to specify the ontology gave birth to Datalog+/-, a framework that has received increasing attention in the last decade, with focus also on decidability and finite controllability to support effective reasoning. Five basic decidable fragments have been singled out: linear, weakly-acyclic, guarded, sticky, and shy. For all these fragments, except shy, the important property of finite controllability has been proved, ensuring that a query is satisfied by all models of the theory iff it is satisfied by all its finite models. In this paper we complete the picture by showing that finite controllability holds also for shy ontologies. The demonstration is based on a number of technical tools which could be used for similar purposes and are valuable per se.

1 Introduction

The problem of answering a Boolean query q against a logical theory consisting of an extensional database D paired with an ontology Σ is attracting the increasing attention of scientists in various fields of Computer Science, ranging from Artificial Intelligence [12, 17] to Database Theory [19, 5] and Logic [4, 20]. This problem, called *ontology-based query answering* (OBQA) [8], is usually stated as $D \cup \Sigma \models q$, and it is equivalent to checking whether q is satisfied by all models of $D \cup \Sigma$ according to the standard approach of first-order logics, yielding an open world semantics.

Description Logics [2] and Datalog$^{\pm}$ [7] have been recognized as the two main families of formal knowledge representation languages to specify Σ, while union of (Boolean) conjunctive queries, U(B)CQs for short, is the most common and studied formalism to express q. For both these families, OBQA is generally undecidable (see, [22] and [6], respectively). Hence, a number of syntactic decidable fragments of the above ontological languages have been singled out. However, decidability alone is not

* The paper has been partially supported by the MISE under project "PIUCultura – Paradigmi Innovativi per l'Utilizzo della Cultura" (n. F/020016/01-02/X27), and under project "Smarter Solutions in the Big Data World (S2BDW)".

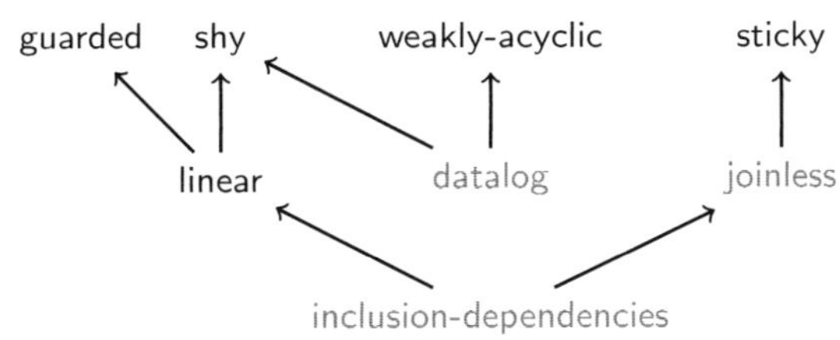

Fig. 1. Taxonomy of the basic Datalog$^{\pm}$ classes.

the only desideratum. For example, a good balance between computational complexity and expressive power is, without any doubt, of high importance too. But there is another property that is turning out to be as interesting as challenging to prove: it goes under the name of *finite controllability* [23]. An ontological fragment $\mathcal{F}$ is said to be finitely controllable if, for each triple $\langle D, \Sigma, q\rangle$ with $\Sigma \in \mathcal{F}$, it holds that $D \cup \Sigma \not\models q$ implies that there exists a finite model M of $D \cup \Sigma$ such that $M \not\models q$. This is usually stated as $D \cup \Sigma \models q$ if, and only if, $D \cup \Sigma \models_{\mathsf{fin}} q$ (where $\models_{\mathsf{fin}}$ stands for entailment under finite models), as the "only if" direction is always trivially true. And there are contexts, like in databases [23, 4], in which reasoning with respect to finite models is preferred.

In this paper we focus on the Datalog$^{\pm}$ family, which has been introduced with the aim of "closing the gap between the Semantic Web and databases" [9] to provide the *Web of Data* with scalable formalisms that can benefit from existing database technologies. In fact, Datalog$^{\pm}$ generalizes two well-known subfamilies of Description Logics called $\mathcal{EL}$ and *DL-Lite*, which collect the basic tractable languages for OBQA in the context of the Semantic Web and databases. In particular, we consider ontologies where Σ is a set of *existential rules*, each of which is a first-order formula ρ of the form $\forall \mathbf{X} \forall \mathbf{Y}(\phi(\mathbf{X},\mathbf{Y}) \rightarrow \exists \mathbf{Z} p(\mathbf{X},\mathbf{Z}))$, where the *body* $\phi(\mathbf{X},\mathbf{Y})$ of ρ is a conjunction of atoms, and the *head* $p(\mathbf{X},\mathbf{Z})$ of ρ is a single atom.

The main decidable Datalog$^{\pm}$ fragments rely on the following five syntactic properties: *weak-acyclicity* [15], *guardedness* [6], *linearity* [9], *stickiness* [10], and *shyness* [21]. And these properties underlie the basic classes of existential rules called weakly-acyclic, guarded, linear, sticky, and shy, respectively. Several variants and combinations of these classes have been defined and studied too [11, 13, 18], as well as semantic properties subsuming the syntactic ones [3, 21].

The five basic classes above are pairwise uncomparable, except for linear which is strictly contained in both guarded and shy, as depicted in Figure 1. Interestingly, both weakly-acyclic and shy strictly contain datalog —the well-known class collecting sets of rules of the form $\forall \mathbf{X} \forall \mathbf{Y}(\phi(\mathbf{X},\mathbf{Y}) \rightarrow p(\mathbf{X}))$, where existential quantification has been dropped. Moreover, sticky strictly contains joinless —the class collecting sets of rules where each body contains no repeated variable. The latter, introduced by Gogacz and Marcinkowski [16] to prove that sticky is finitely controllable, plays a central role also in this paper. Finally, both linear and joinless strictly contain inclusion-dependencies — the well-known class of relational database dependencies collecting sets of rules with one single body atom and no repeated variable.

Under arbitrary models, OBQA can be reduced to the problem of answering q over a universal (or canonical) model U that can be homomorphically embedded into every other model (both finite and infinite) of $D \cup \Sigma$. Therefore, $D \cup \Sigma \models q$ if, and only if, $U \models q$. A way to compute a universal model is to employ the so called *chase* procedure. Starting from D, the chase "repairs" violations of rules by repeatedly adding new atoms —introducing fresh values, called *nulls*, whenever required by an existential variable— until a fixed-point satisfying all rules is reached. In the classical setting, the chase is therefore sound and complete. But when finite model reasoning ($\models_{\mathsf{fin}}$) is required, then the chase is generally uncomplete, unless ontologies are finitely controllable. Hence, proving this property is of utmost importance, especially in contexts where finite model reasoning is relevant, like for databases [23, 4].

Finite controllability of weakly-acyclic comes for free since every ontology here admits a finite universal model, computed by a variant of the chase procedure which goes under the name of *restricted chase* [15]. Conversely, the proof of this property for the subsequent three classes has been a very different matter. Complex, yet intriguing, constructions have been devised for linear [23, 4], guarded [4], and more recently for sticky [16]. To complete the picture, we have addressed the same problem for shy and get the following positive result, which is the main contribution of the paper.

Theorem 1. *Under* shy *ontologies,* $D \cup \Sigma \models q$ *if, and only if,* $D \cup \Sigma \models_{\mathsf{fin}} q$.

For the proof, we design (in Section 3) and exploit (in Section 4) three key technical tools that we consider rather general and that we believe can be useful in the future for similar, or even more general, purposes. In particular, the first (canonical rewriting) and the third one (well-supported finite models) are applicable to every set of existential rules, besides shy ontologies. Finally, we exploit the fact that joinless sets of existential rules are finitely controllable [16]. (Full constructions and proofs are reported in [1].)

2 Ontology-Based Query Answering

Basics. Let $\mathbf{C}$, $\mathbf{N}$ and $\mathbf{V}$ denote pairwise disjoint discrete sets of *constants*, *nulls* and *variables*, respectively. An element t of $\mathbf{T} = \mathbf{C} \cup \mathbf{N} \cup \mathbf{V}$ is called *term*. An *atom* is a labeled tuple $p(t_1, \ldots, t_m)$, where p is a predicate symbol, m is the *arity*, and $t_1, \ldots, t_m$ are terms. An atom is *simple* if it contains no repeated term. We also consider *propositional* atoms, which are simple atoms of arity 0 written without brackets. Given two sets A and B of atoms, a homomorphism from A to B is a mapping $h : \mathbf{T} \to \mathbf{T}$ such that $c \in \mathbf{C}$ implies $h(c) = c$, and also $p(t_1, \ldots, t_m) \in A$ implies $p(h(t_1), \ldots, h(t_m)) \in B$. As usual, $h(A) = \{p(h(t_1), \ldots, h(t_m)) : p(t_1, \ldots, t_m) \in A\} \subseteq B$. An *instance* I is a discrete set of atoms where each term is either a constant or a null.

Syntax. A *database* D is a finite null-free instance. An *(existential) rule* ρ is a first-order formula $\forall \mathbf{X} \forall \mathbf{Y} (\phi(\mathbf{X}, \mathbf{Y}) \to \exists \mathbf{Z} p(\mathbf{X}, \mathbf{Z}))$, where $body(\rho) = \phi(\mathbf{X}, \mathbf{Y})$ is a conjunction of atoms, and $head(\rho) = p(\mathbf{X}, \mathbf{Z})$ is an atom. Constants may occur in ρ. If $\mathbf{Z} = \emptyset$, then ρ is datalog rule. An *ontology* Σ is a set of rules. A *union of Boolean conjunctive query* (UBCQ) q is a first-order expression of the form $\exists \mathbf{Y}_1 \psi_1(\mathbf{Y}_1) \vee \ldots \vee \exists \mathbf{Y}_k \psi_k(\mathbf{Y}_k)$, where each $\psi_j(\mathbf{Y}_j)$ is a conjunction of atoms. Constants may occur also in q. In case $k = 1$, then q is called Boolean conjunctive query, or BCQ for short.

Semantics. Consider a triple $\langle D, \Sigma, q \rangle$ as above. An instance I *satisfies* a rule $\rho \in \Sigma$, denoted by $I \models \rho$, if whenever there is a homomorphism h from $body(\rho)$ to I, then there is a homomorphism $h' \supseteq h|_{\mathbf{X}}$ from $\{head(\rho)\}$ to I. Moreover, I *satisfies* Σ, denoted by $I \models \Sigma$, if I satisfies each rule of Σ. The *models* of $D \cup \Sigma$, denoted by $mods(D,\Sigma)$, consist of the set $\{I : I \supseteq D \text{ and } I \models \Sigma\}$. An instance I *satisfies* q, written $I \models q$, if there is a homomorphism from some $\psi_j(\mathbf{Y}_j)$ to I. Also, q is *true* over $D \cup \Sigma$, written $D \cup \Sigma \models q$, if each model of $D \cup \Sigma$ satisfies q.

The chase. We recall the notion of *chase* [14]. Consider a logical theory $\langle D,\Sigma\rangle$ as above. A rule $\rho \in \Sigma$ is *applicable* to an instance I if there is a homomorphism h from $body(\rho)$ to I. Let $I' = I \cup h'(head(\rho))$, where $h' \supseteq h|_{\mathbf{X}}$ is a homomorphism from $head(\rho)$ to I' such that, for each $Z \in \mathbf{Z}$, $h'(Z)$ is a different fresh null not occurring in I. We will write $\langle \rho,h\rangle(I) = I'$. Indeed, it defines a single *chase step*. The *chase procedure* of $D \cup \Sigma$ is a sequence $I_0 = D \subset I_1 \subset I_2 \subset \ldots \subset I_m \subset \ldots$ of instances obtained by applying exhaustively the rules of Σ in a fair fashion such that, for each $i > 0$, $I_i = \langle \rho,h\rangle(I_{i-1})$, for some rule ρ and homomorphism h from $body(\rho)$ to I_{i-1}. We define $chase(D,\Sigma) = \cup_{i\geq 0} I_i$. It is well-known that $chase(D,\Sigma)$ is a *universal* model of $D \cup \Sigma$. In fact, for each $M \in mods(D,\Sigma)$, there is a homomorphism from $chase(D,\Sigma)$ to M. Hence, given a UBCQ q, it holds that $chase(D,\Sigma) \models q$ if and only if $D \cup \Sigma \models q$ [15].

Shy ontologies. Consider a chase step $\langle \rho,h\rangle(I) = I'$ employed in the construction of $chase(D,\Sigma)$. If Σ is shy, then its underlying properties [21] guarantee that: (1) if X occurs in two different atoms of $body(\rho)$, then $h(X) \in \mathbf{C}$; and (2) if X and Y occur both in $head(\rho)$ and in two different atoms of $body(\rho)$, then $h(X) = h(Y)$ implies $h(X) \in \mathbf{C}$.

Finite controllability. The *finite models* of a theory $D \cup \Sigma$, denoted by *fmods*(D,Σ), are defined as the set of instances $\{I \in mods(D,\Sigma) : |I| \in \mathbb{N}\}$, each of finite size. An ontological fragment $\mathcal{F}$ is said to be *finitely controllable* if, for each database D, for each ontology Σ of $\mathcal{F}$, and for each UBCQ q, it holds that $D \cup \Sigma \not\models q$ implies that there exists a finite model M of $D \cup \Sigma$ such that $M \not\models q$. This is formally stated as $D \cup \Sigma \models q$ if and only if $D \cup \Sigma \models_{\mathsf{fin}} q$, or equivalently $chase(D,\Sigma) \models q$ if and only if $D \cup \Sigma \models_{\mathsf{fin}} q$.

3 Technical Tools

3.1 Canonical Rewriting

From a triple $\langle D,\Sigma,q\rangle$ we build the triple $\langle D^c,\Sigma^c,q^c\rangle$ enjoying the following properties: (1) D^c is propositional database; (2) Σ^c are constant-free rules containing only simple atoms; (3) q^c is a constant-free UBCQ containing only simple atoms; (4) $chase(D^c,\Sigma^c)$ is a constant-free instance containing only simple atoms; (5) there is a "semantic" bijection between $chase(D,\Sigma)$ and $chase(D^c,\Sigma^c)$. By exploiting the above five properties we are able to state the following result.

Theorem 2. *$D \cup \Sigma \models q$ if, and only if, $D^c \cup \Sigma^c \models q^c$.*

Let us now shed some light on our construction. To this aim, consider the ontology $\Sigma = \{person(X) \rightarrow \exists Y\, fatherOf(Y,X); fatherOf(X,Y) \rightarrow person(X)\}$, and the database $D = \{person(tim), person(john), fatherOf(tim,john)\}$. Let p, f, c_1 and c_2 be shorthands of *person*, *fatherOf*, *tim* and *john*, respectively. Hence, $chase(D,\Sigma)$ is $D \cup \{p(n_i)\}_{i>0} \cup \{f(n_1,c_1), f(n_2,c_2)\} \cup \{f(n_{i+2},n_i), f(n_{i+3},n_{i+1})\}_{i>0}$. From D we construct the propositional database $D^c = \{p_{[c_1]},\, p_{[c_2]},\, f_{[c_1,c_2]}\}$ obtained by encoding in the predicates the tuples of D. Then, from Σ we construct Σ^c collecting the following rules:

$$
\begin{array}{llll}
p_{[c_1]} \to \exists Y f_{[1,c_1]}(Y) & f_{[c_1,c_1]} \to p_{[c_1]} & f_{[c_1,1]}(Y) \to p_{[c_1]} & f_{[1,1]}(X) \to p_{[1]}(X) \\
p_{[c_2]} \to \exists Y f_{[1,c_2]}(Y) & f_{[c_1,c_2]} \to p_{[c_1]} & f_{[c_2,1]}(Y) \to p_{[c_2]} & f_{[1,2]}(X,Y) \to p_{[1]}(X) \\
p_{[1]}(X) \to \exists Y f_{[1,2]}(Y,X) & f_{[c_2,c_1]} \to p_{[c_2]} & f_{[1,c_1]}(X) \to p_{[1]}(X) & \\
 & f_{[c_2,c_2]} \to p_{[c_2]} & f_{[1,c_2]}(X) \to p_{[1]}(X) &
\end{array}
$$

The predicates here encode tuples of terms consisting of database constants (c_1 and c_2) and placeholders of nulls (1 and 2). Consider the first rule $\rho : p(X) \to \exists Y f(Y,X)$ applied by the chase over $D \cup \Sigma$, and $h = \{X \mapsto c_1, Y \mapsto n_1\}$ be its associated homomorphism. Hence, $h(body(\rho)) = p(c_1)$ and $h(head(\rho)) = f(n_1, c_1)$. Such an application is mimed by the sister rule $\rho^c : p_{[c_1]} \to \exists Y f_{[1,c_1]}(Y)$. By exploiting the same homomorphism we obtain $h(body(\rho^c)) = p_{[c_1]}$ and $h(head(\rho^c)) = f_{[1,c_1]}(n_1)$. Actually, the encoded tuple $[c_1]$ in $p_{[c_1]}$ says that the original twin atom $p(c_1)$ is unary and its unique term is exactly c_1. Moreover, the encoded tuple $[1, c_1]$ in $f_{[1,c_1]}(n_1)$ says that the original twin atom $f(n_1, c_1)$ is binary, that its first term is a null, and that its second term is exactly the constant c_1. Since from predicate $f_{[1,c_1]}$ we only know that the first term is a null, it must be unary to keep the specific null value.

In the above construction, red rules are those applied by the chase on $D^c \cup \Sigma^c$. For example, rule $f_{[1,c_1]}(X) \to p_{[1]}(X)$ mimics $f(X,Y) \to p(X)$ when X is mapped to a null and Y to c_1; and rule $f_{[1,2]}(X,Y) \to p_{[1]}(X)$ mimics $f(X,Y) \to p(X)$ when X and Y are mapped to different nulls. Hence, $chase(D^c, \Sigma^c) = D^c \cup \{p_{[1]}(n_i)\}_{i>0} \cup \{f_{[1,c_1]}(n_1), f_{[1,c_2]}(n_2)\} \cup \{f_{[1,2]}(n_{i+2}, n_i), f_{[1,2]}(n_{i+3}, n_{i+1})\}_{i>0}$. As a result, the rewriting separates the interaction between the database constants propagated body-to-head via universal variables and the nulls introduced to satisfy existential variables. Also, since the predicates encode the "shapes" of the twin atoms —namely $f_{[1,2]}(X,Y)$ means different nulls while $f_{[1,1]}(X)$ the same null— repeated variables are encoded too.

By following the same approach, we can rewrite also the query. Consider the BCQ $q = \exists X \exists Y r(X,Y) \wedge s(Y, c_1)$. Assume D contains only the constant c_1. Therefore, q^c is the UBCQ $(r_{[c_1,c_1]} \wedge s_{[c_1,c_1]}) \vee (\exists Y r_{[c_1,1]}(Y) \wedge s_{[1,c_1]}(Y)) \vee (\exists X r_{[1,c_1]}(X) \wedge s_{[c_1,c_1]}) \vee (\exists Y r_{[1,1]}(Y) \wedge s_{[1,c_1]}(Y)) \vee (\exists X \exists Y r_{[1,2]}(X,Y) \wedge s_{[1,c_1]}(Y))$.

3.2 Active and Harmless Rules in Shy

Consider a pair $\langle D, \Sigma \rangle$ and the associated pair $\langle D^c, \Sigma^c \rangle$ in canonical form. The final goal of this section is to syntactically identify (and discard) rules of Σ^c that are never applied by the chase. But to be effective here, we need to exploit the key properties of Σ. So, in the rest of this section, let us assume that $\Sigma \in$ shy. First, we observe that the canonical rewriting of a shy ontology is indeed shy. Second, we partition Σ^c in two sets, denoted by Σ^c_a and Σ^c_h, collecting *active* and *harmless* rules, respectively, enjoying the following properties: (1) Σ^c_h are the rules of Σ^c with at least a variable occurring in more than one body atom; (2) $\Sigma^c_a = \Sigma^c \setminus \Sigma^c_h$ is a joinless (and still shy) ontology; and (3) $chase(D^c, \Sigma^c) = chase(D^c, \Sigma^c_a)$. By exploiting the above three properties we are able to state the following result.

Theorem 3. *For each $\Sigma \in$ shy, it holds that $D^c \cup \Sigma^c \models q^c$ if, and only if, $D^c \cup \Sigma^c_a \models q^c$.*

Also in this case, instead of proving formally the above theorem, we provide some insights regarding the way how we partition Σ^c. From the database $D = \{p(c)\}$ and the shy ontology $\Sigma = \{p(X) \to \exists Y\, f(Y,X);\ f(X,Y), p(X) \to p(Y)\}$ we first construct $D^c = \{p_{[c]}\}$ and Σ^c collecting the following rules

$$\begin{array}{rlrl} p_{[c]} & \to \exists Y f_{[1,c]}(Y) & f_{[1,c]}(X), p_{[1]}(X) & \to p_{[c]} \\ p_{[1]}(X) & \to \exists Y f_{[1,2]}(Y,X) & f_{[1,1]}(X), p_{[1]}(X) & \to p_{[1]}(X) \\ f_{[c,c]}, p_{[c]} & \to p_{[c]} & f_{[1,2]}(X,Y), p_{[1]}(X) & \to p_{[1]}(Y) \\ f_{[c,1]}(Y), p_{[c]} & \to p_{[1]}(Y) & & \end{array}$$

Again, red rules are those applied by the chase on $D^c \cup \Sigma^c$. Now we observe that there is no way to trigger the rules in the second column: although the chase does produce an atom $f(t,n_i)$ for some term t and null n_i, it never produces any atom $p(n_i)$. This fact is detected by the syntactic conditions underlying shy, which actually consider variable X as "protected" in $f(X,Y), p(X) \to p(Y)$. Hence, Σ^c_a contains only the joinless rules in the first column, while Σ^c_h contains the remaining "join-rules" in the second column.

3.3 Well-Supported Finite Models

Inspired by the notion of *well-supported interpretations* introduced in the context of general logic programming, we define the notion of *well-supported* finite models of a pair $\langle D, \Sigma \rangle$, denoted by $wsfmods(D,\Sigma)$, which enjoy the following properties: (1) for each $M \in fmods(D,\Sigma)$, there exists a well-supported finite model $M' \subseteq M$; (2) each minimal finite model of $D \cup \Sigma$ is a well-supported finite model. Assuming that the symbol $\models_{\mathsf{wsf}}$ refers to the satisfiability of the query under the well-supported finite models only, by exploiting the above two properties we are able to state the following result.

Theorem 4. *$D \cup \Sigma \models_{\mathsf{fin}} q$, if and only, if $D \cup \Sigma \models_{\mathsf{wsf}} q$.*

Unfortunately, in this case, we cannot avoid defining formally this notion. A finite instance I is called *well-supported* w.r.t. $D \cup \Sigma$ if there exists an ordering $(\alpha_1,\ldots,\alpha_m)$ of its atoms such that, for each $j \in \{1,\ldots,m\}$, at least one of the following two conditions is satisfied: (i) α_j is a database atom of D; or (ii) there exist a rule ρ of Σ and a homomorphism h from the atoms of ρ to $\{\alpha_1,\ldots,\alpha_j\}$ such that $h(head(\rho)) = \{\alpha_j\}$ and $h(body(\rho)) \subseteq \{\alpha_1,\ldots,\alpha_{j-1}\}$.

Interestingly, although each finite model of an ontological theory contains a well-supported finite model of the theory, the reverse inclusion does not hold, as shown in the following example. Consider the father-person ontology Σ given in Section 3.1. $M = D \cup \{f(c_1,c_1), f(c_2,c_1)\}$ is a well-supported finite model of $D \cup \Sigma$. Indeed, for instance, $(p(c_1), p(c_2), f(c_1,c_2), f(c_1,c_1), f(c_2,c_1))$ is a well-supported ordering of M. However, $M \setminus \{f(c_2,c_1)\}$ is a model of $D \cup \Sigma$. Therefore, M is not a minimal model.

4 Finite Controllability of Shy Ontologies

With our technical tools in place, we are now able to prove our main technical result.

Theorem 5. *For each $\Sigma \in$ shy, it holds that $D \cup \Sigma \models_{\mathsf{fin}} q$ if, and only if, $D^c \cup \Sigma^c_a \models_{\mathsf{wsf}} q^c$.*

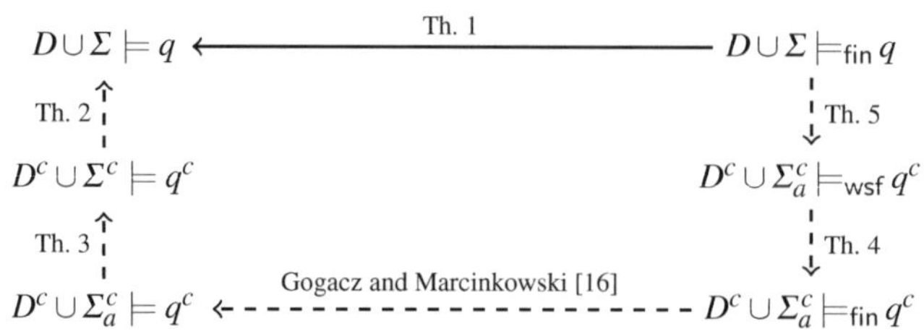

Fig. 2. Chain of implications for the proof of Theorem 1.

For our purposes, the "only if" direction is the most important one. Consider an arbitrary model $M^c \in \mathit{wsfmods}(D^c, \Sigma^c_a)$. Let $\mathit{decode}(M^c)$ be the instance obtained from M^c by decoding its atoms. For example, if $p_{[1,c,1]}(n_i) \in M^c$, then $p(n_i, c, n_i) \in \mathit{decode}(M^c)$. It suffices to prove that there exist $M \in \mathit{fmods}(D, \Sigma)$ and a homomorphism h' s.t. $h'(M) \subseteq \mathit{decode}(M^c)$. Indeed, by hypothesis, there exists a homomorphism h s.t. $h(q) \subseteq M$, and so $(h' \circ h)(q) \subseteq \mathit{decode}(M^c)$. Then, the result follows by the fact that $(h' \circ h)(q^c) \subseteq M^c$.

The difficulty here is that $\mathit{decode}(M^c)$ could not be a model of $D \cup \Sigma$. Consider the database $D = \{s(c)\}$ and the shy ontology $\Sigma = \{s(X) \to \exists Y\, p(Y);\; s(X) \to \exists Y\, r(Y);\; p(X), r(X) \to g(X)\}$. The canonical rewriting is $D^c = \{s_{[c]}\}$ and Σ^c as follows:

$$
\begin{array}{lll}
s_{[c]} \to \exists Y\, p_{[1]}(Y) & s_{[c]} \to \exists Y\, r_{[1]}(Y) & p_{[c]}, r_{[c]} \to g_{[c]} \\
s_{[1]}(X) \to \exists Y\, p_{[1]}(Y) & s_{[1]}(X) \to \exists Y\, r_{[1]}(Y) & p_{[1]}(X), r_{[1]}(X) \to g_{[1]}(X)
\end{array}
$$

One can verify that $M^c = \{s_{[c]}, p_{[1]}(n_1), r_{[1]}(n_1)\}$ is a (minimal) well-supported finite model of $D^c \cup \Sigma^c_a$ since Σ^c_a is obtained from Σ^c by discarding the last harmless rule. However, $\mathit{decode}(M^c) = \{s(c), p(n_1), r(n_1)\}$ is not a model of $D \cup \Sigma$ because the third rule is not satisfied. The idea now is to show how to construct from $\mathit{decode}(M^c)$ a model $M \in \mathit{fmods}(D, \Sigma)$ that can be homomorphically mapped to $\mathit{decode}(M^c)$. Intuitively, we identify the *starting points* in which existentially quantified variables of Σ^c_a have been satisfied and rename the introduced terms using the so-called *propagation ordering*. In the example above, consider the ordering $(s(c), p(n_1), r(n_1))$ of $\mathit{decode}(M^c)$, replace n_1 in $p(n_1)$ by $\langle n_1, 2, 2\rangle$ (null n_1 introduced in the second atom in the second position), and replace n_1 in $r(n_1)$ by $\langle n_1, 3, 2\rangle$ (null n_1 introduced in the third atom in the second position). Then, since M^c is well-supported, we propagate (if needed) these new terms according the supporting ordering. In our case, $M = \{s(c), p(\langle n_1, 2, 2\rangle), r(\langle n_1, 3, 2\rangle)\}$ is now a finite model of $D \cup \Sigma$ that can be mapped to $\mathit{decode}(M^c)$.

Finally, to prove Theorem 1, we can now combine the trivial "only if" implication with the dashed chain of intermediate results given in Figure 2.

5 Conclusion

At this point, also thanks to the results shown in this paper, we know that every basic decidable Datalog$^{\pm}$ class is finitely controllable. However, the problem remains open for extensions and combinations of these classes [11, 13, 18]. For example, it is open whether finite controllability holds for the following classes: (*i*) sticky-join, generalizing sticky and linear; (*ii*) tame, generalizing sticky and guarded; and (*iii*) weakly-sticky-join, generalizing sticky-join, weakly-acyclic and shy. We believe that the techniques developed in this paper can be exploited to give an answer to these questions.

References

1. Amendola, G., Leone, N., Manna, M.: Finite model reasoning over existential rules. Fourthcoming (2017)
2. Baader, F., Calvanese, D., McGuinness, D.L., Nardi, D., Patel-Schneider, P.F. (eds.): The Description Logic Handbook: Theory, Implementation, and Applications. CUP (2003)
3. Baget, J., Leclère, M., Mugnier, M., Salvat, E.: Extending decidable cases for rules with existential variables. In: In Proc. of IJCAI'09. pp. 677–682 (2009)
4. Bárány, V., Gottlob, G., Otto, M.: Querying the guarded fragment. Logical Methods in Computer Science 10(2) (2014)
5. Bourhis, P., Manna, M., Morak, M., Pieris, A.: Guarded-based disjunctive tuple-generating dependencies. ACM TODS 41(4), 27:1–27:45 (2016)
6. Calì, A., Gottlob, G., Kifer, M.: Taming the infinite chase: Query answering under expressive relational constraints. J. Artif. Intell. Res. (JAIR) 48, 115–174 (2013)
7. Calì, A., Gottlob, G., Lukasiewicz, T.: Datalog$^{\pm}$: a unified approach to ontologies and integrity constraints. In: In Proc. of ICDT'09. pp. 14–30 (2009)
8. Calì, A., Gottlob, G., Lukasiewicz, T.: Tractable query answering over ontologies with datalog+/-. In: In Proc. of DL'09 (2009)
9. Calì, A., Gottlob, G., Lukasiewicz, T.: A general datalog-based framework for tractable query answering over ontologies. J. Web Sem. 14, 57–83 (2012)
10. Calì, A., Gottlob, G., Pieris, A.: Advanced processing for ontological queries. PVLDB 3(1), 554–565 (2010)
11. Calì, A., Gottlob, G., Pieris, A.: Towards more expressive ontology languages: The query answering problem. AIJ 193, 87–128 (2012)
12. Calvanese, D., De Giacomo, G., Lembo, D., Lenzerini, M., Rosati, R.: Data complexity of query answering in description logics. AIJ 195, 335–360 (2013)
13. Civili, C., Rosati, R.: A broad class of first-order rewritable tuple-generating dependencies. In: In Proc. of Datalog 2.0. pp. 68–80 (2012)
14. Deutsch, A., Nash, A., Remmel, J.B.: The chase revisited. In: In Proc. of PODS'08. pp. 149–158 (2008)
15. Fagin, R., Kolaitis, P.G., Miller, R.J., Popa, L.: Data exchange: semantics and query answering. TCS 336(1), 89–124 (2005)
16. Gogacz, T., Marcinkowski, J.: Converging to the chase - A tool for finite controllability. In: In Proc. of LICS'13. pp. 540–549 (2013)
17. Gottlob, G., Kikot, S., Kontchakov, R., Podolskii, V.V., Schwentick, T., Zakharyaschev, M.: The price of query rewriting in ontology-based data access. AIJ 213, 42–59 (2014)
18. Gottlob, G., Manna, M., Pieris, A.: Combining decidability paradigms for existential rules. TPLP 13(4-5), 877–892 (2013)
19. Gottlob, G., Orsi, G., Pieris, A.: Query rewriting and optimization for ontological databases. ACM TODS 39(3), 25:1–25:46 (2014)
20. Gottlob, G., Pieris, A., Tendera, L.: Querying the guarded fragment with transitivity. In: In Proc. of ICALP'13. pp. 287–298 (2013)
21. Leone, N., Manna, M., Terracina, G., Veltri, P.: Efficiently computable Datalog$^{\exists}$ programs. In: In Proc. of KR'12 (2012)
22. Rosati, R.: The limits of querying ontologies. In: In Proc. of ICDT'07. pp. 164–178 (2007)
23. Rosati, R.: On the finite controllability of conjunctive query answering in databases under open-world assumption. JCSS 77(3), 572–594 (2011)

Discussion Paper
Prompting the data transformation activities for cluster analysis on collections of documents

Tania Cerquitelli, Evelina Di Corso, Francesco Ventura and Silvia Chiusano

Politecnico di Torino - Dipartimento di Automatica e Informatica
Corso Duca Degli Abruzzi, 24 - 10129 Torino - ITALY
{name.surname}@polito.it

Abstract. In this work we argue towards a new self-learning engine able to suggest to the analyst good transformation methods and weighting schemas for a given data collection. This new generation of systems, named SELF-DATA (SELF-learning DAta TrAnsformation) relies on an engine capable of exploring different data weighting schemas (e.g., normalized term frequencies, logarithmic entropy) and data transformation methods (e.g., PCA, LSI) before applying a given data mining algorithm (e.g., cluster analysis), evaluating and comparing solutions through different quality indices (e.g., weighted Silhouette), and presenting the 3-top solutions to the analyst. SELF-DATA will also include a knowledge database storing results of experiments on previously processed datasets, and a classification algorithm trained on the knowledge base content to forecast the best methods for future analyses.
SELF-DATA's current implementation runs on Apache Spark, a state-of-the-art distributed computing framework. The preliminary validation performed on 4 collections of documents highlights that the TF-IDF and logarithmic entropy weighting methods are effective to measure item relevance with sparse datasets, and the LSI method outperforms PCA in the presence of a larger feature domain.

Keywords: Text mining; parameter-free technique; Big data framework.

1 Introduction

Data-driven analysis is a multi-step process, in which data scientists tackle the complex task of configuring the analytics system to transform data into actionable knowledge. Since collections of textual data are usually characterized by a high variability, the knowledge extraction process is challenging and requires a lot of expertise. The text mining is focused on studying algorithms to find implicit, previously unknown, and potentially high-quality information from a large collection of documents. Text mining activities include: (i) grouping data/documents with similar properties or similar content [3], (ii) topic detection [1], and (iii) document summarizations [5].

Effectively performing the text mining process on textual data requires a multi-step process involving different algorithms and for each one different specific parameters should be manually set by the end-user. Furthermore, different methods exist and the selection of the optimal ones is guided by the expertise of the analyst. Innovative and scalable solutions need to be devised to suggest to the analyst how configure the mining process to relieve the end-user of the burden of selecting proper methods for the overall cluster analysis process [2].

This paper proposes SELF-DATA (SELF-learning DAta TrAnsformation), a distributed engine to suggest to the analyst a good configuration of the mining process to cluster a collection of documents into cohesive and well-separated groups. SELF-DATA relies on different building components that characterize the data distribution of collections of documents and *learn* how configure the analytics process through self-tuning and self-learning strategies. Based on previous processed datasets, SELF-DATA will also be able, in the future, to suggest to the analyst the complete configuration of the mining process after the characterization of the data distribution of a new unexplored dataset. SELF-DATA's current implementation runs on the Apache Spark [8] framework, supporting parallel and scalable processing for analytics activities. A preliminary set of experiments have been performed on four textual data collections to show the potential of some components of SELF-DATA. The experiments highlighted the ability of some of SELF-DATA's components to automatically identify a good weighting schema, a good transformation method, and good values for specific-algorithm parameters.

This paper is organized as follows. Section 2 presents the SELF-DATA envisioned architecture and a brief description of its main building components, while Section 3 discusses the preliminary performed experiments. Finally, Section 4 draws conclusions and presents future developments of this work.

2 The SELF-DATA engine

SELF-DATA (SELF-learning DAta TrAnsformation) is a distributed engine whose aim is to suggest to the analyst a good configuration of the whole mining process to cluster a textual data collection into correlated groups of documents with a similar topic. The components of the SELF-DATA envisioned architecture, as well as the interactions between such components, are shown in Figure 1. It relies on 5 main components exploited in 2 phases, i.e., *learning* and *prediction* phases.

Learning phase. During the learning phase, SELF-DATA learns good configurations of the whole mining process for specifics data distributions of textual data collections from previous processed datasets. To this aim SELF-DATA relies on 4 main components able to (i) automatically configure the complete clustering activity (e.g., selecting the good weighting schema and transformation method, automatically setting the specific-algorithm input parameters) by exploiting self-tuning strategies; (ii) characterize different data distribution through the computation of various indices; (iii) store results of steps (i) and (ii)

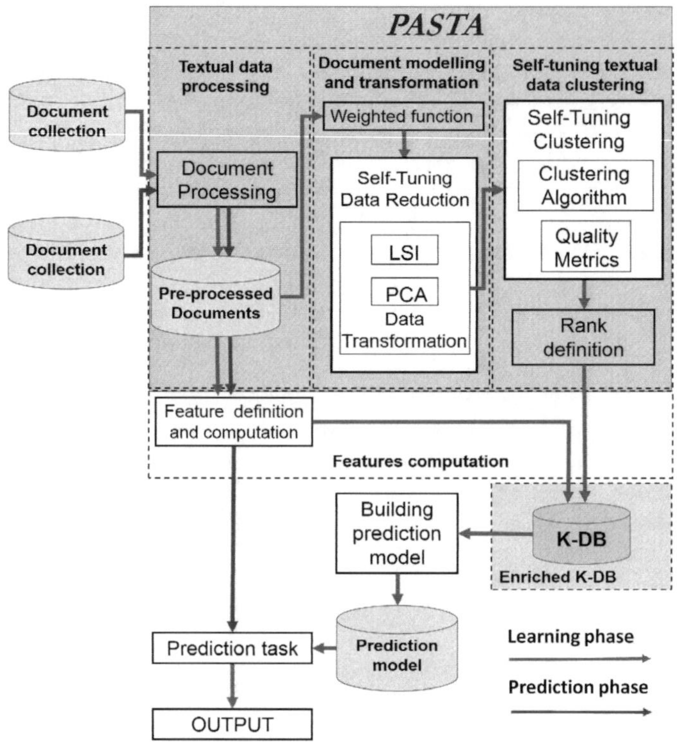

Fig. 1: The SELF-DATA architecture

into a knowledge base; and (iv) exploit the knowledge base to learn which subsets of data distribution indices with the corresponding values are mainly able to forecast the best configuration of the cluster analysis process of textual data collections. Specifically, the following components characterize the SELF-DATA learning phase.

– PASTA (PArameter-free Solutions for Textual Analysis) [4] is *a distributed self-tuning engine* including parameter-setting procedures to relieve the end-user of the burden of selecting proper values for the overall cluster analysis process on a collection of documents. The PASTA engine, reported in Figure 1, includes all the analytics blocks to make the overall analysis problem more effectively tractable and minimize user intervention. Specifically, PASTA includes three main building blocks: (i) *Textual data processing*, (ii) *Document modeling and transformation* including a self-tuning data reduction algorithm, and (iii) *Self-tuning textual data clustering*.
  PASTA explores different suitable data weighting strategies, based on local (*Term-Frequency* (TF) and *Logarithmic term frequency* (Log)) and global

(*Inverse Document Frequency* (IDF)) weights and data transformation methods (e.g., PCA, LSI) before applying a clustering algorithm to gain better insights from the analysis. To streamline the analytics process PASTA includes two procedures to relieve the end-user of the burden of selecting proper values for algorithm-specific parameters. These procedures evaluate and compare solutions through different quality indices (e.g., Silhouette-based indices, rand index, f-measure) to identify a few good configurations (3-top) of the mining process that yield a good partition of the original dataset. PASTA's current implementation runs on the Apache Spark framework, supporting parallel and scalable processing for analytics activities.

- The *Feature computation* component is an engine capable of characterizing the data distribution of a collection of documents (corpus) through various indices including
  - # categories: the original number of topics in the dataset under analysis (if known);
  - Avg frequency terms: the average frequency of a term's occurrence in the corpus;
  - Max frequency: the maximum frequency of a term's occurrence in the corpus;
  - Min frequency: the minimum frequency of a term's occurrence in the corpus;
  - # documents: the number of documents in the corpus;
  - # terms: number of terms in the corpus, with repetitions;
  - Dictionary: the number of different terms in the corpus (without repetition);
  - TTR: the relation between the dictionary variety and the total number of terms in the corpus. It is calculated as a ratio between *Dictionary* and *# terms*;
  - Hapax %: the ratio between number of Hapax (number of terms with one occurrence) and the cardinality of the dictionary;
  - Guiraud Index: the ratio between the cardinality of the dictionary and the square root of *# terms*. It represents the *lexical richness*.
- **K-DB** is a knowledge base storing results of 3-top solutions identified through PASTA on previously processed datasets, including data distribution characterization. Specifically, for each processed dataset K-DB stores one record for each solution selected by PASTA. Each record includes the values of the various indices characterizing the data distribution, the selected weighting schema and transformation method, with the suggested input parameter value for either the LSI or PCA transformation method, and the suggested value for the input parameter of the clustering algorithm (i.e., the desired number of cluster).
- **Building a prediction model** addresses a classification problem trained on the knowledge base content to generate a prediction model to suggest to the analyst a good configuration/setting for the cluster analysis process on a given unexplored dataset. Many different approaches (e.g., data mining approaches, logic programming, statistics models) can be exploited for this complex and challenging task.

Prediction phase. Given a new document collection, SELF-DATA first applies the document processing step and then computes the set of features to characterize data distribution. Given the values of the data distribution indices, the prediction model is exploited to forecast a good configuration of the cluster analysis process. This step suggests to the analyst a good weighting schema (both local and global) and a transformation method, and good values for specific-algorithm input parameters to effectively cluster the data collection into a few well-separated and cohesive groups of documents addressing a similar topic.

3 Preliminary development and results

Here we presented a preliminary implementation of the SELF-DATA system with its preliminary results.

Preliminary development. A preliminary implementation of some components of SELF-DATA has been developed.

The current implementation includes: (1) the feature computation building block able to characterize the data distribution through some basic indices (see Section 2 for further detail) and (2) an extended version of the PASTA component presented in [4]. PASTA includes:

- two local weights (TF and Log) and two global weights (IDF and Entropy) [6] to measure term relevance;
- two data transformation methods LSI and PCA;
- two self-tuning algorithms to automatically select the specific-algorithm parameters of data transformation method (input parameter is K, the number of relevant dimensions to consider) and the K-means algorithm (input parameter is k_{cls}, the desired number of clusters) respectively [4].

PASTA exploits various quality metrics to evaluate different configurations of the mining process.

Silhouette-based indices: purified and weighted Silhouette. The *Silhouette index* [7] measures both intra-cluster cohesion and inter-cluster separation. The *weighted silhouette index* WS [4], computed on a given collection of documents, is the ratio between (i) the sum of the percentage of documents in each positive bin weighted with an integer value (weights in $[w_{min} = 1 - w_{max} = 10]$, where the highest weight is assigned to the first bin [1 - 0.9] and so on) and (ii) the overall sum of weights. The higher the weighted silhouette index, the better the identified partition. The *purified silhouette index* PS [4] disregards documents appearing in singleton clusters to reduce the impact of these documents in the overall Silhouette index.

Classification technique to assess the robustness of a given document partition. PASTA builds a *classifier* using the same input features of the clustering algorithm, and the class label assigned by the clustering algorithm as target. PASTA integrates the random forest method [6] to create the classification model. Quality metrics such as *accuracy and f-measure*[1] are then computed. The higher the classification metrics, the better the overall quality of the clusters.

Preliminary results. We performed preliminary experiments on four real collections of documents (see Table 1) to evaluate (i) the ability of the proposed indices to characterize and differentiate data distributions and (ii) the ability of the PASTA component to correctly identify good configurations for the cluster analysis.

Characterization of the data distribution. Table 1 shows the proposed data distribution indices to characterize data distribution of the considered datasets. The Guirand index is a good parameter to distinguish datasets with a very sparse data distribution (D1 and D2 in Table 1) from less sparse (D3 and D4) datasets. Datasets with high values for lexical richness are usually characterized by a high variability in the data dictionary, thus more sparse data distribution. The TTR index also allows to better differentiate sparse data distribution from more dense data distributions. In fact, the TTR value for D3 is one order of magnitude higher than the TTR values of the others.

Table 1: Datasets

	Wikipedia		Twitter	Reuters
ID	D1	D2	D3	D4
# categories	5	10	-	2
Avg frequency terms	17	23	2	12
Max frequency	8,642	19,437	86	2,605
Min frequency	1	1	1	1
# documents	989	2468	978	1,000
# terms	1,138,570	3,118,499	3,997	80,060
Dictionary	67,539	13,649	1,727	6,453
TTR	0.059	0.044	0.432	0.081
Hapax %	0.505	0.519	0.713	0.371
Guiraud Index	63.3	77.3	27.3	22.8

Selecting good configurations for the whole process of cluster analysis. For each dataset PASTA has been run eight times, once for each combination of a weighting function and a transformation method. Table 2 shows the 3-top solutions identified by PASTA for dataset D1 and by considering the LSI method and all weighting functions. The optimal solution is reported in bold.

For D1 PASTA identifies for K (i.e., number of relevant dimensions for LSI) 34, 37 and 112 dimensions to be considered for the cluster analysis. Given these numbers of dimensions, PASTA selects $k_{cls} = 10$ (input parameter for the K-means algorithm) as the optimal partition. We observed that PASTA usually

[1] It is the weighted harmonic mean of precision and recall

selects as optimal partition the experiment exploiting a low-medium number of dimensions (terms). The higher the K, the more variable the data distribution is and the more complex the cluster activity will be. Thus, the Silhouette-based indices (purified PS and weighted WS) tend to slightly decrease when a large number of terms featuring in each document is analyzed. Furthermore, the results reported in Table 2 highlight that the TF-IDF, Log-IDF and TF-Entropy weighting functions are able to better differentiate the weighting terms, thus identifying a larger number of clusters (associated with different topics in the same category) than the one discovered by Log-Entropy.

Table 2: Results for dataset D1

DId	Trans	Weight	K	k_{cls}	Accuracy	WA-F-Measure	PS	WS
			34	6	0.99	0.99	0.3	0.058
D1	LSI	TF-IDF	**37**	**10**	**0.96**	**0.96**	**0.3**	**0.062**
			112	12	0.91	0.91	0.2	0.039
			19	**7**	**0.95**	**0.95**	**0.3**	**0.068**
D1	LSI	Log-IDF	27	5	0.98	0.98	0.3	0.049
			76	6	0.97	0.97	0.2	0.043
			38	**10**	**0.91**	**0.91**	**0.3**	**0.056**
D1	LSI	TF-Entropy	44	16	0.89	0.89	0.3	0.052
			90	6	0.97	0.96	0.2	0.037
			21	**5**	**0.99**	**0.99**	**0.4**	**0.076**
D1	LSI	Log-Entropy	27	5	0.98	0.98	0.4	0.066
			84	6	0.97	0.97	0.2	0.048

We also compared the optimal configurations selected by PASTA when it explores LSI with respect to the ones obtained with PCA. Table 3 shows the best configuration selected by PASTA for both LSI and PCA and for all weighting functions. Results are obtained on D3 and D4 datasets. For datasets D1 and D2 the LSI method outperforms PCA (detailed results are omitted to lack of space), whereas for dataset D3 and D4 PCA yield a better final partition than LSI. Thus, we can conclude that the LSI method outperforms PCA in the presence of a larger data domain, and usually a more sparse data distribution.

4 Conclusions and future work

This paper presents a challenging vision for a self-learning engine capable of predicting how to configure the cluster analysis process of a collection of textual data. A preliminary implementation of some components has been presented and evaluated on four real collections of documents. We plan to develop the complete SELF-DATA system in a future work.

Table 3: Results for D3 and D4 datasets

DId	Trans	Weight	K	k_{cls}	Accuracy	WA-F-Measure	PS	WS
D3	LSI	TF-IDF	16	20	0.89	0.89	0.4	0.063
		Log-IDF	16	18	0.86	0.86	0.4	0.062
		TF-Entropy	13	20	0.9	0.9	0.4	0.061
		Log-Entropy	12	15	0.86	0.86	0.4	0.059
D3	PCA	TF-IDF	16	17	0.87	0.87	0.3	0.061
		Log-IDF	16	17	0.92	0.92	0.4	0.064
		TF-Entropy	13	20	0.88	0.88	0.3	0.064
		Log-Entropy	12	18	0.9	0.88	0.4	0.062
D4	LSI	TF-IDF	30	3	0.96	0.96	0.3	0.045
		Log-IDF	18	8	0.94	0.94	0.3	0.064
		TF-Entropy	29	7	0.92	0.92	0.3	0.059
		Log-Entropy	18	8	0.94	0.94	0.3	0.063
D4	PCA	TF-IDF	30	3	0.99	0.99	0.3	0.047
		Log-IDF	18	13	0.9	0.9	0.3	0.069
		TF-Entropy	29	3	0.98	0.98	0.3	0.052
		Log-Entropy	18	5	0.95	0.95	0.3	0.058

References

1. Luca Cagliero, Tania Cerquitelli, Paolo Garza, and Luigi Grimaudo. Twitter data analysis by means of strong flipping generalized itemsets. *Journal of Systems and Software*, 94:16–29, 2014.
2. Tania Cerquitelli, Elena Baralis, Lia Morra, and Silvia Chiusano. Data mining for better healthcare: A path towards automated data analysis? In *32nd IEEE International Conference on Data Engineering Workshops, ICDE Workshops 2016, Helsinki, Finland, May 16-20, 2016*, pages 60–63, 2016.
3. Tania Cerquitelli, Silvia Chiusano, and Xin Xiao. Exploiting clustering algorithms in a multiple-level fashion: A comparative study in the medical care scenario. *Expert Syst. Appl.*, 55:297–312, 2016.
4. Evelina Di Corso, Tania Cerquitelli, and Francesco Ventura. Self-tuning techniques for large scale cluster analysis on textual data collections. In *Proceedings of the 32nd Annual ACM Symposium on Applied Computing, Marrakesh, Morocco, April 3rd-7th, 2017*, pages 771–776, 2017.
5. Oskar Gross, Antoine Doucet, and Hannu Toivonen. Language-independent multi-document text summarization with document-specific word associations. In *31st Annual ACM Symposium on Applied Computing*, Pisa, Italy, 2016. ACM, ACM.
6. Pang-Ning T. and Steinbach M. and Kumar V. *Introduction to Data Mining*. Addison-Wesley, 2006.
7. Peter J. Rousseeuw. Silhouettes: A graphical aid to the interpretation and validation of cluster analysis. *Journal of Computational and Applied Mathematics*, 20:53 – 65, 1987.
8. Matei Zaharia, Mosharaf Chowdhury, Tathagata Das, Ankur Dave, Justin Ma, Murphy McCauley, Michael J. Franklin, Scott Shenker, and Ion Stoica. Resilient distributed datasets: A fault-tolerant abstraction for in-memory cluster computing. In *NSDI'12*, 2012.

Effects of Semantic Analysis on Named-Entity Recognition with Conditional Random Fields – Extended Abstract –

Sonia Bergamaschi[1], Andrea Cappelli[2*], Antonio Circiello[1*], Marco Varone[2]

[1]Dipartimento di Ingegneria "Enzo Ferrari"
Università di Modena e Reggio Emilia - Italy
sonia.bergamaschi@unimore.it
a.circiello@outlook.com
[2]Expert System S.p.A.
Modena - Italy
mvarone@expertsystem.com
*affiliation when the work was performed

Abstract. We propose a novel Named Entity Recognition (NER) system based on a machine learning technique and a semantic network. The NER system is able to exploit the advantages of semantic information, coming from Expert System proprietary technology, Cogito. NER is a task of Natural Language Processing (NLP) which consists in detecting, from an unformatted text source and classify, Named Entities (NE), i.e. real-world entities that can be denoted with a rigid designator. To address this problem, the chosen approach is a combination of machine learning and deep semantic processing. The machine learning method used is Conditional Random Fields (CRF).
CRF is particularly suitable for the task because it analyzes an input sequence considering the whole sequence, instead of one item at a time. CRF has been trained not only with classical information, available after a simple computation or anyway with little effort, but with semantic information too. Semantic information is obtained with Sensigrafo and Semantic Disambiguator, which are the proprietary semantic network and semantic engine of Expert System, respectively. The results are encouraging, as we can experimentally prove the improvements in the NER task obtained by exploiting semantics.

1 Introduction

In this work we tackle the Named Entity Recognition (NER) task by combining machine learning with a heuristic disambiguation approach based on deep semantic analysis. NER is a well-known Natural Language Processing (NLP) task consisting in detecting and classifying Named Entities (NE) from free, unstructured text. Named Entities are typically defined as real-world concepts that can be referred to via rigid designators. We address this problem by employing a powerful machine learning algorithm, Conditional Random Fields (CRF), and providing it with data enriched by deep semantic processing. NER can be mapped into a labeling problem. CRF are very well suited to this kind of problems since they can analyze sequences as a whole, choosing labels for the sequence items with globally optimal choices instead of one item at a time. We employ Cogito, Expert System proprietary linguistic analysis technology, to enrich our machine learning pipeline with semantic information. In this work, CRF are fed with both standard linguistic features and semantic information obtained from Sensigrafo and Semantic Disambiguator, the proprietary semantic network and semantic engine of Expert System, respectively.

In this paper, results are presented about the performance improvements obtained by using semantic data together with standard features, as compared with the case in which only traditional features are employed.

Moreover, in the extended version of this paper submitted to the WIMS 2017 conference we performed more experiments varying the size of the corpus used for the analysis and showed the fundamental role semantics plays in many cases.

The rest of the paper is organized as follows.

Section 2 briefly describes our supervised Named Entity Recognition approach that is trained on both standard features and semantic information obtained from text analysis performed with the well-known Cogito linguistic analysis engine, developed by Expert Systems, an international Text Analytics and Cognitive Computing Company. Section 3 is devoted to the Experimental Results obtained on a reduced version of the larger Reuters Corpus, a collection of Reuters news articles. The documents in the corpus are related to various categories, from politics to sports. The training set is composed by one thousand documents while the test set is composed by four hundred documents. Finally, Section 4 outlines conclusions and future work.

2 The Method

The approach we propose is based on a CRF algorithm [11], that is trained on both standard features and semantic information obtained from text analysis performed with the Cogito linguistic analysis engine [3][12].

NER is a field that has been extensively explored in the last years. But the use of Expert System's technology, that is not simple semantic technology, but a complex system aimed, designed and optimized to create an optimal disambiguation process, could lead to very interesting outcomes. Our goal is to combine this resource to the tunability and domain adaptability of a machine learning algorithm such as CRF.

The final goal is to devise a new supervised Named Entity Recognition method, paying attention to the role of semantics in condition of scarse available training data. CRFs are a state-of-the-art class of machine learning algorithms to solve sequence labeling problems. They are part of the more general category of graphical models and are widely used in the domain of NLP, particularly as regards Part-Of-Speech tagging and Named Entity Recognition. Labels are obtained for an input sequence by evaluating label probabilities for a token given

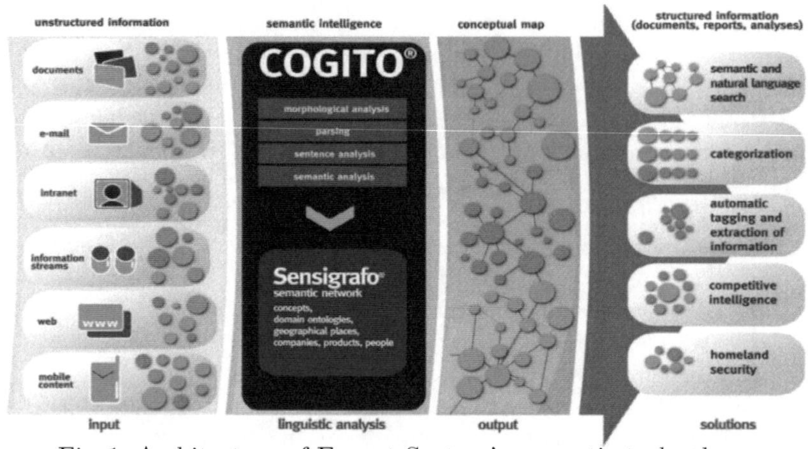

Fig. 1: Architecture of Expert System's semantic technology.

the surrounding tokens, their properties and earlier labels in the sequence. The most likely sequence is finally chosen based on an overall optimization over all possible label sequences.

The semantic analysis of the Cogito component named Semantic Disambiguator allows to associate words in the analysed text to *syncons*, a concept similar to WordNet synsets [8], which are related to each other via semantic links (hyperonymy, meronymy and others) in a proprietary semantic network called Sensigrafo. The linguistic engine is used also for basic linguistic tasks like tokenisation and POS-tagging, and for subject-verb-object relations detection. It also performs text categorisation. All of the information described above is combined in order to get a data matrix of linguistic information for each word in the text [5], so that features can be generated from it to train the CRF and finally detect entities.

Specifically, semantic information was employed to take advantage of the rich hyperonymy/hyponymy relations encoded in the semantic network. For that purpose, some columns of the data matrix were built as follows: for a given word in the text, its meaning ID was retrieved thanks to disambiguation [7][4][10]. Using it, the whole hyperonymy chain for that meaning was obtained, from the concept itself to its more abstract semantic ancestor (i.e. the last of its hypernyms of hypernyms, etc.). Then, moving top-down from that ancestor, up to four levels of ancestors were selected. The choice was limited to some specific nodes of the semantic network that are internally marked as *category nodes*, i.e. well representing a specific class of meanings (e.g.: verbs of communication or invertebrates). Each of such retrieved ancestor meanings (max 4) was used as one separate column in the data matrix. In other words, the four farthest hypernyms of the current meaning were retrieved (if present), that also are marked as "category nodes".

The rationale behind this procedure was to permit the clustering of the meaning of the words in the text at different levels of fine-graining, subsequently leav-

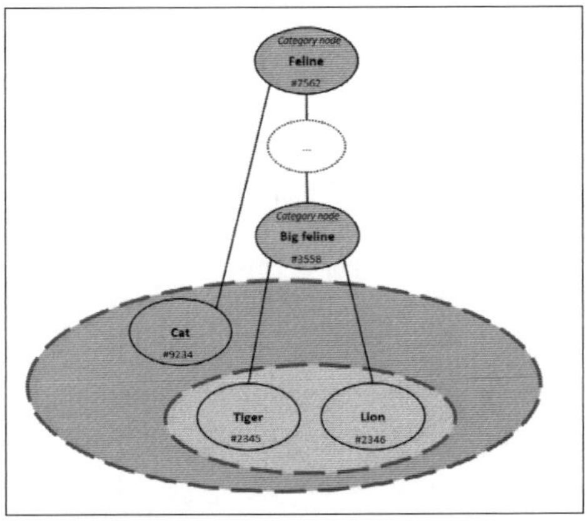

Fig. 2: Example of category nodes. Each node that is under this kind of nodes represents a concepts that semantically belongs to the category expressed by the category node.

ing the CRF the task of deciding which levels to pay more attention to. In this way, e.g., both the word lion and the word tiger are associated with the semantic father *feline* (as well as *vertebrate* and *animal*), and the CRF is enabled to determine the importance of such common property of the two different word, if the training subsequently highlights such importance. The procedure was used for all parts of speech for which a meaning was recognised.

A variation of the meaning clustering algorithm described above was employed for subject-verb and verb-object relations: words that were recognised as subjects or objects of a verb in the text were enriched with up to four more data columns, populated with the semantic ancestors of the verb they were subjects or objects of (the same logic described above applies). This allowed annotating words in the text with classes of verbs they are typically subject or object of. E.g. John plays basketball → John is annotated as a subject of the verb "to play", basketball is annotated as an object of the verb "to play".

Finally, semantic analysis provided categorisation: each document was given a category label (e.g. sports, news, medicine, science, etc.) based on the linguistic engine internal taxonomy. Such tag constituted one more data column for each word found in that document. Such feature was included in order to help recognise the different role of same words in different global context, with the category providing a context discriminator.

Standard data columns used besides semantic ones include: the form with which each word appears in the text, the lemma of the word (its normalised form), the part of speech, a list of regex-based columns (beginsWithUppercase, allUppercase, containsNumbers, allNumbers, etc.), character-type patterns, both extended and reduced (LeBron → extended: AaAaaa, reduced: AaAa; James → extended: Aaaaa, reduced: Aa).

The data matrix constructed with all of these data columns for each word was then used to generate CRF features: for each word, features were generated starting from data for that same word and for surrounding words (typically in a range of -2 to 2 position shifts, -5 to 5 for some cases). For the training phase, true labels in the IOB2 standard [9] were also included in such features. This is done by adding the letters B or I ahead of a label of a word in order not to loose information about multi-word named entities. The standard states that:

- The first word of a named entity is annotated with a B-label;
- Following words of the same entity, if they exist, are annotated with a I-label;
- A word that does not belong to any entity is annotated with O.

" O / A O / U.S. B-LOC /F-14 B-MISC/ military O/ plane O/ while O/ landing O/ at O/ Ben B-LOC/ Gurion I-LOC/ airport O/ blew O/ a O/ wheel O/ and O/ a O/ fire O/ broke O/ out O/, O/ " O/ said O/ spokesman O/ Yehiel B-PER/ Amitai I-PER.

Features were of the label unigram type, in the sense that the correct label of the preceding word was not included in the feature itself, except for the feature composed of the current label and the preceding label alone. As an example, O/O, O/B-LOC and B-LOC/I-LOC could actually occur while O/I-LOC could not, and this feature allowed to account for this. The CRF engine chosen for the experiments was the Wapiti[1] implementation [6]. Elastic-net regularisation was employed [1]. Elastic-net regularisation is a combination of the two regularisations L1 and L2, whose operating parameters are respectively $\rho 1$ and $\rho 2$. Parameters $\rho 1$ and $\rho 2$ were chosen via 10-fold cross-validation. For each fold, 7/10 of the training data were used for training, 2/10 for validation and convergence checks during training, and 1/10 for metric evaluation for the current fold (accuracy in our case, taking care of the macro F-1, the average F-1 score computed across all label types). Predictions were performed using Wapiti's posterior decoding option (some experiments were conducted also with Viterbi decoding, no significant variation was seen).

After parameters selection, quality metrics were assessed over a held out test set, prepared for all corpora used for the experiments.

3 Experimental Results

3.1 Corpus used for the experiments

For these experiments, we used the corpus prepared for the CoNLL 2003 workshop [2]. This corpus is a reduced version of the larger Reuters Corpus, a collection of Reuters news articles. The documents in the corpus are related to various categories, from politics to sports. The training set is composed by one thousand documents while the test set is composed by four hundred documents.

The documents of the CoNLL 2003 corpus are manually annotated (we did not do the annotation) with a label set comprising the following labels:

- PER, tag that represents human beings;

[1] https://wapiti.limsi.fr/

- ORG, tag that indicates companies, industries and other organizations;
- LOC, tag for geographic places;
- MISC, tag that represents other named entities not included in the previous categories;
- O, label that indicates a word not belonging to a named entity.

The training files have been formatted in order to respect the IOB2 format for representing the words belonging to a named entity.

We performed the following experiment on this corpus: A comparison between the performance of CRFs trained with non-semantic features and the performance of CRFs trained adding semantic features to the features set.

The same comparison between the two types of models, this time repeated with models trained on various different sizes of the training corpus (the original corpus has been artificially reduced) and its results are reported in the extended version of this paper, submitted to the 7th ACM International Conference On Web Intelligence, Mining and Semantics.

3.2 Comparison between models trained with and without semantics

The purpose of this experiment is to compare the results obtained with models trained with semantics features and the ones obtained training CRF without the use of semantic technology.

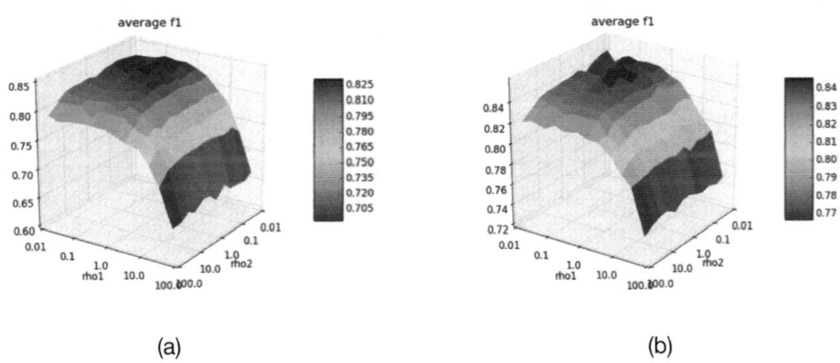

Fig. 3: (a) Case without semantics. (b) Case with semantics. The trends in the figures are similar but the values are different. Specifically, the semantic case leads to better performance, showing increasing values, with a difference of 0.015 - 0.020 with respect to the non-semantic case.

As previously explained, $\rho1$ and $\rho2$ parameters allow to configure the contributions of L1 and L2 regularizations. We trained different models using two ranges of these parameters. Doing this, we aimed at identifying the acceptable values for $\rho 1$ and $\rho 2$ that could lead to better performance of the models. The ranges used for the two parameters are: $\rho 1 = [$ 0.01, 0.02, 0.05, 0.1, 0.2, 0.5, 1.0, 2.0, 5.0, 10.0, 20.0, 50.0 $]$, $\rho 2 = [$ 0.01, 0.02, 0.05, 0.1, 0.2, 0.5, 1.0, 2.0, 5.0, 10.0, 20.0, 50.0 $]$.

This results into 144 different models for each case (semantics and not).

The curves in Figure 3a and Figure 3b show the performance in the two cases. On the x and y axis there are the $\rho 1$ and $\rho 2$ values, while on the z axis there is the macro F-1 measure (calculated on the F-1 measure of each label). Each point in the graph represents a model, trained with the respective values of $\rho 1$ and $\rho 2$.

The better performances are concentrated near the origin of the axis. With ρ values greater than 0.5 the performances get worse. This is clearer with the parameter $\rho 1$, whose bigger values lead to the worst performance.

Figure 4 reports numeric values for each tag in two cases: the best pair of $\rho 1$ and $\rho 2$ for the semantic case and for the non-semantic case. The best pair of ρ is the one which leads to the best result in terms of macro F-1 score.

Both from the plots and from the tables, we can see how the semantic features lead to better performance of the models. The semantic case shows increasing percentages, with a difference of 1.5 - 2 percentage points respect to the non-semantic case.

CoNLL 2003 Corpus	Without semantic features		$\varrho_1 = 0.2$ e $\varrho_2 = 0.1$
	PRECISION	RECALL	F1-SCORE
LOC	0.8786	0.8775	0.8780
PER	0.8780	0.9092	0.8933
ORG	0.8373	0.7379	0.7845
MISC	0.8090	0.7507	0.7787
Average (macro)	0.8507	0.8188	0.8336
Overall (micro)	0.8590	0.8287	0.8441

CoNLL 2003 Corpus	With semantic features		$\varrho_1 = 0.2$ e $\varrho_2 = 0.2$
	PRECISION	RECALL	F1-SCORE
LOC	0.9004	0.8896	0.8950
PER	0.9033	0.9297	0.9163
ORG	0.8250	0.7813	0.8025
MISC	0.8228	0.7564	0.7882
Average (macro)	0.8629	0.8392	0.8505
Overall (micro)	0.8707	0.8526	0.8616

Fig. 4: Numerical results for the comparison between the two cases (with and without semantics). Here we can better see how semantics leads to higher performance, in particular from the last column of the tables, which shows higher values in the semantic case.

With this experiment, we have identified the cases in which the category nodes help to better classify the words. For example, the adjectives of nationality (such as japanese or korean) are labeled as MISC. A simple CRF sees those adjectives as simple words, so if a different adjective of nationality has to be classified (such as chinese), the system will fail to identify the entity. Our NER system, instead, can recognize that those are not simple words, but they belong to a particular category node (the concept adjective of nationality), and that all the concepts belonging to that category node are classified as MISC; thus if a new adjective of nationality is presented in the test phase, the system correctly labels it as MISC. In the case of other MISC entity types (such as tournaments or public events), where fewer or less clear-cut examples are available, this generalization property seems to be less effective. However, generally speaking, this behavior improves performances and is one of the clearest advantages of our system.

4 Conclusions

We proposed a novel Named Entity Recognition (NER) system based on the combination of a machine learning algorithm with the semantic proprietary technology, Cogito, coming from Expert System S.r.l.

NER is the task of Natural Language Processing (NLP) which consists in detecting, from an unformatted text source, and classify Named Entities (NE), real-world entities that can be denoted with a rigid designator. To address this problem, the chosen approach was a combination of machine learning and deep semantic processing. The machine learning method used is Conditional Random Fields (CRF), particularly suitable for the task because it analyzes an input sequence considering it as a whole, instead of one item at a time. CRF has been trained both with classical information, available after a simple computation or anyway with little effort, and with semantic information too. Semantic information comes from Sensigrafo and Semantic Disambiguator, which are the proprietary semantic network and semantic engine of Expert System, respectively. We experimentally evaluated the NER system trained with and without semantic information and compared the results obtained. The results were promising, as we were able to experimentally prove the improvements in the NER task obtained by exploiting semantics. The extended version of this paper submitted to the WIST 2017 conference confirmed and improved these results, showing that when the size of the corpus used for the training is limited, the role of semantics plays is fundamental to improve the NER task.

Our approach can be used to tackle several problems within the category of sequencing problems, as for example, sentiment analysis, text segmentation, direct-speech extraction, etc. We think that, in all these research areas, semantics can help, e.g. by recognizing different words as synonyms or denoting similar concepts, as well as distinguishing different meanings of the same word. Combining words' semantics with machine learning tuning could permit to capture different nuances of words based on context, which might be difficult to model with hand-written rules. Other more general applications domains that can benefit froma our hybrid approach are keyword search on the deep web [4] and Entity Resolution [10].

References

1. http://onlinelibrary.wiley.com/doi/10.1111/j.1467-9868.2005.00503.x/full.

2. http://www.cnts.ua.ac.be/conll2003/ner/.
3. http://www.expertsystem.com/it/.
4. S. Bergamaschi, F. Guerra, M. Interlandi, R. T. Lado, and Y. Velegrakis. QUEST: A keyword search system for relational data based on semantic and machine learning techniques. *PVLDB*, 6(12):1222–1225, 2013.
5. J. D. Lafferty, A. McCallum, and F. C. N. Pereira. Conditional random fields: Probabilistic models for segmenting and labeling sequence data. In *Proceedings of the Eighteenth International Conference on Machine Learning (ICML 2001), Williams College, Williamstown, MA, USA, June 28 - July 1, 2001*, pages 282–289, 2001.
6. T. Lavergne, O. Cappé, and F. Yvon. Practical very large scale CRFs. In *Proceedings the 48th Annual Meeting of the Association for Computational Linguistics (ACL)*, pages 504–513. Association for Computational Linguistics, July 2010.
7. M. Lesk. Automatic sense disambiguation using machine readable dictionaries: how to tell a pine cone from an ice cream cone. In *Proceedings of the 5th Annual International Conference on Systems Documentation, SIGDOC 1986, Toronto, Ontario, Canada, 1986*, pages 24–26, 1986.
8. G. A. Miller, R. Beckwith, C. Fellbaum, D. Gross, and K. J. Miller. Introduction to wordnet: An on-line lexical database. *International journal of lexicography*, 3(4):235–244, 1990.
9. D. Nadeau and S. Sekine. A survey of named entity recognition and classification. *Lingvisticae Investigationes*, 30(1):3–26, 2007.
10. G. Simonini, S. Bergamaschi, and H. V. Jagadish. BLAST: a loosely schema-aware meta-blocking approach for entity resolution. *PVLDB*, 9(12):1173–1184, 2016.
11. C. A. Sutton and A. McCallum. An introduction to conditional random fields. *Foundations and Trends in Machine Learning*, 4(4):267–373, 2012.
12. M. Varone. Method and system for automatically extracting relations between concepts included in text, Mar. 1 2011. US Patent 7,899,666.

Approximation Algorithms for Computing Certain Answers over Incomplete Databases

Sergio Greco, Cristian Molinaro, and Irina Trubitsyna
{greco,cmolinaro,trubitsyna}@dimes.unical.it

DIMES, Università della Calabria, 87036 Rende (CS), Italy

Abstract. Certain answers are a widely accepted semantics of query answering over incomplete databases. Since their computation is a coNP-hard problem, recent research has focused on developing evaluation algorithms with *correctness guarantees*, that is, techniques computing a sound but possibly incomplete set of certain answers.
In this paper, we show how novel evaluation algorithms with correctness guarantees can be developed leveraging conditional tables and the conditional evaluation of queries, while retaining polynomial time data complexity.

1 Introduction

Incomplete information arises naturally in many database applications, such as data integration [16], data exchange [2, 7, 13, 5], inconsistency management [3, 4, 12], data cleaning [8], ontological reasoning [6], and many others.

A principled way of answering queries over incomplete databases is to compute *certain answers*, which are query answers that can be obtained from all the complete databases an incomplete database represents. This central notion is illustrated below.

Example 1. Consider the database D consisting of the two unary relations $R = \{\langle a \rangle\}$ and $S = \{\langle \bot \rangle\}$, where $\bot$ is a null value. Under the missing value interpretation of nulls (i.e., a value for $\bot$ exists but is unknown), D represents all the databases obtained by replacing $\bot$ with an actual value.

A certain answer to a query is a tuple that belongs to the query answers for every database represented by D. For instance, consider the query $\sigma_{\$1=a}(R)$, selecting the tuples in R whose first value is equal to a. The certain answers to the query are $\{\langle a \rangle\}$, because no matter how $\bot$ is replaced, the query answers always contain $\langle a \rangle$. □

For databases containing (labeled) nulls, certain answers to positive queries can be easily computed in polynomial time by applying a "naive" evaluation, that is, treating nulls as standard constants. However, for more general queries with negation the problem becomes coNP-hard. To make query answering feasible in practice, one might resort to SQL's evaluation, but unfortunately, the way SQL behaves in the presence of nulls may result in wrong answers.

Specifically, as evidenced in [18], there are two ways in which certain answers and SQL's evaluation may differ: *(i)* SQL can miss some of the tuples that belong to certain answers, thus producing *false negatives*, or *(ii)* SQL can return some tuples that do not belong to certain answers, that is, *false positives*. While the first case can be seen as an under-approximation of certain answers (a sound but possibly incomplete set of certain answers is returned), the second scenario must be avoided, as the result might contain plain incorrect answers, that is, tuples that are not certain. The experimental analysis in [14] showed that false positive are a real problem for queries involving negation—they were always present and sometimes they constitute almost 100% of the answers.

Example 2. Consider again the database D of Example 1. There are no certain answers to the query $R - S$, as when $\bot$ is replaced with a, the query answers are the empty set.

Assuming that R and S's attribute is called A, the same query can be expressed in SQL as follows:

```
SELECT R.A FROM R WHERE NOT EXISTS (
  SELECT * FROM S WHERE R.A = S.A )
```

However, the answer to the query above is $\langle a \rangle$, which is not a certain answer. The problem with the SQL semantics is that every comparison involving at least one null evaluates to the truth value *unknown*, then 3-valued logic is used to evaluate the classical logical connectives *and*, *or*, and *not*, and eventually only those tuples whose condition evaluates to *true* are kept.

Going back to the query above, the nested subquery compares $\bot$ with a, and since such a comparison evaluates to *unknown* (because a null is involved) then the result of the nested subquery is empty. As a consequence, the final result of the query is $\langle a \rangle$. □

Thus, on the one hand, SQL's evaluation is efficient but flawed, on the other hand, certain answers are a principled semantics but with high complexity. One way of dealing with this issue is to develop polynomial time evaluation algorithms computing approximate certain answers. In this regard, there has been recent work on evaluation algorithms with *correctness guarantees*, that is, techniques providing a sound but possibly incomplete set of certain answers [14, 17, 18]. However, there are still very simple queries for which the approximation can be unsatisfactory.

Example 3. Consider the database D of Example 1 and the query $R - \sigma_{\$1=b}(S)$. In this case, the certain answers are $\{\langle a \rangle\}$. However, the approximation provided by the approach in [14] is the empty set. □

In this paper, we show how conditional tables and the conditional evaluation of queries [15] can be leveraged to develop new approximation algorithms with correctness guarantees. The approach allows us to keep track of useful information that can be profitably used to determine if a tuple is a certain answer. The very basic idea is illustrated in the following example.

Example 4. Consider again the database D of Example 1 and the query $R - \sigma_{\$1=b}(S)$. The conditional evaluation of the query is carried out by applying the "conditional" counterpart of each relational algebra operator. Rather than returning a set of tuples, the conditional evaluation of a relational algebra operator returns pairs of the form $\langle t, \varphi \rangle$, where t is a tuple and φ is an expression stating under which conditions t can be derived.

Considering the query above, first the conditional evaluation of $\sigma_{\$1=b}(S)$ is performed, which gives $\langle \bot, \varphi' \rangle$, where φ' is the condition $(\bot = b)$. Then, the conditional evaluation of the difference operator is carried out, yielding $\langle a, \varphi'' \rangle$, where φ'' is the condition $(\bot \neq a) \vee (\bot \neq b)$. □

Conditions are valuable information that can exploited to determine which tuples are certain answers. For instance, from an analysis of φ'' above, one can realize that the condition is always true—thus, $\langle a \rangle$ is a certain answer. There might be different ways of evaluating tuples' conditions. In this paper, we propose some strategies.

2 Preliminaries

2.1 Incomplete databases

Basics. We assume the existence of the following disjoint countably infinite sets: a set Const of *constants* and a set Null of *(labeled) nulls*. Nulls are denoted by the symbol $\bot$ subscripted. A *tuple* t of arity k is an element of $(\mathsf{Const} \cup \mathsf{Null})^k$, where k is a non-negative integer. The i-th element of t is denoted as $t[i]$, where $1 \leq i \leq k$. Given a possibly empty ordered sequence Z of integers $i_1, \ldots, i_h$ in the range $[1..k]$, we use $t[Z]$ to denote the tuple $\langle t[i_1], \ldots, t[i_h] \rangle$.

A *relation* of arity k is a finite set of tuples of arity k. A *relational schema* is a set of *relation names*, each associated with a non-negative arity. A *database* D associates a relation R^D of arity k with each relation name R of arity k. With a slight abuse of notation, when the database is clear from the context, we simply write R instead of R^D for the relation itself. The arity of R is denoted as $ar(R)$. The sets of all constants and nulls occurring in a database D are denoted by $\mathsf{Const}(D)$ and $\mathsf{Null}(D)$, respectively. The *active domain* of D is $\mathsf{adom}(D) = \mathsf{Const}(D) \cup \mathsf{Null}(D)$. If $\mathsf{Null}(D) = \emptyset$, we say that D is *complete*. Likewise, a relation is *complete* if it does not contain nulls.

A *valuation* ν is a mapping from $\mathsf{Const} \cup \mathsf{Null}$ to Const s.t. $\nu(c) = c$ for every $c \in \mathsf{Const}$. Valuations can be applied to tuples, relations, and databases in the obvious way. For instance, the result of applying ν to a database D, denoted $\nu(D)$, is the complete database obtained from D by replacing every null $\bot_i$ with $\nu(\bot_i)$.

The semantics of a database D is given by the set of complete databases $\{\nu(D) \mid \nu \text{ is a valuation}\}$, also called *possible worlds*.

Query answering. We consider queries expressed with the relational algebra, that is, by means of the following operators: selection σ, projection π, cartesian product $\times$, union $\cup$, intersection $\cap$, and difference $-$. In the rest of the paper, a query is understood to be a relational algebra expression built up from the above operators, unless otherwise indicated. The result of evaluating a query Q on a database D, treating nulls as standard constants (i.e., every (labeled) null or constant is equal to itself and different from every other element of $\mathsf{Const} \cup \mathsf{Null}$), is denoted as $Q(D)$. A query Q returning k-tuples is said to be of arity k, and $ar(Q)$ denotes its arity.

A widely accepted semantics of query answering relies on the notion of a certain answer. The *certain answers* to a query Q on a database D are the tuples in $\bigcap\{Q(\nu(D)) \mid \nu \text{ is a valuation}\}$. Computing certain answers is coNP-hard (data complexity), even when the same null cannot occur multiple times [1].

For query answering, we will use a more general notion first proposed in [19] and called *certain answers with nulls* in [18]. Specifically, given a query Q and a database

D, the *certain answers with nulls* $\mathrm{cert}(Q, D)$ is the set of all tuples t such that $\nu(t) \in Q(\nu(D))$ for every valuation ν.

A query evaluation algorithm has *correctness guarantees* for a query Q if for every database D it returns a subset of $\mathrm{cert}(Q, D)$ [14]. When a query evaluation algorithm has correctness guarantees for every query, we say that it has correctness guarantees.

2.2 Conditional tables

Syntax and semantics. Conditional tables have been proposed in [15]. Essentially, they are relations (as defined in the previous subsection, and thus possibly containing nulls) extended by one additional special column that specifies a "condition" for each tuple. Formally, let $\mathcal{E}$ be the set of all expressions, called *conditions*, that can be built using the standard logical connectives $\wedge$, $\vee$, and $\neg$ with expressions of the form $(\alpha = \beta)$, $(\alpha \neq \beta)$, true, and false, where $\alpha, \beta \in \mathsf{Const} \cup \mathsf{Null}$. We say that a valuation ν *satisfies* a condition φ, denoted $\nu \models \varphi$, if its assignment of constants to nulls makes φ true.

A *conditional tuple* (*c-tuple* for short) of arity k ($k \geq 0$) is a pair $\langle t, \varphi \rangle$, where t is a tuple of arity k and $\varphi \in \mathcal{E}$. Notice that φ may involve nulls and constants not necessarily appearing in t—e.g., t is the tuple $\langle a, \bot_1 \rangle$ and φ is the condition $(\bot_2 = c) \wedge (\bot_1 \neq \bot_3)$.

A *conditional table* (*c-table* for short) of arity k is a finite set of c-tuples of arity k. A *conditional database* C associates a c-table R^C of arity k with each relation name R of arity k. With a slight abuse of notation, when the conditional database is clear from the context, we simply write R instead of R^C for the c-table itself.

The result of applying a valuation ν to a c-table T is $\nu(T) = \{\nu(t) \mid \langle t, \varphi \rangle \in T \text{ and } \nu \models \varphi\}$. Thus, $\nu(T)$ is the complete relation obtained from T by keeping only the c-tuples in T whose condition is satisfied by ν, and applying ν to such c-tuples. The set of complete relations represented by T is $rep(T) = \{\nu(T) \mid \nu \text{ is a valuation}\}$.

Likewise, a conditional database $C = \{T_1, \ldots, T_m\}$ represents the following set of complete databases: $rep(C) = \{\{\nu(T_1), \ldots, \nu(T_m)\} \mid \nu \text{ is a valuation}\}$.

Conditional evaluation. Below we recall the *conditional evaluation* of a query over a conditional database (see [15, 11]). Basically, it consists in evaluating the relational algebra operators so that they can take c-tables as input and return a c-table as output. The conditional evaluation of a query over a conditional database is then simply obtained by applying the conditional evaluation of each operator.

Let T_1 and T_2 be c-tables of arity n and m, respectively. In the definitions below, for the union and difference operators it is assumed that $n = m$. For projection, Z is a possibly empty ordered sequence of integers in the range $[1..n]$. For selection, θ is a Boolean combination of expressions of the form $(\$i = \$j)$, $(\$i = c)$, $(\$i \neq \$j)$, $(\$i \neq c)$, where $1 \leq i, j \leq n$, and $c \in \mathsf{Const}$. The conditional evaluation of a relational algebra operator op is denoted as $\dot{op}$. In the following, given two tuples t_1 and t_2 of arity n, we use $(t_1 = t_2)$ as a shorthand for the condition $\bigwedge_{i \in [1..n]} (t_1[i] = t_2[i])$.

- *Projection:* $\dot{\pi}_Z(T_1) = \{\langle t[Z], \varphi \rangle \mid \langle t, \varphi \rangle \in T_1\}$.
- *Selection:* $\dot{\sigma}_\theta(T_1) = \{\langle t, \varphi' \rangle \mid \langle t, \varphi \rangle \in T_1 \text{ and } \varphi' = \varphi \wedge \theta(t)\}$, where $\theta(t)$ is the condition obtained from θ by replacing every $\$i$ with $t[i]$.
- *Union:* $T_1 \dot{\cup} T_2 = \{\langle t, \varphi \rangle \mid \langle t, \varphi \rangle \in T_1 \text{ or } \langle t, \varphi \rangle \in T_2\}$.

- *Difference:* $T_1 \dot{-} T_2 = \{\langle t_1, \varphi' \rangle \mid \langle t_1, \varphi_1 \rangle \in T_1$ and $\varphi' = \varphi_1 \wedge \varphi_{t_1,T_2}\}$, where $\varphi_{t_1,T_2} = \bigwedge_{\langle t_2,\varphi_2 \rangle \in T_2} \neg(\varphi_2 \wedge (t_1 = t_2))$.
- *Cartesian product:* $T_1 \dot{\times} T_2 = \{\langle t_1 \circ t_2, \varphi_1 \wedge \varphi_2 \rangle \mid \langle t_1, \varphi_1 \rangle \in T_1,\ \langle t_2, \varphi_2 \rangle \in T_2\}$, where $t_1 \circ t_2$ is the tuple obtained as the concatenation of t_1 and t_2.

The result of the conditional evaluation of a query Q over a conditional database C is denoted as $\dot{Q}(C)$. Notice that $\dot{Q}(C)$ is a c-table. For a fixed query Q and a conditional database C, $\dot{Q}(C)$ can be evaluated in polynomial time in the size of C (see [11]).

W.l.o.g., in the rest of the paper we assume that every selection condition is a conjunction of expressions of the form $(\$i = \$j)$, $(\$i = c)$, $(\$i \neq \$j)$, and $(\$i \neq c)$.

3 Approximation Algorithms

In this section, we show how to exploit conditional tables to compute a sound (but possibly incomplete) set of certain answers with nulls. The basic idea is to rely on the conditional evaluation of the relational algebra operators, in order to keep track of how each tuple is derived during query evaluation, and then apply a strategy to evaluate conditions, so that each tuple is eventually associated with a truth value. Tuples that are associated with the condition true are certain answers with nulls.

We start by introducing an explicit conditional evaluation for intersection. In the previous section, we recalled the conditional evaluation of different relational algebra operators. Clearly, even if intersection was not reported, it can be expressed in terms of the other operators. Let T_1 and T_2 be c-tables of arity n. Then,

$$T_1 \dot{\cap} T_2 = \{\langle t_1, \varphi' \rangle \mid \langle t_1, \varphi_1 \rangle \in T_1,\ \langle t_2, \varphi_2 \rangle \in T_2,\ \varphi' = \varphi_1 \wedge \varphi_2 \wedge (t_1 = t_2)\}.$$

We slightly generalize c-tables to allow also unknown as a condition. Thus, from now on, $\mathcal{E}$ is the set of all expressions that can be built using the standard logical connectives with expressions, called *atomic* conditions, of the form $(\alpha = \beta)$, $(\alpha \neq \beta)$, true, false, and unknown, where $\alpha, \beta \in \mathsf{Const} \cup \mathsf{Null}$. We will discuss different strategies to "evaluate" conditions, that is, to reduce them to either true or false or unknown—as shown in the following, tuples having condition true are certain answers with nulls.

We assume the following strict ordering false $<$ unknown $<$ true. The *three-valued evaluation* of a condition $\varphi \in \mathcal{E}$, denoted eval (φ), is defined inductively as follows:

- $\mathsf{eval}\,((\alpha = \beta)) = \begin{cases} \mathsf{true} & \text{if } \alpha = \beta, \\ \mathsf{false} & \text{if } \alpha \neq \beta \text{ and } \alpha, \beta \in \mathsf{Const}, \\ \mathsf{unknown} & \text{otherwise.} \end{cases}$
- $\mathsf{eval}\,((\alpha \neq \beta)) = \begin{cases} \mathsf{true} & \text{if } \alpha \neq \beta \text{ and } \alpha, \beta \in \mathsf{Const}, \\ \mathsf{false} & \text{if } \alpha = \beta, \\ \mathsf{unknown} & \text{otherwise.} \end{cases}$
- $\mathsf{eval}\,((\varphi_1 \wedge \varphi_2)) = \min\{\mathsf{eval}\,(\varphi_1), \mathsf{eval}\,(\varphi_2)\}$.
- $\mathsf{eval}\,((\varphi_1 \vee \varphi_2)) = \max\{\mathsf{eval}\,(\varphi_1), \mathsf{eval}\,(\varphi_2)\}$.

– $\text{eval}((\neg\varphi)) = \begin{cases} \text{true} & \text{if eval}(\varphi) = \text{false}, \\ \text{false} & \text{if eval}(\varphi) = \text{true}, \\ \text{unknown} & \text{otherwise.} \end{cases}$

– $\text{eval}(v) = v$ for $v \in \{\text{true}, \text{unknown}, \text{false}\}$.

The basic idea of our first evaluation algorithm, which we call *naive evaluation*, is to perform the three-valued evaluation of conditions after each relational algebra operator is applied (that is, after its conditional evaluation). One interesting fact about the naive evaluation is that it is equivalent to the evaluation algorithm of [14].

Given a c-tuple $\mathbf{t} = \langle t, \varphi \rangle$, with a slight abuse of notation, we use $\text{eval}(\mathbf{t})$ to denote $\langle t, \text{eval}(\varphi) \rangle$. Likewise, given a conditional table T, $\text{eval}(T)$ denotes $\{\text{eval}(\mathbf{t}) \mid \mathbf{t} \in T\}$.

To define the naive evaluation, we first provide the following definitions:

$$
\begin{aligned}
&\text{Eval}^{\text{n}}(R) = \text{eval}(R) \\
&\text{Eval}^{\text{n}}(Q_1 \cup Q_2) = \text{eval}(\text{Eval}^{\text{n}}(Q_1) \ \dot{\cup} \ \text{Eval}^{\text{n}}(Q_2)) \\
&\text{Eval}^{\text{n}}(Q_1 \cap Q_2) = \text{eval}(\text{Eval}^{\text{n}}(Q_1) \ \dot{\cap} \ \text{Eval}^{\text{n}}(Q_2)) \\
&\text{Eval}^{\text{n}}(Q_1 - Q_2) = \text{eval}\left(\text{Eval}^{\text{n}}(Q_1) \ \dot{-} \ \text{Eval}^{\text{n}}(Q_2)\right) \\
&\text{Eval}^{\text{n}}(Q_1 \times Q_2) = \text{eval}\left(\text{Eval}^{\text{n}}(Q_1) \ \dot{\times} \ \text{Eval}^{\text{n}}(Q_2)\right) \\
&\text{Eval}^{\text{n}}(\sigma_\theta(Q)) = \text{eval}(\dot{\sigma}_\theta(\text{Eval}^{\text{n}}(Q))) \\
&\text{Eval}^{\text{n}}(\pi_Z(Q)) = \text{eval}(\dot{\pi}_Z(\text{Eval}^{\text{n}}(Q)))
\end{aligned}
$$

Given a relation R, we define the c-table $\overline{R} = \{\langle t, \text{true} \rangle \mid t \in R\}$. Analogously, given a database D, we define $\overline{D}$ as the conditional database obtained from D by replacing every relation R of it with $\overline{R}$. Here the basic idea is to convert a database D into a simple conditional database $\overline{D}$ where all conditions are true, so that $\overline{D}$ can be used as the starting point for the conditional evaluation of queries.

Given a query Q and a database D, we use $\text{Eval}^{\text{n}}(Q, D)$ to denote the result of evaluating $\text{Eval}^{\text{n}}(Q)$ over $\overline{D}$. Finally, we define:

$$
\begin{aligned}
&\text{Eval}^{\text{n}}_{\text{t}}(Q, D) = \{t \mid \langle t, \text{true} \rangle \in \text{Eval}^{\text{n}}(Q, D)\}, \\
&\text{Eval}^{\text{n}}_{\text{p}}(Q, D) = \{t \mid \langle t, \varphi \rangle \in \text{Eval}^{\text{n}}(Q, D) \text{ and } \varphi \neq \text{false}\}.
\end{aligned}
$$

Example 5. Consider the database D consisting of the two unary relations $R = \{\langle a \rangle\}$ and $S = \{\langle \bot_1 \rangle\}$. Consider also the query $Q_5 = R - S$. The conditional database $\overline{D}$ consist of the two c-tables $\overline{R} = \{\langle a, \text{true} \rangle\}$ and $\overline{S} = \{\langle \bot_1, \text{true} \rangle\}$. Then,

$$
\begin{aligned}
\text{Eval}^{\text{n}}(Q_5, D) &= \text{eval}\left(\text{eval}\left(\overline{R}\right) \ \dot{-} \ \text{eval}\left(\overline{S}\right)\right) = \text{eval}\left(\overline{R} \ \dot{-} \ \overline{S}\right) \\
&= \text{eval}\left(\{\langle a, \ \text{true} \wedge \neg(\text{true} \wedge (a = \bot_1))\rangle\}\right) = \{\langle a, \text{unknown} \rangle\}.
\end{aligned}
$$

Thus, $\text{Eval}^{\text{n}}_{\text{t}}(Q_5, D) = \emptyset$ and $\text{Eval}^{\text{n}}_{\text{p}}(Q_5, D) = \{\langle a \rangle\}$. □

The following theorem states that the naive evaluation is equivalent to the evaluation algorithm of [14]. We point out that, in the following claim, D is a database (thus, possibly containing nulls), but without conditions. However, the naive evaluation first converts D into a conditional database $\overline{D}$ with all conditions being true, and then performs the evaluation $\text{Eval}^{\text{n}}()$ over $\overline{D}$, so that eventually tuples associated with true are certain answers with nulls, and the remaining ones are possible answers.

Theorem 1. *The naive evaluation is equivalent to the evaluation algorithm of [14].*

Corollary 1. $\mathsf{Eval}^{\mathsf{n}}_{\mathsf{t}}(Q)$ *has correctness guarantees.*

Theorem 2. $\mathsf{Eval}^{\mathsf{n}}(Q, D)$ *can be computed in polynomial time in the size of D, for every query Q and database D.*

The naive evaluation presented above is somehow limited, since it does not use much the power of conditional tables, as shown in the following example.

Example 6. Consider the database D of Example 5 and the query $Q_6 = R - \sigma_{\$1=b}(S)$. Clearly, $\mathsf{cert}(Q_6, D) = \{\langle a \rangle\}$, as the selection returns either $\{\langle b \rangle\}$ or $\emptyset$ in every possible world, and thus the result of the difference is $\{\langle a \rangle\}$ in every possible world. However, the naive evaluation is not able to realize this aspect and behaves as follows:

$$\begin{aligned}
&\mathsf{Eval}^{\mathsf{n}}(Q_6, D) = \\
&\quad = \mathsf{eval}\left(\mathsf{eval}\left(\overline{R}\right) \ \dot{-} \ \mathsf{eval}\left(\dot{\sigma}_{\$1=b}\left(\mathsf{eval}\left(\overline{S}\right)\right)\right)\right) \\
&\quad = \mathsf{eval}\left(\{\langle a, \mathsf{true}\rangle\} \ \dot{-} \ \mathsf{eval}\left(\dot{\sigma}_{\$1=b}\left(\{\langle \bot_1, \mathsf{true}\rangle\}\right)\right)\right) \\
&\quad = \mathsf{eval}\left(\{\langle a, \mathsf{true}\rangle\} \ \dot{-} \ \mathsf{eval}\left(\{\langle \bot_1, \mathsf{true} \wedge (\bot_1 = b)\rangle\}\right)\right) \\
&\quad = \mathsf{eval}\left(\{\langle a, \mathsf{true}\rangle\} \ \dot{-} \ \{\langle \bot_1, \mathsf{unknown}\rangle\}\right) \\
&\quad = \mathsf{eval}\left(\{\langle a, \mathsf{true} \wedge \neg(\mathsf{unknown} \wedge (a = \bot_1))\rangle\}\right) = \{\langle a, \mathsf{unknown}\rangle\}.
\end{aligned}$$

Thus, $\mathsf{Eval}^{\mathsf{n}}_{\mathsf{t}}(Q_6, D) = \emptyset$. In this case, the crucial point is that $\mathsf{eval}\left(\dot{\sigma}_{\$1=b}\left(\mathsf{eval}\left(\overline{S}\right)\right)\right) = \{\langle \bot_1, \mathsf{unknown}\rangle\}$, and the fact that $\bot_1$ can only be equal to b gets lost. □

The previous example suggests that equalities might be exploited to refine the evaluation of conditions, as illustrated in the following example.

Example 7. Consider again the database D of Example 5 and the query Q_6 of Example 6. By "propagating" equalities into conditions and tuples after each relational algebra operator is conditionally evaluated, we get:

$$\begin{aligned}
&\{\langle a, \mathsf{true}\rangle\} \ \dot{-} \ \dot{\sigma}_{\$1=b}(\{\langle \bot_1, \mathsf{true}\rangle\}) = \{\langle a, \mathsf{true}\rangle\} \ \dot{-} \ \{\langle \bot_1, \mathsf{true} \wedge (\bot_1 = b)\rangle\} = \\
&\{\langle a, \mathsf{true}\rangle\} \ \dot{-} \ \{\langle b, \mathsf{unknown}\rangle\} = \{\langle a, \mathsf{true} \wedge \neg(\mathsf{unknown} \wedge (a = b))\rangle\} = \{\langle a, \mathsf{true}\rangle\}.
\end{aligned}$$

Thus, we can conclude that $\langle a \rangle$ is a certain answer with nulls. Recall that $\mathsf{cert}(Q_6, D) = \{\langle a \rangle\}$ and $\mathsf{Eval}^{\mathsf{n}}_{\mathsf{t}}(Q_6, D) = \emptyset$. □

In the previous example, it is interesting to notice that the selection returns the c-tuple $\langle b, \mathsf{unknown}\rangle$, meaning that the only tuple that can be returned (in some cases) is $\langle b \rangle$, and thus providing more accurate information than the naive evaluation.

4 Conclusion

Certain answers are a principled manner to answer queries on incomplete databases. Since their computation is a coNP-hard problem, recent research has focused on polynomial time algorithms providing under-approximations. Leveraging conditional tables, we have shown how new approximation algorithms can be developed.

We are currently working on more refined evaluation strategies which better exploit the power of conditional tables, with the aim of computing more certain answers with nulls. For instance, conditions might be rewritten into a more suitable form (e.g., conjunctive normal form or disjunctive normal form [9, 10]) so as to allow better analyses.

References

1. Serge Abiteboul, Paris C. Kanellakis, and Gösta Grahne. On the representation and querying of sets of possible worlds. *Theoretical Computer Science*, 78(1):158–187, 1991.
2. Marcelo Arenas, Pablo Barceló, Leonid Libkin, and Filip Murlak. *Foundations of Data Exchange*. Cambridge University Press, 2014.
3. Marcelo Arenas, Leopoldo E. Bertossi, and Jan Chomicki. Consistent query answers in inconsistent databases. In *Proc. Symposium on Principles of Database Systems (PODS)*, pages 68–79, 1999.
4. Leopoldo E. Bertossi. *Database Repairing and Consistent Query Answering*. Synthesis Lectures on Data Management. Morgan & Claypool Publishers, 2011.
5. Marco Calautti, Sergio Greco, Cristian Molinaro, and Irina Trubitsyna. Exploiting equality generating dependencies in checking chase termination. *PVLDB*, 9(5):396–407, 2016.
6. Andrea Calì, Georg Gottlob, and Thomas Lukasiewicz. A general datalog-based framework for tractable query answering over ontologies. *Journal of Web Semantics*, 14:57–83, 2012.
7. Ronald Fagin, Phokion G. Kolaitis, Renée J. Miller, and Lucian Popa. Data exchange: semantics and query answering. *Theoretical Computer Science*, 336(1):89–124, 2005.
8. Floris Geerts, Giansalvatore Mecca, Paolo Papotti, and Donatello Santoro. The LLUNATIC data-cleaning framework. *Proceedings of the VLDB Endowment*, 6(9):625–636, 2013.
9. Georg Gottlob and Enrico Malizia. Achieving new upper bounds for the hypergraph duality problem through logic. In *Proc. Symposium on Logic in Computer Science (LICS)*, pages 43:1–43:10, 2014.
10. Georg Gottlob and Enrico Malizia. Achieving new upper bounds for the hypergraph duality problem through logic. *SIAM Journal on Computing*, 2017.
11. Gösta Grahne. *The Problem of Incomplete Information in Relational Databases*, volume 554 of *Lecture Notes in Computer Science*. Springer, 1991.
12. Sergio Greco, Cristian Molinaro, and Francesca Spezzano. *Incomplete Data and Data Dependencies in Relational Databases*. Synthesis Lectures on Data Management. Morgan & Claypool Publishers, 2012.
13. Sergio Greco, Francesca Spezzano, and Irina Trubitsyna. Checking chase termination: Cyclicity analysis and rewriting techniques. *IEEE Transactions on Knowledge and Data Engineering*, 27(3):621–635, 2015.
14. Paolo Guagliardo and Leonid Libkin. Making SQL queries correct on incomplete databases: A feasibility study. In *Proc. Symposium on Principles of Database Systems (PODS)*, pages 211–223, 2016.
15. Tomasz Imielinski and Witold Lipski Jr. Incomplete information in relational databases. *Journal of the ACM*, 31(4):761–791, 1984.
16. Maurizio Lenzerini. Data integration: A theoretical perspective. In *Proc. Symposium on Principles of Database Systems (PODS)*, pages 233–246, 2002.
17. Leonid Libkin. Sql's three-valued logic and certain answers. In *Proc. International Conference on Database Theory (ICDT)*, pages 94–109, 2015.
18. Leonid Libkin. SQL's three-valued logic and certain answers. *ACM Transactions Database Systems*, 41(1):1, 2016.
19. Witold Lipski. On relational algebra with marked nulls. In *Proc. Symposium on Principles of Database Systems (PODS)*, pages 201–203, 1984.

Collective Intelligence support for data service exploration and retrieval (discussion paper)

Devis Bianchini, Valeria De Antonellis, Michele Melchiori

Dept. of Information Engineering University of Brescia
Via Branze, 38 - 25123 Brescia (Italy)
{devis.bianchini|valeria.deantonellis|michele.melchiori}@unibs.it

Abstract. Agile design of data intensive web applications can rely on existing and well-tested third parties data services as components providing access methods to valuable data sources. Producers of real data services are more and more publishing their services in repositories according to light semantic profiles with simple tag-based descriptions. In this paper, we discuss techniques for data service exploration and retrieval that consider service co-usage in existing applications, patterns of tags co-usage, and ratings declared by developers who used a data service in their own development experiences.

Keywords: data service, exploratory search, collective intelligence, web-oriented architecture

1 Introduction

Nowadays, we have been observing a growth of research efforts for explorative techniques and methods to deal with the increasing volume and heterogeneity of information made available over the Web [1]. Building web applications, that integrate information available over the web, increasingly requires frameworks to support the discovery of available services providing access to web data sources.

In literature, service recommendations approaches have been proposed to consider service co-occurrence in existing applications as an implicit measure of relatedness of services [2], or suggest services chosen by similar users in a social network based on their usage information [3]. Considering this scenario, in this paper we discuss techniques for data service exploration and retrieval based on selecting and organizing suitable collective intelligence made available in developers communities. In particular, we consider service co-usage in existing applications, patterns of tags co-usage, and ratings declared by developers who used a data service in their own development experiences. Our contribution with respect to existing service recommendation approaches, including our previous work in [4], is that here we adopt an explorative viewpoint, enabling developers to iteratively discover services of interest and progressively increase their knowledge on available services.

The paper is organized as follows. In Section 2 provides some comparison with related work to underline the specific features of our approach. Section 3

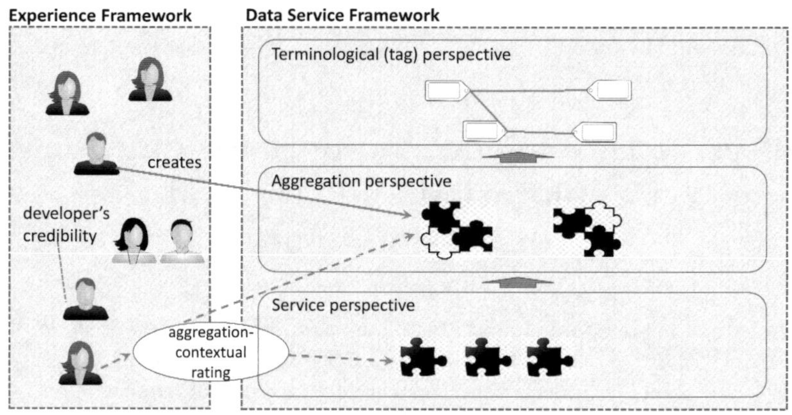

Fig. 1. Overview of the multi-perspective data service model.

describes a multi-perspective data service model. In Section 4 we describe the data service exploration process. Section 5 discusses some preliminary validation. Finally, Section 6 closes the paper with some final remarks.

2 Related work

There are several approaches related to our work. In particular, we mention recent Web service recommendation approaches, that rely on lightweight descriptions of services, such as the ones featuring public repositories (e.g., `ProgrammableWeb` or `Mashape.com`): categories, tags or semantic tags, with the application of advanced IR techniques to enhance topic-based service recommendation [5], natural language API description [6], the number of times a service has been used in the past and the co-occurrence of services in existing applications [2], latent factors (e.g., related to the perceived QoS) that affect users to make service selection, identified mainly using matrix factorization techniques [7]. In this context, approaches like [8] leverage factors to estimate past experiences of data service usage are considered, such as votes/ratings assigned by users to services. These approaches overcome the complexity of traditional state-of-the-art approaches on service discovery (see [9] for a recent survey), that are hampered by the availability of complex, structured service descriptions (e.g., WSDL, WADL and semantic web service formalisms [10]). Compared to these contributions, our aim is to define an explorative approach, exploiting specific collective intelligence, for service recommendation.

Our proposal supports a conversation between the system, used to search for services, and the developer, who is designing a new web application through the selection and aggregation of services.

3 Multi-perspective data service model

We model data services and organize collective intelligence on them by two interconnected frameworks, namely a Data Service Framework and an Experience Framework, that are illustrated in Figure 1 and separately detailed in the next sections. Each framework focuses on specific elements further enriched with cross-framework relationships. Elements considered in such a multi-perspective data service model are the ones included in lightweight descriptions available within most popular repositories (e.g., `Mashape.com`, `ProgrammableWeb.com`).

Service	Service name	Technical features	Tags
s_1	HotWire	$\mathcal{F}_{s_1}^{DataFormat} = \{\texttt{XML,JSON}\}$ $\mathcal{F}_{s_1}^{Protocol} = \{\texttt{RSS, Atom, REST}\}$	{City, Star, Hotel, Travel}
s_2	EasyToBook	$\mathcal{F}_{s_2}^{DataFormat} = \{\texttt{XML}\}$ $\mathcal{F}_{s_2}^{Protocol} = \{\texttt{SOAP}\}$	{City, Hotel, Travel}
s_3	MyAgentDeals	$\mathcal{F}_{s_4}^{DataFormat} = \{\texttt{XML,JSON}\}$ $\mathcal{F}_{s_4}^{Protocol} = \{\texttt{HTTP}\}$	{City, Star, Near, Hotel, Travel}

Fig. 2. Data service descriptions used in the running example.

3.1 Data Service Framework

The Data Service Framework is organized according to three perspectives as shown in Figure 1. Each perspective considers specific elements, namely services, aggregations and terms used to describe them, further described with proper features and relationships between elements.

Service Perspective. This perspective focuses on data services, according to the following definition.

Definition 1. *We define a* <u>*data service*</u> *s (hereafter,* <u>*service*</u>*) as an operation/method/query to access data of a web source, whose underlying data schema might be unknown to those who use the service. Within the scope of this chapter, we model a service s as* $\langle n_s, \mathcal{F}_s, \{t_s\}\rangle$*, where:* n_s *is the service name;* $\mathcal{F}_s$ *is an array of elements, where each element* $\mathcal{F}_s^X$ *represents the technical feature X (e.g., protocols, data formats, authentication mechanisms) and is modeled as a set of allowed values for that feature (e.g., XML or JSON among data formats);* $\{t_s\}$ *is a set of* <u>*tags*</u>*. We denote with* $\mathcal{S}$ *the overall set of available services.*

A *tag* in $\mathcal{T}_s$ may be: (a) a category, taken from a top-down classification imposed within the repository where the data service is stored and advertised[1]; (b) a user tag, that is, a term assigned by developers, aimed at classifying the data service in a folksonomy-like style; (c) a keyword, that is, a recurrent term extracted from the service name and textual description using common IR techniques.
In Figure 2 data services taken from `ProgrammableWeb.com` for the running example are listed.

Aggregation Perspective. Concerning modern application development, to implement a web application starting from available data services, developer has to explore the set of available services, select the most suitable ones, integrate and compose them, in order to deploy the final application. Within the scope of this paper, we focus on the first step, i.e., service exploration for selection purposes, and we talk about service aggregations, instead of web applications that are the final product of the development process. We model aggregations according to the following definition.

Definition 2. *A* <u>*service aggregation*</u> *represents a set of services that can be composed to deploy a Web application. An aggregation g is modeled as a triple* $\langle n_g, \mathcal{S}(g), d\rangle$*, where:* n_g *is the aggregation name;* $\mathcal{S}(g) = \{s_1, \ldots, s_n\}$ *is the set of data services used in g;* $d \in \mathcal{D}$ *is the developer who designed the web application by*

[1] See, for instance, the list of `ProgrammableWeb.com` categories at `http://www.programmableweb.com/category-api`.

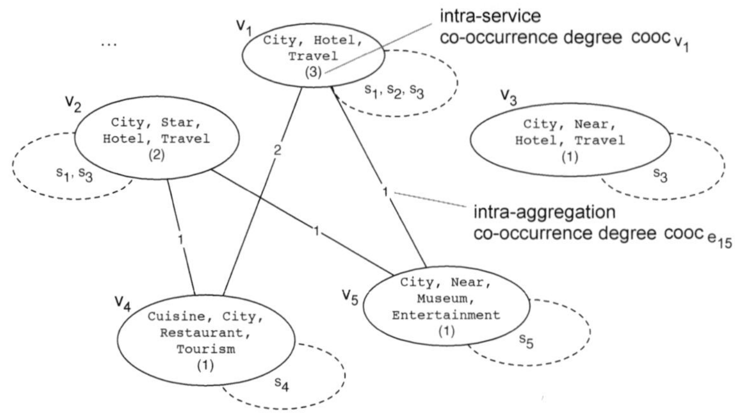

Fig. 3. A portion of the term graph used in the running example; for each node, data services annotated with the node terms are also specified.

composing services in g. We denote with $\mathcal{G}$ the overall set of service aggregations, that is, $g \in \mathcal{G}$, and with $\mathcal{G}(s)$ the set of aggregations where s has been included.

Fictious examples of aggregations are listed in the following.

$g_1 \Rightarrow \langle$ `TravelPlan`, $\mathcal{S}_{g_1} = \{s_1, s_3\}$, d_{g_1} $\rangle$
$g_2 \Rightarrow \langle$ `Stay&Fun`, $\mathcal{S}_{g_2} = \{s_2, s_3\}$, d_{g_2} $\rangle$

Terminological Perspective. The Terminological Perspective collects and organises for supporting service exploration the terminological items used to describe data services. The aim is to provide a *term graph*, described as shown in this section, to start from in order to support data service exploration (see Section 4). We will explain the structure of the graph with the help of the example shown in Figure 3. Formally, the graph is represented as $\langle \mathcal{V}, \mathcal{E} \rangle$, where $\mathcal{V}$ is the set of *nodes* and $\mathcal{E}$ is the set of *edges*. In particular, each node $v_i \in \mathcal{V}$ is formally described as $v_i = \langle \mathcal{T}_{v_i}, cooc_{v_i} \rangle$, where $\mathcal{T}_{v_i}$ is a set of tags jointly used to describe a number $cooc_{v_i}$ of data services (*intra-service term co-occurrence degree*). Each edge $e_{ij} \in \mathcal{E} \subseteq \mathcal{V} \times \mathcal{V} \times \mathbb{N}$ is formally described as $e_{ij} = \langle v_i, v_j, cooc_{e_{ij}} \rangle$, where v_i and v_j are nodes (with corresponding sets of tags $\mathcal{T}_{v_i}$ and $\mathcal{T}_{v_j}$, respectively), such that tags in $\mathcal{T}_{v_i} \cup \mathcal{T}_{v_j}$ have been jointly used within a number $cooc_{e_{ij}}$ of aggregations (*intra-aggregation term co-occurrence degree*). For example in Figure 3, tags in {`City`, `Hotel`, `Travel`} have been used to describe three data services (namely, s_1, s_2 and s_3). The same tags, together with {`Cuisine`,`City`,`Restaurant`,`Tourism`}, are associated with two aggregations (namely, `TravelPlan` and `Stay&Fun`). Tags aim at grouping services that are close from the data viewpoint.

With reference to same figure, $\mathcal{T}_{v_1}$ and $\mathcal{T}_{v_5}$ can be used to suggest developers to aggregate services s_1, s_2 and s_3 with s_5. The framework suggests firstly sets corresponding to an existing aggregation already deployed and tested (let us suppose, $\{s_1, s_5\}$). Other solutions are suggested as well although they do not correspond to existing aggregations (for example $\{s_2, s_5\}$ and $\{s_3, s_5\}$). Therefore, the intra-aggregation term co-occurrence enables developers to explore services that have not been aggregated yet, but can be considered for aggregation because tagged with tags forming patterns used in some existing aggregation. This enables a greater coverage of proposed solutions, at the cost of a lower precision, that however can be acceptable in an explorative process. The term graph can be built and maintained in a fully automatic way.

3.2 Experience Framework

We integrate the Data Service Framework with methods and techniques designed to exploit the experience of developers in selecting data services, thus enabling their ranked recommendation. Such a framework, that in this paper we refer to as *Experience Framework* (EF), has been investigated in our previous work [4, 11]. For the sake of completeness, we report here only few details that are useful to understand the rest of this paper.

The Experience Framework is focused on the set $\mathcal{D}$ of developers. Given a data service $s \in \mathcal{S}$, we denote with $\mu(s, g, d) \in [0, 1]$ the vote assigned to s by a developer $d \in \mathcal{D}$ with reference to the aggregation $g \in \mathcal{G}$ in which s has been used (*aggregation-contextual rating*). Votes are assigned according to the NHLBI 9-point Scoring System[2]. Furthermore, in [11] we included credibility assessment techniques, inspired by the ones defined in [8], with respect to which we introduced the notion of aggregation-contextual rating. In the Experience Framework, a developer is defined according to the following definition.

Definition 3. *A developer represents an actor that is in charge of exploring services and using them to design new aggregations. A developer might also assign aggregation-contextual votes to services. A developer d is modeled as $\langle n_d, c(d) \rangle$, where: (i) n_d is the developer nickname in the considered repository; (ii) $c(d) \in [0, 1]$ is the estimated developer's credibility.*

4 Data service exploration

We envision the service exploration process as a sequence of exploration steps between the developer and the system, used to search for services. The developer starts the exploration by specifying: (i) the set $\mathcal{T}^r$ of terms used within the search request, that provide some initial hints about developer's interests; (ii) the set $\mathcal{F}^r$ of required technical features, for further refining requester's search constraints. Sets $\mathcal{T}^r$ and $\mathcal{F}^r$ compose the service request $\mathcal{R}$, that is completed with the set g^r of services, representing the current composition of the aggregation that is being designed. The framework is equipped with proper wizards (described in [4]), that guide the developer in formulating the request. The system suggests services by computing similarity, filtering and ranking techniques such as the ones introduced in [11] and summarised in the following.

Service similarity evaluation and ranking. A set of similarity metrics have been designed to compare each service description $s \in \mathcal{S}$ extracted from `ProgrammableWeb.com` and the corresponding elements of the request $\mathcal{R}$. The rationale behind these metrics is that the more tags set $\mathcal{T}_s$ of s is similar to $\mathcal{T}^r$, the more technical features $\mathcal{F}_s$ of s are similar to $\mathcal{F}^r$ and the more aggregations where s has been used are similar to the aggregation g^r that is being designed, the more description of service $s \in \mathcal{S}$ fits the request $\mathcal{R}$. The building

[2] `http://www.nhlbi.nih.gov/funding/policies/nine_point_scoring_system_and program_project_review.htm.`

blocks are the *term similarity* ($TermSim() \in [0,1]$), the *technical feature similarity* ($TechSim() \in [0,1]$) and the *aggregation similarity* ($AggSim() \in [0,1]$) metrics that are combined into a overall similarity $Sim(\mathcal{R}, s) \in [0,1]$. We denote the set $\mathcal{S}^e \subseteq \mathcal{S}$ of search results such that $\mathcal{S}^e = \{s_i \in \mathcal{S} | Sim(\mathcal{R}, s_i) \geq \gamma\}$, where $\gamma \in [0,1]$ is a threshold set by the developer.

A ranking function over the set of services in $\mathcal{S}^e$, denoted with $\rho : \mathcal{S}^e \mapsto [0,1]$, is defined as follows:

$$\rho(s_i) = \frac{1}{N} \sum_{N} [\mu(s_i, g_k, d_i) \cdot c(d_i) \cdot AggSim(g^r, g_k)] \tag{1}$$

where N votes have been assigned to s_i, each vote $\mu(s_i, g_k, d_i)$ is weighted with the credibility $c(d_i) \in [0,1]$ of $d_i \in \mathcal{D}$ as computed in [11] and with the aggregation similarity $AggSim(\cdot)$ of g_k with respect to the aggregation g^r that is being developed. The rationale behind Equation (1) is that a service $s_i \in \mathcal{S}$ is ranked better if it received better votes by more credible designers in the context of more similar aggregations. The system reacts to developer's actions by supporting exploration according to the following three modalities.

Exploration by simple search. The system also looks for nodes $v_i \in \mathcal{V}$ such that $\mathcal{T}^r \subseteq \mathcal{T}_{v_i}$. If multiple nodes are found, for each $v_i \in \mathcal{V}$ the system will suggest to the developer additional terms to be included within the set $\mathcal{T}^r$ considering the set $\mathcal{T}_{v_i} \backslash \mathcal{T}^r$. A suggestion is given for each $v_i \in \mathcal{V}$, ranked in decreasing order with respect to the $cooc_{v_i}$ value. The developer can explore these suggestions in order to consider services alternative to $\mathcal{S}^e$ and to formulate a different request. For instance, with reference to Figure 3, if $\mathcal{T}^r = \{\texttt{City}, \texttt{Hotel}, \texttt{Travel}\}$, the system might also suggests as additional terminological item the term $\{\texttt{Star}\}$ first ($cooc_{v_2} = 2$), and $\{\texttt{Near}\}$ as second option ($cooc_{v_3} = 1$). In this way, the developer might realize that hotels can be searched either based on the number of stars or based on the proximity to a given location and he/she might refine the request by choosing one of the two options.

Exploration by proactive completion. The developer selects a subset $\overline{\mathcal{S}^e} \subseteq \mathcal{S}^e$ of services he/she is interested in. The system suggests services that could be used together with services in g^r, by updating the set $\mathcal{S}^e$, according to the *intra-aggregation co-occurrence*. Let's consider the example shown in Figure 4. After performing a search based on $\mathcal{T}^r = \{\texttt{City}, \texttt{Hotel}, \texttt{Travel}\}$, thus obtaining $\mathcal{S}^e = \{s_1, s_2, s_3\}$ as results, the developer chooses s_1 to be included in g^r. With reference to Figure 3, s_1 is associated with v_1 and v_2 nodes. Considering node v_1, other nodes connected to v_1 by graph edges are v_4 (associated with s_4, $cooc_{e_{14}} = 2$) and v_5 (associated with s_5, $cooc_{e_{15}} = 1$). Similarly, considering node v_2, $cooc_{e_{24}} = 1$ and $cooc_{e_{25}} = 1$. Therefore, the system ranks better the service s_4 than s_5, since $cooc_{e_{14}} + cooc_{e_{24}} > cooc_{e_{15}} + cooc_{e_{25}}$. The developer can accept one of these results. If more than one service is included in g^r, the step of retrieving services is repeated for each service in g^r.

Exploration by hybrid completion. This explorative modality is a combination of proactive completion and simple search. After $\mathcal{S}^e$ has been updated, the developer selects a subset $\overline{\mathcal{S}^e} \subseteq \mathcal{S}^e$ of services he/she is interested in, as well as

$\mathcal{T}^e$	$\mathcal{S}^e$	$\mathcal{G}^e$
{City, Hotel, Travel}	s_1 s_2 s_3	s_1

$\Downarrow$ $\Downarrow$

$\mathcal{T}^e$	$\mathcal{S}^e$	$\mathcal{G}^e$
{}	s_4	s_1
$(cooc_{e_{14}} + cooc_{e_{24}} = 3)$		

$\mathcal{T}^e$	$\mathcal{S}^e$	$\mathcal{G}^e$
{}	s_5	s_1
$(cooc_{e_{14}} + cooc_{e_{24}} = 2)$		

Fig. 4. Example of exploration by completion (see also Figure 3 for the intra-aggregation co-occurrences).

he/she specifies a new set $\mathcal{T}^r$ of terms. The system suggests services that could be used together with services in g^r, by updating the set $\mathcal{S}^e$. In order to obtain this set, a proactive completion step on g^r retrieves some services as explained before.

5 Preliminary validation of the framework

The exploration process described in Section 4 calls for a quantitative evaluation of the scalability of the exploration activities and the execution of experiments with developers, to test the effectiveness of the approach in supporting data service exploration. In this section, we present preliminary experiments on scalability, performed on a dataset of 1317 services extracted from `ProgrammableWeb`.

We initially considered a set of service pairs $\langle s_1, s_2\rangle$ in the dataset and we manually compared them according to tags, technical feature and aggregation similarity, considering aggregations where they have been used. We run the similarity evaluator to compute $Sim(s_1, s_2)$ by varying the threshold γ from 0.0 to 1.0 and we chose the value of γ that maximized the F-measure.

Then, experiments have been performed ten times using different requests. To this purpose we randomly retrieved aggregations from the repository and we considered as relevant the services included in the aggregations. We then issued the requests using the features of the services in the selected aggregations and we calculated the precision and recall of search results given by our system. The aim of these preliminary experiments is to confirm the advantages for service search brought by our approach, that considers the elements from the multiple perspectives described in the model. For these reasons, we compared our approach against: (a) the keyword-based search facilities made available within the `ProgrammableWeb` repository; (b) a partial implementation of our system, where we excluded the aggregation similarity from $Sim(\mathcal{R}, s)$ computation. Table 1 shows the precision, recall and F-measure results, the standard deviation and the variance of F-measure for the compared systems. As expected, the complete implementation of the system presents the best F-measure value. Although the exploitation of term and technical feature similarity bring significant improvements compared to the basic searching facilities of the `ProgrammableWeb` repository, it is quite evident as the highest enhancement in F-measure value is due to the integration also of aggregation similarity, that mainly relies on service co-occurrence.

System	F-measure	Precision	Recall	Std deviation	Variance
`ProgrammableWeb`	0,0414	0,03105	0,0621	0,0363	0,0013
WISeR (no *AggSim*)	0,4247	0,5880	0,3324	0,3562	0,1269
WISeR	0,5993	0,7451	0,5012	0,2159	0,0466

Table 1. Results of the experimental evaluation.

6 Concluding remarks

In this paper, we proposed an approach for data service explorative search, based on a multi-perspective model for data services and specific collective intelligence on them. The approach includes proactive search facilities and enables developers to iteratively increase their knowledge on available web data services. Future work will be devoted to the study of techniques for including latent factors (e.g., related to the perceived QoS) in the exploration process. Further open research includes the definition of the visualization interface to further increase the exploration experience of developers.

References

1. S. Idreos, O. Papaemmanouil, S. Chaudhuri, Overview of data exploration techniques, in: ACM Conference on Management of Data (SIGMOD), 2015.
2. W. Gao, L. Chen, J. Wu, A. Bouguettaya, Joint Modeling Users, Services, Mashups and Topics for Service Recommendation, in: Proc. of 23rd International Conference on Web Services (ICWS 2016), 2016.
3. R. Hu, J. Liu, Y. Wen, Y. Mao, USER: A usage-based service recommendation approach, in: Proc. of 23rd International Conference on Web Services (ICWS 2016), 2016.
4. D. Bianchini, V. De Antonellis, M. Melchiori, A Multi-perspective Framework for Web API Search in Enterprise Mashup Design (Best Paper), in: Proc. of 25th Int. Conference on Advanced Information Systems Engineering (CAiSE), Vol. LNCS 7908, 2013, pp. 353–368.
5. B. Cao, X. Liu, B. Li, J. Liu, M. Tang, T. Zhang, Mashup Service Clustering Based on an Integration of Service Content and Network via Exploiting a Two-level Topic Model, in: Proc. of 23rd International Conference on Web Services (ICWS 2016), 2016.
6. W. Xiong, Z. Wu, B. Li, Q. Gu, L. Yuan, B. Hang, Inferring service recommendation from natural language api description, in: Proc. of 23rd International Conference on Web Services (ICWS 2016), 2016.
7. X. Liu, I. Fulia, Incorporating User, Topic, and Service Related Latent Factors into Web Service Recommendation, in: Proc. of IEEE International Conference on Web Services (ICWS 2015), 2015, pp. 185–192.
8. Z. Malik, A. Bouguettaya, RATEWeb: Reputation Assessment for Trust Establishment among Web Services, VLBD Journal 18 (2009) 885–911.
9. S. Pakari, E. Kheirkhah, M. Jalali, Web Service Discovery Methods and Techniques: A Review, Int. Journal of Computer Science, Engineering and Information Technology 4 (1) (2014) 1–14.
10. H. Wang, N. Gibbins, T. Payne, A. Patelli, Y. Wang, A survey of Semantic Web Services formalisms, Concurrency and Computation Practice and Experience.
11. D. Bianchini, V. De Antonellis, M. Melchiori, Capitalizing the Designers' Experience for Improving Web API Selection, in: On the Move to Meaningful Internet Systems: OTM 2014 Conferences, Vol. LNCS 8841, 2014, pp. 364–381.

Tell the student: evidence-based advantages of prerequisites (Discussion Paper)*

Marco Cameranesi[1], Claudia Diamantini[1], Laura Genga[2], and Domenico Potena[1]

[1] Dipartimento di Ingegneria dell'Informazione, Università Politecnica delle Marche, via Brecce Bianche, 60131 Ancona, Italy
[2] Department of Mathematics and Computer Science, Eindhoven University of Technology, 5600 MB Eindhoven, The Netherlands
{m.cameranesi,c.diamantini,d.potena}@univpm.it, {l.genga}@tue.nl

Abstract. When bachelor and master degrees were introduced in the Italian system, the Engineering Faculty of Università Politecnica delle Marche dropped mandatory prerequisites between modules from its degrees. Since then, we periodically witness intense debates among professors, who think this led to unstructured learning practices with consequent performance issues, and students who are concerned of an overly constrained course of study. This paper briefly describes an ex-post analysis of the carriers of students enrolled in the bachelor degree in Computer and Automation Engineering based on process mining techniques, the resulting evidence about typical patterns followed by students, and sketches possible actions that can be put in practice to support students without constraining their course of study.

1 Introduction

Digital technologies in learning received much attention in the last years. In particular, educational data mining is a research field by itself [3]. Leveraged by e-learning environments and MOOC, data mining techniques can be exploited on an increasing amount of digital resources related to almost every step of the learning process, to perform a wide variety of tasks: prediction of future enrollments, abandonments or outcomes; latent knowledge estimation; mining of relations between certain students characteristics and their learning style; clustering of schools, courses or students, just to name a few.

In this paper we briefly describe the application of process mining techniques to the carriers of students enrolled in the bachelor degree in Computer and Automation Engineering, with the aim to understand the typical paths followed by students in taking exams, and their relations with final outcomes. The work is motivated by the intense debate among professors and students that arise from time to time on mandatory prerequisites. Mandatory prerequisites among

* This work has been partially funded by the ITEA2 project M2MGrid (No. 13011).

modules have been dropped from courses of the Faculty of Engineering of the Università Politecnica delle Marche. While somebody would like to re-introduce them in order to limit unstructured learning practices, students are concerned of an overly constrained course of study. The work is part of the monitoring activities in charge of the Faculty committee named "Commissione Paritetica" [5], in which one of the authors is involved. Similar applications of Process Mining techniques exist in the literature. They are mainly devoted to exploit event logs generated by Learning Management Systems like Moodle to discover the workflow of learning activities performed inside a unit of learning, or teaching module (e.g. reading documents, doing assignments, accessing the forum, etc.) [10, 15], or to model patterns of examinee behaviors during assessments [12]. The work in [9] shares some similarities with the present work, in that it tries to find correlations between outcome variables and the sequence of modules, by segmenting traces on the basis of key performance indicators.

The rest of the paper is organized as follows: in Section 2 we provide a brief introduction to Process Mining and techniques used in the paper. Section 3 describes data, their processing and the results of mining activities. Section 4 introduces some reflection and draw future work.

2 Background

Process Mining encompasses a wide range of techniques for the analysis of business processes from run-time information recorded in event logs [1].

A *process* consists of a set of activities that have to be performed by some actors to reach a certain goal. Welfare grant approval is an example of business process, that involves activities like `application_submission`, the analysis of documentation, possibly split in `financial_check` and `check_for_illness_conditions` performed by two different units in parallel, and a final `approval` decision. A *process schema* is a general schema representing the overall control-flow of activities. The main elements of a process schema are activities, and control-flow operators like sequence, parallelization and merging, alternative choices, and loops. Many different process modeling formalisms exist, among them Petri Nets is the best known theoretical model. A *process instance* is a specific execution of the process. In our example, each single welfare grant application represents a process instance. Process instances are recorded by information systems in *event logs* in the form of *traces*, i.e. sequences of events generated by the execution of activities in their strict order of occurrence. The core information recorded in an event log covers the unique id of the event occurred, the associated activity, the time of occurrence and the instance, or case, it belongs to. The name of the actor executing the activity, or its role, can be also reported. Depending on the information system, other information can be recorded, like for instance the data processed by the activity, the case category and so forth. This kind of information is often referred to as data attributes and this kind of logs are also called data annotated logs.

In Process Mining, two major tasks can be recognized:

- Process Discovery: synthesize a process schema from event logs.
- Conformance Checking: analyze the event log to check whether it fits a given process. If the model is a normative or prescriptive (hence a-priori correct) model, conformance checking is interpreted as a way to measure the adherence of real process executions to those prescribed or planned, however it can also be seen as a way to evaluate the accuracy of a model mined by a Process Discovery technique in capturing the content of the event log.

The basic idea of Process Discovery techniques is to exploit event logs to reconstruct causal relations among events that are then used to build a model of the process. In order to deal with variability and noise in real-life logs, *filtering approaches* have been introduced. The infrequent Inductive Miner (iIM) algorithms [11] adopted in this paper belongs to the class of filtering, block-based techniques, that infer a model on the basis of a process tree built on frequent behaviors only. The iIM algorithm adopts an iterative procedure. First, it generates a *directly-follows graph*, i.e. a graph where each node corresponds to an event, and an arc exists between two nodes A and B if event A appears immediately before event B in at least one trace. The number of occurrences of each arc in the log is recorded. The graph is then analyzed to find a *cut*, i.e. a split of activities into disjoint sets such that all the activities in a set are in the same flow relation with all the activities of the other subsets. Sequence, exclusive choice, parallel and loop operators each have their own characteristic cut. If a cut is found then the corresponding operator is chosen as a node of the process tree, and the log is in turn partitioned into sets that reflect the partition choice for the nodes of the graph. The procedure is repeated until each sublog contains only a single event. A user-defined *noise threshold* $0 \leq k \leq 1$ allows to control filtering. For instance, an arc can be removed from the directly-follows graph if the ratio between its number of occurrences and the occurrences of the strongest outgoing arc from the same node is less than k.

Conformance Checking is based on the notion of *replay*: each trace is simulated on the process model one event at a time. When the current event cannot be found at a given step, an *alignment* procedure is adopted to continue the replay procedure, by either skipping the event in the log or the activity in the process schema. Besides, a measure of the fitness of the trace to the model is calculated [13]. In the present work we will adopt the cost-based fitness measures defined in [2].

3 Mining of Students' Careers

The major questions we like to answer can be stated as follows: "Do students take (exams of) modules in the suggested order?" and "Which are *best practices* and *worst practices* followed by students?". The order among teaching modules is related to prerequisites suggested in modules programs, so that module A should be taken before module B if A's contents are fundamental or useful to understand B's contents. Of course there is only a partial order among modules, since courses may deal with different, unrelated topics. Furthermore, best/worst practices are defined with respect to careers performances, as expressed by the final grade mark and length of the period of study.

With these questions in mind, we exploited process mining as a descriptive mining technique to obtain a synthetic view of the paths followed by students from enrollment to bachelor degree, in the form of process schemas. The methodology can be summarized as follows: after some data pre-processing, we obtain a set of traces representing students' careers. Traces are segmented into three disjoint groups depending on the final grade mark and length of the period of study. Then, for each group, a process model is synthesized in the form of Petri Net by the iIM algorithm. Accuracy of the models is assessed by measuring its fitness over the entire set of traces in the group. In the following we provide some details of these steps and of the results obtained.

3.1 Data Selection and Preparation

Data are mainly taken from ESSE3, a software suite commonly adopted by Universities to manage students' careers and in particular registration to exam sessions and record of grades. We focused the analysis on the latest educational system, as defined by D.M. 270/2004, considering students enrolled from Academic year 2009/10 on. This provides us with a set of homogenous curricula. Furthermore only complete and correct curricula are considered, discarding students who have not taken the degree yet, or students with exams confirmed from previous degrees (these exams do not appear as database records, determining oversimplified and short curricula). Further cleaning procedures were necessary in order to deal with inconsistencies and null values generated during database population at the time of ESSE3 software adoption. At the end, the careers of 187 graduated students were available for analysis. In order to reduce noise, a further step was to delete from curricula the diverse modules freely chosen by students from other courses of Università Politecnica delle Marche.

The final dataset is a table with the following attributes: student ID, module name, exam date, exam mark, duration of the period of study (calculated as the difference between the final exam date and the enrollment date, conventionally fixed to the 1st of November of the Academic year of enrollment). The dataset can be interpreted as a very simple event log, where each student is a case, and exam passing is the set of events with their timestamp.

Additional data attributes related to exam mark and duration are exploited to segment the event log. As a matter of fact, a plain application of process mining techniques to the whole event log did not lead to meaningful process schemas. This can be expected, since the many optional choices and the lack of mandatory prerequisites make the course of study very flexibly customized by students according to their needs and contingencies. In order to deal with this kind of unstructured processes, different methodologies have been devised, among which trace clustering and its process cube variant are pre-processing techniques that are related to the approach followed in this study. In both approaches the idea is to generate different groups of traces with homogeneous characteristics such that better models can be obtained for each group. While in trace clustering similarity is based on the sequence of events inside traces (inner or structural trace similarity) [8], the process cube approach segment traces according to common values of data attributes, independently from the trace structure. Data attributes can be organized into hierarchies, thus implementing a multidimensional cube of traces [4]. In order to understand more clearly whether prerequisites have an impact on final performance, we decided to enrich the log with exam mark and duration, and exploit them to segment students' careers into three groups: high performance, medium, and low performance. Table 1 shows the definition of groups and careers distribution within each group. As one can note from the table, the definition of thresholds is such that careers are roughly equally distributed in each group.

Table 1. Data attributes, thresholds and careers distribution. The fraction of year in the second column allows to take into account the last graduation session of each academic year, that usually takes place in February. Dark gray cell: high performance careers. Light grey cells: low performance careers. White cells: medium careers.

		Avg. Mark		
		$m \geq 27/30$	$25 \leq m < 27$	$m < 25$
Study	$d \leq 3.3$	27.27%	12.83%	3.74%
Duration	$3.3 < d \leq 5.3$	7.49%	15.51%	16.58%
(years)	$d > 5.3$	0.53%	4.81%	11.23%

3.2 Experiments

The ProM framework[3] has been adopted to perform experiments, in particular the infrequent Inductive Miner (iIM) and Replay a Log on Petri Net for Conformance Analysis (Replay) plugins. For each group of careers, iIM has been launched with different noise thresholds and the different models obtained have been evaluated on the basis of the fitness value calculated by Replay. In what follows we discuss the best Petri Net models generated for high performance and low performance careers. The former is shown in Figure 1. It is obtained with noise threshold equal to 0.3 and has a fitness equal to 96%. Circles and boxes represents places and transition respectively. In particular white boxes corresponds to events in the log (i.e., exams in our case study), while black boxes are invisible transitions, they do not correspond to real events and are generated by iIM in order to obtain a sound model. We can appreciate in the initial part of the model a fairly structured flow, magnified in Figure 2, followed by a more irregular flow. The process starts with three parallel events, corresponding to exams taken for modules of Algebra Lineare e Geometria, Fisica 1, Analisi Matematica 1. This means that, although there is not a strict precedence relation among these exams in the log, students typically take all the three before moving to

[3] www.promtools.org/prom6

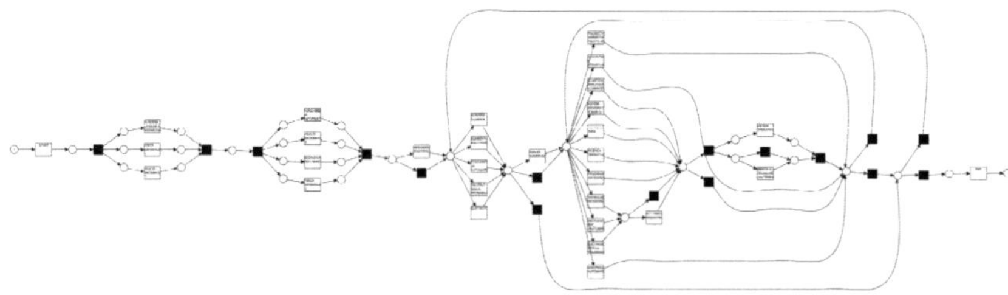

Fig. 1. Process model of best performing students.

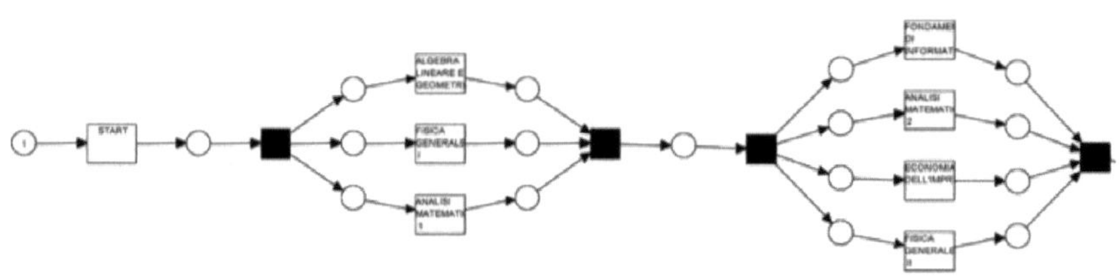

Fig. 2. Process model of best performing students: initial part.

other exams. The three courses are those scheduled during the first semester of the first year. Similarly, the next four parallel events correspond to modules scheduled during the second semester of the first year. Hence, we can see that students with the best careers basically follow the ideal order in taking exams of the first year. Subsequently, the schema shows a less structured flow. This is expected, since free choice modules are introduced from the second year on, due to the presence of two different curricula offered by the course (Computer Engineering and Automation Engineering respectively). Nevertheless, we can still appreciate that the first three groups of events all correspond to modules taught in the second year.

The model is even more interesting when contrasted with that generated from low performing careers, shown in Figure 3. Here, the only regularity is that students choose to take their first exam among six courses taught in the first year (Fisica 2 being the one missed in the list), and that in a number of cases the sequence of exam for Automazione Industriale, Progettazione Assistita da Calcolatore, and Laboratorio di Automazione is followed. No other regularity can be appreciated, suggesting the lack of any criteria in exams flow, and enlightening striking differences in the behaviors of students in the two groups.

4 Discussion

The one presented is a preliminary analysis of students careers, and conclusions must be taken cautiously, in particular for what concerns the cause-effect relationship between high performance and structured course of study: is it that

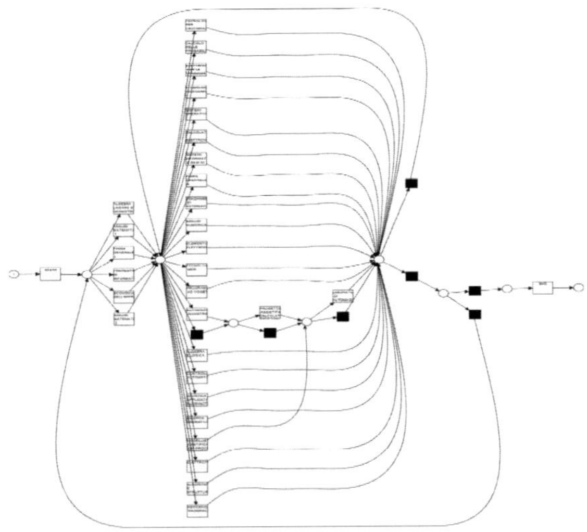

Fig. 3. Process model of worst performing students.

following the "right" order of exams leads students to high performance, or is it the other way around, i.e. students with a natural propensity to computer and automation engineering (which in principle lead to high performance somewhat independently from other factors) have a "structured mindset" and thus follow the order proposed in course regulations? Nevertheless, the evidence of such striking differences between the two groups led us to disseminate results among students, both inside different Faculty committees and during the degree introductory activities, and they have been welcomed by students and professors as the first evidence-based discussion on the advantages of prerequisites. The results also stimulated the board of degree in Computer and Automation Engineering to spread among students information about modules' prerequisites, and to develop actions able to increase awareness on the potential benefits of a thoughtful schedule of exams.

Several further analyses can be performed to support and refine results: first of all, we started replicating the methodology to other degrees, with encouraging results. Second, more refined clustering techniques, based both on finer categories and on structural trace similarity may allow us to discover more precise models. Third, we plan to apply different mining techniques: on the one hand we will consider *local* process mining techniques, tackling unstructuredness of processes by discovering simpler and more precise models of just parts of the process, instead of start-to-end models [6, 7, 14], on the other hand we plan to compare results with those of more traditional data mining techniques, in order to enlighten the advantages of a process perspective of student careers. Finally, information on student's background in terms of secondary school diploma and grade can be exploited to check cause-effect hypotheses. If further analyses will confirm the robustness of the approach, we plan the design of a semi-automatic advisory system, based on mined models, that can inform students when their careers diverge significantly from best practices and/or show some other worrying signs, thus moving from a descriptive to a predictive scenario.

Acknowledgements

We thank the Commissione Paritetica of the Faculty of Engineering, Università Politecnica delle Marche for his support in the development of the analysis presented in this paper. We also wish to thank Dott. Ing. Matteo Marzioli for the work done in carrying out experiments.

References

1. van der Aalst, W.: Process Mining: Discovery, Conformance and Enhancement of Business Processes. Springer (2011)
2. Adriansyah, A., van Dongen, B., van der Aalst, W.: Conformance Checking Using Cost-Based Fitness Analysis. In: 15th IEEE EDOC Conf. pp. 55–64 (2011)
3. Baker, R.S., Inventado, P.S.: Educational Data Mining and Learning Analytics, pp. 61–75 (2014)
4. Bolt, A., van der Aalst, W.: Multidimensional process mining using process cubes. In: Int. Conf. on Enterprise, Business-Process and Information Systems Modeling. pp. 102–116 (2015)
5. Commissione Paritetica per la didattica e il diritto allo studio: Relazione Annuale 2016, Facoltà di Ingegneria, Università Politecnica delle Marche (December 2016)
6. Diamantini, C., Genga, L., Potena, D., van der Aalst, W.: Building instance graphs for highly variable processes. Expert Systems with Applications 59, 101–118 (2016)
7. Diamantini, C., Genga, L., Potena, D., Storti, E.: Pattern discovery from innovation processes. In: Int. Conf. on Collab. Techn. and Sys. pp. 457–464 (2013)
8. Greco, G., Guzzo, A., Pontieri, L., Sacca, D.: Discovering expressive process models by clustering log traces. IEEE Trans. Know. and Data Eng. 18(8), 1010–1027 (2006)
9. Hicheur Cairns, A., Gueni, B., et al.: Custom-Designed Professional Training Contents and Curriculums through Educational Process Mining. In: Fourth Int. Conf. on Advances in Information Mining and Management. pp. 53–58 (2014)
10. Kelly, N., Montenegro, M., et al.: Combining event- and variable-centred approaches to institution-facing learning analytics at the unit of study level. Int. Jour. of Information and Learning Technology 34(1), 63–78 (2017)
11. Leemans, S.J.J., Fahland, D., van der Aalst, W.: Discovering block-structured process models from event logs containing infrequent behaviour. In: Business Process Management Workshops, LNBIP 171. pp. 66–78 (2014)
12. Papamitsiou, Z., Economides, A.A.: Process mining of interactions during computer-based testing for detecting and modelling guessing behavior. In: Third Int. Conf. on Learning and Collaboration Technologies. pp. 437–449 (2016)
13. Rozinat, A., van der Aalst, W.: Conformance checking of processes based on monitoring real behavior. Inf. Sys. 33(1), 64–95 (2008)
14. Tax, N., Sidorova, N., Haakma, R., van der Aalst, W.: Mining local process models. Journal of Innovation in Digital Ecosystems 3(2), 183 – 196 (2016)
15. Vidal, J.C., Vázquez-Barreiros, B., Lama, M., Mucientes, M.: Recompiling learning processes from event logs. Knowledge-Based Systems 100, 160 – 174 (2016)

Interactive Data Repairing: the FALCON Dive

Enzo Veltri[1], Donatello Santoro[1], Giansalvatore Mecca[1],
Paolo Papotti[2], Jian He[3], Gouliang Li[3], and Nan Tang[4]

[1]Università della Basilicata – Potenza, Italy,
[2]Arizona State University, USA
[3]Tsinghua University, China
[4]Qatar Computing Research Institute, HBKU, Qatar

(Discussion Paper)

Abstract. In this paper we discuss FALCON, an *interactive, deterministic, and declarative* data cleaning system. Unlike traditional rule-based system, FALCON does not rely on the existence of a set of pre-defined data quality rules, but it encourages users to explore the data, identify possible problems, and make updates to fix them. The main technical challenge consists in finding a set of rules, expressed as SQL update queries, that are semantically correct and that fixes the largest number of errors in the data. FALCON navigates the lattice by interacting with users to gradually checking the correctness of a set of rules. We have conducted extensive experiments using both real-world and synthetic datasets to show that FALCON can effectively communicate with users in data repairing.

1 Introduction

We address the problem of improving the data cleaning process by involving non-expert users as first-class citizens, and present FALCON [8], a novel system for *interactive* data repairing. FALCON departs from rule-based data repairing [6,7,12,13,16] and other interactive data cleaning systems [5,9,14,15,17], since it brings together a simple, user-oriented interaction paradigm with the benefits of a declarative, *deterministic*, and expressive data quality language – SQL update (SQLU) queries. In fact, the system is bootstrapped by an update to the data made by the user to rectify an error; based on that, it infers a set of SQLU queries that can be used as data quality rules to correct more errors.

Example 1. Table 1 reports a sample real-world dataset T_{drug} for experiments collected from different labs. Each record represents the quantity and date of a test done in a lab over a certain molecule. Errors are highlighted. Consider the following three user updates: Δ_1: $t_3[\mathsf{Laboratory}] \leftarrow$ "New York", Δ_2: $t_3[\mathsf{Quantity}] \leftarrow 100$ and Δ_3: $t_2[\mathsf{Molecule}] \leftarrow$ "$C_{22}H_{28}F$".

There exist multiple interpretations for each update. For instance, two possible semantics behind Δ_1 could be either reformatting all "N.Y." to "New York" as shown in Q_1, or changing all Laboratory values to "New York" as shown in Q'_1, regardless of their original values.

Q_1: UPDATE T_{drug} SET Laboratory = "New York" WHERE Laboratory = "N.Y."
Q'_1: UPDATE T_{drug} SET Laboratory = "New York";

	Date	Molecule	Laboratory	Quantity
t_1	11 Nov	$C_{16}H_{16}Cl$	Austin	200
t_2	12 Nov	statin→$C_{22}H_{28}F$	Austin	200
t_3	12 Nov	$C_{24}H_{75}S_6$	N.Y.→ New York	1000→100
t_4	12 Nov	statin	Boston	200
t_5	13 Nov	statin	Austin	200

Table 1. Dataset T_{drug} with drug tests.

Similarly, one possible interpretation of Δ_2, as given in Q_2, is that it is specific for Molecule and Date. Hence, it is hard to generalize this update to apply it to other tuples.

Q_2: UPDATE T_{drug} SET Quantity = 100 WHERE Molecule = "$C_{24}H_{75}S_6$" AND Date = "12 Nov"

Update Δ_3 is more interesting. Consider the following three interpretations. Q_3 repairs errors in both t_2 and t_5. Q'_3 also repairs both t_2 and t_5, but additionally, it modifies t_4[Molecule] to "$C_{22}H_{28}F$", which is an erroneous update, since in Boston they test a different statin molecule. On the other hand, the tuple-specific query Q''_3 only corrects t_2 but misses the chance to repair t_5.

Q_3: UPDATE T_{drug} SET Mol. = "$C_{22}H_{28}F$" WHERE Mol. = "statin" AND Lab. = "Austin";

Q'_3: UPDATE T_{drug} SET Mol. = "$C_{22}H_{28}F$" WHERE Mol. = "statin";

Q''_3: UPDATE T_{drug} SET Mol. = "$C_{22}H_{28}F$" WHERE Mol. = "statin" AND Lab. = "Austin" AND Date = "12 Nov" AND Qt. = 200;

One may observe that there might exist a large number of SQLU queries. Indeed, this large number is not surprising, as up to thousands of precise and reliable update queries can be needed in real-world settings. However, while an update is a perfect starting point for the process of inferring the general scripts, it comes with new challenges in terms of user interactions. The search space for a new update is exponential to the number of the attributes, and domain experts cannot manually validate each of these SQLU queries. We have to assume that a *budget* (*e.g.*, #-user interactions) is given for a specific update. This *dynamic* behavior, together with the large search space and a budget of user capacity, prevents the use of traditional tools for interactive response, such as precomputing and caching.

Contributions. We present FALCON [8], a novel interactive data cleaning system, with the following contributions: (1) To design data quality rules, we adopt the standard and deterministic language of SQL update statements (Section 2). We discuss how to organize the search space of candidate rules as a lattice, and its pruning principles, by leveraging the properties of the lattice (Section 3). (2) We devise efficient algorithms for selecting candidate queries to effectively interact with the user (Section 4) (3) We have conducted experiments with real-world and synthetic data to show the effectiveness and efficiency of FALCON (Section 5).

2 Problem Statement

SQL Update Queries. We adopt a simple and standard language to repair the database, the language of update statements in SQL (SQLU). An SQLU statement updates records in a table T on attributes $A, B \ldots$, when some conditions hold. We restrict the language to the case where updates are done on one attribute A of table T with only boolean conjunctions:

UPDATE T SET $A = a$ WHERE boolean conjunctions

More specifically, each boolean conjunction is of the form $B = v_B$, where B is an attribute of table T and v_B is a constant value.

Search Space for One Repair. Consider a repair $\Delta : t[A] \leftarrow a'$ that changes the value of $t[A]$ from error a to its correct value a' with $a \neq a'$. We want to generalize this action so as to repair more errors. Naturally, there exist multiple queries to interpret Δ. Implicitly, for each query, the SET clause is $A = a'$. Consider a boolean condition as $B = v_B$, where B could be any attribute in relation R. We adopt a *closed-world* assumption by only using the evidence from tuple t, the tuple that is being repaired. As a special query, we consider $\varnothing$ as *no condition* being enforced in the WHERE clause. Stating in another way, it is to update all A values in T to a'.

In summary, given a repair $t[A] \leftarrow a'$ for tuple t in table T of relation R, the set $\mathcal{Q}$ of all rules for such a repair is:

UPDATE T SET $A = a'$ WHERE $X = t[X]$

where X is an arbitrary subset of R, which can range from the empty set $\varnothing$ to all attributes in R (*i.e.*, $X = R$). Hence, there are $2^{|R|}$ possibilities of X.

Problem Statement Given a repair, one wants to find the queries that are semantically correct so as to repair the database. An SQLU query is *valid* if the query is semantically correct. Since we do not know which queries are valid in advance, we need to ask the user to either validate the query as semantically correct, or invalidate it otherwise. Naturally, we want to find all valid SQLU queries and use them to repair the database. A straightforward strategy is to ask the user to check every possible query. Of course, this method is rather expensive as there could be a large number of possible queries, for which we will use containment relationships among queries to improve the search of queries.

Budget repair problem. Given a set $\mathcal{Q}$ of SQLU queries, a table T, and a budget B for the number of interactions the user can afford, the *budget repair problem* is to select B queries $\mathcal{Q}'$ from $\mathcal{Q}$, so as to maximize $|\bigcup_{Q \in \mathcal{Q}' \wedge \mathsf{valid}(Q) = \mathsf{T}} Q(T)|$.

Here, $\mathsf{valid}(Q)$ is a boolean function that is T (resp. F) if Q is a valid query (resp. not), and $Q(T)$ represents the set of repairs of applying query Q over T. Observe that in the above problem, given a query Q, the validity of Q is unknown, to be verified by the user. Such a problem is typically categorized under the framework of *online algorithms*, where one can process input piece-by-piece in a serial fashion, without having the entire input available.

Offline problem. Its corresponding *offline variant* is the following. Given as input that whether each query Q in $\mathcal{Q}$ is valid or not is known, how to select B queries from $\mathcal{Q}$ to maximize the number of repaired tuples. It is easy to see that the offline problem of its online version (*i.e.*, the budget repair problem) is NP-hard. When the offline variant is NP-hard, there is no efficient algorithm for computing an optimal solution for its online algorithm. In other words, when the offline variant is intractable, there is no hope to find an optimal solution with the cost in a constant factor of the online variant. However, not all is lost. As will be shown later, we can organize all queries in a graphical structure, such that when the user verifies a query Q as valid or invalid, we can even generate more inputs by computing the validity of queries Q' that are related to Q.

3 A Lattice: Falcon Search Space

In this section, we shall present our organization of the search space, so as to enable both efficient and effective search over the candidate rules.

Rule containment. For two rules Q and Q', we say that Q is *contained* by Q', denoted by $Q \preceq Q'$, if for all possible database instances T over the input schema R, the result of $Q(T)$ is a subset of the result of $Q'(T)$. Intuitively, the rule containment captures the semantic relationship among rules. In other words, no matter which database T is used, Q will update a subset of T tuples that Q' will update if $Q \preceq Q'$, since Q is more specific than Q'. It is readily to verify that the query containment "$\preceq$" is a partial order over the set $\mathcal{Q}$ of all possible rules, which is reflexive, antisymmetric, and transitive. For a query Q, we denote by $\mathsf{attr}(Q)$ the set of distinct attributes in its WHERE condition. Note that for each user update, the SQLU queries have the same value constraint on the same attribute, and thus the rule containment verification is *equivalent* to a simpler condition: $Q \preceq Q'$ if $\mathsf{attr}(Q')$ is a subset $\mathsf{attr}(Q)$.

Affected tuples. For each query Q and instance T, we call the tuples in $Q(T)$ *affected tuples*, *i.e.,* the tuples that Q will repair. We also call $|Q(T)|$ the *affected number* of Q, relative to T. Consider Q_3 and T_{drug} in Example 1 for instance. The affected tuples are $Q_3(T_{\mathsf{drug}}) = \{t_2, t_5\}$, and its corresponding affected number is $|Q_3(T_{\mathsf{drug}})| = 2$. Hence, $\mathcal{Q}$ is a *poset* on the partial order $\preceq$ of rule containment. Moreover, consider any two rules Q and Q'. They have a *greatest lower bound*: the most specific query that is contained by both Q and Q'. This query, denoted by $Q \wedge Q'$, is the one *w.r.t.* $\mathsf{attr}(Q) \cup \mathsf{attr}(Q')$. Also, they have a *least upper bound*: the most general query that contains both Q and Q'. This query, denoted by $Q \vee Q'$, is the one *w.r.t.* $\mathsf{attr}(Q) \cap \mathsf{attr}(Q')$. Therefore, we can organize the queries in our search space as a *lattice*.

Query lattice. Given a repair Δ and a database instance T, we denote by $(\mathcal{Q}, \preceq)$ the corresponding lattice. Each node in the lattice corresponds to a query $Q \in \mathcal{Q}$. Each directed edge from node Q to Q' indicates that $Q \preceq Q'$ (Q is contained in Q') and $|\mathsf{attr}(Q)| = |\mathsf{attr}(Q')| + 1$ (with one different attribute). Moreover, the affected number associated with each query is maintained in the lattice.

Valid and maximal valid nodes. Given a lattice $(\mathcal{Q}, \preceq)$, the node relative to a rule Q is *valid* if it is semantically correct, thus should be executed to repair data. In our work, if the validity of a rule is unknown, we rely on the user to verify. Fortunately, if a rule Q is known to be valid, we can infer that Q' is also valid if $Q' \preceq Q$. Moreover, the node relative to a valid rule Q is *maximal valid*, if no Q'' is valid and $Q \preceq Q''$. One nice property of using a lattice is that it provides opportunities to prune nodes to be visited during traversal.

Lattice pruning. If a node Q is valid, by inference, all nodes Q' where $Q' \preceq Q$ are valid. On the other hand, if a node Q is invalid, by inference, all nodes Q'' where $Q \preceq Q''$ are invalid. The rationale behind the above inferences is that: if one query is valid, then any query that is more specific is also valid; conversely, if it is invalid, then any query that is more general is also invalid. We denote by $Q^{\curlyvee}$ (*i.e.*, above Q in the lattice) the queries that Q contains, and $Q_{\curlywedge}$ (*i.e.*, below Q in the lattice) the queries that contain Q. These notations naturally extend to a set of queries, $\mathcal{Q}^{\curlyvee}$ and $\mathcal{Q}_{\curlywedge}$, such that $\mathcal{Q}^{\curlyvee} = \bigcup_{Q \in \mathcal{Q}} Q^{\curlyvee}$ and $\mathcal{Q}_{\curlywedge} = \bigcup_{Q \in \mathcal{Q}} Q_{\curlywedge}$.

4 Algorithms: Falcon in Action

First of all, we notice that traditional traversal algorithms cannot be used to efficiently navigate the lattice $\mathcal{L}$ [8]. In this section we present advanced algorithms to efficiently navigate the search space. Given a budget B, our objective is to define a *divide-and-conquer* strategy that efficiently identifies nodes that are both valid and not very close to the top, so as to maximize the number of tuples to be repaired. To this purpose, we present a strategy, namely *binary jump*, inspired by classical binary search. Roughly speaking, we treat the search space as a linear space (*i.e.*, an array) by sacrificing some structural connections, and sort the nodes based on their associated affected numbers. We can then do multi-hop search to locate a candidate node to be verified with the user. Note that conventionally, *a binary search* finds the position of a target value within a sorted array. Different from it, *binary jump* does not have a target value to be searched. In other words, binary jump is just inspired by binary search by doing half-interval style lattice traversal. We first discuss binary jump over a path. To find the truth with traversal based approaches, we need $O(N)$ questions in average, where N is the length of the path. However, using binary jump will reduce it to $O(\log N)$ questions, which is optimal, by applying inferences of finding all valid/invalid nodes. Straightforwardly, *binary* may refer to the offset as standard binary search. However, we need to incorporate the information of affected number. Hence, the *binary* search could refer to the median number. For binary jump, we introduce a parameter d to bound the search depth, which is the number of iterations one can do binary jump before termination. Given a path $Q_1, Q_2, \cdots, Q_x$, we first ask the middle node $Q_{x/2}$. If the node is valid, we ask the next middle node between $Q_{x/2}$ and Q_x; otherwise, we ask the next middle node between Q_1 and $Q_{x/2}$. After d wrong searches, the process terminates. We refer to this search strategy as BinaryJump(). The rationale behind using the parameter d is that if we are following the wrong direction, we should be aware and go back to the right track. In order to take the advantage of binary jump for lattice traversal, the broad intuition is to do dimension reduction from a lattice to a one-dimensional structure. That is, if we treat all nodes in the lattice uniformly, by sorting them in ascending order on their associated affected numbers, we get a sorted array similar to the one discussed above for the path.

The Dive algorithm. Given a lattice $(\mathcal{Q}, \preceq)$ *w.r.t.* a repair Δ over table T, a budget B for the number of questions the user can answer, the dive algorithm works as follow: 1) at the beginning, the validity of every node is unknown; 2) we sort in ascending order unvalidated nodes $Q^?$ based on their affected numbers. Then we apply BINARYJUMP() over $Q^?$ to select the next node Q to validate by the user; 3) if the user validates Q, we use lattice pruning to infer other valid nodes, and set $Q^? = \mathcal{Q}_\lambda$. 4) it the user rejects Q, then we infer invalid nodes and then we set $Q^? = \mathcal{Q}^\Upsilon$. 5) if user has capacity (number of user interactions is less than B) process will continue in step 2, otherwise it terminates.

Correlation aware binary jump (CoDive). We revise binary jump by using the correlation information between attributes [8, 11], affecting the second step of our Dive algorithm. Note that the function BINARYJUMP() will locate a node Q in the sorted list $\mathcal{Q}^?$. Instead of asking the user to verify Q, we revise it with the following methodology. (1) We pick more nodes around Q in the sorted list, with w on its left and the other w on its right. (2) For the above $2w + 1$ nodes, we compute their scores (affected number multiplies correlation score) and select the one with the largest score, which will then be verified by the user.

5 Experimental Study

Datasets. We used four real-world datasets and one synthetic dataset: Soccer, Hospital, BUS, DBLP and Synth. More details are available in the full paper [8].

Algorithms. We implemented several algorithms for the exploration of the lattice. First, we study our own proposals for multi-hop search. Dive is the binary jump algorithm presented in Section 4. CoDive is its extention to make use of the attributes correlation information, when this is available. These are compared with one-hop search strategies (BFS, DFS and Ducc [10]). As we will show in the results, Ducc is better than BFS and DFS for extensive searches of maximal rules in the lattice, but it was not designed to deal with small values of budget.

Baselines. We compared FALCON with four baselines.

1) *Refine*: Our proposal generalizes the transformation language of existing tools such as OpenRefine and Trifacta Wrangler. These tools enable the inference of only two transformations that are comparable to our language: either the single cell is updated (the top of the lattice) or the erroneous value e is replaced with the new value v for all the occurrences in the attribute.

2) *Rule-Learning Approaches:* Many previous approaches have concentrated on learning data-quality rules (*e.g.,* [2, 4]). In particular (*i*) starting from a dirty database, we asked users to clean a sample of tuples; (*ii*) based on the sample tuples, we used a CFD-miner; and (*iii*) we used the set of SQL-updates to repair the dirty instance, and measured the *benefit* score (see below).

3) *Guided Data Repairs:* To explore the impact of *active learning*, we used GDR [17], that is a recently proposed algorithm that relies on active learning in order to improve the quality of repairs. Given a set of rules, it will incrementally ask users to solicit the right repairs suggested by the rules.

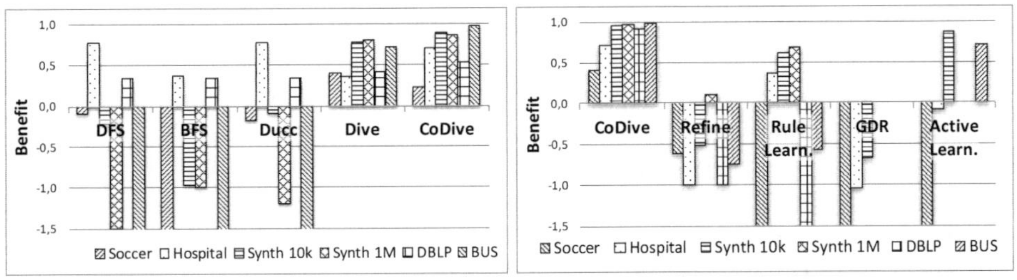

(a) Benefit for the various algorithms. (b) Benefit compared with the baselines.

Fig. 1. Experimental results

4)*Active Learning in Lattice Traversal:* We compared our methods to an active learning variant of our lattice-based approach designed *ad-hoc* for this purpose.

Errors and Metrics. Since the considered datasets are clean, we introduce noise to verify the algorithms behaviour in the cleaning process. To start, we manually defined a set of CFDs [3] and fixing rules [16] for each scenario. Afterwards, we used an error-generation tool to inject errors into the clean instances [1]. We keep running an algorithm until all the introduced errors are fixed either by a rule or by the user updates. Then, we measure the *interaction cost* as the sum between the number of user-provided updates U and the number of users' answers for nodes validation A. In order to have an indicator of the advantage of using interactive cleaning, we also measure the *benefit* of an algorithm in comparison to the manual update of all the errors. We first define the *cost ratio* as the number of actions divided by the number of errors. Given an algorithm α, a dataset D, and the interaction cost T_C to obtain a set of queries $\mathcal{Q}$ covering all introduced errors, we define the *benefit* of the algorithm as $\mathrm{BNF}_\alpha = 1 - T_C/|\mathcal{Q}(D)|$.

Exp-1: Lattice search algorithms. Figure 1(a) reports the benefit of each algorithm for the six datasets with a fixed budget $B = 2$. The proposed algorithms, Dive and CoDive, consistently report a positive gain, which, for CoDive, can be interpreted as a reduction of the total user interaction cost between 22% (Soccer) and 97% (BUS). The plot also reveals that one-hop algorithms fail for the budget exploration of the lattice, with the notable exception of the Hospital dataset. This results is not surprising if we look more closely at this scenario. Hospital schema has a large number of FDs with always one or two attributes in the left hand side (LHS) of the rules. This is reflected in the CFDs that we used to introduce the errors. Rules with one or two LHS attributes are at the bottom of the lattice, and this is the most favourable setting for one-hop based algorithms, since they all start from the bottom. On the other hand, when rules start to have more attributes in the LHS, more nodes must be checked to take a decision, these algorithms fail and Dive and CoDive greatly outperform them.

Exp-2: Comparison to the baselines. Figure 1(b) reports a comparison of our CoDive algorithm to the four baselines discussed above. We fixed a timeout of two hours for all tests. Notice that not all algorithm terminated within the timeout. This accounts for the missing bars in the chart. Our approach significantly outperforms all baselines. CoDive results are significantly better than those based on rule discovery. This suggests that our novel paradigm for data repairing is an improvement *w.r.t.* previous approaches in which quality rules are established upfront. Interestingly, this is confirmed also in the case in which rule discovery is coupled with an interactive algorithm, like GDR. In fact, the additional number of user interactions needed to run GDR brings to even lower benefit. CoDive algorithm outperforms its active learning variant. Since ActiveLearning shares the same infrastructure as CoDive, here results are better *w.r.t.* RuleLearning and GDR. In fact, as for CoDive, whenever it terminated also ActiveLearning was able to repair all errors. CoDive outperforms Refine because of the less expressive language in the latter. Results confirm our intuition that using user updates to lead the discovery of rules in an incremental way yields more complete and effective repairs than state-of-the-art rule-learning algorithms.

References

1. P. C. Arocena, B. Glavic, G. Mecca, R. J. Miller, P. Papotti, and D. Santoro. Messing up with BART: error generation for evaluating data-cleaning algorithms. *PVLDB*, 9(2), 2015.
2. X. Chu, I. F. Ilyas, and P. Papotti. Discovering denial constraints. *PVLDB*, 2013.
3. W. Fan, F. Geerts, X. Jia, and A. Kementsietsidis. Conditional functional dependencies for capturing data inconsistencies. *ACM Trans. Database Syst.*, 2008.
4. W. Fan, F. Geerts, J. Li, and M. Xiong. Discovering conditional functional dependencies. *IEEE Trans. Knowl. Data Eng.*, 23(5), 2011.
5. B. Fazzinga, S. Flesca, F. Furfaro, and F. Parisi. Dart: A data acquisition and repairing tool. EDBT'06, pages 297–317, 2006.
6. F. Geerts, G. Mecca, P. Papotti, and D. Santoro. Mapping and Cleaning. In *ICDE*, pages 232–243, 2014.
7. F. Geerts, G. Mecca, P. Papotti, and D. Santoro. That's all folks! LLUNATIC goes open source. *PVLDB*, 7(13):1565–1568, 2014.
8. J. He, E. Veltri, D. Santoro, G. Li, G. Mecca, P. Papotti, and N. Tang. Interactive and deterministic data cleaning. In *SIGMOD*, pages 893–907, 2016.
9. J. Heer, J. M. Hellerstein, and S. Kandel. Predictive interaction for data transformation. In *CIDR*, 2015.
10. A. Heise, J. Quiané-Ruiz, Z. Abedjan, A. Jentzsch, and F. Naumann. Scalable discovery of unique column combinations. *PVLDB*, 7(4), 2013.
11. I. F. Ilyas, V. Markl, P. J. Haas, P. Brown, and A. Aboulnaga. CORDS: automatic discovery of correlations and soft functional dependencies. In *SIGMOD*, 2004.
12. Z. Khayyat, I. F. Ilyas, A. Jindal, S. Madden, M. Ouzzani, J.-A. Quiane-Ruiz, P. Papotti, N. Tang, and S. Yin. BigDansing: a system for big data cleansing. In *SIGMOD*, 2015.
13. G. Mecca, G. Rull, D. Santoro, and E. Teniente. Semantic-based mappings. In *International Conference on Conceptual Modeling*, ER 2013, pages 255–269, 2013.
14. V. Raman and J. M. Hellerstein. Potter's wheel: An interactive data cleaning system. In *VLDB*, pages 381–390, 2001.
15. M. Volkovs, F. Chiang, J. Szlichta, and R. J. Miller. Continuous data cleaning. In *ICDE*, 2014.
16. J. Wang and N. Tang. Towards dependable data repairing with fixing rules. In *SIGMOD*, 2014.
17. M. Yakout, A. K. Elmagarmid, J. Neville, M. Ouzzani, and I. F. Ilyas. Guided data repair. *PVLDB*, 2011.

A cloud based framework for Emergency Management: experiences in Calabria Region
Extended Abstract

Giuseppe Tradigo‡, Rocco Picarelli‡, Luciano Caropresse‡, Paolo Cappadona∓, Ester Zumpano‡, Andrea Tagarelli‡, Pietro Hiram Guzzi†, Carlo Tansi∓, Angelo Furfaro‡, Pierangelo Veltri†

†University of Catanzaro,
Department of Medical and Surgical Sciences
veltri@unicz.it
‡DIMES, University of Calabria
surname@dimes.unical.it
∓ Protezione Civile Regione Calabria, Cittadella Regionale Catanzaro
name.surname@protezionecivile.regionecalabria.it

Abstract. We present an ongoing project aimed to support the management of the procedures, mainly the handling of emergency calls, for the centralized regional emergency management agency (Protezione Civile Regionale in Italian). The main goal consists in enabling the sharing of information among different active locations that are in charge of acting in any emergency which occurs on the territory. We present a prototype version of the system that has been implemented by following the Calabrian Emergency Management agency specifications. The system is in charge of collecting information regarding various types of emergency such as earthquakes, floods, stormy seas and other extreme weather conditions. In addition, the system offers some functionalities for the management of emergency teams as well as volunteers and available resources (e.g., vehicles) by means of the application of geographical optimization paths. The requirements include also the design and development of a mobile application allowing citizens notify in real-time emergency conditions (e.g., forest fires during summer time).

1 Introduction

The Calabrian Emergency Management Agency (Protezione Civile Calabria, or PCR in short) is in charge of managing all the activities related to the prediction, prevention and emergency management. All the activities for efficient rescue operations, are defined and specified in a national guideline. One of the tasks regards the collection and management of data related to emergency information acquisition (e.g., from citizens' reports arriving via phone calls) and to define activities and apply protocols. The definition of prevention procedures and of emergency plans is one of the main task of PCR to protect and often save human life.

We here present an ongoing project and a system prototype that has been defining with PCR. Recently, PCR decided to make a reorganization of its telecommunications infrastructure, application procedures and communication flows through regional sites and, as a consequence, it has to integrate all the communication facilities through the definition of a centralized structure. The aim is to define a datacenter where information regarding: (i) emergency calls and catastrophe monitoring; (ii) source data management (iii) protocols applications to save life and people as in case of earthquakes or floods or landslides due to heavy rains. The PCR is in charge of apply intervention even in case of car accidents or problems in reaching populations. ICT protocols and infrastructures are in charge of being updated in Calabria Region. We here report about the definition of a new workflow implementing what is currently managed without automatic procedures.

The idea is to define a system able to manage the emergency calls by means of pages and multimedia information that has to be organized by the central operative unit. For instance in the following we report a possible scenario:

1. a citizen is in trouble because of extreme weather conditions;
2. he calls the PCR with an help request;
3. the incident room gets the help request which is assigned an emergency level;
4. a new intervention request is generated and sent to other operative rooms;
5. the nearest operative room identifies a team and the needed resources;
6. the team intervenes and sends feedback back to the incident room;
7. the incident room shares the information with other rooms;
8. eventually the incident is closed and archived.

An efficient emergency response is strongly related to a careful and attentive prevention activity and emergency planning, which are preliminarily carried out before any emergency occurs. In order to predict possible flaws which could occur on the territory, the PCR has many systems and operational sources already working. Some of the preliminary goals of our work with the PCR have been: (i) identification and analysis of the existing components of the PCR information system already in use; (ii) definition and planning of the extraction, transformation and loading procedures from the operational sources towards an integrated database; (iii) definition and implementation of a new information system for the emergency management.

PCR is a Regional Public Administration Unit which is part of a network of other Regional units who refer to the Presidency of the Council of Ministers. It is composed by 180 employees, 91 of which work in the incident rooms (21 for each turn). Each of the incident room dislocated on the territory, is in need to share information about resources, events and updates in real time. Furthermore, due to the inherent complexity and unpredictability of emergency events, the interaction for a human operator with the system has to be minimal and extremely efficient. We decided to design and implement an information system with a lightweight web-based interface implementing an integrated and interactive dashboard for the incident rooms, which allows to perform:

- *scenario analysis and planning* - allowing a PCR operator to acquire and visualize all the data about the event and to plan and enumerate the resources around it;
- *environmental monitoring network* - able to retrieve and visualize real time information from the regional sensor network;
- *models from intervention scenarios* - a system module able to analyze use cases from the past, ranking them by similarity with the current emergency event;
- *inspection reports* - with which PCR operators can obtain detailed reports about present and past emergency events;
- *vehicles and resources management* - a dedicated module for the efficient planning and management of emergency vehicles.

A first conceptualization of the integrated dashboard for emergency data management is depicted in Figure 1, which reports a simulation of an emergency event with its related data aggregated and updated in real time.

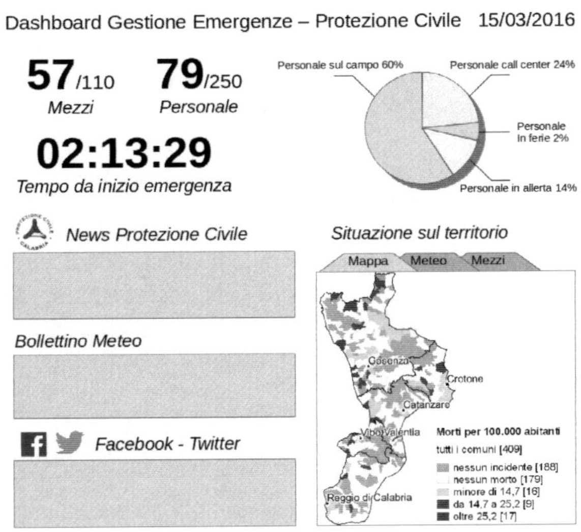

Fig. 1. Dashboard mock-up for the integrated visualization and management of emergency related data and events.

From the initial analysis phase we identified a set of existing systems and information sources in the PCR: (i) SITGE (Sistema Informativo Territoriale per la Gestione delle Emergenze) system, an old and unmaintained web-based geographical information system developed with ESRI technology, containing partial data for the emergency management with particular reference to fire events visualization, (ii) GIOVE (Portale per la Gestione Integrata delle Organizzazioni di Volontariato nelle Emergenze di Protezione Civile) a database containing voluntary associations informations about vehicles and resources, (iii) an hardware/software system for the management of fire emergencies composed of 12 stations with high definition cameras, thermal cameras, humidity, temperature and wind direction sensors implementing a prediction model and a decision support system in the event of a fire; (iv) a regional isofrequency microwave radio network, used for emergency radio communication, covering 80% of the territory with nodes at 10-15 km from each other.

2 Related Work

In [3] a two levels architecture for an Emergency Management System has been presented. It consists of one back-end level for control rooms and one front-end level for teams sent to the affected area. Each of two level is a peer-to-peer (P2P) system. The lack of a fixed infrastructure for P2P systems makes this kind of network suitable in emergency management scenarios where it is needed to quickly deploy a network, but the presence of access points is not guaranteed. This architecture has been developped studying the organizational requirements of Civil Protection Department of Calabria and the *Augustus method* (`https://it.wikipedia.org/wiki/Metodo_Augustus`) that it adopts. As well, since the available bandwidth (roughly 11 Mbps) is enough, MANETs can guarantee a good QoS level. As far as communication of front-end teams with back-end, TETRA seems to be a good choice.

TErrestrial Trunked RAdio (TETRA) is an ETSI standard to build specialist Professional Mobile Networks (`http://www.etsi.org/technologies-clusters/technologies/tetra`). The low frequency used by TETRA guarantees an excellent geographic coverage. TETRA is specifically intended for Police Fire Brigades, Army, etc., and its relays are generally arranged so that, even if some of them go down, the others can cover most of the area.

In [4] an upgrade of the old SITGE system has been presented. The updated system had new features for the computation of indices allowing to identify areas in fire risk.

Each italian region has its own Emergency Management Information System. Usually, a platform of this type has a set of modules allowing to manage the objects of the domain (events, volunteers, vehicles, maps, etc.) and their interactions (e.g. `http://www2.regione.piemonte.it/protezionecivile/index.php/sistema-informativo`).

Similarly, in [5] a model for management of bioemergency is presented. Tools for path optimization and emergency camp positioning is presented. In [6] algorithms for emergency intervention and rescue planning are reported.

The system, here proposed, starts from requirements of the new PCR and it is in plan with respect to new italian reorganization due to recent natural disasters. We plan to include logistic and algorithms to plan rescues, resources according to land orography and streets. The idea is to create an emergency support system for the PCR able to feed a continuously growing database of events and interventions which will be valuable for research because data contains both spatial and temporal dimensions, which can be exploited through spatial and temporal techniques and models (see [7]).

3 System Architecture

We designed a first system prototype by using deployment of components. Figure 2 shows the components layers: (i) the visual part of the emergency management prototype (presentation layer) consists of the JSP pages that contain the views of the data; (ii)the middleware level hosts the web application and data access module and (iii) the database level which is an instance of MySQL database. Figure 2 reports components and their interactions.

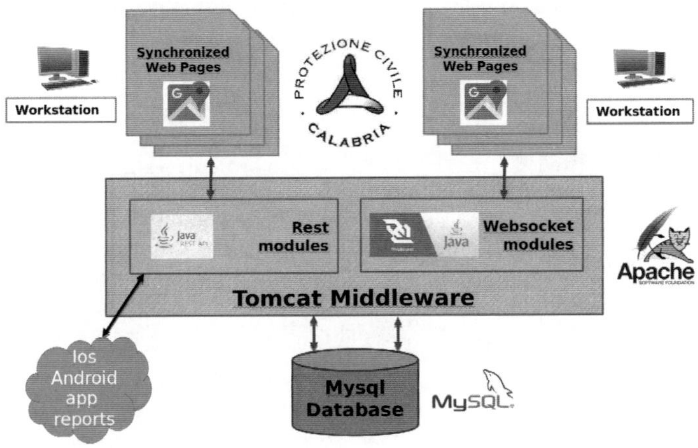

Fig. 2. Functional Architecture of the Emergency Management System

The functionalities regard also the possibility of signalling emergency cases by using a mobile app. A citizen can take a picture and define one of the possible application emergency cases. Citizen position as well as personal data (in case of availability in supporting rescuers) can be sent with simple steps. The system prototype has been implemented in a cloud based environment, to maximize system scalability, availability and redundancy. In order to preserve the integrity and privacy of PCR's own data, we set up an instance of the OwnCloud environment exclusively used by the PCR, to support the functionalities of the presented system, some of which are: (*i*) artifact exchange among incident rooms, (*ii*) end users' data acquisition and storage from the mobile app, (*iii*) storage of daily and periodic reports about PCR emergency management. Nevertheless the adoption of a proprietary cloud environment has some drawbacks. For instance, the limited number of nodes implies some potential problems regarding the application scalability, while the management of the cloud architecture itself can be a costly and complex task to be sustained by the PCR.

Emergency can be managed in one of the operative units by accessing to a web screen where the emergency is verified and validated, and intervention protocols are selected and applied. Resources are also managed as well as the evolution of rescues activities. Consider that in case of emergency the communication activities and signals reach an high frequency in terms of number of call or app instances, thus the system should be able to track the activities. PCR has to both (i) avoid loosing emergency alerts as well as (ii) filter out the less relevant ones. Algorithms to prevent and automatically manage the relevance of alerts can be applied.

Figure 3 reports an example of using the developed application. There are different user profiles. A citizen can apply sending information about emergency situation with pictures and giving the status (e.g., available, not available) in staying on site to give information in case of emergency updates (e.g., fire conditions) in case of safe observation position.

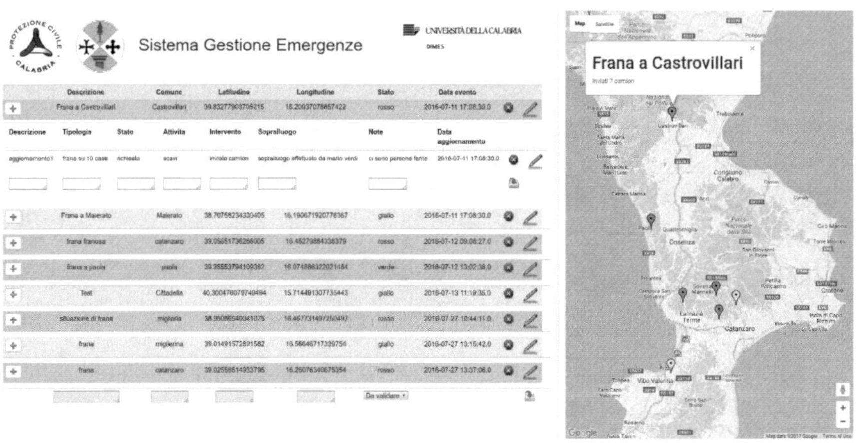

Fig. 3. Web user interface of the implemented Emergency Management Tool prototype

The workflow process has been designed by using a model called rasor model (standing for Rapporto Attivitá Sala Operativa Regionale) which contains information regarding emergency protocols. It contains alerting messages classification, municipality, location and closest emergency team for the event; type and status of the event; rescue team reports and emergency updates; resource details and emergency status time tracking; final reports. The database has been designed using such a schema (a snapshot in italian is reported in Figure 4). It maps the rasor model where emergency signaling regarding reports on new emergency are annotated by PCR operators.

Mod. RA.S.O.R. - VERSIONE INFORMATIZZATA - BOZZA aggiornata al 16 marzo 2016

REPORT SU NUOVE EMERGENZE SEGNALATE DURANTE IL TURNO DI SERVIZIO E AGGIORNAMENTI CIRCA EMERGENZE IN ATTO

DATA Inizio evento	ORA Inizio evento	DATA Ultimo aggiornamento	ORA Ultimo aggiornamento	STATO EVENTO (colorazione che indica la gravità dell'evento all'ultimo aggiornamento)	FONTE Ultimo aggiornamento	COMUNE	PROVINCIA	LOCALITA' LATITUDINE LONGITUDINE	TIPOLOGIA EVENTO, E CRITICITA' PRINCIPALI	Tipologia attività richieste alla SOR	DETTAGLI

Fig. 4. Extract from the Rasor Intervention Model used to map the emergency interventions information

Finally in Figure 5 we report the database schema used to map the information related to the resource and rescue management.

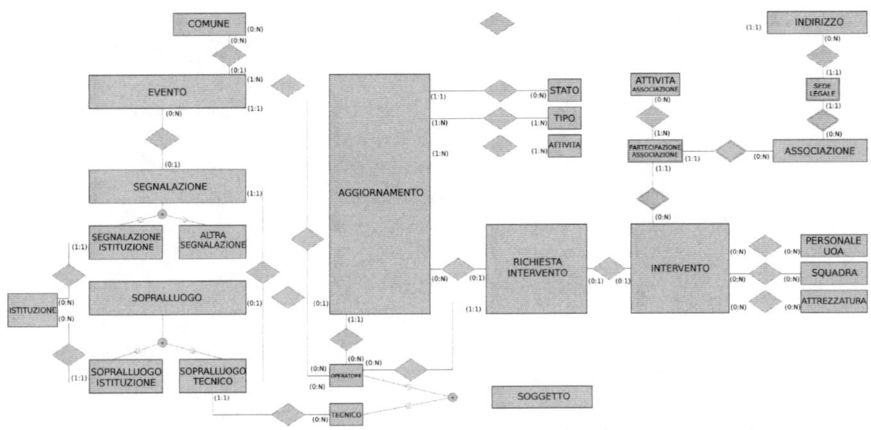

Fig. 5. Extract of the Database Schema to map the emergencies

4 Use Case and applications

Firstly, we report a typical use case implemented by the PCR incident rooms in an emergency, at present time: (*i*) an emergency call arrives at one of the incident rooms by phone; (*ii*) the operator asks for details and compiles the paper registry (which is a non-shared distributed resource); (*iii*) the operator is in charge of distributing the news by phone to the other incident rooms; (*iv*) the decisor (e.g., PCR's Director) plans the intervention(s) and orders the teams to intervene on site; (*v*) the various teams give feedbacks on the intervention status back to the incident room via phone.

We here report some use cases implemented with the system to automatize the use case shown above and others encountered during the requirement analysis for the PCR.

Gathering emergency calls. Currently PCR has already implemented a number of initiatives for the dissemination of competence information through the use of social networks in addition to more traditional communication channels. In order to ensure similar fruition and the maximum possible dissemination of information, the system acquires calls and information coming from web based communication channel (mobile one). Furthermore, the mobile interface will be integrated with the most used social networks (i.e., facebook, twitter) but also the backend will gather comments and enquiries coming from the PCR social network pages and analyze them, rendering ad-hoc statistics on the system dashboard for the PCR management.

Managing resources. As part of the reorganization of the management of mobile vehicles, the system offers a fleet management module to provide an additional flow of information of great importance in the management of emergency situations. Modeling of minimum risk routes is still an open research topic, as well as the development of algorithms to simulate scenarios on networks.

Fire management System. Information regarding fire events, are acquired from an already existing module and the information is mapped on the dashboard with the location as well as the sequence of intervention updates.

References

1. Gunter, T. D., Terry, N. P. (2005). The emergence of national electronic health record architectures in the United States and Australia: models, costs, and questions. Journal of Medical Internet Research, 7(1), e3.
2. Yang, C. C., Veltri, P. (2015). Intelligent healthcare informatics in big data era. Artificial intelligence in medicine, 65(2), 75-77.
3. De Leoni, M., De Rosa, F., Marrella, A., Mecella, M., Poggi, A., Krek, A., Manti F. (2007). Emergency management: from user requirements to a flexible p2p architecture. International Conference on Information Systems for Crisis Response and Management (ISCRAM).
4. Samarelli, S., Manti, F., Span, M., P., (2009). Il SIT di Protezione Civile della Regione Calabria: lutilizzo operativo per la raccolta dati relativi agli incendi di interfaccia e alle Ordinanze di emergenza. Conferenza Nazionale ASITA.
5. Schneider, T., A. R. Mikler, and M. ONeill. "Computational tools for evaluating bioemergency contingency plans." Disaster Management and Human Health Risk: Reducing Risk, Improving Outcomes 110 (2009): 33.
6. Martin, O., Armin R. Mikler, and Tamara Schneider. "An Extensible Software Architecture to Facilitate Disaster Response Planning."
7. Tradigo, G., Pierangelo V., Greco, S. "Geomedica: managing and querying clinical data distributions on geographical database systems." Procedia Computer Science 1.1 (2010): 979-986.

How Planning Techniques Can Help Process Mining: The Conformance-Checking Case

Massimiliano de Leoni[1], Andrea Marrella[2]

[1] Eindhoven University of Technology, The Netherlands
m.d.leoni@tue.nl
[2] Sapienza - University of Rome, Italy
marrella@dis.uniroma1.it

Abstract. Modern organizations execute processes to deliver product and services, whose enactment needs to adhere to laws, regulations and standards. Conformance checking is the problem of pinpointing where deviations are observed in the process event data. Literature proposes solutions for the conformance-checking problem that, in fact, are implementations of planning algorithms built ad-hoc for the specific problem. Unfortunately, in the era of big data, these ad-hoc implementations do not scale sufficiently compared with robust, well-established planning systems. Furthermore, their ad-hoc nature does not allow for seamlessly plugging in new outperforming planning algorithms or heuristics, causing a massive amount of work to be necessary to incorporate and evaluate alternatives. This paper summarizes our last results on how instances of the conformance checking problem can be represented as classical planning problems in PDDL for which planners can find a correct solution in a finite amount of time. If conformance checking problems are converted into planning problems, one can seamlessly update to the recent versions of the best performing automated planners, with evident advantages in term of versatility and customization. Experiments with three different planners highlight this versatility. Furthermore, by employing several processes and event logs of different sizes, we show how our planning-based approach outperforms existing approaches of several order of magnitude and, in certain cases, carries out the task while existing approaches run out of memory.

1 Introduction

Process mining is a discipline that sits between data mining and process modeling and analysis and, hence, can be considered one of the links between data science and process science [1]. The idea of process mining is to discover, monitor and improve the processes by extracting knowledge from the data that are stored in information systems about how these systems are used to carry out processes. Differently from a-priori analysis, the focus is not on the assumed processes but on real processes in the way that they are executed. Therefore, the starting point of process mining is event data, which is analyzed to extract useful insights and recurrent patterns about how processes are executed within organizations.

Within Process Mining, *conformance checking* verifies whether the observed behavior stored in an *event log* is compliant with a process model that encodes how the process is allowed to be executed to ensure that norms and regulations are not violated. As an example, suppose that a process model may indicate that orders for more than

100000 Euros require a double check: conformance checking will check whether the actual executions follows this rule or not.

The notion of *alignment* [1, 2] provides a robust approach to conformance checking, which makes it possible to exactly pinpoint the deviations causing nonconformity with a high degree of detail. An alignment between a recorded process execution (*log trace*) and a process model is a pairwise matching between activities recorded in the log and activities allowed by the model. Sometimes, activities as recorded in the log (*events*) cannot be matched to any of the activities allowed by the model (*process activities*).

In general, a large number of possible alignments exist between a process model and a log trace, since there may exist manifold explanations why a trace is not conforming. It is clear that one is interested in finding the most probable explanation. In [1, 2], an approach is proposed that is based on the principle of the Occam's razor: the most parsimonious explanation is preferable. Therefore, one should not aim to find any alignment but, precisely, one of the alignments with the least expensive deviations (one of the so-called *optimal alignments*).

The work by Adriansyah et al. [2] provide a technique to compute these optimal alignments, based on the A* algorithm and ad-hoc heuristics. However, experiments (also reported in this paper) show that their technique does not scale sufficiently. In the era of big data, scalable approaches are desperately necessary, as also advocated by the IEEE Task Force in Process Mining [3]: "*In some domains, mind-boggling quantities of events are recorded. [...] Therefore, additional efforts are needed to improve performance and scalability.*".

We believe that re-implementing standard planning algorithms, such as A*, for solving specific planning problems in an ad-hoc way is not ideal. First, ad-hoc implementations cannot compare in scalability with well-established planning systems. Second, ad-hoc implementations prevent one from seamlessly plugging in new algorithms or evaluate alternative heuristics. As a consequence, the possibility of evaluating different alternatives is hampered; also, if the literature proposes new algorithms that clearly overtake the existing ones for solving instances of the conformance checking problem, a massive amount of work is needed to modify those ad-hoc implementations.

Hence, in order to facilitate the integration of different planning algorithms, in [4], we illustrate how the problem of computing optimal alignments can be formulated as a planning problem, which can be solved through off-the-shelf PDDL planners.

Here, we summarize the main ideas discussed in [4] and report on the most interesting results from the experiments. The results show that our planning-based approach is versatile, allowing multiple planners to be integrated, and scales better than existing approaches with larger models and event logs.

2 Petri Nets and Event Logs

To model business processes, we opted for Petri nets (see, e.g., [1]), which have proven to be adequate [5] for this purpose. However, the approach described in this paper can be applied to other notations, such as BPMN.

A **Petri net** $N = (P, T, F)$ is a directed graph with a set P of nodes called *places* and a set T of transitions. The nodes are connected via directed arcs $F \subseteq (P \times T) \cup (T \times P)$. Connections between two nodes of the same type are not allowed. Places are represented by circles and transitions by rectangles. Fig. 1 illustrates an example of Petri nets. Given a transition $t \in T$, ${}^\bullet t$ is used to indicate the set of *input places* of t, which are the places p with a directed arc from p to t (i.e., such that $(p, t) \in F$). Similarly, $t^\bullet$ indicates the set of *output places*, namely the places p with a direct arc from t to p. At any time, a place can contain zero or more *tokens*, drawn as black dots. The state of a Petri net, a.k.a. *marking*, is determined by the number of tokens in places. Therefore, a marking m is a function $m : P \rightarrow \mathbb{N}$.

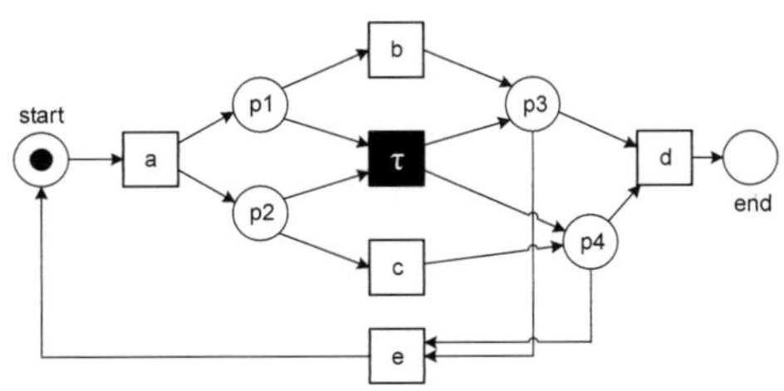

Fig. 1. An example of Petri net.

In any run of a Petri net, the number of tokens in places may change, i.e., the Petri net marking. A transition t is **enabled** at a marking m iff each input place contains at least one token, i.e. $\forall\ p \in {}^\bullet t,\ M(p) > 0$. A transition t can **fire** at a marking m iff it is enabled. As result of firing a transition t, one token is "consumed" from each input place and one is "produced" in each output place. This is denoted as $m \xrightarrow{t} m'$. In the remainder, given a sequence of transition firing $\sigma = \langle t_1, \ldots, t_n \rangle \in T^*$, $m_0 \xrightarrow{\sigma} m_n$ is used to indicate $m_0 \xrightarrow{t_1} m_1 \xrightarrow{t_2} \ldots \xrightarrow{t_n} m_n$.

Event logs are the starting point for process mining. An event log L is is a multi-set of log *traces* $\sigma_L \in T^*$. A trace is a sequence of transition firings and describes the exection of a *process instance* in terms of the executed *activities*.[3] Transition firings in an event log are known as *events*.

Some transitions do not represent process activities but are necessary to correctly represent the business process through Petri nets. These transitions are **invisible transitions** (similar to τ steps) and are not recorded as log events. For the sake of space, we assume here that each activity is mapped to one and only one Petri-net transition and that events are defined over the same alphabet as the Petri-net transitions. In [4], we show how these assumptions can be removed.

3 Alignment between Event Logs and Petri Nets

As mentioned in Section 1, we perform conformance checking by constructing an *alignment* of event log L and process model N [1, 2], which allows us to exactly pinpoint where deviations occur. On this aim, the events in the event log need to be related to transitions in the model, and vice versa. Building this alignment is far from trivial, since the log may deviate from the model at an arbitrary number of places. We need to relate "moves" in the log to "moves" in the model in order to establish an alignment between a process model and an event log. However, it may be that some of the moves in the log cannot be mimicked by the model and vice versa. We explicitly denote such "no moves" by $\gg$.

[3] We use multisets because the same trace can appear multiple times because different process executions can be identical in terms of activities being executed.

Definition 1 (Alignment Moves). *Let $N = (P, T, F)$ be a Petri net and L be an event log. A legal* alignment move *for N and L is represented by a pair $(s_L, s_M) \in (T \cup \{\gg\} \times T \cup \{\gg\}) \setminus \{(\gg, \gg)\}$ such that:*

- *(s_L, s_M) is a* move in log *if $s_L \neq \gg$ and $s_M = \gg$,*
- *(s_L, s_M) is a* move in model *if $s_L = \gg$ and $s_M \in T$,*
- *(s_L, s_M) is a* synchronous move *if $s_L = s_M$.*

An alignment is a sequence of alignment moves:

Definition 2 (Alignment). *Let $N = (P, T, F)$ be a Petri net with an initial marking and final marking denoted with m_i and m_f Let also L be an event log. Let Γ_N be the universe of all alignment moves for N and L. Let $\sigma_L \in L$ be a log trace. Sequence $\gamma \in \Gamma_N^*$ is an* alignment *of N and σ_L if, ignoring all occurrences of $\gg$, the projection on the first element yields σ_L and the projection on the second yields a sequence $\sigma'' \in T^*$ such that $m_i \xrightarrow{\sigma''} m_f$.*

A move in log for a transition t indicates that t occurred when not allowed; a move in model for a visible transition t indicates that t did not occur, when, conversely, expected.

$$\gamma_1 = \begin{array}{|c|c|c|c|c|} a & d & b & c & \gg \\ \hline a & \gg & b & c & d \end{array}$$

$$\gamma_2 = \begin{array}{|c|c|c|c|c|} a & \gg & d & b & c \\ \hline a & \tau & d & \gg & \gg \end{array}$$

$$\gamma_3 = \begin{array}{|c|c|c|c|c|c|c|} a & \gg & d & \gg & b & c & \gg \\ \hline a & \tau & \gg & e & b & c & d \end{array}$$

Fig. 2. Alignments of trace $\langle a, d, b, c \rangle$ and the process model in Fig. 1.

Many alignments are possible for the same trace. For example, Fig. 2 shows three possible alignments for a trace $\sigma_1 = \langle a, d, b, c \rangle$. Note how moves are represented vertically. For example, as shown in Fig. 2, the first move of γ_1 is (a, a), i.e., a synchronous move of a, while the the second and fifth move of γ_1 are a move in log and model, respectively. As discussed in Section 1, we aim at finding a complete alignment of σ_L and N with minimal number of deviations for visible transitions, also known in literature as **optimal alignment**. Aligning an event log L means to compute an optimal alignment for each trace $\sigma_L \in L$. Clearly, different traces in L generally have different alignments, because they contain different events and deviations. With reference to the alignments in Fig. 2, γ_1 and γ_2 have two moves in model and/or log for visible transitions (γ_1 has one move in model for an invisible transition but it does not count for computing optimal alignments). Conversely, γ_3 has three moves for visible transitions, specifically one log move for d (3rd move) and two model moves for e (4th move) and d (last move). Since no alignment exists with only one moves in model and/or log for visible transitions, both γ_1 and γ_2 are optimal alignments and any can equally be returned. For the sake of space, we assume here that all deviations (i.e., moves in model for visible transitions and moves in log) have the same severity. In [4], we show how this assumption can be removed.

4 Encoding the Alignment Problem in PDDL

Planning systems are problem-solving algorithms that operate on explicit representations of states and actions [6]. PDDL [7] is the standard Planning Domain Definition Language; it allows us to formulate a *planning problem* $\mathcal{P} = \langle I, G, \mathcal{P_D} \rangle$, where I is the description of the initial state of the world, G is the desired goal state, and $\mathcal{P_D}$ is the planning domain. $\mathcal{P_D}$ is built from a set of *predicates* and *fluent* describing the state of the world and a set of *actions* that can be executed in the domain.

This section illustrates how, given an event log L and Petri net $N = (P, T, F)$ with given initial and final markings m_i, m_f, the problem of the alignment of N and $\sigma_L = \langle e_1, \ldots, e_n \rangle \in L$ can be encoded as a PDDL planning problem, which can be solved by state-of-the-art planners. The plan synthesized will consist of a sequence of alignment moves that establish an alignment between σ_L and N. As throughout discussed in [4], the proposed encoding of an alignment problem A as planning problem $\mathcal{P}$ is such that one can find a solution for A by solving $\mathcal{P}$. Also, planning algorithms always terminate when the input is a planning problem $\mathcal{P}$ that encodes A according to the procedure proposed in this paper.

In the remainder of this paper, we assume Petri nets to be 1-bounded. This is not a large limitation as the behavior allowed by most of business processes can be represented as 1-bounded Petri nets (see discussion in [4]).

4.1 Predicates and fluents

In the planning domain $\mathcal{P}_\mathcal{D}$, we provide three abstract types called `place`, `transition` and `event`. The types `place` and `transition` represent respectively the places and the transitions of N. The type `event` is used to record the list of events that occur in the specific trace σ_L that must be checked for conformance. For trace $\sigma_1 = \langle a, d, b, c \rangle$ and the Petri net in Fig. 1, the following objects are introduced in $\mathcal{P}$:

```
(:objects a b c d1 e inv - transition
          start p1 p2 p3 p4 end - place
          e1 e2 e3 e4 evEND - event)
```

In addition to the four events, denoted as $e1$, ..., $e4$, we introduce the invisible transition inv and a fictitious $evEND$, which identifies the end of trace. The introduction of this fiction $evEND$ is not specific of this example, but it is general for any instance of the alignment problem.

To capture all possible markings of N and the evolution of σ_L during an alignment, we define four boolean predicates in $\mathcal{P}_\mathcal{D}$, as follows:

token. For each $p \in P$, `(token ?p - place)` holds iff p contains a token in the currently reached marking.

succ. For each $1 \leq n < |\sigma_L|$, `(succ ?e1 - event ?e2 - event)` holds if $e1 = e_i$ and $e2 = e_{i+1}$.

tracePointer. For each event $e \in \sigma_L$, `(tracePointer ?e - event)` holds when, during the computation of the alignment, e is the next trace event to align.

associated. For each event $e \in \sigma_L$, `(associated ?e - event ?t - transition)` holds when $t = e$.

In addition to the predicates above, we introduce a fluent **total-cost** to keep track of the number of deviations found in the alignment till that point. Synchronous moves are associated with no costs and, hence, no fluent needs to be introduced. For trace $\sigma_1 = \langle a, d, b, c \rangle$ and the Petri net in Fig. 1, the initial state of $\mathcal{P}$ with the definition of predicates and fluents is as follows:

```
(:init  (token start) (tracePointer e1) (succ e1 e2) (succ e2 e3) (succ e3 e4)
        (succ e4 evEND) (associated e1 a) (associated e2 d)
        (associated e3 b) (associated e4 c) (= (total-cost) 0))
```

At the end, for the example in question, when the alignment is found, the Petri net needs to be in the final marking, i.e., with one token in place *end* and zero tokens in any other place, and the trace pointer has reached `evEND`:

```
(:goal  (and (tracePointer evEND) (token end) (not (token p1)) (not (token p2))
        (not (token p3)) (not (token p4)) (not (token start))))
```

Readers should notice that, since our purpose is to minimize the total cost of the alignment, the planning problem also contains the following specification: `(:metric minimize (total-cost))`.

4.2 Planning Actions

The plan to reach the final goal from the initial state is constituted by a sequence of alignment moves, each of which is a planning action. Therefore, three classes of actions exist in $\mathcal{P}_{\mathcal{D}}$: synchronous moves, model moves and log moves.

Synchronous moves. A separate action exists for each visible transition $t \in T$ to represent a synchronous move for t. For instance, let us consider transition a of the model in Fig. 1; synchronous move for a is associated with the following action:

```
(:action moveSync-a
 :parameters (?e1 - event ?e2 - event)
 :precondition  (and (token start) (tracePointer ?e1)
                (associated ?e1 a) (succ ?e1 ?e2))
 :effect (and (not (token start)) (token p1) (token p2)
                (not (tracePointer ?e1)) (tracePointer ?e2)))
```

The preconditions of the action are *(i)* that a is enabled (as defined in Section 2): each place $p \in {}^{\bullet}a$ contains a token; *(ii)* $e1$ is the actual event of σ_L under analysis; *(iii)* $e1$ corresponds to the execution of a in σ_L; *(iv)* $e1$ is succeeded by the event $e2$ in σ_L. The effect is such that the trace pointer moves from $e1$ to $e2$ and that the marking changes according to the firing rules: one token in place *start* is consumed and one token is produced in places *p1* and *p2*.

Model moves. A separate action exists for each transition $t \in T$. A model move focuses on making an enabled transition t fire without performing any move in σ_L. For instance, let us consider transition a of the model in Fig. 1; a model move for a is associated with the following action:

```
(:action moveInTheModel-a
 :precondition (token start)
 :effect (and (not (token start)) (token p1) (token p2) (increase (total-cost) 1)))
```

It is worthy observing how the execution of a model move for a makes total cost (of the alignment) increases of a value equal to 1, since a is a visible transition[4]. The effects are accordant to the firing rules: The token in place *start* is consumed and one token is produced in places *p1* and *p2*. The difference with synchronous moves is that the value of any predicate `tracePointer` does not change.

For what concerns invisible transitions, readers should observe that since the executions of invisible transitions are never recorded in event logs, invisible transitions are always involved in move in models, only. However, these model moves are actually not deviations and, hence, the action `moveInTheModel` does not have `(increase (total-cost) 1)` among the effects. E.g., for transition τ in the model in Fig. 1, action `moveInTheModel-tau` will not have the total-cost increase as an effect.

Log moves. All log moves can be represented by a single generic action, which is independent of N and σ_L:

[4] For the sake of simplicity, we are assuming a unitary cost to express the severity of a move in model and/or in log.

	10% noise				20% noise				30% noise			
Petri Net Size	Existing Approach	Fast Downward	SymBA-2*	SPM&S	Existing Approach	Fast Downward	SymBA-2*	SPM&S	Existing Approach	Fast Downward	SymBA-2*	SPM&S
25	**25.85**	84.79	685.35	812.44	**42.8**	86.21	692.97	814.04	**56.87**	88.87	699.42	816.05
36	**11.71**	94.13	767.05	950.25	**19.24**	92.78	785.14	956.19	**28.6**	92.67	793.13	959.25
68	**112.85**	130.68	1,413.85	1,722.13	164.92	**134.57**	1,418.51	1,779.17	278.31	**144.99**	1,419.5	1,808.61
95	**77.56**	123.65	2,048.84	2,431.35	**119.89**	125.78	2,049.14	2,445.66	168.32	**126.82**	2,053.92	2,483.98
115	638.52	**205.47**	2,289.84	2,787.31	966.34	**384.26**	2,291.91	2,817.29	1,987.12	**716.68**	2,352.81	2,868.77
136	304.62	**178.66**	2,752.28	3,282.23	465.97	**182.88**	2,765.14	3,300.87	578.63	**187.17**	2,775.46	3,317.48
175	–	18,759.91	**5,909.46**	6,546.87	–	84,195.41	**6,092.93**	6,837.57	–	$1.71 \cdot 10^5$	**6,259.99**	7,182.13
263	–	**2,343.92**	11,960.84	13,289.56	–	13,524.63	**12,044.67**	13,744.92	–	30,582.11	**12,194.09**	14,075.09

Table 1. Comparison of the experimental results with different planners and with the existing approach of [2], using different models while varying the amount of noise. The values refers to the average time (in ms.) to compute the alignment of a log trace and the respective process model.

```
(:action moveInTheLog
 :parameters (?e1 - event ?e2 - event)
 :precondition (and (tracePointer ?e1) (succ ?e1 ?e2))
 :effect (and (not (tracePointer ?e1))(tracePointer ?e2) (increase (total-cost) 1 )))
```

A log move for any event $e_i \in \sigma_L$ is represented as `(moveInTheLog ?e1 ?e2)` where $e1 = e_i$ and $e2 = e_{i+1}$. The preconditions are that $e2$ follows $e1$, and that $e1$ is the actual event under analysis. The effect is to move the trace pointer from $e1$ to $e2$ and to increase the total cost of the alignment of a value equal to 1.

5 Evaluation and Conclusion

The planning-based alignment tool is publicly available as Java application. Implementation details and information about how to download it are available in [4]. To evaluate the versatility of approach to seamlessly integrate different planners, we employed three different planners: Fast Downward[5], SymBA-2* and SPM&S[6]. These three planning systems were employed with searching algorithms that guarantee the optimality of the solution. Therefore, the returned alignments are always guaranteed to be optimal.

To evaluate the scalability and feasibility of the approaches, we tested our implementation with several combinations of real-life and synthetic event logs and processes. We refer to [4] for a thorough discussions of the experimental test bed and of the results. Here, for the sake of space, we focus on the results on the synthetic process models and event logs. Specifically, we artificially generated different process models of increasing sizes in form of Petri nets to evaluate the scalability of the approach and, for each Petri net, we generated artificial event logs with increasing amount of noise. Established techniques and tools exist for this purpose (see details in [4]). The entire set of artificial models is attached as appendix in [4].

In the remainder, an event log with X% of noise indicates that, starting from an event log where each trace is conforming, an event is swapped with the next event in the trace with a probability of X%. This swapping generally causes the trace to be no more conforming. Note also that multiple events may be swapped in a trace and, also, the same event can be swapped with consecutive events, moving it further apart from the original position in the trace.

[5] `http://www.fast-downward.org/`

[6] SymBA-2* and SPM&S can be downloaded at: `https://helios.hud.ac.uk/scommv/IPC-14/planners_actual.html`

The experiments with these artificial process models are summarized in Table 1. Each row refers to a different Petri net. For each row, the first column indicates the size of the Petri net in term of number of transitions; the subsequent 12 columns refer to the experimental results when the corresponding event log contain 10%, 20% and 30% noise. For each amount of noise, we compared the result of the existing ad-hoc approach by Adriansyah et al. [2] with the results obtained by our approach when integrated with the three planners mentioned above.

The values refer to the average time to alignment and event-log trace with the respective process model. The results show that the existing ad-hoc approach is faster with models of small sizes and/or when using event logs with smaller amount of noise. Conversely, our approach is faster with larger models. In particular, it seems that, generally speaking, Fast Downward performs better with middle-size models whereas SymBA-2* works better with very large models.

To conclude, the existing approach by Adriansyah et al. [2] is confirmed not to sufficiently scale when event logs and process models become very large. As a matter of fact, when testing with the two largest models, the existing approach was not able to align every event-log trace with the corresponding model and was running out of memory, even though we were using a machine with 16 GBs of RAM. Conversely, tracking the memory consumption, all of three employed planners were never using more than 4 GBs of RAM. Even when the existing approach was able to carry out the alignment tasks, it could do it significantly slower. As an example, compare the results for the model with 115 activities and an event log with 30%: On average, the existing approach requires 1987 ms per trace, versus 716 ms for Fast Downward. A saving of 1.2 seconds per trace means that, to align all traces of an event log with, e.g., 100000 traces (not uncommon in real-world case studies), the use of Fast Downward would allow us to save 120000 seconds: 83.3 hours.

References

1. van der Aalst, W.M.P.: Data Science in Action. Springer Berlin Heidelberg, Berlin, Heidelberg (2016)
2. Adriansyah, A., Sidorova, N., van Dongen, B.F.: Cost-based fitness in conformance checking. In: Proc. of Int. Conf. on Application of Concurrency to System Design, IEEE (2011) 57–66
3. Van Der Aalst, W., et al.: Process Mining Manifesto. In: Proc. of the 9th Int. Conf. on Business Process Management (BPM 2011), Springer Berlin Heidelberg (2011) 169–194
4. de Leoni, M., Marrella, A.: Aligning Real Process Executions and Prescriptive Process through Automated Planning. Expert System with Applications **82** (2017) 162 – 183
5. van der Aalst, W.M.P.: The application of petri nets to workflow management. Journal of Circuits, Systems, and Computers **8**(1) (1998) 21–66
6. Ghallab, M., Nau, D.S., Traverso, P.: Automated Planning: Theory and Practice. Morgan Kaufmann (2004)
7. McDermott, D., Ghallab, M., Howe, A., Knoblock, C.A., Ram, A., Veloso, M., Weld, D.S., Wilkins, D.E.: PDDL—The Planning Domain Definition Language. Technical Report DCS TR-1165, Yale Center for Computational Vision and Control, New Haven, Connecticut (1998)

Effectively and Efficiently Supporting Grid and Cloud Integration via a DBMS-based Framework

Alfredo Cuzzocrea[1], Osvaldo Gervasi[2], Mirko Mariotti[3], Flavio Vella[4], and Alessandro Costantini[5]

[1] DIA Dept., University of Trieste and ICAR-CNR, Italy
alfredo.cuzzocrea@dia.units.it
[2] DMI Dept., University of Perugia, Italy
osvaldo.gervasi@unipg.it
[3] FISGEO Dept., University of Perugia, Italy
mirko.mariotti@unipg.it
[4] DI Dept., University of Rome La Sapienza, Italy
vella@di.uniroma1.it
[5] CNAF-INFN, Italy
alessandro.costantini@cnaf.infn.it

Abstract. This paper provides anatomy, models and functionalities of a DBMS-based systems for integrating Grids and Clouds. Our study starts from recognizing the similarity of some axioms of Grid and Cloud computing, still being these computational paradigms very different for what regards both computing and economic models. Our proposed system is centered along a well-designed DBMS schema that allows to obtain a seamless integration between Grids and IaaS Cloud providers. The paper details how images from a Cloud environment are deployed in reply to a specific task execution invoked from the (integrated) Grid environment, as well as other essential components of the proposed architecture (e.g., resource access and grant, user authorization, resource discovery and sharing, job and task management and distribution, integration with other computational platforms, and so forth).

1 Introduction

Nowadays two trends are evident in the way the computational resources are organized and managed to provide users the computing infrastructures adequate for the emerging computing needs. On the one hand, virtualization technologies are massively adopted, based on more and more powerful Cloud systems (Openstack, Opennebula, Eucaliptus, etc.), along with systems for deploying virtual machines and all technologies related to the Cloud scenario. On the other hand, it is clear that in order to increase the performances of the computing systems the best way is to adopt heterogeneous architectures, specializing them on the basis of the requested type of computation from the users. Examples of this type are the usage of GPUs for the fast solution of different problems in computer science like graph analysis [9], cryptography [19, 29, 30] or computational logic[16], the development of innovative architectures, like the Parallella board[24], and the adoption of Field-Programmable Gate Array (FPGA) device as a computing resource[20, 12]. Cloud and Grid computing share some essential driving ideas which led to the construction of both large scale federated Grid infrastructures which can be summarized as follows: (*i*) bring the promise of encapsulating the complexity of hardware resources and make them easily accessible by means of high-level user interfaces; (*ii*) address some form of the intrinsic scalability issues of large scale computational challenges; (*iii*) cope with the need of resources that cannot be hosted on premises.

However, the key differences between Grids and Clouds concern abstractions and compute models adopted by both paradigms [18]. It can be said that Grids are built "bottom up" and are concerned more with federation of static existing resources that typically are legacy clusters built around a Local Resources Management System (LRMS) that exploits the Batch computing model.

The development of applications for Grid environments requires the knowledge of the Grid infrastructure abstractions. This process, aimed at enabling the application to run in such environments, is in fact called "Grid-enabling" and can be rather complex [17]. On the other hand, Cloud users can choose their own compute model, leveraging more general (without the needs of a fine tuning of the environment) interfaces that often lead to simpler interaction and application development [27].

As sketched before, there are several problems that do not play nicely with the heterogeneous nature of aggregated resources in Grids. For example, many scientific applications need different environments (operating systems, libraries) and hardware (i.e., Multicore Processors, FPGA, GPUs, etc.). From a Batch point of view this represents a set of requirements influencing scheduling decisions for both top and local level resource managers. So the Grid sites heterogeneity plays a central role in job distribution (workload) among sites that match the aforementioned requirements.

Furthermore the Grid workload can be often unpredictable and subject to burst increase, that lead to unbalanced distribution in resource usage, and even deterioration of QoS. In this context the Grid workflow represents a weak point for the Batch model in which resources are often statically managed and partitioned, and cannot be adapted in advance to meet possible requirements. Moreover the use of Clouds could allow the extension of private resource pools in number and typology with positive effects on Quality of Service (QoS).

So why do not dismiss Grids and adopt Cloud solutions? There are several reasons: it is not yet clear how some critical issues (data management, security, etc.) are to be dealt with in the Cloud era, while in Grid are well-established. Furthermore, the costs of an eventual shift in technology must be thoroughly investigated. A more reasonable approach is an integration process that combines the features of both.

2 Integration Opportunities

Before the Cloud era, even if these issues were addressed in various works[10, 28, 21], the proposed solutions were often heavy customized and too tightly dependent on particular technological choices.

With the success of Cloud computing through the spread of IaaS providers [7, 2, 3], the development of interfaces for the simplification of virtual management [4, 6] and related libraries (i.e.,[5, 1], etc.) paved the way to several possibilities for Grid and Cloud integration. As a matter of fact, even if Cloud solutions have been, since their first definition[13], primarily driven by business motivations, the IaaS service model seems to respond to some of the Batch model issues and can overcome them with both on-demand and adaptive characteristics.

To the best of our knowledge there are three approaches of site-level integration between the Batch oriented Grid compute model and the service oriented nature of Clouds.

Grid over Clouds. According to this alternative, a whole Grid site is built on top of a public/private Cloud. Through this schema, the Grid infrastructure can be built by instantiating resources according to the real needs of the users. In [8], the authors provided a "Grid as a service" tool in order to create new Grid sites, or to add computational resources to existing Grid sites by exploiting a Platform as a service (PaaS) approach. Similar approach is also adopted in [23].

Hybrid with Batch-Dependent Cloud-Enabled LRMS. In this model a single local Batch system is used to schedule the jobs on a pool of dynamically provisioned resources either on premises or public/private Clouds. For example, in [26], the authors described a solution which enables building dynamical environments through Grid jobs or local Cloud jobs. The solution proposed is built around the LRMS which handles each request. This approach presents manifold limitations. The main drawbacks are the following: *i*) the solution is strongly dependent on a particular technology adopted (i.e. LRMS requires customizations); *ii*) the approach is not *elastic*[11] since it enables the spawn of a virtual environment on local resources only.

Hybrid no Batch-Dependent. In this model the local Grid site spawns resources (even whole clusters) on public/private Clouds on the basis of the jobs requests. The integration is done at the Computing Element level. In this way, several computational resources (i.e. resources available on other computational centers) can be exploited by a fine grained control over virtual instances. In [29], the first solution based on Cloud-over-Grid approach was presented. The authors also validated their solution providing to Grid users special virtual computational resources as GPUs.

The last two approaches can be also identified as two types of "Cloud-over-Grid". In the present work, we describe our solution, that may be used to implement any of the described hybrid approaches with the special attention to the no Batch-dependent model.

3 System Anatomy

The proposed system is based on the adoption of Cloud systems to enable the Grid sites to provide to the users a set of non-traditional resources, like the aforementioned ones and dynamical environments. As an example a Grid user may request to run in a server equipped with a given GPU, or with a particular software library installed or operating system.

Our system has been designed according to the Unix principles: each component is autonomous, independent from the others, specialized in carrying out a named task in a simple way. According to this approach we have chosen to use tags for cataloging the virtual machines that have a certain type of hardware features (such as a named architecture, hybrid systems, GPU, etc.) or software (operating systems, special libraries installed). These tags are published using the standard techniques of the Grid environment, as features implemented and published by a particular site, and which can be specified as requirements by the users when submitting a job. In this way, the Grid information system enable the users to submit jobs requiring special environments, provided only by some Grid sites.

In Figure 1 the project logical schema is sketched. Our solution in built around a DBMS that plays a central role since it contains the configuration of the system, in terms of the connected clusters, the Cloud systems, and their environments and status. The architectural workflow of our solution is implemented by different agents connected to the DBMS each performing a specific action; they will be described in detail later.

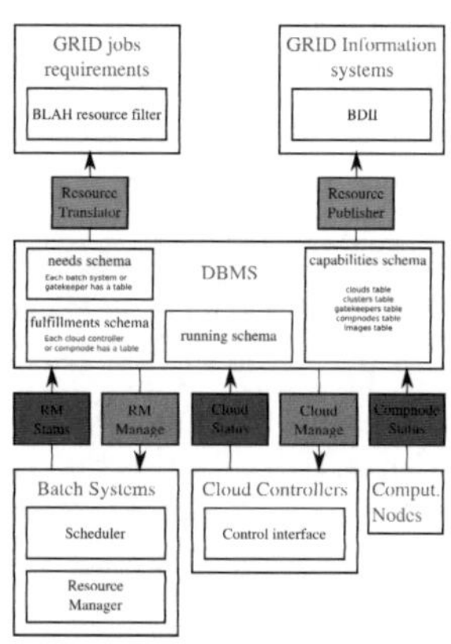

Fig. 1. Description of the Proposed System

In the remaining part of this paper we will use the following terms, and corresponding meaning:

Computing Element (CE): is the set of resources made by the *Gatekeeper* and the *Cluster*.

Gatekeeper: is the system that provides the gateway through which the Grid jobs are submitted to the Batch system running on the local farm nodes;
Cluster: it is a Grid enabled Cluster, i.e. a bunch of *Worker Nodes* (WNs), connected to a Computing Element (CE) and connected to the Grid system. When referring to Clusters we will mean the Cluster Resource Manager.
Cloud: it is a Cloud infrastructure with a Cloud controller like OpenNebula, OpenStack or Eucalyptus.
Computational node: a single server used as target of the incoming Grid job without the use of a Batch system or a Cloud System.
Cloudtag: Tag used to mark the images and to organize the infrastructure resources.

4 DBMS Structure

The information about Clusters and Clouds is collected on a DBMS system. From implementation point of view we have chosen PostgreSQL for this purpose. The informations have been divided into four logic blocks, each one mapped to a DBMS schema:

- The *capabilities* schema contains informations about the Clusters, Cloud Controllers and Virtual Machine images known to the system. It also contains the information about tagging the Virtual Machine images to publish this information through to Grid information system.
- The *needs* schema contains a live view of the *cloudtag* needed by clusters.
- The *fulfillments* schema contains a live view of the *cloudtag* offered by Cloud systems.
- The *running* schema contains the list of the running jobs, with related details.

4.1 The Capabilities Schema

The *capabilities* schema contains the information related to the composition of the various systems. Each software component reads from the DB the necessary information, since the capabilities schema contains all the information related to the structure of the system. The information contained in this schema concern the Cloud, Clusters, Gatekeepers, the Computational nodes connected to the system, and, more important, the Virtual Machine images.

Information on the Active Cloud Systems The table *clouds* of the capabilities schema traces the following information related to the active Cloud systems: (*i*) type of Cloud system (i.e.: OpenStack, OpenNebula or Eucaliptus); (*ii*) the description of the Cloud system; (*iii*) the information on how to interact with the system, which may, or may not, contain authentication information.

Information on the Active Clusters The table *clusters* of the capabilities schema traces the following information related to the Batch system of the active Clusters: (*i*) type of Cluster's Resource Manager (Torque/MAUI, LFS etc); (*ii*) the description of the Cluster; (*iii*) the optional information on how to interact with the Batch system of the Cluster.

Information on Gatekeepers The table *gatekeepers* of the capabilities schema traces the information related to the Gatekeepers of the active Grid nodes. In particular, the more important information are: (*i*) gatekeeper information and the Information System of the Grid site; (*ii*) description of the Grid site; (*iii*) the optional information on how to access the Gatekeeper and/or the Information System.

It is relevant to notice the reason why we implemented two separate tables, one for Gatekeepers and one for the Batch Systems, even if the Grid site is the same, then the CE is listed in the *gatekeepers* table and the Batch System in *clusters* table. We kept separated the two tables because we want to stress the fact that the job path, and the related sequence of events and actions, are different if they are under the control of a Batch System or not.

Information on Standalone Computational nodes The table *compnodes* of the capabilities schema traces the information related to the access to Computational nodes capable of executing jobs. They represent the real or virtual machines not connected to a Batch System, we want to include in our System. The most relevant information are: (*i*) node type; (*ii*) operating system; (*iii*) information related to the access to the node.

Virtual Machine Images A job can be received by a Gatekeeper or by a Batch System and sent to a virtual resource (Cloud) or on a standalone Computational node. The aforementioned resources can be of two types: those that require the fulfillment of a need (Gatekeepers and Clusters) and those that satisfy the need (Clouds and Computational nodes). The association between requests to meet and who can satisfy them is performed inside the table *images*.

The possible job flows originated by this schema are four and they are described in Table 1.

Table 1. Possible Job Flows

Component	**Target**
Gatekeeper	Cloud
Gatekeeper	Computational node
Cluster	Cloud
Cluster	Computational node

The single flows will be discussed in the next sections. The table *images* contains the couple of values *Component* from which the job is coming and *Target*, indicating the job flow in the system, the tag that will be published by the Grid Information System in order to notify the presence of the resource, and a series of information related to the possibility of creating multiple instances. In particular, are advised the following information: (*i*) how many instances may be generated (for a single computational node this value is 1); (*ii*) number of jobs per instance; (*iii*) magnitude and boundaries of the instances; (*iv*) waiting time before destroying the images.

4.2 The Needs Schema

In the *needs* schema the software agents running on Clusters and/or Gatekeepers connected to the system, maintain the status of requests to be satisfied. Each agent has associated a table containing the list of jobs with the related *cloudtags*. The job listed in such tables are all waiting jobs. Running jobs are listed in the *running* schema.

4.3 The Fulfillments Schema

In the *fulfillments* schema are instead listed the resources available to satisfy the requests, so that the systems may know for each *cloudtag* where is located the Cloud or the Computational node.

4.4 The Running Schema

We included in the system also the *running* schema having the purpose of storing the state of running resources.

5 Conclusions and Future Work

In the present work, we have figured out different integration strategies which allow a simple interoperability between Batch-oriented and Service-oriented computing models, namely Computational Grids and Cloud Computing. We provided a straightforward implementation of one of the proposed strategies.

The work may be extended in several ways. The DBMS may be removed from the architecture and the system may be re-engineered to be fully distributed adopting for example the protocol 9P described in [25]. Furthermore we can explore innovative approaches for data and big-data management. In this respect, some interesting directions to be taken into consideration are: (*i*) *fragmentation issues* (e.g., [14]); (*ii*) *uncertain data management issues* (e.g., [22]); (*iii*) *general big data management issues* (e.g., [15]).

References

1. Web site of boto library, a python interface to amazon web services. `https://github.com/boto/boto`. Accessed on 2015-09-09.
2. Web site of eucalyptus. `http://www.eucalyptus.com`. Accessed on 2015-09-09.
3. Web site of nimbus project. `http://www.nimbusproject.org/`. Accessed on 2015-09-09.
4. Web site of the amazon elastic compute cloud (ec2):. `http://aws.amazon.com/ec2/`. Accessed on 2015-09-09.
5. Web site of the fog library sdk, an interface to openstack cloud environment:. `https://github.com/fog/fog/blob/master/lib/fog/openstack/docs/getting_started.md`. Accessed on 2015-09-09.
6. Web site of the open cloud computing interface (occi). `http://occi-wg.org/`. Accessed on 2015-09-09.
7. Web site of the open nebula project. `http://opennebula.org/`. Accessed on 2015-09-09.
8. G. B. Barone, R. Bifulco, V. Boccia, D. Bottalico, R. Canonico, and L. Carracciuolo. Gaas: Customized grids in the clouds. In *Euro-Par 2012: Parallel Processing Workshops*, pages 577–586. Springer, 2013.
9. M. Bernaschi, G. Carbone, E. Mastrostefano, and F. Vella. Solutions to the st-connectivity problem using a gpu-based distributed {BFS}. *Journal of Parallel and Distributed Computing*, 76:145 – 153, 2015. Special Issue on Architecture and Algorithms for Irregular Applications.
10. R. Buyya, D. Abramson, J. Giddy, and H. Stockinger. Economic models for resource management and scheduling in grid computing. *Concurrency and computation: practice and experience*, 14(13-15):1507–1542, 2002.
11. R. Buyya, C. S. Yeo, S. Venugopal, J. Broberg, and I. Brandic. Cloud computing and emerging it platforms: Vision, hype, and reality for delivering computing as the 5th utility. *Future Generation computer systems*, 25(6):599–616, 2009.
12. J. Castillo, . Bosque, C. Pedraza, E. Castillo, P. Huerta, and J. I. Martinez. Low cost high performance reconfigurable computing. In W. Vanderbauwhede and K. Benkrid, editors, *High-Performance Computing Using FPGAs*, pages 453–479. Springer New York, 2013.
13. R. K. Chellappa. "intermediaries in cloud–computing: A new computing paradigm". *INFORMS Meeting*, 1997.
14. A. Cuzzocrea, J. Darmont, and H. Mahboubi. Fragmenting very large XML data warehouses via k-means clustering algorithm. *IJBIDM*, 4(3/4):301–328, 2009.
15. A. Cuzzocrea, D. Saccà, and J. D. Ullman. Big data: a research agenda. In *17th International Database Engineering & Applications Symposium, IDEAS '13, Barcelona, Spain - October 09 - 11, 2013*, pages 198–203, 2013.
16. A. Dovier, E. P. A. Formisano, and F. Vella. Parallel execution of the ASP computation - an investigation on gpus. In *Proceedings of the Technical Communications of the 31st International Conference on Logic Programming (ICLP 2015), Cork, Ireland, August 31 - September 4, 2015.*, 2015.
17. I. Foster, C. Kesselman, and S. Tuecke. The anatomy of the grid. *Berman et al.[2]*, pages 171–197, 2003.
18. I. Foster, Y. Zhao, I. Raicu, and S. Lu. Cloud computing and grid computing 360-degree compared. In *Grid Computing Environments Workshop, 2008. GCE'08*, pages 1–10. Ieee, 2008.

19. O. Gervasi, D. Russo, and F. Vella. The aes implantation based on opencl for multi-/many core architecture. In *Computational Science and Its Applications (ICCSA), 2010 International Conference on*, pages 129–134, 2010.
20. B. Klauer. The convey hybrid-core architecture. In W. Vanderbauwhede and K. Benkrid, editors, *High-Performance Computing Using FPGAs*, pages 431–451. Springer New York, 2013.
21. M. M. L. Servoli and R. M. Cefalà. A proposal to dynamically manage virtual environments in heterogeneous batch systems. In *IEEE Nuclear Science Symposium Conference Record, 2008. NSS08*, pages 823–826, 2008.
22. C. K. Leung, A. Cuzzocrea, and F. Jiang. Discovering frequent patterns from uncertain data streams with time-fading and landmark models. *T. Large-Scale Data- and Knowledge-Centered Systems*, 8:174–196, 2013.
23. C. Loomis, M. Airaj, M. E. Bégin, E. Floros, S. Kenny, and D. O'Callaghan. Stratuslab cloud distribution. *European Research Activities in Cloud Computing*, page 271, 2012.
24. Parallella. Parallella 1-x reference manual, 2014. accessed on July 11, 2015.
25. R. Pike, D. Presotto, K. Thompson, H. Trickey, et al. Plan 9 from bell labs. In *Proceedings of the summer 1990 UKUUG Conference*, pages 1–9. London, UK, 1990.
26. E. Ronchieri, D. Cesini, D. D'Agostino, V. Ciaschini, G. D. Torre, P. Cozzi, D. Salomoni, A. Clematis, L. Milanesi, and I. Merelli. The wnodes cloud virtualization framework: a macromolecular surface analysis application case study. In *Parallel, Distributed and Network-Based Processing (PDP), 2014 22nd Euromicro International Conference on*, pages 218–222. IEEE, 2014.
27. A. M. S. Jha and G. Fox. Using clouds to provide grids with higher levels of abstraction and explicit support for usage modes. *Concurr. Comput.: Pract. Exper.*, 21(8):1087–1108, June 2009.
28. B. Sotomayor, K. Keahey, and I. Foster. Combining batch execution and leasing using virtual machines. In *Proceedings of the 17th international symposium on High performance distributed computing*, pages 87–96. ACM, 2008.
29. F. Vella, R. M. Cefala, A. Costantini, O. Gervasi, and C. Tanci. Gpu computing in egi environment using a cloud approach. In *Computational Science and Its Applications (ICCSA), 2011 International Conference on*, pages 150–155. IEEE, 2011.
30. F. Vella, I. Neri, O. Gervasi, and S. Tasso. A simulation framework for scheduling performance evaluation on cpu-gpu heterogeneous system. In *Proceedings of the 12th International Conference on Computational Science and Its Applications - Volume Part IV*, ICCSA 2012, pages 457–469, Berlin, Heidelberg, 2012. Springer-Verlag.

TourMiner: Effective and Efficient Clustering Big Mobile Social Data for Supporting Advanced Analytics Tools

Gloria Bordogna[1], Alfredo Cuzzocrea[2,3],
Luca Frigerio[1], Giuseppe Psaila[4], Danilo Amendola[5]

[1]CNR-IREA, Milano, Italy
[2]DIA Dept., University of Trieste, Trieste, Italy
[3]ICAR-CNR, Rende, Italy
[4]DIGIP Dept., University of Bergamo, Bergamo, Italy
[5]IRCCS Bonino-Pulejo, Messina, Italy
bordogna.g@irea.cnr.it; alfredo.cuzzocrea@dia.units.it;
frigerio.l@irea.cnr.it; psaila@unibg.it; daniloamendola@gmail.com

Abstract. Nowadays a great deal of attention is devoted to the issue of supporting *big data analytics* over *big mobile social data*. These data are generated by modern emerging social systems like *Twitter*, *Facebook*, *Instagram*, and so forth. *Mining big mobile social data* has been of great interest, as analyzing such data is critical for a wide spectrum of big data applications (e.g., *smart cities*). Among several proposals, *clustering* is a well-known solution for extracting interesting and actionable knowledge from massive amounts of big mobile (geo-located) social data. Inspired by this main thesis, this paper proposes *an effective and efficient similarity-matrix-based algorithm for clustering big mobile social data*, called TourMiner, which is specifically targeted to *clustering trips* extracted from *tweets*, in order to mine *most popular tours*. The main characteristic of TourMiner consists in applying clustering over a well-suited *similarity matrix* computed on top of trips.

1 Introduction

Social networks coupled with the diffusion of *smart mobile devices* equipped with GPS sensors have contributed to generate a big amounts of users-generated contents which are geo-referenced and timestamped. These are recognized in literature as *big mobile social data* (e.g., [1,2,3]). By analizying recent research trends, it follows that, nowadays, a great deal of attention is devoted to the issue of supportingbig mobile social data analytics. These data are generated by modern emerging social systems like *Twitter*, *Facebook*, *Instagram*, and so forth. *Mining big mobile social data* (e.g., [13,14]) has been of great interest, as analyzing such data is critical for a wide spectrum of big data applications (e.g., *smart cities*). The possibility of cross-analyzing geo-references, timestamps, characteristics of content authors, and, last but not least, message contents, poses new challenges to the research community (e.g., [4]). CISCO estimated that data on the Internet will increase at a *Compound Annual Growth Rate* of 25% by the year 2017. Thus, in order to deal with continuously-growing-in-size data sets, it will be necessary to frequently scale-up existing algorithms or to define new paradigms for *big mobile social data analytics* (e.g., [5,6]).

Another aspect to be faced-off is represented by the amenity of *synthesizing* big data collections with the purpose of highlighting *relevant* meanings embedded within them.

Several real-world applications, such as *social network community identification* (e.g., [7]) and their *trajectory summarization* (e.g., [8]), require means to filter-out the communities of users and further to group and represent similar trajectories. This latest task implies scaling-down the collecions of big data by removing noise and redundancies, so that highlighting the main representative *spatio-temporal patterns* (e.g., [9]). *Faceted search* (e.g., [10]) and *clustering techniques* can be used to this purpose since their goal is to identify groups of items within the target data set with common characteristics in a *feature space*, while removing outliers and noise which are considered uninteresting from further analysis.

Inspired by this main thesis, this paper proposes *an efficient implementation of similarity-matrix-based algorithm for clustering big mobile social data*, called TourMiner, which is specifically targeted to *clustering trips* extracted from geo-located *tweets*, in order to mine *most popular tours*. The main characteristic of TourMiner consists in applying clustering (any clustering algorithm) over a well-suited *similarity matrix* (possibly using distinct similarity measures) computed on top of trips.

Looking at specific algorithmic charateristics, TourMiner can be considered as a *hybrid algorithm* as it sequentially applies a "scaling-up" and subsequently a "scaling-down" phase to mine tours. In particular, the first phase applies a scale-up approach in order to identify the community of tourists visiting a region of interest within a big set of Tweet messages, which are collected during a period of time, so that data increasingly scale up with time, thus efficiently improving our previous contribution [15]. The second phase, which is based on *geo-partitioning* and *geo-clustering*, applies a scale-down approach for identifying and synthetising the main tours followed by most of the tourists within the target region, by exploiting low-cost hardware, *GPU-based computing paradigms* (e.g., [16]) and open-source libraries to manage available memory resources, thus significantly extending and further improving our previous contribution [17] and clearly matching the strict computational requirements of big data management by means of low cost hardware (e.g., [18]).

2 TourMiner: An Effective and Efficient Algorithm for Mining Most-Popular Tours from Big Social Media

In this Section, we provide principles and implementation of the proposed algorithm TourMiner. TourMiner comprises three main phases:

1. *Geo-partitioning*: trips extracted from tweets are generated according to different representations so that they are defined as semantic trajectories over a spatial domain ontology, intended as a representation of spatial entities of interest with their geographic footprints;
2. *Computing the pairwise trip similarity matrix*: trips are processed in order to compute a suitable similarity matrix that is the fundamental data structure of our clustering approach;
3. *Trip clustering (based on the similarity matrix)*: finally, on the basis of the similarity matrix, trips are clustered as to extract actionable knowledge from the target big mobile social media data.

In the following, we describe these phases in details.

2.1 Geo-Partitioning

Firstly, each trip is represented by a *semantic trajectory*, i.e., a sequence of IDs $\langle a_1, a_2, \ldots, a_n\rangle$ that identify interesting locations on the spatial domain, such as Points Of Interest (POIs) like restaurants, hotels, museums, etc, or area districts such as city areas, municipalities, etc. An example of semantic trajectory defined by sequence of IDs could be:

<Malpensa Airport, Milano Central Station, Bergamo Railway Station, Piazza Vecchia>

By this representation we may argue that the traveller landed in Malpensa airport, then went to Milano Central Station and from there he travelled by train to Bergamo where he visited the medioeval Piazza Vecchia.

This same trajectory could be represented in a coarsest way bearing more uncertainty on the visited locations, for example by a sequence of municipalities, namely:

<Malpensa, Milano, Bergamo, Bergamo>

In this case, we can just guess the visited cities.

In this phase, one can choose to represent a trip based on the following two kinds of IDs:

a) Categorical IDs: trips are represented in terms of a sequence of *objects of interest* that are implemented as *Point Of Interest* (POI) on the spatial domain or zones such as municipalities, ZIP code areas, NUTS etc. In this case, IDs are categorical and neither a metric, nor an order is defined between them.

b) Numerical IDs: trips are represented in terms of a sequence of *natural numbers* $a_i \in N$ among which a linear order is defined so that $a_i < a_j$ if $i < j$. These IDs identify cells in a *regular tessellation* of the spatial domain, and can be generated by *space filling functions* [12] such as the *Z-Order* and the *Peano* curve. They are named as *GeoHash codes* and a metric over them is defined by a function of kind: $|.|\ N \rightarrow N$ that satisfies the following properties: (*i*) $|a_i - a_i| = 0$; (*ii*) $|a_i - a_j| = |a_j - a_i|$; (*iii*) $|a_i - a_j| + |a_j - a_k| \geq |a_i - a_k|$.

The advantage of using GeoHash codes is represented by the opportunity of using *similarity measures* based on a *metric distance*, thus achieving more accuracy. In fact, when using categorical IDs, the matching operation between two IDs is crisp, they either match or not, and, in this context, it is meaningless to evaluate *fuzzy matching*, since two IDs, e.g. ZIP codes, may differ only by one digit and be distant in space. On the other hand, when using GeoHash codes, one obtains trajectoies whose semantic is both implicit and uncertain with respect to the objects of interest: to explicit the semantics, one should determine which POIs are within each cell identified by the GeoHash codes.

2.2 Computing the Pairwise Trip Similarity Matrix

Computing the pairwise trip similarity matrix depends on the types of IDs used to represent trips (see Section 2.1), i.e. via categorical IDs or numerical IDs. In the following, we address both cases. Before computing such similarity matrix, we first eliminate *redundancies*, i.e. *consecutive duplications* of the same ID in the trip representation. Therefore, a trip of kind:

$$A = \langle ID_1, ID_2, ID_3, ID_3, ID_3, ID_4, ID_3\rangle$$

becomes of kind:

$$A = \langle ID_1, ID_2, ID_3, ID_4, ID_3\rangle$$

after redundancy removal.

Furthermore, *pointwise trips* are deleted. For instance, a trip of kind:

$$B = \langle ID_1, ID_1, ID_1\rangle$$

becomes of kind:

$$B = \langle ID_1\rangle$$

after redundancy removal and then, being pointwise, it is deleted.

The motivation of redundancy removal relies in the idea of not to favor the subsequent grouping of trips into a tour just because many tweets have been sent from the same locality. This usually happens in the airport area, and free WIFI hotspots .

We next describe how the pairwise trip similarity matrix is defined for both cases (i.e., categorical IDs and numerical IDs).

Case 1: Categorical IDs. Let $A = \langle a_1, a_2, \ldots, a_N\rangle$ and $B = \langle b_1, b_2, \ldots, b_M\rangle$ denote a pair of trips of different length, such that $N \neq M$, being a_i and b_j strings that identify categories (i.e., ZIP or NUTS codes). Let $A \cap B$ denote the intersection trip between A and B. We define the cardinality of $A \cap B$, denoted by $|A \cap B|$, as follows:

$$|A\cap B| = \sum_{i=1}^{\min(N,M)} \max_{j=1,\ldots\max(N,M)\ |\ bj \neq ak\ \forall\ k<i} (a_i = b_j) \qquad (1)$$

such that:

$$a_i \in A\ with\ |A| = \min(N,M) \qquad (2)$$

and:

$$b_j \in B\ with\ |B| = \max(N,M) \qquad (3)$$

Formula (1) is computed as follows. We first scan every element of the *shortest* trip A and match it with every element of the *longest* trip B by increasing the counter if there is a new element in the longest trip (not previously matching any other element of B) that matches the current element of A. This way, we constrain an element of B to be selected only once by one single element of A. This measure is *symmetric*. This means that by scanning the longest trip and matching it with every element of the shortest one of the two respective trips we would obtain the *same* result due to the fact that we cancel, at each match, the elements already selected.

Furthermore, the cardinality of intersection trip satisfies the following properties:

$$\begin{gathered} |A \cap B| = |B \cap A| \\ |A \cap A| = |A| \end{gathered} \qquad (4)$$

Finally, in our framework, we exploit the following similarity measures between trips (case of trips modeled in terms of categorical IDs):

$$Fuzzy\_Inclusion(A,B) = |A \subseteq B| = \frac{|A \cap B|}{\min(N,M)}$$
$$Jaccard\_Sim(A,B) = \frac{|A \cap B|}{N + M - |A \cap B|}$$
$$Dice\_Sim(A,B) = 2\frac{|A \cap B|}{N + M} \quad (5)$$
$$Cosine\_Sim(A,B) = \frac{|A \cap B|}{\sqrt{N} * \sqrt{M}}$$
$$Fuzzy\_Sim(A,B) = \frac{1}{2}\left(\frac{|A \cap B|}{N} + \frac{|A \cap B|}{M}\right)$$

These similarity measures are used to enrich the knowledge discovery phase from big social media implemented in our framework.

Case 2: Numerical IDs. Let $A = \langle a_1, a_2, \ldots, a_N \rangle$ and $B = \langle b_1, b_2, \ldots, b_M \rangle$ denote a pair of trips of different length, such that $N \neq M$, being a_i and b_j numbers that identify cells (i.e., GeoHash codes, which we assume to be implemented in terms of Z-Order codes – see Section 2.1). Let *MaxZcode* be the maximum Zcode among those generated, which is defined as follows:

$$MaxZcode = \max(a_N, b_M) \quad (6)$$

Also, let $(A - B)$ denote the difference-trip between A and B, and $|A - B|$ its cardinality, which is defined as follows:

$$|A - B| = \sum_{i=1}^{N} \min_{\substack{j=1,\ldots,M \;| \\ b_j \neq \operatorname{argmin}(|a_k - b_j|) \forall k<i}} (|a_i - b_j|) \quad (7)$$

Furthermore, the cardinality of difference-trip satisfies the following properties:

$$|A - B| = |B - A|$$
$$|A - A| = 0 \quad (8)$$

Finally, in our framework, similarly to the case of trips modeled as categorical IDs, we exploit the following similarity measures between trips (case of trips modeled in terms of numerical IDs):

$$Fuzzy\_Inclusion\_Hash(A,B) = \frac{MaxZcode - \frac{|A - B|}{\min(N,M)}}{MaxZcode}$$
$$Jaccard\_Sim\_Hash(A,B) = \frac{MaxZcode - \frac{|A - B|}{N + M - |A - B|}}{MaxZcode} \quad (9)$$
$$Dice\_Sim\_Hash(A,B) = \frac{MaxZcode - 2\frac{|A - B|}{N + M}}{MaxZcode}$$

$$Cosine\_Sim\_Hash(A,B) = \frac{MaxZcode - \frac{|A-B|}{\sqrt{N}*\sqrt{M}}}{MaxZcode}$$

$$Fuzzy\_Sim\_Hash(A,B) = \frac{MaxZcode - |A-B|}{MaxZcode}$$

These similarity measures, just like to case of trips modeled as categorical IDs, are used to enrich the knowledge discovery phase from big social media implemented in our framework.

On the basis of the definitions above, the pairwise trip similarity matrix *SIM* is introduced as a $D \times D$ matrix such that, for each pair of trips t_i and t_j, the entry $SIM(t_i,t_j)$ satisfies the following properties:

$$i. SIM(t_i, t_i) = 1 \qquad (10)$$
$$ii. SIM(t_i, t_j) = SIM(t_j, t_i)$$

Based on (*ii*), the similarity matrix *SIM* is a *triangular matrix* hence we need to compute only its values below the main diagonal, i.e. $\forall\ i = 1, \ldots, D$. We compute $SIM(t_i,t_j)$ with $j = 1,\ldots, i\text{-}1$ only.

Moreover, since the computation of the similarity between any two trips is independent from the other trips, in our implementation this process has been parallelized by exploiting GPU-based computing paradigms.

2.3 Similarity-Matrix-based Trip Clustering

Here we describe the core strategy of our proposed TourMiner algorithm, i.e. clustering of trips based on the similarity matrix *SIM* (see Section 2.2).

In this phase, clustering is applied to group trips into clusters based on their similarity, and then the biggest clusters are selected as popular tours. In principle, any clustering algorithm based on a similarity matrix could be applied. In our implementation, we tested both the density based *DBSCAN clustering* algorithm, generating a flat partition [24], and the *hierarchical agglomerative complete link clustering* whose main idea consists in generating, at each hierarchical cycle, a new cluster by focusing on the two clusters, said C_i and C_j, with greatest similarity in *SIM*. The *complete link clustering* main steps are the following:

Step 1. Identification of the two clusters to fuse C_i and C_j as follows:

$$\{i, j\} = \text{argmax}(SIM(i, j))\ \ i, j = 1, \ldots, D \qquad (11)$$

Step 2. Computation of the similarity of the actual clusters with respect to the candidate cluster in terms of the *minimum* among the similarities with the elements of the candidate cluster (see formula in step 4.3 in of Algorithm 1). This guarantees that, when a new element or cluster is added to a cluster to form a higher-level cluster, all its (clustered) elements share a *minimum* similarity degree. This allows generating compact clusters.*Step 3.* Selection of the popular tours: they are the first k biggest clusters in partition with minimum similarity ε, being k and ε tunable input parameters. ε identifies the level of the cluster hierarchy, i.e., the cluster partition. k is used to select the clusters with greatest number of trips from this partition.

3 Experimental Assessment and Analysis

In order to prove the effectiveness and the efficiency of our proposed algorithm TourMiner, we designed and developed an experimental campaign, whose results are reported in this Section.

In particular, experiments were aimed at evaluating the proposed clustering approach in terms of both time and memory needed to process the distinct phases (see Section 2). We designed and evaluated optimized solutions for all these phases. We discuss these solutions in the following.

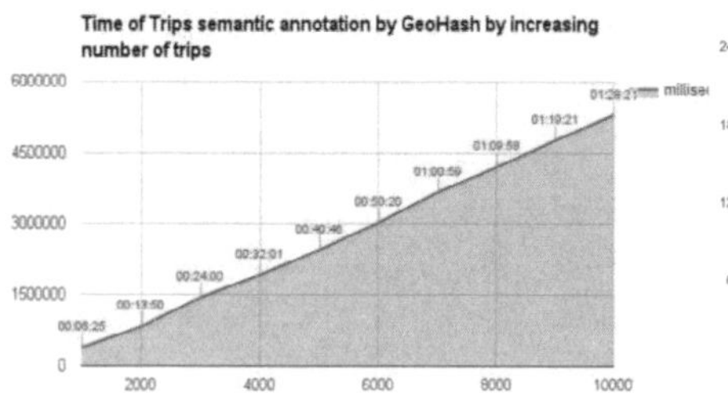

Fig. 1. Tip Creation Time

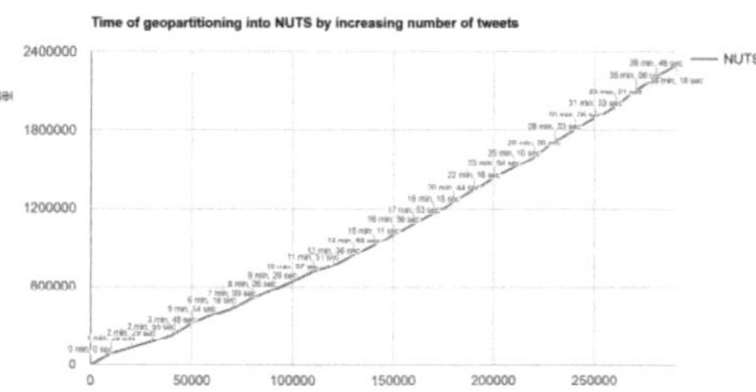

Fig. 2. Geo-Partitioning with NUTS

We developed ad-hoc metrics over such phases, and we studied the evolution of such metrics by increasing the number of tweets and the number of trips. Both parameters well-test the scalability of our proposed algorithm. In the following, we provide our experimental results.

First, in order to have a better understanding on the realibility of our experimental campaign, Fig. 1 shows the time needed to create annotated trips, i.e., semantic trajectories, in terms of GeoHash codes depending on the number of tweets. This, indeed, allows us to better estimate the size of data we deal with, as size is one of the main characteristics of big data to be considered when designing algorithms that run on big data sets.

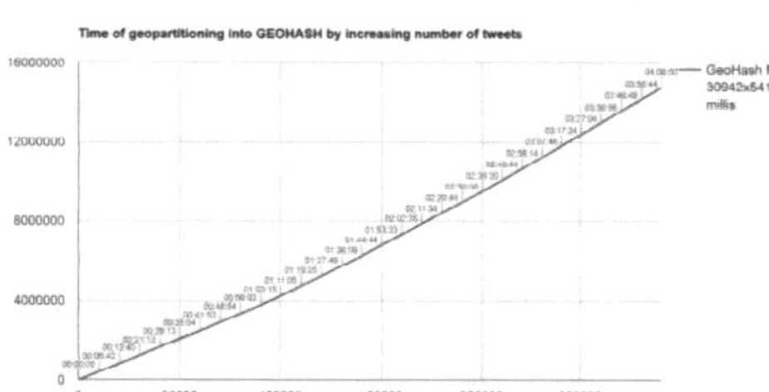

Fig. 3. Geo-Partitioning with GeoHash

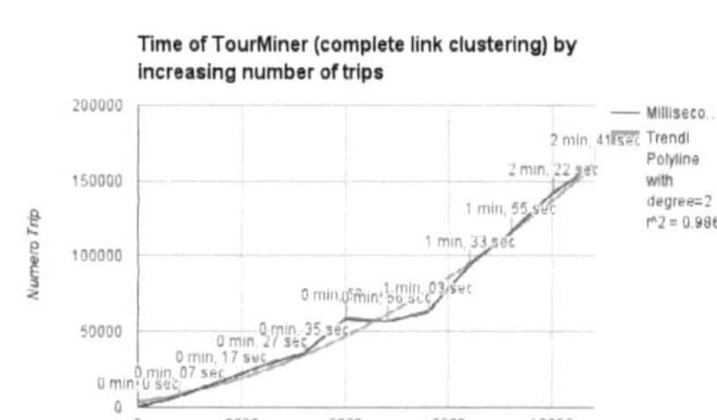

Fig. 4. Temporal Perfomance of the Whole Tour Mining Process with GeoHash and Complete-link Clustering

Fig. 2 and Fig 3 focus, instead, on the geo-partitioning phase of algorithm TourMiner. Here, we report the time needed for computing the geo-partition in the two different cases of NUTS (Fig. 2) and GeoHash (Fig. 3), still with respect to the number of tweets without the parallel optimization.

Fig. 4 reports the time needed for the *whole* tour mining process by using GeoHash codes as semantic annotation of trips and the Complete-link clustering algorithm to identify popular tours. Here, it should be noticed that our introduced optimization support for the geo-partitioning phase (see Section 2) allows us to obtain a polynomial trend with degree 2 instead of 3. This further confirms to us the realibility of our clustering methodology over big mobile social data.

By analyzing the experimental results of our campaign, it clearly follows the efficiency of our proposed algorithm TourMiner for clustering big mobile social data.

4 Conclusions and Future Work

In this paper, we have introduced and experimentally assessed TourMiner, an effective and efficient algorithm for spatially mining big mobile social data about to semantic trajectories. TourMiner implements a clustering procedure that founds on (*i*) suitable semantic representations of trips extracted from Twitter data, alternatively in terms of categorical IDs or numerical IDs, and (*ii*) a well-suited similarity matrix computed on top of such trips. We provided motivations, definitions and analysis of TourMiner, along with its experimental assessment and analysis over Twitter data according to several (experimental) parameters. Results clearly comfirm the benefits coming from our proposal.

Future work is mainly oriented towards enriching our proposed framework with innovative characteristics like *uncertain big data management* (e.g., [19]) and *big data approximation paradigms* (e.g., [27]).

References

[1] S. M. Allen, M. J. Chorley, G. Colombo, E. Jaho, M. Karaliopoulos, I. Stavrakakis, R. M. Whitaker, "Exploiting User Interest Similarity and Social Links for Micro-Blog Forwarding in Mobile Opportunistic Networks", *Pervasive and Mobile Computing 11*, pp. 106–131, 2014

[2] O. Khalid, M. U. S. Khan, S. U. Khan, A. Y. Zomaya, "Omnisuggest: A ubiquitous cloud-based context-aware recommendation system for mobile social networks", *IEEE Transactions on Services Computing 7(3)*, pp. 401–414, 2014

[3] Y. Yu, X. Huang, X. Zhu, G. Wang, "Camel: A journey group t-pattern mining system based on instagram trajectory data", in: *Proceedings of IEEE DASFAA*, pp. 527–530, 2014

[4] M. Balduini, A. Bozzon, E. D. Valle, Y. Huang, G. Houben, "Recommending Venues using Continuous Predictive Social Media Analytics", *IEEE Internet Computing 18(5)*, pp. 28–35, 2014.

[5] Alfredo Cuzzocrea, Domenico Saccà, Jeffrey D. Ullman, "Big data: a research agenda", in: *Proceedings of IDEAS 2013*, pp. 198–203, 2013

[6] A. Cuzzocrea, "Analytics over Big Data: Exploring the Convergence of Data Warehousing, OLAP and Data-Intensive Cloud Infrastructures", in: *Proceedings of COMPSAC 2013*, pp. 481–483, 2013

[7] M. Takaffoli, R. Rabbany, O. R. Zaïane, "Incremental Local Community Identification in Dynamic Social Networks", in: *Proceedings of ASONAM*, pp. 90–94, 2013

[8] H. Su, K. Zheng, K. Zeng, J. Huang, S.W. Sadiq, N.J. Yuan, X. Zhou, "Making Sense of Trajectory Data: A Partition-and-Summarization approach", in: *Proceedings of IEEE ICDE*, pp. 963–974, 2015

[9] H. Jiang, L. Huang, J.J. Zhang, Y. Zhang, D.W. Gao, "Spatialtemporal Characterization of Synchrophasor Measurement Systems – A Big Data Approach for Smart Grid System Situational Awareness", in: *Proceedings of ACSSC*, pp. 750–754, 2014

[10] H. Zhuge, Y. Wilks, "Faceted Search, Social Networking and Interactive Semantics", *World Wide Web 17(4)*, pp. 589–593, 2014

[11] R.C. Daley, J.B. Dennis, "Virtual Memory, Processes, and Sharing in MULTICS", *Communications of the ACM 11(5)*, pp. 306–312, 1968

[12] M.F. Mokbel, W.G. Aref, I. Kamel, "Analysis of Multi-Dimensional Space-Filling Curves", *GeoInformatica 7(3)*, pp. 179–209, 2003

[13] S. Jin, W. Lin, H. Yin, S. Yang, A. Li, B. Deng, "Community Structure Mining in Big Data Social Media Networks with MapReduce", *Cluster Computing 18(3)*, pp. 999–1010, 2015

[14] N.J. Yuan, "Mining Social and Urban Big Data", in: *Proceedings of ACM WWW (Companion Volume)*, p. 1103, 2015

[15] A. Cuzzocrea, G. Psaila, M. Toccu, "An Innovative Framework for Effectively and Efficiently Supporting Big Data Analytics over Geo-Located Mobile Social Media", in: *Proceedings of ACM IDEAS*, 2016

[16] J.A. Cedillo, I. Rivera-Zarate, J.C. Herrera Lozada, M. Olguin-Carbajal, "GPU Programming Paradigm", *Journal of Theoretical and Applied Information Technology*, pp. 133–138, 2009

[17] G. Bordogna, A. Cuzzocrea, L. Frigerio, G. Psaila, "Clustering Geo-Tagged Tweets for Advanced Big Data Analytics", in: *Proceedings of IEEE BigData Congress*, 2016

[18] B. Yu, A. Cuzzocrea, D.H. Jeong, S. Maydebura, "On Managing Very Large Sensor-Network Data Using Bigtable", in: *Proceedings of CCGRID 2012*, pp. 918–922, 2012

[19] A. Cuzzocrea, C.K.S. Leung, R.K. MacKinnon, "Mining Constrained Frequent Itemsets from Distributed Uncertain Data", *Future Generation Computer Systems 37 (1)*, 117–126, 2014

[20] F. Giannotti, M. Nanni, F. Pinelli, D. Pedreschi, "Trajectory Pattern Mining", in: *Proceedings of ACM SIGKDD*, pp. 330–339, 2007

[21] L.O. Alvares, V. Bogorny, B. Kuijpers, J.A.F. de Macedo, B.Moelans, A. Vaisman, "A Model for Enriching Trajectories wth Semantic Geographical Information", in: *Proceedings of ACM GIS*, 2007.

[22] S. Spaccapietra, C. Parent, M.L. Daminai, J.A.F. de Macedo, F. Porto, C. Vangenot, "A Conceptual View on Trajectories", *IEEE Transactions on Knowledge and Data Engineering*, 2008

[23] Z. Yan, D. Chakraborty, C. Parent, S. Spaccapietra, K. Aberer, "Semitri: A Framework for Semantic Annotation of Hetherogeneous Trajectories", in: *Proceedings of EDBT*, 2011

[24] M. Ester, H.P. Kriegel, J. Sander, X. Xu, "A Density-based Algorithm for Discovering Clusters in Large Spatial Databases with Noise", in: *Proceedings of ACM KDD*, 1996

[25] Z. Yin, L. Cao, J. Han, J. Luo, T.S. Huang, "Diversified Trajectory Pattern Ranking in Geo-Tagged Social Media", in: *Proceedings of SDM*, pp. 980–991, 2011

[26] C. Comito, D. Falcone, D. Talia, "Mining Popular Travel Routes from Social Network Geo-Tagged Data", in: *(E. Damiani et al. eds), "Intelligent Interactive Multimedia Systems and Services", Springer*, pp. 81–95, 2015

[27] A. Cuzzocrea, U. Matrangolo, "Analytical synopses for Approximate Query Answering in OLAP Environments", in: *Proceedings of DEXA*, pp. 359–370, 2004

Efficient High Performance Computing by user networks (Extended Abstract)

Nunziato Cassavia[2], Sergio Flesca[1], Michele Ianni[1], Elio Masciari[2], Giuseppe Papuzzo[2], and Chiara Pulice[3]

[1] DIMES, University of Calabria, Italy
[2] ICAR-CNR, Italy
UMIACS, University of Maryland, USA
{flesca,mianni}@dimes.unical.it
{nunziato.cassavia,elio.masciari,giuseppe.papuzzo}@icar.cnr.it
{cpulice}@umiacs.umd.edu

Abstract. The advances in computational techniques both from a software and hardware viewpoint lead to the development of projects whose complexity could be quite challenging, e.g., biomedical simulations. In order to deal with the increased demand of computational power many collaborative approaches have been proposed in order to apply proper partitioning strategy able to assign pieces of execution to a crowd of workers. In this paper, we address this problem in a peer to peer way. We leverage the idling computational resources of users connected to a network. More in detail, we designed a framework that allows users to share their CPU and memory in a secure and efficient way. The latter allows users help each others by asking the network computational resources when they face high computing demanding tasks. As we do not require to power additional resources for solving tasks (we better exploit unused resources *already* powered instead), we hypothesize a remarkable side effect at steady state: energy consumption reduction compared with traditional server farm or cloud based executions.

1 Introduction

Computer Science is a really young discipline whose several branches grew up at impressive rates. Hardware cost is continuously decreasing while its performances are reaching unprecedented levels. Based on the availability of a plethora of powerful (portable) computing devices, new computing tasks have been designed and new data management paradigm emerged (e.g., the well known Big Data metaphore [8, 4, 1, 2]). Even though the advances in computer sciences lead to quite effective solution implementations, several problems still require too much computational resources for a single device execution. Indeed, since the introduction of Linux operating system, the idea of gathering from the crowd the resources for completing a task, have been widely leveraged.

The word Crowdsourcing was first introduced by Howe [5] in order to define the process of outsourcing some jobs to the crowd. It is used for a wide group of activities, as it allows companies to get substantial benefits by solving their problems in effective and efficient way. Indeed, crowd based solutions have been proposed for a wide range of applications as in image tagging [6], or sentiment analysis [3] to cite a few.

Many attempts have been made to properly define the very nature of collaborative distributed systems, however the solution to this apparently trivial task is far from being easy. As a matter of fact, all the successful systems (e.g., Wikipedia[3], Yahoo! Answers[4], Amazon Mechanical Turk[5]) rely on some assumptions: They should be able to involve project contributors, each contributor should solve a specific task, it is mandatory to effectively evaluate single contributions, and they should properly react to possible misconduct. The above mentioned points calls for a good trade-off between openness of the system and quality of service when designing a collaborative environment.

A well known open source framework that is widely used (mainly) for scientific purposes is BOINC (Berkeley Open Infrastructure for Network Computing)[6]. It allows volunteers to contribute to a wide variety of projects. The computing contribution is rewarded by credits for getting to a higher rank in a leaderboard. On the opposite side in recent years a new category of collaborative approaches is born for cryptovalue mining such as Bitcoin [7]. Users aiming at mining new Bitcoins contribute to a decoding task and are rewarded with a portion of the gathered money that is proportional to the effort put in the mining task. Our approach can be seen as a trade-off between BOINC framework implementation and Bitcoin mining.

More in detail, the novelty of our project is the exploitation of a peer to peer approach for reusing resources that users do not fully exploit to provide services that are currently offered by centralized server farm at an high cost with no customization. In particular, current limitation to high performance computing access (high price and difficult customization of resources), could be overcome by using our framework. Users who may need computing power, can simply ask other users that are not fully exploiting the potential of their computing devices (PC, smartphone, smart TV, etc.).

In order to assess the effectiveness of our solution, we analyzed a typical usage pattern for the big market of imaging and animation: the rendering of 3D scenes by a specialized plugin named *Mozaiko*^{TM} [7]. This operation typically engages users computers for several hours. Our experimental analyses evidence that existing solution are slower than our proposal due to their traditional approach to high performance computing and more expensive due to high prices of CPU cycles renting. Our plugin provides high added value to potential customers because it will be faster and cheaper than the competing solution (further details can be found at *www.coremuniti.com*).

Our solution do not require the continuous purchase of new servers, as users continuously provide (up to date) computational power. Finally, the better re-use of already powered resources could induce a beneficial systemic effect by reducing the overall

[3] https://www.wikipedia.org

[4] https://answers.yahoo.com/

[5] https://www.mturk.com

[6] https://boinc.berkeley.edu/

[7] We choose this name as Mozaiko is the Esperanto (a universal language) term denoting a Mosaic that is a good metaphore for our approach that partition a complex task in several sub-tasks that will be re-assembled like mosaic tiles

energy consumption for complex tasks execution. We plan to further investigate our conjecture in a future work as we are not able at this stage to generalize our early results.

Our Contribution. To summarize, we make the following major contributions: 1) We design and implement a hybrid P2P infrastructure that allows collaboration among users by sharing unexploited computational resources; 2) We define a robust model for task partitioning and assignment to network users;

2 Our system in a short

P2P networks features a common goal: the resources of many users and computers can be used in a collaborative way in order to significantly increase the computing power available for the users. In "full" P2P networks computers communicate directly each other thus allowing better bandwidth use. However, there are some inherent drawbacks to P2P solutions that require some functionalities to be centralized. Those systems can be used both for data sharing[10] and distributed computation[9], they are denoted as "hybrid" P2P. Our system, namely *Coremuniti*, falls in the latter category and aims to build a P2P network where users can share their unexploited computing resources. In Fig. 1 we sketched a possible usage scenario for our platform when using Mozaiko plugin. However, we point out that our platform is general purpose thus can be used for solving any complex problem that is parallelizable.

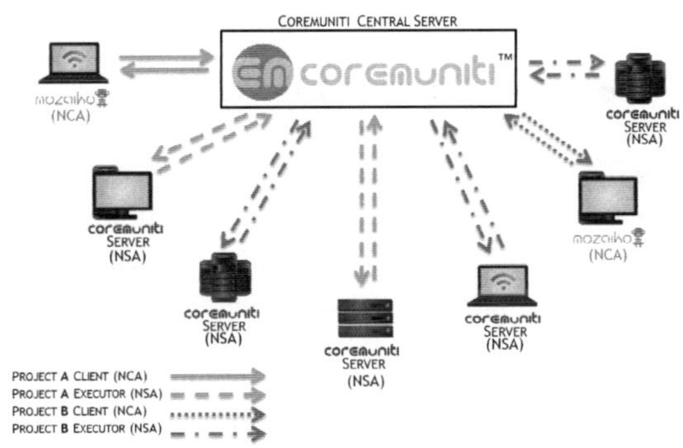

Fig. 1. Coremuniti system at work

Users who want to join our network, will download our software that will install the *Coremuniti server* on their devices (it is worth noticing that our software is platform independent). By running the node server, denoted in Fig. 1 as NSA (Node Server Agent), users can easily set the amount of CPU time they are willing to share with other users in the network. As they allow task execution, they will be rewarded by credits. We point out, that our software is executed in parallel with user own activities without any interaction with them. On the opposite side, users who need additional computing power to complete specialized tasks (in this paper we present the 3D Rendering case study) can install the specific software that is denoted in Fig. 1 as NCA that stands for Node Client Agent (i.e., *Mozaiko* for the rendering case study). As they start a new computing intensive task, they simply issue a request to the network for gathering the required resources. Two cases may occur: 1) they have previously gained (a portion of) the required credits for running the task (e.g., because they acted as servers) or 2) they have bought the required credits. In order, to guarantee a high level of service, we perform the subtask assignment step at the central server. More in detail, to fully take advantage from the capability of our network, we partition the (possibly huge) task in a suitable number of (much smaller) subtasks that can be quickly executed by the server peers.

As subtasks are completed, we check their correctness and reward the participating peers. In the following, we describe our model for subtask assignment that guarantees efficient execution for clients and gave to all peers (even if they have limited computing power) the possibility to be rewarded. Interesting enough, users that are not going to ask for task execution have the chance to accumulate credits that can be redeemed by coins or gadgets. As it will be shown in the experimental section, the latter features makes our framework a more convenient choice w.r.t to other collaborative systems such as cryptovalue miners. Indeed, in the early stage of development of our system we performed some preliminary user analysis by asking 500 students at University of Calabria their interest in joining the network. After specifying our rewarding model all of them agreed to join the network and they are currently beta testing the software. Due to space limitation, we will not describe the architecture details and in hat follows we will describe the most interesting part of our system, i.e. subtask assignment.

3 Subtask Assignment and Credit Rewarding

In this section, we describe our mathematical model for assigning subtask execution to resource providers whose objective is to minimize the expected completion time for the overall task. More in detail, as explained above, when a user asks the network for additional resources, the project s/he is going to execute is partitioned in several subtasks that can be completed using a limited amount of computational resources by every node connected to our P2P network . The obtained results are then combined for producing the project output much as much fast as possible than single machine execution.

The model assumes the presence of a set of available resource providers $\mathcal{RP} = \{rp_1, \ldots, rp_n\}$, and of a function $\lambda_c : \mathcal{RP} \rightarrow N \times N$, that assigns to every resource provider rp a pair $\langle tmin, tmax \rangle$, where $tmin$ (resp. $tmax$) is the minimum (resp. maximum) execution time required by the resource node to complete a subtask.

Furthermore, we leverage a credit assignment function which is based on the "usefulness" of the result yielded by the resource providers. Specifically, let st be a subtask whose execution was assigned c credits and which was assigned to the resource providers $rp_{i_1}, \ldots rp_{i_x}$. We order the resource providers $rp_{i_1}, \ldots rp_{i_x}$ ascending w.r.t. their completion times and store them in a sequence RP_{st}. Resource providers which did not terminate their subtask are put at the end of the sequence RP_{st} ordered according to the percentage of the subtask they completed.

When at least three resource providers completed their work, we assign $\frac{3c}{10}$ of the total credits, paid by the client for running the subtask on the network, to the first three resource providers in RP_{st}, i.e., the resource providers which "step up on the podium" for returning st result. Moreover, we distribute the remaining $\frac{c}{10}$ credits among the other resource provider in RP_{st} as follows. For each $j \in [4..x]$ we assign to $RP_{st}[j]$ the credits given by the following formula

$$\frac{c \cdot Compl(RP_{st}[j])}{10 \cdot \sum_{k=4}^{x} Compl(RP_{st}[k])},$$

where $Compl(rp)$ is the percentage of the subtask st which was completed by rp.

Tasks assignment aims at finding an assignment for resource provider to tasks which minimize the expected completion time while guaranteeing that:

1. every resource provider is assigned at most a subtask, and
2. every resource provider which is assigned a subtask have the possibility to be among the first three resource providers completing the subtask.

Subtask assignment proceeds in two phases. First an initial assignment of the various subtask to resource is yielded (Algorithm 1). Next, at regular intervals, the systems checks for the overall completion of the project and assigns resource providers that are available to new subtasks (Algorithm 2).

Let st be a subtask and $RP = \{rp_1, \ldots, rp_k\}$ be the set of resource providers assigned to st. The expected completion time of st given RP is denoted as $EC_{st,RP}$ and is computed as follows. Let $\boldsymbol{t}_{\downarrow}$ and $\boldsymbol{t}_{\uparrow}$ be two vectors reporting, respectively, the minimum and maximum completion times of the resource providers in RP in increasing order. Let t' denote the value $\boldsymbol{t}_{\downarrow}[\mathbf{2}]$ and t'' denote the value $\boldsymbol{t}_{\uparrow}[\mathbf{2}]$. Let $vect = [t_0 = t', \ldots, t_k = t'']$ be a vector containing all the values in $\boldsymbol{t}_{\downarrow}$ and $\boldsymbol{t}_{\uparrow}$ which lie in the interval $[t', t'']$. Hence, denoting with $F^3(x)$ the probability that at least three resource providers complete their job before time limit x, we have that:

$$\begin{aligned} EC_{st,RP} = \textstyle\int_0^{\infty}(1 - F^3(x))dx = t' + \int_{t'}^{t''}(1 - F^3(x))dx = \\ t' + \textstyle\sum_{i=0}^{k-1} \int_{t_i}^{t_{i+1}}(1 - F_i^3(x))dx = \\ t' + \textstyle\sum_{i=0}^{k-1} FF_i^3(t_i, t_{i+1}), \end{aligned}$$

where $F_i^3(x)$ is the probability that at least three resource providers complete their work before x time limit given that $t_i \leq x \leq t_{i+1}$ and $FF_i^3(t_i, t_{i+1})$ is equal to $\int_{t_i}^{t_{i+1}}(1 - F_i^3(x))dx$. It is easy to see that $FF_i^3(t_i, t_{i+1})$ can be easy derived form the minum and maximum completion times associated to every resource providers by the function λ_c.

Example 1. Consider the case that a set of four resource providers $RP = \{rp_1, \ldots, rp_4\}$ was assigned to st where $\lambda_c(rp_1) = \langle 1, 5\rangle, \lambda_c(rp_2) = \langle 2, 7\rangle, \lambda_c(rp_3) = \langle 6, 7\rangle$ and

$\lambda_c(rp_4) = \langle 4, 8 \rangle$. In this case, $t' = 4$ and $t'' = 7$ and

$$\begin{gathered}
EC_{st,RP} = \\
4 + \int_4^5 (1 - F_0^3(x))dx + \int_5^6 (1 - F_1^3(x))dx + \int_6^7 (1 - F_2^3(x))dx = \\
4 + \int_4^5 (1 - \tfrac{x-1}{5-1} \tfrac{x-2}{7-2} \tfrac{x-4}{8-4})dx + \int_5^6 (1 - \tfrac{x-2}{7-2} \tfrac{x-4}{8-4})dx + \\
\int_6^7 \left(1 - \left(\tfrac{x-2}{7-2} \tfrac{x-6}{7-6} + \tfrac{x-2}{7-2} \left(1 - \tfrac{x-6}{7-6}\right) \tfrac{x-4}{8-4} + \left(1 - \tfrac{x-2}{7-2}\right) \tfrac{x-6}{7-6} \tfrac{x-4}{8-4}\right)\right) dx = \\
4 + \int_4^5 (1 - \tfrac{x-1}{4} \tfrac{x-2}{5} \tfrac{x-4}{4})dx + \int_5^6 (1 - \tfrac{x-2}{5} \tfrac{x-4}{4})dx + \\
\int_6^7 (1 - (\tfrac{x-2}{5} \tfrac{x-6}{1} + \tfrac{x-2}{5} (1 - \tfrac{x-6}{1}) \tfrac{x-4}{4} + (1 - \tfrac{x-2}{5}) \tfrac{x-6}{1} \tfrac{x-4}{4})) dx = \\
4 + \left[\tfrac{11x}{10} - \tfrac{7x^2}{80} + \tfrac{7x^3}{240} - \tfrac{x^4}{320}\right]_4^5 + \left[\tfrac{3x}{5} + \tfrac{3x^2}{20} - \tfrac{x^3}{60}\right]_5^6 \\
+ \left[\tfrac{1}{10}(-126x + 44x^2 - \tfrac{17x^3}{3} + \tfrac{x^4}{4})\right]_6^7 = \\
4 + \tfrac{901}{960} + \tfrac{11}{15} + \tfrac{31}{120} \approx 5.93
\end{gathered}$$

The initial subtask assignment is computed by running Algorithm 1. It works in two phases. First an initial assignment of resource providers to tasks is yielded by assigning a resource provider at a time to the subtask which minimize the maximum expected completion time of all the tasks, considering resource providers in ascending order of their expected completion time (lines 2-8). Next the initial assignment is revised by swapping pairs of resource providers between tasks. The algorithm iteratively selects a pair of assignments $\langle st', rp' \rangle, \langle st'', rp'' \rangle$ which once swapped provide the greatest decrease of the maximum expected completion time (lines 9-12). Finally, the subtask assignment is returned.

Algorithm 1 Initial Assignment

Input: Resource provider sequence $\mathcal{RP}$ of size n
Input: Subtask sequence $\mathcal{ST}$ of size $k < \frac{n}{3}$
Output: Tasks assignment $\mathcal{SA}$
1: $\mathcal{SA} = \emptyset$
2: $\mathcal{RP} =$ *orderOnExpCompl*($\mathcal{RP}$)
3: **for** $i = 1$ to n **do**
4: $\quad st =$ *selectBestFreeST*($\mathcal{ST}, \mathcal{SA}, \mathcal{RP}[i]$)
5: $\quad$ **if** $st \neq$ `null` **then**
6: $\quad\quad \mathcal{SA} = \mathcal{SA} \cup \langle st, \mathcal{RP}[i] \rangle$
7: $\quad$ **end if**
8: **end for**
9: **repeat**
10: $\quad (\langle st', rp' \rangle, \langle st'', rp'' \rangle) =$ *selectBestCandidatePair*($\mathcal{SA}$)
11: $\quad \mathcal{SA} = \mathcal{SA} - \{\langle st', rp' \rangle, \langle st'', rp'' \rangle\} \cup \{\langle st', rp'' \rangle, \langle st'', rp' \rangle\}$
12: **until** *existsACandidatePair*($\mathcal{SA}$)
13: **return** $\mathcal{SA}$

Function *orderOnExpCompl* takes as input a sequence of resource providers $\mathcal{RP}$ and returns $\mathcal{RP}$ ordered ascending w.r.t. the expected resource provider completion time. Function *selectBestFreeST* returns, given a resource provider rp and a subtask assignemnt $\mathcal{SA}$, the subtask $st \in ST$ such that $MaxECP(\mathcal{SA} \cup \{\langle st, rp\rangle\})$ is the minimum, i.e., $st = \arg\min_{st \in \mathcal{ST}}(MaxECP(\mathcal{SA} \cup \{\langle st, rp\rangle\}))$, such that $MaxECP(\mathcal{SA} \cup \{\langle st, rp\rangle\}) < MaxECP(\mathcal{SA})$, `null` otherwise. Since in the initial step of the algorithm it may happen that there is some subtask st in $\mathcal{ST}$ such that $|\mathcal{SA}(st)| = x < 3$, for each subtask st satisfying this constraint, when computing $MaxECT$ function *selectBestFreeST* assumes that $3 - x$ fake resource providers have been assigned to st, where the minimum and maximum completion times of these fake resource providers are $max - 1$ and max, respectively, where max is a constant value (much) greater than the maximum completion time of every the resource provider in $\mathcal{RP}$.

Function *selectBestCandidatePair* returns a pair of assignments $\langle st, rp\rangle$ and $\langle st', rp'\rangle$ in $\mathcal{SA}$ such that there not exist assignment $\langle st'', rp''\rangle$ and $\langle st^*, rp^*\rangle$ in $\mathcal{SA}$ such that $MaxECP(\mathcal{SA} - \{\langle st, rp\rangle, \langle st', rp'\rangle\} \cup \{\langle st, rp'\rangle, \langle st', rp\rangle\}) > MaxECP(\mathcal{SA} - \{\langle st'', rp''\rangle, \langle st^*, rp^*\rangle\} \cup \{\langle st'', rp^*\rangle, \langle st^*, rp''\rangle\})$. Function *existsACandidatePair* returns true if there is a pair of assignments $\langle st, rp\rangle$ and $\langle st', rp'\rangle$ in $\mathcal{SA}$ such that $MaxECP(\mathcal{SA} - \{\langle st, rp\rangle, \langle st', rp'\rangle\} \cup \{\langle st, rp'\rangle, \langle st', rp\rangle\}) < MaxECP(\mathcal{SA})$. Moreover, both functions *selectBestCandidatePair* and *existsACandidatePair* consider only pairs of assignments $\langle st, rp\rangle$ and $\langle st', rp'\rangle$ in $\mathcal{SA}$ such that swapping rp and rp' guarantees that the probability that rp (resp. rp') is among the first three resource providers assigned to st' (resp. st) that complete st is greater than zero.

Our central server runs Algorithm 2 at fixed intervals, in order to check for the overall completion of the project and assigns resource providers, that have completed the assigned tasks, to further tasks whose results are not yet available. Before running this algorithm the system updates the statistics of resource providers which are assigned to a subtask yielding up to date values for the minimum and maximum completion times. Essentially Algorithm 2 first orders the available resource providers ascending w.r.t. their expected completion times and next iteratively assigns each resource provider rp to the subtask st selected by invoking function *selectBest*. Function *selectBest* returns, given a resource provider rp and a subtask assignemnt $\mathcal{SA}$, the subtask $st \in ST$ such that $MaxECP(\mathcal{SA} \cup \langle st, rp\rangle)$ is the minimum, i.e., $st = \arg\min_{st \in \mathcal{ST}}(MaxECP(\mathcal{SA} \cup \langle st, rp\rangle))$, and is such that $MaxECP(\mathcal{SA} \cup \{\langle st, rp\rangle\}) < MaxECP(\mathcal{SA})$, `null` otherwise.

4 Conclusion and Future Work

In this paper, we proposed a hybrid peer to peer architecture for computational resource sharing. By our network users can provide their unexploited computational resource to those users who run computational demanding tasks and they are rewarded for their collaboration. In order to guarantee the efficiency and effectiveness of the computation process, we design a task partitioning and assignment algorithm that reduce the execution times while allowing satisfactory revenues for resource providers.

Acknowledgment

The authors thank the Calabria region that fully funded the project development and the EU commission that awarded our project with a seal of excellence.

Algorithm 2 Incremental Assignment

Input: Available resource providers sequence $\mathcal{RP}$ of size n
Input: Subtask sequence $\mathcal{ST}$
Input: Initial Subtasks assignment $\mathcal{SA}$
Input: Subtasks and Resource Providers constraints STC
Output: Revised Subtasks assignment $\mathcal{SA}$
$\mathcal{RP}$ = *orderOnExpCompl*($\mathcal{RP}$)
for $i = 1$ to n **do**
  st = *selectBest*($\mathcal{ST}, \mathcal{SA}, \mathcal{RP}[i]$)
  if $st \neq$ `null` **then**
    $\mathcal{SA} = \mathcal{SA} \cup \langle st, \mathcal{RP}[i] \rangle$
  end if
end for
return $\mathcal{SA}$

References

1. D. Agrawal et al. Challenges and opportunities with big data. A community white paper developed by leading researchers across the United States. 2012.
2. V. R. Borkar, M. J. Carey, and C. Li. Inside "Big Data Management": Ogres, Onions, or Parfaits? In *International Conference on Extending Database Technology*, pages 3–14, 2012.
3. A. Brew, D. Greene, and P. Cunningham. Using crowdsourcing and active learning to track sentiment in online media. In *Proceedings of the 2010 Conference on ECAI 2010: 19th European Conference on Artificial Intelligence*, pages 145–150, 2010.
4. T. Economist. Data, data everywhere. *The Economist*, Feb 2010.
5. J. Howe. *Crowdsourcing: Why the Power of the Crowd Is Driving the Future of Business*. Crown Publishing Group, New York, NY, USA, 1 edition, 2008.
6. X. Liu, M. Lu, B. C. Ooi, Y. Shen, S. Wu, and M. Zhang. Cdas: A crowdsourcing data analytics system. *Proc. VLDB Endow.*, 5(10):1040–1051, June 2012.
7. S. Nakamoto. Bitcoin: A peer-to-peer electronic cash system. *Freely available on the web*, 2008.
8. Nature. Big data. *Nature*, Sept. 2008.
9. B. Yang and H. Garcia-Molina. Comparing hybrid peer-to-peer systems. In *Proceedings of the 27th International Conference on Very Large Data Bases*, VLDB '01, pages 561–570, San Francisco, CA, USA, 2001. Morgan Kaufmann Publishers Inc.
10. M. Yang and Y. Yang. An efficient hybrid peer-to-peer system for distributed data sharing. *IEEE Transaction on Computer*, 59(9):1158–1171, 2010.

eMiRo: an ontology-based system for clinical data integration and analysis
Discussion Paper

Pietro Cinaglia, Pierangelo Veltri, and Mario Cannataro

Department of Medical and Surgical Science, University of Catanzaro
{surname}@unicz.it

Abstract. Biological experiments and bioinformatics analysis are producing large datasets of omics data (e.g. genomics, proteomics, interactomics, etc.), stored in diversified sources and databases. Biological data and bioinformatics results can be related to various information, such as clinical data (e.g. cancer stage) or environment data (e.g. place where a patient lives), but this requires novel data integration mechanisms and analysis algorithms. Novel data structures are needed for data integration, while efficient algorithms are necessary for managing integrated data and to analyze results in order to extract knowledge and underline correlation with environmental factors. In this paper an ontology-based system for clinical data integration and analysis is presented. The system, called eMiRo (Electronic MedIcal RecOrd), includes geo-reference features for epidemiological analysis based on geographical and clinical information. Using eMiRo, a physician is able to handle and integrate biological data; moreover, the system supports the retrieval of additional information such as ontology terms and information about genes and diseases. When conducting a study, for each gene relevant to the study, biological function and relations with other genes as well as involvement in biological processes is reported.

1 Introduction

The growth of biological resources and information led to the storage of large data, such as: physiological processes, gene patterns, disease-gene associations, clinical trials; in this context it is necessary the development of bioinformatics tools for data management in order to index heterogeneous resources in common structures and to provide a comprehensive view of the state of knowledge. In recent years, many bioinformatics studies have been focused on gene role in biological processes for preventing and treating diseases. Tools for heterogeneous data integration and association are developed to improve knowledge in experiments related to gene samples from Microarray and Next Generation Sequencing (NGS) technologies. In this scenario it is necessary to develop algorithms able to merge data from multiple sources, with heterogeneous models and formats, to obtain a global information which satisfies the requirements formulated by users (e.g. researchers). The literature presents various solutions to improve and to automatize gene data analysis, for example [1] presents a R-based tool for miRNA data analysis and correlation with clinical ontologies related to a study about modeling and management of biological data. Ontologies are used in computer science for knowledge management; its structure is based on information related to each other by Terms (e.g. concepts, processes, and methods). In biology, Gene Ontology (GO) [2] is used by many algorithms and web systems to retrieve biological information such as: molecular functions, biological processes, and subcellular localizations in drug discovery. Analogously, Disease Ontology (DO) [3] correlates human diseases through the cross-mapping of medical vocabularies (e.g. MeSH, ICD, NCI Thesaurus, SNOMED and OMIM); furthermore, it allows the examination and comparison of genetic variations, phenotypes, proteins, and drugs. In genomics, the data heterogeneity is highly grown in conjunction with the new experimental platforms (e.g. microarray experiments) and consequently data size, type and structure is greatly diversified. Data-integration techniques are crucial to obtain an interdisciplinary view which allows, for example, a biologist to retrieve information of interest from large and heterogeneous dataset [4]. Some applications are able to manage several resources (e.g. physiology, pharmacology, clinical data) using ontologies [5] [6] or correlating concepts with information through integration process based on semantic-analysis [7] [8]. In OAHG [9] a correlation among human protein-coding genes (PCGs), miRNAs, and lncRNAs is established in order to generate a comprehensive functional annotation resources; for this purpose, it uses multi-level ontologies, such as: Gene Ontology, Disease Ontology, and Human Phenotype Ontology (HPO) [10]. The semantics analysis of biomedical data is often necessary to integrate the information from sources that use different schemes as in ontology databases, for example: SNOMED CT (Clinical Terms), ICD-9 and ICD-10 (International Classification of Disease), and Human Phenotype Ontology (HPO) [10]. In recent years the interest of Geographic Information System (GIS) technologies are growing in biomedical studies in order to solve health issues, such as: to evaluate the prevalence of diseases, to plan health interventions for epidemiological studies, to perform a geographical analysis for monitoring of population for prevention purposes. In [11] the biological information are integrated with GIS geographic data for the handling and management of microbial genome data.

In this paper we present a system designed to manage clinical and biological data, and to correlate such data by means of available ontologies. The system, called eMiRo, has been developed to manage clinical and genomic data and integrates them using ontologies and genomic information from external sources. Moreover, eMiRo includes a geographical feature for epidemiological analysis.

2 The eMiRo System

We design a system starting by the following requirements: clinical and biological data management, bioinformatics results from ontologies and semantics data, support for geographical data. The actors identified for the system are listed below:

- Physician: all features are available, it is able to manage data patients (using a model configured by the administrator), performs query to filter the informations, consults the geographical analysis results, and requires data integration features for a specific disease; custom access modes are definable for this profile to create sub-profiles.
- Administrator: refers to the user which is able to handle system and its features, as well as user profiles, component configuration, and data.
- Client: identified with a person or service (e.g. an algorithm) which accessed the data-integration function using the genieR as web-service.

2.1 Architecture

System may be roughly divided into three main components, briefly:

- eMiRo (or 'eMiRo-component', to distinguish this from the entire system called with the same name): it handles the biological data and the interactions with users, as well as data exchanges with other modules (genieR and geoP);
- genieR: it concerns data analysis and data-integration features, also supports retrieving and management of unstructured information from external sources (e.g. ontologies);
- geoP: it is related to geographical features: analysis, and geographic coordinates managing (e.g. it converts raw text into coordinates using the Google Maps API).

Figure 1 shows the interactions among the components; external sources and API calling are also shown.

eMiRo-component is the basic module of the system; it is in charge of the following functions:

- graphical front-end management;
- querying;
- biological data handling;
- database connection and components interaction;
- login, security and user roles management;
- analytics.

User is able to access the system through a Web-Panel which, essentially, consists in a set of Graphical User Interfaces (GUI) that are generated dynamically in according to a predefined model for the information required by user. Geographical data are shown to user using a Map-View (from Google Maps API), and a summary table-view to show only the information of interest for the user (e.g. a physician).

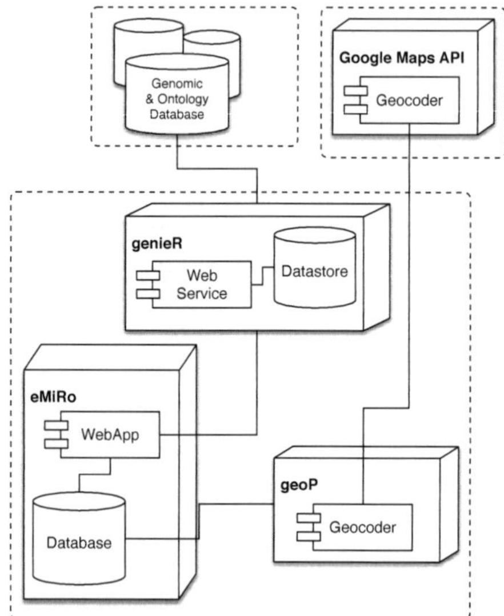

Fig. 1. System deployment

genieR is designed as a web-service to allow external clients (e.g. algorithms or other information systems) to invoke its public functions. This components concerns the data-integration features; specifically it unifies in a custom structure the information given by several external sources. A mapping between Disease Ontology and Gene Ontology is used to integrate annotations in order to obtain the gene-disease associations.

Therefore, it is used for the management and the integration of data from remote genomic and ontology sources. eMiRo supports integration from: Disease Ontology [3], Gene Ontology [2] and DisGenet [12] ("curated gene-disease association" version); others could be added in future updates. The information are structured as objects that structure data using lists and hashmap; this approach allows the management of unstructured data; it is important to emphasize that this component is implemented for deployment on Google App Engine Environment.

genieR main sub-components are:

- GenierServlet: it consists in two modules, dealing respectively to handle requests from clients (even Web-Panel accesses genieR as an external resource) and to structure the output in according to JSON format in order to make faster the data stream and easy the parsing operations.
- Datastore: it periodically retrieves and parse the information from supported external sources and organizes these in a structure compatible with the eMiRo data model.
- DataIntegrator: it is the core module of genieR; it takes care to integrate information in Datastore and to generate an output for the client.

In summary, a physician is able to choose a disease, from a list, to obtain additional information, such as: ontological integration, genes involved for the disease, and meta-data for each gene founded (e.g. description, biological function, biological processes, and relations with other genes). Main commands supported by genieR are 'doget' and 'dolist' ('do': Disease-Object):

- former returns information obtained from data-integration action for a specific Disease Ontology ID (DOID);
- latter gives the list of diseases that system supports for the integration operation.

geoP is able to convert addresses into geographical coordinates using Google Geocoders API; using this approach a geographical coordinates management through GIS systems is allowed. Furthermore, the system supports analytics features to generate statistical information from geographical and biological data mapping (for statistical analysis are supported a set of parameter, such as: range of values, and threshold level).

2.2 Implementation details

eMiRo system is designed for dynamic creation of reports referred to biological information management; this solution allows users to create new examination and handling data models for existing ones. Data-Type supported by the Database Engine are available during models creation.

A 'model' is composed by a set of information related to a graphic layout and its low-level parameters (e.g. field-name, field-data-type, bounds for graphic elements, and the order of the fields in the resulting GUI), furthermore the persistence of models is granted by a Relational Database Management System (RDBMS). In according to this dynamic solution the Figure 2 shows the data structure for a generic examination (named 'Report-1') which consists of three fields ('date' is a default field whose representation is not required); Figure 2-A and 2-D are referred to a specific examination for a given patient; while, 2-B and 2-C contain information related to the model for GUI generation: fields, data-type, and generic meta-data (e.g. field-order, and field-width in pixel). To implement the system are chosen multiple programming languages related to the purpose for each component; this approach optimizes the deployments and the user experience. genieR and geoP are implemented using Servlet technology to deploy Web-Applications [13] and to expose their features as a service (in according with server policy configuration), for genieR the Google Cloud App Engine SDK is also integrated. eMiRo-component has been developed using the PHP and HTML5 languages, the latter extended using Bootstrap and jQuery frameworks in order to support graphical interface with dynamic elements and a responsive design based on CSS and JavaScript. Oracle MySQL has been chosen as RDBMS for biological and geographic data persistence; in addition, it contains information about the structures and the models used by system during GUI generation.

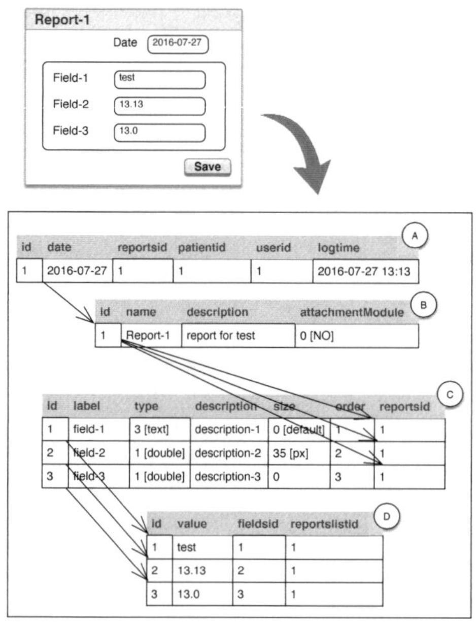

Fig. 2. Data model (low level representation)

2.3 Data-Integration: approach

During the test, the eMiRo data-integration component (named genieR) has been used to retrieve the Open Biological Ontologies datasets from the server of Gene-Ontology, Disease-Ontology, and Disgenet. OBO Foundry initiative supports the evolution of ontologies for biomedical data integration promoting ontologies designed to be interoperable and logically well-formed in order to incorporate accurate representations of biological information [14]. A dataset in OBO format contains several tags (e.g. id, name, description, synonyms, cross-references) organized in Terms linked to each other; thus, a dataset may be represented using, for example, a graph data structure. genieR pipeline is based on two phases: preprocessing and analysis. During Preprocessing the data are integrated and organized in a single structure: (i) the ontological datasets are downloaded on cloud-memory (the data can be refreshed when the sources update their datasets); (ii) subsequently, each dataset is parsed to extract information of interest, and it is collapsed within a single structure with others. Using this approach, genieR is able to create a new large ontology (managed by the Datastore component) that contains the heterogeneous information extracted from each ontological dataset, and the novel relations found among these. Preprocessing reduces the data in the cloud-memory to improve the overall performance during the analysis. For the Analysis phase, genieR implements a component named 'DataIntegrator': when a client requests information about a disease the DataIntegrator performs an analysis of its integrated data (that represents its knowledge), and returns a results in JSON Format. Summing, genieR is able to provide for a specific disease the relevant genes and for each the biological function, and its involvement in biological processes, and the relations with other genes.

3 Security

In eMiRo, the user requests and the access policy are handled by web-application and DBMS Engine [15]; first grants the user access based on his role, second checks the read and write operations by the components, as well as the direct requests to database. The communication between the components (internal and external) is performed through HTTPS protocol which allows server authentication, privacy protection and maintaining data integrity, as well as checks data exchanged between the parts and allows SSL/TLS encryption. Furthermore, account credentials are encrypted using the Secure Hash Algorithm (SHA) before being stored within the database.

4 Conclusion

This paper presents the architecture and the security insights of a cloud-based information system, named eMiRo, for biological data mapping; georeferencing of patients is also supported. A light-beta version is used to handling biological data by infectious diseases group of Magna Graecia University.

References

1. F. Cristiano and et al., "An r-based tool for mirna data analysis and correlation with clinical ontologies," *Proceeding BCB '14 Proceedings of the 5th ACM Conference on Bioinformatics, Computational Biology, and Health Informatics*, 2014.
2. M. Ashburner, C. A. Ball, J. A. Blake, D. Botstein, H. Butler, J. M. Cherry, A. P. Davis, K. Dolinski, S. S. Dwight, J. T. Eppig, M. A. Harris, D. P. Hill, L. Issel-Tarver, A. Kasarskis, S. Lewis, J. C. Matese, J. E. Richardson, M. Ringwald, G. M. Rubin, and G. Sherlock, "Gene ontology: tool for the unification of biology. The Gene Ontology Consortium," *Nat. Genet.*, vol. 25, pp. 25–29, May 2000.
3. DO Official WebSite, *Disease Ontology*, 2016.
4. D. Gomez-Cabrero, I. Abugessaisa, D. Maier, A. Teschendorff, M. Merkenschlager, A. Gisel, E. Ballestar, E. Bongcam-Rudloff, A. Conesa, and J. Tegner, "Data integration in the era of omics: current and future challenges," *BMC Syst Biol*, vol. 8 Suppl 2, p. I1, 2014.
5. S. M. Wimalaratne, P. Grenon, R. Hoehndorf, G. V. Gkoutos, and B. de Bono, "An infrastructure for ontology-based information systems in biomedicine: RICORDO case study," *Bioinformatics*, vol. 28, pp. 448–450, Feb 2012.
6. B. De Bono, R. Hoehndorf, S. Wimalaratne, G. Gkoutos, and P. Grenon, "The RICORDO approach to semantic interoperability for biomedical data and models: strategy, standards and solutions," *BMC Res Notes*, vol. 4, p. 313, 2011.

7. K. M. Livingston, M. Bada, W. A. Baumgartner, and L. E. Hunter, "KaBOB: ontology-based semantic integration of biomedical databases," *BMC Bioinformatics*, vol. 16, p. 126, 2015.
8. C. Pang, A. Sollie, A. Sijtsma, D. Hendriksen, B. Charbon, M. de Haan, T. de Boer, F. Kelpin, J. Jetten, J. K. van der Velde, N. Smidt, R. Sijmons, H. Hillege, and M. A. Swertz, "SORTA: a system for ontology-based re-coding and technical annotation of biomedical phenotype data," *Database (Oxford)*, vol. 2015, 2015.
9. L. Cheng, J. Sun, W. Xu, L. Dong, Y. Hu, and M. Zhou, "Oahg: an integrated resource for annotating human genes with multi-level ontologies," *Sci Rep*, vol. 6, p. 34820, Oct 2016.
10. S. Kohler and at al., "The human phenotype ontology project: linking molecular biology and disease through phenotype data," *Nucl. Acids Res.*, 2014.
11. S. Jelokhani-Niaraki, M. Tahmoorespur, Z. Minuchehr, and M. R. Nassiri, "An Ontology-Based GIS for Genomic Data Management of Rumen Microbes," *Genomics Inform*, vol. 13, pp. 7–14, Mar 2015.
12. J. Pinero, N. Queralt-Rosinach, A. Bravo, J. Deu-Pons, A. Bauer-Mehren, M. Baron, F. Sanz, and L. I. Furlong, "DisGeNET: a discovery platform for the dynamical exploration of human diseases and their genes," *Database (Oxford)*, vol. 2015, 2015.
13. Oracle, *Java Servlet Technology Overview*, 2016.
14. B. Smith, M. Ashburner, C. Rosse, J. Bard, W. Bug, W. Ceusters, L. J. Goldberg, K. Eilbeck, A. Ireland, C. J. Mungall, N. Leontis, P. Rocca-Serra, A. Ruttenberg, S. A. Sansone, R. H. Scheuermann, N. Shah, P. L. Whetzel, and S. Lewis, "The OBO Foundry: coordinated evolution of ontologies to support biomedical data integration," *Nat. Biotechnol.*, vol. 25, pp. 1251–1255, Nov 2007.
15. G. Miklau and D. Suciu, "A formal analysis of information disclosure in data exchange," *J. Comput. Syst. Sci*, 2007.

A WSLA-Extension Supporting Service and Contract Composition Modelling

Antonella Longo[1], Marco Zappatore[1], Mario A. Bochicchio[1], Lucia Vaira[1] and Alfredo Cuzzocrea[2]

[1]Department of Engineering for Innovation, University of Salento, Lecce, Italy
{antonella.longo, marcosalvatore.zappatore, mario.bochicchio, lucia.vaira}@unisalento.it
[2]University of Trieste and ICAR-CNR, Italy
cuzzocrea@icar.cnr.it

Abstract:
When dealing with Cloud Computing Services (CCSs) provisioning and usage, different degrees of complexity can be reached, depending on whether service composition is needed to satisfy users' requests. This scenario demands effective ways for modelling CCSs and corresponding Service Level Agreements (SLAs) in order to facilitate service composition, comparison and monitoring. However, current SLA specifications and tools are not well tailored to service composition. In this paper, starting from WSLA, a widely-known SLA description language, we present an extension aimed at modeling contracts and SLAs suitable to support contract owners during service composition and monitoring phases. The proposed WSLA extension is also supported by a tree-graph based tool that can help during SLA and contract composition phases.

Keywords. SLA Design; SLA Composition; SLA Measurement; Cloud Services.

1 Introduction

Modern Information Technology (IT) environments heavily exploits services according to a provide-and-consume paradigm, allowing users to perform a wide variety of tasks. Service terms have to be rendered as contracts that should be effective and flexible from a strategic point of view as well as workable from an operational perspective. In this scenario, Service Level Agreements (SLAs) [1] play a key-role in describing service relevant features by specifying the agreements between providers and consumers with respect to Quality of Service (QoS), service level guarantees, Service Level Objectives (SLOs), compliance to users' requests, service time-sustainability and so on. Each of these aspects has different levels of complexity. SLAs also define measurements and criteria to be used when services fail or deviate beyond specific tolerability thresholds from the agreed-upon contract terms but such specifications may be qualitative and difficult to be transformed in machine-readable elements. SLAs are: a) flexible and potentially language-independent; b) capable of defining both measurable (e.g., accuracy, availability, latency, cost) and non-measurable aspects (e.g., reputation), therefore can be used for modelling domain information. Normally SLAs refer to single service provisioning and consuming. Cloud Computing Services (CCSs) and Business Process Outsourcing (BPO) represent two typical scenarios where services should be aggregated properly for guaranteeing on-demand access to customizable resources. The available methodologies and frameworks, however, lack in effective formalization of service (and corresponding contracts and SLAs) composition. Therefore, IT managers must a) supervise service functional composition and b) assess precisely Service Levels (SLs) when they design the overall contract for the delivered service. Similarly, consumers usually require rapid service provisioning, reliable resource exploitation, reduced management efforts and frequent interaction with service providers, thus generating a great variety of SLOs that makes more difficult to negotiate and finalize service selection. Moreover, consumers require visibility on SLAs monitoring data and auditing tools. Selected composing contracts and their specifications should allow users to obtain the terms and conditions of the overall contract in a straightforward, non-domain-specific manner; otherwise, these aspects may severely hinder providers' accountability when services do not match with their defined SLs or when services exhibit failures beyond the allowed guarantees after their delivery.

In this research, we present a descriptive template for contract and SLA composition that extends WSLA. WSLA is one the several formal specifications developed so far to model SLAs and their subject of application so far and it has been selected since it is XML-based and sufficiently general to cover different domain scenarios). Its proposed extension overcome its expressivity limitations for service and contract composition scenarios and allows us identifying accountability issues more efficiently in the Cloud scenario. We also propose a tool for easing the design and visualization phases in service contract composition, named Contract-Aware Service COmposer (CASCO), specifically tailored to IT contracts. We validated our model, in a SLA composition scenario, by using the tool to calculate five Key Performance Indicators (KPIs) typically adopted in the CCSs: availability, response time and Mean Time To Response (MTTR), Mean Time Between Failure (MTBF), Mean Time To Failure (MTTF).

The paper is organized as follows. Section 2 analyzes existing works on contract representation and SLA management, Section 3 and 4 present the CASCO tool, its design and implementation. Conclusions are presented in Section 5.

2 Theoretical Background

2.1 SLA for SOAs and WSs

A SLA referring to a specific service should consider: a) description of agreeing parties, QoS and obligations; b) matching with required QoS; c) collected metrics (and when and by whom); d) penalties for failures or unmatched SLs; e) responses to non-deliveries; f) providers' responsibilities; g) effects of technology re-alignments.

SLAs are enforced by management policies, thus ad-hoc frameworks are needed to ensure that applications and services meet the required SLs at deployment, operation, support and maintenance stages [2] and they should be machine-readable, in order to support service discovery, selection and processing with respect to QoS and SLs. This originates numerous language specifications to define SLAs. Some of them adopt a combination of high-level modeling languages and knowledge representation techniques, such as: SLAng [3], where SLAs are defined by mixing natural and object-constraint languages; RBSLA [4], where SLAs are provided as RuleML constructs; PANDA [5], where SLAs are managed by a multi-agent system primarily referred to Enterprise Resource Planning systems (ERPs).

Despite their high-level of expressivity, those approaches are not so suitable for machine processing and for theintegration with Web Services description languages (e.g., WSDL [6]). Thus, XML-based solutions were proposed, such as the Web Service Level Agreement (WSLA) framework [7]. Its main elements are: subjects, services and obligations (which comprise SLOs and action guarantees). Its first prototype was introduced into WSTK [8], an integrated IBM environment for WS design, implementation and management. Although WSLA allows defining, negotiating, deploying, monitoring and enforcing SLAs, it has some limitations: 1) it refers to two-party contracts only; 2) partner responsibilities are described in terms of parameters and metrics, without considering their actions; 3) corrective management actions are not well supported. Subsequently, the WS-Agreement [9] protocol was proposed to facilitate: 1) agreement contextual definition, 2) service attributes definition, 3) customers support (by allowing the XML formalization of service requirements), 4) providers support (by allowing resource monitoring). However, neither third parties' contributions nor service composition monitoring could be modeled. The Cremona architecture [6] by IBM adopted this protocol but neither decision-making capabilities nor support workflow were provided for managing service compositions.

Modeling and monitoring aspects related to service chains and networks in many business ecosystems are usually based on graph models: BPMN [10] and BPEL [11] models represent a viable alternative **Errore. L'origine riferimento non è stata trovata.**for technicians and domain-skilled professionals, but the majority of the stakeholders does not benefit from adequate modeling tools.

Therefore, a standardized model would enable to apply templates to every type of contracts and SLAs, and to categorize contract terms in different services domains. However, despite their usefulness, SLA standardization policies are still in their infancy, thus providing IT professionals with just static or semi-structured information rather than structured contents during the entire service lifecycle [12] (e.g., pre-instantiated, active and terminated SLAs, metrics, service descriptions, guarantees). Moreover, SLA data belong to several domains and the presence of various vocabularies of provisioning terms determines semantic and structural SLA heterogeneity. This hinders the comparison and the efficient SLA manipulation in distributed service markets.

3 The WSLA Model Extension

Contracts for CCSs often result from the composition of underpinning service contracts, thus their specifications refer to those of composing contracts. Starting from them, final providers need to automatically obtain the terms of the overall contract, after defining composition rules. A service-based approach of this problem enables to derive the final contract from service composition rules, and contract specifications from the application of these rules on the parameters of each low-level contract and service. Consequently, services from different providers can be used and composed [13] but service contracts (and SLAs) must be properly defined.

A composed contract is obtained from the integration of other contracts, signed with different providers [14], and its terms and conditions can be derived by applying composition rules to the composing contracts. Similarly, this implies that a provider of a composite contract is able to extract and feed clients with the correct terms from the component contracts. The provider has also to manage responsibilities of underpinning providers if necessary (i.e., service-oriented approach to Contract Management).

In order to model this scenario, we introduce three levels of conceptual abstraction: 1) the *Contracts Layer*, which collects service-provisioning agreements; 2) the *Services Layer*, which gathers the composing services; 3) the *Resources Layer*, which contains IT infrastructure components. The links across levels represent dependencies between contracts and services and between services and resources respectively. The links across the same level represent resources topologically composed to deliver a certain service. Thus, different levels of internal visibility of its composing sub-services are possible for a given service, depending on which kind of details are available about them. For instance, sub-services can be described by using their external parameters only (e.g., availability, response time, MTTF, etc.) or by exposing their internal details, thus enabling more precise monitoring. We decided to consider the Services Layer and the Resources Layer as a unique layer at this stage of our research, in order to strictly focus on highlighting the issues arising in service and SLA aggregation. In this way, we just consider contracts in terms of basic composing elements, thus forwarding the subsequent step of service-to-resource mapping to further research developments.

The aspects described so far cannot be fully described by current SLA models and frameworks, therefore we propose a WSLA extension that introduces SL management aspects, according to [15]. Our template presents contracts as composed by three sections: 1) the Agreement Info, which handles general contract information (e.g., name, description, start and expiry date); 2) the *Agreement Parties*, which models contracting parties and *third parties* (i.e., entities providing goods or services in underpinning contracts that have to support service delivery to final customers); 3) the *Agreement Services*, which manages services information for one or more services. Each service exposes specific properties: a description, a guarantee calendar and its SLA, which is the core element of this component as well as of the entire template. In turn, each SLA exhibits specific features, such as reference period, description, report date and SLA specification. SLAs specifications usually refer to multiple parameters; therefore, we decided to include the following properties:

- Cost (established for a SL with specific parameters);
- Start/End Date;
- Sample Period (used during SL monitoring to make decisions about service times and to improve quality);
- Service Level Objective (SLO): the SL threshold value;

- Working Window: time span for SL generation;
- Penalty: the set of algorithms used when providers fail to meet the agreed SLs;
- Service Level Indicator (SLI): it includes units of measure and algorithms for SLA calculation and service monitoring.

The contract template described so far can be modeled as a directed tree graph (i.e., digraph) where nodes represents template components whilst oriented edges are the available properties. Edges are labeled with corresponding cardinalities (i.e. how many nodes having those properties can be repeated). This approach allows representing data about a single contract, even if with a great level of detail. Therefore, composition topologies and rules have been introduced as additional elements to WSLA, for describing SLA and contract composition. Topologies offer an intuitive way of creating service chains matching users' requests. We adopted four compositional patterns: series (each service starts once the previous one stops), parallel (services work simultaneously), loop (several cycles are needed to complete a service), condition (service execution is oriented by an initial choice) [16]. Topologies can be further composed to create complex systems (in a way similar to circuit elements are cascaded in circuit theory) and the final service is obtained by recursively choosing the available topology patterns.

Fig. 1A depicts the contract template while Fig. 1B and 1C show the composition and rule model, respectively. Listing 1 enlists the formal definitions for all the entities mentioned so far, obtained through sets language.

Definitions
$Agreement := \{AgreementParties_1, AgreementInfo_1, AgreementServices_i\},\quad with\ i \in [1,n]$
$AgreementParties := \left\{Contractor_1, CustomerM_1, \{CustomerS_i\}, \{3rdParty_j\}\right\},\quad with\ i \in [0,n], j \in [0,m]$
$AgreementServices := \{\{Service_i\}\},\quad with\ i \in [0,n]$
$Service := \{\{SLA_i\}, GuaranteeCalendar_1, ServiceInfo_1\},\quad with\ i \in [0,n]$
$GuaranteeCalendar := \{\{IntervalDayYear_i\}\},\ with\ i \in [1,n]$
$SLA := \{\{SLASpecification_i\}\},\ with\ i \in [1,n]$
$SLASpecification := \{\{Penalty_i\}, SLI_1, SLASpecificationInfo_1, WorkingWindow_1\},\quad with\ i \in [0,n]$
$WorkingWindow := \left\{\{IntervalDayWeek_i\}, \{IntervalHour_j\}\right\},\quad with\ i \in [1,n], j \in [1,m]$
$Penalty := \{\{Event_i\}\},\ with\ i \in [0,n]$
$Event := \{Algorithm_1\}$
$Composition := \{\{Service_i\}\},\ with\ i \in [1,n]$
$Service := \{\{Composition\}\},\ with\ i \in [0,1]$
$OutputService := \{\{Composition_i\}\},\ with\ i \in [0,1]$
$ServiceCompositionTopology := \{\{SLACompositionRule_i\}\},\quad with\ i \in [1,n]$
$SLA := \{\{SLACompositionRule_i\}\},\quad with\ i \in [0,n]$
$SLACompositionRule := \left\{\{Series_i\}, \{Parallel_j\}, \{Condition_k\}, \{Loop_l\}\right\}, with\ i,j,k,l \in [0,1] : i+j+k+l = 1$

Listing 1. Contract template (formal definition)

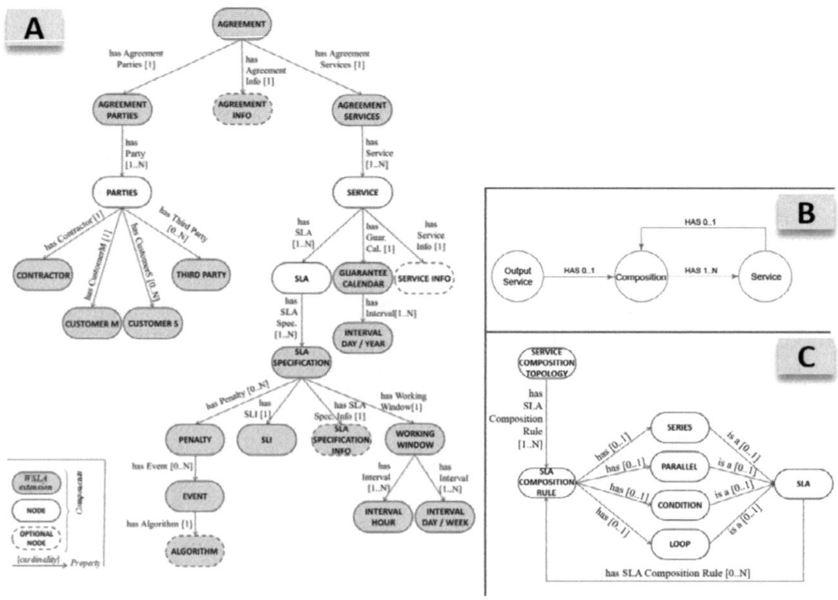

Fig. 1. Contract template as a digraph (A); composition topology (B) and rule (C) models.

4 Tool Description

The main goal of CASCO is to test the model proposed in Section 3 and to help customers and providers in composing SLAs both in design and execution phases. During the design phase, composition can be simulated to verify the compliance with requested SLs, as well as to obtain the SLAs of composed services starting from elemental ones. During the execution phase, the system comes in handy since it offers an engine that is able to calculate the result of composite SLAs. The tool has been designed starting from identifying stakeholders for a generic service providing/consuming firm: both managers (general, technical and business, department, human resources, service and contract) and administration personnel have been considered. Different tasks have been identified during the subsequent goals elicitation. For instance, a service manager can use the tool to: 1) insert contracts signed with other companies to buy primary services; 2) access and visualize the service catalogue; 3) insert new primary services; 4) create a new service by composing services from the catalogue; 5) create new contracts to be signed with other companies or final users. The tool exploits a 3-layer architecture (Fig. 4) to clearly separate data management, business logic and user interface components. Moreover, the application complies with the widely adopted Model-View-Controller (MVC) pattern. In order to separate contract visualization issues from user-agent interaction during composition, the tool splits the front end (Presentation module) and the back end (Business Logic and Data Management module) by using XML files describing agreements, topologies and rules. The Presentation module manages user operations and parses input, in order to generate the XML files (Fig. 3). The *Manager* module is further divided into four subsections. The *Parser* allows extracting and manipulating data from XML files to store them in the graph database (DB). The *Agreement Manager* handles contracts and the operations that have to be performed on them. The *SLA Compositor* creates composed services, defines corresponding measurement metrics and stores output services into the DB. The *SLA Control* allows accessing services information and parameters for resources and services monitoring.

From an implementation point of view, the digraph model has been defined into a NoSQL graph DBMS (Neo4j v.1.9.6/v.2.0.0 [17]), in order to store SLA and contracts information as well as composition topologies and rules. The tool has been developed in PHP with HTML5 compliancy for the front end in order to be natively compatible with mobile devices, and in Java for the back end. We used Spring-data-neo4j (v2.3.4) [18], a framework for mapping classes with the elements stored in Neo4j, and Neo4jPHP (v.0.1.0) [19], a PHP library for accessing Neo4j database. The tool has been used to evaluate and assess SLAs during the design phase of service composition.

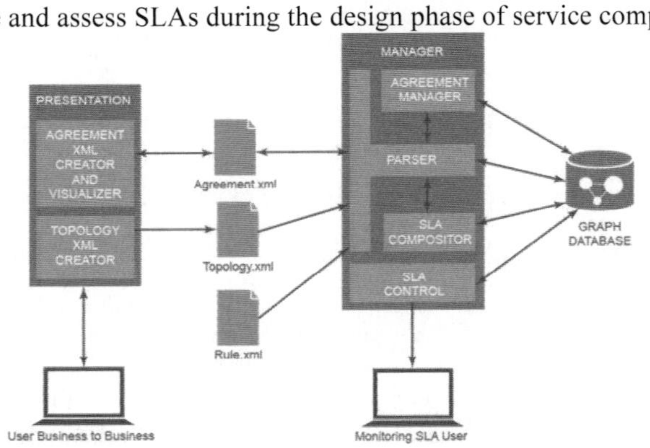

Fig. 2. The CASCO tool architecture in the large

5 Applying The Model To A Real Scenario

5.1 SLA Metrics

Given a specific topology, services are composed and SL specifications are calculated accordingly. To decide the acquisition of a service as part of a final one, a manager needs to know which constraints the final service undergoes. Indeed, this is necessary in order to evaluate the feasibility, the sustainability, the compatibility of the composite service against the requirements. SLA values are calculated with respect to metrics capable of measuring whether a service is compliant with the contract terms and whether the service can achieve the desired business objectives. If we consider a service composition scenario, in order to perform a suitable SLA composition, metrics must be the same and their measurement units must be commensurable and compatible (e.g., all measures have to be time-related or all measures must be percentages, etc.). We considered five metrics exhibiting a great relevance in cloud scenarios to demonstrate the feasibility of the proposed model by using our ad-hoc developed tool. The selected metrics are: Availability, Response Time, Mean Time To Failure (MTTF), Mean Time Between Failures (MTBF), Mean Time To Repair (MTTR).

Fig. 3 introduces some relevant quantities used in calculating the adopted metrics. We refer to *Service Downtime (TSD),* as the time period during which a specific service is not available (i.e., it is the time span between the *i-th* occurrence of a service failure, $t_{d,i}$ and the *i-th* occurrence of its reactivation, $t_{u,i}$). Similarly, *Service Uptime (TSU)*, is the time interval during which a specific service is working (i.e., the time range between the *i-th* occurrence of the service start, $t_{u,i}$, and the *i+1-th* occurrence of its failure $t_{d,i+1}$). The period between two failures (Time Between Failures, *TBF*) is the sum of the time needed to have the service up again (Time To Repair, *TTR*) and the time elapsed before another failure occurs (Time To Failure, *TTF*), that is: *TBF* = *TTR*+*TTF*.

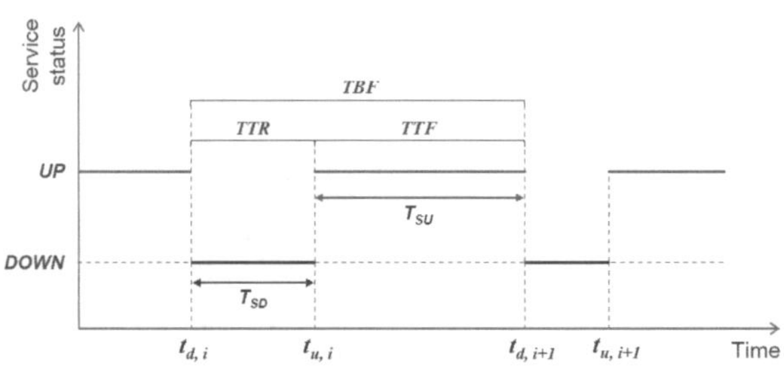

Fig. 3. Significant temporal quantities in service status

Availability: it describes how long a service S_A is available within its temporal window of analysis. Being *TAW* the duration of this temporal window and *TSD* the service downtime period, the availability *A* is expressed as in (1):

$$A(S_A) = (T_{TW} - T_{SD})/T_{TW} \qquad (1)$$

Response Time: it quantifies how long it takes to a service S_A to answer client's interrogation. If we have N interrogations from client, each with its own response time $rt^{S_A}(t)_i$, the overall response time *RT* is the average of the distinct responses *rt*, as in (2):

$$RT(S_A) = \left(\sum_{i=i}^{N} rt^{S_A}(t)_i\right)/N \qquad (2)$$

MTTF: it measures the mean time between two consecutive failures for the same service S_A. If we have N monitored events (i.e., service failures and restorations), $t^{S_A}{}_{u,i}$ indicates the time from which the service is up for the *i-th* time and $t^{S_A}{}_{d,i+1}$ is the time at which the same service fails again, then *MTTF (3)* is:

$$MTTF(S_A) = \left(\sum_{i=1}^{N-1}\left(t^{S_A}{}_{d,i+1} - t^{S_A}{}_{u,i}\right)\right)/N \qquad (3)$$

MTTR: it measures the mean time needed to repair a specific service S_A for N times. Let be $t^{S_A}{}_{d,i}$ the time from which the service is down and $t^{S_A}{}_{u,i}$ the time from which the same service is up again, *MTTR* is given by (4):

$$MTTR(S_A) = \left(\sum_{i=1}^{N-1}\left(t^{S_A}{}_{u,i} - t^{S_A}{}_{d,i}\right)\right)/N \qquad (4)$$

MTBF: it measures the mean time occurred between two consecutive failures of the same service. It can be considered as the sum between (4) and (3), as depicted in (5):

$$MTBF(S_A) = MTTR(S_A) + MTTF(S_A) \qquad (5)$$

5.2 Composition Rules

New services resulting from a process of composition [20] exhibit different metrics, according to the composition rules and topologies selected during the design phase. In order to define such rules, let us refer to series and parallel topologies and let us consider two different services S_A and S_B that have to be composed and whose metrics are known before the composition is performed. By applying math relationships borrowed from circuits theory, the indicators specified in (1)-(5) can be derived for parallel and series topologies, as in parallel and series configurations of circuital elements, thus providing us with the corresponding composition rules. Table I resumes the rules for Availability, Response Time and *MTTF* metrics. For the sake of brevity, their mathematical derivation is not reported in this paper.

TABLE I. COMPOSITION RULES FOR THREE METRICS (SERIES, PARALLEL)

Metric	Series Topology	Parallel Topology
Availability	$A_S = A(S_A) \times A(S_B)$	$A_{//} = 1 - [(1 - (A(S_A)) \times (1 - A(S_B))]$
Response Time	$RT_S = RT(S_A) + RT(S_B)$	$RT_{//} = max\{RT_A, RT_B\}$
MTTF	$MTTF_S = 1/((MTTF(S_A)+MTTF(S_B))$	$MTTF_{//} = MTTF(S_A)+MTTF(S_B) - MTTF_S$

5.3 Validation

Complex modeling approaches typically require a multi-year effort to be validated. Both design- and run-time validation activities against functional and non-functional requirements are required. During validation, specific aspects should be checked, such as the suitability of the model to describe properly a significant variety of SLAs, its amenability to be integrated within information systems, its capability to handle managed resources. Therefore, we started with an internal validation. A set of agreements having as metrics the ones described in Section 5.1 has been simulated. Then, the composition rules described in Section 5.2 have been loaded into the tool (within the corresponding XML file, see Section 4). Specific tests have been executed to both evaluate the template feasibility for modeling SLA aspects and the tool usability for IT managers and contract owners. Therefore, 20 Italian users, aging from 30 to 50 y.o. and belonging to technical and juridical areas, have been selected as testers. The candidates have been assigned with three tasks deemed as representative of a concrete deployment scenario for the application. *Task 1)* to retrieve a service purchased by a company. *Task 2)* to register an agreement and to compose a new output service. *Task 3)* to evaluate the application completeness and user-friendliness.

The users were required to fill a questionnaire in order to assess their mood against the proposed system and the features it exposes. A 10-point psychometric Likert scale has been used to measure users' responses in evaluating each task, according to the easiness in retrieving information, navigational and message clarity, ranging from 1 (i.e., worst evaluation) to 10 (i.e., best evaluation). Table II enlists average scores (*AS*) for the features evaluated when performing a specific task and mean execution times (*MET*) for each task (means are computed across all users). At the end of the questionnaire, users' comments were collected, thus observing their concerns was only about explanatory labels and the localization of the application (which actually is in English to better match references about service contracts and service composition) and do not refer to possible issues in contract and SLA modeling or missing modeling functions.

TABLE II. OVERALL SCORES AND EXECUTION TIMES FROM VOTERS' POOL

Evaluated Feature	AS[1]	Task	MET[2]
Easiness in retrieving information	6.45 / 10	1	42.3[s]
Clarity of navigation and messages	6.8 / 10		
Clarity of agreement registration requests	8.5 / 10	2	183[s]
Easiness of composite service creation	6 / 10		
Clarity of content presentation	9.25 / 10	3	352[s]
Clarity of graphical representation	9,35 / 10		

[1] *AS: Average Score (per feature)* – [2] *MET: Mean Execution Time (per task)*

6 Conclusions

A model for managing SLA information when dealing with contracts and SLA composition in service-based IT environments has been presented in this paper. An extension of the widely known, XML-based WSLA framework [7] has been proposed in order to obtain a flexible template for IT service contracts. We aim at overcoming two main issues in managing SLAs: 1) tackling the lack in standard models representing service contracts and their SLAs in service network environments; 2) making SLAs more machine-readable. The former one is obtained by complementing WSLA with composition topologies and rules, extremely useful when dealing with CCSs (typically provided as compositions of multiple, third-party services). The latter one is achieved by modeling our template as a digraph (implemented in a NoSQL graph DBMS). According to the proposed model, we developed a specific tool named CASCO (Contract-Aware Service COmposer) in order to offer SLA evaluation and assessment capabilities to IT professionals during design phase. Five metrics (i.e., *Availability*, *RT*, *MTTR*, *MTTF*, *MTBF*), typically used in CCSs were selected to evaluate the template feasibility in our tool. We have ascertained that the WSLA extension is suitable to handle all the information needed to describe contracts and SLAs for composed services.

In the near future, this research will be widened and improved by: 1) extending the template (SLAs for BPO contracts); 2) proposing an ontological formalization of the template; 3) adopting rule-based policies to perform real-time monitoring of composed services as in Complex Event Processing (CEP) scenarios.

Acknowledgement

The research has been partially supported by Engineering SpA and Essentia SpA.

References

1. Telemanagement (TM) Forum: SLA Handbook Solution Suite v2.0. (2008)
2. Allen, P.: Service Orientation-Winning Strategies and Best Practices. Cambridge Univ. Press, 2006
3. Paschke, A.: Knowledge Representation Concepts for Automated SLA Management. Decision Support Systems 46(1), 187-205 (2008)
4. Boley, H., Tabet, S., Wagner, G.: Design Rationale of RuleML: A Markup Language for Semantic Web Rules. In : First Semantic Web Working Symposiium (SWWS-2001), pp.381-401 (2001)
5. IST: PANDA: Collaborative Process Automation Support Using Service Level Agreements and Intelligent Dynamic Agents in SME Clusters. PANDA Research Project Report (2007)
6. Ludwig, H., Dan, A., Kearney, R., Heights, Y.: Cremona: an Architecture and Library for Creation and Monitoring of WS Agreements. Research Report, IBM (2004)
7. Keller, A., Ludwig, H.: The WSLA Framework: Specifying and Monitoring Service Level Agreements. Technical Paper RC22456, IBM Research (2002)
8. IBM Corp.: IBM Web Services Toolkit (WSTK) v2006. Available at: http://www.ibm.com
9. Andrieux, A.: Web Services Agreement Specification. Memo GFD-R-P.107, WG (2007)
10. Dijkman, R. M., Dumas, M., Ouyang, C.: Semantics and Analysis of Business Process Models in BPMN. Information and Software Technology 50(12), 1281-1294 (2008)
11. Xiang, F., Tevfik, B., Jianwen, S.: Analysis of Interacting BPEL Web Services. In : 13th Int. Conf. on World Wide Web (WWW'04), pp.621-630 (2004)
12. Stamou, K., Kantere, V., Morin, J. H.: SLA Data Management Criteria. In : IEEE Big Data (2013)
13. Piccinelli, G.: Service Provision and Composition in Virtual Business Communities. HP Technical Report HPL-1999-84, Hewlett-Packard (1999)
14. Bochicchio, M. A., Longo, A., Giacovelli, S.: SARA: a Tool for Service Level Aware Contracts. In : IFIP/IEEE Int. Symp. on Integrated Network Management (2013)
15. Stamou, K., Kantere, V., Morin, J. H.: SLA Template Filtering: a Faceted Approach. In : 4th Int. Conf. on Cloud Computing, GRIDs and Virtualization (2013)
16. Ul Haq, I., Schikuta, E.: Aggregation Patterns of Service Level Agreements. In : 8th Int. Conf. on Frontiers of Information Technology (FIT'10) (2010)
17. Neo4j: Neo4j. Available at: http://www.neo4j.org
18. Spring: spring-data-neo4j. Available at: https://projects.spring.io/spring-data-neo4j
19. Jadell, J.: Neo4jPHP. Available at: https://github.com/jadell/neo4jphp
20. Cardoso, J., Sheth, A., Miller, J., Arnold, J., Kochut, K.: Quality of Service for Workflows and Web Service Processes. J. of Web Semantics 1, 281-308 (2004)

CURRAN ASSOCIATES INC.
proceedings
.com

ISBN 978-1-5108-4725-5

9 781510 847255